Archaeological thought in Am

Archaeological thought in America

Edited by C. C. LAMBERG-KARLOVSKY

Peabody Museum of Archaeology and Ethnology
Harvard University

CAMBRIDGE
UNIVERSITY PRESS

Published by the Press Syndicate of the University of Cambridge
The Pitt Building, Trumpington Street, Cambridge CB2 1RP
40 West 20th Street, New York, NY 10011-4211 USA
10 Stamford Road, Oakleigh, Melbourne 3166, Australia

First published 1989
First paperback edition 1990
Reprinted 1995

Printed in Great Britain by
Athenæum Press Ltd, Gateshead, Tyne & Wear

British Library cataloguing in publication data

Archaeological thought in America
1. Archaeology, American theories
1. Lamberg-Karlovsky, C.C. (Clifford Charles), 1937-
930.1'01

Library of Congress cataloguing in publication data

Archaeological thought in America/edited by C.C. Lamberg-Karlovsky.
    p.   .cm.
Bibliography
Includes index.
ISBN 0 521 35452 8
1. Archaeology – United States.   2. Archaeology – Case studies.
1. Lamberg-Karlovsky, C.C., 1937-
CC95.A73 1988
973.1-dc19   88-7303   CIP

ISBN 0 521 40643 9 paperback

GE

Contents

Contents

Illustrations

Introduction

C. C. LAMBERG-KARLOVSKY

This volume of essays is an unanticipated outcome of a formal archaeological exchange program initiated between the U.S.S.R. and the U.S.A. This collaboration is sponsored by the American Council of Learned Societies and the Soviet Academy of Sciences and is administered in the U.S. by the International Research and Exchange Board. To date three symposia have been held: Cambridge (1981), Samarkand (1983), Washington (1986), and a fourth is to be held in Tbilisi (1988). In addition, collaborative excavations at the Bronze Age site of Sarazm, Tadjikistan, S.S.R., have involved the participation of Philip Kohl, of Wellesley College, and myself. A number of years ago Professor Kohl conceived of the idea to edit a volume of essays addressing aspects of method and theory as practiced and written by Soviet archaeologists. That book, being edited by Philip Kohl, contains over twenty essays, and will be published by Cambridge University Press. There is a widely held belief among American archaeologists that Soviet Archaeology conforms to a particular "school," loosely referred to as Marxist, which implies that all Soviet archaeologists interpret the past according to the evolutionary dictates as set down by Marx and Engels. This is a narrow, ill-informed, perhaps even politically motivated, conception of the real diversity of approaches which characterize Soviet archaeology.

Structural and methodological differences, however, are readily apparent in the archaeological practice of the U.S.S.R and U.S.A. Some of these may be enumerated.

1 Within the Soviet Union there is a greater degree of centralization within archaeological research. Most research and excavation in the U.S.S.R. is carried out by scholars affiliated with Institutes of Archaeology of the Soviet Academy of Sciences. Each of the fifteen Soviet Republics maintains its own Institute of Archaeology or, in its absence, has numerous archaeologists affiliated with the Institutes of History. These centralized institutes, rather than universities as in the U.S.A., coordinate and undertake the majority of archaeological research.

2 Long-term archaeological field programs in the U.S.S.R. representing substantial funding, often for well over a decade, have uncovered broad horizontal exposures from the Paleolithic to Medieval Ages. Soviet archaeologists frequently find Western research programs with their smaller-scale horizontal exposure and statistically derived cultural reconstructions insufficient for meaningful commentary or adequate reconstruction of economic and social organization.

3 Both the U.S.S.R. and U.S.A. maintain varying degrees of interests in (a) an

ecological perspective; (b) the evolution and role of technologies and (c) settlement survey. In reference to (a) there are perhaps more trained paleoethnobotanists, zooarchaeologists, geomorphologists, et al. in the U.S.A. than exist in the U.S.S.R., but interdisciplinary programs are by no means uncommon. In reference to (b) there is an equal concern over the role of technology and social change but the U.S.S.R. is not well developed in archaeometric studies.

4 The U.S.S.R. has not developed a major focus or facility for archaeometry. Few radiocarbon laboratories exist, provenience studies are all but unknown and a strong materials science approach to metals, ceramics, and other organic remains is limited.

5 Sampling strategies, though less frequently adopted within the U.S.S.R., are nevertheless undertaken by Soviet archaeologists. It is difficult to generalize in this instance for there are important regional and problem-specific differences in the archaeology of the U.S.S.R.; some have generated, others eliminated, the adoption of sampling strategies.

6 Though settlement pattern studies have been undertaken in the U.S.S.R., indeed one can make a very strong case that the settlement pattern approach to archaeology was first developed by the Soviets (Tolstov 1948), there remains a strong focus on single sites rather than regions. Spatial information, size, number, and precise locations of sites are often difficult to come by. The extensive and interdisciplinary settlement surveys which characterized the work of R. McC. Adams (1981) in the Near East and MacNeish (1972) in Mexico are all but unknown in the U.S.S.R.

A more complete discussion of Soviet archaeology as specifically practiced in Central Asia is available in Kohl (1984b:237–48). Lastly, we are left to comment briefly on Marxist theory as applicable to archaeology in the U.S.S.R. Too frequently I have heard in the U.S.A. the expressed belief that archaeologists in the U.S.S.R. mindlessly relate the archaeological data to the Marxist model of historical materialism. This is definitely not true, as is readily evident in a major theoretical article on the epistemology of archaeology, co-authored by a Soviet archaeologist and philosopher, in a recent issue of their principal journal *Sovetskaja Archeologija* (Bashilov and Loone 1986:192–208). Soviet archaeology is Marxist in so far as it offers a strongly evolutionary emphasis, concerns itself with aspects of production, technology, and social formations in terms of class relations; in short, it emphasizes a materialist perspective. Its materialist perspective, however, as distinct from that in the U.S.A., is virtually devoid of ecological determinism. Environmental determinism is far more prevalent in the West than in the U.S.S.R. Kohl (1984b:246) in commenting upon Soviet archaeology has written "that ideological practices are emphasized to a degree that seems almost surprising if one expects Marxist-directed or inspired reconstructions to downplay superstructural features . . ." It is not, however, surprising at all if one follows Marx in the belief that material relationships form the basis of mental production (see p. 9); a logic which I find hard to fault. In light of the above, it remains puzzling that American Marxist archaeologists are largely hostile to those who consider ideology a significant force in social formations.

Lastly, from experience based upon our own direct involvement in Soviet archaeology over the past half-decade the following statement by Kohl (1984b:246–7) deserves restatement:

It also must be emphasized . . . that diversity of opinions exist in Soviet archaeology, and one often reads articles highly critical of the works or theories of fellow colleagues. A monolithic structure promoting uniform, dogmatically held policies is a caricature of the real situation and says more about Western stereotypic conceptions of Soviet society than it does about the real nature of Soviet archaeology.

The preparation of the Soviet volume by Philip Kohl led him to suggest that I undertake a companion volume of essays, stressing theory and methodological approaches, as undertaken by archaeologists on this continent. Bruce Trigger, in his chapter for this volume, indicates that: "There is . . . no unity to archaeology as a discipline in the United States." I wholly agree, there is no single dominant paradigm, no "school" which encompasses inelastic theoretical or methodological imperatives within American archaeology. In light of the above, the selection of contributors was necessarily arbitrary, representing a mosaic of different theoretical and methodological approaches in the archaeological undertaking. Nevertheless, each contributor is noted for stressing certain approaches for reconstructing the past; approaches which are not necessarily compatible with each other. This volume does not pretend to provide a "holistic" overview of the archaeological perspectives in the Americas; nor does it pretend to offer geographical or chronological comprehensiveness. The perspectives of American anthropological archaeology dominate the volume; humanist approaches, incorporating art history; classical archaeology, Egyptology and so on are entirely absent.

Initially I formulated a list of twenty contributors, assigning to each of them a topic on which they had made notable contributions. Three of the requested contributors, Robert McC. Adams, Gregory Johnson, and Kent Flannery, declined the invitation in light of prior commitments. All others, somewhat to my astonishment, agreed to participate and all complied to a rigid time schedule, which, in a volume dependant on numerous contributors, was even the more astonishing. It was clear from the start that the volume would not represent all "schools" of thought nor would it strive to promote the mission of a single cause.

Over the past two-and-a-half decades American archaeology has been partially dominated by what Trigger refers to as "the third major paradigm in the history of American archaeology," namely, New or Processual archaeology, which is based on a neoevolutionary perspective (see Trigger, this volume). The materialist bias of this perspective is discussed by Arthur Demarest in chapter 6. Prior to turning to the epistemological framework, in which most of the New Archaeology was initially undertaken, a few comments on its contextual emergence are offered. Recent years have seen an increasing interest in the "uses of the past" as a symbolic resource for legitimizing authority (Fowler 1987). Equally significant is an effort to comprehend the intellectual and sociopolitical contexts in which archaeology is conducted.

It is frequently said that each generation must construct its own interpretation of the historical past. Such a statement is a tacit recognition that interpretations of the past are imbedded in issues and concerns of the present. In this vein it may be of interest to reflect upon the social and intellectual climate in which the New Archaeology emerged. A distance of over twenty years allows for the linearization of perspective. The New Archaeology emerged in this country in the mid-sixties at a time of increasing social turmoil. The younger generation became increasingly distrustful of the views and interpretations being offered by its leaders. The principal issue was, of course, the U.S. government's tragic involvement and defense of its military confrontation in Vietnam. Simultaneously, the injustice of the military draft and the iniquities of race and gender relations set a younger generation in opposition to the "informed wisdom"; that is, the perception and guidance of its elders, including within the family unit. Struggle, opposition and mistrust of the traditional, indeed revolution characterized the 1960s and early 1970s. A younger generation had successfully confronted the establishment and won, at least partially, the directive of its causes. It was within this social milieu that the New Archaeology was born. It was explicit in castigating all that came before it as an inadequate, misconceived "traditional" archaeology. Certain elders of the "traditional" approach were caricatured as mentalists communicating with sherds. The New Archaeology was trumpeted as a "paradigm shift," in the Kuhnian sense, totally replacing the archaism of the "traditional." Its participants were involved with a revolutionary struggle directed toward the total displacement of a previously "informed wisdom." Leslie White (with his materialist and evolutionary perspective) and Albert Spaulding (advocating a quantitative methodological rigor) were the ancestral Darwins and Lew Binford their self-appointed Huxley (see Binford 1972:13). To the above was added an epistemological approach for the undertaking of science; the philosopher of science Carl Hempel's nomothetic deductive (N–D) positivism became the *sine qua non* for advancing the New Archaeology as a science revitalized.

No one can doubt that the New Archaeology has advanced the discipline. I dare say that there is not a contributor to this volume who does not owe the New Archaeology a substantial debt. It has, however, fallen far short of being a "paradigm shift." In fact, it could never have become such due to its exclusive dependency on the N–D theories of explanation and cause. It should have been recognized, and, indeed, it was by a few archaeologists, and a great many philosophers of science, that the N–D theory of scientific explanation was deeply flawed. The archaeologists who contested this model of scientific method were deemed "traditional" and the philosophers of science who challenged the primacy of the N–D model, or presented other models of scientific explanation, were simply ignored in the archaeological literature. The commitment to the Hempelian model remained at the very basis of the New Archaeology – it was, and remains, in its exclusionary commitment to this model of science quite simply wrong! Before commenting further on the N–D aspect of archaeological science, one other aspect for the contextualization of the New Archaeology deserves comment: the job market. The 1960s and early 1970s saw an increase in jobs within academe – a time of promised "guns and butter." Departments of Anthropology were splitting off from Sociology – as I myself first experienced at Franklin and Marshall College in 1964 –

creating new jobs in anthropology. Additionally, entire universities, indeed entire university systems, were being created, as, for example, the state university system in New York at Binghampton, Stonybrook, Albany, and so on. The newly formed Departments of Anthropology, as well as departments already established (usually dominated by social anthropologists) found an undeniable appeal in an archaeologist participating in a would-be paradigm shift; suggesting their greater relevance toward an understanding and explanation of social anthropological systems. Their failure to deliver this "paradigm shift" involves the commitment of the New Archaeology to the N–D model.

That there is an amelioration in the rigidity toward explanation and the use of the N–D model in archaeology can be perceived in the following passages (Redman 1987):

It is widely recognized that a project should have a problem orientation and almost every research proposal written is replete with goals. What often happens is that goals are indeed put forward, but they are too general, too numerous, and too unrealistic. Other scholars take a different position and argue that our interpretive goals should emanate from our work, not be formed in advance. This is a more complicated issue than was acknowledged by new archaeologists who years ago downgraded the latter position as "narrow inductivism" . . . I agree, but only in part, with the position of new archaeologists that one needs specific hypotheses in order to define relevant data to collect (p. 257).
Nevertheless, I also think that to speak to the entire discipline, not just to those who adhere to a new archaeology position, we should acknowledge that, in fact, much good work is done without *a priori* problem definition and without explicit concern with middle-range theory (p. 259).

These passages, written by Professor Redman, appear to temper the views expressed in his earlier work (Watson et al. 1971) in which there was advanced one path, and only one path, toward explanation in archaeology, namely the Deductive-Nomological model as advanced by the philosopher of science Carl G. Hempel. Hempel's approach to science, the approach adopted by the New Archaeologists, was advocated by L. R. Binford in the influential volume *New Perspectives in Archaeology* (Binford and Binford 1968). What was "new," and perhaps all that was "new," was the dependence on an epistemology derived from Carl Hempel. Binford (1968:17) put it this way:

The changes in archaeology which are documented in this book are more than simply new methods and new theories: the changes consist of theories and methods developed in the context of a *new epistemological perspective on such basic issues as the appropriate scientific procedures* to be followed in investigating the past (emphasis mine).

The "appropriate scientific procedures" were those advocated by Hempel. If archaeologists followed those procedures they could become "scientists" – explaining the past and predicting the future. "By use of scientific laws and theories, explanations can be given and predictions made" (Redman 1971:vii). Much of the contemporary dispute in archaeology – over hard versus soft paradigms and methods – is part of an older and larger conflict: the confrontation between positivism and romanticism. Today this debate in archaeology has passed the point of diminishing returns; further heat has yielded less and less light. This is not the place to review or outline Hempel's model (Hempel 1966). Suffice it to say that according to Hempel's (1948) classic account to explain a fact is to show how, under specific circumstances, it was only to be expected. This is accomplished by deducing a specific fact from different premises about the prevailing conditions and laws of nature. It is astonishing that Binford's "appropriate scientific procedure," which depended exclusively upon Hempel's model was, already, in the early 1960s a philosophical approach in deep trouble! Hempel's model, first adumbrated in the early 1940s, was being attacked already in the 1950s. Under this attack Hempel was forced to modify his model and offered numerous exceptions to his general theory – all of which went unnoticed in the archaeological literature. (For an analytical and historical view of the Hempel model see the various essays in Feigl and Brodbeck 1953; the chapters on "Explanation and Laws" in Gardiner 1959; Dray 1966; and Hexter 1971.)

Today it is possible to say, "it is well-known that the D–N (deductive nomological) model is wrong" due to, in part, "its implicit commitment to a defective theory of causation" (Horwich 1987:9,143). It is ironic that the general model of science which the New Archaeologists adopted, the D–N model, on which they predicted a paradigm shift, is defective in detailing cause – precisely the aspect which together with explanation was the New Archaeology's paramount concern. Fortunately, not all archaeologists embraced the rigors of the D–N model. Many, early on, shared the sentiment that "Unfortunately, his [Binford's] students and followers have been overimpressed with the great simplicity and apparent logical power of the deductive-nomological paradigm of scientific explanation and have pushed the discipline in a questionable direction" (Sabloff, Beale and Kurland 1973:105).

The unreflective nature of the New Archaeology was astonishing but not more so than its almost anti-intellectual insistence upon the absolute truth of a single epistemological framework of science. There is further irony in the fact that the whole-cloth adoption of this epistemology became, in practice, less of a method than an ideology, an attribute of culture which was all but banished from archaeological discourse. The D–N model became, in fact, a commodity reduced to a fetish; it became something quite fashionable which without presented alternatives was responded to by "I'll buy that!" Its purchase provided instant membership in a self-proclaimed paradigm shift. Never mind that no-one explicated what its shift was directed toward, other than a concatenated scientism. By the mid-1970s the "school" of New Archaeology had become so absolutist that one of the major government funding agencies favored only proposals whose research design was framed according to explicit deductive-nomological hypothesis-testing approaches. In discussing the New Archaeology and the Hempelian model two British archaeologists have recently observed: "The unfortunate spectacle is one of archaeology embracing thoroughly discredited and outmoded ideas as the framework for its own advances" (Shanks and Tilley 1987:32).

The New Archaeology is not only comprehensible in the context of the above discussed sociology of the mid-1960s but also in the logic of post-modernist construction, namely, that which makes a community is its specific form of "sociality" (see Kroker and Cook 1986). What counts is if a commodity sells, if it is popular, if it's the in-thing – not whether it is credible, correct or even comprehensible. The construction of the New Archaeology community, its "sociality", was explicitly configured: "We had fun that night. All my students were there . . . People from other places who were doing innovative things were at the party . . . We laughed, we sang, we joked . . . Change could occur. The younger students began to refer to us as the 'Mafia'" (Binford 1972:13).

The rapid spread within archaeology of the "culture of narcissism" so fundamental an aspect of post-modernist society, quickly reached England and is well captured in an essay by Kohl (1985:107): "Thus, Renfrew slapped his American counterpart, Binford, on the back and in an obsequious foreword to an 'outstandingly important book' by the 'outstanding archaeological thinker of our time . . .'" The result has been what some have come to refer to as the Anglo-American school of archaeology.

Today a new wind is passing over archaeology. Typically, what is new to archaeology is passing into old age within Anthropology or related disciplines (Leone 1972) – once again, reflexive evidence that archaeology derives its method on how it is to view the past from related disciplines. Archaeology appears to be consistently a consumer, rather than a producer, of perspectives, theory and methods derived from other fields. There is nothing inherently wrong with this but one must wonder why the perspectives, theories and/or methods take a decade to percolate into the archaeological consciousness. Today archaeologists are turning toward "symbolic" or "interpretive" modes in which, it is argued, the discipline must move to "hermeneutic, interpretive processes, dialectics, praxis and archaeology as cultural critique" (Shanks and Tilley 1987:243). This perspective, advanced most articulately by Hodder (1982b, 1986), returns to idealist constructs (see Demarest's chapter in this volume) in which the "meaning" of the past is to be seen as a Geertzian "text" of contextualized relativism. As in the manner of hermeneutics we are now informed that each interpretation creates a new meaning. Within two decades archaeologists have gone from a formal rigor of methodological scientism to archaeology as "interpretive quest." One is reminded of the lapel button: "Roses are red; violets are blue; I'm schizophrenic and so am I." Today with such "interpretive quests," which relativize all categories as mere symbols, denying even their material content, we are informed that even power doesn't exist, that it was always only a "perspectival simulation" of itself (Baudrillard 1980). This form of self-indulgence, in which anthropology is reduced to a relativism of interpretive quest, is a greater immaculate deception than what preceded it. Archaeologists swing between the polar oppositions of a crude scientism in which culture is only comprehensible as a mechanical adaptive process to a culturalist flattening of the world into "symbol" and "text."

Colin Renfrew, who has carried the drum for Binford's bandwagon and early identified the decade of the 1980s as one of "Cognitive Archaeology," now carries the drum for Ian Hodder (Renfrew 1982b). In his inaugural address, "Towards an

Archaeology of Mind," Renfrew (1982b:1) begins with the current fascination for relativist positions:

Each age and every society has its own image of the human past; an image which shapes its attitudes to the present and governs the nature of what is seen to be possible and appropriate action in the world.

There is a curious mirroring within archaeology of the debate which characterized the field of history in the 1930s (!) in the conflict between the "New Historians," the "Scientific Historians," and the emergence of "Historical Relativism" linked to the names of the historians Carl Becker and Charles Beard. As Becker (1932:253) put it: "Every generation, our own included, will, must, inevitably understand the past . . . in the light of its own experience": and, as Beard (1934:220) wrote:

Each historian who writes is a product of his age, and his work reflects the spirit of the times, of a nation, race, group, class or section . . . Every student of history knows that his colleagues have been influenced in their selection and ordering of materials by their biases, beliefs, affections, general upbringing and experience.

The disturbingly recent recognition of this reality has directed archaeological thought toward an increasingly idealist and relativist position wherein all objects are merely symbols and these symbols offer a subjective "text" of meaning. In this approach propositions become true or false only in reference to the assumed state of the world rather than to objective knowledge. If archaeology in past decades stood in danger of being a bad science in adopting the rigors of a Hempelian model, it stands today in equal danger of being a poor philosophy in the call to "move beyond the opposition of subjectivity and objectivity to a hermeneutic interpretative process" (Shanks and Tilley 1987).

  That American archaeological thought has, nonetheless, not become buried in an epistemological vice nor a philosophical quagmire is well evidenced in the following chapters. The obligatory reference to Hempel, the penchant to offer a test of a specific hypothesis, the elucidation of a newly discovered general law of cultural process, or the post-modernist obsession slowly creeping into archaeology which attempts to discover the relevance of Wittgenstein or Critical Theory are all but absent. This is not to say that the authors are unaware of the above – it does suggest, however, that they are willing to leave to others the residue of intellectual "showboating" in the "hermeneutic circle."

  The majority of chapters in this volume offer a formal argument applied to a concrete work. The Maya, the Inka, China, Mesopotamia and the Paleolithic are all represented. Conclusions from single instances or arguments based on single factor causes are absent, as are "explanations" based on origins. There are few, if any, American archaeologists who would agree with Peter Winch's (1958) wrong-headed belief that because we are "cognizers and agents we can ignore nature." To a certain extent archaeology today in the U.S. offers no explicit creed, only aids toward learning; no universal principle except "It all depends . . ." George Cowgill and before him Albert Spaulding have sensitized a generation to the importance of the careful application of statistical techniques to elucidate patterns. Cowgill's cautionary advice forewarns those who too readily would see a social "reality" behind a numerical "fact."

Numerous chapters in this volume point out that materialist approaches have dominated American archaeology over the past several decades. More recently, as argued most explicitly by Demarest, the materialist emphasis must be tempered by considering the role of ideology. Gilman advances Marxist perspectives critical of "adaptationist" and positivist approaches and avoids the issue of the role of ideology in generating change. In light of the ongoing debate this is somewhat surprising, for Marx was very explicit concerning the role of ideology within a materialist framework. The importance of ideas to material production, of increasing concern within the materialist versus idealist debate in archaeology, merits our recalling the full quote from Marx (Marx and Engels 1970:64):

The ideas of the ruling class are in every epoch the ruling ideas, i.e. the class which is the ruling material force of society is at the same time its ruling, intellectual force. The class which has the means of material production at its disposal has control at the same time over the means of mental production, so that thereby, generally speaking, the ideas of those who lack the means of mental production are subject to it. The ruling ideas are nothing more than the ideal expression of the dominant material relationships, the dominant material relationships grasped as ideas . . .

This passage leaves little doubt that material relationships, as conceived by Marx, are the basis for "mental production." Max Weber added to this the notion that every system of power, authority, or whatever, strives to *legitimate* itself through an ideology.

The question becomes, of course, whether we can put the role of legitimation and ideology in terms of causation – the causality of the infrastructure on the superstructure – or is it to be expressed by another conceptual framework? It remains one of the challenges for a Marxist history of ideas to relate a more plausible connection between a system of *interests* and a system of *thought*. It is essential to articulate the relationship between an interest and its expression in ideas within a system of legitimization. Such a framework must then introduce the notion of motivation in attempts to justify a system of authority (for the complexity of the process see Ricoeur 1986:68–102). Explanation in terms of motives is not the same as explanation in terms of causes. Motives or intentions do not "cause" actions; they do, however, provide a teleological account of them.

Gilman is, I believe, correct in pointing out that "differences between Marxist and non-Marxist work are often slight." His observation, however, that most recent American Marxist archaeologists "received their intellectual formation during the Vietnam war years" and reflect "the need of younger scholars to establish distinctive niches in the academic struggle for survival" appears to duplicate, but with a different voice, what we referred to in speaking of the New Archaeology as a "community of sociality." This appears to be particularly true in the penchant for Marxist archae-ologists to quote each other's work in a favorable light and to discover in those works, to the elimination of other obviously relevant and prior studies, the starting point of all important perspectives. At times this ideological tribalism resembles a form of intellectual Darwinism – a communal solidarity of shared intellectual ideas engaged in the struggle for survival against competing attitudes. Gilman's chapter is unique in his startling requirement for a political commitment to the Marxist intellectual frame-work: "The critical definitive criterion is, then, political commitment." As one who has gained a very great deal from the Marxist framework is it naive to ask, "A political commitment to what?"

Archaeology in the Americas is increasingly characterized by rationalizations of its application to society. Perhaps in reaction to the past emphases on materialist "explanations" and the scientism of the "New Archaeology," a fundamental conflict is once again emerging between scientism and humanism, between rational calculations and humane values.

In archaeology this conflict appears in the dispute between praxis-oriented versus value-neutral explanations. In its more committed form deterministic theories of structure are opposed to voluntaristic theories of consciousness. Perhaps each gener-ation must confront, with varying degrees of scholasticism, this presumed polariz-ation. Archaeology today begins to grapple with the old-fashioned hermeneutics of Wilhelm Dilthey (Makkreel 1975), who asserted that human action can only be understood through an interpretive rather than through the causal logic which explains the natural world. It seems to me that numerous archaeologists, not only in this country but also abroad, are undertaking floral arrangements of ideas which have little more than a metaphysical connection to archaeology (for its exaggerated practice see Shanks and Tilley 1987). One is reminded of Gellner's (1987) apt phrase, "All or most of us in the academic profession are guilty of some humbug some of the time." From an earlier period of archaeologists offering very factual facts to the present where "facts" are not even believed to exist (Sabloff, Binford and McAnany 1987) is an archaeological sojourn of less than twenty years.

Today, as Demarest points out in his chapter, there is an increasing polarization between idealist versus materialist perspectives. Such a dichotomy falsifies their dialectical relationship. The construction of meaning and the use of symbols is inherently a matter entailing the construction of political and economic interests while the concerns of a political economy are inherently conflicts over meanings and symbols.

In the provocative book *Anthropology as Cultural Critique* by George Marcus and Michael Fisher (1987), the authors note that anthropology moves away from the conception of a "natural science of society" toward anthropology as an interpretive quest in search of meaning, symbol and language. Within this country, of recent years, there are increasing evidences for the use of archaeology as "cultural critique." The study of Mark Leone at Annapolis; William Rathje's various Garbage Projects utilizing archaeological methods for the study of present-day consumption patterns, class structure, etc., and James Deetz's various studies of colonial America serve as excellent examples of archaeology as "cultural critique." Such approaches, selective from a variety of choices, indicate a discipline whose ideas are free of authoritative paradigms or any single hegemonic hold of an agreed-upon single grand theory or method. A healthy pluralism of methods and theories co-exist which do not appear to advocate a particular "ism" or "ic." In this sense archaeology, like social/cultural anthropology, attains a period which is best characterized as "post-paradigm." The advocacy of authority imposed by deductive-nomological positivism, ecological materialism, or for that matter any other "ism," no longer holds complete conviction as a deliverance from an indeterminate past. Of course, there do remain shrill voices advocating different "isms." Such views, as in the past, typically begin by declaring that all past methods and theories in archaeology are dead wrong, announce the presence of a "methodological crisis," and then point the way to the newly received wisdom. In a recently published paper of this genre the authors banish the presence of "facts" (as "given empirical truths") from archaeology and suggest that within the archaeological discourse "knowledge cannot come from archaeological facts but must be derived from ethnographic or historic research" (Sabloff, Binford and McAnany 1987). Somehow the authors believe that given the lack of "facts" in archaeology one can turn to the "independently derived" facts of history and ethnology to make sense out of archaeological objects and cultural processes. It is difficult to comprehend by which epistemological act of faith history and ethnology are believed to contain the "facts" which archaeology lacks and which then enable a reading of the archaeological record. A cursory examination of the Freeman–Mead controversy over Samoan ethnography or Hayden White's *Metahistory* should be enough to disabuse one of any belief in the existence of these types of "facts" in history or ethnography as well. More importantly, such exclusivist views which take the point of view that there is but one truth are intellectually reactionary in their constant search for a single monolithic paradigm which will place law and order on the comprehension of all cultural processes. A pluralist understanding, an appreciation for principles of indeterminacy and equifinality, simply are seen as having no meaning.

A pluralistic thinker does not retreat to the security of an exclusivist position in believing a singular truth. Nor is pluralism uncritical relativism in which all perspectives are equally good – as in the lowest common denominator. Pluralism does simultaneously recognize the significance of difference and particularity in the comparative study of social process. Commonality and difference are held in tension: an indispensable aspect of dialogue. Dialogue becomes the instrument for the creation of relationships, not for the achievement of a uniformitarian understanding of cultural evolution.

Today within archaeology there are numerous scholars (both in the Americas and abroad) assuming what has been called a symbolic realist approach to social theory (Clifford and Marcus 1986). In the present volume this approach is entertained by Conkey and Demarest. The idea that all knowledge, whether formal or common-sensical, is symbolic construction brings with it the possibility of multiple realities, each with its own model of articulation. That all representations of human nature are symbolically mediated finds support in philosophers as diverse as James and Russell.

Symbolic realism today permeates virtually all aspects of postmodern thought. It has been briefly accounted for in the following manner (Brown 1978:29–30):

In sum, then, on the one side are old-fashioned positivists who want not only explanatory laws to which everyone must agree, but laws that assume a purely material world and deny all subjective reality, including even that of the theorist. Opposing them are romantic subjectivists who want not laws, but experience and intuitions that, they claim, are a higher kind of science. Transcending the views of both these groups is that which seeks generalized explanations of the natural as well as the human world, including subjectivity, without a materialist bias. This view finds its justification in a post-positivist, post-romantic, dialectical, symbolic realist theory of knowledge. In such a view all knowledge is symbolic construction: Causal lawlike explanation is itself an interpretive procedure, and interpretation itself can be a rigorous way of knowing.

The chapters in this volume abound with interpretations, forming iterated examples of closely argued positions; a unity of substantive control and theoretical position. In the aggregate they represent a characteristic pluralism of approach which today dominates American archaeology. Virtually all chapters avoid theoretical bombast which advocates single-minded methods. Archaeology today can be conjunctive, behavioral, ecological, cognitive, New, processual, historical, Marxist, analytical, symbolic, and so forth. The bombast of the past which heralded each of the above "ideal types" as a shift in paradigm is perhaps the most important feature of archaeologists' "loss of innocence." Archaeology is no longer reduced to a faddish jingoism which must be reconstituted every few years by a new terminology, or an adopted philosopher, to resolve paradigm problems, methodological crises, or paradigmatic thinking, all of which was analogous to charismatics, pentecostals and fundamentalists arguing for hegemony over a false reality. Years ago Kent Flannery (1976) introduced three types of American archaeologists: the Great Synthesizer, the Field Archaeologist and the Skeptical Graduate Student. To these I would add a fourth – the Sirens: those archaeologists continuously sounding a cacophonous noise, advocating new advances or crises in theoretical and/or methodological approaches in an effort to divert the course of the field toward their staked-out territory.

Archaeologists can close the humor gap between science and society by wearing T. S. Kuhn T-shirts displaying a pair-of-dimes or simply stating "Paradigms Lost." Archaeologists, nevertheless, seem to be unnecessarily troubled by "critical theory," the role of ideology, or even the quackery of post-modernism, by what physics, that bench-mark science against which all others seem to be measured, has long recognized, namely that the existence of the world depends on consciousness, that, indeed, reality is a mental construct. (The reference here is to the Bohr–Einstein debate in quantum mechanics; Fine 1987.) The reasoning of physics (quantum theory) as in anthropology (as cultural critique), that the observer is inextricably linked to the observed and changes the experiment can be, and has been, carried to absurdity. The astrophysicists John Barrow and Frank Tipler were serious when they wrote that nothing is real "until all sequences of observation by all observers of all intelligent species that have ever existed and ever will exist, of all events that have ever occurred and will ever occur are finally joined together by the Final Observation by the Ultimate Observer." The absurdity of the position of post-modernists is that nothing is meaningful that relates to what Cowgill refers to in his chapter as "out there," while everything one does say has only an interpretive relevance.

As archaeologists in the U.S. have typically followed the notions of what their fellow social anthropologists are directed toward, it is important to not only be aware of their post-modern "crises," or present "revolution," but to avoid it! Post-modern anthropology is perceived as a "game" to be played out, the appropriate genre is not representation but the "representation of representations" (Rabinow 1986:250), in which one deliberately "plays" with context, all is seen as "irony" and as "fictional accounts" in which one is "self-consciously in writerly control." The Anthropologist as scientist is transformed into a spell-binding writer of fiction offering us such exemplary vignettes as:

Context is neither a transcendental signifier nor a transcendental signified, for it emerges only within and by means of the contexts it creates as it is created by them. So, the context is neither there already nor not there, and that is why postmodernism is not ironic; irony requires an outside, a place to step back from the context, a *topos* where impartial, objective narrators are not already figured in the ironies that figure them. Except as illusion, no moment of pure freedom enables authors to *de*-scribe as they de-*scribe* or grants texts immunities from communities of readers. Just as there is no place outside the text that does not already implicate the text, there is no text that does not implicate the outside that implicates its implicating it. And so neither texts nor authors break free of the con-texts they can but parody.

(Tyler and Marcus 1987:276)

The proliferation of such twaddle is perhaps only comprehensible in the narcissistic appreciation of self – a strong component of all that passes for "post-modern." One can only hope that such inane, post-modernist, reflexive, critical, post-structuralist abscesses do not affect archaeology. The reciprocity which should exist between analysis and narrative must enjoin a particular point of view rather than an "anti-anti-relativism" (rejecting something without committing oneself to what that something has rejected: see Geertz 1984). The point, of course, is that archaeology embodies a number of approaches; the field is large enough to embrace them all – but the prevailing method, whatever it be, simply must involve a point of view directed to the discovery of what is "out there" (in Cowgill's sense). Archaeology by its very nature strives to be a holistic discipline. It benefits by following the twin banners of Art and Science in reflecting upon humanities' inner nature. Cyril S. Smith, whose reflections upon the archaeological artifact have profoundly influenced our appreciation of both past and self, has captured the duality of art and science within archaeology:

Everything that we can talk about involves the relationship of a human
mind to other humans, to the things they have made, or to nature.
Without internal experience there could be no external communication.
The mind is more complex than the brain; the response of the whole body
influences both experience and memory. Understanding, even scientific
understanding as distinct from analytical proof and extension, seems to be
in a large part emotional, for it involves an interplay between what the
senses can feel and what the mind can think about – movement,
resistance, and the interlock of parts into patterns. Perception is the
discovery of a link between sensable quality and conceivable structure.
One cannot know the meaning until one has had the experience.

   Both as individuals and as societies we first explore the world sensually
(aesthetically at the higher points); then we seek to explain and exploit
what we have discovered by finding replicable relationships between as
many parts as possible; finally we move beyond this to emotionally
satisfying understanding. Both the initial discovery of anything and the
final stages of adjustment at maturity seem to involve more of what we call
"art" than does the intermediate stage of logical growth.

> (Smith 1980:117, see also Smith 1981)

The present lack of consensus as to what archaeology is manifests itself in the
proliferation of our almost indefinite number of "types" of archaeology, each bearing
its own specific qualifier: cognitive, behavioral, new, critical, and so on and so forth.
Archaeology, like Anthropology, appears to be suffering from a "chronic discontinuity" (Dumont 1986:203). Gilman offers, in his chapter, a possible explanation for
this phenomenon: "Its specific character is, however, the result not of political
activism but of disciplinary competition, of the need of younger scholars to establish
distinctive niches in the academic struggle for survival" (emphasis mine). Louis
Dumont (1986:203) is perhaps more specific, but echoes Gilman's thought in
reflecting upon the causes of this "chronic discontinuity":

This is a trait which may come from the United States, where transitory
fashions rapidly succeed each other in an ideological and institutional
climate of competition which favors overbidding, but it is a fact often
encountered in modern thought, though the intensity may vary.

   From this stems his conclusion that according to all appearances we are living, at
least within our discipline, in a "permanent revolution." More charitably it might be
as Marcel Mauss believed, namely, that we are a "science in process of becoming."
The scope of archaeology's ambition is enormous and there is no surprise that tensions
should exist, healthy ones, in search for a seamless totality.

   The pages in this volume indicate numerous convergences and a not wholly
unexpected divergence. Yellen and Conkey point to an emergent tension between
ethnography and archaeology; Kohl and Trigger agree upon the notion that archaeologists have perpetuated a "grossly misleading caricature of history," while Trigger

and Binford share the view that culture history is an "idealist" approach to understanding. Yellen argues forcefully for the importance of the "specific historical context." Binford suggests what the post-modernists in anthropology have indicated for ethnography, namely that "archeology became essentially a game" and continues to advocate the adoption of "law using" approaches to avoid the charade. Binford points to three agendas within the New Archaeology, all dealing with comprehending "variability." Dunnell wholly agrees with the importance Binford accords to an understanding of variation, stating that "evolutionary theory hinges on variation." Yet Dunnell speaks of the New Archaeology as "demonstrably defective as science on methodological and substantive grounds." Cowgill–Binford–Dunnell all point to the poor quality of our data and offer differing paths toward "models of the world that increasingly approximate how it really is, even if we can never get beyond approximation" (Cowgill). Gilman and Trigger, and implicitly Kohl, converge in their appeal for a clearer Marxist "praxis" in archaeology, while Chang points out that Western historiography when tested against the Chinese record for the rise of civilization "fails the test." Demarest and Chang both point to the importance of ideology and concur that it is not a prime mover but "one of the principal instruments" (Chang) in culture change. While Chang emphasizes "political culture" as more significant than economic/technological, Kohl, Wright and Zagarell emphasize the economic, which is perhaps resolvable through accepting Chang's belief that different factors of paramount importance dominated different civilizations. Willey, influenced by the recent advances in the reading of Maya "texts," warns against the reconstruction of state polities from settlement data alone. In this respect Mesoamerican archaeology, with its advances in detailing an understanding of the glyphs, begins to balance the typically precarious interrelationships that characterize the archaeological artifact and the written word.

The chapters by Yellen, Kohl, Earle and D'Altroy, Wright, Chang, and myself all share the recognition of the importance of the "dialectical interplay of regional and supraregional forces" (Chang). This recognition, won largely by the results of new and extensive excavations in areas previously little explored, has led to important new insights of the interdependence of cultural processes which relate "cores" to "peripheries." Metropolitan centers and "cradles of civilization" have been the focus of most previous research, whether along the river banks of the Nile, Tigris–Euphrates, Indus, Yellow River, or the Lowlands of the Maya. They have commanded the major attention of both archaeology and its public. Today, with extensive research in wholly new and largely unexplored territories a view confirmatory of McNeill's (1986a:6) postulate, that "marginality and pluralism were and are the norm of civilized existence," is being confirmed for antiquity. Archaeological field research continues to elucidate the nature and structure of that "marginality" and the degree of its "pluralism."

It has often been asserted that new archaeological data are not what is needed but that theory and method are paramount! Theory divorced from data or data in the absence of theory is not only boring but vacuous. As Cowgill points out, the quality of our data is poor, but it should also be recognized that the amount of our data is, in fact, minimal even for "idealist" culture history. The *extraordinary* accomplishments of field archaeology in China, Central Asia, South Asia, Mesoamerica, Peru, the Near East and Europe have dramatically changed our understanding of entire regions, often through the excavation of a *single* site. These changed conceptions, whether culture-historical or based on theory, i.e. "core-periphery" relations, would not have been predicted by theory or realized by other methods. In my own area of concern the excavations at the single site of Ebla in Syria or the discovery of the existence of the "Bactrian Civilization" are cases in point of revolutionary changes emanating from regions already known archaeologically, while the new field of Arabian archaeology, where excavations are hardly a decade old, offers an initial glimpse at an archaeological *terra incognita*. The accumulation of "quality" data will, even if derived by rigorous methods which offer the potential to answer questions, still require asking of the data an appropriate question. Without a dialectical interaction of method–theory–data one may well write a dictionary believing it contains a plot. Rather than thinking dictionaries useless, however, it is better to perceive them as the building blocks on which a multiplicity of plots can be written.

The reader is invited to go beyond the marginality of these introductory comments and view the pluralism and vigor of the archaeological practice as undertaken by a diverse, but exceptionally able, cohort from this continent.

Part I: History, method, and theory

I

History and contemporary American archaeology: a critical analysis

BRUCE G. TRIGGER

Extraordinary as it may seem to those who have been trained in the Western European and Soviet traditions of archaeological research, history, both as a discipline and as a methodology, has always been viewed as largely irrelevant to prehistoric archaeology in the United States. Prehistoric archaeologists have recognized only a narrow thematic overlap between their discipline, which as a branch of anthropology examines the prehistoric remains of American Indians, and history, which studies the actions of Europeans and Euro-Americans (Fitzhugh 1985). Nor have prehistoric archaeologists seen historiographical methods as having any special relevance for their work. Prehistoric archaeology has been characterized by dramatic oscillations between evolutionary and anti-evolutionary perspectives and by a general failure to recognize that history and evolution are complementary rather than antithetical concepts. The reasons for this are to be found in archaeology's relations to Euro-American society and its values. A brief examination of the history of these relations is therefore necessary to understand recent developments. The connection is of particular interest because for the most part until recently it has been an unselfconscious one.

One of the important factors affecting this relationship has been the low prestige accorded to history in the United States during the twentieth century; an attitude epitomized by the remark of the industrialist Henry Ford that "History is bunk." Commentators have noted the "present-mindedness" of American culture, which they associate with the belief of Americans that they have freed themselves from the legacy of their European past (Kroker 1984:8). History in the United States has traditionally focused on political narrative and been cultivated as a humanistic and literary genre; while the more recently developed social and economic histories, which have turned increasingly to studying women and minority groups, are viewed as a radical critique of American society that is being made by dissident academics (Bender 1985; McNeill 1986b:3–22).

The social sciences, by contrast, have largely dissociated themselves from history and sought prestige and respectability by formulating general laws of human behavior that can claim utilitarian value in a "technocratic" society (Kolakowski 1976:229). Their prestige roughly parallels that of the applied physical and biological sciences, which have enjoyed greater esteem than their pure science counterparts because they are seen to contribute more directly to economic growth (Bronowski 1971). In addition to divorcing themselves from history, the social sciences in America pursue their search for knowledge of human behavior in relative isolation from each other. To a large degree political science explores problems of power without direct reference to economics; economics studies commercial behavior in isolation from considerations of power and social control; and sociology prescribes techniques for coping with social problems while avoiding examination of their political and economic context. Over the years anthropologists have attempted to determine how American society could deal most effectively with native ones, first within the territory of the United States, then in Cuba, the Philippines, and other American colonies, and finally throughout the world (Wolf 1982:7–19). Successive divisions along disciplinary lines have been lauded as evidence of growing specialization and progress in social science research, while only inconsequential attention has been paid to their harmful effects (Kuttner 1985). Under these circumstances there has been no role for history or prehistory to play as disciplines unifying the social sciences.

There is also no unity to archaeology as a discipline in the United States. Prehistoric archaeology has always been classified as a branch of anthropology; classical, Egyptian, and Mesopotamian archaeology have been attached to specialized human-istic disciplines; and historical or colonial archaeology, which studies Euro-American sites, has developed only slowly and with uneasy ties to both history and prehistoric archaeology (Noël Hume 1969; South 1977).

Historical background
American archaeology began to develop in the nineteenth century, during the final and most dramatic phase of Euro-American colonization of the lands west of the Mississippi River that were occupied by native people and Mexican settlers. The study of the ancient civilizations of the Old World and to a lesser degree of Mesoamerica and Peru was favored by rich American patrons as a means of raising the cultural level of Euro-American society (Hinsley 1985). Prehistoric archaeology developed, with considerable support from American federal government agencies such as the Smithsonian Institution and the Bureau of American Ethnology, within the context of an evolutionary anthropology that attributed Euro-American hegemony to their racial and cultural superiority over native peoples (Hinsley 1981; Meltzer 1983). The subjugation and anticipated disappearance of Indian groups was thus attributed not to Euro-American violence and aggression but to the alleged failure of native peoples to evolve over thousands of years prior to the arrival of European colonists.

The initial paradigm of American archaeology assumed that native cultures would be found to have developed or changed little, if at all, in prehistoric times and hence that archaeological discoveries in each part of the United States would closely resemble native cultures described by ethnologists for the same areas. There was therefore a general tendency to study archaeological material on a regional basis without paying much attention to temporal differences or making any systematic effort to construct general chronologies. Where changes were observed in the archae-ological record they were attributed wherever possible to migrations of new ethnic groups into a region (Willey and Sabloff 1980:34–82). Archaeological finds that lacked convincing ethnographic analogues were frequently attributed to extinct non-Indian peoples, especially if they appeared to be very old or relatively advanced in terms of cultural development. This was the case with sites of alleged Paleolithic age (Meltzer 1983) and also with the Adena-Hopewell and Mississippian cultures that had flourished in the Ohio and Mississippi Valleys between 500 B.C. and A.D. 1500. These later cultures, with their large burial and temple mounds, exotic raw materials, and elaborate material cultures, were attributed to a "Moundbuilder people," who were variously speculated to have been of Scandinavian, Welsh, Mexican, Siberian, or South Asian origin and were thought to have been either exterminated or driven out of eastern North America by hordes of savage Indians (Silverberg 1968). These speculations further vilified the Indians as inveterate enemies of civilization in the opinion of Indian-hating Euro-Americans. While Moundbuilder theories were given the form of historical narratives, they supported a static view of native Americans by assigning some of their most important cultural achievements to a fictitious non-Indian people. Archaeological findings therefore reinforced the belief that only people of European origin were progressive enough to be suitable for historical study, while Indians along with other "people without history" became the subject matter of anthropology (Wolf 1982). Prehistoric archaeology was thus established in North America as a branch of anthropology and clearly separated from American history, which chronicled the Euro-American occupation of the continent. Even when native people were discussed in histories of colonization, it was as a biologically inferior race that evolutionary processes had doomed to vanish as a result of the spread of civilization and as an element of the primeval world that European settlers had to sweep aside. Thus native peoples were denied an active role in American history at the same time that they were being relegated, as a conquered people, to the lowest rung in American society (Berkhofer 1978; Drinnon 1980).

By the end of the nineteenth century this initial paradigm was being challenged by accumulating evidence of changes in the archaeological record that could not be explained by migrations as well as by changing views of the American Indians, who were now living on reservations and were no longer perceived as a significant threat to Euro-Americans. The German-trained ethnologist Franz Boas successfully combatted the racist views that had been prevalent in American anthropology and drew attention to the ability of native cultures to change (Stocking 1974). As an anti-evolutionist he stressed, as did Friedrich Ratzel and other German theorists, the unpredictability of cultural change, which he attributed for the most part to the fortuitous operation of diffusion. In accepting his ideas American archaeologists and ethnologists embraced the doctrine of cultural relativism, which denied that any culture could be evaluated by a standard external to itself, such as a cultural evolutionary scale. Boas also supported the related doctrine of historical particularism, which rejected claims that there were any inevitable or even highly probable trends in cultural development.

These doctrines, which obfuscated the true nature of the domination of native societies by Euro-Americans, formed the basis of the second major paradigm in American prehistoric archaeology, the culture-historical approach. Archaeologists began to define chronological sequences, and later mosaics, of archaeological cultures for the various natural regions of North America and interpreted each culture as the material remains of a way of life that differed to varying degrees from those known in historical times (Martin, Quimby and Collier 1946). Change was now explained in terms of the diffusion of innovations from one culture to another as well as migrations. Nevertheless most important innovations, such as food crops, pottery, burial mounds, and knowledge of metallurgy, were stated to have reached North America either from Mesoamerica or Siberia (Willey and Sabloff 1980:116–20). Culture-historical archaeologists acknowledged the capacity of North American Indians to change their ways of life but continued to minimize their creativity by portraying them as cultural borrowers rather than innovators (Trigger 1980:669).

Everywhere, except in the southwestern United States, where beginning in the 1920s dendrochronology provided accurate dating for sites as far back as the beginning of the Christian era, short chronologies, which suggested that major changes in Indian life-styles had occurred in rapid succession, both reflected and reinforced the idea that migration and diffusion were the major forces bringing these changes about (cf. Ritchie 1944 and 1965). These short chronologies persisted until radiocarbon dating revealed their erroneousness. Although this approach was labelled culture-historical, it had little in common with true history. Its only significant historical attribute was a concern with chronology. Change was attributed almost entirely to external factors. Nevertheless the culture-historical approach marked a definitive advance by comparison with the preceding paradigm inasmuch as it allowed archaeologists to take account of temporal as well as spatial variations in the archaeological record.

Beginning in the 1930s American archaeologists and ethnologists became increasingly disillusioned with the sterility of historical particularism. A small but influential minority advocated trying to discover laws governing human behavior and cultural change. Ethnologists, such as Clyde Kluckhohn (1940), and archaeologists, such as Walter Taylor (1948:156–67), Gordon Willey and Philip Phillips (1958:5–6), proclaimed the search for such generalizations to be a common goal uniting archaeology and ethnology as branches of anthropology. This orientation favored the development of neoevolutionism, which saw human behavior as highly patterned and largely governed by materialistic constraints. The ethnologist Leslie White (1949, 1959a) treated technological change as the principal factor shaping the social organization and ideologies of cultures, while Julian Steward (1955) advocated an ecological approach to understanding human behavior. He contrasted a scientific concern to explain the regularities in human behavior with an unscientific preoccupation with stylistic variations and other cultural traits that were shaped by historical accidents. He and the archaeologist F. M. Setzler argued that the main variables that accounted for cultural change could be studied by archaeologists if they shifted their attention from typology to subsistence and settlement patterns (Steward and Setzler 1938). As a result of such arguments, a growing number of archaeologists identified scientific studies with generalizations, evolutionism, and ecology, while history was equated with a mechanical interest in chronologies and with attributing changes to historical accidents. Hence history came to be viewed as the opposite of science; and as descriptive rather than explanatory.

Processual archaeology

Joseph Caldwell (1958, 1959) and Lewis R. Binford (1962, 1965, 1972) built upon these developments to create the third major paradigm in the history of American archaeology: New or processual archaeology. The New Archaeology was based on neoevolutionism, which received considerable support among American anthropologists during the two decades of American economic and political self-confidence that followed World War II (Sahlins and Service 1960; Sahlins 1968; Service 1971, 1975), although it never became a dominant position among ethnologists, many of whom observed that it was unable to account for the diversity found in living cultures. Archaeologists who were influenced by neoevolutionism stressed some form of technological, ecological, demographic, or economic determinism, or all four approaches as they were synthesized in Marvin Harris's (1979) cultural materialism. Some archaeologists also attempted to explain cultural change in specifically Darwinian terms, thereby rejecting the need for any separate theory of social evolution (Dunnell 1980). Most of them, however, adopted Steward's ecological point of view, defining culture as humanity's extrasomatic means of adapting to the environment. All of these views implied a mechanically deterministic perspective concerning how these forces shaped society rather than a humanly centered, dialectical one. New Archaeologists rejected as hopelessly teleological the nineteenth-century view that cultural change occurred as a result of individual human beings using their capacity to reason and plan to gain greater control over the natural environment. Instead cultural systems were held to remain in equilibrium provided that no changes occurred in the relations between them and their ecosystemic context. Change was therefore attributed to the operation of adaptive forces and human behavior was maintained to be passively molded by these forces (Watson et al. 1971:88–107). This diminished view of the role played by human beings in bringing about cultural change reflected the altering views of the historical role of individuals that accompanied the gradual replacement of many small competing industries by large, bureaucratically controlled multinational conglomerates in American society. Yet this new interest in how changes in the adjustment of cultural systems to the broader ecosystem of which they were part brought about corresponding changes in their economic relations, social and political organization, and ideology encouraged American archaeologists for the first time to try to understand the systemic relations that existed within individual societies or cultures. As a result diffusion and migration became less important as explanations of cultural changes and were dismissed by some anthropologists as irrelevant. Many archaeologists assumed that societies would invent appropriate traits as these were required by their evolving systems and hence that borrowing was no different from independent invention (Binford 1968a; Chang 1962:190–1). The basic claim was that as a result of ecological constraints, societies did not develop differently in the presence of external stimuli from how they would have developed in their absence. It was also assumed that cultural patterns contained much random variation which provided them with the resources to cope with changing ecosystemic relations (Martin and Plog 1973; Cordell and Plog 1979).

The emphasis of New Archaeologists on ecologically induced cultural changes added a new dimension to the understanding of the flexibility and adaptive capacity of native peoples in prehistoric times. There was also a strong emphasis on the integrated nature of cultural systems as well as on material factors as a primary source of change. The expectation of major cross-cultural regularities also encouraged a deductive approach towards the explanation of the archaeological record. Archaeology was seen as a means of testing generalizations about human behavior, especially about changes that occurred over long periods of time (Watson et al. 1971:1–57; Salmon 1982:34–42). In his own work Binford (1983a) has emphasized evolutionary changes, especially the impact of new technologies and population pressure on the development of hunter-gatherer cultures, and processes leading to the development of food-production and complex societies. Specific historical sequences were treated as case studies to be used as a basis for testing such generalizations rather than as being of significance in their own right. Like Steward, the New Archaeologists showed only minimal interest in features that were unique to specific instances of cultural development. This encouraged a major devaluation of an already weak historical perspective in favor of an evolutionary one.

This devaluation has led to a growing emphasis on social rather than cultural systems, since the former are seen as more susceptible to generalizations than the latter (Murdock 1959b). In a societal approach, networks of social, political, and economic relations linked to technology are seen as the basis of human adaptations to the natural environment. Culture is interpreted as knowledge related to these activities, which acquires its functional significance only in relation to social action. This view began to influence archaeology through Childe's (1951b, 1958) latest writings and with settlement archaeology in the decade before the rise of the New Archaeology (Willey 1953). Only later did the view of social relations as the systemic aspect of human behavior become an alternative to cultural systems within the general context of processual archaeology (Redman et al. 1978). While Binford (1983b:229–41) has objected that this view of culture is a repudiation of ecological materialism, it has been adopted by many processual archaeologists (Schiffer 1976).

In the course of the 1960s the New Archaeology won many adherents, especially among younger archaeologists, and its supporters began to control major committees that allocate research funding. Its principal intellectual attraction was that it offered an escape from the conceptual poverty of American culture-historical archaeology. Generalizations were emphasized as a source of prestige in a society that valued technical knowledge far more than it did philosophical and historical understanding; especially by insisting that only the positivist equation of explanation and prediction provided a scientific basis for interpreting archaeological data (Spaulding 1968; Watson et al. 1971:3–57). Ecological generalizations were claimed to be a useful source of information for the management of modern ecosystems (Ford 1973; Fritz 1973). On a more abstract level, Paul Martin and Fred Plog (1973:364–8) argued that understanding how the prehistoric societies of Arizona had responded to various types of ecological stress would help to predict how underprivileged Blacks and Mexicanos might behave in urban ghettos. This generalizing approach to analyzing archaeological data left little scope for viewing archaeology as a source of information about native prehistory. Instead archaeologists sought to use products of native history to create generalizations that were useful to modern Euro-American society. Thus, despite an enhanced awareness of the flexibility and adaptiveness of prehistoric North American cultures, the alienation of Euro-American archaeologists from native people grew ever greater.

The retreat from neoevolutionism

The conceptual unity of processual archaeology began to break down in the 1970s, as the approach itself continued to grow more popular. At the same time there was a rapid increase in the number of professional archaeologists, the funding available for archaeological research, and the number of universities where post-graduate training in archaeology was offered. This encouraged the diversification of archaeological theory and interpretation along lines that had long-term significance for conceptualizing the relations between history and evolution.

General systems theory was soon found to enhance the systemic view of culture that had been adopted by processual archaeology. It was used to give structural and quantitative rigor to explanations of changes, by ascertaining the direction and strength of positive and negative feedback connections between the components of cultural systems (Flannery 1967; Watson et al. 1971:61–87). Yet this approach quickly encouraged a more skeptical and inductive attitude towards problems of causality. Some archaeologists have concluded that instead of assuming how prehistoric cultures worked, they should carry out detailed case studies, in the tradition of social anthropology, to determine how individual cultures actually had functioned. This approach can claim greater scientific rigor from a Baconian point of view, as it assumes less; although hard-line deductivists regard this as a lamentable revival of Boasian historical particularism (Leone 1975). While many interpretations of archaeological data continue to reflect the influence of ecological determinism, other archaeologists have returned to the view that ecological factors constrain rather than determine human behavior (Friedman and Rowlands 1978b:203–4). The latter view acknowledges that factors other than ecological ones play a significant role in shaping such behavior. The problem of demonstrating the determining role of ecology has been discussed by Sanders et al. (1979:360); although they had anticipated that four or five major ecological factors might account for 80 percent of the variability in their detailed settlement pattern data for the Valley of Mexico, they were unable to demonstrate such relations.

On the other hand the application of General Systems Theory suggested unexpected constraints on human behavior. These constraints take the form of new structures for information processing and decision making that must evolve if the scale of the society (Flannery 1972a; Johnson 1973; Rathje 1975), or the number of units requiring coordination (Johnson 1981), is to increase. Such theories do not explain why political or social changes occur but suggest limitations on the forms these changes can take as the scale of social integration increases.

There is also a growing tendency to study cultural systems as open not only to the environment but also to neighboring cultural systems. This openness was countenanced by the early New Archaeology, especially in terms of Caldwell's (1964) concept of interaction spheres, which sought to explain the Hopewell manifestation in the central United States as a series of cultures linked by trade and ritual exchanges related to a shared burial cult (Binford 1972:204). Yet, as diffusion and migration came to be viewed as irrelevant for understanding cultural change, each culture tended to be studied as an independent adaptation to the natural environment and there was growing emphasis on independent inventions and parallel evolution. Now there is once again a tendency to examine how cultures influence each other's development (Flannery and Marcus 1983). The Near East has been viewed as a network of economic interaction in which later centers of civilization did not necessarily have a special role to play in early times (Lamberg-Karlovsky 1975; Kohl 1978; Alden 1982). Sanders, Parsons and Santley (1979) saw the need to study the whole of the Valley of Mexico in order to understand what happened to its various sectors. Now archaeologists argue that the whole of Mesoamerica developed as an interaction sphere in which prestige goods were exchanged among regional elites. Hence they need to know the archaeological record for large areas before they can determine if regional population fluctuations represent actual increases or decreases in population or merely movements from one region to another as economic and political conditions changed (Blanton et al. 1981). Large-scale archaeological data are also required to determine the economic relations between hegemonous and subordinate political units in Mesoamerica (Price 1977; Parsons et al. 1982). Similar concepts of "peer polity" interaction are also being applied to explain the archaeological record for Bronze Age Europe (Renfrew 1982a; Renfrew and Shennan 1982; Renfrew and Cherry 1986).

Some archaeologists have attempted to provide these analyses with a sounder theoretical basis by employing Immanuel Wallerstein's (1974) world-systems theory (Kohl 1979, 1981a; Blanton et al. 1981). This theory, as applied to modern capitalist societies, assumes large-scale, supranational spatial systems, an intraregional division of labor in which peripheries supply core areas with raw materials, that cores are politically and economically dominant, and that the social and economic development of all regions is constrained by the changing roles they play in the system. There is at present no agreement about what kind of world systems existed in ancient times and to what extent they resembled those of more recent mercantile and capitalist economies. Answering this question is a major object of much recent research.

A growing appreciation of the extent of interaction between neighboring societies also calls into question the appropriateness of the analogies used in neoevolutionary studies (Fried 1975). Hunter-gatherer societies were inevitably linked in a variety of ways to industrial or neighboring tribal ones prior to ethnographic study (Wobst 1978; Schrire 1984). The degree to which various economic ties, such as the fur trade or opportunities for occasional wage labor, and missionary efforts transformed these non-literate societies prior to study is a question that can only be answered archaeologically. There is certainly a possibility that aspects of their economies, settlement patterns, and value systems were altered in significant ways as a result of relations with non-hunter-gatherers. It is not known, for example, to what extent the modern hunting patterns of northern peoples, which Binford (1980b) has interpreted as an ecological adaptation to high latitude environments, are a product of a recent adaptation to the capitalist fur trade throughout the northern circumpolar zone. This raises the question of whether modern hunter-gatherer societies can be treated as analogues for understanding prehistoric hunter-gatherer ones, as processual archaeologists assume (Jochim 1976; Yellen 1977; Binford 1978). How alike they are is a subject for archaeological investigation, not something to be assumed.

There is also now an unprecedented emphasis on the large amount of variation in the archaeological record. This trend was initiated by the New Archaeology's emphasis on studying variation within cultural systems. Initially this meant that archaeologists sought to study the total range of sites associated with seasonal movements or sociopolitical hierarchies in prehistoric cultures. Yet in the southwestern United States, a well developed area of archaeological research, archaeologists now recognize that there was a much greater range of variation in prehistoric subsistence and settlement patterns at any one time than was noted in the past and that cultural change did not occur uniformly over large areas. It is argued that adaptation takes place at the level of the individual human being or local group coping with the local natural and cultural environment and that general trends are the statistical outcome of a plethora of individual decisions, some of which worked and some of which did not (Cordell and Plog 1979).

This growing awareness of the interrelations between neighboring societies and of the complexity of internal cultural change has promoted increasing concern with the complexity of the archaeological record. What have to be understood in the first instance are specific situations that are influenced by a large number of factors. These factors include environmental constraints, internal dynamics, cultural traditions, competition with neighboring cultures, and innovations of internal or external origin. This complexity of causal factors resembles that studied by historians. Evolution is no longer seen as a unilinear sequence, as neoevolutionists viewed it, or as a set of multilinear sequences, each correlated with a different type of natural environment, as Steward did. It is not enough to explain how societies evolved from one level to another; archaeologists must also explain how each society has been influenced by its relations with its neighbors. What is known in the way of generalizations about human behavior and cultural change must be used, as far as possible, to try to explain individual situations that in their specific detail are unique. If historians, after generations of intensive research, continue to debate the reasons for the disintegration of the Roman Empire, it is surely unrealistic for archaeologists to believe either that complex processes can be explained by simplistic formulations or that complexity necessarily precludes understanding. This historical approach also raises a whole series of questions ignored by processual archaeologists.

Among these is the question of the degree to which cultures or societies truly constitute systems: are they tightly integrated, as neoevolutionists believe, or do they merely have to fulfil a limited number of cultural prerequisites necessary to sustain themselves, while the rest of their content can vary relatively freely and hence is open to being significantly influenced by ideas from neighboring cultures (Aberle et al.

1950)? The latter view of culture is close to that of historical particularism. While few archaeologists have abandoned the terminology of a systems view of culture, many would no longer agree with Steward's (1955:182) claim that diffusion can only duplicate internal processes of cause and effect and Harris's (1968:377–8) view that it is a non-explanation. There is now a tendency to agree that societies are altered not only by political and economic pressures from neighboring ones but also by ideas that are borrowed from these societies to the extent that they develop in ways they would not have done had these specific external stimuli not been present. There is also growing concern with the roles played by religious beliefs in bringing about social change, some of which represents the revival of an explicitly idealist position. What is more significant than extreme materialist or idealist positions is that most archaeologists refuse to adhere to either one of these positions. Increasingly they are seen not as points of departure but as questions that in due course may be answered inductively. These views bring archaeology into line with the standard eclectic and inductive position of most American ethnologists (Trigger 1982).

Contextualism

The rejection of neoevolutionism has been provided with a new focus in recent years by Ian Hodder's contextual approach. Although Hodder is British, his ideas have attracted growing minority support in the United States and are now recognized as a specific challenge and rival paradigm to processual archaeology (Binford 1986). Basic to contextualism is Hodder's ethnographically well-documented claim that material culture is not merely a reflection of ecological adaptations or sociopolitical organization but an active element in human relations and that it can be used to disguise as well as reflect social relations (Hodder 1982a). This view runs counter to the Binfordian position that the relative amount of wealth consumed in burial rituals in a particular society reflects the degree of social differentiation within that society (Brown 1971; O'Shea 1984). Hodder and his supporters argue that in some cases burial customs may reflect an ideal of simplicity not practiced in everyday life or other concepts related to hygiene or status competition (Chapman et al. 1981; Pearson 1982). It is maintained that it would become clear, if archaeologists discovered evidence of palaces as well as hovels, that egalitarian burial practices reflected a social ideal rather than social reality. On these grounds contextualists argue that it is necessary to examine all possible aspects of an archaeological culture in order to understand the significance of each part. Yet, while contextualists may assume that the discrepancy between simple burials and palaces would reveal the ideological basis of these burial practices, in the absence of written records an archaeologist might alternatively conclude that the high-status burials had not yet been found. Considerations such as this result in many American archaeologists viewing Hodder's ideas about material culture primarily as a caveat against a simplistic interpretation of archaeological evidence.

The contextual view also denies the validity of the distinction between what is culturally specific and what is cross-culturally general; which was the basis of Steward's dichotomy between history and science. It validates an interest in culturally-specific topics, such as art styles, cosmology, religious beliefs, and astro-nomical knowledge. These were topics that were studied on the fringes of processual archaeology during the 1960s and 1970s but were treated by it as matters of little importance because they could not be integrated into its ecological concerns. By contrast, contextual archaeologists, who are searching for order within individual cultures, are strongly interested in cultural phenomena of this sort. There is much admiration for the pioneering work of the recently deceased French archaeologist André Leroi-Gourhan (1968), who demonstrated patterns in the way paintings of different animal species were distributed in relation to each other and located in different parts of caves in Western Europe during the Upper Paleolithic period; and for Alexander Marshack's (1972) evidence of seasonal patterns in associated mobiliary art. The contextual approach has encouraged the analysis of a wider range of patterning in the archaeological record, such as the orientation of Neolithic tombs in Europe (Tilley 1984) and similarities in tomb and house patterns in particular cultures (Hodder 1982a:218–29; 1984), which were ignored by processual archaeology. Yet no way has been found to move beyond speculation in interpreting the meaning of such regularities when only archaeological data are available. Archaeologists have had more success in relating the designs of houses and gardens in colonial New England and Virginia to values and class attitudes documented in historical texts (Glassie 1975; Deetz 1977). The situation is similar to that encountered by art historians, who can find order in the themes and style of Greek statuary and in the way these changed over time. Yet while they can formulate these changes in aesthetic terms, without written records they could not understand their cultural meaning to the Greeks.

The study of patterning in material culture is strongly influenced by the structural approach of the French anthropologist Claude Lévi-Strauss, especially his study of the relations underlying themes of native American mythology. Ernest Gellner (1982) has drawn an elegant contrast between disciplines, such as ecology and economics, which study the order resulting from the scarcity of resources, and the structural approach, which studies the order that human beings impose on those areas of their lives which by virtue of their symbolic nature are subject to no natural scarcity. Yet what is the relation of the symbolic order to economic and adaptive behavior? It is no longer possible to maintain that the symbolic aspects of material culture are merely a reflection of the economic and social order, but to what extent are they free from the latter? How can it be determined if specific cases are reflections, inversions, or some other transformations of economic and political relations? Hodder is interested in seeing if cross-cultural regularities can be found in such aspects of behavior as attitudes towards dirt or the elaboration of pottery decoration (Hodder 1982b). If such regularities exist, they would probably have their basis in uniformities of human psychology. They would constitute the basis of more extensive patterning in human behavior than most anthropologists now recognize and require significant additions to Gellner's concept of two types of uniformity.

The contextual approach also stresses the importance of cultural traditions as factors playing an active role in structuring cultural change. These traditions account for a major part of the knowledge, beliefs, and values that members of a particular group share at any one time. If environmental factors, technology, changing relations of production, and ideas of external origin play significant roles in bringing about cultural change, the latter requires reworking, redefining, or obliterating selected aspects of historical traditions. The traditions themselves can also play an active role in resisting or promoting changes. Because it is impossible to determine, on the basis of general principles, the specific content of a cultural tradition at any one point in time, archaeologists cannot predict detailed trajectories for specific prehistoric cultures. Yet when these traditions are known, they can increase the archaeologist's ability to account for what is happening. Under these circumstances, it is no longer possible to maintain that all explanation is equivalent to prediction. There is growing acceptance that some explanation takes the form of a statistical-relevance model, whereby an event is explained when all the factors statistically relevant to its occurrence or non-occurrence are assembled and an appropriate probability value for its occurrence is determined in the light of these factors (Salmon 1982:109). What is not added is that this method closely resembles the traditional one used for sound historical explanation (Dray 1957). Moreover, not all the factors involved in explaining complex situations are equally rigorous from a scientific point of view. The historical characteristics of archaeology do not rule out its value for producing broad generalizations concerning the direction in which specific classes of societies might be expected to evolve in the long term or as a basis for planning for the future. Nevertheless, predictions for specific societies must be based on detailed factual knowledge as well as on the best currently accepted social science theories, and even then allowance must be made for unexpected factors.

Yet American prehistoric archaeology has not moved in a historical direction to the extent that it has begun seriously to integrate native prehistory into a more comprehensive history of North America. The main weaknesses of current historical syntheses of archaeological data are their continuing domination by ecological approaches and lack of attention to culturally specific regularities (Snow 1980; Milanich and Fairbanks 1980; Mason 1981). Archaeology has also not begun to see itself as a methodology for studying the past within a broader discipline of prehistory; a view commonly held by British archaeologists and advocated in the United States by Irving Rouse (1972). There is now growing a realization that the anatomical and chemical analyses of human skeletal remains may reveal as much about prehistoric diets as floral and faunal analysis and even more about band exogamy than does the study of artifact styles (Katzenberg 1984; Kennedy 1981). Yet in studies of native American prehistory there seems to be less awareness than ever of the value of combining the study of archaeological data with the findings of historical linguistics, oral traditions, historical ethnography, and historical records, although it is clear that many problems about prehistory can be resolved in this fashion. Nor is it clear how studies of primate behavior can be combined with the ethnology of modern hunter-gatherer societies and with archaeological evidence to resolve problems of hominid behavior (Isaac 1971; Binford 1984; Cartmill et al. 1986). Yet the growing emphasis on inductive approaches and on understanding the development of specific historical sequences is gradually weakening the disinclination of many archaeologists for interdisciplinary studies of this sort. In American studies of African prehistory there is a strong tradition of such studies stemming from G. P. Murdock's (1959a) historical-ethnological research, and the example set by British archaeologists working in Africa, many of whom have come to teach in American universities (McCall 1964). There is also a tradition of collaborative research in studying Polynesian prehistory, which began during the culture-historical period (Jennings 1979); while Joyce Marcus (1983a) has recently argued the advantages of such an approach for Mayan archae-ology. The resistance relates mainly to the widely held view of processual archae-ologists that their discipline is a science based on the study of material culture, which they interpret as a challenge to do as much as possible with archaeological data. Most processual archaeologists, who maintain that their ultimate goal is to study human behavior and cultural change, seek to maximize the autonomy of archaeology by relying only on universal generalizations about relations between material remains and human behavior to translate archaeological data into information about human activities. The realization that many aspects of human behavior cannot be understood by means of universal generalizations reveals the limitations of this approach and may in due course encourage the employment by archaeologists of a broader range of techniques for understanding the past.

Critique of positivism

The questioning of positivism has produced a relativistic awareness that the questions archaeologists ask and the answers that they judge to be acceptable are influenced by their personal beliefs and attitudes and those of the society in which they live. This has encouraged studies which reveal the degree to which interpretations of archae-ological evidence have unconsciously expressed contemporary social values or been deliberate attempts to impose these values on the past (Gero et al. 1983). Other studies have documented how wealthy patrons (Hinsley 1985) or government funding agencies (Patterson 1986b) have shaped the development of archaeology through selective support of research or how sexual stereotypes have biased the interpretation of archaeological data (Conkey and Spector 1984). As a result of these studies there is more awareness that archaeological interpretation must be understood in relation to the social, political, and historical context in which it occurs. Relativists argue that even archaeological data are mental constructs and hence not independent of the presuppositions of the milieu in which they are utilized (Wylie 1982, 1985c). These views are directly contrary to the positivistic outlook of the New Archaeology. The latter maintains that while the questions asked by archaeologists may reflect contem-porary social conditions, provided that archaeologists have sufficient data and follow sound analytical procedures, the results will be a scientific statement that is uncon-taminated by ideology or personal prejudice. Relativists disagree about whether archaeological interpretations can ever be more than an expression of ideology and personal opinion or knowledge of the subjective factors influencing their thinking can help archaeologists to transcend these limitations and achieve greater objectivity in their work (Miller and Tilley 1984: 151; Leone 1982). This is an old and unresolved debate among professional historians.

It is clear that the movement towards greater historicity in American archaeology has been influenced by Marxist concepts, particularly within the context of symbolic, structural, and critical archaeology. Most of these ideas have been mediated through the para-Marxist Frankfurt School, the structural Marxism of Louis Althusser, and French Marxist anthropology (Bloch 1983:141–72) and have reached the United States largely through the work of younger British archaeologists (Spriggs 1977, 1984; Miller and Tilley 1984). There is little interest by self-styled Marxist archaeologists in either America or Britain in the theoretical views of Soviet archaeologists, which are summarily dismissed as sterile, or in the writings of Gordon Childe, who was the only Western archaeologist of his generation who seriously assessed the work of his Soviet colleagues (Trigger 1984c, 1985).

The most important "borrowing" from Marxism is the realization that conflicts that develop within societies concerning the ability of different social groups to control the production and allocation of goods and services is a major internal stimulus to change. This dialectical view, which is the antithesis of the ecological determinism of the New Archaeology, puts human beings at the center of social change in a totally different form from non-Marxist efforts to lessen the rigidity of ecological determinism by broadening the range of external factors that determine human behavior. Following the lead of French Marxist anthropologists, some American archaeologists have treated conflict between men and women, age groups, and clans as sources of change in pre-class societies that are analogous to class conflict in more complex ones (Miller and Tilley 1984; Spriggs 1984). Also explicitly Marxist is the view of ideology as a factor masking unequal social relations and therefore seeking to diffuse social conflict. This view is now being applied to understanding both how ancient societies operated and how archaeological evidence is interpreted (Miller and Tilley 1984).

Other views have been influenced at least in part by Marxist concepts. The idea that each prehistoric society was in some irreducible fashion a unique entity and that its origins must therefore be explained in a historically specific way echoes Marx's observation that what are transformed at every stage of history by the changing relations of production are the existing conventions of societies. Childe (1936 [1965 ed.: 100]) elaborated this point for archaeologists when he argued that the nature of parliamentary government in Britain in the nineteenth century could not be predicted from generalizations about the nature of capitalist societies. Instead it was a historical precipitate of British institutions altered by changing economic and political relations which had brought new classes into political power. Likewise, relativistic views of social science knowledge have close affinities to Marxist views, although they also appeal to those who are sympathetic to the hyper-empirical historiography of the now old-fashioned von Ranke school, which stressed the value of facts and tended to regard interpretations as little more than expressions of personal opinion (Carr 1962:2–3; Mandelbaum 1977). They also have affinities with the views of the British archaeologists Stuart Piggott (1950) and Glyn Daniel (1950), who have related archaeological interpretations to changing intellectual fashions, such as rationalism and romanticism. The writings of both archaeologists, which express views that have much in common with historical particularism, have been widely read in the United States.

The utilization of Marxist concepts by American archaeologists corresponds with Leszek Kolakowski's (1978:524–5) observation that Marxist ideas, whether recognized as such or not, are widespread in Western intellectual life, but at the same time have become disembedded from a broader Marxist framework. It is therefore doubtful that Marxism as an integrated philosophy exerts any significant influence in American archaeology. The strongly idealistic emphasis in much American self-styled Marxist archaeology is not in keeping with the orthodox Marxism of the Second International or of Soviet social science. These archaeologists ground their work on the sound principle that no one denies that the essence of human life is simultaneously both material and symbolic (Conkey and Spector 1984:24). Yet some of them seize upon Engels's observation that "the various elements of the superstructure . . . also exercise their influence upon the course of the historical struggles and in many cases preponderate in determining their form" (Marx and Engels 1962, 2:488) to argue further as the French anthropologist Maurice Godelier (1977, 1984) does, that in specific cases politics or religion can play a dominant role in shaping social change. While such arguments help to move archaeological interpretations away from the vulgar materialism of processual archaeology and encourage a more historical perspective, they repudiate the basic Marxist principle that "the mode of production in material life determines the general character of the social, political, and intellectual processes of life" (Marx and Engels 1962, 1:363). Hence such interpretations have only tenuous claims to be regarded as Marxist. They ignore the Marxist view that while human groups make their own history in terms of pre-existing values and ideas no less than in terms of nature and technology, these values and ideas have themselves been shaped by economic activity (Kohl 1981a:112). They also ignore Childe's (1942) well-documented argument that while the superstructure has historical significance, its influence is mainly negative. Although political manipulation or ideological obfuscation can slow or halt change, progress can result only from changes in the means and relations of production. There is also no clear exposition in American "Marxist" archaeology of the complementarity of evolutionary theory and detailed historical analysis, as found in the writings of Marx and Engels, and little awareness of the unity of theory and practice as exemplified in the life's work of V. I. Lenin.

Discussion

The new trends in American prehistoric archaeology do not represent a movement in the direction of historical materialism, but rather a drift towards historical particularism, a doctrine in keeping with the intellectual obfuscation currently rampant in American popular culture (Harris 1981). Regardless of the sophistication of the contextual and Marxist-influenced approaches, extreme forms of these views are encouraging a return to an analytical position that anthropologists long ago abandoned as sterile. They also ignore the implications of data concerning human behavior collected over the last two centuries. If the new historicism rightly tries to account for cultural variations ignored by the neoevolutionary New Archaeology, there is a danger that it may ignore the considerable regularities that neoevolutionism has documented.

Yet it does not appear likely that American archaeology will sacrifice the accomplishments of the last thirty years to embrace a neo-Boasian historical particularism. What kind of compromise is likely to emerge? Archaeologists will probably abandon the idea that only traits that are cross-culturally recurrent are worth understanding. They will also try to understand specific sequences of development in their complexity and will reject the view that prediction is the only form of explanation. It is unclear if American archaeologists will recognize this as historical explanation, although that is what it will be. At the same time archaeologists will continue to delineate and explain cross-cultural regularities in human behavior. They will probably seek to construct an evolutionary theory that is concerned not only with the regularities exhibited as societies develop from stage to stage but also with how interacting societies at differing levels of complexity influence one another. For the first time archaeologists would be employing an evolutionism that seeks to take account of colonial relations past and present. Finally American archaeologists are likely to become more aware of the intellectual links between individuals and societies that study the past and how they view that past. This will make them more aware of the nature of United States society at the same time that it may allow a more objective understanding of the past.

It is harder to predict how American archaeologists will handle the issue of causality. If even a moderate emphasis on understanding cross-cultural regularities continues, material factors will likely still be regarded as significant constraints on human behavior and therefore as major factors influencing cultural development. It is likely, however, that there will be less emphasis on specifically ecological or technological factors as major constraints and more on broader economic factors, such as relations of production. Attention will also be paid to the constraints imposed on social and political organization by general-systems factors. Ideologies and beliefs will likely be viewed as far from passive aspects of the system within which economic change occurs. What is unclear is the importance that will be accorded to ideological variables and the extent to which they will be seen only as negative factors blocking change or as factors promoting it in an independent fashion.

Whatever happens with respect to views of causality, the growing sense of the unity and complementarity of history and evolutionism in American archaeology should allow it to develop beyond the vulgar materialism of processual archaeology, the idealism of historical particularism, and the ersatz Marxism of critical, symbolic, and structural archaeology. The result is not likely to be an ideological convergence between Soviet and American archaeology. Hopefully, however, it may permit a constructive debate between Soviet and American archaeologists centering on the interpretation of cultural change as well as exchanges of specific data and discussions of what these data mean in terms of human behavior.

2

Aspects of the application of evolutionary theory in archaeology

R. C. DUNNELL

Setting aside the general developmental idea with which the term evolution is associated in English, there are two distinctly different explanatory systems that bear this label and that are current in American archaeology. One, of course, is the methodology initiated by Darwin (1859) in the mid-nineteenth century, linked to genetics in the mid-twentieth century (e.g. Fisher 1930; Haldane 1932), and which today constitutes the foundation for the scientific understanding of the organic world and its diversity. The second explanatory system called evolution is more commonly identified as cultural evolution. Although it is frequently conceived as the application of principles of biological evolution to cultural phenomena (e.g. Yoffee 1979), even cursory examination demonstrates that it is a fundamentally different methodology (Blute 1979; Dunnell 1980). Cultural evolution, as a system of explanation, is far more ancient than biological evolution. Its rigorous expression as a "theory" is usually traced to Spencer (e.g. 1857), at about the same time as Darwin was forwarding his methodology. As was also true of biological evolution, cultural evolution fell from favor in academic circles in the early twentieth century, not to be revived until mid-century largely by the work of White (1949). White (1959b) plainly recognized that his position was at variance with evolution in the natural sciences as did many other early workers (e.g. Carneiro 1967; Sahlins and Service 1960). This revival of Spencerian evolution was initially limited to sociocultural anthropology; archaeologists found little of value in it at first (Willey 1961). Its first, and most lasting, archaeological impact has come in the study of complex society. In this context, Flannery (1972a; cf. 1983) has been the most rigorous and systematic proponent. However, the societal types or stages associated with cultural evolution (e.g. Fried 1967; Service 1962) have seen much broader use in recent years (e.g. Bender 1985; Braun and Plog 1982), even though the origin and implications of these constructs have not always been recognized.

As a result of the homonymic terminology and the common objective of explaining the course of human development, the two systems had been so thoroughly conflated that Blute (1979) could accurately label biological evolution as an "untried theory" in American anthropology. The picture is but slightly different today. Although methodological discussions (e.g. Blute 1979; Dunnell 1980, 1982) have raised professional consciousness and stimulated some attempts at theory development (e.g. Leonard and Jones 1986; Marks and Staski 1986), actual use of a Darwinian evolutionary theory has been exceedingly limited (e.g. Boyd 1986). Certainly the most comprehensive attempts have been those of Rindos (1980, 1984) in explaining the development of agriculture.

Given the confusion that surrounds the term evolution in American archaeology, it is critical that the two kinds of explanatory systems be differentiated clearly and their relation to scientific inquiry understood. I have undertaken this task elsewhere in some detail (Dunnell 1980) so only an outline of that analysis need be presented here. The body of this chapter is directed toward elucidating the application of scientific evolutionary theory, as a generalization of biological evolutionary theory, to archaeology. In the process, I hope to show why scientific evolution has been slow to be implemented by archaeologists and suggest some of the directions that theory development must take for it to become effective in the archaeological context. I conclude with an example to demonstrate its current value.

What is evolutionary theory?
Scientific theory
Scientific theories are self-contained systems for explanation of empirical phenomena. They contain two elements, a set of primitive definitions or basic concepts and a set of rules or laws which relate the concepts axiomatically. The concepts generate a data language, a set of terms, that dictate how phenomena must be described in order to be explained by the laws (Lewontin 1974a). The same concepts also structure how research questions are posed. Theory functions to generate hypotheses, models of the empirical world, that can be falsified by comparing the models with descriptions of phenomena.

Science does not "interpret" experience apprehended *a priori*; it constructs an experience that is explained axiomatically by its laws. Cause is lodged in the axiomatic relations among concepts rather than in the empirical world (Willer and Willer 1974). The link between cause and phenomena is accomplished by positing mechanisms sufficient to produce the observed result.

The systematic element characteristic of scientific knowledge arises because all hypotheses are generated by the same theory within a given field. Thus the results obtained in testing one proposition have direct, explicit implications for all other propositions in the field. The cumulative character of scientific knowledge is a consequence of using a single epistemology, an empirical standard of truth (Hesse 1978), in accepting or rejecting all results.

Cultural evolution
Cultural evolution, when measured against this standard, is not scientific. Its "theory" is constituted by empirical generalizations about the course of human history or, more accurately, what is believed to have been the course of human history. The "believed-to-be" part is significant because archaeology had a negligible role in the development of the cultural evolution methodology; it was created largely from data on contemporary peoples to explain contemporary peoples. Developmental relations, ancestor–descendant relationships, are thus not part of the empirical basis of cultural evolution. They are imputed *ex post facto*.

More importantly, cultural evolution is, by virtue of this construction, tautological, not just in the self-contained sense of all theory, but in a substantive sense. The rules which are said to explain the human record are rephrasings of intuitive observations made about the record. Progress, or some other assumed model of history, is cast as the cause of cultural evolution, rather than an observation about history. This characteristic compels cultural evolution to be vitalistic, that is, to attribute cause to the phenomena being studied, rather than locating cause in the theoretical system. The course of human history is the way it is believed to be because people made it that way. Human intention becomes the only proximate cause of human phenomena. Apart from excluding cultural evolution from the family of sciences, vitalism has numerous other implications for cultural evolution and its relation to the rest of knowledge. For example, if human intentions cause human history and diversity, then do we suppose that squirrel history and diversity, or oak tree history and diversity, or star history and diversity are the consequence of squirrel intentions, oak tree intentions, or star intentions? Generally not. These phenomena are understood without recourse to vitalism, and successfully so to judge from our ability to manipulate large segments of the world around us. Recourse to vitalism effectively isolates the study of any phenomena associated with people from all other scientific knowledge. In more substantive terms it draws an inviolate man/nature dichotomy that compels the view that people are unrelated to the rest of the natural world. How we came to be human is enigmatic by definition; people are a special creation, not because of empirical evidence but because we are constrained to think so by the cultural evolution methodology.

What makes this approach superficially plausible is a confusion between reason giving and scientific cause. We all have reasons, or at least suppose we do, for our actions, things that stimulate us, motivate us to action. In the context of daily life we regard reasons as causative, and, indeed, to the extent they are accurate and motivational, they are causative *but not in a scientific sense*. Scientific cause attends why people walk across streets, or murder, or whatever, not why a particular individual decided to do any of these things. Scientific cause as contained in a theoretical system does not motivate anything to action. Einstein's theory of relativity did not change how matter and energy, time and space, interact. It explains physical forms and processes in a useful way.

There is, of course, no reason to suppose that a large variety of animals in various lineages have not developed a system of motivation similar to our own. We cannot study their motivational systems, however, because we have no access to them. This confusion between reason and cause has made cultural evolution attractive; it allows archaeologists to account for the record in exactly the same way they account for themselves – they just imagine what they would do or should do were they there.

Substantive tautology also has another debilitating effect. It precludes empirical testing and forces its users into an interpretive mode. Since its "theory" is also its conclusions, the possibility of being wrong empirically cannot arise. Particular interpretations can be more or less popular, but there is no definitive way to show that one is better than another. So archaeology and other disciplines that use such a methodology find themselves wandering from one interpretive fad to another, the popularity of which is mainly dictated by attitudes in the larger society rather than any increase in empirical control of the subject matter.

Although not entailed by the methodological elements already mentioned, cultural evolution, particularly in the form adopted sporadically in archaeology, also takes a particular ontological position on the significance of variation usually called essentialism or typological thinking (Mayr 1959; Sober 1980). History is conceived in the same manner as synchronous phenomena. The phenomenological world is constituted by "types" or "kinds," variation within which is not accorded explanatory significance. This attitude is objectified in stages, phases, and foci which are accorded empirical status. Explanation consequently focuses on the transformation of one "box" into another. Change is compressed into the lines separating units. This feature of cultural evolution is not important because it contrasts with scientific ontologies. It does not. Many sciences, physics and chemistry to name but two, are precisely of this sort. However, it is in marked contrast with Darwinian evolution where the adoption of a new metaphysical position, materialism, was requisite to extending science from the historical realm of physics to the study of change (Lewontin 1974b).

Cultural evolution, as an explanatory system, is not bad in some absolute sense; it is, however, fundamentally different from those systems of explanation grouped as sciences. It employs different notions of cause, lacks theory in the usual sense of the word, and employs an entirely different research strategy.

Biological evolution

Biological evolution is, on the other hand, an unusual but nonetheless scientific theory. It is unusual because it addresses questions of ultimate causation (why things exist) rather than functional causation (how things work). In common with other scientific theories it makes empirical claims that are falsifiable, treats cause as theoretical, and supplies mechanisms sufficient to account for its observations. Because evolutionary theory explains kind as a consequence of change rather than difference, its methodological focus is on variation.

Biological evolutionary theory is founded in two simple observations: organisms find themselves in a finite world, finite in terms of energy and space; and, organisms are not identical, they embody variation. It takes the ontological position that kind is explicable by change, that things above the scale of individual are transitory configurations of greater or lesser stability in continuously changing populations of organisms. Evolutionary theory provides a set of mechanisms that relate variation to kind through change. It is fundamentally concerned with information or character reproduction and it is in this that it differs from all other scientific theories.

Structurally, biological evolution is strictly applicable only to phenomena that reproduce. In biological evolution, trait transmission is usually seen as effected by a single system of transmission – genetics. Consequently, evolution is frequently defined as change in gene frequencies. There are two sets of mechanisms that operate on trait transmission; one generates variations and the other structures them. At the genetic level, variation is generated by *mutation*; at the organismic level, *recombination* and its attendant mechanics add to this source of variation in sexually reproducing organisms. The principal mechanism responsible for structuring variation is *natural selection*. Selection is objectified in differential reproduction and is the theoretical expression of the finite world observation much in the same manner as mutation gives theoretical expression to the observation of variation. Because no two organisms are identical and because there are limits on energy and space, organisms compete. The outcome of such competition inevitably leads some individuals to reproduce more effectively than others. If the basis of individual variation is heritable, that is, transmitted from individual to individual, differential reproduction will lead to patterns in variation over time. There are other mechanisms, of course, such as drift, immigration, and emigration that play a role in the structuring of variation, but, in general, their role is minor in relation to that of selection.

Two grand variations of evolutionary theory are recognized, Darwinism and Lamarckism. They differ on one fundamental point (Gould 1979). In Darwinian evolution, the generation of variation is independent of selective conditions. The factors that control variation are different from those which create patterns in the variation. Darwinian evolution is a two-step process. In the Lamarckian version the generation of variation is controlled by the selective force such that change is a one-step process, with the role of selection reduced to that of removing mistakes. Lamarckian evolution is not used in contemporary science simply because no mechanisms have been identified that allow selective conditions to generate variation. The key point is, however, that Lamarckian evolution is not inherently unscientific; it is rejected because current understanding of mechanisms renders it unparsimonious in relation to the Darwinian model. The choice between the two is empirically founded. Should a general mechanism for generating directed variation be documented, Lamarckian evolution would become just as valuable to science as Darwinism has proved to be. The popular notion that Lamarckism is distinguished from Darwinism because it operates on "acquired" traits is fallacious and arises from the confusion between reason-giving and cause noted earlier. All biological evolution operates on traits "acquired" from ancestors.

While the main features as outlined are not controversial and are capable of generating a vast range of explanations of living phenomena, there are areas of general importance still poorly developed, most especially determining what empirical entities constitute individuals in evolutionary theory (alternatively, at what scale[s] does selection act) (e.g. Lewontin 1970; Maynard Smith 1976; Stanley 1979) and in relation to specific questions such as the cause of speciation (e.g. S. J. Gould 1980; Stebbins and Ayala 1981). The scale of selection issue has already been identified as critical to any extension of biological theory to people (e.g. Dunnell 1980; Marks and Staski 1986). These issues are too complex to more than mention in a brief chapter such as this; however, it is important to recognize that biological evolutionary theory is not complete and remains controversial in some important aspects.

Is scientific evolutionary theory applicable to people?

There is no *a priori* reason why people cannot be treated scientifically. The only requirement of a subject matter by science is that it be empirical; if there is an empirical subject matter, then a science can be constructed for it. People have been and are often treated in non-scientific ways, but no one would contend that people lack empirical substance. So the real issue is not whether people can be studied scientifically but the applicability of evolutionary theory.

Strategies for application

Biological evolution is just that. It is a theory that developed in the context of biology. It is designed to explain a particular range of phenomena of concern to that field. In consequence, one cannot simply assert it is applicable to cultural phenomena un-critically. There are two general strategies that have been employed in the extension of evolutionary theory to people.

The simplest strategy is to assert that people are not qualitatively different from any other organism and therefore biological evolution is directly applicable to cultural phenomena. While it is exceedingly difficult to fault the general assertion on empirical grounds, as humbling as it might be emotionally, using this proposition as the basis for the application of biological theory in archaeology and anthropology presumes that biological evolution has been unaffected in its conceptual structure by its historical focus on a non-human subject matter.

Sociobiology (e.g. Alexander 1974, 1975, 1979; Lumsden and Wilson 1981; Van den Berghe and Barash 1977; Wilson 1975, 1978) represents just such an attempt. The liabilities of the general approach are well exposed by sociobiology. As I have already noted, biological theory relies on a single mechanism of trait transmission, genetics. In consequence, direct application of biological evolution to cultural phenomena *requires* genetic transmission of all parts of the human phenotype. In particular, it assumes genetic determination, either directly or indirectly, of human behavior. It further assumes that transmission operates on particulate "bodies" analogous to genes (e.g. the "memes" of Dawkins [1976] and the "culturgens" of Lumsden and Wilson [1981]).

Plainly, these assumptions are not justified. A large fraction of the human pheno-type, including most behavior, is demonstrably the product of a different system of transmission, cultural transmission. Individuals learn behaviors from their parents and unrelated conspecifics (see Boyd and Richerson [1985:46–53] for a review of empirical studies). This observation is *not*, however, a warrant for regarding people as qualitatively distinct from other animals. As Bonner (1980) has assayed in some detail, many other animals transmit significant, but much smaller, segments of their pheno-types culturally as well. Further, no one has suggested any plausible empirical analogs to genes that could be regarded as empirical interpretations of "culturgens." Because cultural transmission plays a small role in non-human species, a role that could not even be investigated until biology took a serious interest in animal behavior, it is not surprising that biology could operate effectively for a long time using only genetic transmission. For these reasons, among others (e.g. Maynard Smith and Warren 1982), evolutionary theory as used in biology and strictly applied to cultural phenom-ena has relatively low explanatory power. Sociobiology has, of course, had many benefits in the form of insights about behavior generally and that of people in particular, but it is not a general strategy likely to maximize the potential of evolutionary theory.

The second strategy has taken the form of generalizing biological theory, principally by recognizing the existence of cultural as well as genetic transmission (e.g. Boyd and Richerson 1985; Cavalli-Sforza and Feldman 1981), although the significance attributed to cultural transmission varies (cf. Durham 1976). The theory's development has been carried primarily by people with interests in cultural phenomena, rather than biologists as is the case with sociobiology. As a result, the expansion of evolutionary theory has been guided, at least initially, by seeking analogies between the units and processes of the biological theory and cultural phenomena. This strategy has yet to produce a complete, robust theory. Some of the lacunae are probably a function of the analogic approach itself. For example, some authors (e.g. Rindos 1986a) suggest that, in addition to a new transmission mechanism, a more general theory will also include an additional mechanism of selection, "cultural selection." In my view, this is premature and not warranted by cultural data as yet; however, its importance is ambiguous because of the unresolved nature of the scale of selection and how it is to be measured in biological theory. More concretely, one of the major sources of insight in such works as Cavalli-Sforza and Feldman (1981) and Boyd and Richerson (1985) lies in the use of simple mathematical models of transmission. When these models draw upon generations as the basis of computation, one of the most important reasons for holding cultural transmission distinct from genetic transmission is negated. Cultural transmission can and does take place throughout the lifetimes of individuals, albeit at different rates. It is difficult to see how ignoring this is any less pernicious than continuing to insist that cultural transmission operates on particulate "memes."

What has clearly emerged from these efforts, however, is a general recognition that genetic transmission is not inherent in, nor essential to, evolutionary theory. It is but one empirical expression of trait transmission. All that is required by the theory is that phenotypic traits be heritable, that is, transmitted, and not that this is accomplished by any particular mechanism. Selection, the principal mechanism for producing patterns in variation, lacks any means to differentiate traits inherited through different mechanisms. This does not mean that the mechanism of transmission is irrelevant. I have already noted that cultural transmission mitigates many of the effects of generations. Lower fidelity of transmission likewise must have major effects, dominantly in rates of change. Generally, as Boyd and Richerson (1985:240) note, "similar selective regimes may result in very different equilibria." The key point, however, is that evolution theory is just as effective with multiple mechanisms of inheritance as it is with one and that the existence of cultural transmission does not mandate the construction of a parallel but separate "cultural evolution." Cultural transmission is just as relevant theoretically to biology as genetic transmission is to the study of people.

Anthropologists and archaeologists have intuitively appreciated the significance of cultural transmission for a long time. Although culture is a rather nebulous "concept" in anthropology because of the variety of different concepts that share this label (e.g. Kroeber and Kluckhohn 1952), one of the principal notions holds that culture is the transmission of traits by learning, often mediated by symbols. In archaeology, this view of culture can be traced explicitly at least as far back as Rouse's (1939) early explications of culture historical method. If culture is taken to be a transmission mechanism, then "cultural phenomena" can be specifically interpreted as those elements of the human phenotype that are generated by this kind of transmission process rather than simply calling any behavioral trait associated with people cultural. Boyd and Richerson (1985:34–6) provide an insightful discussion of the importance of this distinction. One of the more exciting early results from these efforts at theory construction is the possibility of explaining how culture as a transmission mechanism may have itself evolved (Rindos 1986b), a point on which traditional cultural evolution must remain enigmatic.

Increasing the number of mechanisms of trait transmission may prove to be the only major alteration required to convert evolutionary theory from a strictly biological theory to a general scientific theory. There are, however, a number of secondary consequences with important ramifications. Cultural transmission, for example, reopens the possibility of Lamarckian-type evolution by providing, at least intuitively, a mechanism that might link the generation of variation to selective conditions. This point, however, requires careful *empirical* study, if only because folk wisdom, as represented in the "necessity is the mother of invention" cliché, takes a decidedly Lamarckian tone. Similarly, cultural transmission opens the real possibility that under certain conditions, selection may exert its greatest influence on individuals larger than the organism bounded by a skin by providing a mechanism by which organisms are functionally bound into larger *reproductive* units (e.g. Boyd and Richerson 1985; Dunnell 1978a; Marks and Staski 1986). Elsewhere, for example, (Dunnell 1978a, 1978b; Dunnell and Wenke 1980) I have suggested that complex society, a perennial focus of both anthropological and archaeological interest, may be little more than the manifestation of a shift in the scale at which selection is most effective.

Even though one cannot point to a complete and robust theory at this point in time, I think it is clear that evolutionary theory is applicable to people. Further, it is also clear that simply borrowing biological evolution or constructing simple analogies with it is not going to prove very profitable, however useful these approaches may have been in the initial stages. The modern thrust is to rewrite biological evolution in more general terms so that it is applicable to all living things including people. Even though considerable progress has been made in the last five years (e.g. Boyd and Richerson 1985; Cavalli-Sforza and Feldman 1981), there are still important theoretical issues that require resolution.

Application to the archaeological record

There are two features of the modern theoretical development which are easily overlooked but critical if one's interests lie in using evolutionary theory in an archaeological context. First, most efforts have been directed, as was the previous section of this chapter, to showing that people, as creatures, present no unique problems for evolutionary theory once our emotional investments are discarded and the theory itself relieved of its historical constraints. Second, these efforts have been carried out in a contemporary context and treat behavioral variables directly. Such demonstrations are essential, but they are a long way from showing that evolutionary theory, even in a general scientific form, has any potential for archaeology.

The archaeological record may have been produced by the actions of people but, whatever else might be said about it, the archaeological record is not people nor is it human behavior. In fact, it is the absence of behavior that allows us to identify the archaeological record as the archaeological record. It does not move or interact in any way other than that characteristic of sedimentary particles. So showing that evolutionary theory is applicable in some general way, even powerful, when applied to contemporary cultural phenomena, says nothing whatsoever about its applicability in archaeology.

Reconstruction

The great temptation is to ignore this fact, or try to overcome it by manufacturing reconstructions. In essence, reconstruction creates a set of "facts" analogous to those on which evolutionary theory would operate in contemporary circumstance. Although reconstruction has been the principal activity of many, many archaeologists for a long period of time and the main thrust of the new archaeology, it is demonstrably defective as science on two counts, one methodological and one substantive.

First, and perhaps most obviously, the reconstructions are not generated by the theory that will be used to explain them. Consequently, they constitute *ad hoc* conceptions of the phenomena of the archaeological record in respect to evolutionary or any other theory designed to operate on behavior. A reconstruction is not a categorization of phenomena in a way to make it explicable; it contains information not contained in the empirical record. In short, it is an inference about the record, and it is these inferences, not the phenomena, that would be the subject of explanation. In recent years propositions used to generate the reconstructions have been formally recognized in "middle range theory" (e.g. Binford 1977, 1980a), propositions which we are told *should* be different from those used to explain it. It is obviously underlain by a belief in objective knowledge, that the external world can be known independently of the means of knowing it. This is a position that has not been philosophically respectable for 35 years (Hanson 1958). Even if this were not the case, the reconstruction approach simply negates any effort at testing through falsification. Does a lack of isomorphism between model and description arise because the model is incorrect or the reconstruction constituting the description is incorrect?

Reconstruction is flawed even more fundamentally. To create a behavioral reconstruction, one has to associate certain behaviors with the time transgressive objects and their locations that constitute the contemporary archaeological record. This is formally recognized in "actualistic research" and ethnoarchaeology (Binford 1980a). Relations between behavior and material must be invariant if they are to serve as timeless, spaceless rules for reconstruction. This amounts to an assertion that behavior cannot change. Behavioral change, however, is precisely what archaeologists hope to describe and explain. In the last analysis reconstruction employs an essentialist or typological metaphysic that is inimical to explaining change because it eliminates change. This is precisely why biological evolution had to embrace a materialist metaphysical position (e.g. Lewontin 1974b; Mayr 1959).

Of course, valuable insights have come from these efforts, but so long as archaeology desires to be scientific or is interested in explaining change, reconstruction, no matter how rigorous, is defective. Reconstruction is attractive for only one reason (Dunnell 1982). In the absence of archaeological theory, common sense, our own cultural system, provides the means of explaining the archaeological record. Common sense operates on ordinary English terms so it requires that the archaeological record be translated into everyday terms.

An evolutionary view of the archaeological record

Scientific explanation requires that the discipline's theory generate its own data. So the real question is, can evolutionary theory be used to describe the archaeological record directly? The ultimate applicability of the theory hinges on just this point. If the terms used by evolutionary theory cannot be used to describe the archaeological record, then the archaeological record cannot, ever, be explained using that kind of theory. What then is the status of the rocks and bones and sticks and stones that constitute the record in evolutionary theory?

In a critique of the then popular pseudo-Linnean hierarchy of cultural units in the southwest, Brew (1946:44–6) once contended, "potsherds don't breed." For Brew, as for many others, this observation forever closed the door on evolutionary applications in archaeology. What is expressed in this statement is a point made earlier – analogic approaches to the application of evolutionary theory are doomed to failure. A nonevolutionary construct "potsherd" is found to be inconsistent with evolutionary theory. This could have been known *a priori*.

Selection, the principal mechanism imparting pattern to variation, operates on phenotypes. The human phenotype, just as the phenotype of any other organism, has two analytically separate components: the materials bounded by the individual's skin and its behavior (Mayr 1970:442). In the standard genetic view of transmission, both parts of the phenotype are generated from information contained in the genetic code. In a more expanded scientific view, cultural transmission as well as genetic transmission are responsible for the phenotype in both human beings and other animals. These codes also contain the information for maintaining the individual, for replicating various elements, like body cells, at different rates.

Artifacts are the hard parts of the behavioral segment of phenotypes. Artifacts are not unique as a class to human beings. Lots of organisms build things, from shells, to nests, to dens and dams. Further, like people, some of their behaviors leave traces that would be called sites (e.g. the shell middens accumulated by muskrats provide an obvious example – Binford's *Bones* [1980a] supplies many more). So while it is true that potsherds do not evolve, it is true only in the same sense that bones do not evolve or brains do not evolve. Note, too, that the mode of transmission is not necessarily linked to a particular phenotypic segment. Birds' nests are probably largely determined genetically (though only in a general way, given the kinds of modifications in materials and shapes individuals employ in particular circumstances), but much of their behavior is culturally transmitted. You cannot generate a robin solely from a robin egg; you have to have robin parents as well.

The point is simple if somewhat counter-intuitive at first. Artifacts do not "represent" or "reflect" something else that is amenable to evolutionary theory; they *are* part of the human phenotype. Consequently, artifact frequencies are explicable by the same processes as those in biology (Leonard and Jones 1986).

People produce many more artifacts under a wider range of conditions than do other animals. Rather than setting people apart, artifacts may play a critical role in understanding organic evolution generally simply because they provide empirical access to the behavioral part of animal phenotypes. Thus anthropology may well become an important contributor to, rather than just user of, evolutionary theory.

Development and use of evolutionary theory in archaeology

There are many implications of this view for the conduct and structure of archaeology. If evolutionary theory is to be used as more than just another interpretive algorithm, "business as usual" with a new vocabulary, then the very foundations of archaeology as it is presently constituted must be changed.

The magnitude of the change required is much greater than that which Kuhn (1962) identified with scientific revolutions. Use of evolutionary theory not only requires construction of a new theory, the kind of thing on which Kuhn focuses, but also adoption of a new materialistic metaphysic and a new empirical epistemological standard. Above all else evolutionary theory hinges on variation. The materialistic view of variation mandates the abandonment of modal descriptions that suppress variation, including such archaeological favorites as phases, cultures, and periods. Archaeological types, variously regarded as empirical (e.g. Spaulding 1953) or analytical (e.g. Ford 1954) in traditional archaeology, must be restricted to the latter role. For the same reasons, behavioral reconstruction, as a methodological tool, must be abandoned, for not only is it defective, but its functions, translating the archaeological record into English or anthropological terms, will be usurped by evolutionary theory.

These are truly wholesale changes. Some of them have already been suggested in the Americanist literature (e.g. Binford [1968a] on the importance of variation; Plog [1974] on the liabilities of phases), but to date nothing like an integrated revision of the discipline has taken place along these lines, partly because of the influence of cultural evolution.

At the theoretical level, a new systematics that categorizes the archaeological record in terms that can be explained is essential. Elsewhere (Dunnell 1978b) I suggest that the first step in this process must be the separation of those elements which are measurably affected by selection (functional attributes) from those which are conditioned only by the process of cultural transmission (stylistic attributes in traditional archaeological usage, though not synonymous with analyses of "style" in some contemporary works where style is the English word rather than a particular

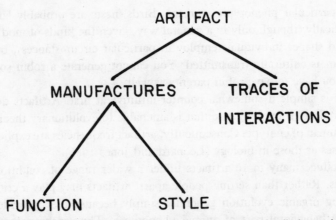

Fig. 2.1. Archaeological systematics required by evolutionary theory. "Artifact," when understood as anything which has one or more artificial attributes, must first be subdivided to isolate those components which are part of the human phenotype (manufactures) from those other elements of the environment modified by human activity (traces of interactions). Phenotypic elements must be further differentiated into components affected by selection (function) and components conditioned only by cultural transmission (style).

concept embedded in a larger theory). A further implication is that the traditional use of artifact to identify all objects that display evidence of human activity must be divided to distinguish those elements which are strictly part of the human phenotype and those which have arisen incidental to the interaction of people and their environment (Fig. 2.1). A key contrast with traditional categories is that theoretically informed systematics carry with them empirical expectations about distributional characteristics (e.g. Dunnell 1978b; Leonard and Jones in press) that allow one to determine definitively whether, for example, a given element is style or function in a particular context.

Evolutionary theory is not, at present, capable of explaining much of the archaeological record. The outstanding successes such as Rindos's (1984) account of the origins of agriculture are possible only in limited areas that require dominantly non-human data. Even in cases such as this, the theory is not used to account for specific data because the relevant variables have yet to be described. Archaeology finds itself in much the same position as biology some decades ago. As Lewontin (1974a:8) notes, one cannot describe the empirical world in any old fashion and then expect to be able to explain it with a particular theory. The descriptive terms must be the terms used in the theory's laws and processes. The construction of an evolutionary archaeology is going to require a lengthy settling-in period during which reformulating processes will lead to better description and better descriptions will inform on how to improve the construction of theory.

As the foregoing implies, the principal reason why detailed applications of evolutionary theory are lacking lies in the quality of data archaeologists have amassed from the record. Guided by approaches underlain by essentialist views on the nature of variability, types, phases, and cultures rather than descriptions of variation structure our data. Until this is corrected on a large scale, no serious progress in using evolutionary theory or understanding change can take place. Nonetheless, evolutionary theory can suggest ways to understand existing data, if only grossly. One example may serve to suggest something of its importance in this role.

Cultural climaxes and waste

Not all of an organism's energy is devoted directly to reproduction or maintenance of individuals until reproduction has taken place. Some energy, for example, may be converted into body fat which, because the chemical process is reversible, represents stored energy against unforeseen environmental perturbations. The net loss in numbers of offspring, which must accompany such uses of energy, is apparently offset by the increased likelihood of survival of those which are produced, much in the manner in which parental care acts to increase overall fitness at some expense to simple reproduction. One immediate benefit of viewing organisms in this fashion is that it points out the signal importance of energy storage regardless of the particular mechanism that may have evolved to provide this capacity. Archaeologists have, in fact, already realized this important issue in its most direct expression (e.g. Rindos 1984; Stiles 1979). There are, however, decided physical limits to which storage can be put to offset environmental perturbation, be its manifestation body fat, oil reserves, or stored food.

The behavioral component of the phenotype offers similar and additional potential when energy is expended in activities that do not enhance the rate of reproduction, activities that might be conceptualized as "waste" from a strictly reproductive point of view (Isbell 1978). Energy so expended, however, cannot be recovered at a later date, so these mechanisms are less efficient as adaptations for environmental perturbation. In this regard, waste-type behavior is similar to morphological structures created by irreversible chemical processes (e.g. the antlers of the Irish elk which are usually "explained" by functional scenarios that draw upon such untestable notions as a function in attracting females). The role of waste in coping with environmental perturbation is twofold: (1) the use of energy itself necessarily lowers the birth rate (e.g. Harner 1970); and (2) it provides, through its temporary abatement, a reservoir of time that an organism can devote to subsistence and/or reproduction in difficult conditions. It is easy, thus, to see how waste-type behavior can be fixed by natural selection under specific sets of circumstances (Fig. 2.2). When environmental perturbations are modest and/or predictable, larger numbers of offspring will enhance fitness, but when perturbations are severe and/or unpredictable, then waste will be fixed commonly by selection.

Because of the scale at which these phenomena are manifest, they can be translated directly into archaeological terms. Cultural elaborations (cultural "climaxes"), for example, are frequently explained by increasing subsistence development (e.g. appearance of agriculture) or by the accumulation and redistribution of "surpluses." If this were the case, then one would expect elaborations to show a steady increase through time and occur in the geographic centers of adaptations. These expectations, however, are often not realized. The Woodland period in the midwestern United States is a good example. Its earliest segments are distinguished by the presence of a

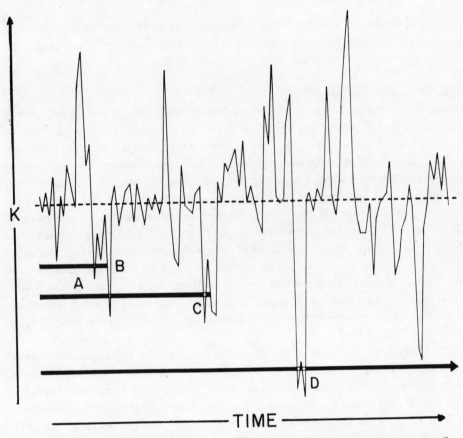

Fig. 2.2. Simplified model of the selection of "waste." Mean carrying capacity (———) is held constant (i.e. no environmental trends and no change or difference in subsistence). Three heavy bars represent different populations in equilibrium at different sizes (i.e. size differences are due to different efficiencies or amounts of "waste"). All populations can persist through minor short-term shortfalls in productivity (A); however, drastic shortfalls (B) and/or repetitive shortfalls (C) will cause emigration or extinction. In the short run, larger populations are more fit but, in environments which experience large unpredictable fluctuations in carrying capacity, populations stabilized at smaller sizes by waste-type behavior will be at an advantage not only because of the smaller size but also because temporary abandonment of waste provides a reservoir of time to allow "intensification" (D).

mortuary cult that frequently entails the laborious construction of earthen mounds and the manufacture and disposal of vast quantities of goods, many of which are costly imports. The traditional position is that it represents a climax associated with at least the beginnings of agriculture (e.g. Willey 1966). The "collapse" of this phenomenon, represented by lackluster Late Woodland phases, poses an explanatory problem of significant proportion; explanations usually call upon environmental change and its supposed effects on the supposed agricultural system (Griffin 1960; Gunn and Adams 1981).

Taking the mortuary cult to be an expression of waste, a rather different picture emerges. First, its origins should lie on the periphery of the Woodland, a fact confirmed by Dragoo (1963). Secondly, investigators who looked at subsistence data (e.g. Caldwell 1958; Dunnell 1972) found no reason to regard Woodland phases as agricultural (in contrast to mainstream archaeological thought that linked elaboration to subsistence and thus was compelled to conclude that agriculture in some form was required to account for the appearance of the mortuary cult). Recent isotopic fractionation studies have confirmed the non-agricultural status of the Woodland associated with the mortuary cult (e.g. Bender et al. 1981). Rather, agriculture makes its appearance in the Late Woodland. Agriculture increases the carrying capacity and in so doing lowers the fitness of waste-type behavior in relation to higher birth rates. Thus the loss of waste does not represent some kind of collapse or "devolution" but the predictable effects of the appearance of agricultural subsistence.

Scenarios such as this have limited value. They serve to suggest the potential of evolutionary theory and they suggest some of the variables that are critical for documentation. The dangers are, however, great. It is all too easy to regard them as full-fledged evolutionary explanations, rather than simply as a warrant to pursue the documentation of variability in cultural phenomena. To the extent that they are so regarded, they will obstruct the development of evolutionary theory and its use in archaeology.

Summary

Evolutionary theory has seen limited use in American archaeology for a number of reasons. Initially, confusion with Spencerian cultural evolution was the principal impediment. Once this was recognized, it became apparent that evolutionary theory as employed in biology could not simply be transferred to the cultural realm. In turn, this recognition has stimulated efforts to generalize the biological theory so that it is applicable to all living things, not just the genetically transmitted component of non-human species. As the outline of a more robust theory has begun to take shape, it is also apparent that the way in which archaeologists have typically acquired and described their data precludes the use of even a general evolutionary theory because of the typological metaphysic that underlies traditional practice. Variation, not modal description, is required in an evolutionary view.

It is clear that evolutionary theory can be applied in the archaeological context. It is also clear that its application would greatly change our understanding of human development while at the same time firmly ground archaeology in science and lead to cumulative knowledge. It is not clear, however, that American archaeologists are willing to make the kind of effort that is required to accomplish this goal when "interpreting" the archaeological record yields immediate, intuitively satisfying results.

3

The "New Archaeology," then and now

LEWIS R. BINFORD

A review of the arguments and developments that characterized American archaeology during the late 1950s and early 1960s shows that several basic positions were
being advocated, and, as a result, subsequent archaeological work has pursued several
different directions. Central to the arguments advanced by so-called New Archaeologists in America was the issue of *how to accurately give meaning* to archaeological
observations. This concern, at least during the 1960s, was embedded within arguments that addressed how archaeologists had traditionally given meaning to the
archaeological record. The early years of this discussion, which opponents called the
"New Archaeology" (generally said with scathing sarcasm), were characterized by
attempts to evaluate the validity or accuracy of the propositions that had guided the
interpretation of (and the assignment of meaning to) archaeological remains by the
leading archaeologists who had been our teachers. The ideas that the New Archaeologists criticized might be thought of as basic aspects of the culture-history view of
culture, which dominated the writings of archaeologists during the 1930s, 1940s, and
1950s.

Culture history is first and foremost an idealistic approach to understanding. By
idealism I mean "any system or doctrine whose fundamental interpretative principle is
ideal" (Runes 1962:136–7). Most anthropologists and archaeologists were not mentalists in that they acknowledged a reality (e.g. historical or environmental) outside of
their own minds, but they were idealists in the sense that culture was considered to be
a product of the workings of individual minds as those individuals reacted to the
events of cultural and natural history. If any order in culture history could be
demonstrated or any predictive knowledge could be gained about culture, it was
thought that a greater understanding of individual psychology was the key.

It is not possible to predict the behavior resulting from historical events
that made the people what they are. The problem is essentially a
psychological one and beset with all the difficulties inherent in the
investigation of complex mental phenomena of the lives of individuals.

(Boas 1938:5–6)

At the same time that culture was seen as being understandable in idealistic terms
there was a tendency to distrust the methods of the natural sciences as they had been
developed by the end of the nineteenth century. Part of this distrust lay in the reaction

against "analogies" or the selective study of similarities (in modern parlance, the use of etic categories). This Boasian shaping of American anthropology and its subfield, archaeology, has been summarized as follows:

> The second issue on which historians and physicists differed was the legitimacy of the study of phenomena having "a merely subjective" as opposed to an "objective" unity. Physicists would grant the legitimacy of certain types of historical studies. But even here, the physicist does not study "the whole phenomenon" as it represents itself to the human mind, but resolves it into its elements, which he investigates separately; and insofar as he was interested in the history of these elements, it was in order to create a "systematical arrangement" whose order was "objective." On the other hand, the historian insisted on equal scientific validity of the study of more complex phenomena whose elements "seem to be connected only in the mind of the observer"; and in studying them, he was interested not in elements but in the "whole phenomenon."   (Stocking 1974:10)

Searching for similarities – analogies, as they were commonly labeled – violated an important tenet of the idealistic philosophy with which Boas-influenced culture historians worked. Things that to us appear to be similar may have been dissimilar by virtue of the idealistic integration achieved for those phenomena in the minds of the ancients. Understanding this integration was viewed as the only "correct" way to understand varying cultural responses to environmental and historical stimuli. One had to uncover the underlying cultural context that conditioned the way past individuals reacted to external events and stimuli.

In such an environment of thought, archaeology was in a very paradoxical position. The materials remaining from the past were seen as the only sources of potential knowledge about the past, yet the causes of those remains, the way the world had worked, was a knowledge inaccessible to the archaeologist using only those material remains. Past dynamics were seen as the consequences of unique interactions achieved in ancient holistic cultural contexts operating in conjunction with the "laws of the human mind," which together conditioned how individuals reacted to events in their social and natural environments. Since the causes were said to be idealistic, the archaeologist saw only material by-products as they had been structured by ancient idealistic forces. Because no further understanding seemed possible, archaeologists did not search for theories to explicate the actual workings of those dynamics. There was no way to anticipate relationships between the character of the alleged causes and the character of material remains that might have been idealistically structured in the past. There was no apparent way to recover the intellectual contexts or to formulate laws of the human mind, since it was essentially denied that these "variables" would condition in regular ways properties of artifacts and other material remains archaeologists might find. Archaeologists operated with a theory that basically claimed its irrelevance to the things that archaeologists studied!

An archaeologist may recover material but not the substance of aboriginal artifacts. The exact meanings of any particular object for the living group or individual is forever lost, and the real significance or lack of importance of any object in an ethnological sense has disappeared by the time it becomes a part of an archaeologist's catalogue of finds.   (Griffin 1943:340)

Traditional archaeology could not address itself to the testing of theory since relevant information on assumed seats of causation was not preserved. In addition, the results of the operation of causal forces could only be described and systematized but could not be investigated since there were thought to be no regular relationships between similar material things and the meanings – the cultural contexts – in terms of which they were integrated in the minds of past man. The paradox of adopting a strict empiricist's view of science while at the same time adopting an idealist's theory of causation, where the "black box" – the minds of the ancients – was not available for investigation, placed archaeology in a strange position indeed.

Strict empiricism argued against inference and interpretation, yet the past was gone and could only be known through inference from the remnants surviving in the present! The position adopted by traditional archaeologists publicly assumed that similarities did not necessarily imply similar causal conditions. Inference was therefore only justifiable when continuity and stability could be assumed between the past and the present. Under these conditions these modern contexts could be used to guide interpretation. Such beliefs by the archaeologists left the remote past, for which no "historical" connection could be demonstrated between the archaeological remains and contemporary peoples, seemingly beyond the pale of archaeological illumination. Nevertheless, archaeologists studying the remote past did offer inferences and interpretations. When they did so they appealed to "the other half" of the traditionalist's view of cultural causality – the concept of human nature as elaborated by an assumed understanding of "culture" viewed as a unique by-product of that underlying human nature. This particular approach to archaeological interpretation was suspected by New Archaeologists as being a sterile and misleading convention.

First and foremost, traditional archaeologists side-stepped the problems of inference by adopting a set of conventions for assigning meanings to their data. They committed what in any science would be considered a basic error: they stipulated the meaning to be given to generalizations made from their data. They did not seek to know the world in its terms; they assumed they knew what the world of culture was like, and they proceeded to order the world of archaeological experience in these *a priori* terms. In a productive science the aim is to learn something of the limitations and inadequacies of one's received knowledge. The tactics of traditional archaeology prevented the archaeologists from availing themselves of this possibility.

Perhaps the most explicit and understandable exposition of the strategy of traditional archaeology has been given by Robert Dunnell (1971). He provides one of the best discussions of what traditional archaeologists did and also what they thought they were doing that I have been able to find. Dunnell correctly suggests that a very simple argument permitted traditional archaeologists to link their observations of phenomena (their data) to the *a priori* ideas they held about that data.

The field is that encompassed by the concept *artifact*, objects which owe
some of their attributes to human activity. The problem similarly is to
provide categories for these data that are cultural, for the ultimate purpose
of explaining the products of human behavior and with them the behavior
that created them in terms of ideas held in common by the makers and
users.   (Dunnell 1971:130)

At the root of this argument is the idealist assumption that the causes of the
archaeological record, and any derivative information obtained therefrom, were the
ideas held in the minds of past people.

Prehistory assumes that attributes which are the products of human
activity and which recur over a series of artifacts . . . can be treated as
manifestations of ideas held in common by makers and users of those
artifacts.   (Dunnell 1971:132)

In other words, traditional archaeologists forged an analytical linkage, by stipulation,
between the generalizations archaeologists might make from their data, commonly
called patterns, and the alleged causes, the shared ideas held by past peoples.

If the attributes considered are only those which are the products of
human endeavor, it follows that any explanation of these attributes is
necessarily done in human rather than natural terms. If their
distinctiveness lies in their humanness, then so does their explanation.
Further, given our assumptions about the uniqueness of the
phenomenological world, recurrence or sharing necessitates an ideational
element in the explanation.   (Dunnell 1971:133)

If several objects hold features in common, and those features are of
human origin, there is but a single plausible account. Intentionally or
unintentionally, consciously or unconsciously, the objects were made to
look alike by people who can be treated as possessing similar ideas about
them and who have the same categories of features and ways of articulating
the features into whole artifacts. In short, the objects can be treated as
expressions of the same mental template.   (Dunnell 1971:132)

The definition of culture not only stipulates the element of human
involvement (ideas) but restricts this general field to that set of ideas which
can be assumed to be shared. This is a most crucial point, for it is here that
the articulation of phenomena with concepts is made. This connection
necessarily must be made by means of assumption . . . Prehistory assumes
that attributes which are the products of human activity and which recur
over a series of artifacts . . . can be treated as manifestations of ideas held
in common by makers and users of those artifacts. Thus the link is made
between the phenomenological and the ideational.   (Dunnell 1971:133)

In fact, the archaeologists were not linking the archaeological record with the *ancients'* ideational milieu but with their own. In addition, this link between the phenomeno-logical (the world of experience) and the ideational (the ideas about that world) was made, as Dunnell noted, by assumption. The world of experience was assimilated directly with the archaeologists' prior beliefs about the world, and thus experience could never be used to expose limitations in our beliefs and ideas, nor could it be used to guide evaluations of their utility or accuracy. The goals of science as a learning process were effectively cut off, closed to participation by archaeologists.

Under the above solution to the "archaeologists' paradox" – namely, working with a contemporary world of material phenomena and believing that it was to be understood in terms of an idealist past – the practice of archaeology became essentially a game. Just as one plays a game within the framework of stipulated rules for participation, so did the traditional archaeologists. Their energies were directed toward competing, using their personal skill linked with their knowledge of archaeological data, within the framework of the prescribed rules of the game. Little puzzles were recognized during the course of playing the game, and much energy was directed toward their solution. In reality this activity took the form of an endless and energetic search for new observations on the archaeological record, since only the generalizations made directly from the data could change the views of the past proposed by archaeologists. Their interpretative procedures were a closed system of stipulations not subject to evaluation from experience, that is, not subject to tests using the data. The under-standing of the past was changed by archaeologists as a simple function of changes in the amount and quality of data available for generalization. New discoveries were the means to fame and recognition, not critically designed research aimed at evaluating ideas (theories) used in interpreting such discoveries. This was an intellectual climate in which archaic empiricists' ideas thrived. The good archaeologist was the one who could synthesize observations and generate defensible generalizations seemingly directly from the phenomenological world of artifacts. Once done, the interpretation seemed to flow self-evidently from the facts. Truth about the past seemingly came directly from the remains of the past; the role of all those stipulated meanings used in interpretation was largely not acknowledged by archaeologists who were "playing the game." Those who were sarcastically referred to as New Archaeologists questioned the utility of the game for gaining a knowledge of the past by questioning the accuracy and adequacy of the stipulations used in assigning meanings to archaeological observations.

The situation in traditional archaeology was a classic example of history as described by Bruce Trigger (1978:26–7):

History differs from the generalizing social sciences only in that its
primary aim is to explain individual situations in all their complexity
rather than to formulate general laws for indefinitely repeatable events and
processes. That is what is meant by saying that history is ideographic, the
social sciences monothetic . . . This does not mean that historians deny
the existence of general rules; rather they seek to employ them to gain an
understanding of individual (i.e. unique and non-recurrent) situations.

The generalizing social sciences, on the other hand, extract recurrent variables from their socio-cultural matrix so that relationships of general validity can be established between them.

Traditional archaeology was a "law-using" (rather than law-formulating) field addressing itself to the interpretation and elucidation of unique events and conditions of the past. To New Archaeologists, the problem seemed to be clear: where did these laws used for historical interpretations come from, and were they valid? Another problem might be recognized by asking whether archaeology was "historical" by virtue of its law-using posture or by virtue of its desire to know about the past. Did the latter interest limit our methods for learning to the law-using posture? Oddly enough, a historical discipline like geology did not seem to be so limited! To many New Archaeologists the answer to this question was a resounding no.

The use of general rules to explain a concrete situation is no less an act of creative skill than is the formulation of such rules to explain repeated correlations. Because the aim is to explain a particular situation in all its complexity, the application of such rules serves as a test of theory, and because a variety of different bodies of theory may have to be applied in conjunction with one another, historical interpretation serves as an interdisciplinary arena in which the explanatory power of different theoretical approaches may be ascertained.   (Trigger 1978:27)

The situation in traditional archaeology did not seem conducive even to the demands of valid inductive argument, which as suggested above is basic to the study of history. Archaeological laws were stipulations about the meaning of properties of the archaeological record in general, and they never seemed to lead to the explanation of "particular situations in all their complexity." Inferential assessments, such as whether people were culturally similar or different, whether a migration or invasion of culturally distinct peoples occurred, or whether one ethnically distinct people differentially "influenced" surrounding peoples as judged from measures of similarity viewed through time, did not seem to measure up to the goal of "explain[ing] particular situations in all their complexity." As traditional archaeology was practiced its historical orientation never led to the testing of theories, which as stated above is a component of "good" history. All archaeologists' interpretations were either theory-dependent or *ad hoc* inferences, and in both cases the world of experience was accommodated to the theory through the stipulations or accommodative arguments offered as to the meanings of observations. It seemed quite possible, and even necessary, for archaeology to maintain its goals for the growth of historical knowledge, but the methods advocated by "culture historians" did not seem to be appropriate given those interests; there had to be better ways of learning about the past.

Because our criticisms of traditional archaeology were so strong, the challenge facing the New Archaeology appeared overwhelming to many of us. We began in obvious ways. First, it was recognized that *generalization* was the basic source of new views of the past arising from traditional approaches. We began to explore the methods of generalization, emphasizing sampling strategies and more sophisticated methods for pattern recognition. At the same time, we wanted to know if the stipulated links between archaeological experience and interpretation were accurate and valid. We had to know how to interpret patterns once valid generalizations could be made. This problem seemed to demand a testing program aimed at evaluating the utility and accuracy of ideas. This procedure was science. The scientific method was never a component of traditional archaeology; only the fit between generalization and the data was commonly evaluated under the older procedures. It was in this context of problem recognition that we began to explore the epistemological procedures available to us for evaluating ideas. Emphasis was placed on deductive forms of reasoning since the problem as it was perceived in the 1960s was one of evaluating the utility of ideas already in existence. There was never a claim for the absolute priority of deduction over induction, as many critics have asserted. We fully acknowledged the crucial role of induction, while at the same time we realized that inductive arguments were not "verifiable" by simple reference back to the manner in which they may have been constructed in the first place.

What is argued here is that the generation of inferences regarding the past should not be the end-product of the archaeologist's work . . . The main point of our argument is that independent means of testing propositions about the past must be developed. Such means must be considerably more rigorous than evaluating an author's proposition by judging his professional competence or intellectual honesty.   (Binford 1968a:17)

Given the situation as it was perceived in the 1960s, it was the propositions basic to traditional archaeology that were in need of validation independent of the seeming "strength" with which they had been presented by authorities. Deductive argument seemed an important avenue to explore.

Second, it was argued that the acknowledged "law"-dependent status of history was inappropriate to archaeology. Historians are said to draw upon the "sciences" for their theories utilized in interpreting historical documents. Our "historical documents" were archaeological remains, and we could find no scientists who were already studying such phenomena. We could find no rules being produced by other scientists that informed us about what our phenomena, pottery sherds, house remains, garbage, and so on, might mean in either historical or processual terms. We concluded that archaeologists themselves had to accept the challenge of theory development; we had to develop and evaluate the rules used for interpreting our data. Archaeology had to become a science concerned with understanding the significance of patterning observed in the archaeological record. Importantly, it also had to evaluate the ideas it used when interpreting observations and patterning. No other science was addressing our phenomena or our problems.

Finally, it was argued that in so far as the character of the past was an inference from contemporary observations made on the archaeological record, the archaeologists had to decide "which past" should be the target of their inferential constructions. In any concrete archaeological situation the archaeologist faced some segment of the archaeological record, some "site" or collection of archaeological materials from a region. The situation represented the potentially unique, discrete characteristics of past dynamics. Since dynamics could be manifest at different levels or scales (e.g. varying but cyclical phenomena or variable but internally differentiated phenomena not indicative of organizational change or variability between systems), before archaeologists could cite formal variability in the archaeological record as indicative of large-scale processes, evolution, systems change, ethnicity, or even such historical events as migrations, we had to be able to diagnose the archaeological record at differing organizational scales. Variability in the archaeological record did not necessarily have reference to a single scale of dynamics. Variability was not directly referable to modifying processes; it may equally and ambiguously refer to stable but internally complex processes. Variability in the archaeological record may have reference to multiple and differing causes and conditioning phenomena. The archaeologists not only had to diagnose the statics of the archaeological record in dynamic terms, but in addition they had to diagnose the relevance of those dynamics with respect to differing goals of knowledge seeking. These three general points of view conditioned and guided the development of research by New Archaeologists.

During the 1960s, research and argument was begun on two of these points. The factors that might be internal to a system and yet condition variability among archaeological sites with reference to pottery styles were explored (Longacre 1963; Hill 1965). At roughly the same time arguments were initiated regarding the "meaning" of seemingly anomalous patterning (with respect to traditional assumptions) in lithic materials documented within the Mousterian sequences of the Old World (Binford and Binford 1966). These early researchers were working from the perspective of the third approach described above, but the presentation was commonly made as if we were "testing" the validity of the stipulated meanings traditionally used by earlier archaeologists and/or the propositions that made possible alternative arguments. Unfortunately this posture was adopted by some who focused on the testing aspects (Fritz and Plog 1970; Watson et al. 1971) that New Archaeologists saw as a necessary component of archaeological activity. It was clear that if we were to succeed in confronting the issue of the accurate linkage between our observations and our ideas, testing had to be accomplished. Ironically, most of this early research did not succeed in testing traditional arguments but instead dissolved into what I have called "arguments of relevance" (Binford 1983b:3–20). The validity of propositions was not being evaluated directly – only the relevance of those propositions to certain specific cases.

This was an important learning experience for most of us. It brought home forcefully the need to confront directly the second point listed above, namely to be engaged directly in theory building and to accept the scientific responsibility for the growth of our understanding of the archaeological record itself. The attempts by some to propose and test theory simultaneously were clearly misleading (see Binford's [1983b:14–17] discussion of Plog's work). Rather than testing the traditional propositions, the tempo of the field shifted very quickly to a demand for new theory and finished historical models. Clearly, in this posture the idea of testing the traditional propositions appeared to be a waste of time. Given this shift in emphasis from the early testing attempts to the more ambitious need to develop our own science aimed at understanding the archaeological record itself, both testing and the growth of knowledge were linked in a new and fascinating manner.

When I went north to study the Nunamiut, I sallied forth as a beneficiary of the learning that the early days of the New Archaeology had provided. My Nunamiut research was certainly a testing of the traditional archaeologists' stipulations as to the significance of variability in the archaeological record, but it was more. It was an attempt to develop a methodology for evaluating from archaeological remains the relevance and meaning of variability in the archaeological record, which could then be used in evaluating or rendering judgments of relevance for the organizational knowledge gained from the Nunamiut experience. I emphasized these aspects of the research because I felt that the discussion on testing had at that time become extremely confused. My research rested on the recognition of what any good designer of scientific experiments already knows: a general theory cannot be tested on the assumption that all cases (or experiments) are equally relevant to the testing. The scientist engaged in testing theories must be able to unambiguously isolate critical and relevant experiences – any experience *per se* is not necessarily relevant.

From my perspective, a good example of the use of irrelevant arguments (in this case propositions rather than experiences) is provided by Ian Hodder. Although Hodder maintains that ideas cannot be tested or evaluated by scientific means, he ironically claims that he has tested (and discounted) the general approaches of the New Archaeology by virtue of having demonstrated that humans act intentionally! Was denial of the ability of humans to act intentionally ever a proposition critical to the positions advocated by the New Archaeology? No. The only argument advanced by New Archaeologists of which I am aware was that apparent free will and volitional action by individuals was not the explanation for long-term historical processes. Intentional action was never denied; it was only suggested that human actions could be explained as manifestations of other causal forces, and it was maintained that intentional acts were not *the* causal force standing behind history.

The problem of relevance for the archaeologist is central and crucial. This arises from the fact that all interpretations of archaeological observations are inductive arguments of some kind. Importantly, the successive introduction of propositions into an inductive argument requires that two features be sustainable: (a) the propositions are accurate, and (b) they are relevant to the materials being interpreted. A proposition may be accurate but irrelevant, inaccurate and irrelevant, inaccurate and relevant, or accurate and relevant. Evaluations must be made with regard to the above possibilities before the strength of an inductive argument can be judged. It is the strength of such arguments that determines the accuracy of the past we infer from our observations. Such judgments cannot be made simply from evaluations of how good the argument fits the facts. The accuracy of component propositions must be evaluated independently of the accommodative argument made to advocate their relevance and link them to a conclusion. In turn, the relevance must be judged independently of arguments offered as to the accuracy of components introduced into argument. The demonstration of the accuracy of the proposition that man acts intentionally does not establish the relevance of this fact to the explanation of a given body of humanly produced materials; intentionality may well be conditioned. In fact, one could argue that I demonstrated this in my Nunamiut study!

It was in this context of appreciation for the problem of interpretation facing archaeologists that I advocated the conscious investment in *middle-range research* as being basic to the development of archaeology (Binford 1977, 1980a). This is not the place to discuss this suggestion at length; it should be noted, however, that all inductive argument draws upon "source-side" knowledge (Watson 1979) in building arguments about its subject. Archaeologists have not pursued the study of source-side knowledge, even though it is crucial to interpretations of their subject matter. Most inductive arguments are forged by archaeologists from propositions having differing referents to domains of knowledge and areas of phenomena extant in the archaeological record. The claims to knowledge and the meanings given to observations are not all justified by reference to a given theory or paradigm; instead these archaeologists commonly appeal to many different theories and interpretative principles. The claim of many that all inferences are "paradigm-dependent" and hence tautological is not sustained by most concrete examples in inductive argument. Middle-range research is proposed as a means of developing secure and intellectually independent interpretative principles and of expanding our knowledge of phenomena of relevance to our interpretative task.

Let me see if I can illustrate the importance of this research with some concrete examples. An examination of some of the propositions basic to traditional archaeology renders the activities of New Archaeologists quite understandable. "If the attributes considered are only those which are the products of human endeavor, it follows that any explanation of these attributes is necessarily done in human rather than natural terms" (Dunnell 1971:133).

This proposition has certainly been basic to the interpretations that traditional archaeologists have offered regarding our past. It sounds very clear and unambiguous to the traditional believer. Let's see what happens to this basic proposition in scientific practice. "If the attributes considered are only those which are the products of human endeavor" is a stipulation of relevance as discussed above. How have archaeologists traditionally dealt with this stipulation? Certainly it is defensible to generalize that archaeologists developed "rules of thumb" for meeting this criterion of relevance. For instance, until quite recently animal bones were considered to be attributes of the natural world. They were not artifacts and were therefore not analyzed except as potential sources of information regarding past environments or climates or at best as clues to "food preferences" conceived as idealistically guided customs of past peoples. One can search in vain for any type of analysis other than species lists appearing as appendices to traditional archaeological reports. In short, a categorical approach was taken; animals were natural, and thus their bones were not "products of human endeavor." The archaeologist needed a "natural scientist" to deal with these aspects of the archaeological record. If a similar approach had been taken to stones, clearly "natural" phenomena, our field might never have developed! What was needed was not a judgment of relevance, but instead concrete investigations aimed at uncovering the *attributes* of relevance for our science. This was my middle-range approach to the study of animal bones documented in the Nunamiut book (Binford 1978). I sought to investigate the linkages between natural elements incorporated within a cultural system and attributes thereof, which could carry significant and relevant information for the archaeologist seeking to understand how a cultural system was organized.

The other side of this coin is illustrated in *Bones: Ancient Men and Modern Myths* (Binford 1980a). There I explored the willingness of archaeologists to accept categorically animal bones in the archaeological record as "products of human endeavor." In the *Bones* book I argued that there are many situations and contexts in which patterned associations may exist in nature that in no way implicate "human endeavor." It is interesting that while my Nunamiut research, the positive side of the coin, largely fell on deaf ears, the response to the *Bones* book was loud and outraged. There, of course, I had been arguing that archaeologists had made poor and inaccurate judgments of relevance, while in the Nunamiut book I was suggesting how we might make new and potentially informative arguments of relevance! In both books I was strongly advocating the fact that advances in archaeology are dependent upon archaeologists accepting the responsibility for developing their own criteria of relevance and, by extension, their own theories for meanings that could be reliably assigned to observations. I think it is sad that the most productive consequences for the field have stemmed from the *Bones* book. Many archaeologists began middle-range research not because they considered it basic to the field but because they wanted to defend their personal positions.

Let's explore another aspect of this same proposition: "if the attributes considered are only those which are the products of human endeavor." What is human? Is it the behavior considered unique to our species? If so, and if one can demonstrate in the behavior of our ancestors some property previously considered unique to our species, does it follow that the ancient actors, not members of our species, were also human? Of course I am referring here to the problem that traditional archaeology dictated for the archaeologist of the Middle and Lower Paleolithic. As outlined by Dunnell, "it follows that any explanation of these attributes is necessarily done in human rather than natural terms." As I suggested above, traditional archaeologists interested in the very ancient past could only appeal to laws of human nature when interpreting their observations. These laws nearly always took the same form as those used by any other archaeologist – interpretations of culture history in terms of the stipulations or meanings referable to culture. If we as archaeologists accept conventions of relevance, such as "man the tool maker," or arguments to the effect that an archaeological record is necessarily a *cultural* record, we are creating a past stipulated in cultural terms that may not have a historical reality. Archaeologists must accept the middle-range research challenge of investigating the unambiguous indicators for culture rather than simply accepting the old convention of equating patterned behavior, which is clearly also a product of the animal world, with cultural behavior.

If we acknowledge the possibility that our ancient ancestors, who were demonstrably different species, may well have left an archaeological record but may not have been culture bearers, then all the conventions for the interpretation of the ancient archaeological record in culture-historical terms quickly become irrelevant. Even if we accepted traditional conventions as accurate for "humans," the archaeologist of the Lower Paleolithic would be at best investigating *when* these conventions may have become relevant. Traditional archaeology provided no guidelines on this issue.

An additional problem that the fundamental principles of traditional archaeology dictated for the Lower Paleolithic archaeologist is seen in the second phrase of Dunnell's fundamental statement: "explanation . . . is necessarily done in human rather than natural terms" (Dunnell 1971:133). Of course, what the traditional archaeologists had in mind was that *culture* was the "human terms" within which explanation was to be sought. By virtue of accepting these basic tenets, Paleolithic archaeologists were in the interesting position of never being able to investigate the origins of or the conditions for the emergence of culture itself. As suggested above, if we can imagine a time when hominids produced an archaeological record yet did not yet possess the capacity for culture, then it would be both possible and important to seek an understanding of the very appearance of culture itself. Could we expect the appearance of culture to be explicable in cultural terms? Of course not. Since we cannot rule out the possibility that hominids produced artifacts but not cultural records, then clearly the basic arguments of relevance establishing the boundary conditions for traditional archaeological explanation are false, misleading, and if accepted uncritically, certain to produce conventionalism rather than research.

Many more propositions of traditional archaeology require discussion and investigation at the middle range. Investigations in contemporary archaeology of the accuracy, utility, and relevance of basic propositions introduced in inferential argument are leading to a growth in our understanding of the archaeological record. This was the goal of New Archaeology, and this goal is being pursued with productive results in contemporary archaeology.

Unfortunately, not all contemporary archaeology is productive. There are many reactionary movements advocating the use of propositions and beliefs of traditional archaeology whose limited utility has already been demonstrated. We see Richard Gould (1980) advocating the "law"-dependent status for archaeology, and at the same time advocating an idealist philosophy of culture. We see James Sackett (1977, 1982, 1986a, 1986b) seeking to subsume functional variability into his unique characterization of style, thus limiting the possibility of explaining cultural variability to the traditional view that people behave the way they do because their grandfathers behaved that way. We see Ian Hodder (1982a) and the "coggies" rediscovering traditional archaeology as if it were new and innovative. We see a new skepticism linked to the Frankfurt school of philosophy, which essentially claims that we cannot learn about a past reality – we can only create a past in "our image," so we should shift our concerns to social criticism (Saitta 1983). Finally, we have been introduced to the wonders of the "power motive" as the driving force of human nature, dictating a dialectical history and serving as the basis for appreciating our past as a guide to contemporary political truths (Miller and Tilley 1984).

As Gellner (1985:8) has said, the theoretical "barrel" is never empty. Removing bad apples does not ensure against further decay occurring in similar ways or in new and innovative ways. Throwing ideas out of the barrel, or clutching them to one's heart, does not permit evaluation – only judgment. Science is a learning process. Scientists pursue knowledge through the evaluation of ideas. Unfortunately, as we should know by now, the simple accumulation of knowledge is not sufficient to explain the cultural process. Our contemporary culture of archaeology goes on in terms frequently quite independent of science and its goals. Students of contemporary archaeology must concern themselves with much more than seeking an understanding of the archaeological record. Nevertheless, archaeology will progress as a simple function of increases in our understanding. This growth can be enhanced by the scientific evaluation of ideas, as I have illustrated here, whether or not the original ideas were "true," accurate, or ultimately proven useful. Learning goes on as we seriously investigate the properties of our own ideas as they condition the way we treat our experiences. This investigation can only be accomplished in the context of intellectual independence between our tools for experiencing and our tools for explaining. Not only is this procedure possible; it is done all the time in science. Much of contemporary archaeology appears to be engaged in a search for "truth" judged in terms of extrascientific criteria, and not in the serious job of doing scientific archaeology. This smacks of religion to me, but regardless of its connotations, it will not advance the field of archaeology. The New Archaeology was dedicated to the scientific growth of knowledge; this goes on today in spite of much opposition.

4

Marxism in American archaeology

ANTONIO GILMAN

Introduction

When Philip Kohl and I sought to organize a session on "Marxist approaches to archaeological research" for the 1974 meetings of the American Anthropological Association, we faced the problem of identifying American archaeologists who were Marxists. Numbers of anthropological archaeologists had done work which might be related to Marxist approaches, but this research did not in any explicit way acknowledge its debt to a theoretical perspective emphasizing the primary significance of the relations of production to the dynamics of social change. Indeed, more than one of those whom we invited to participate in the session responded that they were unfamiliar with Marxist theory and its possible relation to their work. As Spriggs (1984: 7) has commented:

It is only since the mid-1970s that an appreciable number of Western archaeologists have stated their interest in Marxist theory. There have of course been many other "closet" or "hidden" Marxists: those using theories clearly derived from Marxism but who have not chosen to identify the source of their ideas. It is not my intention to "expose" these authors but included among their number are several of the better-known archaeologists of the 1960s and 1970s.

The marginal position of Marxism in American archaeology even now is well expressed in the somewhat apologetic title of Spriggs's article ("Another way of telling . . .").[1] This marginality derives from various circumstances.

One significant factor has been the lack of a broad context of interest in Marxist ideas. Lowie (1937: 54) commented that, as a result of Morgan's adoption by Marx and Engels, "German workingmen would sometimes reveal an uncanny familiarity with the Hawaiian and Iroquois mode of designating kin, matters not obviously connected with a proletarian revolution." In the United States, however, the effective absence of any independent working-class political party and labor movement has meant the absence of any large audience for Marxist thinking in anthropology or any other field. Marxism has only found a place in the university, and even there its influence has been limited by the individual isolation of its proponents and by the disciplinary segmentation of the social sciences.[2] Even within universities, furthermore, overt use of Marxist theory has been limited by the pressure of colleagues and administrators. As the McCarthy period demonstrated, universities are hardly insulated from the prevailing political climate (cf. Caute 1978: 403–30), which is generally hostile to Marxism. Opler's (1961: 13) attack on the cultural materialism of Meggers ("the 'practical tool kit' Dr. Meggers urges upon the field anthropologists is not quite so new as she represents, and its main contents seem to be a somewhat shopworn hammer and sickle") would only have been harsher had his target supported a dialectical materialism. The entrance into the universities of younger people trained during the turmoil of the late 1960s and early 1970s has only partially modified the regard for self-preservation which earlier led scholars to shun Marxist positions or to take them up inexplicitly at best. That archaeologists (unlike economists, political scientists, or even social anthropologists) work in an arena relatively remote from issues that might require a direct political commitment has only made their avoidance of explicit Marxist theory easier. Be that as it may, a prudent concern for political dangers is no doubt at the root of the disclaimers placed at the conclusion of some of the archaeological studies which *have* used Marxist concepts.

Calling the [National Air and Space] Museum an ideological artifact and analyzing it in this fashion should not cause alarm; this is not a call to revolution. An analysis of this sort can be apolitical.

(Meltzer 1981: 125)

It is better to label such ideas [the Marxist notion of ideology] as materialist and leave the political involvement associated with Marxism behind . . . The ideas can then be regarded most usefully as extensions of the successful materialist approach of the new archaeology, a move which will abandon the cumbersome and emotion-laden parts of Marxism.

(Leone 1982: 757)

Given such clarion calls to intellectual action, it is hardly surprising that the impact of Marxist thinking on American archaeology has remained limited.

The most important reason for the restricted interest which Marxist ideas have had for American archaeologists, however, is the nature of the prevailing theoretical framework within which most of the archaeological work of the past generation has been conducted. When Leone presents his views as extensions of the New Archaeology of the 1960s and 1970s, this reflects the extent to which the mainstream of American archaeology has preempted much of the theoretical ground on which Marxist approaches to prehistory have been built elsewhere.

The New Archaeology has, as Flannery (1972b) has noted, two principal strands. The first involves the adoption of explicitly positivist scientific procedures in archaeological research, the use of "a consciously deductive philosophy, with the attendant emphasis on the verification of propositions through hypothesis testing" (Binford 1968a: 18; cf. Watson et al. 1971). The second involves the explanation of contrasts in the archaeological record within a cultural ecological framework ("it is to be hoped that the explanations offered [for similarities in the archaeological record] would deal with cultural or ecological processes operative in the past" [Binford 1968a: 15]). This latter aspect of the New Archaeology necessarily involves a materialist approach to the explanation of the contrasts documented in the material record of the past. That approach can avoid political complications by pointing to Darwin rather than to Marx as its source, however. Just as Bulkin et al. (1982) can claim archaeological ecology as an integral part of a Marxist approach to prehistory in the Soviet Union, just so the vast majority of American archaeologists can view the analysis of the social relations of production as an integral part of a Darwinist approach to prehistory.

Under these circumstances it is hardly surprising that only a few American archaeologists have made explicit use of Marxist concepts. Usually working in isolation,[3] these individuals have developed their ideas in the context, not of a broader political movement, but of their own research. Their work is best seen as a somewhat piecemeal, if critical, intradisciplinary commentary on certain of the deficiencies of the positivist, adaptationist cultural ecological approaches that have become hegemonic in the American archaeology of the 1980s. They have addressed two main issues – the questionable historical realism of certain aspects of the New Archaeology's ecological functionalism and the pretensions to objectivity inherent in the New Archaeology's scientism.

Marxist criticism of adaptationist ecology

The New Archaeology seeks an ecological explanation for the variability of the archaeological record. Human cultures are viewed as extrasomatic means of adaptation. Similarities and differences between contemporary archaeological complexes are seen as differences in their respective systems of homeostatic regulation. Accordingly, in a given archaeological complex, "change should be considered to occur only when the homeostatic mechanisms . . . fail to work adequately" (Hill 1977: 64). The stress which causes such change is thought necessarily to be external to the cultural system. As the same prominent practitioner of the New Archaeology has stated: "I fail to understand how a system can have internal sources of stress. There *must* be something external to the system, with which it is interacting, that causes a subsystem to malfunction in the first place" (Hill 1977: 69–70).[4] Because of the Darwinian model of adaptation underlying this approach, the external source of stress is usually considered to consist of the pressure resulting from the imbalance between a population and the resources upon which it depends. Since cultures are viewed as functionally integrated systems of homeostatic regulation, their social organization and ideology are either interpreted as facilitating that integration or (if such an interpretation seems far-fetched) dismissed as "random noise" (Higgs and Jarman 1975: 3). To give weight to the conscious intentions of individuals is "needlessly teleological" since "many system states and adaptive responses in societies are not conscious to many or most of the people involved – they are in no useful sense goal oriented" (Hill 1977: 66–7).[5] Given the immediacy of the infrastructural determination which explains similarities and differences between archaeological complexes over time and space, such complexes tend to be viewed as separate cases, largely independent both from their past and from their contemporaries. This straightforward cultural materialism provides a practical and clear sociological model, which archaeologists can use to guide them in their recovery and interpretation of evidence.

A number of American archaeologists have used Marxist principles to criticize the interpretations of prehistory put forward by their colleagues who subscribe to the dominant paradigm I have just summarized. These criticisms come into clearest focus in considerations of the nature and origins of complex class societies. From a cultural ecological perspective the leaders of complex societies function as higher-order regulators whose activities confer adaptive benefits on the mass of their followers. This view fails, however, to explain how rulers *retain* their positions even when they withhold a substantial surplus for their own use and very often provide no services to their followers (Gilman 1981). From a Marxist perspective the long-term hereditary tenure of superordinate social positions by the elites of complex societies can only be explained by the capacity of that elite to extract and retain a surplus from their subjects, that is, to exploit their subjects, a capacity variously considered to be based on the control rulers can exercise over interregional exchange (Kohl 1978) or on the rent rulers can extort from peasants committed to an intensified agriculture (Gilman 1976, 1981; Gilman and Thornes 1985; Muller 1985).

The ecological approach sees the evolution of the institutions of complex societies develop under the stimulus of the pressure of human populations against a limited resource base. As Brumfiel (1983: 263) has noted, however:

Cases of state formation in the absence of population pressure have been particularly vexing. Most ecological models of state formation have relied on positive feedback through the channels of population growth and recurring population pressure to maintain the system in a state of evolutionary change. But if state formation occurs in the absence of a serious disparity between population and resources, it seems necessary to search for some other source of systematic dynamic.

Brumfiel uses Engels as a starting point for the formulation of an approach to the origins and development of states, emphasizing their internal structural conflicts over political power based on the ability to exact tribute:

Structurally induced social conflict . . . is a three-party affair where commoners exploit elite rivalries to lighten their tribute demands, while rival elites exploit commoner discontent to gain access to office, and the ruling paramount uses whatever strategies he can devise to secure his own position against both commoners and elite rivals.

(Brumfiel 1983: 265)

Such a class analysis is developed in more explicitly Marxist terms by Zagarell (1986a) in his analysis of the early development of Mesopotamian civilization. Internal and external competition over resources develops in the context of the contradiction between "centralized government and the constraints of the dispersed power of kinship dominance" (Zagarell 1986a: 157). Zagarell (1986b) sees the further development of Mesopotamian social institutions as the result of the dynamic interaction between landholders holding their titles as members of corporate kin groups, owners of large private estates, and administrators of temple and palace estates. The potential of the last to expand their operations by exploiting the slave labor of women captured during state-sponsored warfare and using the products of such labor as commodities in long-distance exchange networks leads to the possibility of concentrating wealth outside of the network of kin obligations. State institutions develop, then, not due to causes exogenous to the social system, but in the context of class struggles within that system.

This view of matters tends, of course, to undermine the cultural ecological tendency to view societies as isolated cases responding to local environmental constraints. Just as elites seek to increase their wealth by increasing the surplus captured from subordinates within their societies, just so they seek to profit from commerce and warfare with their neighbors. Kohl's (1975, 1978, 1984a) analyses of inter-societal emulation, commerce, and conflict on the Iranian plateau and in central Asia attempts to develop perspectives analogous to Marxist studies of core–periphery relations in the modern world.[6] Such studies are at the root of Paynter's (1985) analysis of changing settlement patterns in western Massachusetts during the nineteenth century in terms of the relations between primary producers, regional elites, and homeland elites.

A cultural ecological approach to societies without social classes is fully compatible with a classical Marxist orientation. As Marx (1965 [1857–8]: 68–9) puts it:

Once men finally settle down, the way in which to a smaller degree this
original community is modified, will depend on various external, climatic,
geographical, physical, etc. conditions as well as on their special natural
make-up – their tribal character . . . The earth is the great laboratory, the
arsenal which provides both the means and the materials of labour, and
also the location, the *basis* of the community.[7]

In an effort to understand the changes that kinship-organized societies underwent prior to the emergence of social classes, American Marxist archaeologists have sought, however, to introduce a greater sensitivity to the social tensions (that is, to the contradictions) within them. The homeostatic functionalist approach sees social organization as facilitating techno-environmental practice or resulting from it. Thus, for example, the development of style zones demarcating ethnic groupings in the Upper Paleolithic has been seen as assisting the development of the cooperation required for hunting migratory herds of big game (Wobst 1976). In contrast, Gilman (1984) sees that development as a response to the lessened need for mutual assistance resultant from the development of more effective subsistence strategies. Again, the development of specialized production and long-distance trading networks during the transition from foraging to farming in the Near East has been seen as a result of the increasing importance of surplus banking in human adaptive strategies (Flannery 1965), where Kohl and Wright (1977) seek to develop a view in which exchange and competition between social groups is antecedent to the development of food production and extensive surplus banking.[8] Within a framework of analysis which is consistent with cultural ecology, Marxists thus seek to give greater causative weight to the social relations of production.

American archaeologists using Marxist approaches have developed similar positions with respect to the interpretation of ideological aspects of the archaeological record. The adaptationist mainstream of the New Archaeology sees ideational systems as the information regulating the adaptive responses of a social group to its natural and human environment. In cruder versions, Aztec ritual cannibalism is seen as a response to the protein shortages caused by population pressure (Harner 1977). In more sophisticated versions, Paleolithic art is seen as "part of the processes of boundary formation, mediation and maintenance . . . concerned with constituting the continuities and discontinuities of the human social world" (Conkey 1982: 117–18). As Leone (1982: 747) points out, even this more reasonable approach "depart[s] very little from a functionalist viewpoint which argues that recognizable information passed via religion or art assists in communication, which is basically practical."

Now, a view which sees the ideas of a social group as reflecting and facilitating their environmental and social activity is certainly compatible with a straightforward reading of certain passages in Marx's work.[9] In the interests of revolutionary practice, however, Marx must and does go beyond this to concede causatory independence to human ideas: philosophy can be used to change the world, as the Eleventh Thesis on Feuerbach (Marx 1968a [1845]: 30) points out. A complete Marxist view of ideology sees systems of ideas as means by which competing classes and interest groups present their views and justify them, so as to manipulate and control others. American archaeologists recently have used such ideas to expand upon the mainstream's tendency to reduce ideology to sociology. General programmatic statements (e.g. Leone 1982, Kus 1984) have been amplified by particular case studies. Thus, Kus (1982, 1983) sees the principles of statecraft put forward by the founder of the Merina state embodied in the layout of the capital of Ambohimanga. Patterson (1986a: 82) argues that "the new ideological forms and practices of the Inka state were intended to obscure the new relations of exploitation" attendant on Inka conquest and subjugation of previously independent groups. Leone interprets the design of the William Paca garden in Annapolis as an active effort to mask the contradictions of late eighteenth-century Maryland society:

> The order of Tidewater society faced a fundamental dilemma in the 1760s and 1770s of upholding traditional authority and supporting popular sovereignty . . . [The garden] was not passive; it was very active, for by walking in it, building it, looking at it, admiring and discussing it, and using it in any way, its contemporaries could take themselves and their position as granted and convince others that the way things are is the way they always had been and should remain.
>
> (Leone 1984: 34)

It is significant that these concrete exemplifications of how ideological constructs are deployed in the struggle of ruling classes to implement their dominion all depend on extensive historic and ethnohistoric documentation of the meanings expressed by material symbols. Gilman (1976) discusses the elaboration of burial ritual in the Copper Age of southeast Spain in terms of the tensions generated by the development of differential wealth in nominally egalitarian social contexts, but such "readings" of prehistoric ideologies necessarily must remain rather general, since they lack the bilinguals with which to assign specific meanings to the symbols they interpret.[10]

Marxist criticism of positivism

The New Archaeology seeks to investigate prehistoric cultural ecology by explicitly scientific methods (e.g. Binford 1968a; Fritz and Plog 1970; Watson et al. 1971). As Binford (1983a: 22) recently has reiterated:

I have always advocated that archaeology should adopt the methods of the natural sciences. They are the only techniques of which I am aware that can help the archaeologist in his special and peculiar dilemma: the availability only of contemporary observations about material things whose causes are unavailable for observation.

Just as astronomy depends upon the laws of physics to explain the variability of the light in the heavens, just so archaeology must depend on laws of human behavior to understand the variability of the artifacts in the ground. The objective formulation of such laws is to be done through model-building and hypothesis-testing, that is, through the adoption of a logical positivist scientific philosophy.

This research program necessarily is in conflict with the Marxist notion of ideology that I have just discussed. Archaeology is a body of knowledge built up by social actors in accordance with their interests. As Gero (1985: 342) puts it, "Archaeology is fundamentally and uniquely an institution of state-level society. It is only the state that can support, and that requires the services of, elite specialists to produce and control the past." In accordance with such an outlook, American Marxist archaeologists have sought to show how the reconstructions, presentations, and practices of their profession are the products of capitalism.[11]

Thus, the models archaeologists use to reconstruct the past are seen as validations of present-day views of social problems. In general terms, Kohl (1981a: 92) argues that:

The dominant materialist models stressing environmental mismanagement or the inevitability of long-term population growth mirror the difficulties of the contemporary world as advanced nations attempt to obtain scarce resources and control the numbers of people residing on spaceship Earth.

More specifically, Handsman (1980, 1981) suggests that interpretation of the settlement patterns of colonial New England in terms of modern economic rationales obscures the importance of kinship in structuring residential decisions. Similarly, Keene (1983: 148) cautions against uncritical acceptance of optimal foraging theory's premise, derived from capitalist micro-economics, that "prehistoric foragers were consumers in the environmental market."

From this perspective, presentation of archaeological materials in museum exhibits or popularized writings are "ideotechnic" artifacts intended to demonstrate the necessity of modern social relations by their existence in the past. Leone's (1981a, 1981b) discussions of the Colonial Williamsburg and Shakertown outdoor museums indicate how these mask the reality they purport to exhibit objectively by presenting it in terms of present-day rationality.

Finally, critical archaeologists seek to show how far the practice of the discipline is governed, not by value-free scientific goals, but by social and economic constraints of its setting. Gero (1983) argues that the gender bias prevalent in American ideology tends to exclude women from funded field research and that the greater tendency toward such exclusion in archaeology relative to other social science disciplines reflects the fact that "archaeologists are charged with reproducing and legitimating the present in the past" (Gero 1985: 347). Paynter (1983) suggests that the increasing specialization of archaeological work, especially in contract archaeology conducted under the constraints of profit-making, reflects not only the division of labor objectively required by large-scale scientific operations but also managerial interest in de-skilling the labor force the better to control it (cf. Braverman 1974).

Suggestions along these lines would be more persuasive in the context of a general analysis of the class character of American archaeology. Patterson has attempted to produce just such a general account. As he sees matters,

There have been two interpretative communities represented among
Americanist archaeologists in the United States. These reflect the cultures
of the national and international capitalists and their allies: the Core
Culture and Eastern Establishment, respectively.

(Patterson 1986b: 21)

In the absence of detailed documentation of the articulation between the source of funding for archaeological research and publication and the work of particular archaeologists, such broad conclusions are not entirely persuasive, however. Schuyler's (1976) discussion of the influence of patronage on archaeological research in historical archaeology (cf. Raab et al. 1980) and Gero and Root's (1986) discussion of the leadership of the National Geographic Society and its use of archaeology to legitimize the United States' global dominion indicate how one can construct the detailed articulation of class interest and ideological production required by a Marxist analysis of the development of American archaeology. Until such links are developed in detail, the identification of more general correspondences between state or class ideology and archaeological research, such as the nationalist, colonialist, and imperialist archaeologies identified by Trigger (1984a), may be as far as a Marxist approach in these matters can go.

The central idea of the Marxist view of science is that claims about knowledge necessarily reflect the interests of those advancing such claims. The danger of such a view is a self-defeating relativism that sees Marxism as only one "way of telling" among many, a way which can only be judged on its own terms. What is only implicit in the title of Spriggs's (1984) article is fully accepted by some "critical" archaeologists:

From the standpoint of dialectical materialism the knowledge-claims
delivered by *any* theory (including those informed by a dialectical
materialist epistemology) can only be considered "true" insofar as their
own validity criteria are concerned; that is, they are relative truths.[12]

(Saitta 1983: 301)

The reaction to such an abnegation of scientific principles has been explosive, even
(perhaps especially) among scholars who respect and are influenced by Marxist
theory):

No Marxist denies that the position of scholars in society shapes their
understanding of the present and the past. Yet, through their extreme
attacks on positivism and empiricism, the grotesque views of the [neo-
Marxists] not only fail to strengthen Marxism by liberating it from the
constraints of orthodoxy but also are promoting a new intellectual dark
age.[13]

(Trigger 1985: 122)

In fact, the relativism of some Marxist scholars only reflects their lack of a concrete
program of social action which would demand their coming to terms with the world as
it exists, as it were, positively and empirically. Instead of taking the Marxist view of
ideology as a license to lapse into a logically satisfactory but sterile relativism,
Marxists should see the critical evaluation of theory as an opportunity to approach
scientific truth more effectively than through a naive positivism. As Wylie (1985b:
142) has stated:

The recognition that interests may distort knowledge claims simply
serves . . . to direct attention to a new source of error that the scientific
research process should undertake to control; it is not taken to imply that
knowledge claims are so irrevocably tied to interests that they are
impervious to rational, empirical methods of criticism.

A philosophy which seeks to change the world must necessarily deal with it scientifically. The world can be dealt with scientifically without subscribing to the type of
positivism advocated by the more innocent exponents of the New Archaeology,
however (cf. Wylie 1985a).

Discussion

It is fair to say that, prior to the emergence of the New Archaeology in the 1960s, the
only Western archaeologist to make explicit use of Marxist concepts was V. Gordon
Childe. The increasing interest in such concepts over the past twenty years responds
partly to political concerns (most of the recent users of Marxism received their
intellectual formation during the Vietnam War years) and partly to the relaxation of
political controls in the greatly expanded American university systems during the
1960s and 1970s. Its specific character is, however, the result not of political activism
but of disciplinary competition, of the need of younger scholars to establish distinctive

niches in the academic struggle for survival. American use of Marxist concepts in archaeology reacts to the deficiencies of the New Archaeology, an approach to research whose closeness to much of Marxism makes it amenable to a Marxist critique.

In the absence of clear political goals it is easy for such a reaction to become reactionary.[14] It is a short step from the respect Kohl and Wright (1977) have for the old-fashioned historicism of Mellaart (1975) to the anti-materialist historicism of Conrad and Demarest (1984). Similarly, the structural Marxism of Kus's (1982, 1983) and Leone's (1984) above-cited analyses of architectural layouts is very close to the structural idealism of Fritz's (1986) discussion of the design of the Hindu capital of Vijayanagara, a discussion which would fit comfortably into the mainstream of Classical archaeology (cf. McDonald 1965). We have already seen how "critical theory" can bring about a return to the relativism traditional in American anthropological studies (Geertz 1984), a relativism whose political implications are hardly progressive (Keesing 1987). For American archaeologists the road from Marxism to conservatism is open and easy to take.

At the same time that Marxism is easily set aside in the American academic context, Marxism is easy to practice without acknowledgement.[15] I take the center of a Marxist approach to the analysis of social history to be summarized in the famous passage from volume 3 of *Capital*:

The specific economic form in which unpaid surplus-labour is pumped out of direct producers determines the relation of rulers and ruled . . . Upon this . . . is founded the entire formation of the economic community . . . [and] thereby simultaneously its specific political form. It is always the relationship of the owners . . . to the direct producers . . . which reveals the innermost secret, the hidden basis of the entire social structure.

(Marx 1967 [1894]: 791)

On this account, the work of many of the more sophisticated practitioners of cultural ecology is fully compatible with Marxist approaches to analogous problems. Henry Wright's shift from emphasizing the function of elites as managers (1977) to stressing their role as tribute-capturers (1984) is representative of an increasingly widespread recognition among the more recent cohort of cultural ecologists that an analysis of modes of exploitation is critical to understanding social complexity (Brumfiel 1980, 1987; Earle 1977, 1978; D'Altroy and Earle 1985; Kirch 1984; McGovern 1980), a recognition whose convergence with Marxism is at times explicitly recognized (Brumfiel and Earle 1987; Haas 1982). Such an approach has, of course, a considerable history among American archaeologists, the most distinguished contribution being that of Robert McC. Adams (1966), whose emphasis on land tenure as the nexus between ecological and social relations presages many of the overtly Marxist contributions I have mentioned.[16]

The closeness between Marxism and the mainstream of American archaeological research is particularly striking at the level of practice. In fact, nothing distinguishes the concrete data recovery procedures of more vulgar and more dialectical materialists. As we have just seen, even at the level of research design and interpretation, differences between Marxist and non-Marxist work are often slight. The critical definitive criterion is, then, political commitment. If some American prehistorians wish to refer to Marx and Engels as explicit influences on their work, it is because they wish to associate that work with the emancipatory thrust which the founders of historical materialism gave to the social sciences.

Notes

1 That Trigger's (1984b) review of Marxist approaches in archaeology contains no mention of recent North American work speaks directly to the position of such work within the discipline. Patterson's (1986b) identification of a Marxist "interpretative community" in American archaeology constitutes, at this time at least, wishful thinking.

2 These conditions reproduce at the modest scale of the university the "embourgeoisement" and fragmentation which have inhibited the expression of working-class consciousness in the country as a whole (cf. Oppenheimer 1985: 23–42).

3 The main exception to this is the nucleus of archaeologists working at the University of Massachusetts at Amherst. There Arthur Keene, Robert Paynter, and their students (Joan Gero, Dean Saitta, and Dolores Root, among others) have been able to develop a mutually beneficial dialogue building on Marxist ideas. Their intellectual work has, of course, been assisted by the group of radical political economists also working at that institution.

4 Italics are in the original.

5 I have quoted Hill extensively because he expresses with commendable clarity a viewpoint widespread in the literature: for similar viewpoints see, for example, Athens (1977), Gall and Saxe (1977) or Isbell (1978) among many others.

6 These perspectives have been given great emphasis by Western European Marxist prehistorians: see, for example, Frankenstein and Rowlands (1978) or Kristiansen (1981).

7 Italics are in the original.

8 This view has been extensively developed in Britain by Bender (1978, 1981).

9 "The mode of production of material life conditions the social, political and intellectual life process in general. It is not the consciousness of men that determines their being, but, on the contrary their social being that determines their consciousness" (Marx 1968b [1859]: 182).

10 Various British scholars have used Marxist approaches in presenting concrete interpretations of the ideologies of particular European prehistoric contexts (e.g. Miller and Tilley 1984: 51–146), but, as Earle and Preucel (1987:501–38) point out, their "only apparent method . . . is to project [themselves] into a past cultural context. The dangers of ethnocentrism and imaginative myth making should be apparent."

11 The derivation of "critical theory" in American archaeology from Marx by way of Habermas (1971) and others of the Frankfurt School is discussed by Wylie (1985b).

12 Italics are in the original. Views like Saitta's have been extensively developed by various British "critical" archaeologists. See, for example, Miller and Tilley (1984: 151).

13 See Kohl (1985) for a more sympathetic presentation of the same criticisms.

14 In Britain, Hodder (1982d) has made an explicit virtue of this tendency.

15 The ready assimilation of the "critical theory" strand of Marxist thinking into the mainstream is a particularly striking example of this phenomenon: Conkey and Spector (1984), Fowler (1987).

16 Thus, R. McC. Adams's (1977: 271) statement that "higher levels of [societal] integration cannot be understood without reference to the quite asymmetrical, which is to say often downright unpleasant, relations of political and economic power on which they ultimately depend" is also the thrust of the argument presented in Gilman (1981). Adams's emphasis on entrepreneurship in ancient trade (1974a) forms the starting point of Kohl's (1975) discussion of that subject. His suggestions about the changing role of women in Early Dynastic Mesopotamia (1984) presages Zagarell's (1986b) treatment of the same subject.

5

Formal approaches in archaeology

GEORGE L. COWGILL

In this chapter I offer some methodological and theoretical perspectives on the current state of formal methods in archaeology. Such methods are often referred to as "quantitative," but that term is inappropriate for several reasons. It is difficult to do anything archaeological that is not "quantitative" in the sense that counts or measurements of something are made and discussed. However, work that does not go much beyond simply tabulating and inspecting some numbers, although often very useful, is not what I have in mind. Doran (1986:21) defines formal methods as "mathematical, statistical and computer-based," and says that "rather than being merely quantitative, formal methods are characterised by a combination of abstraction, systematisation and exactness."

I will begin by summarizing important points in an earlier review of this topic (Cowgill 1986). The tone of my earlier chapter was predominantly critical. In this chapter I will try to get that part over with quickly, and turn, in a more positive mood, to some approaches that I think will repay more attention in the near future.

In my earlier chapter I proposed that we structure our thinking in terms of three broad categories: archaeological observations (that is, data), analytical methods (which provide connections between observations and theory), and sociocultural theory (Cowgill 1986:369). I said that mathematical and formal techniques mostly belong in the category of analytical methods, and while there is room for improvement in these techniques, what is most needed is better sociocultural theory, improved data, and better understandings of the connections between archaeological evidence and past behavior (that is, better "middle-range" theory) (Cowgill 1986:370, 390).

One set of commentators interpreted this as only a call for better theory and ignored my emphasis on the need for better data as well (Meltzer et al. 1986:14). This suggests that many archaeologists have a mind-set that makes them complacent about the quality of their data, so that they focus their attention on new theory and have trouble "hearing" the message that the quality of the data themselves is often problematic.

To be sure, at least one reviewer understood my point about data (Fagan 1986:211–12), and perhaps I exaggerate the problem. Nevertheless, I will repeat it in a way that should be impossible to ignore. It is a variation on the old themes "garbage in, garbage out" and "You can't make a silk purse from a sow's ear." These statements do not mean that if we don't have nearly perfect data we should simply give up. The message is that archaeological data are usually marginal in quality, relevance, and quantity for most of the really interesting topics in sociocultural theory. We are unavoidably in the business of refining low-grade data to win something of value. One can think of it as tuning our detection gear ever so finely to try to decode voices that are faint, alien, distorted, and almost drowned out by irrelevant messages and random noise. To do this very well we need all the help we can get. Formal approaches are one very important source of help, but they do not substitute for anything else. My point about data was, and remains, that more or less elaborate analyses (non-formal as well as formal) are often applied to data bases whose weakness does not seem to be a matter of concern. In an era of rapid site destruction and scarce funding, such data are sometimes the best we can hope for. But insensitivity to problems about quality of data will do nothing toward improving the situation, and awareness of the problem is at least a beginning.

In my 1986 paper I noted several specific kinds of trouble with data that can be alleviated by better methods. It is a mistake to think that a survey is ever "total"; more intensive survey will always identify additional archaeological occurrences. I argued further that even the best spatial sampling schemes are inferior substitutes for doing a survey that is as intensive and comprehensive as possible, especially because spatial sampling is apt to miss occurrences that are inconspicuous but very important and because spatial sampling makes it almost impossible to correctly recognize spatial patterns unless they are much smaller than the sampling units employed. I do not think spatial sampling can be regarded as a way to avoid unprofitable redundancy in regional survey, because it is highly probable that fuller survey will yield unexpected important new information. Sampling should be used for regional survey only when one is forced to it by shortage of time and resources. Nance (1983) provides a very useful review of regional sampling.

I also pointed out that it is a mistake to think that a collection is ever "total." There must always be some cutoff below which objects are ignored because they are considered too unimportant (usually because they are too small and featureless). The composition of collections can be significantly affected by these cutoffs. Since we cannot really collect everything, we should use consistent criteria for what to ignore, and report these criteria routinely and carefully (Cowgill 1986:382–3).

I criticized the term "controlled collection" because it is often used to suggest that collection procedures were highly reliable – that is, that what one field worker collected one day from a site is highly similar to what would have been collected on any other day by any other member of the same project. In fact, the term is nearly meaningless unless one carefully explains what steps were taken to achieve high reliability (Cowgill 1986:382–3). These steps should include some repeated collections made by different workers under different circumstances from the same sites, in order to provide an empirical basis for assessing reliability.

I was especially critical of the notion that "around 100 objects" is a good target for collection sizes. Unless the material in question is remarkably lacking in diversity, some categories are bound to be represented by small numbers in such collections. For example, if there are twenty categories of interest, all approximately equally common, then on the average each will be represented by about one-twentieth of each collection, or about 5 objects in a collection of 100 objects. One is then faced with the difficult problem of deciding whether a count of 2 or 8 really means something, since deviations that large can easily occur by chance when the true proportion (in the population of objects sampled by a specific collection) is really $1/20$. If instead one had a collection of 400 objects, obtained as an approximately random sample from a population where the true proportion of a given category is $1/20$, one would expect a count of around 20 of that category in the collection. An observed count of 8 would provide strong evidence that the true population proportion was distinctly less than $1/20$ and was more likely around $1/50$, while an observed count of 32 would provide strong evidence that the proportion was greater than $1/20$ and more likely around $8/100$.

A further problem with a small collection is that it is likely to underrepresent the true diversity of the population represented by the collection (Jones et al. 1983; Kintigh 1984; Jones and Leonard in press). Comparisons of assemblage diversity are misleading unless collection size is taken into account, and larger collections give more reliable estimates of true diversity. Finally, correlations between either counts or percents of categories are not merely unreliable, they are systematically biased toward zero if they are based on data from collections so small that there are never more than a few objects belonging to the relevant categories in any one collection. For all these reasons, collections of only around 100 objects are usually hard to deal with statistically. Often we have no choice and must make the best use we can of small collections. But it would be better to make collections of several hundred objects, if this is at all feasible (Cowgill 1986:383–4).

I ended my criticism of data quality by saying that excavation techniques still often leave much to be desired. Few will admit to ignoring distinct layers when they are observed, but there are still tremendous differences in the extent to which care and skill in recognizing layers is emphasized in archaeological training and practice. There are also sometimes surprising deficiencies in drawing profiles and other aspects of data recording. Elaboration of formal methods (or of archaeological theory) does not mean that we are somehow beyond all that tedious attention to excavation technique. It means, instead, that there is more need than ever for good technique, and more point to it (Cowgill 1986:385–6).

In an earlier section of the paper I talked about the relationship between archaeological data and sociocultural theory. Although there are a number of formal techniques that are intended to aid in building models that parsimoniously and effectively *describe* data, it is incorrect to equate this process with the building of explanatory theory. It is, instead, only one component, albeit a very important one, in the creation, testing, and improvement of theory (Cowgill 1986:371–8).

At various places in the paper I noted that formal methods have been used for the design of research (data collection), for summarization and exploration of data, and as aids in efforts to connect data with sociocultural theory, but that there was still remarkably little relevant sociocultural theory that was itself expressed in formal terms. Many of the most important concepts in theory seem fully expressible by very simple formal relationships (such as "greater than" and "less than," "highly probable" and "quite improbable"). What is most important are concepts coming from sources such as ethnography, social anthropology, and social history. I said that "richness of mathematical concepts cannot remedy poverty of sociocultural concepts" (Cowgill 1986:374). This is worth emphasizing because, after having just argued that we must be superb technicians, I am now arguing that we must also be widely and perceptively acquainted with knowledge that is only remotely connected with the materials we study directly. If this seems too much for any one person, I can only reply that we must do it, or at least people who do different parts of it must communicate in genuinely effective ways, if archaeology is to progress.

Attempts to express sociocultural theory in formal terms are commonly vitiated by the shallowness, naivety, or ethnocentrism of the sociocultural "data" and assumptions embodied in the formal model. This deficiency is by no means distinctive of archaeologists. Many of the worst offenses are committed by economists and political scientists, who often show a quite bizarre willingness to base their understandings on official statistics and interviews with elites, even when they could collect the kind of ethnographic data archaeologists would give their eye teeth for.[1] Rather than "thick" description, they seem content with descriptions so thin that they border on the ectoplasmic.

Is the "thinness" and ethnocentrism of the inputs characteristic of formal models an unavoidable consequence of the abstraction these models require, or is it something else? The ethnocentrism could be considerably reduced by proper regard for ethnographic knowledge. Would this suffice for the production of formal models that are abstract and yet apt and relevant enough to be of value? Or is the problem, which is that of taking adequate account of ideational realms that are rich and powerful but very different from the ideational realm within which the formal models are created, very much more intractable? Many readers may already have their minds made up on this issue. But to me it is an open question, and one that I pose as a challenge.

With this, I turn to several specific topics to which I want to call attention because, in my judgment, it will be profitable in the near future to pursue work along these lines. I emphasize especially matters omitted from my earlier chapter. Several of these are still relatively unknown to archaeologists.

Bayesian approaches

The "Bayesian" approach is named after Thomas Bayes, author of a theorem basic for its formalization that was published posthumously in 1763. The mood of the approach is, however, perhaps best introduced by a relatively informal example. The date of the earliest human occupation of the New World is controversial. Some archaeologists doubt if it was much more than 12,000 years before the present, while others favor a far earlier date. On brief reflection and introspection, I find that I can quite comfortably sketch my own current opinions (though certainly not the reasons for those opinions) by means of a simple table.

The second column of Table 5.1 can be thought of as a basis for the betting odds I would give at present for different possible dates, if I were a betting person. Other archaeologists who have given any attention at all to the problem are not likely to agree entirely with my probabilities. Some may even insist that they cannot meaning-

Table 5.1 *Personal prior probabilities of the author and two hypothetical other archaeologists ("E" and "L") for the presence of humans in the New World by various dates*

Date (years B.P.)	Prior probabilities		
	GLC	E	L
30,000	0.01	0.99	0.00
20,000	0.05	1.00	0.01
15,000	0.90	1.00	0.50
12,000	1.00	1.00	0.99

Note: Probabilities are rounded to two decimal places. Probabilities shown as 0.00 and 1.00 do not necessarily mean absolute certainty.

fully assign any numbers at all to their own views. However, I think it unlikely that even they will remain neutral about Table 5.1. Some will feel quite strongly that I have assigned much too low a probability to the earlier dates. Others may feel that my probabilities are about right. At least a few will think I have given too high a probability to early dates. We can imagine two other archaeologists; E, who favors an early date, and L, who is even more skeptical of an early date than I am. The probabilities that reflect the views of E and L are summarized in columns 3 and 4 of Table 5.1.

Suppose a new site is found in North America, with really good evidence of human occupation and several radiocarbon dates that are consistent, widely agreed to be unproblematically associated with the human occupation, and cluster around 20,000 B.P. Even one such case without any "weak link" in the evidence would suffice to cause me to revise considerably the views represented in Table 5.1, which is a *prior* probability distribution ("prior" because it is prior to taking into account some specific body of new evidence). My *posterior* probability for humans in the New World by 20,000 B.P. might jump from 0.05 to as high as 0.95. There are many instances where skeptics have seen some body of really strong evidence and changed their minds. This happened, for example, in the late 1920s when American archaeologists first became persuaded of the reality of the human occupations that are now dated around 10,000 to 12,000 B.P.

Other archaeologists will react differently to the new data. E was already practically certain people were here 20,000 years ago, and his/her opinion will be unaffected. L, however, might still be unwilling to assign a higher posterior probability than 0.05 for humans in the New World by 20,000 B.P., and might think it more likely that "something is wrong" with the data on the newly reported site.

All this may seem woefully unscientific. Surely we are all supposed to be "objective" and to draw identical conclusions from any particular body of evidence. If we allow the opinions we held prior to examining the evidence to influence our subsequent opinions, do we not open the door to anarchy?

The answer many statisticians have given to this question is that to pretend that our prior views do not influence what we think the data mean does not enable us to be objective; instead it confuses us about what we really do, and encourages us to reason illogically and ineffectively. Furthermore, if our prior views are not wholly incompatible, examination of a given body of new evidence will lead to posterior views that are less divergent than the prior views were.

This last proviso is important, and I think it could be paraphrased by saying that for people's posterior views to converge, they must begin by at least sharing the same *paradigm*. For example, it is not likely that any amount of new evidence will lead to convergence between the views of "creation scientists" and evolutionary biologists, because they begin with incompatible assumptions. On the other hand, archaeologists who argue heatedly about whether humans were in the New World long before 30,000 B.P. or not before 12,000 B.P. conduct their arguments in the context of a large body of shared assumptions. When there is broad agreement about the nature of reality and the modes of reasoning that are valid, then it is possible for disagreements on specific points to be resolved, or at least greatly reduced, by consideration of new evidence.

It may be objected that people don't really behave like the hypothetical archaeologist L. In particular, L may actually be far less willing to change his or her mind than the prior probability of 0.01, which is small but not extremely small, would suggest. But if that is the case, then either L was not realistic about his or her prior probability, or there is a clear sense in which L is behaving illogically. As expressed in qualitative terms, the "Bayesian mood" seems to me partly a way of thinking about how we really behave, and partly a sensible prescription for how we ought to behave, at least for "normal science." Kuhnian revolutions are perhaps another matter.

One possible misunderstanding needs to be cleared up at once. The viewpoint that I advocate is totally opposed to the notion that there is no such thing as absolute truth, and that any person's opinion is just as good and just as "true" as anyone else's. To be sure, there are any number of different socially constituted realities, and we fall short in understanding ourselves to the extent that we cannot enter the ideational realms of others and understand their own underlying assumptions, logic, and preoccupations. Nevertheless, a deep assumption of my native culture is that there is something "out there" that exists and has properties independently of our awareness of it. How we perceive what is "out there" is the result of a complex interaction between what is outside us and the very complex apparatus of prior knowledge and sensitivities by which we experience things. I believe it is possible to construct models of the world that increasingly approximate how it really is, even if we can never get beyond approximations. I also think that doing science is a distinctive and unusually effective way of improving our approximations, in large part because doing science involves systematically subjecting our ideas to challenge and being prepared to change ideas that do not stand up to these challenges. The "Bayesian mood" sketches some good guidelines for ways to modify ideas. It is, thus, not a denial that there is something definite "out there," but rather a way to facilitate the approximation of our models to that something definite.

To make this argument more specific, if we consider any region of the New World, I have no doubt that there was a definite date when the first humans set foot in it. It is highly unlikely that we will ever be able to determine such a date with complete certainty and accuracy. Nevertheless, it is both likely and desirable that archaeologists will arrive at a far narrower range of estimates agreed to be plausible than is the case at present.

In this first example, it does not seem to be feasible to replace what I have called the "Bayesian mood" with specific Bayesian techniques, because, even if we had the hypothetical new site with "very good" evidence of occupation at 20,000 B.P., it is not clear how that "very good" evidence could be equated with some specific numerical probability. In other cases, however, there are reasonable ways to do this. I will illustrate this with a second example. In the nineteenth century the "Long Count" of the Classic Maya calendar was deciphered, and this made it possible to determine with great confidence the exact number of days between two dates recorded by the Maya. However, the correlation between the Long Count and the European calendar remained controversial for many years and is still not settled to the satisfaction of all competent scholars. For technical reasons only a limited number of correlations are plausible, and those considered most plausible occur at intervals of about 256 years. For simplicity, consider just the two most popular, which I will call "early" and "late." Suppose a stela is found, with a Long Count date that correlates either with A.D. 400 (early) or A.D. 656 (late). Suppose also that a calibrated radiocarbon date of A.D. 600 is obtained from material that indisputably ceased to metabolize at just about the time recorded by the stela date. Unfortunately, the date was determined by antiquated equipment and it comes with a standard error of 250 years. For purposes of illustration, assume that the probability distribution of the date nearly follows a Normal (i.e. Gaussian) curve (the distribution is actually Poisson, which is slightly different). A standard statistical approach would then be to say that the late correlation implies a date that is $(656 - 600)/250$ or 0.224 standard errors later than the "best" radiocarbon estimate. Consultation of the table of areas under the Normal curve that is to be found in every introductory statistics text shows that a deviation as large as this, or larger, is to be expected in about 82 percent of cases where the hypothesis (that the true date is A.D. 656) is correct. On the other hand, the "early" correlation implies a date that is $(600 - 400)/250$ or 0.80 standard errors earlier than the radiocarbon estimate. The probability of a deviation this large or larger is about 42 percent. Another approach is to compute a "confidence interval" about the radiocarbon date. For example, statistical theory tells us that if we construct an interval that extends 1.645 times the standard error above and below the best estimate, 90 percent of such intervals will include the true value. In this case, $1.645 \times 250 = 411$, and we get a 90 percent confidence interval that runs from A.D. 189 $(600 - 411)$ to A.D. 1011 $(600 + 411)$. This interval, of course, comfortably includes both A.D. 400 and A.D. 656.

By any correct way of looking at it, the radiocarbon date has not helped noticeably. To be sure, 600 is considerably closer to 656 than to 400, but the very large uncertainty in the date means that accepting the radiocarbon evidence does not require one to regard either correlation as particularly implausible. Perhaps the greatest danger is that a statistically naive advocate of the late correlation might argue that since the radiocarbon date is highly consistent with the late correlation, it adds meaningful support to that correlation. But a naive advocate of the early correlation could say that the date is highly consistent with *that* correlation, and therefore highly supportive of *it*. The fact is, of course, that the date comes with such a large standard error that it is highly ambiguous, and thus provides almost no evidence one way or the other. For such poor evidence, it may be reasonable to leave it at that.

Suppose now that the radiocarbon date is redetermined with better equipment and that it happens to yield the same value, A.D. 600, but now with a standard error of only 80 years. The late correlation date is $(656 - 600)/80 = 0.70$ standard deviations high, and if A.D. 656 were the true date a deviation this large or larger is to be expected in about 48 percent of samples. However, the early date is $(600 - 400)/80 = 2.50$ standard deviations low, and if A.D. 400 were the true date, a deviation this large or larger would be expected in barely more than 1 percent of samples. The 90 per cent confidence interval spans the range A.D. 468 to 732, and even the 95 percent interval is only from A.D. 443 to 757. This new evidence considerably favors the late correlation. According to the prevailing custom of treating the 5 percent significance level as an unerring guide for decisions, we could say that the hypothesis that the early correlation is correct can be rejected at the 5 percent level, and there is an end to the matter . . . or at least an end until new evidence appears.

But is this really the end? Should advocates of the early correlation give up that easily? *Will* they, whether they should or shouldn't? According to a common but incorrect understanding of the "hypothesis testing" approach, the late correlation must be "provisionally accepted" and the early correlation rejected. More correctly, advocates of the early correlation are put on the defensive but not required to abandon their position. They ought perhaps to hold it with less confidence than before, but conventional statistical analysis gives no guidance beyond that vague suggestion (Cowgill 1977).

A Bayesian approach offers considerably more help. If one can give a rough quantification of one's prior probabilities for the competing hypotheses, then the radiocarbon evidence can be used to give an unambiguous set of posterior probabilities. This was not possible in the earlier example because the new evidence could not be expressed in a definite quantitative form. In the present example, the mean of the radiocarbon date, its standard deviation, and the fact that the distribution is approximately Normal are sufficient information to permit the computation of definite posterior probabilities. To illustrate this, imagine again two archaeologists, A and B, whose prior probabilities are shown in column 2 of Table 5.2. A's prior probabilities are 0.10 for the early correlation, and 0.90 for the late. That is, s/he leans toward the late, but figures there is about one chance in ten that the early correlation may be correct. B, on the other hand, holds prior probabilities of 0.99 for the early correlation and only 0.01 for the late correlation. B is a very strong advocate of the early correlation and quite skeptical of the late correlation, though willing to admit that it just might be correct. By simple computations that take only a few minutes by

Table 5.2 *Prior and posterior personal probabilities for two individuals ("A" and "B") concerning two possible correlations of the Maya and European calendars, before and after taking into account the evidence of a single new radiocarbon date*

Individual	Prior probability for "late"	Posterior probability after taking into account a radiocarbon date of A.D. 600 with standard error of:		
		250 years	80 years	50 years
A	0.90	0.92	0.99	1.00
B	0.01	0.01	0.15	0.94

Note: Probabilities for the "late" correlation are shown. Probabilities for the "early" correlation can be found by subtracting "late" probabilities from one.

pocket calculator, the result of taking into account the first radiocarbon determination, with a standard error of 250 years, leads to posterior probabilities for A of about 0.08 for the early correlation and 0.92 for the late correlation. For B, the posterior probabilities come out to about 0.99 and 0.01. In other words, the radiocarbon evidence was so ambiguous that it has had almost no impact on the prior probabilities. However, the effect of a radiocarbon determination with a standard error of only 80 years is very different. It leads to posterior probabilities for archaeologist A of 0.01 and 0.99. This is a substantial further shift in favor of the late correlation. The posterior probabilities for B are 0.85 for the early correlation and 0.15 for the late. This is also a substantial shift toward the late correlation, but B could rationally still give odds of 0.85 to 0.15, that is, 17 to 3, in favor of the early correlation.

At this point it may seem that the Bayesian approach is little better than the conventional approach, since A and B began by disagreeing and they still disagree. But suppose the radiocarbon date had a standard error of only 50 years. Bayesian computations show that A can now feel virtually certain that the late correlation is correct, while the posterior probabilities for B are about 0.06 for the early correlation and 0.94 for the late correlation, as shown in the last column of Table 5.2. In other words, the rational thing for a person who holds B's prior probabilities to do, in the light of the radiocarbon evidence, is to switch from a very strong belief in the early correlation to moderately strong belief in the late correlation.

All these posterior probabilities can be used as prior probabilities whenever further evidence is obtained, in a cyclic interaction between beliefs and further evidence. The stronger the evidence, the greater the narrowing of the gap between initially diverse personal views.

A real archaeologist who originally assigned a probability of 0.01 to the late correlation, when confronted with a single radiocarbon date of A.D. 600 with a standard error of 50 years, might not actually be willing to switch to a posterior probability of 0.94 for the late correlation. However, this unwillingness could only be based on (a) hitherto unexpressed suspicions that the true uncertainty in the radiocarbon date was much greater than the 50-year standard error implies, (b) an admission that his or her true prior probability was really considerably less than 0.01, or (c) indefensible irrationality.

This is only a sketch of one way in which Bayesian methods can be used, to avoid the obfuscation of our actual reasoning processes encouraged by the "hypothesis testing" approach, and to help us make our reasoning more explicit, more coherent, and more powerful.

There are many other possible applications and many specific Bayesian techniques. "Empirical" Bayesian methods can be used, for example, to make estimates of population parameters that are better than those made by more conventional approaches. I believe that Chernoff (1982) is the first to have applied empirical Bayesian techniques to an archaeological problem. Iversen (1984) gives a brief and relatively simple introduction to Bayesian statistical inference. Box and Tiao (1973) is a more advanced text on Bayesian methods.

Activity signatures and intrasite spatial analysis

Figuring out the activities represented by an archaeological occurrence is basic for good interpretation. If the occurrence covers more than a tiny area, it is also desirable to infer as much as possible about the spatial patterning of activities. Ideally, there should be good diagnostics of different activities. By a "good diagnostic" I mean a kind of evidence that is relatively durable and is consistently left behind by a certain type of activity in quantities sufficient so that more than a very little bit of the activity will practically always leave behind a detectable amount of evidence. It is also important that no other type of activity should generate much, if any, of this kind of evidence. Examples of things that are sometimes good diagnostics are specific artifact categories, distinctive kinds of waste or by-products, discarded tools with distinctive types of wear or damage, special kinds of immobile facilities or features, and distinctive alterations to land surfaces or layers (such as high-temperature burning). If there is at least one good diagnostic for an activity, then the activity leaves behind a relatively clear "signature." If the diagnostics are immovable or if there is reason to think they have not been moved from the spot where the activity took place, they also provide fairly straightforward evidence about the spatial pattern of the activity. If there is reason to think that the good diagnostics were tossed, dumped, or otherwise moved away from the spot where the activity took place, it is harder to tell much about the spatial pattern of the activity but it can at least be inferred that the activity took place nearby. Specialized tools, even if they are used for only a single type of activity, cannot be good diagnostics if they are usually "curated" and rarely discarded or lost at the spot where the activity took place.

In the absence of identified good diagnostics, can anything useful be done? Much effort has been devoted to aspects of this problem. Noteworthy recent examples include Kintigh and Ammerman (1982), Whallon (1984), and many of the chapters in Carr (1985). I think the model that is at least implicit in most of this work is that activities are distinguishable by different *proportions* of different types of remains. That is, although no one category of remains is a good diagnostic of any of the activities, at least some activities are distinguishable from other activities by propen-

Table 5.3 *Example of a situation where there are no "good diagnostics" of any activity, but different propensities to leave behind different proportions of different categories of remains leave contrasting signatures of three activities*

	Average proportions of categories in material left behind (%)				
Activity	Category v	Category w	Category x	Category y	Category z
a	5	10	20	40	25
b	30	20	10	10	30
c	15	5	40	30	10

sities to generate different proportions of different categories of remains. For example, if there are five categories of interest, say v, w, x, y, and z; and three activities, say a, b, and c; then perhaps activity a tends to generate residues consisting of, on the average, about 5 percent v, 10 percent w, 20 per cent x, 40 percent y, and 25 percent z, while activities b and c tend to generate different average proportions, as illustrated in Table 5.3. No single category is diagnostic of any specific activity, but the activities still have distinctive "signatures," because each generates a characteristic *proportion* of the different categories of remains. If we somehow knew what the characteristic proportions were for each type of activity, and if each archaeological occurrence reflected only a single activity, we would be able to infer the activity represented by each occurrence. The problems are that we do not know in advance the characteristic proportions, and a single archaeological occurrence, even with the best possible stratigraphic control, is usually a palimpsest of the signatures of multiple activities. This is especially true if the occurrence is large and concentrated enough to be termed a "site." Confronted with these problems, can anything at all be done?

The answer, perhaps surprisingly, is that quite a lot can be done if the individual signatures are fairly consistent and if the various signatures are not uniformly distributed over the whole occurrence. In an earlier paper (Cowgill in press) I showed, with invented data, that a seemingly natural principal components approach to this situation gives results that are not technically incorrect, but are limited and prone to misinterpretation, while a cluster analysis approach runs into serious trouble when signatures overlie one another. I tried a different multivariate approach, that begins by postulating activity signatures and then explores the implications in order to find limits on the ranges of possible signatures and proportions of these signatures in different site segments. Some possible signatures or proportions of signatures are ruled out because they imply impossible values (less than zero or greater than one) for other proportions. I was able to show that some limits can be established, but there remains an unavoidable indeterminacy because, for a given set of site segments, more than one set of signatures and proportions of signatures is consistent with the observed data. These include the "true" values (built into this artificial example) but also a range of other possibilities. However, it seemed likely that, given a large enough number of site segments and at least a few segments that differ markedly from one another in the mixes of activities represented, the indeterminacy in the solution could be made small enough so that the result would be quite useful.

This was as far as I was able to carry the matter when (thanks to Ron Bishop of the Smithsonian Institution) I discovered that there is already a sizable literature by geologists and mathematicians concerned with an analogous problem, referred to as "linear unmixing." This deals with the situation where a data set "can be viewed as a collection of samples representing mixtures of a relatively small number of end members" but where the end members themselves are not necessarily present in the set of samples (Full et al. 1982). What they call "end members" are the same as what I call "activity signatures" here. To say that an end member is not present in the sample is the same as to say that no site segment represents the pure signature of a given activity. Full et al. (1982) use a "fuzzy subsets" technique (Zadeh 1965) to deal with the problem of noisy data – essentially to make the reconstruction of end members considerably more robust in the face of data errors, samples that do not belong (e.g. a site segment that actually pertains to a culturally different occupation), and so on. So far as I know, linear unmixing has not yet been applied to archaeological data. However, I think it by far the most promising solution available to the problem of inferring activity signatures in the absence of good diagnostics.

This is not to say that the linear unmixing approach is guaranteed to give good results. For one thing, the whole concept of activity signatures remains shaky. If there is not much consistency from one time to the next in the proportions of things left behind by people engaged in a certain type of activity – in other words, if the variances in proportions actually left behind in specific instances are too large relative to differences between average proportions left behind – then linear unmixing probably will not give good results. However, if activities do not leave reasonably consistent signatures, I cannot imagine any other approach that would work better.

Linear unmixing should be able to deal with situations where a fraction of the material left behind by an activity is left in place and another fraction is tossed or dumped. All that is needed is that the propensities for dropping, tossing, and/or dumping should not have variances that are too large. If that condition is satisfied, one could identify a "dropping signature" for a given activity, a "dumping signature" for the same activity, and so on.

The dilemma of whether to use counts or proportions afflicts R-mode principal components approaches. Using raw counts causes correlations to be undesirably influenced by differences in absolute quantities of material in different site segments, while standardizing by converting to proportions introduces complex constraints in correlations because the proportions in a segment must sum to unity. A very attractive feature of linear unmixing is that it is untroubled by this problem.

Finally, linear unmixing is probably fairly insensitive to the size and shape of the site segments used. The signatures of different activities in a site may result in scatters of material that are very diverse in size, shape, and density (Whallon 1984) and this has been a vexing problem for efforts to infer activities and their spatial distribution, if no good diagnostics are identified. For linear unmixing, it is only necessary that the site segments represent a fairly wide range of proportionate mixes of the signatures of different activities. It is not necessary that a site segment be homogeneous in the signatures present, or that the boundaries of the segment have any relationship to the edges of any particular signature. If site segments are too large they will not differ enough from one another for linear unmixing to work well, and also the spatial resolution will be poor. If segments are too small, they will tend to contain very small quantities of material and random statistical errors will be too large. But it seems that, between these extremes, there will be a fairly wide range of sizes and shapes of site segments for which linear unmixing will work well, if well-defined activity signatures exist at all. It would be logical to use segments as small as they can be made without making random errors in counts within each segment too large. I see no reason why all the segments have to be the same size. If linear unmixing enables one to infer activity signatures reasonably well, the proportion of a given signature in each site segment could be plotted (like the factor scores in a principal components study) in order to show the spatial distribution of that activity signature. The size and shape of the signature would emerge naturally from such a plot, with a resolution determined by the sizes of the site segments.

Typology and systematics

Most formal approaches to typology or classification have been preoccupied with the problem of finding a way to divide a set of objects into subsets that are in some sense optimal clusters or groups. The general idea is that each subset should consist of objects that are relatively similar to one another and relatively different from all the objects in other subsets. This problem is interesting mathematically and there is a large literature on it, much of it in biology and other non-archaeological fields, which attests to the belief that it also has great practical importance. Undoubtedly this is so, and continued archaeological pursuit of this problem seems worthwhile. But I urge that we also work on the formalization of other aspects of systematics. I am thinking of situations where objects differ enough so that they unquestionably belong in different classes (in the sense of Dunnell 1971, 1986), yet show a "family resemblance"[2] that cannot plausibly be accidental. For example, cylindrical vases with flat bottoms, vertical or slightly concave walls, and slab-like tripod supports are very widespread in Mesoamerica between about A.D. 200 and 600. They share a general resemblance that is surely not accidental, and their presence at a site has sometimes been interpreted as reflecting direct and strong "influence" from some single center, such as Teotihuacan. More than superficial study of the objects shows, however, that there are a number of regional and temporal variants, as well as great differences in pastes and techniques and styles of decoration. It is likely that closer comparison of many examples would reveal complexly intertwined patterns of imitation and innovation, with interesting implications about interactions between Mesoamerican societies. However, attempts to optimize discovery of the "best" clusters do not seem highly relevant for unravelling these relationships. To be sure, clusters can be organized hierarchically into clusters of clusters, clusters of clusters of clusters, and so on, but these hierarchies themselves are rigid and can only express certain resemblances at the expense of others. The "fuzzy subset" concept (Zadeh 1965; Bezdek

1981) may be helpful, since it does not require an object to be wholly a member of only one cluster. Instead, it can be, for example, 70 percent a member of cluster A, 20 percent a member of cluster B, and 10 percent a member of cluster C. However, this still requires that the intricate pattern of partial resemblances between an object and a subset of other objects be reduced to a single number, and this is probably too drastic an abstraction from the observed data.

In order to deal adequately with these "family resemblance" problems it is clearly necessary to do a good deal of painstaking and rather old-fashioned comparison, relying far more on specific attributes and "modes" than on class definitions. It may be that that will be sufficient, as well as necessary. I suspect, however, that there are ways to formalize such investigations that will be very helpful. For example, the "design grammar" approach (Chippindale and Hassan, in preparation) offers ways to formalize the description of local styles, and comparisons of such styles will probably be facilitated by phrasing them as comparisons between the design grammars.

The problem of identifying patterns of imitation and innovation within a corpus of material that is obviously related (though perhaps often distantly) seems to have much in common with that of working out the relationships between different manuscript versions of an ancient text, and even more in common with the interplay of diverse influences and new ideas in the history of an artistic style. All this points vaguely in the direction of data bases with sophisticated and flexible organizations. Some steps in this direction have already been taken (e.g. Gardin 1980; Langley 1986). I urge that much more attention be given to such approaches.

Some brief notices
Space does not suffice to deal adequately with all important formal approaches in archaeology. There are three more, however, that require at least brief mention.

Discrete multivariate analysis
Cross-tabulations of pairs of nominal scale variables and associated statistics, such as chi-square, are relatively familiar. Extensions of this approach to consider the joint effects and interactions of a number of nominal scale variables has flourished only in the past two or three decades. In spite of a number of archaeological papers on the methods (Spaulding 1976, 1977; Read 1974; Clark 1976; Lewis 1986), there have as yet been relatively few archaeological applications. This is perhaps because even with only four or five variables the simplest models that satisfactorily summarize the data may seem disturbingly complex, and it may also be that many archaeologists have not seen, from the examples presented, how to make the approach bear directly on the problems that most interest them. I predict, however, that in the near future discrete multivariate analysis will find many applications in archaeology.

Exploratory data analysis
This label refers to a diversity of techniques that share the attitude of looking without too many preconceptions at a "batch" of data in various ways to try to see what structure or pattern may lurk within, and a concern with "robust" methods that are

not much disturbed by a few aberrant or erroneous data values or by serious departure of the data from traditionally popular assumptions such as approximate Normality. Many of the techniques offer very welcome alternatives to "standard" procedures described in elementary statistics texts, and with good reason they are becoming very popular in archaeology. They are increasingly available in common statistical systems for computers. They do not, of course, supersede other techniques that require stronger assumptions about the data and "cleaner" data, but they are extremely valuable additions to the repertoire of techniques, especially in earlier stages of an analysis. Many of the techniques and concepts are relatively simple, and all archaeologists should become acquainted with them. Tukey (1977) and Mosteller and Tukey (1977) are good introductions.

Artificial intelligence and expert systems

I have had no direct experience with this field, and I rely largely on a recent discussion by Doran, who argues that these non-numerical but formal methods will be particularly effective in suggesting "new forms of theory, both sociocultural and middle-range, precisely because they already, and in practice, bridge the gap between data and process models" (Doran 1986:32). Clearly a great deal more work needs to be done, and Doran cautions that "progress will not be easy" (Doran 1986:32). But, to return to the Bayesian mood, I think the odds that something important will come from this direction are good enough to warrant careful attention to it.

Notes

1   Binford (1986:463–4) charges that some archaeologists seem to think of themselves as merely disadvantaged ethnographers. Clearly we should not think of ourselves that way. To do so carries the tacit implication that if only we had access to the kinds of information on ancient societies that an ethnographer can get on contemporary societies, all our questions would be answered, whereas the magnitude of unsolved theoretical questions about ethnographically accessible societies is only too apparent. Furthermore, archaeologists can get kinds of information, especially about changes over time, that are rarely available to ethnographers. Nevertheless, the kinds of highly relevant information that we cannot get, or can only infer with great difficulty, remain very frustrating. Our understanding is greatly aided when archaeological data on a society can be combined with documentary and/or ethnographic data on the same society.

2   This use of the term "family resemblance" comes from Wittgenstein and has been taken up in social anthropology by Needham and others (Benson Saler, personal communication).

6

Ideology and evolutionism in American archaeology: looking beyond the economic base

ARTHUR A. DEMAREST

Even with contemporary societies the analysis of religion presents formidable conceptual, epistemological, and methodological obstacles. It is not surprising then that extensive studies of ideology in archaeology have traditionally been largely derived from historical and proto-historic sources rather than prehistoric evidence. The study of prehistoric religion and ideology in Old World archaeology relied heavily upon Biblical texts, Mesopotamian tablets, Classical mythology, and other historic and proto-historic sources. Similarly, in American archaeology and anthropology most early analyses of New World religious systems were based directly or indirectly on written records (Demarest 1987). Studies of the religious systems of historic and proto-historic peoples (Aztec, Inka, Post-Classic Maya) were based on the Precolumbian codices, the conquistadors' chronicles, church and government surveys, and archives of legal records (e.g. Seler 1960–1; Caso 1945; Nicholson 1971; Leon-Portilla 1963, 1968a; Rowe 1946). Studies of religion in the prehistoric period were derived primarily from the art and iconography which, in turn, was interpreted through comparison to these same Conquest period sources (e.g., Covarrubias 1957; Leon-Portilla 1968b; Morley 1956; Joralemon 1971; Coe 1968:111–15, 1978). Such studies were sometimes successful in describing Precolumbian pantheons, rituals, and cosmologies, especially elite religious ideology. Beyond the direct historical approach, analysis of fully prehistoric ideology was left to those who were willing to apply unsystematic and subjective interpretations to ancient art or artifacts.

Most of the studies of Precolumbian religion, moreover, had little relevance to the broader issues of the study of general cultural evolution that were reemerging in the 1960s and 70s. In American archaeology the return of evolutionism came together with the introduction of culture ecology, and quasi-Marxist concepts in the work of Leslie White (1959a), Julian Steward (1955), and others. Ideology was explicitly viewed as a trivial, secondary, or "epiphenomenal" force in this reemerging evolutionism, at least in the reinterpretations of White and Steward by the cultural materialists that followed them (Harris 1964, 1968; Sanders and Price 1968).

Such a position found a receptive audience among American field archaeologists for a number of reasons. The many methodological and technical breakthroughs of the 50s, 60s, and 70s related primarily to chronology and recovery of subsistence evidence (see for example Brothwell and Higgs 1970; Butzer 1982). So, it was the economic base that captured the interest and efforts of most archaeologists. There seemed to be a (largely implicit) consensus that religious behavior was too complex, idiosyncratic, or obscure to be perceived in the archaeological record. Thus, both explicit theoretical stances and methodological expediency guided evolutionary anthropologists away from ideology and toward the cultural materialist approach. Demographic pressure, hydraulic systems, marketing networks, and conflict over limited resources were among the economic factors investigated as major forces in cultural evolution.

The growing interest in ideology in American archaeology

The reappearance of a major interest in ideology and religion in American evolutionary anthropology came from a number of different sources. The self-designated "New Archaeology" of the 60s was generally interested in ancient economic and ecological analyses. But it also incorporated high methodological aspirations. Among these were Binford's assertions (1962, 1965) that by using a scientific deductive approach archaeologists could move beyond culture-history to reconstruct aspects of social and even ideological systems. Following Binford's lead a number of archaeologists in the 70s addressed broad patterns in ancient ideology through intensive analysis (often statistically aided) of patterning in distributions and associations of architecture, artifacts, or design elements (e.g. Drennan 1976; Fritz 1978; Flannery and Marcus 1976a, 1976b; Pyne 1976). Other intensive studies of distributions and correlations in artifact types, attributes, and design elements reopened an archaeological focus on style as a means of defining information networks and interregional interaction (e.g. Plog 1976, 1978, 1980; Wobst 1977). Such researches led inevitably to a realization of the importance of ideological systems in defining both culture areas and the interaction networks that transcended them (e.g. Demarest 1978, 1986; Freidel 1979, 1981; Ashmore 1986). Thus, one of the original sources of American archaeology's renewed interest in ideology arose ultimately from the New Archaeology's concern with extending the interpretive limits of the analysis of patterning in the archaeological record. It is interesting that the most recent neo-Marxist analyses of prehistoric ideology have drawn heavily upon the New Archaeology's ambitious approach to statistical patterning as a methodological tool (see for example, Miller and Tilley 1984: 1–15).

Archaeological applications of systems theory were also important in the return of ideology to the debate on cultural evolution. Systems theory emphasizes the interrelationships between all institutions in the functioning of social and political systems. It follows that no major institution or aspect of society – including ritual and religion – can be considered a wholly dependent or "epiphenomenal" variable in culture change. In the article that introduced many New World archaeologists to systems thinking, Kent Flannery asserted that "Archaeologists must cease to regard art, religion and ideology as mere 'epiphenomena' without causal significance . . . such 'epiphenomena' . . . lie at the heart of society's environmental and interpersonal regulation, and as such cannot be omitted from any comprehensive ecological analysis . . ." (Flannery 1972a:400). Rappaport (1978), Whyte (1978), and other systems theorists addressed the issue of the role of ideology in cultural maladaptation and collapse. Such systems approaches were among the influences in a series of interpretations of the rise and fall of Precolumbian civilizations that incorporated ideology, especially state religion, as a major causative factor (e.g. Demarest 1976; Cowgill 1979; Freidel 1981a; Drennan 1976; Flannery and Marcus 1976b).

The current intense interest in ideology's role in cultural evolution can also be traced to a third thread in the weave of influences on American archaeology in the 1970s and early 80s. Ironically it was renewed European interest in Marxism, the most important school of *economic* history, that led to intense interest in ideology in archaeology and to the most direct confrontation with cultural materialism and ecological functionalism that had dominated American archaeology for decades. While asserting the primacy of the infrastructural base, Marxist theory also provided a role for ideology in legitimation of authority, a particularly critical factor in the fragile power relations of emerging chiefdoms and archaic states. Friedman (1974, 1975), Godelier (1977, 1978a, 1978b, 1978c), Terray (1978), Legros (1977; Legros et al. 1979), and others went further to argue for more complex interpretations of the causal relationships, relative importance, and interplay between infrastructural economic factors and higher level sociopolitical institutions (structure or superstructure). To structural Marxists it was perfectly conceivable that ideological or social factors could play a dominant role in a specific historical transformation:

A change in dominance can be explained only by taking the whole social
formation into account, for if we restrict ourselves to the infrastructural
level alone, we exclude the possibility that a formerly super-structural
element will become part of the relations of production, a phenomenon
which characterizes the great majority of historical transformations.

(Friedman 1975:198)

In a specific application, Godelier asserted that Inka state religion did more than merely legitimate or reflect economic relations: "But, in this context, we see that religious ideology is not merely the superficial, phantasmic reflection of social relations. It is an element internal to the social relations of production . . ." (Godelier 1978a:8–10).

So, by the late 1970s the aging "New Archaeology," ecologically oriented systems theory, and structural-Marxism were all leading a minority of American archaeologists toward an appreciation of the complex relationships possible between economic, social, political, and ideological forces in cultural evolution. Unfortunately, trends in field archaeology and archaeological funding had moved in the opposite direction, toward an ever more entrenched materialism.

The trials and tribulations of cultural materialism
By the 1970s cultural materialist thinking had come to dominate evolutionary thinking in American archaeology. Frankly, most American field archaeology continued to be at least explicitly atheoretical. However, when broad level theory was invoked it was usually a form of cultural materialism (see for example, Wolf 1976; Palerm 1972; Parsons 1974; Sanders 1968, 1972; Isbell 1978; Paulsen 1976). Harris (1964, 1968, 1974, 1977, 1979) had popularized a theory of cultural evolution that was

explicitly reductionist, seeking ultimately to explain all culture change in terms of technological responses to environmental change, demographic pressure, and protein deficiency:

I believe that the analogue of the Darwinian strategy in the realm of sociocultural phenomena is the principle of techno-environmental and techno-economic determinism. This principle holds that similar technologies applied to similar environments tend to produce similar arrangements of labor in production and distribution, and that these in turn call forth similar kinds of social groupings, which justify and coordinate their activities by means of similar systems of values and beliefs.

(Harris 1968:4)

The appeal of such a philosophy to American archaeology should be apparent. The most accessible kinds of evidence that had been the focus of decades of research (subsistence data, ecological reconstructions, hydraulic systems, and so on) were now designated as theoretically the only significant independent factors:

Translated into research strategy, the principle of techno-environmental, techno-economic determinism assigns priority to the study of material conditions of sociocultural life, much as the principle of natural selection assigns priority to the study of differential reproductive success.

(Harris 1968:4)

In presentations in cultural anthropology, cultural materialism has taken two forms. Broad works have tried to explain general evolution and culture change in terms of social responses to ecological pressures resulting in increasing "energy-efficiency" and population growth (e.g. Harris 1979; Sanders and Price 1968). A more common presentation of cultural materialist interpretations is in the form of essays that purport to discover the hidden economic rationality in apparently irrational religious institutions such as the sacred cow of India, Islamic prohibitions on pork, or Aztec human sacrifice and cannibalism (e.g. Harris 1974, 1977; Harner 1977). These exercises represent reductionism in its purest form, as each cultural feature or institution is literally translated into a disguised mechanism to increase agricultural productivity, supplement protein resources, or respond to demographic pressure. Religious behavior was not merely limited to a role of legitimating authority, but was redefined as a package of supplemental subsistence techniques thinly disguised as sacred principles.

In application to field archaeology cultural materialism and culture-ecology provided a *post hoc* theoretical environment for the studies of population trends and agricultural intensification that were the most significant areas of successful research in American archaeology from the late 50s to the end of the 1970s. Inspired by early innovative approaches to settlement patterns in archaeology and ethnography (Steward 1937, 1955; Willey 1953), American archaeology had concentrated on the recording of settlement distributions and the interpretation of such patterns in terms of irrigation systems, population dynamics, and exchange systems (e.g. R. McC. Adams 1965b; Wolf 1976; Wright and Johnson 1975; Deevey et al. 1979; Harrison and Turner, eds. 1978; Sanders et al. 1979). The archaeological findings of such projects were used to construct regional cultural materialist histories with an emphasis on population growth in relation to limited resources (see, for example, Spooner 1972; R. E. W. Adams 1977; Sanders and Price 1968; Webster 1976; Carneiro 1970).

Yet even before the confrontation with the developing interests in ideology discussed above, there were empirical problems arising within the field data from such ecologically oriented projects. After extensive settlement pattern studies and historical analysis (Adams 1965b; Adams and Nissen 1972), Adams concluded that in Mesopotamia irrigation and population dynamics could not be considered the "prime movers" in cultural change. Rather, a complex interaction between social, political, and ecological factors helped to bring about the need, conditions, and the organizational capacity involved in developing major hydraulic systems (Adams 1966, 1969, 1972). Furthermore, historical and archaeological data indicated that the methodological focus on individual basins, valleys, or other topographically defined ecological zones was inadequate, since interregional, interethnic, and even "international" interaction appeared to be critical in the development of complex society in the Near East (R. McC. Adams 1981; Lamberg-Karlovsky 1974, 1975; Wright 1985).

In the New World the results of intensive settlement studies in Central Mexico were interpreted according to the materialist hypothesis of interaction between population pressure, irrigation, and intercommunity economic symbiosis (Sanders 1968; Wolf 1976). However there was disagreement among the archaeologists working in Central Mexico as to whether the proposed ecological hypothesis had been verified or negated by the results. Blanton (1976a, 1976b) argued that neither the timing nor scale of demographic pressures and economic symbiosis could explain the major political transformations in the Valley of Mexico. He later concluded that in the Valley of Oaxaca population pressure and agricultural intensification were not the major factors in urbanism at Monte Alban (1978, 1980). Parsons (1976; Sanders et al. 1979:281) concluded that the most massive transformation of the Central Mexican intensive agricultural systems occurred *after* rather than before the formation of the Aztec empire, an inversion of Wittfogel's causal order for hydraulics parallel to Adams's findings in the Near East. Millon, excavator of the preeminent Central Mexican city of Teotihuacan, believed that the identified pre-Aztec hydraulic systems of the Valley were few and unimpressive. Millon suspected that state formation and urbanism at Teotihuacan were more closely related to the site's early role as a pilgrimage, market, and craft center (1973). Brumfiel reinterpreted the Valley of Mexico settlement patterns (1976), noting that the site locations during the period of transition to the state were in ecologically redundant settings contradicting the hypothesis of "economic symbiosis" and inter-village exchange of goods. Overall the application of cultural materialist theory in Mexico had not succeeded in producing a credible evolutionary reconstruction.

Meanwhile, in other regions of the New World, enthusiastic applications of cultural ecology had run into similar difficulties. In the Maya area social circumscription, demographic pressure, and warfare had been applied to explain state formation in the

Caribbean limestone plain of the Peten jungle and Yucatan (Carneiro 1970; Webster 1977; Sanders 1977; Ball 1977). However, discoveries subsequent to these interpretations pushed back the chronology of the florescence of Maya civilization by four to five centuries rendering the proposed demographic trends and evidence of conflict irrelevant to the initial formation of the Maya state (Freidel 1979, 1981a; Matheny 1980; Demarest 1984, 1986). Similar difficulties arose in Peru where the chronology for the formation of complex society was pushed back well before irrigation, warfare, and, arguably, even major staple agriculture (Moseley 1975, 1978; cf. Wilson 1981; Quilter and Stocker 1983).

Two decades of cultural ecological approaches in American archaeology had revolutionized our understanding of culture-history and the subsistence systems that sustained the New World civilizations. Yet it was equally clear from the recovered evidence that the materialist interpretive framework was, at best, incomplete. Hypotheses mechanically deriving early political systems from demographic pressures and economic responses had generally failed to fit the form or the timing of early state formation.

The confrontation over ecological determinism

In the 1970s a period of polemic debate began over cultural materialist theory and the nature of the causal forces involved in cultural transformations. A climate for confrontation was set by the beginnings of an interest in ideology coming from the New Archaeology, some systems approaches, and structural Marxism – together with the field results, discussed above, that failed to convincingly support cultural materialist interpretations. By the mid-70s even conservative field archaeologists, whose work rested on a kind of implicit culture ecology, were prepared to question the completeness of the culture materialist paradigm and seek more holistic explanations:

If thinking human beings are the generators, as well as the carriers, of culture it seems highly probable that, from very early on, ideas provided controls for and gave distinctive forms to the materialist base and to culture, and that these ideas then took on a kind of existence of their own, influencing, as well as being influenced by, other cultural systems. If this is so, then it is of interest and importance to try to see how ideas were interrelated with other parts of culture and how they helped direct the trajectories of cultural and civilizational growth.

(Willey 1976:205)

The most aggressive challenges, however, to culture materialism and strictly ecological analysis came in rejections of specific essays and theories of Marvin Harris and his adherents. The often acrid tone of debate was induced by the materialist works themselves which tended to label other approaches interested in ideology as "reactionary" or "obscurantist" (see for example Harris 1979) and rejected most Marxist analyses because of their emphasis on the dialectic, the "Hegelian monkey" on their backs. Despite such bitter defenses, it became clear to many scholars that there were basic problems with the evidence cited in support of many materialist explanations. Attacks from specialists in India, the Near East, and Mesoamerica exposed basic errors in the cultural materialist explanations, especially failure to examine known historical sources concerning the chronological order of events and factors involved in the creation of the sacred cow, pork taboos, Aztec cannibalism, and other rituals. Anthropologists pointed to specific historical sequences of events that created these institutions in response to a variety of forces (e.g. Diener, Nonini and Robkin 1978, 1980; Diener, Moore and Mutaw 1980; Simoons 1973, 1979; Azzi 1974). In retrospect it is clear that most of the anecdotal materialist "solutions" to specific riddles of culture had committed the simplest form of functionalist fallacy by substituting hypotheses that an institution is ecologically adaptive for the actual historical documentation of origins: "A specific fallacious form of explanation which has plagued functional-ecological investigation in anthropology, as it plagued classical functionalism before it, involves the improper accounting for historical origins by reference to observed or assumed functions" (Diener et al. 1978:223).

Additional problems were found in the mechanics of specific materialist explanations. In most cases, rituals or religious institutions had been reduced to culturally disguised examples of ecological engineering. But anthropologists more familiar with each culture under discussion usually found ample evidence that the proposed increased productivity, alleviation of protein deficiency or other positive economic effects would *not*, in fact, have occurred. For example, a number of studies demonstrated that Aztec sacrifice and cannibalism would have been counterproductive as a response to protein or food shortage, while other studies pointed out that there were, in fact, no such protein shortages (Garn 1979; Garn and Block 1970; Berdan 1975:304; Price 1978a; Ortiz de Montellano 1978; Diener, Nonini and Robkin 1980; Demarest 1984). It could also be shown that warfare would not be an effective means of stabilizing population resource imbalances as cultural materialists had proposed (Cook 1946; Paulsen 1976). Indeed, the death of warrior/farmers in their prime would have greatly exacerbated resource deficiencies (Berdan 1975:304; Demarest 1984; Conrad and Demarest 1984:165–70; Conrad 1981a, 1981b; Price 1978a). Similarly, Old World scholars pointed out that the sacred taboos identified in the Old World would not have produced the proposed protein maximizing effect (Simoons 1973, 1979; Diener and Robkin 1978).

An area of broader criticisms against cultural materialism attacked the simplistic assumptions it made about human demography. Most cultural materialist explanations (almost all of those applied in American archaeology) were based upon the assumption that human "population growth is a general phenomenon and that human reproductive behavior generally is unlike that of most other species only in its tendency towards sustained growth" (Sanders et al. 1979:364). Apart from the apparent dismissal of human consciousness, will, and imagination as unique features, the fundamental assertion that the species blindly outbreeds its resources has been thoroughly rejected in regional and cross-cultural demographic studies based on direct ethnographic data (e.g. Lee 1972; Wagley 1973; Cowgill 1975a, 1975b; Nardi 1981; Wrigley 1969; Polgar 1971, 1972, 1975; Langer 1974; Himes 1963). These studies have demonstrated that "fertility regulation is a virtually universal phenomenon" (Nardi 1981:31). Infanticide, abortion, post-partum taboos, celibate sectors of society, homosexuality, coitus interruptus, periodic abstinence, and other forms of birth control exist in some degree in all societies. Indeed, as Cowgill has pointed out (1975a, b) anthropologists need to explain *why* demographic growth occurs when it does, since culturally unrestrained reproduction is more the exception than the rule.

From systems theory, Marxism, and even cultural ecology another series of criticisms accused cultural materialists and most cultural ecologists of having committed the so-called "organic fallacy," another common ailment of functionalist explanations. The Marxists were most aggressive in pointing out that society does not consist of a coordinated uniform organism responding to environmental pressures. Rather, it consists of conflicting individuals, groups, families, and classes whose goals are not necessarily identical and whose interests (and actions) are often not in agreement with the "adaptive" or "functional" needs of the cultural system as a whole. The unequal distribution of power in complex societies can often result in the dominance of interests of specific individuals or small elites, even in cases where these interests are maladaptive for the society as a whole.

The inability to deal with maladaptation and collapse became another common criticism of most of the "adaptive" functionalist interpretations prevalent in archaeology. Marxists and systems theorists criticized such "vulgar" materialist approaches for their failure to recognize the conflicting forces within society which were, ultimately, the cause of most systemic collapses of civilizations. As Friedman (1974:466) has noted, "History is built upon the failure of social forms as much as on their success." The assumption that institutions and societies are ecologically adaptive only allows for "conquest" (in a Darwinian usage) as an explanation of collapse. Yet it is clear from history that internal maladaptation, conflict, and inefficiency have more often been the cause of the disintegration of civilizations.

Integrating ideology into reconstructions of culture change: the search for an approach

By the late 1970s and into the 80s those rejecting strictly ecological interpretations began to face the more difficult task of proposing alternatives. The goal in each case has been to discover interpretive frameworks that would not rigidly preassign chronological or causal priority for economic, social, and political institutions and that would incorporate internal societal diversity, human volition, and ideology in theories on culture change. Initial gropings toward such complex models faced great obstacles.

There were, of course, methodological difficulties to be faced in reconstructing ideological systems. But even more formidable were the conceptual and epistemological problems involved in understanding systems now acknowledged to involve conscious actors. Ecological models addressing decision-making processes, Marxist analyses, some recent systems approaches, and eclectic holistic reconstructions shared an ambition to incorporate human consciousness, self-interest, free will, and even irrationality into historical or evolutionary explanation. By moving away from a strict economic or ecological determinism, Marxists, culture ecologists, and others began to find common ground in the thorough interpretation of societies as collections of heterogeneous interests (*cf.* Orlove 1980; Rodin et al. 1978; Rappaport 1978; White-brook 1976; Cohen 1981). Ideology in such analyses could be seen as a major component which affects the decision-making processes (in both maladaptive and adaptive ways) and which motivates, legitimates, and, at times, shapes human social action.

Following the traditional direction of Marxism, most neo-Marxists or structural-Marxist analyses emphasized the role of ideology in the legitimation of authority and iniquitous arrangements of wealth and power. In 1978, Claessen and Skalnik edited an influential collection of essays on the early state that examined prehistoric, proto-historic, and historic states from a somewhat flexible Marxist theoretical perspective. In that same year a volume edited by Carrasco and Broda (1978) focused on Marxist approaches to ancient Mesoamerican state institutions. In these analyses ideology was given a major role in social formations, but that role is rather narrowly limited to legitimation. Analyses of the Aztec state by Kurtz (1978) and Bray (1978) emphasized the state use of ideology to legitimate the authority of the elite through myth and dogma, while exercising "political intimidation" through the grisly religious rituals of mass human sacrifice. According to Kurtz (1978:85) the "inchoate, uncentralized form of the Aztec state necessitated a heavy reliance on religious justification to acquire legitimacy and maintain a tenuous control."

While early states certainly did legitimate their authority through religion, it is a mistake to restrict interpretations to such a role. In analyses of Aztec human sacrifice, I have emphasized that the central cult of the Mexica state was politically manipulated, at least initially, to overturn the existing social order, motivate endemic warfare, and subsequently institutionalize a perpetual state of war (Demarest 1976, 1984; Demarest and Conrad 1983; Conrad and Demarest 1984: ch. 2, 4). Thus, in this case ideology functions as a dynamic element in the reformulation of a new social order. Ultimately the manipulation of the state religion can be traced to elite interest groups, but they did far more than reaffirm the status quo. In the end the ideological revisions they instituted became a force for expansionism that they neither understood nor could control (Conrad and Demarest 1984: ch. 2). In fact, the decentralized "inchoate" nature of the state referred to by Kurtz was more a result than a cause of their manipulations of state ideology (Demarest 1984).

Such a dynamic role for ideology has been seen in Andean societies as well, in analyses by Schaedel (1978), Godelier (1978a), Conrad (1981a), Haas (1982) and myself (Demarest 1981). Schaedel emphasizes both the high economic costs of Inka religious ritual and its active role in integrating social, political, and economic networks in that society. Godelier explicitly argues that the Inka cult of Inti "was not merely a legitimizing ideology, after the fact, for the relations of production; it was a part of the internal armature of these relations of production" (Godelier 1978a:10). In my own analysis of the Inka upper pantheon (Demarest 1981) I saw continuous state revision of the mythology of the high gods as an instrument used by the elites to *change* existing economic strategies. Murra (1960, 1980) had demonstrated a parallel manipulation of rituals – again to shift, as much as to legitimate, economic behavior. Finally, Conrad and I (1984: ch. 3, 4; Demarest and Conrad 1983; Conrad 1981a) have tried to demonstrate that Inka property rights of the dead and split inheritance, while instituted originally to legitimate authority, had far more sweeping economic and political consequences.

In studies of the Maya civilization there also has been a parallel trend in interpretations of ideology. State religion and rituals are no longer viewed as after-the-fact legitimation but rather are believed to have been a dynamic force, one of the major sources of the initial formation of the distinctive state institutions of that society. Recent hieroglyphic decipherments have confirmed the longstanding impression that Maya kings held sway more through their role in ritual than through economic or coercive power (e.g. Schele and Miller 1986; Schele 1984; Freidel and Schele 1986). Even the endemic warfare among the Maya was so ritually defined and channeled as to serve a function closer to one of social and political interaction and alliance (Demarest 1978; Freidel 1986). Recent archaeological and iconographic evidence indicates that early religious cults and their transformation played a major role in the initial formation of the Maya state, its dispersed "galactic" political structure, and its uniquely charismatic and shamanistic form of kingship (Freidel 1981a, 1981b, in press; Demarest 1984, 1986, in press; Matheny 1987).

The fact is that analyses that rigidly limit the role of ideology to legitimation commit some of the same fallacies as earlier cultural materialist studies. They impose *a priori* a causal and chronological order, at times ignoring evidence to the contrary. For the Aztec and Inka, and perhaps now for the Maya, religious reformations and cults not only legitimated existing economic and power relations, but reshaped and even overturned existing political institutions. Ideology was a source of power, power that could be legitimating or that could be utilized by individuals or institutions as a disruptive or revisionary force. Clearly, its effectiveness is greatest when religious and economic power coincide. As Haas (1982:196) has argued regarding the earliest complex centers in coastal Peru, their formation "cannot be accounted for strictly in terms of the exercise of either economic or ideological bases alone; rather it can only be accounted for in terms of the combination of both types of power."

The most recent published studies on ideology have pursued the issue of the relationship between legitimation, ideology, and power. Volumes edited by Hodder (1982a), Miller and Tilley (1984), and Demarest and Conrad (in press) are collections of essays addressing these issues for specific prehistoric societies in Europe and the New World, respectively. These most recent collections embody both the promise and the problems of our current struggle for an approach to ancient ideologies. The discussions by European scholars in the first two volumes espouse an explicitly Marxist orientation again emphasizing the legitimating role of ideology. Nonetheless, the emphasis is on power relations and it is clearly understood by the analysts that ideology can be a dynamic element in such relations: "ideology and power are inextricably bound up with social practices; they are a component of human *praxis*, by which is to be understood the actions of agents on and in the world, serving as an integral element in the production, reproduction and transformation of the social" (Miller and Tilley 1984:14).

Drawing on discussion of these issues in European history (e.g. Larrain 1979;

Sumner 1979; Duby 1985), these studies also acknowledged the existence of different, at times conflicting, ideologies within a single society. They explored the ways in which such conflicting ideologies actively represent, or rather misrepresent, the relations of groups within it. Miller and Tilley (1984:1–15) argued that the distinction between representation, reality, and social action is blurred in diachronic analyses of ideology, since representation itself generates actions that can transform the realities of existing power relations.

However, in these recent neo-Marxist interpretations there is somewhat of a disjunction between the lofty theoretical debate and the specific applications to archaeological evidence on prehistoric societies. For the prehistoric European societies Shanks and Tilley (1982), Shennan (1982), Braithwaite (1984), and Tilley (1984) examined cultural transformations apparent in the remains of Bronze Age and Neolithic sites. They saw changes in ideological systems both reflecting and helping to cause major realignments in power relations between social groups within these societies. However, as with the New Archaeology's first discussions of "ideofacts" in the 1960s (Binford 1962), their primary evidence involved the statistical patterning of artifact types, especially funerary goods, tombs, and so on. In each case, the correlation between the ideological artifact and the interest group identified must, to some extent, be assumed. The chronologies for the social transformations do not seem to be sufficiently precise to elucidate the causal order involved in the power/ideology equation. Furthermore, alternative interpretations could be given for most of the artifact patterns discussed. Still, these are hardly damning criticisms from such innovative initial attempts to address ideology in fully *pre*historic contexts. I suspect that such ambiguities will always exist in studies of prehistoric ideology, given the nature of the archaeological data base and the complexities of human ritual and religious behavior. I have somewhat more serious reservations about the continued emphasis on legitimation, even "active" legitimation, as the nearly exclusive role for religion.

The very latest major contribution to this formative field of prehistoric ideology is the School of American Research Advanced Seminar on the role of Precolumbian ideology in cultural evolution (Demarest and Conrad in press). Essays by Cowgill, Grove, Freidal, Kolata, Wilson, Conrad, and myself addressed specific examples of the role of ideology in cultural transformations and state formation in the states of Teotihuacan, the Maya, the Aztec, Inka, Initial Period Peru, and Tiahuanaco. Theoretical counterpoints, ethnographic comparisons were given by Helms, Carneiro, Haas, and Adams. It is remarkable that this American symposium on the study of ancient ideology in cultural evolution contrasts in so many respects with the recent European contributions.

On the positive side, these new American studies are freed from the need to conform to a Marxist paradigm that I believe is, at times, restrictive. There is no compunction about moving well beyond a legitimating function in describing ancient ideologies. Another strength, one that allows more sophisticated and convincing analyses, is due to the far richer data base available to Mesoamerican and Andean archaeologists. As in the past, the interpretations of ancient ideology are almost entirely derived from the historic materials of the Conquest period and their projection back in time is via iconography and a greatly expanded corpus of deciphered hieroglyphic texts. In contrast to the fully prehistoric European studies there is almost no use of the more ambiguous statistical interpretation of patterning in artifact and grave good distributions. While this continued use of the direct-historical approach in the Precolumbian studies allows for more detailed and convincing studies of ancient ideology, it is an implicit admission of the inability of American archaeologists to develop a methodology for addressing fully prehistoric evidence on ideology.

Another surprising flaw is that the American archaeologists seem to be less fully informed about the methodological and epistemological literature on ideology that exists in the field of European historiography (e.g. LeGoff and Nora 1985; Larrain 1979). In only a few cases does there seem to be a usage or perhaps even awareness of the structural-Marxist approaches to ideology. This limited communication between American and European scholarship is particularly surprising given that most of the recent major volumes on prehistoric ideology were published by the same press (Cambridge University Press: Hodder 1982a, 1982c; Conrad and Demarest 1984; Miller and Tilley 1984; Renfrew and Cherry 1986; Demarest and Conrad in press). However, from the results of recent symposia and from volumes such as this one, communication between the American and structural-Marxist "schools" on ideology is beginning. Perhaps a sharing of concepts will correct both the theoretical rigidity of the Marxist framework and the ethnohistorical dependency of the American studies.

Reactions and response

Needless to say, these forays into the issues of ideology's role in cultural evolution have not always been positively received. Some cultural ecologists and cultural materialists have rejected any significant role for ideology as a causal force in cultural evolution or historical transformations.

The criticisms of the new approaches fall into two types. One argument is that while holists and structural-Marxists have successfully challenged the determinism of cultural materialism, we have not yet ourselves been able to present a clear, methodologically integrated, and uniform theoretical alternative (e.g. Bray 1984, Charlton 1986). These criticisms are clearly valid. We have demonstrated the importance of ideology but we are still struggling for a semblance of a methodology to approach it. However, this criticism expresses an unfair impatience given the almost total absence of discussion of the *evolutionary* impact of ideology prior to the 1970s.

A second set of negative responses has far less validity. These are the reactions of materialists who accuse these studies of ancient ideology of merely positing religion as the "prime mover" of social change in place of the materialists' use of subsistence technology or demographic pressure (e.g. Mignon 1986; Smith 1986). Such assertions are simply untrue. Not one of the recent studies of ideology mentioned above sees ideology as a prime mover. Indeed, every study openly acknowledges that ultimately most major trends in cultural evolution "can be said to reside in the materialist matrix. This is where life begins, where populations are sustained, and where certain limits are set on sizes and groupings of human societies" (Willey 1976:205). Most of the recent discussions of ideology have directly addressed the ways in which it modifies and reshapes a trajectory of cultural evolution whose broadest parameters were set by economic and ecological forces (see especially Conrad and Demarest 1984: ch. 4; Miller and Tilley 1984).

These condemnations of the recent researches as ideologically deterministic merely reflect the rigidity of cultural materialist dogma and a clinging to the worst scientific pretensions of the New Archaeology of the 1960s. It is a simplistic logic which demands that institutions, subfields of society, and causal forces be reduced to fully independent or fully dependent variables in a pseudo-mathematical equation. Such a reductionism ignores both the complexities of the causal relationships between institutions and the terminological and philosophical problems raised by their labeling.

In one example of such a blind reaction, Smith (1986:83) accuses Conrad, myself, and others of arguing that the rise of the Mexica state was due to "intangible factors like destiny, personality, or ideology" and that we believe that Mexica success was due to "intrinsic characteristics of the Mexica populace," especially "religious fanaticism." Yet even a casual reading of any of our analyses of Aztec imperialism would reveal that our argument views Mexica state religion as an instrument manipulated for political ends by the military elite. Such manipulations were among the factors that produced economic, political, and ideological incentives for continual warfare – incentives that operated at the level of both class and individual decision-making strategy (Conrad and Demarest 1984: ch. 4). Economic and status incentives, together with the overt propaganda of the state cosmology, motivated Mexica warriors to the unrelenting efforts and savagery well testified to in the chronicles and direct ethnohistorical reports of their neighbors. So, while a portion of our analysis does deal with religious fanaticism, it views it as a conscious creation of a self-interested social class. Group personality, irrationality, or mysticism are not involved. Once generated, the fanaticism of the Aztecs was critical in their military success.

Those who feel that discussions of the role of fanaticism in military successes are "mystical" or "intangible" need only to read a bit about the Nazi movement in the 1930s and 40s or about the Islamic conquests of the seventh and eighth centuries, or even the ongoing wave assaults by hords of untrained adolescents in the mudflats of contemporary Mesopotamia. There seems to be an immediate assumption by some materialists that almost any discussion of the role of ideology as a causal force is forbidden by scientific rationality. In view of the powerful ideological forces in recent Western history and in the world today, such an attitude can itself be labeled an unrealistic, almost "mystic," philosophy.

While the responses by some materialists have been bitter and polemic, the new approaches to ideology have in general been very well received. It seems that most field archaeologists practicing culture ecology never really espoused the rigid paradigms constructed by the philosophers of that school: the focus on ecological parameters was largely due to the inaccessibility of most data on ideological or cultural institutions. Culture-ecologists and Marxists are now among those most active in the ongoing studies of ideology. As Orlove had accurately predicted, the issue of ideology has actually tended to pull together "idealist" and materialist approaches to cultural evolution: "As this work progresses, materialist and idealist approaches in anthropology are likely to find more common ground through a more thorough interpretation of culture and ideology as systems which mediate between actors and environments through the construction of behavioral alternatives" (Orlove 1980:262).

I think that the innovative approaches and intense debate of the past five years demonstrate that our disorganized assault on this inscrutable issue is yielding a fruitful dialogue as well as some initial understandings. We should not be naive, however, about the continued difficulties that we will face in addressing issues of ancient ideology. In the field of European history, scholars interested in ideology, mentalities, and attitudes as historical forces admit that they have not yet succeeded in forging a coherent, systematic approach to this issue (e.g. LeGoff 1985; Duby 1985). Their problems in historiography, methodology, and epistemology exist despite decades of research and an evidential record far more complete than exists for any Precolumbian period. Archaeologists, as of yet, have not, and perhaps cannot, address the issues raised by these historians regarding the impact of internally contradictory social values on individual decision-making, the existence of unrecorded and unrepresented heretical ideologies, and the constant interplay between a culture's internal ideology and the foreign concepts which continually affect it (see especially LeGoff and Nora 1985). As always, archaeologists should be humbled by the contrast between the vast scale of the explanations they seek and the feebleness and unreliability of the evidence, their means of recovering it, and their tools of interpretation. We should not, however, be discouraged; those interested in the study of long-term cultural evolution must resolve themselves to the broad strokes and flawed canvases of our art.

7

The present and the future of hunter-gatherer studies

JOHN E. YELLEN

As the concept of a world system has expanded beyond the historical context from which it originally derived and has gained increasing favor in anthropological analysis, the notion that any hunting and gathering group can stand, be "explained" or "understood" in seemingly untouched isolation becomes increasingly tenuous. Although this basic issue – the definition of analytic units and the relationship between such units – is far from new in anthropology, the focus has until recently been directed towards relatively complex societies where ties with a market economy were clear. Recent hunters and gatherers have rarely been considered in this light because they exist in geographically remote areas as isolates surrounded by empty or sparsely inhabited space. In this context the symbiotic relationships long noted between Central African pigmy groups and their Bantu neighbors were seen more as exceptions than the rule. In the last several years however the tide has strongly turned and it is increasingly argued not only that contemporary foragers can only be "understood" in terms of a more encompassing network of human interaction but also that such a stricture holds for past counterparts who existed in a post-Neolithic world. For example recent studies of Ife (pigmy) and Lese (neighboring Bantu agriculturalists) suggest that the Central African rainforest lacks sufficient resources to support hominid foragers and thus the pigmy hunting and gathering adaptation both post-dates and is dependent upon the expansion of agriculturalists into the Congo basin. If this hypothesis is correct, it suggests that the tropical foraging groups of Southeast Asia should be revaluated in the same light. The rainforest case is but the most explicit example of a broader trend which clearly calls into question the value of much past ethnographic as well as archaeological work. The issue merits careful consideration. It affects the value of past research and calls into question the extent to which data from any extant society can increase the understanding of the pre-Neolithic hominid past.

This chapter adopts a regional perspective and takes as its focus the Zu/twasi or !Kung, a San (Bushman) people of Africa's northern Kalahari desert. Within this context it considers whether it is possible to gain insight into hominid foraging strategies from extant part-time foragers and, if so, how this may best be done. Three reasons recommend the northern Kalahari as an area for such examination. In addition to personal familiarity, the published data base, which includes archaeological and ethno-historical as well as ethnographic information, is excellent. Of equal importance is the fact that the proponents of a world system view have focused on the Kalahari San using anthropological studies of them as examples of a naive isolationist approach.

In 1980, Schrire, using data from the distant and ecologically distinct Cape Province of South Africa, noted the long history of interaction between supposed hunting and gathering and non-hunting and gathering groups and explicitly questioned whether in the twentieth century any San foragers maintained sufficient cultural integrity to stand as proxy for Pleistocene hunter gatherers. This challenge was directed explicitly at the northern Kalahari region where first the Marshalls (Marshall 1976) and then DeVore, Lee and their students continued to work. (Schrire's article can be considered a turning point in northern Kalahari research. For sake of convenience, 1980 is taken as a breakpoint and work conducted before this time is referred to as "traditional Kalahari research." Because research focused on San groups at the Dobe and /xai /xai waterholes it is convenient to label the entire region "the Dobe /xai /xai area.") According to Schrire's characterization, the Marshall and Lee–DeVore researchers assumed that San contact with non-foragers was recent and superficial: a gloss that could easily be wiped away. Schrire disagreed and the effect of her initial argument, and the supporting papers which followed it, has been such that Howell, a demographer and member of the original Kalahari research group, has repudiated much of her earlier work. She states that she now recognizes its historical shortcomings and questions its value.

Because of recent, and ongoing, archaeological and ethno-historical research our understanding of the northern Kalahari's history and prehistory is much greater today than when the first wave of Lee–DeVore research was published in the early and mid-1970s. Such new data provide some basis in fact for Schrire's arguments and Howell's recantation and both authors draw heavily on this information. However, a counter argument can be advanced that this new view of Kalahari foragers derives not from new data but rather a new research agenda, a different set of questions which fall far outside the evolutionary framework which guided the traditional research. To advance this thesis, however, one must first consider the factual base. It is necessary to discuss what is now known about the northern Kalahari's past and how this changes the pre-1980 picture.

The past in the Dobe/xai /xai area

Archaeological excavation at a number of sites in the Dobe /xai /xai region of Western Ngamiland Botswana, where Marshall, and subsequently DeVore–Lee et al. conducted original research, yields a consistent picture (Yellen 1971; Wilmsen 1978; Brooks et al. 1979; Denbow and Wilmsen 1986). A large suite of unpublished radiocarbon dates has been obtained from a stratified site located on a sand ridge adjacent to the /xai /xai waterhole. It records the first evidence in the region of a Late Stone Age (LSA) Wilton industry at 3645 ± 100 B.P. Although detailed analysis of stone tools may eventually show some time-dependent change, the assemblage appears the same from the lowest levels to the top and this implies a single cultural tradition. A sample near the top of the sequence gives a date of 280 ± 70 B.P. At the site of ǂ gi, located in the same general region, a radiocarbon date of 110 ± 50 B.P. indicates that this tradition continued into the nineteenth century. /xai /xai, ǂ gi and other sites with LSA material are located in the same general areas extensively utilized by present-day San. With the exception of rhinoceros, which disappeared in the nineteenth century, LSA fauna consists of animals which are present in the region today. Stone implements comprise the overwhelming proportion of the LSA artifacts; at all sites these account for more than 99.5 percent of the non-faunal assemblage. Also present at most sites are small amounts of ceramics, and rare bits of metal. The fauna indicate a complete or nearly complete dependence on non-domestic species. Although Wilmsen has argued for the at least sporadic presence of cattle at /xai /xai, and other archaeologists have strongly disputed this claim, the overwhelming dependence on hunted game is clear. Similar sites are found over much of southern Africa and archaeologists believe these represent a presumably Khoisan tradition which can be traced back at least 10,000 years. Thus evidence indicates pre- and proto-historic people from the Dobe /xai /xai region were primarily, or I would argue solely, hunters and gatherers until relatively recently. Rare finds of metal and pottery indicate definite but weak links with non-foraging peoples. Given the mid-nineteenth century date at ǂgi, local contemporary San are almost certainly directly descended from those stone-using Wilton groups (although no living San can remember the use of chipped stone tools). Faunal remains excavated by Yellen from Dobe camps occupied in the early 1940s show that reliance on non-domestic species continued well into this century (Yellen 1986).

Archaeological evidence is mute on the issue of when direct and sustained contact with non-hunting and gathering peoples began in the Dobe /xai /xai area. In the early 1900s Herero pastoralists fled eastward through this region after their defeat by the Germans in Namibia (German Southwest Africa) and over time these contacts increased. However, for the pre-1900 period there is no archaeological evidence to indicate the presence of any other than "Wilton peoples."

An archaeological synthesis of these results has yet to be published. Brief site descriptions and overviews (Brooks et al. 1979; Wilmsen 1978; Yellen 1971) have appeared in print but only in specialized regional journals which are hard to locate and unavailable to a general anthropological audience. Schrire in her 1980 article relies on evidence from the Cape Province and does not include local archaeological data. Therefore, although it is important to be aware of these data and what they imply, from another perspective they are irrelevant. The shift in how these northern Kalahari San are viewed has little to do with new data *per se* but rather results from a quite different set of factors. To support this argument it is useful to examine what was known during the 1960s about the Dobe /xai /xai past, "the early years" in which Lee–DeVore et al. conducted their first research. At that time non-San people – primarily members of the Bantu-speaking pastoralist Herero tribe – were present at /xai /xai and at all of the waterholes in the Dobe region with the exception of Dobe itself. Informants made clear that Herero had lived at Dobe until driven from the waterhole by the South African police. Elderly Herero could recount their migration from Namibia and a Herero presence in the region since the turn of the century was well established. Lee explicitly discusses this history in his major monograph (1979).

Several of DeVore and Lee's main informants had lived and worked in a Bantu village during the 1950s and this fact was also learned in the course of their original fieldwork.

Lee's classic monograph, which exemplifies a "traditionalist" approach and has served as a focus of attack, was published in 1979. It is useful to see what information has emerged since then to change our understanding of the Dobe /xai /xai area's past. New data fall in two general categories. First, a series of archaeological excavations by Denbow and Wilmsen (1986) has documented an extensive Early Iron Age (EIA) occupation which centers on the margins of the Okavango swamps approximately 100 km to the east of Dobe. These well-dated and excavated sites show the presence by the sixth century A.D. of people who made pottery of the kind which appears in small amounts at /xai /xai. These Okavango groups smelted copper and iron, herded cattle and grew pearl millet and sorghum. While the cultural affiliations of the earliest EIA people are unknown, analysis of ceramics from later EIA sites suggests ties with Zambia and northeastern Botswana.

Documentary analysis provides the second source of new information. Gordon (1984) has examined the role of !Kung-speaking San in the nineteenth and early twentieth centuries in long-distance exchange. The geographic focus of Gordon's work is well to the west of the Dobe /xai /xai area but it shows that !Kung-speaking San were involved in a mercantile economy. Some groups mined and traded copper, sold tanned skins and ostrich feathers and as participants in the ivory trade hunted elephant with rifles. While there is no direct evidence for this at Dobe or /xai /xai, documents examined by Gordon show that by the early 1900s traders of the Bantu-speaking Tswana tribe regularly trekked into the area from the east to graze cattle, hunt and trade. This confirms Lee's (1979) informant-derived accounts of Tswana contact.

However interesting this recent work may be (and it is extremely important), one must question whether it significantly affects the kinds of pre-watershed studies which are the focus of Schrire's concern. Much of that literature viewed the !Kung as foragers and examined them from an evolutionary perspective. If one accepted that approach in the 1970s, should the more recent archaeological and ethnohistorical data lead to an abandonment of that position? The answer is no. By the early 1960s, as anthropologists realized at that time, three generations of Dobe /xai /xai San had been exposed to Tswana and Herero influence. They used ceramics, and had iron spears and knives. Although the group at Dobe subsisted by hunting and gathering, some men knew how to tend livestock and to plant and harvest fields. Clearly this group was not composed of "pristine" hunters and gatherers. In the face of these facts, the new historic and archaeological data do not significantly alter the basic picture.

American anthropology in the 1980s: evolutionary and historical approaches

If new data *per se* have not caused a change in perception in how these northern Kalahari people are viewed, then what forces are responsible? On the narrowest level, within the discipline of archaeology one can observe a progressive retreat from the optimism which characterized the late 1960s and much of the next decade. What has dissipated is not only a view of archaeology as "science" with an accompanying "scientific methodology," but more importantly the sense of optimism this entailed. Individual sites – archaeological counterparts to individual societies such as the !Kung – and collections of stone tools or ceramics had been seen as direct windows to what archaeologists considered the most basic, the most important questions. But great answers to significant questions such as the nature of cultural evolution proved elusive. The term "middle-range theory" was introduced and it provided at least a tacit admission that the New Archaeology goals had been set too high, that the nature of archaeological data limited what could be learned from an individual site.

This change in archaeological perspective can best be viewed within a broader intellectual and chronological context. Early in the history of American anthropology Boas contrasted a physics-like approach (which emphasized general and abstract principles at the expense of discrete phenomena) with an historical one (which preserved the particular within a broader framework of understanding). Although it is a far from straightforward enterprise, the course of American anthropology can be charted in relation to these two extremes (see for example Spiro 1986). After World War II cultural anthropology moved away from the then dominant historical ideal which Boas had championed and towards increasing integration with social sciences such as sociology and psychology. From an institutional perspective this shift is reflected in the establishment of Harvard University's Department of Social Relations (which included elements of all three disciplines) and the Human Relations Area Files at Yale. In the late 1960s and early 1970s – heyday of northern Kalahari research – both Lee and DeVore were affiliated with the Social Relations Department at Harvard.

By the 1980s, however, the tide had turned and archaeology reflected, in attenuated form, what was evident across much of anthropology where advocates of a hermeneutic position argued that the broad generalizing "scientific" approach was antithetical to what they conceived as anthropological understanding. Powerful case studies by anthropologists such as Wolf (1982), Mintz (1985) and Fox (1985) have made it clear that specific ethnographic situations can only be fully appreciated in their specific historical context. This emphasis on the full understanding, the insistence that the ethnographic particular must be set in a broader framework of both space and time, the insistence on the consideration of historical context and antecedents, provide the broader intellectual basis for the criticism raised against traditional San research. What also unites the Mintz–Wolf–Fox approach and the specific Kalahari exemplar is the belief that the present structure of third-world societies can be understood as responses to Western domination. And in fact this assumption does provide a powerful perspective from which to examine northern Kalahari peoples.

In this context much of the traditional Kalahari work can appear almost hopelessly old-fashioned and out of date. It is easy to understand how Schrire in her criticism of this approach can write:

It is as though contemporary hunter gatherers have been catapulted from a timeless and stable past into a turbulent, labile present, with ancient

adaptations crammed into a dissonant framework. Scholars imagine
themselves as standing on the interface of past and present, watching
former hunters teetering on the cusp as they hurtle into modernity with no
previous experience of change and no lessons gained from the past
(1984:1).

In the context of mid-1980s anthropology such a criticism against "traditional"
hunter-gatherer research is understandable. It is also undeniable that all northern
Kalahari San are affected by economic and political decisions made in both national
and international contexts and therefore a world systems approach may provide a
powerful analytical tool. To what extent, however, do these facts negate the value of
the earlier work? I believe that one can accept the power of a world systems approach
and still use Kalahari data to shed light on pre-Neolithic forager adaptations. Neither
logic nor other necessity argues otherwise. This issue is of central importance to
students of prehistory and deserves direct scrutiny. At the outset, one can recognize
some justice in Schrire's remarks, since the pre-1980s genre of research emphasizes
"traditional" elements of culture. This basic position is clearly reflected in the
introduction to Lee's monograph:

. . . we must acknowledge that nowhere today do we find, in Sahlins' apt
phrase, hunters living in a world of hunters. All contemporary hunters are
in contact with agricultural, pastoral, or industrial societies and are
affected by them. Therefore, the first order of business is carefully to
account for the effects of contact on their way of life. Only after the most
meticulous assessment of the impact of commercial, governmental, and
other outside interests can we justify making statements about the
"hunter-gatherers'" evolutionary significance (1979:2).

While Schrire may argue that it is impossible to factor out, as Lee proposes, such
outside impacts, her position rests on no stronger ground than her assertion that such
is the case. It lacks an objective or well-articulated standard against which to evaluate
the adequacy of traditional forager research. The basic charge which seems to be
leveled against a Lee approach involves a systematic selectivity in which a researcher
focuses on certain bodies of data at the expense of others. Yet selectivity characterizes
any research enterprise, be it set in a "scientific" or historic context and that *per se* does
not render conclusions incorrect. Methods by definition are means to an end and to
select between alternative methods without consideration of an intended goal is often
a fruitless exercise. Where recent historicist criticisms of traditional Kalahari research
fall short are their almost total neglect of this broader context. One can easily argue
that northern Kalahari San are not totally faithful representatives of a pre-Neolithic
way of life, but this does not necessarily mean that they cannot provide insight into
such a condition. As the above statement by Lee indicates, the goal of much
traditional hunter and gatherer research has been explicitly stated: to make statements
of evolutionary significance; to use what can be observed in the ethnographic present
to elucidate a set of processes which operated in the past. One can question whether
such a research agenda is worth pursuing and whether it can be obtained. However,

its goal is specifically and succinctly stated. Non-essentialist or historical attacks of this traditional approach fall short because they criticize it not in the context of the traditional questions towards which it is directed but within the context of a very different set of concerns. Rather than understanding the past through study of the present, the historicist goal is the very different one of "elucidating the present in terms of the past" (Schrire 1984:2). Since "elucidating" is used in its broadest sense, then clearly both historical minutiae and contemporary world context become essential elements in any analysis. But, at the same time, the confrontation between the "historical" and the "traditional" or "evolutionary" approaches becomes less direct and dissolves, for the most part, into the unanswerable question of which alternate (and not necessarily conflicting) goal is most worthy of anthropological pursuit.

There are other reasons why such condemnations of traditional research fall wide of the mark. For example, if one takes a broader view of the human past and recognizes that the archaeological record covers a span of just over two million years, historical criticisms become curiously myopic. This near-sightedness merits examination because as well as pointing out the most serious problems of evolutionary reconstruction it also suggests a way around them. Consider Denbow's statement:

While the inhabitants of the Kalahari 5000 years ago were undoubtedly
hunters living in a world of hunters, over the past 2000 years all cultural
and ethnic groups in the region have been in some form of contact with
food-producing peoples, with the result that the economic and social
decisions of all groups have become, to some degree, interdependent.
Even though hunting and gathering continued to be the primary basis for
subsistence among some Late Stone Age groups throughout this period,
the potential influence of other activities cannot be ignored . . .
Anthropologists have tried to get around this problem by searching for
independent foraging groups, but in fact there has probably been no such
thing here, in an historical or processual sense, for almost 1500 years
(1984: 188).

The fallacy in this statement lies in the assumption that before 1500 years ago an entity labeled an "independent foraging group" might in fact have existed. The level of caution and critical evaluation which Denbow applies to the recent past disappears when he refers to the vast earlier span of time when hunters lived in a world of hunters and for this reason it is myopic. If one applies to pre-Neolithic societies the fine level of examination which allows each contemporary group to be classed as unique, then the same will almost certainly hold for the earlier time period as well. It is a mistake to oversimplify that more distant past. Archaeological evidence clearly attests to behaviorial change over time and the first stone-tool-using hominids from Kobi Fora certainly acted in ways which were distinct from the Mesolithic hunters and gatherers who occupied the same lakeshore over a million years later. By the middle Pleistocene hominids had expanded across much of Europe and Asia and in the process they adapted to markedly different environments. As Middle Stone Age heavy and light tool traditions indicate, even within a single chronological horizon regional differences are evident. That complex relationships between groups existed during the Paleo-lithic is demonstrated by both Old and New World data. Analysis of Upper Paleolithic art provides evidence of an interaction sphere which extended from the European Atlantic coast to the plains of Central Russia. Sourcing studies show that in the New World chert was exchanged over long distances and several cultural boundaries. The ethnographic record reveals instances in which foraging societies of different levels of complexity existed side by side and undoubtedly the same was true prehistorically. Both the California acorn-gathering deer-hunting societies and their Great Basin counterparts to the east who lived in smaller more mobile groups represent ways of life which extend thousands of years back into the past. It is difficult to believe that similar juxtapositions were unusual in the more distant past or that no interactions crossed cultural boundaries.

Two implications may be drawn from this more realistic view of the pre-Neolithic past. On the one hand the concept of this "past" as a monolithic entity dissolves and it becomes even more difficult to apply, in any simplistic way, patterns observed in extant foraging groups. This problem was clearly recognized over twenty years ago in discussions at the Man the Hunter Conference in Chicago (Freeman 1968), and it raises the major stumbling block to the use of ethnographic data for "evolutionary" goals. In this context, the fact that northern Kalahari San traded with Early Iron Age peoples fades to insignificance.

On the other hand, the existence of Paleolithic complexity destroys the argument that contemporary hunters who live in a non-hunter world can shed little light on a distant Paleolithic past. The historicist position reflected in the Denbow passage quoted above rests on a supposed dichotomy which categorizes the pre-Neolithic as "simple" and post-Neolithic as "complex." Such an absolute distinction precludes generalization. When, however, one recognizes that the distant past was also complex, the criticism falls away. Quite possibly ethnographically known foragers, because of the historically complex world which they inhabit, provide better models for the Upper Paleolithic than some mythically isolated and untouched group of hunters and gatherers. Rather than adopt a misconceived notion of "purity" and bemoan the absence of "pure" hunting and gathering groups today, one can use this perceived liability to analytic advantage.

Contemporary foragers in evolutionary perspective

As Boas used the term, "history" which is by nature particularizing stands in opposition to a generalizing or "scientific" approach. However, it is possible to recognize the importance of specific events, to work within a historical framework, yet avoid this potential dichotomy. Geertz (1980), for example, has argued that individual societies are characterized by basic structures. For Geertz, these structures are determined by environmental and demographic variables. Through time as a society responds to specific events internal change can occur, but the essential structure remains constant. For the prehistorian who uses the present in an attempt to understand the past such an approach is particularly congenial. Not only does it allow one to broaden one's horizon beyond the description of particular situations and specific sequences of events, but it also provides guidelines for broader inquiry. It implies that basic structure may be most clearly revealed during change and thus rather than seeking "timeless" or static situations (which do not exist in any case) one should search for dynamic contexts, for groups which are buffeted, which are forced to adapt to changing external conditions. Groups such as these are widely in evidence today. This kind of approach to understanding the past deserves careful examination because it can serve as a productive context for future evolutionarily oriented foragers.

If one accepts this line of argument, it is necessary to consider what kinds of extant societies are most likely to provide information which can be generalized to the distant past. Because no known human groups obtain their diet only from hunted and gathered resources it is impossible to limit inquiry to strictly defined foragers. Likewise no extant society exhibits a pre-Neolithic technology; no groups lack both metal and ceramics. Thus a list of material traits cannot serve to establish distinguishing criteria: organizational characteristics, however, can.

Although others may also exist, two crucial defining criteria may be posited for pre-Neolithic hominids. The first involves extent of environmental buffering. No humanly habitable environment is unchanging and all are unpredictable to a greater or lesser degree. In all, resources vary over both time and space and all human societies must adapt to or buffer this environmental reality. (Storage, individual mobility, transport of goods and increased variety of diet all may serve as buffering mechanisms.) These buffering mechanisms may vary from simple to complex and, in theory at least, be ranged along a single axis. How different groups use geographic networks to buffer the effects of rainfall unpredictability in semi-arid environments provides a concrete example of difference in degree. Total rainfall in semi-arid regions is not only, on the average, low, but it varies in dramatic and unpredictable ways not only from year to year but also from region to region within a single year. For the northern Kalahari individual !Kung were mobile and this allowed the population to shift in response to rainfall controlled resource variability. Through a network based both on kinship and reciprocal exchange individuals acquired rights in a number of areas. When the rains were poor in one area, an individual or family could determine where the grass was literally greener, and claim residence rights accordingly. In this case it is individuals or small groups of people which move rather than goods or entire bands. The distances involved rarely if ever exceed 100 km and the rules which determine areal rights are embedded primarily within the kinship system and do not constitute a separate formalized body of knowledge.

Bantu-speaking Tswana and Herero pastoralists who share this same northern Kalahari environment buffer against fluctuation quite differently. Dependent on livestock, they employ a highly formalized system in which an individual divides his cattle into groups and he then distributes them among tribesmen who may live hundreds of kilometers away. Thus a single herd is usually an agglomeration of animals owned by many individuals. The herdsman in turn may have only a small number of his own animals directly under his supervision because most are distributed over a number of locations. Herdsmen recognize that rainfall is spatially variable, that diseases which afflict cattle may be localized and that large predators such as lion and hyena are also not evenly distributed across the landscape. Through division of stock, they minimize the likelihood of catastrophic loss. This Tswana–Herero system of buffering emphasizes the movement of goods rather than individuals; it operates under the authority of a chief or headman who must approve the movement of livestock from one waterhole to another. It spans distances measured in hundreds of kilometers.

Gould (personal communication) describes a similar situation in Australia where sheep ranchers divide their herds to guard against drought. In this instance animals are moved by truck across the continent and the obligations of owners and caretakers specified by contract. If one defines a continuum which extends in this way from Kalahari San to Australian ranchers, societies with simple buffering mechanisms can be seen as similar or perhaps virtually identical to pre-Neolithic counterparts. The more simple the contemporary buffering mechanism, the more useful the potential comparison becomes.

A second criterion which may serve to distinguish more from less appropriate analogs involves the extent to which social networks are formalized and subject to centralized control. This concept is an old one and has provided the basis for many evolutionary schemes. What has been less considered, however, is the extent to which the degree of centralized authority affects how groups respond to environmental variation. (The role of irrigation, which has received careful scrutiny, provides an exception to this generalization.) An interesting comparison exists between the northern Kalahari San and Chacoan peoples of the southwestern United States, who also occupied a semi-arid environment. In the Kalahari, ethnographic observations would predict that at times of greatest environmental variation individual mobility would be at its height and group membership the most unstable. In the Chacoan case, however, archaeological evidence indicates that just the opposite occurred. Excellent climatic data derived from dendrochronological analysis and a large archaeological data base allow climatological cause to be correlated with cultural response (Plog 1986). It is just during the periods of greatest variability that Chacoan organization appears the most highly structured, most subregionally distinct. It has been suggested that during such periods the movement of foodstuffs served to buffer local groups and that it required the assertion of centralized authority to put this system in effect. The San–Chacoan comparison is illuminating because it illustrates alternative buffering strategies: in the first people move to resources; in the second (possibly) it is the resources not the people which move. Although the first can work in a situation with either acephalous or centralized authority, the second requires centralized authority to succeed. And by this standard some groups provide better analogs for the pre-Neolithic past than others.

Although two criteria have been suggested to sort contemporary societies, such an approach in the absence of specific questions will prove primarily of heuristic value. Criteria can best be established in light of specific questions. For example, presently many archaeologists are interested in how human societies adapt to specific conditions of resource availability and distribution. To determine which, if any, contemporary societies may provide potentially useful insights, it is valuable to examine variables such as degree of buffering and centralization of authority. To understand the evolution of symbolic behavior, however, quite likely very different criteria should be applied. What makes the discussion of buffering and centralization valuable is the demonstration that useful pre-Neolithic analogs can be defined on the basis of organizational principles rather than material traits. This seems a more fruitful and valid approach than one which employs trait purity as the basis for deciding which groups can or cannot be useful in understanding the distant past.

This implies that the standard concept of hunter gatherer should be revised. The traditional category of "hunter gatherers," although clearly defined, is perhaps too broad since it includes groups as diverse as central Australian aborigines and the native American inhabitants of the northwest coast. In terms of political centraliz-ation, for example, these latter groups fall closer to many non-foragers than to their Australian counterparts. On the other hand, such groups as the central Kalahari Balakahadi and the northern Kalahari San, although they incorporate livestock in their subsistence repertoire, still act more as foragers than as traditional pastoralists. From this perspective goats and cattle do not stand in opposition to warthog and wildebeest but can best be seen as two specific food items within a much broader range.

The Dobe example
In this chapter two main arguments have been developed. First, that structure may both be maintained and revealed through adaptation to external change. Secondly, that if carefully chosen, societies which incorporate post-Neolithic elements of diet and technology still may illumine more general hominid patterns. A brief case study serves to illustrate these points. In the early 1960s, Lee and DeVore camped with San at Dobe and both they and their students returned repeatedly to this small northern Kalahari waterhole.

Because Dobe provides year-round water in all but the most severe periods of drought, it serves as a focus for settlement and the association of some San families which currently live near the waterhole can be traced back into the 1940s. It has been possible to locate and accurately date occupation sites which span this four-decade period, to reconstruct history through interviews with the original inhabitants, and to use archaeological techniques to recover quantitative information on both settlement pattern and diet. About midway in this period the protectorate of Bechuanaland received its independence from Britain and assumed its present name of Botswana. In the years which immediately followed, the pace of change in the Dobe area quickened perceptibly. A general store, a school and dispensary were built within one day's walk of Dobe and a more formal administrative structure for the district was established. The Dobe San were directly affected by a number of government programs. Families were provided with seed, donkeys, and technical assistance and were encouraged to plant fields. Under UN sponsorship Botswana established a craft marketing organiz-ation and San were given direct access to a cash economy through sale of traditional items such as bows and arrows, and necklaces strung with ostrich egg shell beads. In the late 1970s a well which provided a plentiful supply of potable water was dug and as

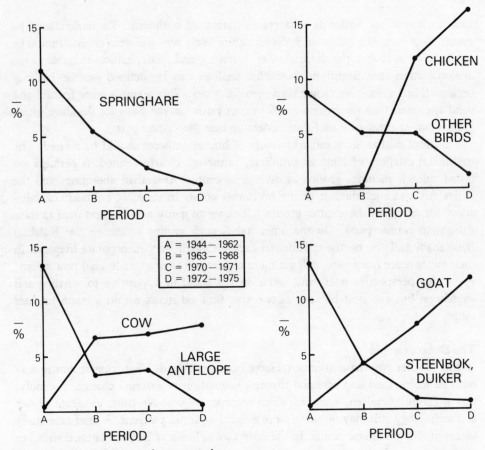

Fig. 7.1. Changes in frequency for seven species.

a consequence both Herero and Tswana established settlements at Dobe and based livestock there. In South African controlled Namibia, just a kilometer west of Dobe, a fence was erected to mark the border and a good dirt road constructed to permit easy access. With changes in the military situation in Namibia traffic to the border increased and contact between Dobe residents and their kin at Cum!kwe (a Namibian mission station and military base) also increased.

As one might imagine, the cumulative effect on the Dobe San was great. Individuals acquired herds of goats, some acquired cows, and many planted fields. Mud-walled huts replaced their smaller grass-walled counterparts and the traditional share and "travel light" philosophy so well described in many ethnographies was supplanted as many individuals hoarded in tin trunks surprisingly large stashes of privately owned goods (Brooks et al. 1984).

In this context of rapid change it is instructive to examine shifts in the pattern of faunal exploitation. The data presented in Table 7.1 and Figures 7.1 and 7.2 derive from a study of Dobe settlement pattern. A series of camps occupied over four decades by members of a single extended family were located, mapped and then partially excavated. (Basic data and detailed interpretation are presented in Yellen

Table 7.1 *Average number of species per site by size and time period*

Time period	Average number of species				
	Large mammals	Medium mammals	Small mammals	Reptiles/ amphibians	Birds
A (1944–62)	1.40	2.40	1.80	0.80	1.20
B (1963–8)	2.86	2.86	2.14	1.71	1.86
C (1970–1)	2.33	3.33	2.33	1.67	1.33
D (1972–5)	2.00	2.75	2.00	1.25	2.25

1986.) While it is impossible to generalize from this limited faunal sample the amount of meat consumed, one can make valid comparisons within this series itself, since analysis indicates that differential bone destruction is minimal over time. As Fig. 7.1 indicates, major changes occur in faunal utilization over this 32-year period. As contact with a non-San world increased, domesticates became concomitantly more important. While cows, goats, and chickens were minimally represented before the mid-1960s, by the next decade they had assumed a position of dominance. However, it is fascinating to note that although cows replaced large antelope and the amount of steenbok and duiker (both small antelopes) declined as goats increased in importance, the basic structure of the assemblage remained unchanged. As Table 7.1 indicates, the representation of different classes of vertebrates remained basically the same and these data imply that from a San perspective a cow counts as just another large mammal, and a goat as just another medium-sized one. Figure 7.2 shows that Simpson's "D", when calculated for each assemblage, does not vary unilinearly over time. Simpson's "D", which ranges from 0 to 1, provides a measure of species diversity. The greater

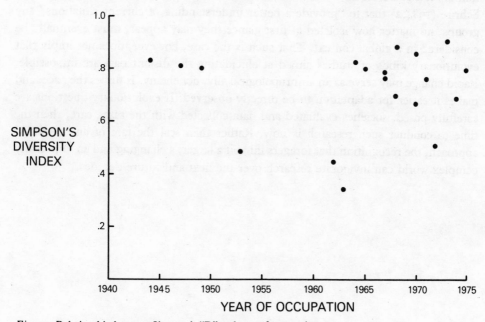

Fig. 7.2. Relationship between Simpson's "D" and year of occupation.

the number of species present in an assemblage and the more even the distribution of individuals among those species, the more nearly Simpson's "D" approaches 1. Figure 7.2 demonstrates that all Dobe San assemblages exhibit a very high level of species diversity; it also shows that it is maintained whether or not domesticates are present. It has been argued (Yellen 1986) that in the face of a highly unpredictable environment, !Kung act to minimize risk rather than maximize return and these data support such an interpretation.

These graphs serve to illustrate two additional points. First, the shift from "purer" to "less pure" foraging need not lead to basic structural change. A Geertzian view of history as a process in which basic structure remains intact is exemplified by these data. In fact it is through change, through history itself that this underlying pattern of organization is most clearly revealed. Secondly, if one were to subdivide the data into an earlier marginal contact and later extensive contact groups and analyzed each separately, both would yield the same result. Lee, as the earlier quotation demonstrates, argues that to understand evolutionary significance the effects of recent change must be carefully peeled away. What this example shows is that such a stringent criterion need not necessarily apply. An analysis of goats, cows, and chickens reveals the same structure as one based on warthog, kudu, and guinea fowl.

Conclusion

The argument has often been made that anthropologists carried by the advancing wave of Western civilization always arrived to study hunters and gatherers just a bit too late. What the Dobe data imply is that such may not be the case. Granted all societies are, and for some time have been, part of a world system. "Pure" societies of hunters and gatherers have long since ceased to exist. One can also readily agree with Schrire (1984:2) that to "provide a better understanding of current situations" any groups, no matter how isolated at first glance they may appear, must eventually be considered in a global context. That such is the case, however, does not imply that evolutionary kinds of studies aimed at elucidating the distant past are impossible. Rapid change may serve as an anthropological ally, not enemy. It forces the pace, and makes it easier for adaptation to be directly observed. If evolutionary questions are carefully posed, societies evaluated and data collected with the same care, then the time to conduct such research is now. Rather than seal the fate of an outmoded approach, the recognition that foragers inhabit a larger, a changing and an impossibly complex world can invigorate research over the next and future decades.

8

Paleopathology and the interpretation of economic change in prehistory

MARK N. COHEN

One of the most important trends in archaeology in the 1980s has been the emergence of human osteology and paleopathology as means of testing hitherto untested (and often, supposedly "untestable") theories about the meaning of prehistoric events. A number of controversies about prehistory are now (at least potentially) amenable to resolution because opposing theories explicitly or implicitly offer conflicting predictions about changes in human health and nutrition.

The emerging importance of these new lines of inquiry is based in part on an explosive increase in the attention paid to human remains from archaeological sites and in part on significant changes which have occurred in the style of paleopathological research. Despite the work of some early pioneers, much of the work in paleopathology prior to the last decade focused on the diagnosis and description of specific examples of pathological conditions in individual skeletons. Early workers in the field were medical specialists often lacking sophistication about social issues. Much of what they reported was of little more than anecdotal value to other prehistorians. The tendency of pathologists to focus on rare diseases and spectacular examples of illness resulted in diagnoses which proved the antiquity of certain types of illness, but told us little about the relationship of health and disease to surrounding economic and social conditions.

In recent years there has been a marked shift in the balance of personnel in the field of paleopathology. A larger number of the individuals involved are coming from training in anthropology which supplements their medical or osteological training. As a result, the field as a whole has shifted in important ways. (See Buikstra and Cook 1980; Cohen and Armelagos 1984.)

First, there has been a shift from focus on diagnosis and disease history *per se* to broader concern with issues of prehistory and anthropology. Patterns of health and disease are now seen as analytical tools that afford increasing accuracy in the elucidation of other aspects of human behavior – subsistence economy, the structure of settlements, warfare, division of labor, social class structure and the division of economic goods, trade networks, and the centralization of power, to name only a few examples.

Second, as an inevitable consequence of this changing interest, there has been a shift in the focus of paleopathological study away from rare or extreme conditions toward evaluation of comparatively common and often relatively mild disorders.

There has also been a shift toward evaluation of conditions that imply behavioral or nutritional differences between individuals or populations but that are not strictly "pathological" at all.

Third, interest has begun to focus less on the simple identification or diagnosis of disease and more on the description of their pattern of occurrence within a population or analysis of the differences in their occurrence in two or more populations. Paleopathology has become a quantitative, statistically oriented science.

Modes of analysis in paleopathology

A brief summation of the kinds of analysis now being performed must suffice as background to the discussion of issues in archaeology. (More complete description of the techniques in skeletal analysis is provided by various sources: Steinbock 1976; Ortner and Putschar 1981; Cohen and Armelagos 1984; Goodman et al. 1984b; Huss Ashmore et al. 1982; Buikstra and Cook 1980; Gilbert and Mielke 1985; Shipman et al. 1985.)

(1) A range of techniques are now in use by which the constituents of prehistoric diet can be identified with increasing precision from the skeleton. These include the identification of microwear patterns and of macro-level wear and caries on teeth. Also included are the analysis of bones and teeth to determine the proportions of trace elements such as strontium, zinc, magnesium, copper (Sillen and Kavanaugh 1982; Lambert et al. 1984; Bumstead et al. 1986); or the proportions of various isotopes of elements (carbon, nitrogen, strontium) thought to act as signatures of the foods eaten (Norr 1984; Nelson et al. 1986; Schoeninger et al. 1983).

(2) A number of techniques now permit us to assess the nutritional status of individuals (and thus of classes or whole populations of individuals). Specific dietary deficiencies can be assessed. (More properly speaking we can assess the net availability of nutrients which reflects not only dietary intake but also secondary loss to parasites or to special demands such as growth, healing, pregnancy and lactation.) The individual elements of the diet most commonly evaluated include iron, zinc, calcium, magnesium and vitamins C and D. In addition, undernutrition, protein deficiency and/or protein calorie malnutrition have been identified in prehistoric skeletons using a number of indicators including changes in adult stature or other skeletal measurements, reduction in the cortical area and density of bone, reduction in the size of teeth (particularly deciduous teeth); and patterns of delayed growth (or reduced length and cross sectional areas of bones relative to dental age) in children.

(3) Paleopathologists can describe the frequency and distribution of infection in prehistoric groups. Some individual diseases which are of considerable historical importance can be identified because they leave diagnostic traces in the skeleton. These include tuberculosis, treponemal infections (yaws or syphilis), leprosy and, more controversially, smallpox. (As Allison [1984] and others have shown, where mummies are preserved, a far broader range of specific infections can be identified.) Perhaps more important from the anthropological point of view (because they are far more common), it is possible to identify and quantify the occurrence of low-grade or chronic infection or inflammation in the skeleton even when the specific pathogenic

agent cannot be identified. Such lesions are referred to as periostitis or periosteal reactions when they affect only bone surfaces or as osteitis or osteomyelitis when they involve progressively deeper penetration of bone.

(4) It is possible to identify trauma (fractures, dislocations to the skeletons) and analyze a population in terms of the frequency and distribution of trauma (see especially Lovejoy and Heiple 1981). Since the pattern of trauma often provides clues to the nature of the traumatic event, patterns of behavior which place individuals at risk of particular types of accident – or intentional violence – can often be identified.

(5) It is possible to assess the nature and severity of the workload in which an individual has engaged. A heavy workload (particularly high peaks of physical demand) is recorded in the skeleton both in the form of arthritic changes in stressed joints and in the form of increased muscular development.

(6) It is possible to identify the occurrence of episodes of growth-disrupting or growth-retarding biological stress to which individuals were exposed during childhood. Harris lines or transverse lines of dense bone visible in radiographs of long bones of the body are thought to indicate such growth arrest. Stress related defects of teeth include enamel hypoplasia (surface defects visible to the naked eye) and Wilson's bands and pathological striae of retzius observable in cross sections of teeth viewed at various powers of magnification. Such markers can be produced in the skeleton by a variety of stressors including starvation, severe malnutrition, or severe infection. As a result neither Harris lines nor dental defects permit specific diagnosis of disease. Their importance is that they record the frequency of stress in individuals (and therefore in populations or subpopulations) and permit crude quantitative comparisons of the degree to which particular life-styles exposed individuals to stressful episodes or buffered them against those episodes.

(7) (and most controversial) It is possible to determine the age at death of an individual (fairly accurately among children, more crudely – and perhaps only very crudely – among adults: see Lovejoy et al. 1985). Such individual assessments can then be converted to various statistical descriptions of patterns of death in the population (Acsadi and Nemeskeri 1970; Goodman et al. 1984a; Mensforth n.d.; Van Gerven and Armelagos 1983; Lovejoy et al. 1977; Buikstra and Konigsberg 1985; but cf. Boquet-Appel and Masset 1982, 1985; Sattenspiel and Harpending 1983; Howell 1982).

In short, paleopathological data provide clues to a number of significant aspects of prehistoric human experience: patterns of work; diet and dietary shortcomings; risk of violence, accident and disease; cultural buffering or lack of buffering against episodes of stress; survivorship and death. These patterns permit us to evaluate the real human impact of economic, political and social changes which scholars otherwise have often evaluated on indirect – and often strictly ideological – grounds. Before proceeding to an analysis of some applications of these modes of analysis, however, it is necessary to call attention to some shortcomings of the existing data.

First, of course, the study of archaeological skeletons shares the kinds of sampling problems which affect the field of archaeology as a whole and which particularly affect the analysis of any perishable organic remains. Good skeletal samples are few, and are unevenly distributed in time and space. At present good samples are conspicuously concentrated in Europe and North America. Like all organic remains, skeletons are also conspicuously concentrated in the recent phases of prehistory and in climates and soil regimes conducive to organic preservation. Like all archaeological samples, moreover, skeletal populations provide nothing more than brief glimpses at the archaeological record, "snapshots" of what would more accurately be portrayed as a moving picture; and like the snapshots of an amateur photographer the existing samples often fail to focus precisely on key moments and episodes of change.

But skeletal samples also suffer from two other kinds of distortion which may not be immediately obvious to archaeologists working with other materials. First, skeletons are inherently limited (and perhaps biased) representations of life processes. The skeleton records only a limited subset of the stresses to which the body is exposed. In particular, with the exception of certain types of violent death or trauma, it tends to record chronic rather than acute conditions – conditions persisting long enough in the body to display a cumulative effect on bones and teeth. Moreover the skeleton has a limited range of recording techniques, tending to lump together diverse stresses into a small number of categories whose poor definition may mask real and important changes in health or behavior. Second, cemetery samples (whether they reflect formal or informal collections of the dead) are also likely to be biased samples of the once-living group. Some of the biases are obvious. Individuals may be left out of the cemetery sample fortuitously (for example, because they died too far away from home to be recovered) and they may be left out systematically as a function of specific social or demographic characteristics: age, sex, or class. The youngest infants are not found in many cemetery samples; and the elderly are often not represented (or not correctly identified). A more subtle point is that even when all deaths can be accounted for, the cemetery may provide a misleading picture of life. The proportion of children who died with a certain pathological condition is not likely to be the same as the proportion of children who lived at the same age with that pathology; and the distribution of ages at death in the population may provide a distorted picture of life expectancy in the living group. In sum, like all archaeologists, paleopathologists are having to come to grips with the fact that what they observe is not strictly speaking what prehistoric people were, but rather what they left behind.

Paleopathological tests of theories of prehistory

In an explicit attempt to apply paleopathological data as a test of cultural evolutionary theory on a cross-cultural basis, Cohen and Armelagos (1984) collected a world sample of existing data. Because the coding of paleopathologies suffers from a lack of standardization (and because variations in the natural environment cloud the effects of cultural choices in determining health) we eschewed simple numerical comparisons between the published reports of other scholars. Instead we focused as much as possible on *the relative frequency of various classes of pathology as reported by the same individual or team from sequential populations* (at different stages of economic development) in particular parts of the world. In short we looked for trends in pathology in the course of cultural evolution within different world areas. In an attempt to circumvent problems of sampling error that complicate all interpretation of individual archaeological sequences, we also focused on replicated patterns, that is, on trends shared by several sequences that might therefore be viewed as regular, cross-cultural patterns or tendencies rather than as peculiar outcomes engendered either by poor sampling or by local cultural idiosyncrasies. The data from that collection, supplemented by other published studies and reinterpreted in light of recent argument, provides the bulk of the discussion which follows.

The health and "affluence" of hunter gatherers

During the 1960s, work with a number of contemporary foraging groups (most notably the African !Kung San and Hadza) led to a reassessment of the health, workload and nutritional status of hunter gatherers. Richard Lee (Lee and DeVore 1968), James Woodburn (1968), and Marshall Sahlins (1972), among others, suggested that such groups enjoyed good health and nutrition and reliable food supplies based on comparatively light workloads when compared to their agricultural neighbors. Their assertions have played a significant role in the molding of anthropological theory because they challenged prevailing stereotypes of "primitive" life-styles. Moreover, because contemporary foragers were assumed to provide representative examples of an ancient way of life, these studies raised questions about prevailing models of economic change and cultural evolution in prehistory.

The image of hunter-gatherer well-being and its application to the interpretation of prehistory has been subject to controversy on at least two levels, however. Various workers have suggested that Lee's !Kung San and other contemporary examples of the hunting and gathering way of life may not be so well-off as Lee or Woodburn portrayed them (e.g. Hawkes and O'Connell 1985). In addition, several recent scholars (e.g. Schrire 1984) have pointed out that many, if not all, of these groups, including the !Kung, are not simply remnants of an ancient life-style, but are in fact twentieth-century people making twentieth-century adaptations to difficult but potentially rewarding circumstances which inevitably include interaction with other, larger societies. They argue that contemporary foragers may therefore tell us little if anything about our own prehistory.

The data of paleopathology obviously provide a key test of the image of hunter-gatherer well-being in prehistory. The existing data do not support an image of "affluence" in the sense that we usually apply the word. Although the results are mixed, the data do suggest, however, that prehistoric hunter gatherers were often (perhaps even most commonly) relatively healthy people in comparison to the average of later and more advanced prehistoric groups, in keeping with models stimulated by Lee's work.

(1) The data do not support Lee's contention that prehistoric hunter gatherers enjoyed light workloads; but neither do they suggest that farming and/or the emergence of civilization consistently reduced workloads. Cohen and Armelagos found a slight preponderance of more severe arthritis and more robust muscular development among hunting and gathering populations than among subsequent farmers, although the trend was mixed. Studies by Kennedy (1984), Larsen (1984),

Perzigian et al. (1984), Smith et al. (1984), and Meiklejohn et al. (1984) displayed a decline in arthritis and/or robusticity through time. Studies by Goodman et al. (1984a), by Cook (1984), and by Cassidy (1984) suggested in contrast that arthritis was more severe and/or robusticity greater among farmers. The latter trend is also reported in some other recent studies including Koerner and Blakely (1985) and Bridges (1983). Rathbun (1984) and Rose et al. (1984) reported complex patterns of change. (However, as suggested above, these skeletal indicators say more about the size of peaks of physical demand on muscles and joints than about hours of labor exerted. They tend to suggest that certain populations work hard, not necessarily that they work long hours.)

(2) Although comparative studies are few (surprisingly few considering the relative ease with which analysis can be done), the data do not support the expectation that rates of skeletal trauma were high among hunter gatherers or that they regularly declined with adoption of farming. Rathbun (1984), Perzigian et al. (1984), and Meiklejohn et al. (1984) report a decline through time; Goodman et al. (1984a), Kennedy (1984), and Cook (1984) reported the opposite trend as has Bennike (1985). (See also Donisi [1983], who suggests that there is little to distinguish Archaic and Mississippian populations in Alabama.) The data suggest that we may be over-stating the physical risk associated with hunting and gathering (a point which can be confirmed by reference to various ethnographically described groups (Cohen in preparation). The data also make no clear cross-cultural statement about presumed hunter-gatherer non-violence or about the role of violence at various stages of cultural evolution in general, although they obviously can speak to peaks of violence surrounding specific historical events. Cook (1984), for example, suggests very tentatively that there may have been an increase in violence in Illinois in the Late Woodland period during the transition from hunting and gathering to agriculture. Some clear cultural foci of violence can be found, such as the Mississippian Period Averbuch site in Tennessee (Eisenberg 1986).

(3) Rates of infection in skeletal populations appear fairly commonly to have increased as farming was adopted and intensified – although most scholars associate increased rates of infectious pathology with increasing population density, increasing sedentism and increasing nucleation of populations rather than farming *per se*. Goodman et al. (1984a), Cook (1984), Ubelaker (1984), Perzigian et al. (1984), Meiklejohn et al. (1984), Cassidy (1984), Rose et al. (1984), and Norr (1984) all report generally upward trends in rates of infection although the trend is not always simple or uniform. Rathbun (1984) surprisingly suggests that infections are relatively uncommon in later periods in Iran. Most reports refer only to the general category of "unspecified" infection or to treponemal disease. (It is interesting from an epidemiological point of view that the relative freedom of hunter gatherers from disease appears to extend not only to "crowd" diseases which various scholars have predicted would be found to appear recently in human history but also to apparently chronic infections which are thought to have plagued human beings since earliest times. See Cockburn 1971; Black et al. 1974.)

Several scholars have further suggested that tuberculosis first appears, or at least is most common, in recent, relatively dense populations in various parts of the world (Cook 1984; Perzigian 1984; see also Buikstra 1981; Pfeiffer 1984; Robbins 1978; Hartney 1981; Bennike 1985; Zivanovic 1982; but cf. Williams 1985). Using mummies, Allison (1984) has also been able to demonstrate an increase in specific intestinal bacteria (salmonella) with the adoption of sedentism, although he found that rates of pneumonic infections were not affected.

(4) Most comparative studies suggest that hunter gatherers enjoyed better quality nutrition than did later farmers. For example, the most commonly reported nutritional index, porotic hyperostosis suggestive of anemia, almost invariably increases with the adoption of farming (Cook 1984; Goodman et al. 1984a; Cassidy 1984; Palkovich 1984; Norr 1984; Angel 1984; Perzigian et al. 1984). Originally attributed to the iron-absorption inhibiting properties of cereals such as maize (see El Najjar 1977), porotic hyperostosis is now increasingly thought to be associated (at least in some cases) with increasing infection rates (which results in secondary iron loss) or with the withholding of iron by the body (Stuart-Macadam 1986; Walker 1986; Cook 1984); with altered cooking styles (Walker 1985); or with cereal processing such as tortilla making (White 1986). Whatever the combination of causes, however, the net result appears to be a common reduction in available iron with the adoption of sedentary farming economies.

Other indices of nutrition, less frequently reported, also appear to suggest a decline in the quality of nutrition among farmers compared to earlier hunter gatherers: bone cortical area and maintenance are often reduced among farmers (Goodman et al. 1984a; Smith et al. 1984; Cook 1984; Cassidy 1984; Pfeiffer 1984; Stout 1978; Nelson 1984; individual childhood growth is retarded (Goodman et al. 1984; Martin et al. 1984); the size and robusticity of adult individuals is reduced (Larsen 1984; Angel 1984; Kennedy 1984; Meiklejohn et al. 1984); specific skeletal dimensions such as pelvic inlet and skull base height are reduced (Angel 1984); the size of deciduous teeth declines (Larsen 1983); increasing rates of prenatal stress on infants are though to indicate increasing rates of maternal malnutrition (Cassidy 1984). Finally, specific vitamin and mineral deficiencies such as scurvy and rickets which become common in the civilized world are remarkably infrequent among hunter gatherers, and often early farmers as well (e.g. Meiklejohn et al. 1984; cf. Zivanovic 1982).

(5) Indicators of childhood stress suggest that hunter gatherers were probably at least as well buffered against episodes of severe stress by their economy and culture as were later populations, although they may suggest that the Neolithic revolution was often accompanied by a shift in the nature and distribution of stress events to which individuals were exposed. The two most commonly used indices of stress, Harris lines and enamel defects of teeth, give apparently contradictory results. Harris lines more often are less common in farming populations than in earlier hunter gatherers (Goodman et al. 1984a; Cassidy 1984; Rose et al. 1984; Perzigian et al. 1984; Cook 1984; but cf. Rathbun 1984). Robert Benfer (1986), however, has recently argued that, although less frequent among formative maize dependent farmers on the Peru coast than in earlier hunting and gathering populations, Harris lines in the later period

display a severity rarely if ever equaled among the earlier groups. Benfer suggests that later populations experienced fewer lean seasons than their forebears but incurred more episodes of severe stress.

In contrast to Harris lines, enamel hypoplasias and other dental defects almost invariably become more frequent and/or more severe as farming replaces hunting and gathering as a way of life (Goodman et al. 1984a; Cook 1984; Cassidy 1984; Allison 1984; Smith et al. 1984; Angel 1984; Kennedy 1984; Perzigian et al. 1984; Ubelaker 1984; see also Y'edynak and Fleisch 1983; Sciulli 1977, 1978; but cf. Molnar and Molnar 1985 and Brothwell 1963). The contrasting trends raise the possibility that hunter gatherers commonly traded one type of stress for another with the adoption of farming – possibly, as Cassidy (1984) has suggested, a trade of seasonal hunger (represented by Harris lines) for less regular but more severe stress episodes associated with starvation and epidemics. However, various recent studies (e.g. Symes 1984; Murchison et al. 1983); have found Harris lines unreliable as an indicator of stress because they do not form unless an individual is otherwise well nourished and/or because they are subject to subsequent erasure after formation. (The causes of the erasure of Harris lines are not fully understood but one good possibility is that accelerated rates of bone remodeling associated with high-cereal diets may make such erasure more common among farmers than among hunter gatherers.) The conflicting data provided by Harris lines and dental defects might then reflect a change in the type of stresses experienced; but it might reflect, at least in part, the fact that poor background nutrition and/or subsequent erasure tend to interfere with the expression of Harris lines in farming populations, whose high rates of enamel defects point to the true, higher frequency of severe stress which they experienced.

(6) The data appear to suggest at face value that hunter gatherers fared relatively well in terms of mortality and survivorship compared at least to early farming populations. First, in the few cases where samples are complete enough so that individuals or teams felt comfortable offering estimates of infant and child mortality, hunter gatherers often appear to have lost relatively small proportions of children prematurely compared to later archaeological populations and even to historically reported rates of pre-adult mortality (Goodman et al. 1984a; Cook 1984; Cassidy 1984; Lovejoy et al. 1977; Mensforth 1985, n.d.; Ubelaker 1984; cf. Storey 1985; Acsadi and Nemeskeri 1970; Cohen in preparation). In addition, where average ages at death for adults are recorded, that average appears more often than not to go down with the adoption of agriculture, often only rebounding in later stages of civilization (Angel 1984; Goodman et al. 1984a; Cassidy 1984; Ubelaker 1984; Kennedy 1984; Kobayashi 1967; Blakely 1971; Welinder 1979; see also the more eclectic samples of Acsadi and Nemeskeri 1970; Weiss 1973).

Two problems are clearly involved in the interpretation of these demographic data: the problem of sampling and the problem of population growth. Infant and child mortality may appear low because of natural low childhood mortality or because cemeteries are incomplete (Lovejoy et al. 1977; cf. Howell 1982). Moreover, accelerating population growth may produce a cemetery with an increased percentage of children or a declining average age at death even though no decrease in individual life expectancy has occurred (Sattenspiel and Harpending 1983; Johansson and Horowitz 1986). Thus the increased number of children and the lower average adult ages in some Neolithic cemeteries might reflect the fact that the cemeteries are more complete or the fact that they represent faster growing populations than those of the Paleolithic or Mesolithic (as is commonly assumed).

However, several points must be raised before the demographic data are simply discarded. First, of course, the lower rate of mortality among hunter gatherers is what we ought in fact to expect given the observed rates of pathology just discussed. Second, whatever their faults, those prehistoric hunter-gatherer cemeteries described as complete are providing estimates of infant and childhood mortality that are not out of line with ethnographic observations of hunter gatherers. The studies cited – suggesting infant mortality averaging approximately 20 percent and pre-adult mortality totalling 40 to 50 per cent – are not markedly different from the estimates of Howell (1979) for the contemporary !Kung (which in turn are not exceptional compared to other existing ethnographic measures or estimates of infant and child mortality among hunter gatherers: see data collected by Cohen in preparation). These figures are in turn only moderate rates of loss by historic standards. In addition, as Howell herself suggests (see also Cohen in preparation), these rates of loss are appropriate to balance low hunter-gatherer child production whether resulting from natural infertility or purposeful child spacing (however, cf. Campbell and Wood in press).

Third, we should not overstate the distorting effects of population growth (or migration) on cemeteries even though we recognize those effects. Accelerating population growth can reduce average age at death and thus create an "artificial" appearance of reduced life expectancy; but such an acceleration cannot simply be assumed; and even where demonstrated it may not account entirely for the changes observed in the death profile. Johansson and Horowitz (1986) argue, for example, that the apparent decline in life expectancy through three sequential populations at Dickson Mounds reported by Goodman et al. (1984a) may be an artifact of accelerating population growth, which they argue has a profound effect on estimates of life expectancy, particularly in the middle or transitional period; but even after re-evaluating the data they conclude that life expectancy was actually less in the latest (Mississippian Period) population than in the earliest population (albeit by a smaller margin than originally calculated).

Moreover, population growth rates cannot affect death profiles on any significant scale unless the acceleration of population growth rates is itself fairly marked and sustained. Such effects cannot have been widespread or long-lasting during the Neolithic, given estimates of average population growth which suggest at best a trivial average acceleration in growth with the adoption of farming. Typical estimates of population growth of 0.1 percent per year for the Neolithic and for early civilizations (e.g. Hassan 1981) do not imply a rate of growth sufficient to have a widespread distorting effect on average adult age at death (cf. Coale and Demeny 1983). The very wide geographical distribution of the decline in average age at death at the beginning of farming suggests that we are seeing a real increase in mortality.

At present, the best model is one in which we assume that foragers did in fact enjoy relatively low infant and child mortality and moderate average ages at death as adults. With the beginnings of farming, I suspect that infant and child mortality increased and adult longevity decreased as a matter of fact and not just as an artifact of accelerating population growth. In later populations (cf. Acsadi and Nemeskeri 1970; Weiss 1973) adult life expectancy clearly often rebounded back past Neolithic levels and ultimately beyond Paleolithic levels as well – but infant and child mortality may commonly have remained at or above hunter-gatherer levels until relatively recent historic times.

Such speculation aside, one other point needs to be made in this context. There is neither empirical evidence nor theoretical basis for the assumption that high rates of infant and childhood mortality explain the appearance of good health among prehistoric hunter gatherers (that is, that prehistoric hunter gatherers appear "healthy" because they died before their skeletons could record biological stress). If the Neolithic acceleration in population growth reflects increased fertility or relaxed birth control as many authorities have argued (e.g. Hassan 1981; Handwerker 1983; Howell 1986; Roth 1985; but cf. Campbell and Wood in press), then the acceleration could easily have been achieved despite higher mortality among later groups as the skeletal data appear to imply. But, even if the acceleration in population growth were due entirely to improved survivorship (with no change in the production of children), the slight acceleration in growth (from near zero to 0.1 percent) implies only a very small improvement in survivorship. If for the sake of argument we use Howell's !Kung data as a basis for analysis, an increase from 44 to 45 percent survival to the mean age of maternity (approximately age 30) would explain the Neolithic acceleration – a percentage of change far too small to suggest that reported increases in rates of pathology can be explained by the improved survival rate of stressed individuals.

The net import of all of these data appears to be that although the !Kung and other contemporary peoples may be misleading examples; and although it may be inappropriate to refer to hunter gatherers as "affluent," there is substantial evidence that they enjoyed comparatively good health and nutrition in comparison to the average of subsequent farming populations and that they enjoyed better life expectancies than early farmers.

The Boserupian model of agricultural origins

One corollary of the image of hunter-gatherer affluence which emerged in the 1960s was a reconsideration of the Neolithic Revolution. A number of scholars (Flannery 1969; Binford 1968b; Cohen 1977) combined the new image of hunting and gathering with the economic model proposed by Ester Boserup (1965) and argued that the adoption of farming, rather than being a technological "advance" was in fact a technological adjustment to stress – probably to growing population. We argued that the new economy undoubtedly succeeded in feeding more people and supporting larger populations but probably did so only at the cost of diminishing returns for labor both in the quality and quantity of food available. I have added two further extensions of the Boserupian argument, suggesting that not only the adoption of farming but also the "intensification" of Mesolithic and Archaic economies, that is, the "broad spectrum revolution," was also the product of population pressure among prehistoric foragers (Cohen 1977). I suggested that the adoption of shellfish oriented economies, of fishing, of the hunting and trapping of small animals and birds, and the utilization of small seeds were all strategies of necessity rather than choice. I also suggested that the emergence of complex political institutions among recent hunter gatherers such as those of California and the Pacific northwest probably resulted more from the pressure of larger populations on resources and the logistic problems of managing those resources than on the "affluence" to which they had traditionally been attributed (Cohen 1981, 1985b). This analysis of the broad spectrum revolution has been contested by a number of authorities including Hayden (1981), who has reasserted the image of technological progress in the interpretation of broad spectrum economies.

The data from paleopathology concerning the comparative health of hunter gatherers and farmers summarized above does, I believe, tend on balance to accord with the predictions of Boserupian models of the origins of agriculture. The skeletons do not support the contention that labor costs increased with farming; but the apparent reduction in nutritional quality when farmers are compared to earlier hunters does fit the Boserupian model. So, too, I believe do the data on infections. Infection, of course is a function of group size and sedentism and not strictly of economic choices *per se*; so its relationship to the Boserupian argument is indirect. Nonetheless, the increase in rates of infection is likely to have been a regular, fairly immediate, and generally palpable consequence of settling down in large group aggregates. As such it would have been a significant disincentive to sedentism, supporting the argument (Cohen 1977, 1985b) that sedentism is most often a strategy of last resort among foraging populations.

The key to the test of the population pressure model of agricultural origins, however, really depends on trends identifiable in the record among hunter gatherers *before* the beginning of farming.

Recent work evaluating exploitative efficiency of various foraging tasks – work stimulated by interest in optimal foraging models – appears generally to support the Boserupian interpretation. Although there are variations from environment to environment, efficiency studies in a wide range of environments appear to suggest that the hunting of large game animals is in fact a relatively efficient activity in energetic terms and that other aspects of broad spectrum foraging such as gathering shellfish, hunting small animals or birds, and collecting small seeds are commonly less efficient. (The tests also suggest that the relative advantages of hunting large game would have been even greater for populations, in a world richer in game, equipped only with Stone Age equipment, than for modern foragers with metal tools.) The implication is that the Mesolithic expansion of foraging economies away from an early focus on larger game animals probably implied diminishing returns for labor (see Cohen 1985b, 1987) and is probably a strategy of necessity, not one of choice.

The data from paleopathology, although mixed, also appear increasingly to support this model. Cohen and Armelagos obtained mixed results in comparing early and later hunter gatherers for signs of progress or decline in health and argued that they could not conclusively test the population pressure model based on the fragmentary paleopathological data available. Various scholars in the study described a decline in human body size throughout the Old World which began before the adoption of farming. The trend was reported in India (Kennedy 1984); in the Aegean (Angel 1984); in the Levant (Smith et al. 1984) and in Western Europe (Meiklejohn et al. 1984). The meaning of this trend is ambiguous, however. In keeping with historic and modern interpretation of stature changes the trend might well indicate declining nutrition (as both Angel and Kennedy assert). Angel in particular argued that the reduction in stature was accompanied by other changes in the skeleton specifically diagnostic of declining nutrition. However, the trend might also be a function of changing climate or it might be a function of changing foraging activities (Frayer 1981).

Only two studies compared the frequency of acute stress episodes recorded among early and late hunter gatherers in the Old World. Smith et al. (1984) found no trend in tooth enamel defects when Paleolithic and Mesolithic populations were compared; Brothwell (1963) had earlier found increased rates of enamel defects in Mesolithic as compared to Paleolithic samples in Europe. In sum there is suggestive but not conclusive evidence of declining nutrition in Mesolithic populations in the Old World; there is little or no evidence to suggest improved nutrition, better health or more reliable food supplies.

In the New World, the picture is also complicated. In central California, Dickel et al. (1984) reported that rates of Harris lines declined through time suggesting improvements in cultural buffering against episodes of stress; but they also reported that enamel hypoplasias show a net increase through time, stature a slight decline. Dickel (1985), adopting one of the techniques of Angel, has more recently argued that skull measurements among California Indians suggest a decline through time in the quality of nutrition. Working with populations from southern California, Phil Walker (n.d.) has now also suggested that enamel hypoplasias are more common in later populations although his conclusions about the quality of background nutrition differ from Dickel's. Walker (1985, 1986; Walker and de Niro 1986) suggests that there was an increase in protein consumption through time. His theories predict that porotic hyperostosis should increase through time as a function of increasing dependence on aquatic resources and as a function of increasing group size and sedentism promoting infection. But at present his data are mixed.

In contrast, Robert Benfer (1984), working in Peru, has found that the Archaic Paloma site displayed a progressive improvement in stature over time and a reduction in the frequency of Harris lines. He also found that the natural environment of the site was being progressively degraded, suggestive of a population out of balance with its resources. In more recent work (1986) he has also found that enamel hypoplasia increased through the sequence as did the rates of wear on teeth. Coprolite studies suggested that an expanding array of plant foods was being consumed, including a number of increasingly coarse and fibrous foods. In later coastal sites of the Cotton Preceramic Period he found Harris lines to be less frequent but more massive, suggesting that the latest hunter gatherers in the region may already have traded mild seasonal hunger for more occasional periods of severe stress.

Robert Mensforth (1985, 1986) has undertaken a comparison between an earlier Archaic site (BT5) in Kentucky and the later, larger, and more sedentary Woodland Libben hunting and gathering population in Ohio. Mensforth was concerned with evaluating contrasting styles of foraging independent of the adoption of agriculture. He found that the later, Libben population displayed more frequent growth retardation and shorter diaphyseal bone length for age in children, higher rates of infection and higher rates of porotic hyperostosis than the earlier site. He also found that Libben, although displaying slightly lower rates of infant mortality than BT5, also displayed higher rates of mortality at all ages from one to fifteen, such that the Libben population reared a smaller proportion of its infants to age fifteen (52 vs 62 per cent). (Mensforth argues, however, that differences reflect primarily the increasing burden of infectious disease, not declining adequacy of nutritional intake.)

One other new set of data appear to support the implication that the intensification of hunting and gathering may have had negative rather than positive health consequences. Recent work by Australian prehistorians such as Harry Lourandos (1985), Robert Beaton (1983, 1985), and Josephine Flood (1976) has demonstrated that contrary to Birdsell's (1968) models of population equilibrium among Aborigines, the Australian continent displays a history of intensification of use similar to that of other continents. In addition, Australian scholars are now arguing that portions of Australia supported late, large, dense and relatively sedentary populations in some locations.

Stephen Webb (1984) has recently compared rates of pathology among different prehistoric Aboriginal groups. Unfortunately his samples can only occasionally be controlled for time depth. Webb reports one well-defined early sample from the terminal Pleistocene which exhibits relatively high rates of arthritis but low frequencies of enamel hypoplasias and porotic hyperostosis compared to more recent aboriginal groups. He also reports that the early group displays no hypoplasia of the third molar, suggesting that childhood stresses did not extend as late in life as they did in later populations. Webb also reports that rates of several categories of pathologies (infections, porotic hyperostosis, enamel hypoplasias) are relatively high in those recent populations which were thought to have lived in large, sedentary (that is, "affluent") foraging settlements, many of which display rates of pathology comparable to rates in more settled groups elsewhere.

The paleopathological data may also begin to address variations among Boserupian models. Marvin Harris (1977) has proposed a model for the interaction of economic change and population growth which parallels my own but differs in one important respect. Harris suggests that incipient agriculture may have relieved demographic stress on hunter gatherers temporarily, providing a short-lived period of relative prosperity before population growth again created stress. Some archaeological sequences do in fact provide glimpses of such temporary periods of well-being. In the Levant, for example, Smith et al. (1984) argue that pre-pottery Neolithic B with incipient domestication of animals displays reduced strontium content in bone, suggesting increasing per capita availability of animal products. This change is associated with an increase in body size, suggesting a short-lived improvement in nutrition – although Neolithic and later populations generally appear less well nourished than their hunting and gathering forebears. Similarly, Cassidy suggests that in Kentucky, early pre-maize horticulturalists, only glimpsed in the record of paleopathology, may have enjoyed good health relative to hunter gatherers but particularly relative to established maize farming populations. Perzigian et al. (1984) also suggest that transitional populations in Ohio may have enjoyed a temporary nutritional advantage reflected in their stature at the same time that they appear to have experienced particularly high rates of infection. On the other hand, Angel's (1984) reconstruction of Aegean prehistory suggests that Neolithic populations were more stressed than either earlier hunter gatherers or later groups. Goodman et al. (1984a) suggest that transitional populations at Dickson Mounds participated in the gradual decline in health that characterizes the history of the site; and elsewhere in Illinois, Cook (1984) suggests that transitional populations were more stressed than either earlier or later groups.

Trends in human health after the adoption of agriculture
Although the data have not yet systematically been gathered, evidence from paleo-pathology has begun to provide hints about the impact of the intensification of agriculture and the emergence of centralized political institutions on human health and nutrition. We can begin to evaluate conflicting images of the evolution of complex society and its impact on individuals (Childe 1951a; cf. Fried 1967, Cohen in preparation). We should ultimately be able to use paleopathological data also to help sort out more detailed competing hypotheses about the processes of evolution of complex societies.

At present, however, the most prominent "pattern" to these data is the striking contrasts between the existing studies and the conclusions they draw. Angel, for example, suggested that nutrition and health rebounded among Bronze Age and later Aegean populations following the "bottoming out" of most health trends in the Neolithic. On the other hand, Martin et al. (1984) as well as Rudney (1983) suggest that nutrition and health in Nubia declined in proportion to the intensification of agriculture and the inclusion of Nubia in the sphere of larger political societies. And Smith et al. suggest that in the Levant signs of anemia, cortical thinning of bone and enamel hypoplasia often appear most severe in Chalcolithic, Bronze Age, or later populations.

In the New World, Cook (1984) and Buikstra (1984; Buikstra and Van der Merwe 1986) suggest that Mississippian Period health was comparatively good in the Illinois Valley despite the appearance of "a tuberculosis-like" pathology. Similarly, Powell suggests that Mississippian Period health was comparatively good at Moundville in Alabama despite the common presence of low-grade infection; and Blakely found health to be good in Mississippian Period Etowah. However, Goodman et al. (1984a) suggest that almost all indicators point to a decline of health and longevity extending into the Mississippian Period at Dickson Mounds. Similarly Cassidy reports the Mississippian Period population of Kentucky to show high degrees of stress. Other workers in the eastern United States have also reported high levels of pathology or stress in Mississippian sites (Robbins 1978; Perzigian et al. 1984; Eisenberg 1985, 1986). Stodder (1986) has recently reported that health and survivorship declined significantly in the later prehistory of the Anasazi region of the American southwest.

Rebecca Storey (1985) has also reported exceptionally high levels of stress associated with urbanization in both Copan (Honduras) and Teotihuacan. She argues that these sites display levels of mortality which are not matched in other New World archaeological populations with the exception of the Mississippian Period Hiwasee Dallas site in Tennessee. In addition, in Mesoamerica, various sources (Haviland 1967; Saul 1972; Nickens 1976) report on stature decline and increase in dietary stress continuing from Preclassic to Postclassic Periods; and White (1986) has recently reported that the highest rates of porotic hyperostosis within the long sequence of Lamanai in Belize are from the Postclassic and Colonial Periods.

These apparent contradictions may resolve themselves into patterns as more data emerge. The fragments so far described suggest that we may be seeing the outlines of a pattern in which biological stress is partitioned both along lines of social class and along lines of the specialization of settlements within social networks. Angel, for example, suggests that the Bronze Age rebound in health in the Aegean is accompanied by the appearance of social class-associated differences in stature and other indicators of class-differentiated health and nutrition. Acsadi and Nemeskeri (1970) find sharp distinctions in mortality in early civilizations based not only on class but on the type of settlement, urban areas including Rome displaying comparatively low apparent life expectancies. Martin et al. (1984) have argued that the decline in nutrition in Nubia reflects the marginal status of Nubian communities in the trade networks of larger empires.

Similarly, Haviland suggested some years ago that the stature decline among Maya during Classic and Postclassic Periods was not shared by the Mayan elite. Storey's description of particularly acute stress in an urban ward in Teotihuacan would appear to foreshadow the kinds of biological stress reported historically among the poor in urban environments.

The varied experience of Mississippian populations in North America may ultimately have to be plotted against maps of the boundaries of political empires and economic exchange networks before they can be fully understood. Koerner and Blakely (1985) and Blakely and Detweiler (1986) have reported that health and nutrition were not as good among villagers in (relatively central) Etowah as among those living in the contemporary outlying King site within the Mississippian Coosa chiefdom. Conversely, Goodman et al. suggest that the poor health of Mississippian populations at Dickson Mounds (in contrast to the Mississippian rebound reported elsewhere in Illinois) may be a function of Dickson's marginal political position in a trade network dominated by Cahokia. The implication is that the redistributive mechanisms of centralized political society may be working more to the detriment than to the benefit of the latter population. Buikstra (Buikstra and Van der Merwe 1986) has recently offered an alternate hypothesis suggesting that severely stressed

Mississippian Period populations in Tennessee were on political frontiers, their stress secondary to fortification.

The patterns of affluence and stress associated with early civilization are not yet clear. What is clear from the data on recent prehistory is that, whatever their benefits, these civilizations clearly were capable of generating high levels of biological stress and of focusing stress on segments of the population in a manner rarely experienced by earlier groups. To judge by some recent work in the paleopathology of modern societies, including Black American populations of the last 150 years (e.g. Rose 1985), such foci of extreme biological stress persisted well into the twentieth century.

PART II: Archaeology in the Americas and beyond

9

The structural analysis of Paleolithic art

MARGARET W. CONKEY

Introduction

This chapter is about the application of structuralist ideas to the study of a particular
archaeological phenomenon that we have labeled "Paleolithic art."[1] It is ambitious to
take on structuralism in general in a single chapter. Although some general background on structuralism is presented, I will focus on structuralist approaches in
Paleolithic art, particularly that of Leroi-Gourhan (e.g. 1965, 1972), who elucidated
what he believed to be a set of underlying structural or generative principles for the
making and placing of specific images on cave walls. It is thoroughly appropriate to
consider structuralist perspectives in the archaeology of the Upper Paleolithic because
a pioneering structuralist analysis in archaeology as a whole is widely recognized to
have been this work of Leroi-Gourhan. Furthermore, this study, which will be
considered below, remains one of the more extensive applications of structuralism to
archaeological data, particularly from a prehistoric (as contrasted with historic)
context.

The object of structural analysis that is being considered here is "Paleolithic art."
By this term we refer to an amazingly wide and diverse range of imagery and material
culture: geometrically incised bone and antler implements; pieces of bone and antler
with representational imagery (often animals); carved or sculpted images – in bone,
stone, antler, ivory – that include humans and animals; bas-reliefs on stone blocks;
engravings on cave walls or plaquettes of stone – sometimes hundreds of images
overlain in a single 'panel' or space; and perhaps the most famous imagery – the
paintings or drawings on cave walls.

These images derive from archaeological contexts of the late Pleistocene that we
refer to as Upper Paleolithic: from about 35,000 to 10,000 years B.P. The geographic
and temporal distributions of these images and objects are highly variable. Whereas
cave painting appears to have flourished during the last 8–10,000 years of this period
and to be concentrated in limestone caves of southwestern Europe (especially
southwestern France and north coastal Spain), most of the famous female statuettes
appear referable only to a 6000-year period within the Upper Paleolithic or to two
temporal subsets (Gravettian and Magdalenian [Delporte 1979:12], although given
the dating and provenience problems these are hardly definitive), and have been
recovered at locales as far east as into Russia and as far west as the French Atlantic
Pyrenees.

We are reasonably sure that these materials are the handiwork of anatomically modern humans, *Homo sapiens sapiens* (or Cro-Magnon peoples, as they are called in Europe at this period). Because we have labeled these materials "art" and because this European Upper Paleolithic sequence and associated fossils of early modern peoples were defined very early in the development of prehistory, these materials and images have occupied a most privileged position in our evolutionary scenarios: the images are said to be the "origins" of art, testimony to the achievement of "fully symbolic behavior" by modern humans, and the cultures that produced them have been considered as a "slice of ethnography."

Although some discussion of prevailing twentieth-century accounts for the imagery – prior to the application of structuralism – will be given below, it is relevant to keep in mind that such accounts are inextricably a part of the development of the field of prehistory (see, e.g., Sackett 1983), and of the emergent tension between archaeology and ethnography; most of the early interpretations were derived from direct parallels with (not even analogies to) ethnographic groups observed in the nineteenth and twentieth centuries (for example, as reported by Spencer and Gillen 1899). Further-more, because of this early "discovery" of prehistoric art of hunter gatherers, the interpretive paradigm for rock art anywhere (for instance, for that of southern Africa) was that which was put forth for the Franco-Cantabrian materials. Thus, the impact of the early interpretations and the way in which such imagery was conceived – as a class of archaeological data – extended far beyond the immediate sociohistorical contexts of Upper Paleolithic Europe. It is only now, in the 1980s, that important challenges to that transhistorical paradigm are being successfully put forth (e.g. Lewis-Williams 1982, 1983a).

Prior to the work of André Leroi-Gourhan in the late 1950s and 1960s the prevailing account for the Paleolithic images – especially those on cave walls, which was the preferred and favored medium for study – was one that appealed to premises of sympathetic magic. Specifically, it was held that the predominantly animal images had been painted/engraved as part of sympathetic magic designed to ensure success in the hunt (for bison, horse, deer, reindeer, mammoth, ibex) or to successfully challenge dangerous animals (cave lion, rhinoceros, cave bear). Whereas the imagery was thought to be 'read' directly (those animals depicted were those preferred for food; geometric markings with animals were variously 'read' as wounds, arrows, traps, or hunter's huts), the peoples producing the images were thought to be hunter gatherers (amd mostly hunters) who were *not* like modern humans of the civilized world; they were pre-scientific, pre-religious and not to be 'read' in the same terms and concepts. Many of the tenets of a structuralist perspective, as summarized below, directly challenge such 'readings', and although Leroi-Gourhan's structuralist study of Paleolithic art also produced a monolithic, inclusive interpretation (which is what the sympathetic magic one is as well) for an extremely diverse corpus of imagery that may span some 20,000 years (1000 generations!), there is no doubt that the structur-alist approach was revolutionary in its implications for the study of archaeological materials, even those from contexts other than the Upper Paleolithic (see Hodder 1982d:7–9; Leone 1982: 743–4).

Some observations on structuralism

Although often thought of as a relatively recent intellectual development, the fundamental ideas behind structuralism may be several centuries old. Hawkes's reading of Vico's *The New Science* (1725) suggests that one can find here the basic structuralist ideas that humans "construct the myths, the social institutions, virtually the whole world" as they perceive it, and in so doing humans construct themselves (Hawkes 1977: 14). In Hawkes's twentieth-century terms what Vico wrote is that "particular forms of humanity are determined by particular social relations and systems of human institutions." This process of making is a process that we would now call "structuring". The "mental language common to all nations" that Vico (1725: 161) insisted on is the universal human capacity to simultaneously formulate structures and to submit to them: "to be human . . . is to be a structuralist" (Hawkes 1977: 15). But structuralist perspectives and *being* a structuralist have meant many things over the last decades, as structuralism has come to be explicitly formulated. In fact, this variation and the accompanying lack of coherence that has characterized structuralism may be one factor contributing to the relatively slow arrival of structuralist studies in such fields as archaeology (Hodder 1986: 34).

In providing some sort of overview of structuralism, I will stress those attributes and aspects that can be most directly linked to the ways in which structuralist notions have been applied to archaeological inquiry without replicating, I hope, what has already been suggested by Hodder (1982d), Leone (1982) and Wylie (1982). The rich and complex history of discourse on structuralism can only be implied; there has even developed a recognized intellectual movement labeled "post-structuralism," given that structuralism, as an intellectual movement, was effectively over in Europe some years ago (see, for example, Eagleton 1983:127–50). Overviews of structuralism include those by Caws (1968), De George and Fernande (1972), Eagleton (1983), Ehrmann (1970), Hawkes (1977), Lane (1970), Piaget (1968) and Robey (1973). Other critiques and edited volumes of commentary include Gardner (1973), Macksey and Donato (1970), Pettit's inquiry into the philosophical premises of structuralism (1977), and Culler's (1975) introduction to the field of structuralist criticism. Within anthropology there is Leach's (1976) useful discussion of the anthropological basis of structuralism, Gellner's (1982) overview, and, of course, the primary texts by Lévi-Strauss (e.g. 1958, 1962a, 1962b, 1964). Recent critiques of structuralism in anthropology of particular relevance for archaeologists are those by Ortner (1984) and Fabian (1984), because of their concerns with history and the construct of time.

Within archaeology, one might begin with the volume edited by Hodder (1982c), and especially the essays by Hodder (1982d) and Wylie (1982). At least two major structuralist analyses comprise the primary examples (Deetz 1977; Glassie 1975; see also Leone 1977), other than the earlier work of Leroi-Gourhan (e.g. 1965). Among the shorter case studies of structural analysis of archaeological materials are those of architecture and space by Fritz (1978), Isbell (1976) and Huffman (1981); Clarke's study (1972) of structural transformations at an Iron Age site; Muller's analyses of material culture from the prehistoric U.S. southeast (e.g. 1971, 1977); Washburn's formal structuralist analyses of symmetry principles for ceramic designs (e.g. 1977;

1983); Wynn's attempt to apply Piagetian notions of cognitive structures to early stone tool manufacture (e.g. 1979); and McGhee's (1977) very contextualized structural analysis of the prehistoric Thule (arctic Canada). Other most useful sources are Leone (1982) and the most recent call for structuralist analysis in archaeology by Hodder (1986). But what is structuralism all about; why is it appealing or compelling to archaeologists, and what has been gained by structuralism in studies of Paleolithic art?

Hawkes (1977:17) has noted that structuralism has involved a "momentous historic shift in the nature of perception"; this involves the realization that the world does *not* consist of objects that exist independently, objects with concrete features that can be perceived clearly and individually and whose nature can be classified accordingly. The nature of things "may be said to lie not in things themselves, but in the relationships which we construct, and then perceive, *between* them. This new concept, that the world is made up of relationships, rather than things, constitutes the first principle of that way of thinking which can be properly called 'structuralist'" (Hawkes 1977:17–18).

Classic structuralism, then, set forth that the individual units of any system have meaning only by virtue of their relation to one another. Although the "ultimate quarry of structuralist thinking may be the permanent structures into which individual human acts and perceptions fit" (Hawkes 1977:18) – and from which they derive their final nature – much structuralist analysis has worked away at accessing less ambitious structures than those assumed to be not only permanent but even universal. Leone (1982: 743), however, has made a good case that because of the idea of universal structures as part of classic structuralism, the structuralist approach in archaeology has been able to address aspects of "recovering mind" – a topic that had been summarily banned by the programmatics of the New Archaeology (e.g. Binford 1965:203–10).

Historically, structuralism derived from linguistics and made one of its biggest impacts in the field of anthropology. It has been described as "an attempt to rethink everything through once again in terms of linguistics" (Jameson 1972: vii, as cited by Eagleton 1983: 97). From the pioneering structural linguist, deSaussure, came the synchronic emphasis of structuralism: to study language as a system of signs at a given point in time. The primacy of relationships in structuralism allowed for an emphasis on the *connectedness* and the '*constructedness*' of human meaning; such meaning is the product of certain shared systems of signification. And although there was the potential for a historical and social theory of meaning, the emphasis on synchronicity on the one hand, and the universalisms of structures that were held by "hard" or classic structuralists on the other, militated against any development of such a social and historical theory. Although sign systems were seen to be culturally variable, the deep laws governing the working of these systems were not. As a result, classic structuralism was "hair-raisingly unhistorical" (Eagleton 1983:109).

Fundamental to structural anthropology (and the structural linguistics from which it derives) has been a challenge to the reigning notion that a "transparent one-to-one correspondence exists between a work of art (*sensu latu*) and the 'reality' or nature to which that work of art is presupposed to 'refer'" (Hawkes 1977:55). It is from this structuralist challenge to "realism" and "naturalism" that the analyst or reader of cultural "texts" (myths, visual images, architecture, etc.) must recognize that art (*sensu latu*) "acts as a mediating, molding force in society rather than an agency which merely reflects or records" (Hawkes 1977:56). That is, the empiricist/rationalist view of language (and other cultural products) "suffered severely at the hands of structuralism" : in the structuralist view, reality is not reflected (or expressed) by language but *produced* by it. And yet, although challenging what Lévi-Strauss called "sterile empiricism," this view that reality is essentially a product of language still fits within the quite classic doctrine of idealism, which holds that the world is constituted by human consciousness (Eagleton 1983:108). The application of structuralism to Paleolithic art has had an appeal to those who are inherently idealists for just this very reason. That is, by showing that the imagery – the so-called "first art" – made by early modern humans (and in Europe, no less) some 20–30,000 years ago created a reality, in much the same way as language does, fully supports, and gives evolutionary depth to, this idealist doctrine that the world was constituted by human consciousness.

The structuralist method, in general, brackets off content and focuses on form: it is the structure of relations that are scrutinized. The method, furthermore, is said to be "quite indifferent" to the cultural value of the text: it is an analytical, not evaluative method (Eagleton 1983:96). Furthermore, as a result of the challenge to "realism," analysis "does not take the text at face value, but 'displaces' it into quite a different object"; "it is a calculated affront to common sense" (Eagleton 1983:96).

Two other general aspects of method are worth noting. First, there is the link between structuralism and semiotics; the latter has been called, simplistically, "a science of signs." Semiotics is a field of study that uses structuralist methods; structuralism treats something that is not usually thought of as a system of signs as if it were one. As will be noted, this is what happened with Leroi-Gourhan's application of structuralist methods to Paleolithic art; the images, by means of structuralist analysis, were now treated as a system of signs. Thus, attempts at reading signification were then possible.

Second, one result of structuralism has been, however, that the individual subject is no longer seen as the source or end of meaning; the individual subject is "decentered," and "to say that structuralism has a problem with the individual subject is to put it mildly" (Eagleton 1983:112–13). The new subject becomes the system itself; structuralism can be charged with being anti-humanist in the sense that the individual human subject – like the "real object" (language, architecture, art, or whatever) – is bracketed off. The structuralist project does not refer to an object nor to the expression of an individual subject; "what is left hanging in the air between them (the object and the individual) is a system of rules" (Eagleton 1983:112). To view language, art, architecture – or whatever cultural text is the object of structuralist scrutiny – as more than the mere "expression" of the human mind is indeed recognized as a "valuable advance," but the structuralist picture, as originally framed, leaves out both the human subjects and their intentions.

Various archaeological modifications on structuralism try to address this weakness (e.g. Hodder 1982d; 1986), but in the pioneering application of structuralism to Paleolithic materials by Leroi-Gourhan there is no doubt that among the missing are individuals, intentions, and an inquiry into the *contexts* of making and using imagery that follows from a concern with intentions. But this is to get ahead of the discussion and to anticipate the retrospectives of the 1980s on inquiry of the 1960s; this is to see "art-making" as a practice rather than as an object, which would not have been possible without what we might call the "structuralist break-out," particularly as generated by Leroi-Gourhan's study of Paleolithic cave art.

Leroi-Gourhan and the "structuralist break-out"

In contradistinction to his intellectual predecessors in the field of Paleolithic art, Leroi-Gourhan assumed that the cave wall images were not randomly placed on sacred wall locales but were, instead, deliberately selected images placed in deliberate locales within the cave and in specific relations among each other. In other words, he assumed there was an underlying structure or set of structural principles that generated the resultant imagery. One of the gains of his structuralist approach to paleolithic cave art was the demystification of the art which (to paraphrase Eagleton's [1983:106] observations on literature when subjected to structuralist scrutiny) becomes a *construct* whose mechanisms could be classified and analyzed like the object of any other science. And yet the art – by means of structuralist analysis – is then treated by Leroi-Gourhan as a system of signs, and attempts at reading signification are then possible. The cave is "as text"; to Leroi-Gourhan, it is a "mythological vessel." In this regard, it could be argued that Leroi-Gourhan's work "redefined the prehistorian's enterprise" (Michelson 1986:3).

Although Leroi-Gourhan's inclusive structural analysis was set forth in full by 1965, there were several preliminary articles (e.g. 1958) that began to explore the patterning. At the same time, a colleague of his had also begun to develop a structural approach that was prodding the question of signification (Laming-Empèraire 1962). A particularly informative essay on how he viewed this enterprise was written by Leroi-Gourhan in 1966 (and reprinted in Leroi-Gourhan 1983; in translation by Michelson 1986).[2] Here it is clear that all along he had as a goal "accessing traces of metaphysical thought." In the early 1960s this was strikingly incompatible with the emergence in the Anglo-American world of the New Archaeology and its denial of "mind." The now tragic irony (tragic because of the recent [February 1986] death of Leroi-Gourhan) is that this New Archaeology had grounded its claims in anthropology and yet it missed the link with the most anthropological of Europe's prehistorians, Leroi-Gourhan. Because of his recent death, it is appropriate – particularly in a review of structural studies in Paleolithic art – to consider more fully Leroi-Gourhan's structuralist project.

There are four particularly interesting aspects of Leroi-Gourhan's 1966 essay, "The religion of the caves: magic or metaphysics?" that inform on his structuralist study: (1) why he felt it was possible in the 1950s to embark on a "general investigation"; (2) why he chose the wall paintings; (3) why he came to believe that a certain syntax must have been at work; and (4) why his 1965 treatise was, to him, only a "clearing of terrain" *and* able to show the cave as a myth-container, as a mythological vessel. Although numerous summaries and synopses (e.g. Leone 1982) of his structuralist enterprise have been published, many are explicitly a critique of all (e.g. Ucko and Rosenfeld 1967) or just a part of his analysis or interpretation (e.g. Parkington 1969; Stevens 1975). Leroi-Gourhan's 1966 article, however, offers a particularly incisive summary of his own work and will form here the basis for exposing the major features of his structuralist endeavor. As one translator has written, this 1966 essay offers the "theoretical grounding for his radical revision of its [Paleolithic art's] decipherment and interpretation . . . Locating a central generalized mythogram, it proposes a general intelligibility of paleolithic culture . . ." (Michelson 1986:3).

Michelson makes one further interesting point that, if one accepts it, actualizes the structuralist premise (noted above) on the "constructedness" of meaning in human life. In the introduction to her translation, which she entitles "In praise of horizon-tality", Michelson discusses Leroi-Gourhan's adoption of an excavation technique for the Upper Paleolithic (Magdalenian) site of Pincevent that was strikingly different from the vertical and stratigraphic techniques developed by most French pre-historians: the horizontal exposure, or a "planographic" method.

The axis of inquiry was, quite literally, rotated, and the horizontal cut
replaced the vertical . . . This rotation . . . facilitated the reading of a
terrain in terms of its inner relationships . . .

> (Michelson 1986:4)

Leroi-Gourhan himself noted that the consequence of this method – in particular the way in which it allowed for plotting the "liaisons" among the flint and hearthstones – was the way in which it could reveal "latent structures" that were otherwise not accessible given the apparent disorder (Leroi-Gourhan 1983:134).

Michelson goes on to suggest that we can see in Leroi-Gourhan's excavation technique

the exact and concrete grounding of theory in praxis, for the rotation of
the digging axis, the replacement of the stratigraphic by the planographic,
rehearses for us that privileging of synchronic over diachronic in relational
analysis of cultural texts which characterizes the structuralist enterprise.

> (Michelson 1986:4)

In retrospect, it is paradoxical that the structural "break-out" or liberation from the sympathetic hunting magic hypothesis was achieved by means of statistical and quantitative analysis. Indeed, it was Leroi-Gourhan's use of key sorting to chart the distributions of specific animal species depicted and the locales for their depictions within caves and in relation to other animal images that gave his structuralist analysis a fundamental prop: there *were* demonstrable patterns, and these – unlike many higher order inferences about the "meaning" of the patterns – were potentially verifiable patterns. In both Paleolithic art studies and in those of southern African rock art, the 1960s witnessed these quantitative studies (see Vinnicombe 1967, 1976 on the southern African imagery), which seems to have been the best language through which to effect a reorientation of the prevailing interpretive framework. The *consequence* of this quantitative method – which was fully acceptable in the 1960s – being applied to a very new data set was, paradoxically, "a move away from the empiricist paradigm to an exploration of anthropological theory" (Lewis-Williams 1983a:5). In southern African rock art studies, researchers have turned to the previously untapped sources of ethnography and ethnohistory and found a rich and ampliative set of connections that has allowed metaphoric readings of the rock art as constituting and being constituted by trance experiences (Lewis-Williams 1982; 1983b).

In studies of Paleolithic art, Leroi-Gourhan felt that his predecessors (the prehistorians of Breuil's generation) lacked not only "distance" but also an inventory: "it took three-quarters of a century to acquire the thousands of examples which authorize a general investigation" (Leroi-Gourhan 1986:9). Furthermore, these predecessors were closely – too closely – dependent upon the evolution of ethnological theory. Leroi-Gourhan's quantitative analysis in Paleolithic art studies moved the field away from empiricism and away from ethnological theory to structuralism and to semiotics, towards art as a system of signs, towards asking, "what does it signify?"

Leroi-Gourhan saw his work of the early 1960s as a "simultaneous study of chronology and content in paleolithic imagery" (1986:9). At one level, this is not in strict keeping with structuralism in that in a classic structuralist approach the content is bracketed off; it is the form that matters. But Leroi-Gourhan used content (especially his "readings" of the geometric "signs") to inform his form. It is in this regard that he leaned towards the semiotic link with structuralism; his structuralism treats the imagery as a system of signs. Furthermore, although he claims chronology as a goal – and indeed one of his more enduring contributions as far as most European prehistorians have been concerned has been his definition of four sequential styles (I–IV) – he produced a *continuous* evolutionary schema of style that involved no change in structure (form) or content. The consequence is an inherently synchronic view; since his structuralist analysis or "reading" could account for variations and details in time and place – as variations on a master pattern of "art-making" – the analysis presumes that the structure or basic organization of a culture is continuous (Leone 1982:744). Leroi-Gourhan's structuralist study took the one class of cultural products (cave wall art) as it was distributed through time and space and argued for a unity because a single structure can be inferred across that temporal and spatial spread. But why would the wall paintings be a medium amenable to structural analysis and likely to inform on the "metaphysics" of the makers?

Leroi-Gourhan considered a well-preserved cave to be a message (cave-as-text) with elements (frame and figures); and these elements, he notes, are in the very position chosen by the author of the figures. "Whether the figures correspond to magical or any other sort of religious intention, the order and frequency of these figures were bound . . . to express the image – even if unconsciously or incompletely formulated – which their maker had of the world upon which those practices were exercised" (Leroi-Gourhan 1986: 10). From this it follows that, unless it could be shown that the figures were completely independent of each other, a "certain syntax must have governed the arrangement of images considered as symbols" (Leroi-Gourhan 1986: 10).

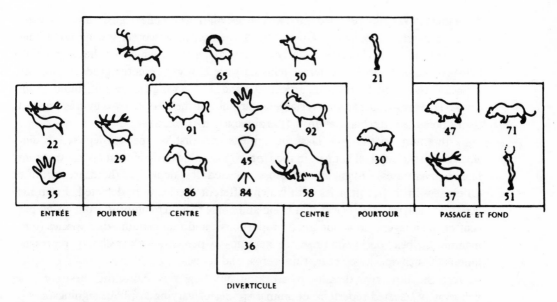

ENTRÉE   POURTOUR   CENTRE   CENTRE   POURTOUR   PASSAGE ET FOND

DIVERTICULE

Fig. 9.1. Leroi-Gourhan's diagram to illustrate the ideal arrangement for a "Paleolithic sanctuary." The numbers below each figure are percentages based on 865 subjects in 62 caves. Thus, 86 per cent of the horses depicted in caves will be found in the center panels ("centre"), or 71 per cent of the cave lion depictions will be in passages and the back ends of caves ("passage et fond") (after Sieveking 1979:57).

In confirmation of his concept of cave-as-text and of his semiotic leanings, Leroi-Gourhan explains his procedure for decoding as one that is related to those used to interpret unknown systems of writing: "each figure is considered a signifying part disposed in an order provided by the very configuration of the cave" (Leroi-Gourhan 1986:12). A point not often stressed by those who focus on Leroi-Gourhan's resultant formula for the placement of images, on the mythogram he claimed, or on his "ideal sanctuary" plan (Fig. 9. 1), is that the cave itself in topography and form is part of the structure. Leroi-Gourhan went on to argue that the role of the cave itself is "non-fortuitous," the cave was an "active participant," its very configuration played a part in the *choice* of site to be decorated, and the cave lent itself to the "placing of a preconceived arrangement . . . a traditionally shaped intellectual schema" (Leroi-Gourhan 1986:14). Despite the Paleolithic preoccupation with the expression of volume (Leroi-Gourhan 1982:9), and despite the non-fortuitous role of the cave, the very existence and abundance of the mobiliary materials and engraved blocks in daylit shelters – whose imagery, he argues, has mythogrammatic consistencies with that on cave walls – shows that the "ideological framework of the works was not exclusively linked to the cave" (Leroi-Gourhan 1982:58).

Assuming then that the figures in the cave were an assemblage of graphic symbols, and that the assemblage was neither writing nor pictogram, Leroi-Gourhan suggested that the mode governing the assemblage was that of a *mythogram* in which the figures are arranged around a central point, as in a picture. On one set of key-punch cards he reproduced the topographic divisions of the caves (entry, first recess, chamber, other recesses, galleries, terminuses). On another set he established his "vocabulary" of more than 2000 figures divided into two classes: animals, in one; signs, human shapes, stenciled hands in the other. Given this distinction into two classes, he notes that imagery from both classes are always in any given cave, which implied a relation between them. However, whereas animals were always present, figures within the second class might be missing: stenciled hands, for example, are not found in all caves. To Leroi-Gourhan this variable occurrence of these (class two) figures implied their "possible interchangeability" (Leroi-Gourhan 1986:12).

Furthermore, within the class of animals, the list of species depicted is not equivalent to a list of all animals in the Upper Paleolithic environment (as known from faunal inventories). Even among those selected for depiction there are striking differences in the frequencies with which different species were depicted. From his very first analysis, it was clear that bison and horse together comprise from 60–70 per cent of the imagery (in about equal proportions), and that certain other species (e.g. mammoth, ibex, deer) comprise the next 20–30 percent, with declining representations of such species as bear, rhinoceros, and felines.

Over the next two decades of working out how this Paleolithic bestiary – a deliberately selected repertoire of animal species of varying symbolic significances – was played out topographically, Leroi-Gourhan finally (1972, 1982) came to account for the mythogram as images hierarchically coordinated according to a certain formula: two major classes of animals, A (horse) and B (bison-aurochs), which are the central figures of any composition, and which comprise 60 percent of the animal depictions. By formula, they are complemented by the complementary animals, C – stag, hind, mammoth, ibex, or reindeer – that comprise 30 percent of the depicted species. Animals of type D (rhino, bear, feline) comprise the remaining 10 percent and are remote in relation to the composition as well as within the cave. The application of this formula to various panels and compositions is most explicitly developed in his contribution to the monograph on Lascaux (in Leroi-Gourhan and Allain 1979:343–66, esp. 348).

In his initial formulations of the mythogram, Leroi-Gourhan sought further patterning and signification among the second class of images: geometric signs, human shapes, and stenciled hands. By drawing on what he could identify as the maleness/femaleness of the humans (but see Ucko and Rosenfeld 1972), on the presumed identification of many signs as male or especially as female genitalia (but see Bahn 1986), on the determination of other signs as "wounds", and on the division of other geometric signs into the two categories of "full" (ovals, triangles, rectangles, "read" female) and "thin" (lines that are straight, hooked, branched, or a series of dots, "read" male) (see Leroi-Gourhan 1978; 1986:12–13), Leroi-Gourhan felt he could reflect upon the possible content of the assemblage of figures:

Most succinctly put, it comes down to the co-presence of male and female
figures, of horse and bison (or of wild cow), with the addition of a third
animal (ibex, mammoth, or deer) and a fourth possible animal (feline or
rhinoceros). The steadiness of arrangement implies a determinate
association between the couplings of the assemblage.

(Leroi-Gourhan 1986:15)

The constant coexistence of bovines and horse was initially seen not just as a pairing but of an order comparable to that of female/male in the signs. And, to Leroi-Gourhan, the "realistic sexual symbols were numerous enough that, even without the help of abstract signs, the presence of sexual polarization is evident" (Leroi-Gourhan 1986:16).

It is possible – as Leone has done – to extrapolate a classic structural accounting from Leroi-Gourhan's original (1965) treatise:

Leroi-Gourhan found that the standard Upper Paleolithic cave contained statements that life and death depend on each other: that males, weapons, and death-dealing animals are opposed to females, animals traditionally hunted by Paleolithic peoples, and wounded and dying people or animals. The two fundamental assumptions, one *inflicting* pain and death, and the other *suffering* pain and death, are essential to each other in providing life. Thus, Magdalenian logic linked women and wounded bison, horses, and ibex, and counterposed them to men, lion, and bears, while seeing all within a single paradigm, not as scattered unrelated items of sympathetic magic.

(Leone 1982:744)

Thus, what Leroi-Gourhan has done has been to produce an accounting for 20,000 (or more) years of image-making; he *does* include the mobiliary materials in a general and inclusive way (e.g. 1986:15) and, in fact, some of the initial stimulus for a sexual symbolism derived from what he saw as direct readings of such on several specific engraved bones and antlers (Leroi-Gourhan 1965: 137). This accounting is structuralist in many ways, including the following: (1) the individual units have meaning only by virtue of their relations to one another: the images do not have a "substantial" meaning, only a "relational" one; (2) the actual content of the art is, for the most part, bracketed off: the bison and horse, full sign and thin sign, could be replaced with entirely different elements and the same mythogram could be there; (3) the "obvious" meaning of the art and imagery is refused and certain "deep" structures, not apparent on the surface, were sought; and (4) since the particular contents are, in theory, replaceable (and this was shown within the second class of figures: signs, humans, hands), there is a sense in which one can say that the "content" of the art is its structure: thus, in a way, the imagery is about itself (Eagleton 1983:96).

There is no doubt that Leroi-Gourhan succumbed to many of the analytical problems for which structuralist analyses are criticized: he does not consider some of the fundamental variables of archaeological inquiry such as time, place, ecology, or artifacts, that is, context. There is no referential context of social action, no actors, intentions, reasons, or query into why this particular kind of structural mythogram might have been meaningful to these particular makers–users–viewers. Particularly to the world of Paleolithic prehistorians whose concerns have been so predominantly typological, chronostratigraphic, and with issues of time-space systematics, the Leroi-Gourhan structuralism *is* "hair-raisingly unhistorical," only deceptively concerned with chronology, which is itself based on "soft" notions of stylistic evolution without the "hard" support of absolute, or even relative, dates. And, of course, there is the challenge not just to the verifiability of the mythogram but to its verification, as numerous critics have suggested (e.g. Ucko and Rosenfeld 1967; Parkington 1969; Stevens 1975).

It is important to point out that Leroi-Gourhan did not put forth this structural account in 1965 and let it stand. As he himself suggests in 1966, this was only a "clearing of terrain," revealing not only a more complex Paleolithic thought than traditional interpretation had led us to believe – that the images were only traces of isolated magical operations – but also that "the cave's decor does really form a decor, that is to say, a framework within which something magically or mythically unfolds" (Leroi-Gourhan 1986:10). The system that he originally elucidated corresponds more closely, he suggested, to the framework of myth than to the traces of magical operations. But from the very beginning he did *not* claim that it was a mythological *content* that he had elucidated; rather, it was a container, a "mythographic vessel" or an infrastructural figurative framework that could serve – over many millennia and many kilometers – not as an articulation of identical concepts, but as a basis for an infinite number of detailed moral symbols and practices. The details of these we may never know, and to the structuralist reading they are subsidiary, if relevant at all.

By the 1982 publication of his next book devoted to European cave art Leroi-Gourhan shows little concern with the sexual polarization of his earlier work. Only the cave itself retains sexual connotations, in whole (as female) or in part (as male or female). The structural pairing of animal species is reaffirmed, but no value is implied, and the classic structuralist pairings, of a binary opposition sort, are not invoked:

The metaphysical alternation of the horse and the bison cannot be better expressed than in these two groups of painting (Le Portel, Lascaux), each exchanging one of its symbols for one of the other's. The risks of explanation are always great and it does not seem possible at the present time to suggest anything other than this fundamental liaison between animals (horse-bison) which alternate, having as a possible partner the ibex (Le Portel, Niaux, Les Trois Frères); the stag is quantitatively secondary and is in a lateral position.

(Leroi-Gourhan 1982:60–1)

Some preliminary assessment and some other structuralisms
There is little doubt that one must have serious reservations about the neat packaging of Paleolithic cave art presented by Leroi-Gourhan; there are justifiable concerns with the statistics, with the divisions of the very complex limestone caves into comparable topographical entities, with the counting of individual figures, and with the determinations for signs and what constitutes an association. These are justifiable concerns for the empiricist in most of us. After all, as Eagleton questions regarding structuralism in general: "How, for example, did the structuralist identify the various 'signifying units' of the text in the first place? How did he or she decide that a specific sign or set of signs constituted such a basic unit, without recourse to frames of cultural

assumption which structuralism in its strictest form wished to ignore?" (Eagleton 1983:122).

There is, on the other hand, also little doubt that Leroi-Gourhan has demanded some reorientation of Paleolithic research in ways that its practitioners are probably unaware; some of these will be developed in the concluding section. Certainly, he engaged prehistorians in a class of data ("Paleolithic art") that they have preferred to marginalize as "too humanistic" (for scientific inquiry) and "too decontextualized" (for the writing of chrono-"cultural" narratives).

The intellectual climate of opinion that was spawned, in part, by Leroi-Gourhan's structuralist accounting has demanded that Upper Paleolithic research be grounded in the acceptance of the cognitive complexity and comparability (to that of ourselves) of Upper Paleolithic peoples (as in the research of Marshack, e.g. 1972). This climate has also demanded that "Paleolithic art" – whether one agrees or not with the particular demystification that Leroi-Gourhan proposes – can be an object and a construct of archaeological inquiry, no matter what one's paradigm might be. Since the 1970s, for example, there have been numerous attempts to account for various kinds of Paleolithic art in terms of the adaptive systems/art-and-style-as-information paradigm characteristic of 1970s Anglo-American archaeology (e.g. Conkey 1978a; Gamble 1982; Jochim 1983; Pfeiffer 1982).

It took more than a decade for the ambitious structuralist enterprise of the sort undertaken by Leroi-Gourhan to penetrate "the hard positivist armor" (after Kohl 1985:105) of the scientistic New Archaeology. These extensive structuralist analyses (e.g. Deetz 1977) were often more ampliative (that is, considered more than one cultural product or text) than Leroi-Gourhan's and, not surprisingly, were usually rooted in historical – not prehistorical – contexts, where arguments and measures of plausibility mediated the skepticism (e.g. Glassie 1975; Leone 1977). It is not surprising that perhaps the first kind of structuralism to penetrate Americanist archaeological research is what has been called "formalist structuralism." Among these studies (e.g. Friedrich 1970; Washburn 1977) have been my own attempts (Conkey 1978b; 1980a; 1980b; 1981; 1982) to elucidate the design structure of engraved bone and antler objects (part of the corpus of "portable art") from Magdalenian Upper Paleolithic sites in Cantabrian Spain. Just a few comments on this kind of structural study in Paleolithic art.

As Hodder (1982d; 1986:36–40) has suggested, the formal structural analysis of archaeological materials could be integrated within the positivistic paradigm of the New Archaeology because in claiming that analysts could "discover" an underlying structure (to the designs on pots, or on bones) and by showing how this structure varied in correlation with social units, it appears as if the analyst is being objective and systematic in the measurement of "relevant variables" and it appears as if the correlations, often across time and space, can serve as "tests" for such anthropologically valued questions as how social groups are differentiated or integrated.

With the advent of structuralism, it was not only the *structured* nature of human material culture that was highlighted for archaeologists, but it was the ancillary supposition: that the broader cultural systems, of which material culture was a part

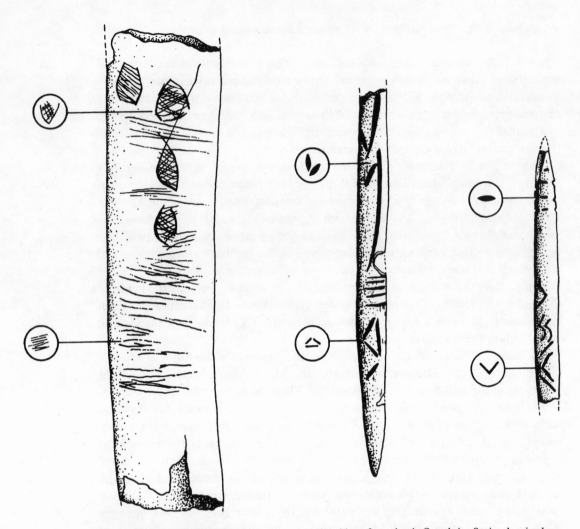

Fig. 9.2. Several engraved Magdalenian bone or antler objects from sites in Cantabrian Spain, showing how some geometric design elements might be inferred from the engravings (from Conkey 1978b).

and which material culture may well construct or constitute, were themselves structured. *If* systems of meaning or orientational constructs of human life are realized by the objects or landscapes that humans create, these meanings or constructs should be observable, in some form, in the processes that produce the objects. Drawing then, in part, from structural linguistics and the idea of generative structures, formal structuralist analyses of archaeological materials intended to elucidate the structures or structural principles that brought artifacts, and their varying attributes, into existence in the first place. Furthermore, it was assumed that if artifact style were rooted in the deep semantic structure of a cultural system, and because the structure of artifact style is potentially observable in the processes of production and use, that is, in human performance, then there is a more substantive basis for the pursuit of style as part of the processes of (social) boundary formation, mediation, and maintenance. That is, structural studies of artifact style appeared to be a more sophisticated way of accessing what had long been an accepted and highly valued goal of anthropological archaeology: the identification of prehistoric social groups.

Design structural analyses, inspired primarily by the linguistically informed study of Margaret Hardin (Friedrich 1970), were carried out on a range of archaeological materials, including engraved bones and antlers from Upper Paleolithic contexts. In my own work on these specific Paleolithic materials (see also Chollot 1964; 1980), thousands of engraved bones were studied and from them a set of fundamental design elements were inferred. Although some design structure studies have claimed a kind of objectivity for their analytical units (such as Washburn's symmetry studies, e.g. 1977, 1983), those design elements identified for Magdalenian engraved bones from sites in Cantabrian Spain (Fig. 9.2) were not claimed to be *the* elements that Magdalenian makers and users also "saw" and differentiated. However, one of the analytical and interpretive *consequences* of a design element structural study of this sort is that the subjectively sorted elements take on a meaning; usually they come to be considered as the units or elements actually selected by prehistoric peoples.

The intent of such design structural studies is to reveal not only the differential patterns in the selection and use of the design elements, but also how they are combined and recombined, perhaps according to some set(s) of generative rules. Again, drawing from ethnographic studies, it was often argued that variation in overall designs that would serve as good indicators of "group" were variations not in selection of design elements but in the combinations or generative structural principles guiding the use of design elements. That is, it is the relations among the parts that were important; it is the form, not the content. In fact, many structural design studies were explicitly heralded as grammars (e.g. Muller 1966; 1979).

The analysis of design structure among 1200 geometrically incised bones and antlers led to the identification of 57 design element classes that were drawn from the 264 different elements incised on the bones and antlers; these 264 elements had been organized hierarchically into nine different sets (see one such set in Fig. 9.3) based on the (engraving) stroke operations. Furthermore, fifteen different structural principles that could have been followed to generate many, but not all, of the engraved objects were inferred, and some of Washburn's classes of symmetry principles were shown to underlie the generation of "designs." The analysis of patterning of design element classes, of structural principles, and of symmetry classes among and within engraved materials from twenty Magdalenian levels led to a variety of interpretations about Magdalenian engraving activities and about why some sites had more engraved materials of greater diversity than did other sites (e.g. Conkey 1980b). *If* one accepts the design element identifications, the analysis showed that the engravers throughout the region all used a set of core elements, and that additions to this repertoire showed no clear-cut patterning that could be referable to different engraving styles and social groups. Several sites showed a marked diversity in the engraving structures, and, drawing on other kinds of archaeological evidence (such as fauna) it was hypothesized that these sites (especially Altamira) may have been locales where otherwise dispersed hunter gatherers congregated, leaving a diverse inventory of engraved materials, as

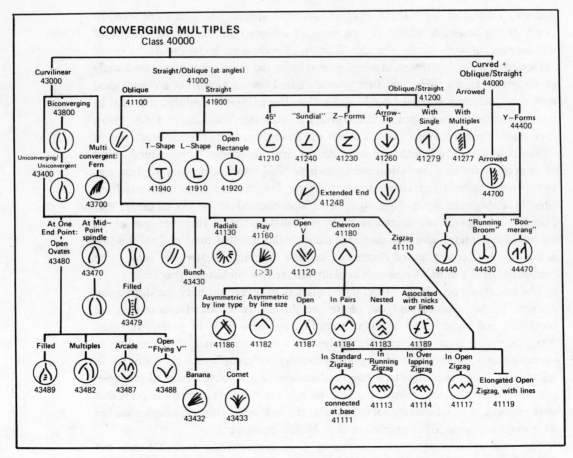

Fig. 9.3. One of nine different sets of design element hierarchies inferred from the study of 1221 engraved bones and antlers from Magdalenian levels in Cantabrian Spain. Each of the nine sets of hierarchically organized elements is based on different (incising) strokes that might have been used to generate the elements; this particular set is based on the use of converging strokes (from Conkey 1978b).

well as an abundance of red deer bone and shells from shellfish (Conkey 1980b).

There are many problems with both the analyses and interpretive hypotheses; these have to do with the issue of subjectivity in the identification of elements and structures, as noted above, as well as with the poor archaeological resolution of some sites that were excavated a century ago or more. However, for the purposes of assessing the gains of structural analysis in studies of Paleolithic art, the study of Paleolithic design structure and the kind of structural analysis carried out by Leroi-Gourhan have, together, had several implications. These include a theoretical shift in how archaeological data – especially human material culture – are conceptualized. As Leroi-Gourhan himself noted, the structuralist enterprise was only the pursuit of a method that would lead to a better definition of the problems.

Some conclusions: the production of meaning and structuralism as practice

The application of a structuralist method to a wide range of phenomena – from the usual literary text to artforms of the northwest Coast Indians (Lévi-Strauss 1958) – allowed for a reconceptualization of such phenomena in the processes whereby humans construct meaning from experience. As Pettit has noted, the objects in the new field (for example, myths, masks, poetry) are "semiological": they are cultural constructs that have "meaning effects" due to the arrangement of their component elements. The structuralist view of a field is that it is meaning structured or meaning-bearing (Pettit 1977:109).

For the archaeologist, this means that "various aspects of material reality . . . have been 'made cultural,' appropriated by the cultural system, and, in this, transformed, made orderly and intersubjectively meaningful through the imposition (or objectification) of established 'models of intelligibility' . . ." (Wylie 1982:40). Material culture – such as that which comprises the archaeological record – is thus not neutral; it is meaning determined and can be examined as a structured set. It is the product of human categorization processes, it is active, and it is constituting. As such, material culture has a central role in the ideological representation of social relations (Hodder 1982d). The logical extension of this, as structuralism has argued, is that the meaningfully constituted material record is not an "expression" or "reflection," nor even a "record," but an active, constructing, constituting agency, which does not express meaning, but produces it.

Thus, with the structuralist project, all sorts of human phenomena can be admitted as an object or construct in this new field, and, as we have noted, a certain demystification is allowed. In the case of "Paleolithic art," there have been at least three interesting results of the demystification engendered by Leroi-Gourhan's quantitative and structural analysis. First, as noted, "art" became an object for scrutiny under alternative "paradigms." With those studies that attempted to account for the art as part of the ways in which Upper Paleolithic peoples resolved certain demographic and socioecological stresses (Conkey 1978a; Gamble 1982; Jochim 1983), something that was missing from the Leroi-Gourhan structuralism is introduced: context. By attempting to evaluate how the art (or different media, such as female figurines [Gamble 1982] or cave art [Jochim 1983]) "fit" certain socioecological contexts, these archaeologies of an anthropological sort attempt to provide a genuinely social analysis of particular cultural products/artifacts (W. Davis, personal communication).

Furthermore, what Leroi-Gourhan has done has been to show that the wall art, in particular, appears to be a "culturally standardized system of visual representation" (after Munn 1962). The design structure analyses (e.g. Conkey 1978b) also show the possibility of *another* kind of culturally standardized set of visual representations. Although the original Leroi-Gourhan analysis claims a widespread and uniform mythogram, when one pursues a lower-level structural question, "what generative and productive processes brought the artifacts into existence in the first place?", there are numerous other standardized sets of visual imagery: the female statuettes, the middle Magdalenian "spearthrowers" from the Pyrenees, and the *découpés* (bone cutouts of animal heads), which appear to have been made in close conformance with specific design targets and according to certain (different) principles (Conkey 1985). Thus, although it is not the same "conclusion" as that reached by Leroi-Gourhan, it is now possible to suggest that what we have lumped under the label "Paleolithic art" may well be not just one, but "several – perhaps interpenetrating – sign systems" (Davis 1986:202).

Certainly a major critique of structuralism has been its avoidance of context; in the case of image-making – specifically in the case of Leroi-Gourhan's study of Paleolithic image-making – where is the notion of that making as a *social practice*, as a form of *production*? Structuralism could dissect the product but it refused to inquire into the material conditions of its making (Eagleton 1983:112). The "materiality" of the "text" itself and its detailed "artistic processes" were in danger.

But the Leroi-Gourham structuralism and the design structural analyses actually set the stage for such questions to be addressed. For example, structural analysis does displace the question of meaning from the individual boundaries of particular images (such as what does the image of a "horse" mean?) to the relationships of elements among images. One can displace the question of meaning in a different direction, as well: from the individual boundaries of particular images to the *productive contexts* within which the imagery came to be invested with meaning. Recent studies of the technologies of painting, based on experiments and replications (e.g. Lorblanchet 1980; Vandiver n.d.) are part of this inquiry into productive contexts (see Conkey n.d. for a review).

Current perspectives on structuralism seek not just the "structure" behind the object, but have come to be increasingly concerned with the "referential context of social action" (Hodder 1982b:8). Thus, there is movement away from structural*ism* to a structural *analysis* that can elucidate how structures "make sense" in particular historical contexts of social action. Thus, there would be new questions generated from the design structure analysis that hypothesized Altamira to have been a hunter-gatherer aggregation site. The question is not the (functional) determination of Altamira as an aggregation site, but (1) what is it about the context(s) of the site that led to the differential accumulation of engraved bones there, and not so much elsewhere (why the difference?); and (2) what is it about the engraved bones and antlers that would have made them meaning*ful* in the supposed aggregation context of social action? The abstract formal analysis (of design structure) must be made relevant to a particular social and historical context, and the same could be said for other studies that have now admitted the "art" as constructs: what is it about the painting of cave walls that would have made this meaningful in a context of demographic stress (Jochim 1983)? what is it about female figurines that would have made them efficacious in a context of regional alliance networks (Gamble 1982)?

Structuralism of the sort pursued by Leroi-Gourhan did not concern itself with the "intentions" of cultural products, but it did allow such questions to be asked in a different way. To understand "intentions" is *not* to "get into the mind of the maker"; rather, to understand the intentions of a cultural product is "to interpret it as being in some sense oriented, structured to achieve certain effects" (Eagleton 1983:114). This cannot be grasped, Eagleton goes on to argue, apart from the *practical* conditions in which image-making/using operates. To understand intentions is to see "art" as a practice rather than as an object, and "there are, of course, no practices without human subjects" (Eagleton 1983:114).

Structuralism itself is a cultural practice. What it has done, of course, has been to demonstrate that "there is nothing innocent about codes; but there is nothing innocent about taking them as the object of one's study either" (Eagleton 1983:124). A few concluding comments to address this – what is the point of doing structural analysis? whose interests are served? – are in order. Certainly structuralism seemed to make the texts and images it "foregrounded" a window onto the universal mind. Certainly, in the case of the images of Paleolithic art that were "foregrounded" in the work of Leroi-Gourhan, this played into the on-going process whereby the Eurocentric Upper Paleolithic *stage* was being reified as *the* achievement of full human-ness and modernity. Europe – with its "successful, art-making" hunter gatherers – became an evolutionary and temporal stage: the Upper Paleolithic time period, when fully-modern humans became established, was spatialized (Eurocentrically).

The readings of Paleolithic art as structured, as the products of the kind of structuring characteristic of civilized "man," have not been neutral readings. It may not be so fortuitous that Leroi-Gourhan was working on the structure of Paleolithic art at the same time that Lévi-Strauss, in the early 1960s, was developing the arguments about the "savage mind" that would come to undermine the long-held distinctions between the "primitive" and the "civilized." A realignment of "difference" was being produced. The structural reading of Paleolithic art, as developed by Leroi-Gourhan, confirmed and extended the universal underpinnings of fully-human thought back into the Upper Paleolithic. The necessary "difference" has subsequently been shifted: from prehistoric-primitive/civilized to pre-Upper Paleolithic (that is, Neanderthal)/Upper Paleolithic-and-since, which is why the Upper Paleolithic came to be called a "slice of ethnography." It may be why, in part, one of the most unruly archaeological debates of our time (the last two decades) has been the so-called "Mousterian problem" and the discussion on the Middle/Upper Paleolithic transition. Here is where "difference" is being negotiated. As a recent cover of *Newsweek* (November 12, 1986) announces in its story on Upper Paleolithic art and life: (this is) The Way We Were.

Although structuralism as an intellectual movement has effectively been over in Europe for some years now, various genres of structural analysis are still being debated and proposed (e.g. Giddens 1984; Hodder 1986:34–54). It can be argued that design structure analyses, as spawned by formal structural analysis, have – as with Leroi-Gourhan's work – demystified such materials as "art," and allow for the dual analysis of Paleolithic pictures as artifacts/tools *and* as images/texts. The definition of culturally standardized systems of visual representation sets the stage for a next round of inquiry: what is the relation of these particular cultural products, particular meanings, and particular conditions of existence? Having accepted that these are meaningfully constituted cultural products, can we access the referential context(s) of social action within which they were made and used?

There is little doubt that the structuralist study of Leroi-Gourhan has had a variety of impacts not just on the relatively narrow domain of European prehistory but on the practice and use of archaeological interpretation. It is perhaps more meaningful to consider the "gains" of structuralism to be, however, not so much in the domain of having fostered or increased our knowledge about the past. Rather, one could argue that Leroi-Gourhan's structuralist insights have restructured our own experience and cultural positioning. It may be more a means of contemporary human experience than a record of past human life.

Notes

1 My thanks go to C. C. Lamberg-Karlovsky for assigning me so challenging a topic, and to the editors of *October* for having so fortuitously sent me the Michelson translations of Leroi-Gourhan (1966). Thanks also go to the unwitting students in my SUNY-Binghamton graduate seminar on Material Culture Studies in Anthropology for tolerating my trying out some of these ideas on them.

2 When quoting from the original 1966 article of Leroi-Gourhan, I will use here the 1986 English translation by Annette Michelson of the French version that is reprinted in Leroi-Gourhan (1983). I have checked her English translation with the French in the 1983 volume and find it a very good one. Thus, her English translation of Leroi-Gourhan will be cited in the text as Leroi-Gourhan (1986) to remind readers that although this is what Leroi-Gourhan wrote, it is the 1986 English version that is being cited rather than extensive passages in the original French. For all correct citations to Leroi-Gourhan (1966, 1983) and to Michelson (1986) see References.

10

Ancient China and its anthropological significance

KWANG-CHIH CHANG

In demanding that humankind be examined not merely in a single manifestation but "in all its variation" (Kluckhohn 1955:320), American anthropology has as one of its main objectives the formulation of true universals that may exist in the process of the evolution of cultures and societies. In this regard one of the major accomplishments of American anthropology is in our understanding of how civilizations arose in the New World as an indigenous and independent process and of how this process both resembles and differs from similar processes in the Old World. An examination of the ancient Chinese civilization serves a similar purpose.

Ancient China is unique for the study of cultural and social evolution, for only in this area of the world do we have at our disposal a combination of several kinds of data that are not available together elsewhere: abundant archaeological material, mostly brought to light in the last thirty to forty years; enormous quantities of textual and inscriptional material left from and pertaining to the earliest Chinese civilizations; and a vast continuum of history from the first civilizations to the present day, which provides us with endless opportunities to apply the methods of ethnoarchaeology and the direct historical approach. From these sources a reasonably complete picture of the beginning of Chinese civilization has now emerged.

Beginning of Chinese civilization

Authentic written records from ancient China begin with the Shang (c. 1750–1100 B.C.) and Zhou (c. 1100–220 B.C.) dynasties, and both dynasties have been archaeologically substantiated (see, e.g., Chang 1980). The Xia dynasty, preceding the Shang, is on the verge of being identified with archaeological sites (Chang 1983a). Prior to the advent of modern archaeology in China in the 1920s, the Three Dynasties – Xia, Shang, and Zhou – were in turn preceded historiographically by a series of legendary heroes and sages, but prehistoric archaeology during the last sixty years has supplanted this legendary history with scientifically established cultural phases from the early stages of the Neolithic farmers through the dawn of the Chinese civilization. Close examinations of these prehistoric cultural phases reveal significant patterns pertaining to a dialectic interplay of internal and external factors for cultural and social development, or, to put it differently, to a dialectic interplay of regional and supraregional forces. Readers of traditional Chinese fiction will be familiar with the proverbial phrase, *tianxia dashi: fenjiu bihe hejiu bifen*, or, "the overarching trend of

Table 10.1 *Upper Paleolithic regional cultures*

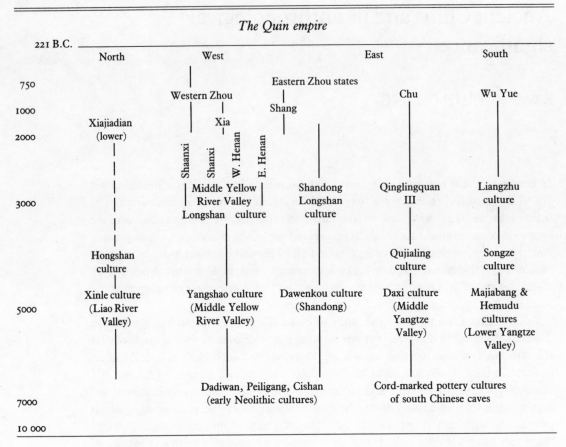

	The Quin empire		
221 B.C.			
North	West	East	South

the world is such that when it has long been divided it will unite and when it has long been united it will divide." If we look at the developmental trend of Chinese prehistory and early history (Table 10.1), we find that this phrase may not be as simplistic as it may appear literally.[1]

Chinese civilization began as several regional cultures that were scattered throughout the land area now known as China proper. First appearing in the archaeological record around 7000 B.C. and firmly and richly established according to archaeological evidence by 5000 B.C., each of these regional cultures is believed to be an indigenous development out of that region's own Paleolithic foundation. The best known of these Neolithic cultures are the Yangshao culture of the middle Yellow River Valley, the Dawenkou culture of Shandong peninsula, the Xinle culture of the Liao River Valley of southern Manchuria, the Majiabang culture of the Huai River Valley and the lower Yangtze River Valley, the Hemudu culture south of Hangzhou Bay, the Daxi culture of the middle Yangtze River Valley, and the Dapenkeng culture of the southeastern coastal areas. Each of these cultures is characterized by a distinctive assemblage of ceramics and other artifacts, although all of them had fairly advanced agriculture – that of the millets in the north and of rice in the south.

The beginning of the fourth millennium B.C. witnessed the spatial expansion of the regional cultures and their resultant contact and interaction. While during the previous millennium the regional cultures were mutually distinctive, now they all share conspicuous and significant cultural traits, above all ceramic types such as tripods and bowls on pedestals, which, together with other types, constituted a "Longshanoid horizon" that ran north to south and east to west. Thus, what had been independent regional systems are by this time – 4000 B.C. – interlinked into a common sphere of interaction. From the point of view of each of the regional systems that constitute this interaction sphere, its subsequent developments were to depend both upon factors internal to the system and external relationships with other systems within the interaction sphere.

This interplay of internal and external factors becomes evident during the third millennium B.C. when a Longshan culture developed within each regional system at about the same time across the interaction sphere. These regional Longshan cultures share not only a number of stylistic elements but also many similar societal character-istics. These characteristics make it clear that after 3000 B.C. the growth and development of Chinese civilization took place in three distinctively recognizable stages: (1) Longshan (3000–2000 B.C.); (2) the Three Dynasties, to the middle of Eastern Zhou (2000–650); and (3) Late Eastern Zhou (650–221 B.C.). Brief character-izations of Chinese civilization in these three stages will show the process of the emergence of that civilization very clearly.

The most significant finds of the Longshan period in terms of the light they throw upon contemporary social organization are town walls and cemeteries. The town walls are the markers of the powerful people who had now emerged, and the cemetery finds indicate the birth of the wealthy class. Significantly, for Longshan-period China the powerful were the wealthy, and the interplay of power and wealth from now on becomes a core feature of Chinese civilization.

The cemetery finds not only indicate that the Longshan period saw the strong development of social stratification but also give a clear hint about the nature of the social strata. At the Chengzi cemetery in Zhucheng, in Shandong province, eastern north China, 87 Longshan-period burials were brought to light in the 1976–7 season of excavations. These burials are grouped into no fewer than four classes, according to the degree of elaboration of tomb construction and of the abundance and quality of tomb goods. Furthermore, the 87 burials were clustered in three well-defined areas of the cemetery, but each cluster had its own rank order of rich to poor graves (*Kaogu Xuebao* 1980). This is one of the earliest examples of a burial pattern associated with the stratified lineage society of ancient China that we are going to see often from now on. At the Taosi cemetery in Xiangfen, southern Shanxi, over one thousand graves from the Longshan period have been excavated. Again these graves appear to be arranged within the cemetery in two or more clusters, and within each cluster they are again grouped according to some order. According to the construction of the tombs and the quantity and quality of their contents, once more a minimum of three classes is distinguishable (*Kaogu* 1980, 1983, 1984). These burial patterns, in light of the known prevalence of the segmentary lineage system in ancient Chinese society (see, e.g. Chang 1976a:ch. 5), unmistakably point to a system of social divisions which were based in significant part upon a system of stratified segmentary lineages.

In early historic China one of the characteristic features of the segmentary lineages is the special role individual lineages often assumed in handicrafts. The Longshan period saw a degree of craft specialization that enabled the making of copper objects (trinkets and small tools) and of wheel-thrown pottery. Some of the pottery is so thin and so well polished that it was impractical and probably served ritual purposes.

Ritual undoubtedly played a prominent role in Longshan society. At Yangshao sites in the Yellow River Valley we have already seen motifs of pottery art that point to shamanism in contemporary society – an X-ray or skeletal rendition of a human figure, a bisexual human figure, recurrent human faces with a fish at each ear, and a row of dancing human figures (Chang 1987a:150). By Longshan times, the role of religious personnel in contemporary society must have increased substantially, for material manifestations of ritual are now everywhere. We have already mentioned pottery types that are both ultra-fine and impractical. There are also at this time widespread remains of oracle bones, shoulder-blades of deer, cattle, and sheep, that show burn marks, undoubtedly burned to produce cracks for purposes of divination. This practice – scapulimancy – foreshadowed the all-important oracle bones of the Shang dynasty, bones associated with the earliest Chinese inscriptions.

The most striking finds from the Longshan period in recent years are objects of ritual art. Using many media – pottery, wood, and jade, among archaeologically recovered objects – the Longshan artists began to employ designs of fantastic or mythical animals on their objects of ritual. These include a fine red pottery plate, on which a black dragon was painted, found at the Taosi site; jade spatulas carved with human faces associated with animals and birds, found at the Rizhao site in coastal Shandong; and, in particular, numerous jade tubes – called *cong* in Chinese antiquarianism – carved with animal masks, consisting of pairs of eyes and mouths, and, sometimes, birds, found at a number of sites in the Liangzhu culture, a version of the Longshan culture in the Lake Taihu region of southern Jiangsu. These *cong* tubes, incidentally, are rounded on the inside and square on the outside. In ancient China a circle shape was often associated with heaven and a square shape with earth, and the *cong* tube, which manifests the interpenetration of heaven and earth, is believed to be a microcosmic *axis mundi* (Chang 1987b:252–60).

In a series of related writings (synthesized in Chang 1983b), I have attempted to demonstrate that ancient Chinese art, especially bronze art, was intimately relatable to politics: ancient art, with its emphasis on animals and birds, which served as mediums or agents between the different world layers, was essentially shamanistic paraphernalia, and the possessor of the art treasures was, thus, the possessor of the instrument to heaven, viz, to wisdom and to foreknowledge. The possessor of such knowledge had the right and the power to rule. We will elaborate upon this point presently, but here we will note that recent archaeological discoveries of the ritual art of the Longshan period have served to push the same system of political culture back from the Bronze Age or the Three Dynasties to the Longshan period.

Longshan society now manifests great political power in the same way that power is so manifested in the Three Dynasties. It resided in the walled towns, and the violence it wrought is archaeologically revealed in remains of raids and battles. Stone arrowheads are found lodged in human bones, human skulls show scars of scalpings, and skeletons were thrown into water wells. These are all indications of that all-consuming political power, which above all must account for the new way to manage human labor in relation to natural resources so that enormous wealth could be produced, on the basis of the same Neolithic technology for food production. Longshan agricultural implements remained the same stone, bone, shell, and (presumably) wooden implements that had been in use since the early Neolithic.

Shortly before 2000 B.C. Chinese civilization crossed the next threshold and entered the so-called Three Dynasties. The first unmistakable manifestation of the new regime is the coming into use of bronze. Chinese bronzes are copper-tin alloys, cast in the characteristic "piece-molds" (for the classic treatise see Barnard 1961). But the most characteristic feature of all of the ancient Chinese bronzes pertains to the principal types of artifacts bronze was made into: ritual food and drink vessels, musical instruments, and weapons. It is stated in *Zuozhuan*, under the entry for 579 B.C., that the two "principal affairs of the state were ritual and warfare." Bronze artifacts were manufactured to serve these affairs of the state. There are finds of bronze implements, tools, ornaments, and the like, but these are extremely few. The agricultural implements, the center of the productive technology of the Three Dynasties, were still made of wood, bone, antler, shell, and, above all, stone. Thus, the major technological breakthrough – bronze metallurgy – that dawned with the beginning of the Three Dynasties period of ancient China did not perform a consequential service in the productive realm of contemporary society; rather, it was associated with a major change in the political realm of contemporary society, namely, the emergence of a powerful kingship.

We know a certain amount about the Three Dynasties kingship system because kingship is now at the center of three new institutions that mark off the Three Dynasties from the Longshan period. These are the city, the state, and writing. The terms "city," "state," and "writing" are common enough terms, but each is associated with a definition that has been codified on the experience of the history of Western civilization, together with its Near Eastern antecedents. The most widely used definition of the city, that by V. Gordon Childe (1950), stresses population size and density and the city's economic roles in craft specialization and trade. The Bronze Age cities of China, on the other hand, are like modern Chinese cities as characterized by Fei Hsiao-t'ung: "an instrument of the ruling classes in a political system where power resides in force. [The city] is the symbol of power and also a necessary tool for the maintenance of power" (Fei 1952:95). The archaeological manifestation of the early Chinese city consists of massive walls of stamped earth and imposing "palatial" structures which dominated the cityscape (see, e.g., Chang 1985:61–7, 1976b:61–71).

The term "state" is defined in American anthropological literature in various ways, but Kent V. Flannery's characterization is often quoted as a universal category:

The state is a type of very strong, unusually highly centralized government, with a professional ruling class, largely divorced from the

bonds of kinship which characterize simpler societies. It is highly stratified
and extremely diversified internally, with residential patterns often based
on occupational specialization rather than blood or affinal relationship.
The state attempts to maintain a monopoly of force, and is characterized
by true law . . . While individual citizens must forego violence, the state
can wage war; it can also draft soldiers, levy taxes, and exact tributes.

(Flannery 1972a: 403–4)

The Chinese state of the Three Dynasties, which did possess both law and military
force, was, nevertheless, built upon a hierarchical system of segmentary lineages, where
the distance away from the main line of patrilineal descent determined political status
and the share of political power. Members of these lineages inhabited the walled
towns, which constituted stratified networks ruled by the state government. The king
sat at the top of the conical clan and, at the same time, at the top of the hierarchical
state.

The states of the Three Dynasties period constituted information networks strung
together with written messages, but the messages, as they are now seen on the
available written materials, such as oracle bones (Keightley 1978) and bronze inscriptions, pertained, not to the records of economic transactions, which are common in
the ancient Near East and the Aegean inscriptions, but to affairs of the state, ritual
and warfare.

Permit me to generalize a little at this point. It is clear that in ancient Chinese
civilization and in its formative process, from the Longshan period to the Three
Dynasties, political culture was a dominant element. Chinese civilization, like all
other civilizations, was built upon the basis of enormous wealth absolutely and on the
basis of concentrated wealth relatively. The archaeological and historical study of this
civilization makes it clear that the accumulation and concentration of wealth in
ancient China were accomplished through intensified manipulation of the labor force,
or, in other words, accomplished more in the domain of politics than in the domain of
technology and economics. In ancient China, in crossing the civilizational threshold,
neither productive technology nor trade of strategic resources appear to have played
predominant roles.

Both productive technology and strategic trade had their turn in the next phase of
Chinese civilization. Beginning in the seventh and sixth centuries B.C., cast iron came
into rapid and universal use, and it came into use immediately in the sphere of food
production. From then on, archaeological remains of iron plowshares, tools, and
implements are found universally at archaeological sites (Needham 1958). Cities
increased in size, and markets and workshops as well as palaces were enclosed within
stamped earth walls. Kinship bonds began to diminish or even break down, and
territorial units and bureaucracies gained in eminence.

Did urbanism and state society come late in China, around 650 B.C., with the
emergence of the Iron Age? Was the Three Dynasties period that of "proto-urbanism"
and "proto-state"? If we use these labels because we feel ancient Chinese civilization
did not in some way live up to our expectations, by comparison with the process of

development of China's near or far neighbors, then we would, I believe, be committing the fallacy of "cutting the feet to fit the shoes," to borrow a traditional Chinese phrase. In terms of the internal sequence of development of Chinese civilization as briefly reviewed above, Longshan, the Three Dynasties, and late Eastern Zhou each marks a qualitative threshold. The Three Dynasties segment possesses some of the characteristic features of the other ancient civilizations – among them the nucleation of settlements, the formation of the state government invested with force and law, a sophisticated writing system, and great art. If some of the major factors of social and cultural change that can be isolated to explain the emergence of this civilization appear to differ, fundamentally or in trivial respects, from those of some other civilizations, it may be that in different civilizations different factors assumed paramount importance.

It is in instances like these that the study of ancient China assumes its anthropological significance. More than a quarter-century ago, the late Mary Wright posed a sinologist's challenge to the social scientists: "If the aim of social scientists is to establish the broadest generalizations obtainable, and if the breadth of any generalization depends on the range of phenomena to which it is applied, do the intellectual demands of their own research not lead them to the study of the appropriate portions of the Chinese record?" (Wright 1961:220–1). Wright was referring to the enormous Chinese historical record, but archaeological excavations and research in the last 38 years have further expanded that record by several thousand years into the past. The time has come for the social scientists to take the Chinese experience into account in formulating and/or testing their generalizations.

Continuity and rupture: sketching a new paradigm for the rise of civilizations[2]

As we come to see how civilization, urbanism, and the state form of society arose in China, we also begin to realize what ancient Chinese historiography can do for social science generalizations. China provides a significant data base for the testing of social science hypotheses that have been formulated on the basis of Western historiography; and we find that some important hypotheses on the rise of civilizations have failed the test. Then, China provides the data base sufficient in its own right from which new social science hypotheses can be generated. A good example pertains to how civilization began here, as just described. These two issues – first that some Western generalizations on the rise of civilization do not apply to China, and second that China offers its own generalization – are, of course, related. A preliminary comparative study (Chang in preparation), involving China, the Maya, and the Sumerian civilizations, shows that the Chinese pattern was probably the prevailing pattern in the transformation to civilizations everywhere, whereas the Western pattern was rather the exception. I refer to the Chinese pattern as one of *continuity* and the Western pattern as one of *rupture*.

What may be seen as the most striking feature of ancient Chinese civilization is that ideologically speaking it was created within a framework of cosmogonic holism. In the words of Frederick Mote, "the genuine Chinese cosmogony is that of organismic process, meaning that all of the parts of the entire cosmos belong to one organic whole and that they all interact as participants in one spontaneously self-generating life process" (Mote 1971:19). This organismic process, Tu Wei-ming amplifies, "exhibits three basic motifs: continuity, wholeness, and dynamism. All modalities of being, from a rock to heaven, are integral parts of a continuum . . . Since nothing is outside of this continuum, the chain of being is never broken. A linkage will always be found between any given pair of things in the universe" (Tu 1985:38). This ancient Chinese world view, sometimes referred to as "correlative cosmology" (Schwartz 1985:350), is surely not unique; in essence it represents the substratum of the human view of the world found widely among primitive societies (see, e.g., Lévi-Strauss 1966). What is uniquely significant about its presence in ancient China is the fact that a veritable civilization was built on top of and within its confines. Ancient Chinese civilization was a civilization of continuity.

The significance of this fact becomes clearer as we move east across the Pacific and find a number of New World civilizations that were built upon and within the confines of the same cosmological substratum. In a 1972 study of shamanism and hallucinogens among American Indians, Weston LaBarre proposed that American Indian religions generally retain diagnostic features – prominent among them being an emphasis on the ecstatic experience – of an archaic Paleolithic and Mesolithic substratum which their ancestors brought on their entry into the New World from their Asian homelands (Furst 1972:261–78). Following upon the same theme on the basis of Mesoamerican studies, Peter T. Furst has reconstructed "the ideological content of [an] Asian–American shamanism" (Furst 1976:149–57) as follows:

(1) The shamanic universe is a magical one, and the phenomena of the natural and supernatural environments are the consequence of magical transformation, not creation *ex nihilo*, as they are in Judeo-Christian tradition.

(2) The universe is typically multi-layered or stratified, with an underworld below and an upperworld above the middle level as principal divisions. Underworld and upperworld are often further divided into several layers, which usually have their respective spirit rulers and supernatural denizens. There may also be gods of the cardinal directions or world quarters, and supreme spirits who rule over the celestial and chthonic spheres respectively. While some of these deities control the fate of humanity and other forms of life, they are also subject to manipulation, for example, through sacrifice. The several levels of the universe are connected by a central axis (*axis mundi*), and merge conceptually and practically with the shaman's various symbols of ascent and descent to the upper and underworlds. Shamans' trees or world trees are typically surmounted by a bird, symbol of celestial flight and transcendence. Again, the world is divided into quarters, bisected by a horizontal north–south and east–west axis, and there are frequently color associations for the different directions.

(3) It is further axiomatic of the intellectual universe of shamanism that man and animal are qualitatively equivalent, and that man is "never the lord of creation but always a pensioner of natural bounty," in the words of Herbert Spinden.

(4) Closely tied to the concept of qualitative man–animal equivalence is that of man–animal transformation – that is, a primordial capability of people and animals to assume each other's forms. Man–animal equivalence also expresses itself in animal alter egos and companion animals; further, shamans typically have animal spirit

helpers. Shamans and other participants in a shaman-led ritual also symbolize transformation into their animal counterparts by donning skins, masks, and other characteristics of these animals.

(5) All phenomena in the environment are animated by a life force, or soul; hence, there is in the shamanistic universe no such thing as an "inanimate" object in our sense.

(6) In humans and animals the soul, or essential life force, characteristically resides in the bones, often those of the head. Humans and animals are reborn from their bones. Shamanistic skeletonization – the shaman's ritual initiatory death and rebirth in his ecstatic trance from his skeletal state, sometimes enacted by self-starvation to the point of near-skeletonization and commonly depicted symbolically among the shaman's paraphernalia and in his art – likewise is tied to these concepts.

(7) The soul is detachable from the body and may travel over the earth or to other worlds; it may also be abducted by hostile spirits or sorcerers, and retrieved by the shaman. Soul loss is a common source of illness, and so is the intrusion of foreign objects into the body from a hostile environment. In fact most illnesses are of magical origin, and their diagnosis and cure are the shaman's special province.

(8) Finally, we have the phenomenon of the ecstatic trance, often, but by no means always and everywhere, induced by means of hallucinogenic plants.

Having characterized the shamanic world view, Furst made the further observation that

much of the above applies no less to civilized prehispanic Mesoamerica
and its symbolic systems, insofar as we know them, than to the more
classic kinds of shamanism among less complex societies. Origin through
transformation or metamorphosis, rather than creation in the Biblical
sense, is the hallmark of Mesoamerican religion. The stratified universe
with its respective spirit rulers, world axis, world trees with birds, world
mountains, world quarters and color directions – all these and more are
surely Mesoamerican, as are qualitative equivalence of man and animal,
naguals or alter egos, companion animals, the use of animal skins, claws,
teeth, masks and other parts to symbolize or effect transformation, etc.

(Furst 1976:153)

I have quoted Peter Furst at some length (see also Furst 1973–4:33–60), because much of it, perhaps all of it, applies no less to early Chinese civilization than to civilized prehispanic Mesoamerica. We have in mind such conspicuous though fragmentary remnants of the ancient Chinese symbol and belief systems as the skeletal art of the Yangshao culture mentioned earlier; the jade *cong* tubes, with their animal mask and bird imageries; the offerings to natural bodies, the world quarters, the winds and spirits of the four directions, and the reference to birds as divine agents in the oracle bone inscriptions of the Shang dynasty; the animal imageries on the ritual vessels of the Shang and Zhou dynasties; the belief in the ancient Chinese mind in "the continuous presence of *qi* (the vital force) in all modalities of being" (Tu 1985:38); the shamanistic poems in *Chuci* of Eastern Zhou, their descriptions of shamans and their ascent and descent, and their summons to the lost souls. These and many more pieces of evidence point to an ancient Chinese shamanism at the core of ancient Chinese belief and ritual systems, which were preoccupied with the inter-penetration of heaven and earth. In fact, the word for shaman in the oracle bone and bronze inscription, wu ✢ , is itself seen as depicting the use of a square-rule, the fundamental instrument in the mastery of the circle (heaven) and the square (earth) (Chang 1987b). Even the ecstatic aspect of shamanism is suggested by the close association of ritual with alcohol and by the early use (at least as early as Eastern Han) of the hallucinogenic plant *Cannabis sativa* (Li 1974:195).

A detailed reconstruction of the ancient Chinese shamanism (Chang 1983b; in preparation) is not the purpose of this chapter. It should, however, be clear that the Furst reconstruction of an Asian–American shamanistic substratum and the profile of an ancient Chinese world view are both correlative cosmologies, and that both in China and in the New World high civilizations with urbanism and state society were formed at comparable thresholds without doing violence to the "continuity of being."

When at the beginning of this section we stated that Chinese civilization was distinctive in being created within a framework of cosmogonic holism, we did not mean to give ideology the role of the prime mover. The characteristic feature of the Chinese rise to civilization – and the rise of comparable civilizations – is that ideology was one of the principal instruments whereby the society's economic relations were realigned to create the concentration of wealth necessary for civilizations. Specifically, our new paradigm contains the following elements essential in the rise of the civilization.

(1) The concentration of wealth that is manifested in the archaeological civilizations was, in our paradigm, not accomplished through such commonly recognized devices for the increase and circulation of wealth as innovations in productive technology and trade. It was almost entirely accomplished through the manipulation of the productive labor force. Productivity was increased through the increase of the labor force (effected by demographic increases and by conscription of war captives), through the apportionment of increasing numbers of the labor force to production, and through more effective management techniques. In other words, wealth was accumulated in both relative and absolute terms primarily *through the political process.*

(2) One important manifestation of the dominance of the political process is the fact that trade was largely confined to that of prestige goods, while the circulation of strategic resources was more often effected by war.

(3) Because the concentration of wealth was accomplished through the political (man–man) and not the technological and mercantile (man–nature) process, the rise of the civilizations exerted no violence to the existing ecological balance and could be achieved within a continuing cosmological framework.

(4) In fact the existing cosmological as well as social systems provided the instru-ment for political manipulation. The key to the manipulation lies in social and economic stratification, which in the Chinese case is manifested in three archae-ologically and textually verifiable areas: lineage segmentation, settlement hierarchy (which led to urbanism and state organization), and monopoly of the shamans as a class and the shamanistic paraphernalia, including the art treasures.

(5) Of the above, only the third point requires brief additional comment. In the stratified universe ancestors and deities inhabited the upper levels. Living men communicated with them only through shamans or like personnel with the help of animal agents and shamanistic paraphernalia – including ritual implements and vessels adorned with pertinent animal images. In a civilization like that of the Chinese, where the bestowal of ancestral and divine wisdom and the right to rule were equatable, the monopolistic services of the shamans and the possession of art treasures (shamanistic paraphernalia) were essential qualifications of the upper crust of society. In this sense the correlative cosmology of the Asian–American substratum was itself the ideological system that enabled the rulers to manipulate the labor force and to realign the interrelationship of man and his natural resources.

Chinese civilization is presumably but one of the numerous ancient civilizations that came out of the ancient Asian–American substratum by means of the political process China exemplifies. To the social scientist seasoned in the theories of Marx, Engels, Weber, Childe, and others with regard to social evolution and the rise of urbanism and state society, however, the Chinese road to civilization appears to be an aberration – often called the "Asiatic" aberration. It is an aberration precisely because it continued to carry forward so much from its antecedence. As the name implies, at the stage of "civilization" (so these theories go) man had attained civility and urbanity, "as distinct from [the culture] of the barbarian – the agricultural rustic" (Daniel 1968:19). By definition, civilized people were city-dwellers – refined, sophisticated, artistically accomplished, in contrast to the country dwellers and the prehistoric barbarous forebears. This city-countryside contrast means, at a deeper level, a contrast between culture and nature:

We can see the process of the growth of a civilisation as the gradual
creation by man of a larger and more complex environment, not only in
the natural field through increasing exploitation of a wider range of
resources of the ecosystem, but also in the social and spiritual fields. And,
whereas the savage hunter lives in an environment not so different in many
ways from that of other animals, although enlarged already by the use of
language and of a whole range of other artefacts in the culture, civilised
man lives in an environment very much of his own creation. Civilisation,
in this sense, is the self-made environment of man, which he has fashioned
to insulate himself from the primeval environment of nature alone.

(Renfrew 1972:11)

This definition points to the essence of a common belief that, when the threshold from barbarism to civilization is crossed, man passes from a world of nature he shared with his animal friends to a world of his own making, in which he surrounds himself with artifacts that insulate him from, and elevate him above, his animal friends – monumental architecture, writing, a great art style, and a new religion.

This common definition of civilization stands in sharp contrast to the kind of civilization we have been discussing, the civilization of continuity – continuity between man and animal, between earth and heaven, and between culture and nature.

Nothing exposes this contrast more quickly than when the two types of civilization came into direct contact:

> The Mexica saw the relationship between their city [Tenochtitlan] and its environment as an integrated cosmological structure – an ordered universe within which the natural phenomena were regarded as intrinsically sacred, alive, and intimately relatable to the activities of man. This outlook contrasted with that of the Europeans, who saw cities as artifacts of civilization – places where religions and legal institutions sharply distinguished man's identity from that of untamed nature. The Spanish friars and soldiers automatically placed themselves as human beings on a higher level than other forms of life in a hierarchy of Creation. But the Indians approached the phenomena of nature with a sense of participation: the universe was seen as reflections of relationship between life forces, and every aspect of life was part of an interpenetrating cosmic system.
>
> (Townsend 1979:9)

The Aztec–Spanish contrast – or, indeed, the Asian–American substratum versus Western social science theories contrast – alerts us to two important implications of our new paradigm. First, Western social science theories have typically been generated from the historic experience of Western civilization, and they may or may not be applicable to non-Western experiences. Second, and this is far more important, the Western experience that gave rise to generalizations that characterize a new social order must have represented from its beginning a qualitative break from the ancient substratum common to the lot of the rest of men. As we examine the prehistory of that experience that has been traced to the Near East, we indeed see the formation of a type of civilization that was characterized, not by continuity, but by rupture – rupture of that cosmic holism – and by the demarcation between man and his natural resourses. Civilizations on this route were built by wealth accumulated through innovations in productive technology and importation of new resources by trade. This route can better be traced not by me but by students of Western civilization, who must face the daunting task of characterizing and explaining mankind's initial breakout from the Asian–American substratum, but such searches for similarities and differences are central to the formulation of universal theories in American anthropology.

Notes

1 The following summary of Chinese prehistory and the dawn of Chinese civilization is based on Chang 1987a.
2 This section was presented before the International Conference on Ancient China and Social Science Generalizations, held in June 1986 under the sponsorship of the Committee for Scholarly Communication with the People's Republic of China, National Academy of Sciences, and the Wang Institute of Graduate Studies.

Settlement pattern studies and evidences for intensive agriculture in the Maya Lowlands

GORDON R. WILLEY

Settlement patterns and agricultural practices are obviously interrelated subjects so that it is fitting that they be treated jointly. This is especially so in a context of Lowland Maya archaeology for in the last three decades ancient settlement patterns and Prehispanic agriculture have been closely related research concerns. Questions and findings about one have prompted queries and discoveries about the other in an interrelated research circle. This present chapter is an attempt to summarize some of that research.

It will be my aim to present basic data on settlement and agriculture and inferences deriving from these about ancient Maya demography and sociopolitical structure. These presentations and inferences will compose the larger part of what I have to say, but, in addition, I would like to consider some recent translations of Maya hieroglyphic texts which provide information that bear upon old Maya political structure and territoriality. While this information supplements the inferences drawn from settlement patterns, it also offers some interesting contradictions.

Introductory background

The Lowland Maya archaeological area includes the Guatemalan Department of Peten, bordering portions of the Mexican states of Chiapas and Tabasco, all of the Mexican Yucatan peninsula, the Republic of Belize, and a small fringe of western Honduras (see map, Fig. 11.1). This is territory that was occupied by Maya-speaking peoples from remote prehistoric times until today – specifically by the Yucatec, Chol, and Chortian branches of that large language family.

The area, is, for the most part, low-lying terrain – generally below 300 m in elevation. The geological understructure is largely limestone. Much of the country is low, rolling hill topography although large sections are flat. There are a number of rivers, draining into both the Gulf of Mexico and the Caribbean; some of these rise in the Guatemalan Highlands to the south; others are of local, lowland origin. Small lakes occur in the Peten and in the southern part of the Yucatan peninsula. Rainfall is seasonal (December–May), being very heavy in the more southerly latitudes but less so in the north. Climates are tropical. The tropical vegetation varies from a high tree cover, especially in the south, to somewhat lower, more sparse forests in the north. Large patches of savanna grasslands occur in places, as do swamps or *bajos*.

While there are overall cultural similarities which bind this archaeological area

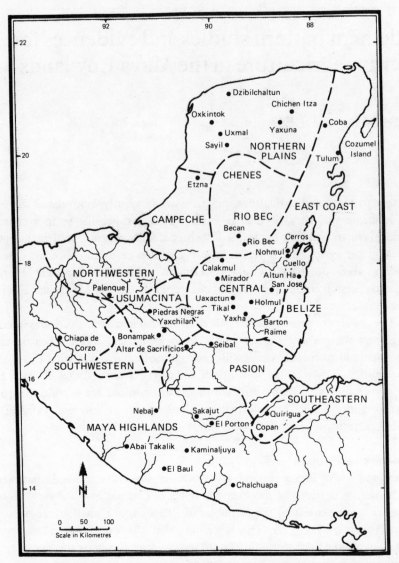

Fig. 11.1. Map of the Maya area, showing cultural regions of the Lowlands and archaeological sites (redrawn from Hammond and Ashmore 1981, Fig. 2.1).

together – similarities and a shared cultural tradition in basic economy, ceramics, architecture, high arts, iconographic symbolism, writing, calendrics – there are also regional differences expressed in stylistic variations in these several trait categories. While such traits can be used to define a number of regions (Fig. 11.1), the differences are most striking between the southern and northern regions.

The culture history of the Maya Lowlands, as this can be reconstructed from archaeology, opens with scattered and as yet rather poorly defined evidences of early hunting-collecting populations (MacNeish et al. 1980). After this, an Early Preclassic Period (*c.* 2000–1000 B.C.) is marked by the first appearances of sedentary village farming and ceramics; however, this period, too, is known only from limited information (Hammond et al. 1979). It is only with the Middle Preclassic Period (1000–300 B.C.) that our story of settlement and agriculture can begin to be traced in any detail. Middle Preclassic sites have been found all over the Lowlands. Communities at this time, although widely scattered throughout the area, were relatively few and mostly simple villages or hamlets; however, in some of the larger villages the first evidences of special buildings – little temples and, perhaps, elite residences – appear.

With the Late Preclassic Period (300 B.C.–A.D. 250), the number of communities increased several times over, and these were considerably larger than they had been previously. Large constructions – massive temple pyramids and huge palace platforms and acropoleis – now appear in great numbers at sites in all parts of the area. Elite craft goods appear – carved jades, marine shells, specially ornamented ceramics. These objects were found with burials of what were obviously privileged or upper-class individuals. By this time there is no doubt that Lowland Maya society had grown complex and non-egalitarian (Adams 1977).

An Early Classic Period (A.D. 250–600) followed in which population growth and expansion seems to have slowed, stopped, or possibly even reversed itself in some regions and localities; nevertheless, this was an important period for elite class developments. The great Late Preclassic ceremonial or politico-religious centers, with their imposing pyramids and platforms, were often added to in the Early Classic, and, in addition, new centers were founded. Maya sculptural art came into full flower, and Maya hieroglyphic writing, which had only been foreshadowed in the Later Preclassic, now enjoyed a full development.

After what appears to have been a short period of disruption, at least in some regions, in the latter part of the sixth century A.D., Maya civilization resumed its full vigor in the Late Classic Period (A.D. 600–800). Many new centers were constructed; earlier ones were built over; and a proliferation of residential communities signals a Precolumbian population peak for the Maya Lowland area.

A period of decline set in at about A.D. 800, with the abandonment of many of the southern centers and depopulation in many sections of the south. This is the "Maya Collapse" of the Terminal Classic Period (A.D. 800–900) (Culbert 1973). At one time, archaeologists thought that this "collapse" or "time of troubles" was a more or less synchronous phenomenon for the entire Lowland Maya area. Now it would appear, however, that the northern Lowlands did not experience this same ninth-century "collapse" but, instead, enjoyed for a time a florescence in architectural construction and densely populated centers. Just how long this northern florescence lasted is arguable, but most authorities are inclined to see it extending well beyond A.D. 1000 and into what traditionally has been set as the Postclassic Period (A.D. 900–1520) (Sabloff and Andrews 1986). In the south, the entire Postclassic Period, while not being one of complete dissolution and abandonment, saw relatively little in the way of large center construction that would compare with the previous Classic Periods (Chase and Rice 1985). In the north, the Terminal Classic Period florescence continued with the construction of the great site of Chichen Itza which, for perhaps two centuries or more, dominated the northern part of the Yucatan peninsula. Chichen Itza was abandoned as an important center in about 1250. Following this, the northern Lowlands, unlike the southern Lowlands, remained densely populated. Mayapan (Pollock et al. 1962) was the largest politico-religious center of the time, and it was also a walled city. Mayapan was deserted in the mid-fifteenth century, but many other smaller centers continued to thrive in the north until the Spanish *entradas* of the sixteenth century.

Settlement patterns

Although there had been some occasional earlier attention paid to aspects of settlement in Lowland Maya archaeology (Ashmore and Willey 1981), the first research project which took the nature and arrangement of settlements – or a comprehensive view of settlement patterning – as its primary theme was the investigation carried out at Barton Ramie in the Belize Valley in the mid-1950s (Willey 1956; Willey et al. 1965). Since then, similar surveys have been made at Tikal (Haviland 1965, 1966), Seibal (Tourtellot 1970), in the Rio Bec region (Adams 1981; Thomas 1981), in southern Quintana Roo (Harrison 1981), and at Dzibilchaltun in the northern Yucatecan plains (Kurjack and Garza 1981) – to offer only a partial list (see Ashmore 1981b, for more detail). The significant innovation in all of these studies – at least in the context of Maya archaeology as then practiced – was a concern with total settlement, especially with ordinary residential structures, as well as with the more imposing temple and palace architecture of the great centers. The theoretical implications of this are obvious. All-inclusive settlement pattern study was an attempt to prepare a groundwork for an archaeological reconstruction that would approximate a total society, not just the elite segment of that society.

In the following, let us review what is known of the principal elements of Lowland Maya archaeological settlement and their patternings.

Residential units

Residential units are one of the two basic elements of Lowland Maya settlement patterns, the other being the politico-religious centers. On a primary level of inference, archaeologists refer to residential units as "households" (Ashmore 1981a; Rice and Puleston 1981; Kurjack and Garza 1981; Willey 1981). The archaeological remains of such "households" may be either a single small platform mound or two or more (usually from three to six) such platforms which are grouped around a small central patio. The latter, called patio-groups, are much the more common of the two household types. A single mound or platform household is generally conceded to have been occupied by a single biological family. The patio-group household is thought of as having housed two, or perhaps as many as three, biological families, of being, in fact, an "extended family" group residence.

These sociological interpretations of the archaeological data are aided by ethnohistoric sources or modern ethnological observations of Lowland Maya residences where such familial-household arrangements are the norm. We know from such sources and observations that Maya Lowland residential units were patrilocal and the kinship system a patrilineal one, and it is inferred that such kin-residence prevailed in Precolumbian times. From these same ethnohistoric or ethnological sources, we know that some of the platforms in the patio-group household units were often used for other than sleeping buildings – as kitchens or places for storage – and this has been confirmed archaeologically.

The residential household platforms are made of earth or rubble – often faced with masonry retaining walls and surfaced with plaster-gravel floors. There is considerable variation in the height of the platforms, varying from less than 1 m to as much as 3 m; however, the lower platforms are the more common. Platforms are oblong-rectangular in form, both at base and summit, and usually range from about 6 to 9 m in length and 4 to 7 m in width. The house superstructures on the platforms, also usually oblong-rectangular but sometimes apsidal, measured somewhat less than this. It has been suggested that these houses had a minimum of about 20 m of roofed space (Ashmore 1981a). They were one- or two-roomed as a rule. When two-roomed, the rooms were longitudinally arranged with the front room often open, in porch-like fashion, on the front side. The back room, entered through a small doorway, served as the sleeping quarter, and frequently had an earth or stone bench built along the back wall. In construction, houses were most often of perishable wooden poles and thatch although sometimes they had masonry walls and even vaulted stone roofs. Such constructional differences in the houses, as well as the height and masonry quality of the platforms on which they stood, undoubtedly reflected the status and wealth of the inhabitants.

Both single house structures and patio-group house structures were frequently found in clusters of from five to twelve residential units in all, and such clusters would be separated from each other by open spaces. In bringing the "cluster" in at this point in the discussion, we are anticipating settlement disposition and patterning to a degree, but the cluster is a low-level settlement unit and one which is found throughout the area. It is speculated that these residential clusters also may have had kin correlates or kin significance. It is customary in such a cluster that one residential unit, usually a patio-group, is larger than the others in the cluster, and this patio-group will have in it a larger and more imposing building than any in the entire cluster. One can conceive of such a building as the "palace," "shrine," or "office" of the lineage head of the cluster. A good example of this would be the large patio-group CV-43 in a cluster on the outskirts of the main Copan center. It had within it a large platform surmounted by a masonry building with a carved hieroglyphic bench (Willey, Leventhal, and Fash 1978).

Politico-religious centers

As noted, politico-religious centers are the other major formal element in Lowland Maya archaeological settlement. Formerly called "ceremonial centers," they are now more frequently referred to as "politico-religious" or "organizational centers," or just "centers." It seems fairly obvious that they were places of administration as well as religious ritual; indeed, with the ancient Maya it probably would have been impossible to disentangle religious from political authority. The centers, with their tall pyramids and temples, huge platforms and palaces, and carved stone reliefs and stelae, were the first sites in the lowland jungles to catch the eye of early explorers and, later, to attract the attention of archaeological scholars. For a long time, they were what Maya archaeology was all about. When one referred to Tikal, Copan, Palenque, or any of the other famous Maya sites, the reference was to the center. As noted, it was only with regional settlement pattern studies that the residential aspects of Lowland Maya sites came into consideration.

While the centers and the residential units may be viewed as analytically distinct, it is unrealistic to carry the dichotomy too far. Usually residential units are found on the outskirts of the architectural nuclei of the centers, but they also may be located within the center's temple-palace precincts. Also, there are clear relationships between residential constructions and major constructions of the centers. This is seen in the large patio-group residences with their special buildings, as in the previously mentioned Copan CV-43 example. The CV-43 "special building" has to be conceived of at least as a minor palace or temple. As such, it is an architectural counterpart to the big structures of the centers, and this implies functional relationships. Another example of the way residential units may grade into small temple-and-palace complexes is seen in the "Plaza Plan-2" arrangements of structures at Tikal (Becker 1986).

The functions of centers, as implied in the "politico-religious" or "organizational center" designations, must have included both political and religious governance. Craftspeople and craft products were certainly focused in or around the centers. This does not mean that all manufactories were located within a major center, proper. As a contradictory example, we know that the pottery of Palenque and its surrounding region was not made within the great site itself but in other, lesser, nearby centers or satellites of Palenque (Rands 1967, 1969). Or, to take a different kind of example, we know that the relatively small site of Colha, in northern Belize, was not a major political center but was an important manufactory of chert tools. In the local regional site hierarchy, it would appear to have been a tributary of the much larger center of Nohmul (Gibson 1986). Nevertheless, it is highly likely that the major politico-religious centers – in these cases, Palenque and Nohmul – were the places which controlled goods production in their respective domains.

The Maya centers also must have served as points of goods exchange, either through a distributional system, a market system, or some combination of both.

While some Lowland Maya centers are fortified (Webster 1977), most of them are not so we cannot make a ready generalization that they had defensive functions; nevertheless, there is sufficient evidence of various kinds, including hieroglyphic texts (Houston and Mathews 1985; Mathews and Willey 1986), to make the reasonable speculation that centers served as "strong points" or "rallying points" for the more or less endemic warfare that characterized much of the Maya Classic Period.

Although the degree to which Lowland Maya centers were "urban" has been a longstanding debate (see Sanders and Price 1968; Sanders 1981; Willey 1981; Marcus 1983b; Bray 1983), it seems fairly clear that their functions were essentially the same as those of cities in other parts of the world and in other early civilizations. They served, in effect, as the governmental "capitals" or the political and defensive "strongpoints" in the emergent state; they were the foci of organized religion;

political and religious leaders and other elite lived in them; the great palaces and temples were located in them; they were places of work for artisans and for those who traded in or distributed goods; and, last but not least, they were places of residence for large numbers of people. This last characteristic is to many the crucial diagnostic of the urban condition, or the definitive quality of the "city." It needs further examination in the Maya Lowlands. We will return to it.

A survey of politico-religious centers in the Maya Lowlands reveals considerable variation in architectural styles. The buildings of, for example, Palenque in the west, Tikal in the northeastern Peten, and Copan in the far southeast are strikingly different in ornamentation – as all of these are from structures of the Rio Bec region or of northern Yucatan. There are also regional differences in the layout of centers as well as in the architectural features of their buildings. Thus, centers in the south tend to have more compact arrangements of buildings: structures are close together and plazas are often contingent or interconnected. Northern Lowland centers, in contrast, are usually more spread out, with integrative acropoleis and plazas often lacking.

Time trends within the centers are nicely traced in the architectural stratigraphy that has been obtained in the excavations of many of them – Uaxactun (A. L. Smith 1950), Tikal (W. R. Coe 1965), Dzibilchaltun (Andrews and Andrews 1980), Altar de Sacrificios (A. L. Smith 1972), to name but a few. These trends run from relatively small and simple temple or palace structures of the Middle Preclassic through larger and more elaborate Late Preclassic and Classic buildings, frequently constructed one on top of the other. Thus, these site stratigraphies often show that the size of many of the Classic structures owes much to the earlier building of the Late Preclassic for the later Classic pyramids and platforms were sometimes little more than a veneer of the earlier ones. A number of architectural changes characterize the sequence. Thus, the corbelled vault does not appear until the Early Classic Period, and multi-roomed palace buildings do not have their inception until the Late Classic.

Settlement disposition and patterning

A major concern in Lowland Maya settlement patterning has always been the relationship of residential units to centers. As previously stated, some residential units occur within centers; greater numbers appear on the immediate peripheries of centers; and many are found on more distant peripheries of centers, or in locations that might be defined as being between centers. What was the nature of these center-and-residential relationships? At what distances did the presumed elite leadership of a center control the lives and activities of its outlying supporting residential population? How did these center-plus-residential territories relate to each other? With such questions, we begin to move to inferences about sociopolitical units or territorial polities and possible hierarchies of such polities.

In a previous article (Willey 1981) I attempted to distinguish between what I referred to as "micropattern" and "macropattern" settlement assemblages. This is a difficult task because of the necessarily subjective decisions one has to make in drawing the line between the two. The "micropattern" concept was aimed at defining the "community," the "macropattern" at the relationships of one community to another. But what is a community? What are community boundaries? At the smaller end of the scale, we might define a cluster of residential mounds as a community; or, at the larger end of the scale, the great site of Tikal might be so designated. If we make the latter choice, how far may we go from the Tikal main center and still remain within the community?

Let us pursue the Tikal example. Settlement density in the surrounding regions of that center perhaps provides a clue to community delimitation. Settlement survey showed that the occurrences of residential mounds around the Tikal center were fairly constant in their density for a radius of about 6 km around the city center, numbering 100 to the sq. km. Beyond this 6 km radius, residential mounds did continue to occur but in markedly fewer numbers. In addition to this, the Tikal archaeologists also located earthen walls or embankment constructions at just about this 6 km distance to the north and south of the main center. The purpose of the walls is uncertain; they may have been defensive constructions, or they may have served to control the movement of traders entering the city. In any event, the settlement density and the walls suggest what might be called Greater Tikal community limits. Using this radius of 6 km, Haviland (1969; see also Willey 1981) drew a circle from a Tikal center, and within this circumscribed territory of 120 sq. km he estimated, on the basis of mapped samples, close to 12,000 residences. This included those within the center proper and those on the periphery. This residential mound figure would convert to about 72,000 persons for Greater Tikal.

A digression is in order at this point. Ethnographic data have indicated that averages of from four to seven persons lived in an ordinary Maya Lowland household. The lower figure is more consistent with the single-house household, the higher figure with that of a patio-group household. The Tikal estimate is projected for six persons per household, a conservative figure when one takes into account that many of the patio-group households within the Tikal center probably housed a great many more than six persons.

But to return to the Greater Tikal community or "microstructure," it is to be noted that there were a good many peripheral "residential units" that could be viewed as something considerably more than residences. While they probably had residential functions, these could also be looked upon as small temple pyramid-palace complexes – in effect, small politico-religious centers of a "secondary" or "tertiary" class – having governmental or ritual functions as satellites to the main Tikal center.

Seen in this way, the Greater Tikal community, consisting of the main center, the satellite secondary and tertiary centers of the peripheries, and the numerous residential units of these peripheries within the 120 sq.km zone, would be one settlement "microstructure," and perhaps the most populous of any in the Maya Lowlands during the Classic Period. It should be added that the settlement and population projections made here for Tikal pertain primarily to the late Classic Period, the time of the population maximum for the Maya Lowlands as a whole; however, in this connection, it must also be noted that chronology – and the problems of chronological differentiation of residential, as well as larger, structures – remains a complicating factor in settlement study and one that will be with us for some time to come.

But to continue with our settlement "microstructure," or community, theme, another site for which we have substantial survey data is that of Seibal, on the Rio Pasion in the southern Peten (Willey et al. 1975). Seibal is a smaller politico-religious center than Tikal. The main center proper covers only a single sq.km, in contrast to Tikal's 4 sq.km, and the temple and palace structures within the center are less densely packed and generally smaller than those of Tikal. Tourtellot's (in press) house mound counts and population estimates give a figure of 10,000 persons living within the center and a surrounding zone of 25 sq.km in the Late Classic Period. Dotted throughout this surrounding zone are not only the numerous residential structures but several minor centers, similar to the satellite centers within the greater Tikal community.

The community pattern at Copan is also comparable, except that here one definition of the larger community, or "microstructure," is provided by the natural boundaries of the hills bordering an alluvial pocket in the river valley in which the Copan center lies. The total area of the pocket is 12 by 4 km, or approximately 50 sq.km. Residential-mound counting provides the basis for an estimate of about 12,000 to 17,000 persons during the Late Classic occupation of the pocket (Fash 1983; Webster 1987). As at Tikal or Seibal, there are several smaller elite-type complexes within the pocket which would appear to be minor administrative centers (Fash 1983). One question arises in connection with the Copan community, however, in that survey beyond the pocket, into other reaches of the Copan Valley, suggests that a Copan polity – ruled from the main Copan center – might have been extended over a larger territory than that of the pocket and have encompassed perhaps twice the population of the pocket itself. But this kind of question leads us into the next level of settlement disposition and patterning, that of the "macrostructure."

In considering settlement "macrostructures" or "macropatterns" we are confronted with the question of just how densely were the entire Maya Lowlands settled. Can the Tikal, Seibal, or Copan microstructural densities be projected to the Lowlands at large? "Was there a virtual sea of continuous residential settlement over all reasonably habitable land in the entire lowlands, with this sea dotted by the many 'islands,' large and small, of the architectural nuclei of centers?" (Willey 1981:401). From the knowledge that we have now, it seems unlikely this was the case. We have already noted the lessening of residential mounds as one goes out beyond the Tikal 6 km radius. In surveys between Tikal and Uaxactun – the latter a center 18 km to the north – there is no house-mound density comparable to that of the Tikal microstructure, and the same is true of the territory between Tikal and Yaxha, a center located 20 km to the southeast of Tikal (Willey 1981; Puleston 1974). Further, in other parts of the Lowlands surveys have revealed substantial stretches of territory between centers with few or no mounds (Harrison 1981). This suggests that territorial polities may have been relatively small in geographic scope – perhaps no more than 10 or 12 km in diameter, as implied by the settlement density of the Tikal community. Bullard, on the basis of surveys in the northeastern Peten, offered some such model a good many years ago (Bullard 1960). Working from the bottom up, so to speak, he designated *clusters* of residences occupying a little area 200 to 300 m in diameter; a dozen or so such *clusters* in an area of about a sq.km then formed a *zone*, and each zone was also the seat of a minor politico-religious center; at the top of a hierarchy was a *district*, composed of several zones, extending over about 100 sq.km, and having a major center as its capital. Was this the top of the hierarchy? Bullard did not speculate further, but his use of the term *district* might be taken to imply that he was thinking of a still larger polity made up of several districts.

In the 1960s and 1970s, I believe that most of us in Maya archaeology did think in terms of rather grand hierarchies, composed of a good many large politico-religious centers, secondary and tertiary centers, and extensive territories of residential settlement. To some extent, this was conditioned by the central-place theory of the economic geographers (Haggett 1966). Flannery (1972a), Hammond (1974), and Marcus (1973, 1976) all advanced models of this nature, with politico-religious centers serving as the central points of hexagonal territories in lattice-like networks. The variation in the sizes of the politico-religious centers, computed from architectural volumetrics and counts of courtyard arrangements within the sites, also allowed for hierarchy building (Turner et al. 1981; Adams and Jones 1981). Marcus (1973, 1976) added another dimension to these site hierarchies, or implied polities, with the suggestion that the use of site "Emblem glyphs," as these had been defined by Berlin (1958), gave the clues to dominance–subservience relationships among politico-religious centers. Briefly, she held that tributary centers would cite the Emblem glyph of cities to which they owed allegiance but that the dominant site would never display the Emblem glyph of the vassal city. Combining this with site sizes, she diagrammed lattice arrangements, or hexagons, of Maya cities. Each major hexagon had a primary central city, such as Tikal, Naranjo, or Calakmul, and equidistant from this central city, and from each other, were six secondary cities. Such hexagons measured about 40 to 60 km in diameter. In considering the polities which Marcus was suggesting by her Tikal, Naranjo, or Calakmul hexagons, we are probably on a higher territorial level than that which Bullard was designating as a "district." The capitals of Bullard's "districts" would more likely be on the site hierarchical level of the secondary centers in Marcus's Tikal or Naranjo spheres of influence. In a very recent article, Adams (1986: see map, p. 437) has offered his opinions of the territories and territorial sizes of "regional states" in the Maya Lowlands, and these are all of considerable geographical range.

Marcus, however, has suggested still larger political territories for the Lowland Maya, arguing, from combined settlement, Emblem glyph, and ethnohistoric legendary accounts, that the Maya had four great regional "capitals" – Tikal, Palenque, Copan, and Calakmul. Each of these cities then had at least three tiers of smaller centers under their hierarchical control. In such an arrangement, Naranjo, a quite major center, would have been under the direction of Tikal; and the four regional capitals would each have governed over a very large territory. Continuing with such speculations, particularly as these might be stimulated by site sizes and settlement hierarchical patternings, we might project that Tikal, as the largest of all of the southern Classic Period centers, was the "capital" of a very sizable territorial state. We will come back for a more critical look at this matter of the sizes of territorial polities later. Let us break off for the moment and have a look at the Lowland Maya agriculture which sustained the peoples of these emerging states.

Agriculture

Settlement and agriculture
Ancient Maya settlement distributions and densities definitely relate to suitable land for maize farming. Both residential distributions and the centers or cities are found on or near lands which have an agricultural potential. The only other natural factor of equal importance in determining most settlement location is the availability of potable water.

The most extensive terrain type that is well suited to agriculture without intensive man-made modifications comprises well drained lands of moderate slope. These were clearly favored for settlement, as witnessed by the extensive archaeological remains of residential communities and politico-religious centers found upon them. Such lands were fertile, but their thin soils were often subject to cultivation exhaustion and erosion. Because of this they were farmed by swidden, or seasonal slash-and-burn methods. These varied from short-fallow swiddening, or two or three year rotation of fields, to long-fallowing periods of up to as much as ten years. Regions of this kind of farming are found throughout the Maya Lowlands. Some of the best known are in the hill-country in the northeast Peten, but they occur in many other places. Usually, such lands are in gently rolling hill country; however, the flat northern Yucatecan plains also had very thin fertile soils – sometimes little more than pockets of clay over a limestone base. These, too, must have been successfully cultivated by swidden methods, judging from the density of settlement in these regions.

Riverside locations were also favored for settlement. Indeed, the alluvial soils in the river valleys were no doubt more choice locations for farming than the hillslopes, for their deeper and seasonally replenished soils could be tilled without fallowing; however, such riverine alluvial tracts are relatively limited in area in the Maya Lowlands, and, often, as in the Copan Valley (Fash 1983), or in the Belize Valley (Ford 1985), the surrounding hills were farmed, as well as the valley flats – presumably to take care of the growing populations of the Late Classic Period.

The grassland savannas, which occur in various places in the Maya Lowlands, were not well-suited for agriculture, and, for the most part, settlement was not dense in such environments.

The remaining major terrain type within the Maya Lowlands is the swamp or *bajo* country. Such *bajos* are found scattered through much of the area, principally in its southern half. Settlements, in the sense of dwellings or politico-religious centers, are not found in them. For a long time it was thought that they were virtually worthless to the Maya; more recently there has been a revision of this idea, but this takes us into intensive cultivation.

Potable water was mentioned as a settlement necessity. For sites along rivers or on lake shores it was no problem, but for those not so situated, as for instance in the interior of the northeast Peten, it was necessary to depend upon water-holes or *aguadas*. Often these *aguadas* were reduced in size during the dry season, and, apparently to counteract this, the Maya frequently enlarged and sometimes paved them so that they served as effective catchments for rain as well as sources for ground water. In the north, in Yucatan, limestone sinks or *cenotes* took the place of the *aguadas*.

Research into intensive agriculture

Settlement research actually touched off questions about ancient Maya farming as early as the 1930s. This was done when Ricketson (Ricketson and Ricketson 1937) made a settlement survey on the peripheries of the Uaxactun politico-religious center. His counts of residential mounds in this survey indicated a settlement and population density too great to have been sustained by long-fallow swidden farming alone. From this Ricketson went on to argue that the inhabitants of Uaxactun, and the northeast Peten in general, had probably practiced more intensive cultivation on the hillslopes and high ground of the region. Such intensification, in his opinion, had been annual planting, or at least short-fallow swidden farming, on these relatively fertile soils. He went on from this to advance the hypothesis, in conjunction with C. W. Cooke (see Ricketson and Ricketson 1937; also Cooke 1931), that such attempts at intensive or short-fallow farming had set in train serious erosion and degradation of the topsoils, washing these sediments into the *bajos*, and leaving the formerly cultivated hills denuded and unfit for cultivation. Indeed, this Cooke–Ricketson hypothesis was seen by him as the causal chain of the Classic Maya "collapse." But Ricketson's ideas had little influence upon Maya archaeologists at the time. His settlement survey, which was the first of its kind, was of limited scope and not followed up, and the notion of long-fallow swidden farming, documented as it was by Maya history and ethnography, was not easily dislodged.

The change in attitudes came about in the 1970s. By that time, as the result of extensive settlement surveys in many parts of the Lowlands, it had become obvious that the productivity of long-fallow swidden cultivation could not have sustained the populations indicated by the house-mound counts, no matter how conservatively these population figures were computed (Willey 1978; Harris 1978; Turner and Harrison 1978). It was now incumbent upon Maya archaeologists, aided by agronomists, botanists, and others, to come up with some new ideas about agricultural and general subsistence intensification in Precolumbian times. The response to the situation in the last decade and a half has been a strong one, and it can be only very briefly summarized here (see, especially, Harrison and Turner 1978 and Pohl 1985b for collections of papers devoted to various aspects of the subject).

Essentially, three lines of investigation have been pursued. Perhaps the most dramatic and revolutionary of these has been the discovery and definition of artificial raised fields. Siemens and Puleston (1972) called attention to these along the Candelaria River in southern Campeche. In wet lands along the sluggish course of the river, beds or banks of sediment had been piled up to form series of rectangular patches of ground that had apparently been used in the past for intensive farming. Comparable to the *chinampas*, or "floating gardens," in the Valley of Mexico lake beds, such artificial gardens, frequently replenished with muck from the river or lake bottoms, could sustain several crops a year. A variety of crops could be grown on them, and we know from pollen studies in the Maya lowlands that maize (*Zea mays*) was one of these. Since the Rio Candelaria discoveries, additional fields have been discovered and explored in various parts of the Maya Lowlands, including northern Belize (Turner 1974; Turner and Harrison 1983) and Quintano Roo (Harrison 1978). Moreover, it now seems quite likely that many of the *bajos* or swamps of the Maya Lowlands were once (R. E. W. Adams 1980; Adams et al. 1981) laced with artificial canals and the raised fields which they drained. As is evident, these findings put ancient Maya agriculture in a new light. R. E. W. Adams (1980, 1983) has attempted to relate greater settlement densities to nearby raised field cultivation plots, but he has done this only in a preliminary way, and it is a line of research that needs further exploration.

Artificial terracing for agriculture has been a second line of investigation. Occasional terracings or "silt-traps" had been reported upon in earlier Maya archaeology (Thompson 1931; Lundell 1940), but the most detailed recent coverage of the subject is an article by Turner (1979), in which, among other regions, he describes the complex systems of agricultural terrace walls of stone found in the Rio Bec territory, and he has gone on to describe settlement in conjunction with such systems.

Both raised fields and terraces would have demanded considerable labor investment to construct and to maintain. For the ancient Maya there was undoubtedly a "trade-off" here between larger subsistence yields, larger populations, and greater labor investment on the one hand, and smaller yields, populations, and labor costs on the other. Clearly, the Classic Maya opted for the first course.

What might be considered a third, and less-focused, line of investigation into Maya subsistence intensification would include a number of strategies. One of these would be the short-fallow swidden procedures referred to earlier (Pohl and Mikcisek 1985). As noted, these could have been carried out on alluvial soils or on favored hillslope or upland soils. Such activity is difficult to trace archaeologically and is largely inferential from natural environmental conditions. Household or "kitchen" gardens (Netting 1977; Bronson 1978) maintained near the residence were almost certainly a subsistence strategy. A variety of crops could have been grown in these, including sweet manioc (Bronson 1966). Orchards and tree harvesting would have been a part of this strategy (Puleston 1978). The range and variety of cultivated and "semi-cultivated" food plants was great and went far beyond the maize–beans–squash staples (see Pohl and Mikcisek 1985, for a listing). Finally, the Maya depended to an important extent on animal foods. Deer, the prime game, seems to have been a prerogative of the aristocracy, at least by Classic times (Pohl 1985a); however, smaller land animals and turtle, fish, and shellfish, in those locations where they existed, all made up a part of the diet (Lange 1971; Hamblin 1985).

Contemporaneous hieroglyphic textual evidence
Recent translations of Maya hieroglyphic texts, as contemporaneous documents of some of the events described in them, have thrown interesting light on old Maya

political life. While documents make no references to agriculture, many of them relate to settlement and the political implications of settlement patterns. These hieroglyphic texts, found on stelae and other monuments in the politico-religious centers, tell us of the histories of dynasties, of wars between centers or cities, of royal or aristocratic marriages, of births and deaths, and of the dominance of certain centers over others (Kelley 1976; Schele 1976). With these histories as a guide, let us turn back to where we left our settlement pattern discussions of political territories.

There we spoke of Marcus's (1976) use of the Emblem glyphs in conjunction with settlement hierarchies, and together with the aid of central place theory, in an attempt to arrive at some conclusions about how the ancient Maya exercised political power. These trial examinations of Marcus's tended to favor the former existence of fairly large territorial states in the Lowlands, but a more detailed reading of the hieroglyphic texts, as these have been recovered now from a number of sites, prompts a reversal of this interpretive trend toward territorial bigness to one suggesting that the Lowland Maya polities were of relatively small size. As such, they would have included only a single sizable center, perhaps a few very small satellites, and their surrounding residential populations. Going back to some of Marcus's (1976: 26–7) diagrams, sites such as Dos Aguadas, Yaxha, and Nakum, which she had placed within the hexagon, and polity, of Naranjo, would now be conceived of as independent polities in their own right. This revised view of the small polity unit, as opposed to the larger regional state, is now favored by the majority of opinion of Maya hieroglyphic experts (personal communication, L. Schele, P. Mathews, and C. Jones, Santa Fe, New Mexico, 1986). In their opinion, the Maya preoccupation, or obsession, with the hieroglyphic recording of political matters, especially with wars, conquests, and conditions of dominance and subservience, renders it highly unlikely that polities as large and powerful as some of the regional states suggested by Marcus (1976) or Adams (1986) were ever in existence. Certainly, there is no reference to such political giants in any of the known monumental inscriptions.

A detailed survey of sites and hieroglyphic texts in the Pasion Valley in the southern Peten (Mathews and Willey 1986) supports the idea of small territorial polities although, at the same time, it does lend some support to the idea that the Maya themselves were constantly struggling to increase the sizes of their small domains, however geographically limited and chronologically unstable these "would-be" conquest states might have been. In an area along the Pasion, which measures about 100 km in its L-shaped drainage, from Cancuen in the southeast to Altar de Sacrificios to the northwest, there are at least 25 sites which set up carved stelae or other hieroglyphic monuments. Some of these sites were of relatively minor size, and, judging from their locations near much larger centers and from the specific information in the inscriptions found on their monuments, these were not centers of independent polities. Still, among these 25 sites at least 11 had been independent statelets at some time during the Late Classic Period. We know that for a while, in the latter part of the seventh and during most of the eighth centuries, one of these centers – Dos Pilas – dominated some of the others as the result of both military conquests and strategic dynastic marriages. But this Dos Pilas expanded state was still of rather modest geographical proportions; Altar de Sacrificios, which is only 25 km west of Dos Pilas, apparently continued to maintain its independence, as did Machaquila, somewhat farther to the east. This little Dos Pilas "empire" was short-lived, falling apart soon after A.D. 800 (Houston and Mathews 1985; Johnston 1985; Mathews and Willey 1986). Mathews (personal communication, 1986) has stated that the Dos Pilas seventh to eighth century attempt at state enlargement, or modest empire building, is unique to the Maya Lowlands, at least in so far as hieroglyphic texts have informed us.

To sum up, the contemporary hieroglyphic record, as these are now known from the northeast Peten and the Pasion, as well as from the Copan and Usumacinta regions, indicate Lowland Maya polities to have been normatively rather small territories, perhaps no more than 30 to 50 km in diameter, and to have been ruled from a single independent center in each, indeed, usually the only large center in the particular territory. This center was the seat of the ruling dynasty or lineage, and its power was made manifest throughout the polity by its hieroglyphic monuments. This condition of many small, independent polities, judging from the translated hieroglyphic texts now available, prevailed during the Late Classic Period (A.D. 600–800). There is no good evidence that the situation was significantly different during the preceding Early Classic Period. In the Terminal Classic in the southern Lowlands there seems to have been some consolidation of state power; however, by this time a general cultural and population decline had set in (Mathews and Willey 1986).

All of this should give us pause, as archaeologists, as we try to reconstruct ancient Maya states and polities from settlement data alone. I do not think we can ignore settlement data in our attempts to talk about Prehispanic Maya politics; certainly texts will not give us the whole story. Some texts may omit pieces of history that were not to rulers' likings; others may add to or embellish the facts of political successes. For a while, at least, and perhaps always, our strategy will have to be one of playing settlement and other archaeological information against the information from the hieroglyphic texts and vice versa. In this way, we will move forward most soundly and successfully in our attempts to understand the Precolumbian political history of the Lowland Maya.

Summary

The last 30 years have seen rapid advances in our knowledge of Lowland Maya archaeological settlement. This has meant that ancient Maya communities now are known not only from their spectacular great architectural achievements – the temple pyramids and great palaces of what were, in effect, the politico-religious or administrative centers of these former societies – but from the numerous residential mounds and residential quarters that are found surrounding such centers. These findings have permitted population estimates to be made for both centers and for sustaining territories. They also have made possible the plotting of regional site hierarchies. These two kinds of inferences – demographic and socio-political – have changed our image of ancient Maya civilization.

Closely allied with this settlement pattern research, and to an important degree stimulated by it, have been the still more recent investigations into Maya subsistence. How were the very large populations, as these have been inferred from settlement surveys, fed and sustained? In what ways was swidden cultivation of maize – undoubtedly one important long-lived subsistence strategy – supplemented or replaced by more intensive food production methods? In answer to these questions, archaeologists have brought to light evidences of intensive agricultural techniques: artificial raised fields and terrace constructions of truly extensive scope. These discoveries have been made and described in the last fifteen years. Besides this, both direct findings and inferential reasoning and analogy have demonstrated, at a very high level of probability, that ancient Maya diet was further supplemented in important ways through "kitchen gardens," root crops, and arboriculture.

Finally, we come to a most recent series of positive developments in the translation of Maya hieroglyphic texts from site monuments. These relate very obviously to our settlement findings of site sizes, to hierarchies among centers, and to population densities. They offer us some idea of what the Maya themselves thought about, or how they acted upon, such things. To some degree, they confirm some of our interpretations and suppositions drawn from the material remains and dispositions of settlement alone; but they also tell us that the forms of settlement as we see them upon the landscape do not hold all of the answers to ancient political history.

12

The political economy of the Inka empire: the archaeology of power and finance

TIMOTHY K. EARLE and TERENCE N. D'ALTROY

Since late prehistory, empires have developed and expanded to dominate extensive territories and large populations.[1] The scale of even archaic empires is remarkable, as they sometimes incorporated millions of people from ethnically diverse backgrounds. To secure control and to finance their activities, these polities fashioned institutional means of rule that typically included administrations for decision-making and mobilization of resources, state religions to foster local consent, and militaries for expansion, protection, and suppression. Explaining the repeated expansions of empires challenges historians, sociologists, and anthropologists, but there have been surprisingly few attempts to analyze such evolutionary developments with archaeological data, with some notable exceptions (e.g. R. McC. Adams 1965a, 1981; Sanders et al. 1979). As we hope to show, however, the ample diachronic data of archaeology provide rich opportunities for studying the development of early empires. Of equal significance is the alternative perspective that archaeology provides to the early documentary evidence from the early complex societies themselves.

Archaic empires, existing prior to mercantilism and the industrial revolution, were fashioned by conquest and incorporation of other societies, initially often competitors for power. As in the Inka case, empires arose out of the same conditions of "peer-polity" competition and alliance that characterized the evolution of states (cf. Price 1978b, 1982; Renfrew and Cherry 1986), ultimately succeeding by exerting effective control over diverse and less organized societies beyond the political core.

Our perspective in addressing this development is materialistic, focusing attention on the energetics of a society that contributed directly to its viability and capability to maintain and extend itself. This implies that a primary evolutionary interest should be the relationship between social complexity and the channeling of energy (see Steward 1955; R. N. Adams 1976; Price 1978b, 1982). Accordingly, our analysis concerns the institutions that manage matter, energy and information exchange and the political power derived from that management (see Flannery 1972a; Wright 1984).

Two interlocked transformations seem central to the issue of imperial development, one political and one economic. The first lies in the core's extension of control of sovereignty over subject polities by establishing a monopoly of force and by appropriating decision-making through a state bureaucracy. The second lies in the reorganization of the economy – notably labor and exchange – within the subject populations and, to a lesser extent, within the core polity. The purposes of these economic transformations are to mobilize resources for state finance and to solidify control over the subject populations. As should be apparent, these political and economic processes are interdependent. While the ability to apply power effectively derives from the concentration and strategic allocation of economic resources (cf. Webster 1977), the reasons to concentrate economic production and flow are, in premarket societies, largely political (Brumfiel and Earle 1987).

In this chapter, we focus on the strategies of expansion and incorporation adopted by the Inka state. The implementation of these strategies varied considerably according to the existing social, political, and economic character of conquered polities. However, the goals were similar – maintenance of security and generation of revenues for imperial support. The research questions here are concerned with finance, the strategic collection and allotment of resources for institutional support. To provide a concrete example of the complexities of the problem, we will concentrate our attention on the strategy of Inka finance in one central highland province, in the Upper Mantaro Valley of Peru.

A brief historical sketch of the Inka empire may help the reader understand the more detailed archaeological case that we analyze momentarily. The initial growth of the empire was explosive. At the end of the Late Intermediate Period in the fifteenth century A.D., the Andean highlands were fragmented among many competing chieftains and small states, each with limited territories and supporting populations (Rowe 1946:274; Krzanowski 1978; Earle et al. 1980; Salomon 1986). The Inkas were very much part of this milieu. Their territory was restricted, covering probably no more than 1000 sq.km, and their population comprised perhaps twenty or thirty thousand people. According to oral tradition, leadership was based largely on military prowess and effectiveness, characteristics essential for defense of territory. Initial military success for the Inkas, in what was apparently a defensive war against an aggressive neighbor, set the stage for rapid expansion of the Inka polity during successive reigns by three strong lords. In less than one hundred years, they fashioned the largest empire in the New World and probably the largest polity with a Bronze Age technology ever to have existed (Conrad and Demarest 1984:84). The Inkas conquered the coastal and mountain peoples stretching from what is now Chile and Argentina on the south, through Bolivia and Peru, to Ecuador and southern Colombia incorporating nearly a million square kilometers and six to twelve million subjects (Fig. 12.1). How was this possible?

A partial answer to this question lies in the Inkas' ability to fashion effective institutions of integration and control. The military organization was unquestionably of primary initial importance. Combining an elite royal corps and specialized commanders with inductees drawn from all local communities (Rowe 1946:278), the Inkas assembled a fighting force effective more because of its sheer size and tenacity than innovative tactics. In a world of small polities that, in most instances, could field a fighting force of only a few thousand, the Inka army of twenty to thirty thousand or more would be literally overwhelming. In a vivid description of the Inka conquest of the Mantaro Valley, a Wanka lord recounted the strategy of coercive diplomacy and outright conquest employed by the invading army.

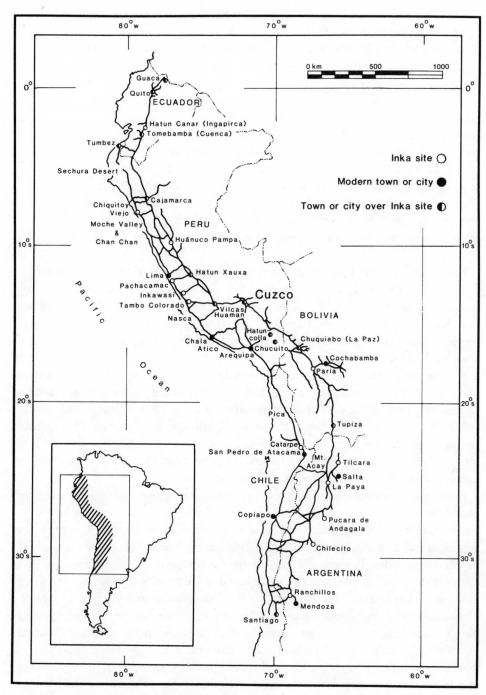

Fig. 12.1. The Inka empire, showing the principal roads (after Hyslop 1984: frontispiece).

[This] witness heard said . . . that when [Topa] Inka came to conquer and rule this land, he positioned himself on a hill in this territory with the people that he brought, who were ten thousand soldiers, called an *hunu* in his language; and that his great-grandfather, named Apoguala, went there and pledged obedience and bowed down . . . the said great-grandfather arrived to speak with said Inka and to subject himself to him and that the other Indians that he took with him arrived with him and the others remained hidden; and said Topa Inka, this witness heard, had given to his great-grandfather some elegant shirts and blankets and some drinking cups called *aquilla*, among them . . . and said Inka told him that they were to go with him to Quito and that he heard said that they would give him obedience there and that he made war on and subjected those who did not obey him nor came to bow down, killing some and taking their lands and others who came to give him obedience he received . . .[2]

Following conquest, areas were integrated into the empire, often with a remarkable investment in state facilities. The scope of the Inka effort can best be appreciated by considering the 30,000 km of roads that united the empire, the nearly one hundred new administrative and urban centers spaced along the roads, the vast storage complexes, and the extensive areas of newly created farming terraces, many of which were fed by irrigation canals.

A debate has surfaced recently in the literature over the extent of Inka intervention into local affairs. Some authors have argued for extensive and profound reorganization of economic relations as part of the imposed state economy (e.g. Rowe 1982; Julien 1982). Others have played down the impact, emphasizing a retention of long-held Andean patterns of production and exchange (e.g. Pease 1982; Murra 1982). As is so often the case, both perspectives have considerable merit and can be reconciled by understanding two strategic aspects of Inka rule.

First, the structural relationships between state and local community must be understood in their ideological role. They did not simply represent and order reality but were intended to legitimize and make a system of domination appear to be the natural order. The organization of the empire was represented as an extension of the proper world order. Consent of those dominated was nurtured by making the Inka state appear to be an enlarged chiefdom based on principles of those societies that previously characterized the Andean world. That administrative centers, such as Huánuco Pampa, were involved heavily in feasting activities was surely meant to portray the state–local relationship as an extension of chief–commoner reciprocity (Wachtel 1976:61–84; Morris 1982). At least some of these centers were overtly conceived as microcosms of the world, "New Cuzcos" spatially laid out according to Inka principles of cosmology and society, as was the imperial capital. Among these intrusive, planned settlements were Quito and Tomebamba in Ecuador (Cieza de León 1967:lvii, 190; see Salomon 1986:144–8, 174), Inkawasi in the coastal Cañete Valley (Cieza de León 1984:lxiii:217; Hyslop 1984), and Huánuco Pampa in the Peruvian highlands (Morris and Thompson 1985; Morris in press). The state religion was carefully groomed to delineate the cosmic sanctions for the new order on which local fertility depended, and local religions were explicitly incorporated into state practice. In many regions, local leaders were retained and incorporated into the lower levels of the state decimal hierarchy by which labor was recruited (D'Altroy 1981; Julien 1982; LeVine 1987). Thus an ideology of continuity was used to ease the massive reorganization.

Second, the actual basis and extent of incorporation varied widely among subject territories. Areas of the empire conquered at different periods required varying strategies because of differences in resources, population size, existing organization, and the broader imperial needs for security and integration. The means of incorporation for the large coastal states such as Chimor (Netherly 1978), for the populous polities of the Bolivian altiplano (Diez de San Miguel 1964), for the complex highland chiefdoms such as the Wankas (D'Altroy 1981), or for the simpler chiefdoms in Ecuador (Salomon 1986) were expectedly quite different.

Inka strategies of incorporation can be seen as arranged along a continuum with hegemonic and territorial control to either extreme (D'Altroy 1987; cf. Luttwak 1976; Hassig 1985). With *hegemonic control*, the core Inka polity ruled indirectly, through clients who retained considerable autonomy in management of local affairs, but were forced to accept military submission, tributary payments in labor and special products, and truncation of economic relations with neighboring ethnic groups. For the core, the advantages of such hegemonic relationships were found in the relatively low costs of control and in the minimal internal security duties. Control was maintained by the threat of attack and by economic penetration through the client elites, which affected interest relationships in the periphery. Disadvantages of such relationships were found in the limits to potential extraction of goods and in the greater likelihood of repeated rebellions, fostered by the high degree of subject autonomy. In contrast, with *territorial control*, the core Inka polity extended direct state presence into the dominated regions through a comprehensive restructuring of economic and political relationships, a supervisory administrative presence, and often a series of dramatic cultural changes. Control was high, permitting a high level of extraction, but the degree of intervention was tempered by the high costs of direct administration.

Variation along this continuum from hegemonic to territorial control reflected at least three basic conditions of incorporation. First was the time of incorporation with respect to imperial development. During the initial phase of rapid expansion, emphasis on indirect rule (hegemonic control) would have minimized administrative costs and permitted the empire to direct a high proportion of resources into military conquest. However, as the opportunities or needs for conquest declined and costs of control escalated, an increased emphasis on direct administration would have become necessary to expand resource extraction and guarantee continued domination.

Second, the intensity of control reflected the economic and logistical position of the dominated societies within the structure of the empire. Core areas in the central highlands of Peru and Bolivia were controlled directly because of their proximity to Cuzco and the corresponding needs for security and intensive use of available resources. In contrast, peripheral areas, such as the central and northern highlands of Ecuador, were minimally incorporated and the emphasis was on manipulation of existing sociopolitical and economic structures to impose state control. A case in point is the state's use of exchange specialists to extend relationships with the peoples of the Amazon and the Ecuadorian coast, two regions that were never successfully brought under the Inka aegis (Salomon 1987).

Third, the complexity of existing societal organization could have facilitated or provided impediments to imperial incorporation. In the core, simply organized populations were swept away (Wachtel 1982; Lavallée and Julien 1983:35–40) or ignored (Krzanowski 1978), depending on the resource potential of their region. More complex societies were heavily incorporated, as we will discuss for the Wanka case, but the local divisions according to ethnicity and eliteness were recognized and used. In this light, the renowned self-sufficiency of local communities, often spoken of as a long-held Andean ideal, may rather be seen as a means to increase the vertical dependence of the communities on the state in lieu of horizontal ties with other highland communities (Earle 1985; see also Murra 1975, 1980; Salomon 1986). Around the peripheries, control was characteristically indirect, using existing leadership where possible and creating this leadership where tribute extraction was desirable. Perhaps surprisingly, indirect rule appears to have been implemented in a large proportion of the Peruvian coastal valleys, some of which were politically decentralized following conquest and ruled from a slightly removed distance (see, for example, Netherly 1978; Conrad 1977).

Inka rule in the Upper Mantaro Valley

In order to provide a more concrete examination of the nature and extent of local Inka involvement, we will summarize the relevant data collected recently by the Upper Mantaro Archaeological Research Project (UMARP). Our project has studied the late prehistoric periods of the intermontane Mantaro Valley in the central highlands of Peru. The alluvial plain of the Mantaro (3200–3400 m above sea level) is a rich maize-producing ground. Bordering the plains are bare hillslopes and rolling uplands that produce rich yields of Andean tubers and other high elevation plants such as *quinoa*. Still higher (above 3700 m) is the grassland *puna* that provides pasture for herds of llama and alpaca.

From 1977–9, UMARP established the late prehistoric chronology and settlement pattern changes, including the construction of the intrusive Inka imperial facilities (Earle et al. 1980; D'Altroy 1981). In 1982–3, UMARP excavated six sites in order to investigate in greater detail the impact of Inka imperial expansion on the native Wanka ethnic group (Earle et al. 1987). The late prehistoric sites of the Yanamarca Valley, where the excavations were conducted, present an unusual opportunity for archaeological research. Rapid sociopolitical change in the region prior to the Spanish conquest caused radical shifts in settlement locations; as a result, late prehistoric sites are typically single component. Additionally, because site locations are fairly high (above 3600 m) and are located on rugged limestone outcrops, architecture is well-preserved and visible on the surface. The short occupation and good preservation are ideally suited to the type of archaeology that we planned.

Our field research has permitted us to identify two phases of interest to the present discussion. Wanka II (A.D. 1350–1460) was a time of balkanized society in the region immediately preceding Inka conquest. The sociopolitical landscape was occupied by several competing chiefdoms, each dominated by a major center with at least 8000 inhabitants. Smaller communities of a thousand or more were linked politically to each center. Settlements were located on high ridges and protected by fortification walls. Within the walls, densely packed residential structures clustered around private patio spaces, interconnected by a maze of pathways. Centers were distinguished from satellite towns and villages by public plazas and complexes of relatively large central buildings. During Wanka III (A.D. 1460–1533), the Wankas were conquered and incorporated into the Inka empire. Most large settlements were abandoned and much of the population was resettled in smaller communities located near agricultural land that was more productive in the preferred maize-complex crops. A settlement hierarchy continued, but settlement populations ranged from several hundred to several thousand.

The imperial presence was established in the form of a major administrative center (Hatun Xauxa), secondary administrative facilities (e.g. J63), extensive warehousing complexes, and the road system. The importance of Hatun Xauxa lay partially in its logistical position at the juncture of the main highland highway and major passes to the coast and to the jungle. The productivity of the valley and its location may have played major roles in the emperor Huascar's choice of Hatun Xauxa as his preferred seat of government (see Guaman Poma 1980: I, f. 116:94).

To obtain information from Wanka II settlements, UMARP excavated at Tunanmarca (J7) and Umpamalca (J41). Marca (J54), Chucchus (J74), and Huancas de la Cruz (J59) were excavated for Wanka III, and the multicomponent site of Hatunmarca (J2) yielded data on both phases (Fig. 12.2). The sites excavated for Wanka II comprised two centers (Tunanmarca and Hatunmarca) and a dependent settlement (Umpamalca). For Wanka III, the excavated sites were ruins of two towns with central functions (Hatunmarca and Marca) and two villages (Chucchus and Huancas de la Cruz). A Wanka III hamlet (Pancan: J1), excavated in 1977 and 1979, is included in our discussion where pertinent.

At these sites, we excavated in a total sample of 29 patio groups. These consist of sets of residential structures facing onto private, open spaces set off by walls and terraces. To judge both from consistencies in the household assemblages recovered during field work and from early Spanish inspections of comparable highland regions (e.g. Ortiz de Zúñiga 1967), we believe that the patio group represents a household, the minimal unit of economic and social cooperation. The excellent architectural preservation permitted us to delimit these compounds prior to excavation and to classify them preliminarily into elite and commoner statuses based on size, architectural quality, and location. The sample was therefore divided approximately evenly between phases and between statuses (see Earle et al. 1987).

In order to discuss the nature and extent of Inka penetration into the economic activities of the Wankas, we will review the available archaeological data concerning four critical processes: (1) the organization of labor to extract a staple surplus for imperial finance; (2) the storage and disposal of the goods extracted; (3) the organiz-

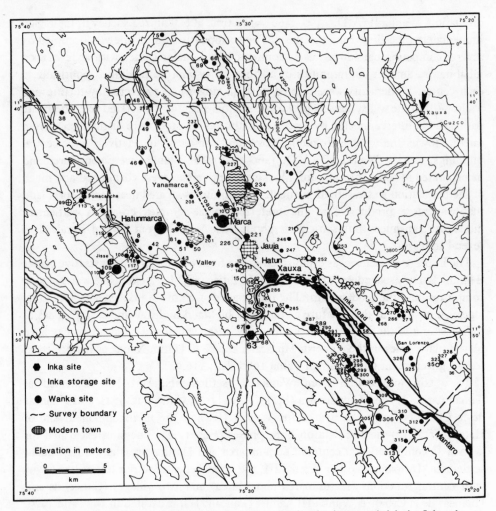

Fig. 12.2. The northern end of the Upper Mantaro Valley, showing the sites occupied during Inka rule.

ation of exchange relationships; and (4) the manipulation of the sociopolitical system through control over wealth. A major theme of this presentation will be the archaeological methods available to study these critical aspects of finance and the broader political economy.

The organization of labor

As numerous authors have observed (e.g. Childe 1951a; Adams 1965a), the evolution of social complexity depends on systems of finance to extract a disposable surplus. With the imposition of Inka imperial control, the labor of subject populations was partially reorganized to accomplish this end. Over their century of power, the Inkas moved from indirect to direct control over labor as the demands on imperial rule shifted from conquest to consolidation (see Murra 1980). Extraction of support in a non-market economy can be accomplished most easily through staple finance, in which staple products (main foods) are mobilized and used directly to support state personnel (D'Altroy and Earle 1985). The simplest form of direct control over agricultural labor in a staple finance system involves state ownership of land and its allocation to local communities in return for peasant labor on state lands. In the Inka empire, the state assumed ownership of land and other natural resources through right of conquest. Lands were then reassigned to the local communities in return for regular labor service required of each household on state lands and other state projects, on both permanent and rotating bases.

Archaeological evidence of such a labor organization is subtle. Perhaps the most effective demonstration would be to show that the basic contexts of production, within the household and community, were little changed except for an increase in the intensity of work needed to generate the demanded surplus. Data from the Upper Mantaro Valley can be used to address this problem. During the last century prior to the Inka conquest, much of the production for the subsistence economy appears to have taken place within a household context. In the seventeen Wanka II patio groups excavated, production was generalized, as indicated by the distribution of characteristic tools and waste used for agriculture (sickle-gloss blades and hoes), stone tool manufacture (cores and debitage), spinning (whorls), and ceramic manufacture (wasters).

Table 12.1 *Summary of Wanka III production indices*

Site	Household	Status	Hoe density[a]	Waster index[b]	Blade prod. index[c]	Whorl density[d]
Hatunmarca	2=1	elite	0.25	0.09	2.74	7.64
(J2)	2=2	commoner	0.00	0.17	1.62	2.97
	2=3	elite	0.34	0.06	2.20	6.60
	2=5	elite	0.17	0.17	0.71	8.59
Marca (J54)	54=2	commoner	4.72	0.51	0.06	8.76
	54=4	elite	5.83	0.76	0.31	6.19
	54=7	elite	0.91	2.30	0.20	1.18
	54=9	commoner	10.78	0.68	1.05	21.98
	54=10	commoner	5.64	1.22	0.60	7.92
Wankas de la Cruz (J59)	59=1	commoner	1.70	0.07	1.00	0.85
Chucchus	74=1	commoner	8.90	0.00	0.00	3.42
(J74)	74=2	commoner	8.07	0.00	0.00	0.00
Pancan (J1)	n/a	n/a	n/a	0.00	0.50	n/a

[a] *Hoe density:* frequency of hoes/m^3.
[b] *Waster index:* 100 × frequency of wasters/frequency of total sherds.
[c] *Blade production index:* frequency of unused blades/frequency of used blades.
[d] *Whorl density:* frequency of spindle whorls/m^3.

During Wanka III, this pattern of generalized household production continued at some settlements, especially the larger towns such as Marca (J54) and Hatunmarca

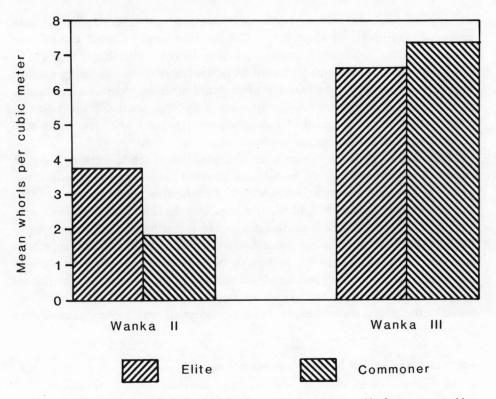

Fig. *12.3*. Standardized counts of spindle whorls by phase and status, represented by frequency per cubic meter excavated. The data are from Costin (1984).

(J2). The possible increase of agricultural activity under the Inkas is hard to document with household evidence. Changes in agriculture dramatically shifted the tools used, from sickle-gloss blades to hoes, indicative of the shift to maize agriculture resulting from state demands and the movement to lower elevation settlements. It is worth noting in this regard that the commoner households in Wanka III yielded a much higher density of hoes than did the elite households (Table 12.1). At present, we hypothesize that this is attributable to a disproportionate levying of agricultural labor duties on the general populace (Russell 1985).

More substantive information is available for the intensification of spinning. Murra (1962; see Diez de San Miguel 1964:39) has described how each family was required to spin and weave a certain amount of cloth as part of its annual corvée labor obligation to the state. In the Mantaro Valley excavations, spindle whorls were commonly recovered from household refuse. Household excavations in Wanka II deposits yielded two to four whorls per cubic meter (Fig. 12.3). The density did not vary markedly among households of the same social status, although elite households had nearly twice the density of whorls as did commoners. This most likely was a result of the production of cloth in elite households for either higher internal use of cloth or broader distribution. During Wanka III, with about seven whorls recovered per cubic meter, spinning activity apparently doubled, with the additional cloth probably mobilized by the state. Note that although both elite and common households experienced an increase in spinning, the larger increase was clearly in commoner households (Wanka II: 1.8 whorls/m³; Wanka III: 7.2 whorls/m³).

The extraction of surplus by requiring increased work within existing social contexts was surely important in Inka finance. However, the state also reorganized labor to centralize control and to guarantee increased income flows. It has been recognized for some time that major shifts of populations were implemented within the Inka empire as a means, among other things, to increase production in prime agricultural areas. These movements of *mitmaqkuna* (internal state-relocated colonists) were often associated with the creation of new agricultural lands through terracing and irrigation. In the region of Huancavelica, just south of our region, some of the relatively low-density, decentralized, indigenous populations were swept away and partly replaced by *mitmaqkuna* (Lavallée and Julien 1983:35–40). The most famous case is that of Cochabamba in Bolivia, a fertile maize producing highland valley (2400–2600 m) located about 800 km southeast of Cuzco. The emperor Wayna Q"apaq removed most of the local population, expropriated all agricultural land in the valley, and subdivided it into strips farmed by temporary multi-ethnic corvée laborers and managed by a permanent *mitmaq* population. The huge maize harvests were then temporarily stored at Cotapachi before being transported by llama caravan to Cuzco where the maize was used to support the state's military personnel (see Wachtel 1982). The scale of this state enterprise is exemplified by the archaeological remains of approximately 2400 storehouses. Such comprehensive restructuring of agricultural production, which has been documented at a lesser scale for Abancay (Espinoza Soriano 1973) and other areas, has recently been described as the development of state farms to support the extensive needs of the empire's military campaigns (La Lone and La Lone 1987).

In the Mantaro Valley, evidence for the reorganization of agricultural labor is less clear, but still suggestive. It is reasonable to assume that the potential productivity of this agriculturally rich zone would have been eyed with considerable interest by the Inkas. In the Wanka II phase, the river plain soils were apparently almost completely abandoned as the populations settled in fortified communities on high ridges, such as those encircling the Yanamarca Valley. This pattern, generated by intense intravalley warfare (Toledo 1940:18, 22, 27–8, 30, 33–4), created a population vacuum in the most productive agricultural areas, and would have provided motivation for resettlement at lower elevations to facilitate intensification of agriculture. At least part of this resettlement was by Cañari, Chachapoya, and Llaguas *mitmaqkuna* (Toledo 1940:22). Irrigation agriculture in this area may also have been expanded at this time (Hastorf and Earle 1985).

Excavations at two Wanka III sites indicate that the state may have established specialized farming villages in areas close to the administrative center and the major storage facilities (Fig. 12.2). Chucchus (J74) was a village of perhaps 1800 people located on the rolling uplands above the Inka administrative center, while Pancan (J1) was a smaller hamlet located on rich maize-producing soils. Analysis of both surface-collected and excavated Wanka III artifacts displays some striking patterns. Standard

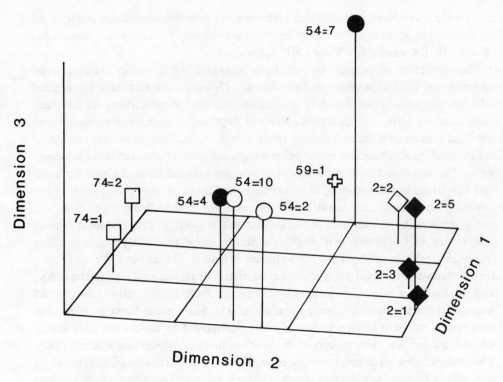

Fig. 12.4. Three-dimensional plot of similarities among Wanka III households, based on production indices. Solid symbols are elite households; open symbols are commoners. J2: diamonds; J54: circles; J59: cross; J74: squares.

household activities are indicated by ceramic vessels used for cooking and storage, grinding stones, and normal flaked tools. Hoe frequency was unusually high at both sites, indicating the importance of agricultural activities. In contrast, evidence for other production activities is remarkably low (Table 12.1). At Chucchus, we recovered virtually no evidence for ceramic or textile manufacture. This suggests that, as agricultural production became intensified at certain villages, other productive activities were reduced. This sort of community labor specialization may be analogous to that of other groups whose members were relieved of general corvée exactions because of their contributions in other kinds of labor, such as masonry construction or textile manufacture (see Julien 1982; LeVine 1987).

In Figures 12.4 and 12.5, we summarize graphically the evidence for agricultural, ceramic, lithic, and textile production at the Wanka III households excavated by UMARP. To generate these two figures, we plotted the relationships among households, based on the production index values in Table 12.1.[3] In these plots, each point represents a single household; distances between points represent the differences between households in overall production activities. In Fig. 12.4, the relationships are shown in three dimensions, while Fig. 12.5 shows only the second and third dimensions of the same relationship. In both figures, it can be seen that the households from each site cluster together, separated primarily along Dimension 2.

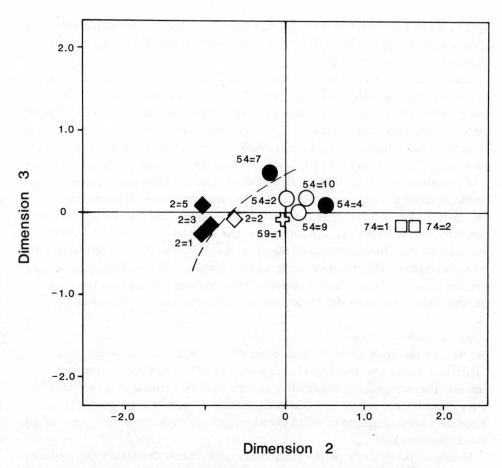

Fig. 12.5. Plot of second and third dimensions of Fig. 12.4, showing distinctions between elite and commoner Wanka households, based on production indices. Solid symbols are elite households; open symbols are commoners. J2: diamonds; J54: circles; J59: cross; J74: squares.

The household clusters grade from J74, through J59 and J54, to J2, with the values for hoe density, whorl density, and blade production primarily responsible for the gradation. From an alternative perspective, the sites simultaneously grade from the lowest to highest in elevation (maize to tubers) and by distance from Hatun Xauxa. The high values of the J54 households along Dimension 3 are a result of a high level of ceramic production. Overall, this plot shows how households within communities were engaged in similar kinds of productive activities and how production activities differed among communities. (It should be noted that household J54=9 is not included in this plot, because it is an outlier with respect to both hoe density and whorl density; see Table 12.1.)

The plot shown in Fig. 12.5 allows us to separate the elite from the commoner households. With the exception of household J54=4, the elite households lie above and to the left of the dashed line. The separation of the elite from commoner here is clearly a reflection of the relative participation of members of the two statuses in maize agriculture. With respect to J54=4, it may be the case that our *a priori* architectural classification was in error or that the residents were unusually heavily involved in production for an elite group.

This evidence for production suggests that, in the Mantaro Valley, the Inkas mobilized surplus both indirectly, through corvée labor requirements levied on communities and constituent households, and directly, by creating small specialized farming communities producing for the state. This raises a key question: how and at what level were decisions made concerning the organization of labor within the province? While the data on this issue are scarce for the Mantaro region, LeVine's (1987) analysis of a detailed inspection of the Huánuco region about 250 km to the north (Ortiz de Zúñiga 1967) shows that the native lords were intimately involved in the mobilization of labor both for production of goods and provision of services. Similarly, the Wanka elites' assignment to state decimal offices and their ability to maintain the state storage system for about twenty years after the Inka demise indicate great familiarity with the state staple finance system. The reorganization of agricultural labor in the Mantaro is therefore part of what we see as a more general imperial strategy to exert direct controls over highly productive core areas.

The management of surplus

As well as the Inka labor taxation program was organized, it would have been ineffectual unless the goods produced were available when and where they were needed. The storage and transportation systems were thus critical to the success of the state staple finance system. Because both of these aspects of Inka logistical organization have been examined in detail elsewhere, we will summarize only some of the major elements here.

Hyslop's (1984) study of the road system documents the state's extraordinary exertions in integrating already extant transport routes and in constructing new roads. Over 30,000 kilometers of road were tied together, based on the two major parallel highways along the coast and the spine of the Andes and a series of cross routes joining them (Fig. 12. 1). The system provided benefits in communication and transportation of goods and personnel, as well as significant advantages for the military. Reports of the state's transport of goods over long distances along this network have drawn considerable attention. Peasants' testimony in early Spanish inspections recounted numerous examples of long-distance transport of staple goods and sumptuary raw materials and finished products, both by llama caravan and human porter (e.g. Diez de San Miguel 1964:81, 92, 116; Ortiz de Zúñiga 1967: 37, 47, 59). The most remarkable example of the movement of staple goods was the previously mentioned llama transport of maize from Cochabamba, Bolivia, to support Wayna Q"apaq's military personnel in Cuzco. The movement of sumptuary materials to and from Cuzco was also a central feature of the political economy, since ceremonial consumption was high and goods redistributed from Cuzco gained considerably in importance (Morris 1986:64).

The Inka willingness to move goods has led to the perception that somehow the state was not affected by cost-benefit calculations in its economic activities (e.g. Murra

1985:200). We feel, to the contrary, that several lines of evidence suggest that the Inkas worked out a balance between the costs of investment and security of control in the state political economy. The state's shift toward a high cost/high control strategy of labor organization, as described above, is indicative of this kind of determination. A similar conclusion may be drawn from the fact that the state seems to have calculated much of its labor tax based on needed output in material goods, such as food and cloth (e.g. Diez de San Miguel 1964:31, 39, 92; see D'Altroy and Earle 1985:190).

Analysis of the massive state storage system also provides insight into the logistics of the staple finance system and state considerations of costs and benefits (see Morris 1967, 1982, 1986). The Inkas mobilized massive amounts of goods that were stored locally and regionally to support imperial activities, including maintenance of full-time state personnel, such as administrators, religious staff, and craft specialists at provincial centers; part-time workers, such as corvée laborers; itinerant state personnel; and the military. The storage system was a key element in the Inka hard-point military strategy, which depended on containment and massive retaliation. Food, utilitarian items, and craft goods were stored in such huge quantities that the Spaniards were repeatedly amazed at the volume and variety at the state's disposal (e.g. Cieza del León 1984;xliii:143–4).

With respect to storage, the agriculturally rich and centrally located Mantaro Valley was critical to Inka imperial strategies. At present, we know of roughly 3000 storage structures within the valley, distributed among about fifty complexes. The approximately 2000 structures in the northern half of the valley, which corresponds to UMARP's research area, had the capacity to hold in excess of 120,000 m³ of food and other goods (for details, see D'Altroy 1981; Earle and D'Altroy 1982; D'Altroy and Hastorf 1984). About half of the storehouses were concentrated in a few complexes within one kilometer of Hatun Xauxa, with the remainder scattered throughout the valley, in smaller facilities (Fig. 12.2). Buildings were laid out in neat rows that followed the contours of the hillslopes on which they were placed. The storehouses, which were either rectangular or circular in floor plan, were usually arranged in groups according to shape. As Morris (1967) has suggested, these arrangements were probably designed to facilitate accounting conventions.

While the size of storage complexes ranged from 8 structures with an estimated total volume of 313 m³ (J30), to 479 structures with a volume of 27,075 m³ (J17; Fig. 12.6), the buildings themselves were extremely standardized architecturally within sites and often between them. For instance, measurement of the interior diameters of a random sample of structures with circular floor plans at J16 and J17 yielded means of 4.74 m (s=0.50 m; N=22) and 4.46 m (s=0.77 m; N=29), respectively. Interior measurements of rectangular buildings at the same sites yielded lengths of 5.88 m (s=0.65 m; N=27) at J16 and 6.24 m (s=1.40 m; N=23) at J17, with widths of 3.26 (s=0.43) and 3.12 m (0.38 m), respectively (D'Altroy 1981:481–6; D'Altroy and Hastorf 1984:338). For the entire study region, we estimate mean volumes (based on an estimated height of 3.5 m to roofline) for structures with circular floor plans to have been about 52 m³ and, for rectangular structures, about 71 m³.

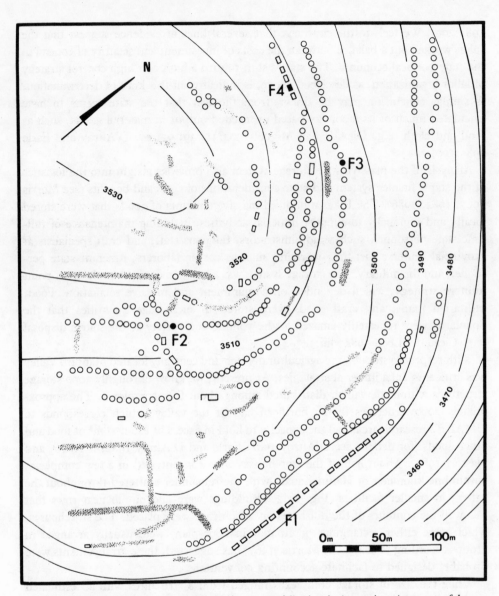

Fig. 12.6. State storage site J17, showing lines of structures following the (approximate) contours of the hillslope. Structures F1–F4 were excavated.

The distribution of these storehouses provides some insight into the political economy. First, central concentration of stored goods seems to have been an over-riding concern for the state. Several advantages accrued to this organization, whose relative importance is still unclear. In the Upper Mantaro and Huánuco to the north, by far the majority of the goods were apparently intended for use at the provincial centers. Growing, crafting, and storing goods near the center thus kept the costs of the transport of goods to a minimum at the same time that it ensured security. Second, the concentration at nodes along the road network ensured that goods could be drawn on by the military for billeting, for nearby ventures, or for transport to other locations. Third, the storehouses were dispersed throughout the northern part of the Mantaro Valley such that the amount of storage space available was inversely proportional to the log of the distance from the capital (Earle and D'Altroy 1982:284). This implies either that the costs of transportation to final point of consumption were significant in the state's distribution of the storage facilities, or that the state's control over production decreased as a function of distance from the provincial center. These last two points, of course, are not mutually exclusive.

What is clear from the organization of the transportation and storage aspects of the Inka political economy is that the state was willing to invest vast amounts of peasant labor throughout the empire in a strategy of increasing control over time. However, that investment was differentially applied across space, so that the Inkas' capacity to mobilize the products of their staple finance system varied a great deal even within the most intensively incorporated provinces of the empire.

The organization of exchange

Many researchers see an intimate link between the expansion of exchange and state formation. It has been argued, for example, that states either were required to maintain a regional peace for expanding exchange (Sanders 1957) or created the regional peace that permitted the growth of markets. Alternatively, markets have been seen as part of a state's financial strategy to convert a currency used in payment for services into staple products (Brumfiel 1980). In the Andes, however, it has been persuasively argued from historical data that markets did not exist to any appreciable extent in the central area (Murra 1980; La Lone 1982). This was possible, of course, to the degree that state activities were diversified and personnel working for the state could be supported directly by mobilized staples.

The recent archaeological data collected by UMARP support the ethnohistoric argument that market exchange in subsistence or utilitarian goods was comparatively unimportant in the Mantaro Valley, although some intercommunity exchange did occur in goods of specialized manufacture. Despite the enforced peace introduced by the imposition of the Inka state, the amount of goods exchanged apparently changed very little from Wanka II to III. In order to record the extent of exchange archaeologically, we have argued elsewhere for a simple quantification by percent of assemblages, according to the distance that material moved from its probable source to its final resting spot in a settlement's refuse (Earle 1985). For analytical purposes, the assemblages from the Mantaro were divided into staple goods (plant and animal products), tools and implements (lithics, ceramics), and wealth objects (especially metal and shell used in decoration). Distance from source was represented simply according to three zones of procurement, each potentially associated with different mechanisms of exchange: 1) local procurement (<10 km) permitting either direct access by a household or simple reciprocal exchange with other households in its community or an immediately neighboring community; 2) regional exchange (10–50 km), probably employing fairly simple down-the-line exchange, perhaps involving organized intercommunity expeditions or trade events; and 3) long-distance exchange

Table 12.2 *Summary of rough percentages of materials, based on weights, according to distance from source. In parentheses are the changes from Wanka II to Wanka III*

	Local < 10 km (WII–WIII)	Regional 10–50 km (WII–WIII)	Long-distance > 50 km (WII–WIII)
Food goods	90[a]	10	trace
Lithics	83 (79–86)	17 (14–21)	trace
Ceramics	60 (53–67) 0–50 km = 31	6 (5–6) (22–39)	4 (3–5)
Metals	0	80[b] (70–100)	20 (0–30)
Shell	0	0	100
Stone goodies	9 (4–22)	90 (78–96)	0

[a] At present, these figures are estimates of magnitude.
[b] From Earle (1985).

(>50 km), requiring exchange across several territorial divisions and characteristically involving some entrepreneurial or administered activity.

As seen clearly in Table 12.2, most goods other than wealth goods were almost certainly obtained locally or at least regionally. Virtually all foods were locally procured and most implements were also so obtained. This is not to say that exchange was non-existent, only that it was highly localized. Most interestingly, the amount of goods exchanged changed remarkably little from Wanka II to Wanka III. The only significant change appears to be in the amount of regionally traded ceramics, especially the Inka pottery that was produced and distributed under direct state supervision, discussed below (Costin 1986; D'Altroy and Bishop n.d.).

The localized production of agricultural goods is supported by three lines of evidence. First, predictions of catchment productivity for each site in the study region corresponded very closely to botanical remains recovered in excavations for both Wanka II and III (Hastorf 1983). Second, changes in bone isotope ratios indicate a shift from a diet heavy in tuber complex crops to maize complex crops from Wanka II to III (Hastorf and DeNiro 1985). This change in diet corresponds to the shift in settlement pattern, under Inka rule, from the tuber production areas to maize areas. Third, virtually no remains were recovered from plants, such as capsicum pepper or fruits, known to have come from lower elevations. Local production of ceramics is supported by (1) stylistic differences between Yanamarca Valley ceramics and those farther south in the Mantaro Valley, (2) differences in the styles and fabrics of ceramics used by local settlement groups within the Yanamarca itself, and (3) concentrations of wasters (overfired sherds) at Wanka communities (LeBlanc 1981; Costin 1986). Similarly, analysis of the ratios of finished lithic tools to manufacturing waste demonstrates that chert-blade tools were produced by a couple of Wanka communities near a major quarry and then exchanged to neighbors both prior to and under the Inkas (Russell 1985). Except for the odd blade, chert from this source rarely moved beyond 15 km.

Changes in exchange patterns from Wanka II to III were very subtle and it can be argued that the state strategically discouraged any expansion in exchange in an effort to maintain close control. Without a market system, a local group would have been dependent on the state to obtain products not produced within its community boundaries. This was offset by allowing communities to establish distant colonies to procure needed products, but would still have made the community heavily dependent on the state for status objects obtained from a distance. In addition, the minimization of intercommunity exchange would also have made it practical to isolate communities and thus reduce chances for large-scale rebellions. Ethnic differences were emphasized by the state, and a pragmatic divide-and-rule philosophy was a central precept in Inka statecraft. In this light, the evidence for no change or even a reduction in exchanged products makes sense, *despite* the apparent increased opportunities for exchange that would be an expected outcome of the stable and prolonged peace.

Manipulation of the sociopolitical ideology

As alluded to earlier, the Inkas employed various techniques to legitimize their rule and culturally integrate subject populations (see Rowe 1982), in the process reducing the threat of rebellion and the costs of administration. One approach was to incorporate the religions of their subjects into the state religion, in part by transporting sacred objects to Cuzco where they were held as venerated hostages. The enculturation of the sons of provincial elites at Cuzco also served to increase allegiance to the central powers. But perhaps the most effective tactic was to control the production and distribution of goods that signalled both the status of the owner and his affiliation with the empire. To this end, vast quantities of raw materials and craft goods, from feathers and *Spondylus* shell to precious metals and stones, were shipped to Cuzco for redistribution (see Morris 1986). Cloth, often manufactured by specialists, played a central role in political ceremony and status legitimation (Murra 1962). Because cloth does not preserve well in most archaeological contexts, however, we have to rely on other materials to address the problems of state activities in this area of the political economy.

In the Mantaro Valley, both prior to and under Inka rule, Wanka elite households were clearly distinguished archaeologically by the concentration in their refuse of long-distance trade items (e.g. ocean shell), metal (silver and copper), and high-status ceramic forms (e.g. Inka state vessels). Such objects were items of wealth important in status display and a wide range of social and political exchanges. In the century before the Inka conquest, elite households characteristically had more wealth objects than did commoners. This concentration may be measured archaeologically by tabulating the percentage of excavated proveniences with a certain class of objects (*ubiquity*) (Monk and Fasham 1980). As seen in Table 12.3, ubiquity for silver and copper in elite households is two and five times that in commoner contexts, respectively.

Under Inka domination (Wanka III), elite households continued to be distinguished, but the goods changed in ways indicative of a state impact on the Wanka political economy and status legitimation. In the case of metals (Table 12.3), the relative advantage of elite households remained largely unchanged, but silver became scarcer overall at the same time that the amount of copper increased significantly and lead remained little changed. The change in the relative abundance of silver and lead provides insight into the Inkas' effects on the production and consumption of status goods. Silver, used exclusively in such objects of display as pins and disks sewn onto clothing, was identified symbolically in the Andes with the moon, a major deity (Lechtman 1984). This metal probably identified elite status and legitimized social inequality as a part of a religiously sanctioned natural order. In contrast, lead was used for such comparatively trivial objects as *bola* weights and pot mends. Because its menial uses would not have justified the complicated procedures needed to smelt it from galena, a sulfide ore, lead is most likely to have been procured as a waste product of silver manufacture. Its frequency in Wanka III contexts suggests a slight increase in the intensity of silver manufacture from Wanka II to Wanka III at the same time that local silver consumption declined by half. The obvious inference is that locally produced silver – so important in status display and legitimation – was being removed by the state. The continued concentration of silver in elite households, however, suggests either that Wanka elites had access to their own mines (see Berthelot 1986) or that the Inkas granted Wanka lords silver objects as part of the insignia of status.

Table 12.3 *Ubiquities of silver, copper, and lead by status and period*[a]

	Silver	Copper	Lead
Wanka II			
elite	4.3	2.1	0.8
commoner	0.8	1.0	0.5
Wanka III			
elite	2.2	12.1	0.8
commoner	0.5	4.5	1.0

[a] From Owen (1986: Table 6).

Changes in the distribution of lead may provide some insight into the Inka use of labor in subject communities. At the same time that the ubiquity of silver dropped about 50 per cent in Wanka III, there was a doubling of the number of proveniences with lead in commoner households (Table 12.3). Wanka III commoner households thus show a higher ubiquity of lead than do elite households, while the reverse was true prior to the Inka conquest. Because metallurgical waste was rarely recovered in our excavations, we believe that production took place off site. While the presence of lead does not, therefore, indicate locations of manufacture, it does probably indicate involvement in the production process. The increase in lead in commoner households could be indicative of their work in smelting as the close control over metals production by the local elites broke down.

The dramatic increase in use of copper under Inka domination involved many display objects (pins, pendants, and disks) that appear to have partially replaced the elite silver items made in local context. As was true throughout the empire generally (Lechtman 1984), the Wanka III copper objects are actually a tin bronze (Owen 1986), in contrast to the arsenic bronzes of Wanka II. Since tin is not available locally (its nearest sources were apparently in southern Peru and Bolivia), it must have been obtained through long-distance exchange. Tin was, in fact, the only durable, long-distance exchange good that seems to have been imported into the Upper Mantaro in amounts significantly above pre-Inka levels. Because tin bronze was found throughout the empire and because the shift to its use was sudden, it is probable that its production was introduced by the Inkas, who would have controlled manufacture by regulating the distribution of the tin.

With respect to ceramics, the locally produced decorated pottery styles ceased to distinguish elite status. They were found in essentially equal mean densities in both elite and commoner contexts (Earle and Costin 1986). The only ceramics to differentiate the elites symbolically were the standardized Inka vessels manufactured by state workshops and most probably distributed by the state, perhaps at special feasting ceremonies periodically held at the administrative centers (Morris 1982). Trace element characterization of Inka and Wanka ceramics from the UMARP study area shows that the state apparently controlled the production of its pottery and that Wanka access to state vessels may have varied along both social and spatial lines (D'Altroy and Costin 1983; D'Altroy and Bishop n.d.). Inka pottery in the UMARP study region was produced from at least two sources that were both internally homogeneous and distinct from the local pottery. However, the distribution of the ceramics from these sources corresponds best to spatial groupings in the region, *not* to distinctions between Inka and Wanka settlements. Residents of some Wanka settlements, such as Marca, were receiving most of their Inka ceramics from the same source as that which provided the provincial capital with its pottery. Other settlements, such as Hatunmarca, got their state vessels primarily from another source. While these studies are only an early step in reconstructing state–local interaction, they do suggest that the relationships were intricate and pervasive.

The adoption of Inka status markers by Wanka elites is seen further in a shift in architectural style. In Wanka II, virtually all structures were circular stone structures typical of the central highlands. Differences between elite and commoner housing lay primarily in the fineness of the masonry and the size and number of buildings in residential compounds. In Wanka III, while commoner housing continued largely unchanged, elites began building larger rectangular structures with trapezoidal niches in direct imitation of the Inka architectural style.

To summarize, eliteness among the Wanka had, prior to Inka conquest, been signalled in part by items of local symbolic significance, the manufacture of which could have been handled simply by specialists attached to elite households. Following conquest, however, eliteness became marked by reference to Inka imperial style and by access to goods of imperial manufacture. Social inequality became legitimized not by local referents but by identification with the dominant imperial order. At the very least, the state exerted considerable economic control over the local status systems by controlling the manufacture of state ceramics directly and by manipulating metal production.

Conclusions

The Inka empire was financed by massive quantities of staple goods mobilized from its support population. In the Mantaro Valley, a rich agricultural zone centrally located on the imperial road system, this mobilization involved both a surplus generated from Wanka communities and a partial but important reorganization of labor. The reorganization of some of the populace into specialized agricultural communities may have been quite common, especially later in the empire's history as it became important to consolidate control within the central regions of the empire so as to increase productivity.

In contrast, reorganization of exchange in subsistence and utilitarian goods appears to have been unimportant probably because of the widespread imperial institutions that could rely on local systems of production for support. Archaeologically, we can recognize some changes in the sumptuary aspects of the political economy, notably in the production and distribution of metals and fancy ceramics. Silver was removed from local use, probably to be moved to the capital Cuzco, and tin, used in bronze, was distributed throughout the empire for manufacture of status objects and metal tools. The production of ceramics made in the imperial style was controlled by the state and their distribution, while widespread within the province, seems to have been carefully controlled as well. These changes suggest a purposeful control over the production and distribution of wealth that permitted some measure of imperial control over local political and social relationships.

The Inka empire's remarkable success thus depended on a flexible but at times intense intervention into the many economies that it dominated. Alongside the extensive data obtained through documentary analyses, archaeology is now providing critical information for studying the details of how this incorporation was carved out.

Notes

1 We would like to thank our colleagues on the Upper Mantaro Archaeological Research Project – co-principal investigator Christine Hastorf, Cathy Costin, Glenn Russell, and Bruce Owen – who provided many of the previously unpublished data on plant use, spinning and ceramics, lithics, and metals, respectively. Glenn assisted particularly in the creation of Table 12.1. We are also grateful to Terry LeVine for comments on an early draft of the chapter. Gregory Ruf and Walter Bourne assisted in the preparation of Figs. 12.1 and 12.4, respectively. Additional thanks go to the Instituto Nacional de Cultura in Lima, Peru, which granted permission to conduct the field research, and to the students from San Marcos and Trujillo Universities, who assisted in the field and laboratory research. The Mantaro Valley research has been supported principally by a grant from the National Science Foundation (grant No. BNS 82 03723), with additional funding for the junior author being provided by the Columbia Council on the Social Sciences.

2 Translated from Toledo (1940:19–20).

3 The production index values in Table 12.1 were used to create a Euclidean correlation coefficient matrix, using the Minkowski metric in the SAS procedure PROX. This matrix was then used as input into the SAS multidimensional scaling procedure ALSCAL, using Kruskal's (1964) least-squares monotonic transformation (Joyner 1983). A Euclidean distance model was used to generate the distances between points. The dimensions in Fig. 12.4 have been rotated for maximal visibility of the separation of sites.

13

An epigenetic view of the Harappan culture

W. A. FAIRSERVIS

The Harappan civilization first became known during the early part of the twentieth century because of the discovery of two urban sites, Harappa and Mohenjo Daro, by the members of the Archaeological Survey of India. Its character was amplified by subsequent surveys and excavation by Majumdar (1934) and Mackay (1938:II, 1943). All of this work took place during the last years of the British Raj. In consequence, interpretations of the Indus civilization largely rested with the British archaeologists, Marshall (1931) and Mackay (1948). At the close of World War II and the departure of the British from rulership on the subcontinent, Wheeler (1953, 1968a), Piggott (1950b), Gordon (1958), and Childe (1952) (some of whose experience was of the Raj) were the new interpreters. From the very first discovery of the age and apparent character of the Indus civilization, starting with Marshall's clarion call to Meso-potamian archaeologists for help in identifying the time and relationships of the ancient culture, up to the death of Wheeler in 1975, the model used in representing the style of Harappan culture has been that of Near Eastern and Classical civilization. Thus Piggott wrote of a state with twin capitals. Childe described empire, and Wheeler's labels, such as "citadel," "serried ranks of coolies," evoked despotic monarchy.

Archaeological research in India and Pakistan since World War II has both extended and amplified our knowledge of the Harappans. So much so that we are now in a position to review the older model and in consequence construct a newer model, or at the least modify the older one. To do this, however, there is a constraint in the interpretation of the term *civilization* which is not simply a matter of semantics.

The model of civilization which emerges from the study of the indigenous or primary civilizations of the Old World is manifestly a two-stage affair. The first stage is largely a socioeconomic-technological one, which sees control over natural resources by increasingly complex and centralizing societies. This consequence of a cycle of technological innovation, resource exploitation, and social challenge, becomes more and more institutionalized as communities cluster, subsistence and other resource sources amplify to create surpluses by which non-subsistence populations are main-tained and the coherence of a substantive redistributional system necessitated, then insured. The coherence vital to the well-being of these communities is instrumented initially by sodality cooperation and moves to controls by class with lineage preference gained by the need for successful leadership on the one side and the acquisition of power through wealth and authoritarian charisma on the other. Ideologically the taxonomic classification of the cosmos via the creation of pantheistic world views rooted in the natural vulnerabilities and advantages of sedentism moves to include secular leadership and thus the emergence of monarchies of divine or semi-divine character. With this the sacred city, one acknowledging by ritual a patron deity (or deities), is institutionalized and serves the polity. What is particularly significant to this primary stage of civilization is the elaboration of graphic symbolism which permits an acceleration of sophistication in record-keeping (from tokens to written sign) with an efficient system of numeration. Accompanying this are systems of naming which evolve from the "his mark" stage to one where either by elaborated iconography or more importantly via largely rebus principles of syllabization the individual is named; this for purposes of identifying ownership or station. Standardization of weights and measures, high-level craftsmanship, functional graphic expression, and a substantive bureaucracy lucidly mark this level. It is demonstrated in most of its aspects in the Proto-Literate and the early phases of Early Dynastic Sumer, the Gerzean – Early Archaic developments in Egypt, and the San Dai in early China.

Economic determinism, which has today replaced British classicism (largely owing to Marx and Western exponents of market-oriented cultural development), has made trade and the identification of the proprietors and profiteers of production critical in the judgment of the occurrence and character of this stage of civilization. This emphasis is amplified by international eagerness to convert artifacts and settlement, and thus human behavior, to data which provide for complex manipulation commensurate, it would appear, with the subject. The computer age reinforces this approach. However, the study of culture as much as the study of history minimizes quantitative methodologies, or ought to. At the very most, economic determinism has its value only in the case of the first stages in the development of civilization.

It is the second stage which is most clearly the determinant of civilization, for certainly numerous societies reached the first stage in one way or another and went no further. The second stage is characterized by the appearance of higher abstract thought, with great consequences in the development of human cognition. Significantly this stage appears during, or as a consequence of, a period of trouble in which warfare has a significant part. The concern is for the human condition when the order of society is changed, threatened or broken down. The question of personal and social identity and the relationship of people to nature, whether in terms of deism, metaphysics or ethical principle, is the common theme. With this comes the development of literature and science as the writing system becomes logo-syllabic, since the relationship of writing to language is graphically implemented. Syntax is utilized and the resulting clarity of written expression creates a memory bank which provides for historical records, didactic literature, scientific or subjective observations of nature, and even of jurisprudence, and has the advantage of a developmental feedback into the advances of the first stage. An aesthetic style reflective of abstract conceptions also emerges, as does urbanization involving state polities, imperialism, and sophisticated market economies and a densely populated residential area. This second stage is necessary to confirm the altruism by which the term "to be civilized" is best defined.

It is demonstrated in Old Kingdom Egypt with conceptions of a pharaonic moral order, ma'at; in late Early Dynastic Sumer with the appearance of law codes and the speculations apparent in the Epic of Gilgamesh and other such accounts; in China with the developments in the Chou that led to the ethical concerns of Confucius, Mencius, and Mo-Ti and the religious concepts of Lao-tzu and Chuang-tzu.

With the above two-stage model of primary early civilization we have a standard by which to measure the candidacy of Harappan culture as a civilization. The evidence we do have is largely archaeological (Allchin and Allchin 1982: 131–228), but a vital element can now be added because of significant understanding at this date of the Harappan writing system.[1] Several salient features are immediately obvious.

(1) Recent work in the Indus River Valley, the presumed homeland of the Harappans, particularly by the French at Mehrgarh (Jarrige and Lechevallier 1979) and Naushauro but supported in general by surveys and excavations elsewhere, evidences that the Harappan culture was the result of a long indigenous development. The Harappan cultural style, as Kroeber (1948) defined style, is unique to that culture but it is the consequence of that development.

(2) Though there is evidence for possible ethnic variety within the boundaries of the Harappan world in general there appears to be a compelling uniformity of the Harappan style wherever it occurs.

(3) Harappan sites usually demonstrate short periods of occupation, less than 150 years. Even the "urban" sites were probably occupied for less than 300 years.

(4) Harappan sites are found all over Western Indo-Pakistan from the vicinity of Delhi to the proximity of the western Narbada river drainage.

(5) Harappan sites, as a whole, are located close to rivers and streams but in a variety of ecological settings.

(6) With considerable certainty it can be said that the Harappan core language was a form of early Dravidian with, however, lexemes from Indo-Aryan and probably some substratum tongues (Fairservis and Southworth 1986).

With these characteristic features as background we can proceed to examine Harappan culture in some detail.

There appears to have been a basic myth critical to Harappan polity (Fig. 13.1). A Herculean male of Gilgamesh form, sometimes referred to as "Kavir" or "Seizer of Two" (tigers) impregnates a female named "Ambara." Their union results in the birth of a "mutali" or "first paramount chief." The chiefdom thereby had a divine or semi-divine origin. The paramount chief was referred to as "Tōn-nel Piran" or "Lord of the Harvest," and as "An-il Piran" or "The High-placed Lord." As such, he was dominant over the sodalities which characterized Harappan social organization. These sodalities were likely totemic clans divided into two moieties. One of these was represented by domestic or semi-domestic animals: zebu, gaur, bovid bull, goat; the other by wild and often dangerous animals: rhinoceros, elephant, buffalo and tiger. Inter-moiety marriage was common.

The evidence suggests that the so-called seals of the Harappans, while occasionally used for stamping, had a prime function as a marriage badge, or tāli. More than 95 percent of all these "seals" were found in habitational debris, strongly suggesting that

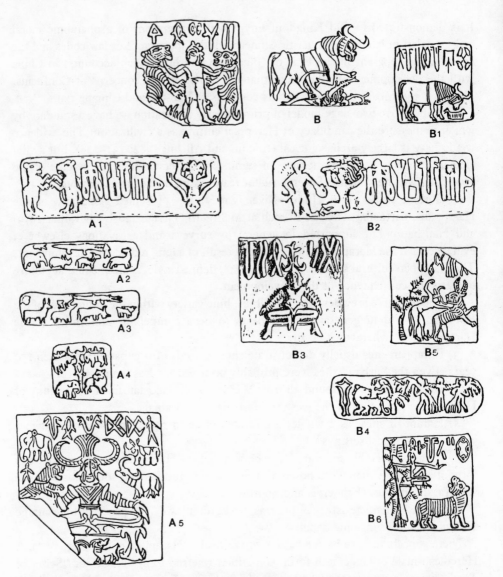

Fig. 13.1. Origin of the Harappan chiefs. There are two aspects to the presumed founder of the Harappan chiefdom, the Herculean hero (A) and the powerful gaur (B).

For the first aspect we can trace the hero grasping two tigers on the bar "seal" (A1-B2). Here the hero has apparently impregnated a female who bears him a gavial (A1). The inscription reads "Ambara mag aṇ-il toṇ-nel kāvaḍi(y)āl," or "Ambara, Child of the High-Placed Guardian of the Harvest." The gavial is seen on the prism (A2-A3) (the third side is not shown due to its poor condition). In A2 the gavial is depicted above the wild animals: elephant, rhino, buffalo and tiger. At his jaw is the twist sign meaning "pir" or "chief." On the A3 side the gavial is shown above the domesticated or semi-domesticated animals: zebu, "unicorn" bull, gaur and goat. The gavial is a homophone for "paramount chief," "mutali." He is sometimes shown with horns when with the wild animals as in A4. As paramount chief he is known as "Aṇ-il Piraṇ," "The High-placed Lord" (A5), and is shown with a gaur crown seated on a dais amid the wild or dangerous animals which represent sodalities or clans, for which they are totemic.

As gaur (B – B1) he impregnates a female who wears a floral crown.[2] She is seen seated before the Herculean hero (B2). The inscription, identical with that on the A1 side, indicates that "Ambara" or "Arambu" was the daughter of the hero as well, probably as his consort. The floral crown appears on a chief they were common attributes of household activity. In addition, while some "seals" show considerable wear, a majority are fresh in character which would not occur if the steatite of which they were manufactured was regularly dipped in moist clay. The "seals" normally have a boss at the back which was pierced to hold a suspension cord.

Marriage, as one of the most important aspects of interfamilial and interclan relationships, has much ethnohistorical documentation and no less so with the Harappans. Aspects of the wedding are depicted and have ready parallels in ethnography (Fig. 13.2). There was a wedding procession with individuals carrying the involved totemic standards, ribboned poles, and the wedding post. The last, a common motif of the "seals," consists of a basin and above it a filter or basket cover, both connected by a central pole. The wedding ceremony took place under a pandal of pipal leaves and branches. The groom stood in the midst of that shed wearing a buffalo or gaur horn headdress, and before him the bride, wearing a nearly identical crown, knelt. She offered a goat to her groom, and other offerings made to one or another were heaped on a low table in the wedding place. Auspicious signs like the swastika and the endless knot were placed here and there. The proof of the woman's new status was the presentation to her of the tāli, which was to be worn on her person.

The tāli characteristically has two motifs; the totemic animal representing the groom's sodality or of the joining of sodalities, symbolized by the so-called "mythological" animals (where an elephant's trunk is attached to a bull-bovid, and so on); the second motif was a written statement of the groom's name, occupation and place in the Harappan geography. This statement consists of conventions of title regularly represented in the "seals" and the more specific identity of the individual involved. From these statements we learn a great deal about Harappan social and political organization.

The Harappan leadership was that of chiefs or "pirs" organized into a political unity: the "vēlir" or "velāra." These chiefs in turn were divided into "talpirs", or head chiefs, a title applicable to the leader of a settlement, "marupir" or "margh-pir," literally "horned chiefs," most probably priests or ritual leaders; "acci(accu)pir" or elder, and ordinary chiefs, "pirs." Where a number of "seals" are found on a site all of these chiefs are usually represented. In some cases we learn from the correlation of "talpirs" with the other "pirs" that there were head chiefs in each category of chief.

Beneath these leaders were the "kāvadi(y)ār" or administrators whose job was to implement or guard the affairs of the settlement. Among their tasks was the control of storage. To obtain a substantive image of Harappan storage and its administration it is important to consider both the characteristic settlement patterns and the economic emphases.

There is modern evidence for a wet and dry season agricultural year.[3] The dry season runs for about nine months, from September to May. It is the time for the

(B3) known as "Pir-a Nīraṇ," or literally "Chief of water." He is seated on a dais with bovid legs.

In B4 the Herculean hero confronts two "giants" who have torn up acacia trees, which are associated with a bovid female who taunts tigers. This figure is represented in several forms, B4, B5, and B6. In B5 the small pot to the left of the tiger is homophonic to words meaning "to destroy," (caṭṭu-caṭṭu), and the implication is clear.

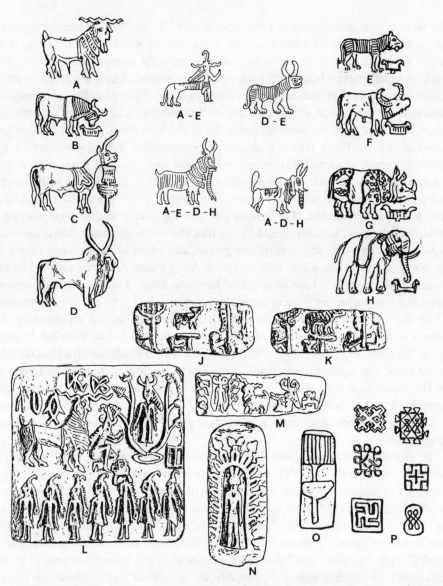

Fig. 13.2. Harappan chiefdoms. The marriage and wedding evidence critical to the cohesiveness of Harappan chiefdom(s) was the relationship of the totemic sodalities which fall into a moiety: the domestic animals (AD), the wild or dangerous animals (EH). Marriage was arranged via specific intermoiety clans or according to phratry. For example, ram (A) to tiger (E); tiger (E) to zebu (D) or ram–tiger–zebu–elephant (A-E-D-H); or ram–zebu–elephant (A-D-H).

The wedding itself involved a procession (JK) with the marriage pole (O) and the totemic emblems. Sacrificial or gift animals were decorated by painting or decked with collars or cloths (A,C,H). The wedding ceremony (L) included the presence of women decorated with peacock-feather headdresses; a sacrificial or gift animal (A in this example); the bride wearing a floral crown as in the myth (Fig. 13.1) or a gaur crown (M) knelt before the groom, who wears the gaur crown, and who stands in a pandal (N). An offering table (L, M) was also involved. Auspicious signs were employed (P). The relationship to the myth (Fig. 13.1) and statements of invocation as in the offering "aya" (L – tray above woman on extreme right) indicate the religious nature of the joining of the sodalities through marriage. The seals (A-D, E-H) are "tāli" or statements of the marriage contract.

growth, cultivation, and harvest of the grain crops, wheat and barley. In the monsoonal summer, from June to September, cotton and sesamum were cultivated. In each season garden keeping was practiced. The plow and the harrow are attested. Storage of grain and cotton was in baskets as a rule. These basket containers were of standard size based on a precise knowledge of measurement that in the economic sector marks the Harappan style.[4]

The Harappans used a base-eight in the number system. The signs involved cumulative strokes through seven and a rebus symbolism for numbers from eight through ten. The latter number was represented by the harrow ("pala"), meaning many or ten.

The lunar year was probably recorded through a mechanism akin to an abacus. By sliding grooved ivory or wooden pieces along cords according to a noon-to-noon daily sequence the lunar month was traced. Intercalary days were included to bring the lunar year in line with the solar (Fairservis 1977).

The cubit (c. 20″) was the standard of linear measurement and was used as a measure of capacity in the case of storage. The storage basket had a linear height of one cubit and its diameter was three-quarters of a cubit. At Harappa a large number of stone tokens have been found. These are small objects (1 inch by ½–¾ inches by ¼–¾ inches) with the name of the individual token owner, or the commodity involved (or both) on one side and on the other the basket measure established in units from one to four. One can envision record keeping by which individuals left (or gave) in storage so many cubit baskets of a given commodity and received (or gave) tokens as statements of account. This principle is also signified by the small clay carts which, rather than the playthings which they are regularly labelled, were simply tokens used to account for so many "carts-full." This was established either by using the individual model carts as tokens or by clay bicones (or balls) tossed into baskets; so many bicones – so many carts-full.

Copper was a valued commodity and was measured by weight. It had, however, its own scale known probably as "kor" and was marked by incising fingernail-like crescents into the metal object. Measurement by weight of small amounts of a commodity (spices, rare stones and metals, and so on) were on a two-pan scale with standardized square stone weights arranged in an essentially binary system.

This emphasis upon precision is also manifest in the system of drains, sluices and wells characteristic of Harappan sites, as well as in the construction of brick platforms and superimposed structures found at the "urban" sites. Indeed the "seals" with text and main motifs set in carefully arranged and aesthetically pleasant order also mark the Harappan obsession with exactitude. In this phenomenon there is little reason to doubt that a powerful centralization was at work. Wheeler's (1968a) determination of granaries at Harappa and Mohenjo Daro, the possibility of their presence at Lothal (Rao 1973), Kalibangan (Thapar 1973), Ganweriwala (Mughal 1982: 92) and Allahdino (Fairservis 1982: 107), supports the notion of a substantive redistributional system which reinforced chiefly authority both at the local level and in the case of the paramount chiefs interregionally. The evidence for a reasonably complex bureaucracy confirms this notion.

Occupational variety is attested for the Harappan and includes, in addition to the "vēlir" and the "kāvadiyar", scribes, herdsmen, hydraulic engineers, hunters, metal smiths, fishermen, captains of boats, architects/builders, potters, weavers, measurers (recorders), cotton and grain growers, and so on.

There is a good possibility that the Harappans invented the windmill, but though they built dams or kach basins in the Kohistan they appear not to have developed irrigation beyond short inundation canals, and the channeling of well water to the fields utilizing artificial slopes. They did, however, employ the shaduf. In all, the Harappans maintained an efficient agricultural operation on the floodplains or local banks of rivers. That they were able to maintain a large-scale food surplus capable of sustaining a sizable population of non-subsistence producers is amply clear (Vishnu-Mittre and Savithri 1982). One might expect in turn, and in view of the fertility of the riverine environment in western India–Pakistan, that a number of urban communities like those of Mesopotamia would emerge. On the contrary this is not the case nor do we have, as in Egypt and China, evidence for communities with a long history of culturally homogeneous existence. Sites such as Dabar Kot, Amri, Kot Diji, Bala Kot, and Kalibangan demonstrate a superimposition of the Harappan style with perhaps some integration with the indigenous culture and then a short period of occupation often probably of only a century or less. Clearly agricultural development was not central to the Harappan chiefdom(s).

What was central was most emphatically cattle. The seal motifs, the abundance of cattle figurines, the faunal evidence, and the character of Harappan settlements underlines the emphasis. Cattle were eaten, used as draught animals, cattle had representation in religion. Most obvious is the emphasis upon cattle as wealth, and in consequence of power. This affected the settlement pattern both as to location and as to kind.

Recent surveys in the Cholistan (Mughal 1982), western Sind (Flam 1984), the Karachi region (Fairservis 1982: 107) and Gujarat (Possehl 1980) evidence that the characteristic Harappan settlement was a dispersed one with a variety of functional nuclei, some of which were industrial in function. It does appear that in the Indus floodplain the large urban sites were the centers about which were scattered house-holds rather than nucleated villages. One can envision extended families resident in the midst of agricultural fields bringing surplus to some central place which in turn had ties to the larger centers such as Mohenjo Daro, the whole extending as a network over an entire region. Means of transport included riverine vessels with square rigged sails for movement up-river; the backs of donkeys, water-buffalo and possibly elephant for the conveyance of some loads; cattle-drawn carts and, of course, the shoulder yoke for men to carry liquid-filled vessels (honey, wine, and so on). While this situation existed for the Indus River plain the hinterland settlements were of a different type. They came into being as a consequence of the need to balance agriculture with animal husbandry.

The problem is an old one. How to integrate the demands of agriculture, which require the extensive use of fertile soil and a regular water supply, with pastoralism which needs productive extensive grazing land, fodder out of season, and also a regular source of water. Large herds of cattle imperil growing crops, while the cultivation of land in turn reduces grazing land. When numbers of cattle are considered the basis of wealth there is a regular threat to subsistence farming.

It is difficult, if not impossible, to balance these challenges over the years in consideration of the vagaries of the seasons and the fluctuations of population. An obvious solution is migration away from the agricultural centers and the establishment of new settlements elsewhere, settlements which would still maintain the chieftain polity and at the same time be profitably responsive to local ecologies.[5] The hinterland settlements everywhere consisted of cattle camps, dispersed agricultural households, industrial sites, and administrative centers. The last provided for central processing: grinding and storing. The advance into a new region was initially made by cattle herders whose animals in general belonged to chiefs and their followers. At Allahdino, for example, there is possible evidence for corrals at the earliest Harappan levels (Shaffer 1974:19). Settlement occurred where there was a secure supply of water, grazing land, some agricultural land, and critical natural resources such as clay, flint, wood, and at the least native copper. The agricultural land, if necessary, was made productive by controlling the water supply through a system of kachs or by wells, where diameter caused a rise in hydrostatic level substantially higher than the local water table. The settlement was bound by the centralization of agricultural produce in storage at the administrative center. This center was directly under the control of the "Talpir" or head chief, and the subsidiary chiefs; the whole operating through the bureaucracy previously outlined. Essential occupations such as smithing, pottery manufacture, or cotton weaving were carried on by kin-related practitioners who acted in symbiosis with the polity.[6]

Cattle added to the accumulation of commodities through meat, hide, and milk production. Milk goats were also herded. Conical dairies, somewhat like those of the Toda, were storage places for dairy products.

Each hinterland settlement owed a percentage of its production to the paramount chiefs at the large centers of the floodplain, probably on an annual basis. Furthermore, there was high prestige associated with luxury items, which were much in demand by the chiefdom(s). In addition to good copper, there was always a need for gold, silver, jasper, agate, carnelian, azurite, lapis, antimony, fine shell, steatite, ivory, peacock feathers, and the objects manufactured or ornamented from or with these materials. Certain Harappan sites were located far from the Indus Valley in response to these needs. Sutkagan Dor in Makran, Bala Kot in Las Bela, Lothal in Gujarat, Dabar Kot in Loralai, Shortughai in Badakhshan exemplify these outposts. In the south, Harappans came into contact with itinerant traders from the Persian Gulf and occasionally some Harappan traders even resided in Mesopotamia, at Kish, Ur, Umma, or Irbil; but this far-flung contact was minimal and there is no substantive evidence either for extensive commerce or the market economy necessary to international trade.

However it is fair to note that the writing of the Harappans was largely based on a borrowed script, hybrid in origin. Of the 400 odd signs known for the script over half are identical with proto-Elamite and proto-Sumerian examples. The remainder are apparently of indigenous origin. The proto-Elamite habit of affixing signs is also followed by the Harappans. It appears that in the latter part of the third millennium B.C. a lingua franca of sorts was developing along the Arab-Persian gulf and a hybrid script emerged from which the Harappans borrowed. The borrowing was, however, in line with the need for the precision and order characteristic of the culture. Thus the script which they adopted was largely used for accounting purposes and the identification (status, place, lineage, occupation, proper name) of the individual. There is no indication of a literary tradition of any kind. Indeed the script arrived full-blown with the Harappans and, except for a few signs maintained as graffiti in central and south India, died out with their demise.

The evidence of the writing on the seal-tāli is that the names inscribed are masculine. There is the repeated use of the honorific third-person masculine ending "-an" and "-ār" or even "-āl": man, male. This poses two possible interpretations. The first is that the man's name was used to designate to whom the woman wearing the tāli belonged by marriage. The second, that the woman, by wearing the inscribed tāli with her husband's name upon it, was designating her husband's affiliation to herself and her own family.

There are three pieces of evidence which added to the above hint at Harappan social organization. The first is that the main seal-tāli motifs refer to sodalities and not directly to families, even though some of the writing describes affiliations to lineages ("kal"), of sun, moon, stars, monsoon, and so on. It is entirely possible then that sodality membership came through women, the tāli bearers being something of an elite class. However, if the characteristic Harappan settlement was made up largely of scattered households, our second piece of evidence, it is more than likely that some form of bilateral residency and inheritance was followed in order to insure the labor pool, in this case because of the exigencies of herding cattle, of males. Third, Trautman (1981) has described Dravidian kinship as cross-cousin. In other words, one may marry one's mother's brother's children or father's sister's children. Since the plow and cattle herding give precedence to men as inheritors of property (Murdock 1949: 206), the tendency was probably towards patrilocal–patrilineal kinship and thus, most likely, to father's sister's children in crossness. The clan affiliation, in turn, may well have emphasized matrilateralism in the case of the elite. In any case, there does seem to be some class division with a suggestion of differing social organization that was rooted in both socioeconomic roles and membership in sodalities.

Harappan religion was characterized by an emphasis upon the division of the wild and the domestic, the dry season and the wet, and perhaps other dualities. There is no evidence for pantheistic taxonomies by which the natural world was classified. There is a strong indication of an "ara-amban," or "Royal Mother," which can be presumed to be in sexual relationship to the Herculean deity father of paramount chiefs already alluded to, one called "Aṇ-il Piraṇ," or in other contexts, "Irukavar," the Seizer of Two (tigers). There may also have been a water deity, "Nīran." Most depicted among Harappan "deities" is the hoofed and sometimes horned female anthropomorph usually shown in an acacia tree taunting a tiger or even attacking one. The association with the acacia suggests the dry parklands where grazing was good in season but where cattle could be prey to predators. Interestingly for those who adhere to the Harappans as a source for aspects of later Hinduism, there is a possible linguistic (Dravidian) association of "kāli" – cow or herd of cows – with "cāli" – acacia (Fig. 13.2).

The archaeological evidence for Harappan religion is very poor. Claims have been made for phallic worship, fire altars, temple platforms, and so on, but this is purely speculative. The fact is that in the present state of these studies there is a lack of any substantive evidence for highly institutionalized religious activity at the level of a state cult. That there were religious practitioners is quite clear. The so-called "margh-pir" or "marupir" qualifies as an example and the "ara-amban" qualifies also. The "mutali," or paramount chief, had at least a semi-divine status based on the myth of his origins. But in all it seems clear that Harappan religion had a form more akin to a tribal world than to a civilized one.

In sum, if we compare the evidence for the Harappan culture with that for the indigenous primary civilizations of China, Mesopotamia, and Egypt, we find comparable material only for the first stage of development. Even at that stage there are decided differences. While the Harappans did practice an intensive agronomy, pastoralism was more important as a status foundation. There was no large-scale building on a par with the Near East; the platform for the great temple of Erech, for example, was larger than the whole "citadel" at Mohenjo Daro. There is no evidence for alien states which had to be fought, no soldiers, and the bureaucracy it appears was concerned largely with redistribution. There is some suggestion of social division by wealth but more typical is sodality membership. There were no kings, or large priesthoods; the "urban" centers were short-lived and though well laid out do not seem to have housed a large number of specialists concerned with the variety consequent on urban life, for those that we can identify are for the most part typical of Harappan settlements everywhere, including those in a non-urban context. Finally, the writing system was directly concerned with accounting and naming, and beyond this it did not go.

In short, though much of Harappan culture is of the first stage it does not qualify as the first stage in the direction to new civilization as the Near Eastern and Chinese models define that stage. The second stage, defined by the presence of higher abstract thought, is not at all attested in the Harappan culture. What we do have evidenced by the Harappans is a unique culture which owes its uniqueness to indigenous influences. These influences can be summed up in a single process, that of "Indianization."

Indianization is a process by which essentially highland–lowland cultures in the Indo-Iranian borderlands were converted to a subcontinental style. There is little doubt at this date that the genesis of sedentary village farming in these borderlands was largely due to the diffusion of Iranian-type village sedentism into the region, beginning as early as the sixth millennium B.C. There appear to have been several stages in this development, which began with simple cultures whose subsistence occupations included small-field grain agronomy and the pastoralism of goats and cattle, the latter requiring transhumant movement seasonally between the uplands and the Indus and adjacent lowland plains. In time, permanent settlement in village clusters was manifested in the lowlands, probably because of social fission occurring in the highlands owing to the pressures caused by limited field and pasture resources combined with improving technology and increased population. Some symbiosis remained between highland and lowland cultures, however (Amri–Nal, Mehrgarh–Kechi Beg, Zhob–Rahman Dheri, Baluchistan–Early Kulli, and so on). Lowland sedentism required cultural adaptations, reflected both in the indigenous cultures and in their counterparts in the highlands. These adaptations, some of which had a long developmental history, included the breeding of humped cattle, the domestication of the water buffalo and possibly the elephant, cotton, sesamum agronomy, and the adoption of highland grains (emmer wheat, barley) to the hot Indus plains, emphasis on milk goats for dairy products along with cattle, the shaduf and possibly the windmill, graphic motifs which reflect a structural duality probably generic to the dry–wet seasons of western India/Pakistan: acacia/pipal, florid scenes/geometric series, upriver (north)/down-river (south), sunrise (east)/sunset (west), sun (dry, light)/monsoon (dark, wet), grain/cotton, wild animals/domestic animals. Other Indianization features include heavily bangled and necklaced female decoration, tiger motifs, the gavial as symbol, turbans, buffalo horn headdresses, the wedding pandal, the tāli, the swastika auspicious sign, drains and hydraulic devices (especially gabar-bands or kachs), the conical dairy, cross-footed seated male anthropomorphs, "toy" carts as accounting devices, fired-brick platforms to support buildings in the flood-plain, and cattle iconography. These Indianization traits characterize the Harappan development. With them we see the demise of the highland culture orientation found in the pre-Harappan cultures of Kot Diji, Mehrgarh, Sarai Kola, Rahman Dheri, Amri, and Kalibangan I, which have a somewhat Iranian aspect. Indeed the highland cultures now assume an Indianized aspect reflective of the developments within the Indus system: the center drain platforms, dissolution of the strict geometry of vessel painting, humped cattle herds, the pipal as a decorative motif, large "town" centers perhaps in keeping with the "urban" redistributional centers of the Harappans and the related polity (Quetta Miri, Edith Shahr, Duki Mound) and so on.

Indianization, for the Harappans, placed great emphasis upon cattle as wealth. Since cattle were now adapted to the Indus environment, highland transhumance was impractical. Pasturage was to be found in hills and open normally arid plains where rainfall provided for grass in season. The search for pasturage created lateral move-ment and temporary settlement characterized by migrations south into Gujarat and beyond, east into Rajasthan and northeast into Ganges–Jumna Doab. Agriculture and cottage industries, while still important and indeed essential to Harappan settlement everywhere, were nonetheless secondary to cattle husbandry. Thus some fertile soil for crops and access to natural resources for materials had always to be considered in arriving at settlement locations, but cattle pasturage was the primary goal in the Harappan movement in western India/Pakistan. This very movement, which caused settlement far from the generic and developed homeland in the Indus Valley, eventuated in the gradual demise of the Harappan cultural style and the emergence of what might be cultural hybrids created by the integration of that style with indigenous cultural development whose genesis was non-Harappan.

In short, our model admits highland to lowland movement of Iranian style village-farming cultures into the Indus River Valley at least as early as the sixth millennium B.C, and their gradual Indianization until by the middle of the third millennium B.C. the Harappans emerged as the most important representative of the full-blown type. But what emerges is substantively subcontinental in aspect and almost entirely different from early primary civilizations elsewhere. Indeed it cannot be regarded as a civilization on their terms; it is more akin to what Service has called chieftainships (Service 1962).

True civilization comes to India later, when the tension of wars among the Vedic Aryans led to inquiries about man, existence, and the cosmos, as symbolized in the Bhagavadgita, the life of Buddha, of the cult of Mahavira, and eventually of the Arthasastra. The Harappans were one among numerous cultures of the borderlands who laid the basis of village farming on the Indian subcontinent, but their organizational advances were eventually more directed to pastoralism which of itself has never been the foundation for civilization.

Notes

1 The work on the Harappan script is an ongoing process. What is presented here utilizes the latest developments (Fairservis 1976, 1982; Fairservis and Southworth, 1986) and Mahadevan (1970).

2 This interpretation was pointed out to me by R. Allchin, personal communication.

3 There is no indication of a substantive climatic difference between the Harappan period and the modern (but see Singh 1974).

4 A study of Harappan measurement, measuring devices, and the number system is forthcoming (see Fairservis 1988).

5 My use of the term "chiefdom" in this context is based on the work of Elman Service (1962), in particular his definition " . . . particularly distinguish from tribes by the presence of centers which coordinate economic, social and religious activities" (p. 143), and "Chiefdoms are redistributional societies with a permanent central agency of coordination" (p. 144). However, since the research on the polity and social organization of the Harappans is an ongoing matter the term "chiefdom" may in the end not be suitable. This is particularly true in view of the Harappan combination of sedentism and pastoralism, which is not typical for Service's case examples.

6 Note J. M. Kenoyer's observation that shell working, for example, was the product of a "distinct social group" (Kenoyer 1984: 62).

14

The use and abuse of world systems theory: the case of the "pristine" West Asian state[1]

PHILIP L. KOHL

Recently archaeologists working in the Anglo-American regional tradition of archaeology have become increasingly critical of neo-evolutionary formulations for the
development of complex society that stress internal, frequently ecological factors to
the exclusion or near-exclusion of features relating to interaction and exchange among
disparate societies at different levels of cultural development.[2] Fried's concepts of a
"pristine" social formation or society considered almost in isolation from other
societies has been criticized as never operative or too ideal and misleading a type to be
useful.[3] Whether one prefers to refer to "peer polity," "cluster," or some other form
of intersocietal interaction (Renfrew 1982a; Price 1977), the basic fact remains that the
development or cultural evolution of any society is dependent upon its relations with
other societies; that cultures are open, not closed, systems; and that studies – be they
based on excavations of a site or settlement data from surveys of precisely defined,
well-demarcated, but bounded areas – that fail to consider broader patterns of
interaction are necessarily incomplete and partial. A boundary problem, in short,
exists for prehistory that is every bit as real as that which besets later historical studies
or analyses of the contemporary world.

One stimulating solution to this problem of defining the proper unit for social
analysis, which, to date, has seen relatively limited application in prehistory,[4] is the
model of a world system developed by I. Wallerstein and his followers for explaining
the emergence and current state of the modern world.[5] Prehistorians, as well as
ancient and medieval historians, have been less drawn into the creative furor
stimulated by Wallerstein's study for the simple reason that the societies archaeologists and early historians study are explicitly regarded by Wallerstein as not being
constrained or influenced by a world system. For Wallerstein, the "Great Transformation" or divide that separates human history into pre-modern and modern epochs
occurred during the sixteenth century A.D. with the emergence of the modern world
system; a distinction is drawn between earlier world empires that existed in various
places at different times extending back to the dawn of history or the beginnings of
state societies and the modern world system defined as a unique product of European
civilization that has developed over the past 500 years. Wallerstein's distinction is
explicit:

Empires were a constant feature of the world scene for 5000 years. There
were continuously several such empires in various parts of the world at any

given point of time. The political centralization of an empire was at one and the same time its strength and weakness . . . Political empires are a primitive means of economic domination. It is the social achievement of the modern world, if you will, to have invented the *technology that makes it possible* to increase the flow of the surplus from the lower strata to the upper strata, from the periphery to the center, from the majority to the minority by eliminating the "waste" of too cumbersome a political structure.

(1974; 15–16, emphasis added)

The modern world system is distinguished by primarily economic, as opposed to political, cultural, or presumably even ideological linkages among its constituent parts. Political diversity, primacy of the economic sphere, and control and development of a technology capable of supporting and expanding such a system are the critical variables, according to Wallerstein, that distinguish the modern era from ancient and medieval times. The modern world system also is characterized by a highly complex global division of labor that results in major regional differences: some areas become exporters of primary resources, while others produce and successfully market industrial products. The exchange uniting different regions is not symmetrical but structurally weighted or tipped in favor of the politically more powerful and technologically advanced core states of the West. The exchange relations that develop are thus beneficial to the core areas and detrimental to the peripheries, which essentially are exploited or "underdeveloped" by these relations. Wallerstein's model becomes even more complex when he shows how specific nation-states' core status shifts over time and how certain countries, termed semi-peripheries, provide a built-in flexibility to the world system.

Development of the world systems concept was clearly related to the writings of dependency theorists, such as Amin (1974) and Frank (1967), but was distinguished by its longer and more detailed historical perspective. As has been explicitly acknowledged, Wallerstein's model was also indebted to the writings of *Annales* historians, particularly the macro-historical pathbreaking study of F. Braudel on the Mediterranean world in the sixteenth century (Braudel 1966).[6]

Wallerstein has refined and clarified his model in later writings. Now he considers a system as referring to a structure exhibiting a division of labor over time within some set of spatial boundaries that change or fluctuate. According to Wallerstein (personal communication), human history can be divided into three eras that were characterized successively by three types of "systems": mini-systems; world empires; and world economies. His second era, which concerns us in this chapter and which lasted until c.1500 A.D., contained numerous examples of all three systems, but was typically dominated by world empires that expanded through the political incorporation of mini-systems and nascent world economies. The validity of this grossly schematic perspective as it pertains to the ancient Near East will be discussed below. Here it is important to observe that Wallerstein freely admits the existence of countless earlier "world economies" and "world systems," while at the same time he insists that the *modern* world system is qualitatively distinct.

World systems analysis and prehistory: its potential value

The purpose of this chapter is not to evaluate the utility of the world systems concept for explaining the peculiarities of modern times but to assess its relevance, if any, for understanding the emergence of complex society; particularly, its value for elucidating the best documented and possibly only genuine "pristine" Old World state formation, that which occurred in West Asia during the fourth and third millennia B.C. Some possible objections to this borrowing or extension of the world systems concept must be anticipated and answered at the outset. Most significantly the Wallersteinian formulation for the beginnings of the modern era has encountered substantive empirical and theoretical criticisms from a broad array of historians, sociologists, and anthropologists which deserve most serious consideration.[7] If the concept of a world system is problematic at best for explaining modern times, what possibly can be gained by extending its range backwards to encompass developments explicitly rejected by its founder and most ardent advocate? Since archaeologists already can dip into a well-stocked conceptual bag replete with models for explaining intersocietal interactions from the earlier notions of various types of diffusion[8] to the more recent peer polity and cluster interaction concepts, why introduce a new buzz word? If contemporary Anglo-American archaeology suffers from a certain narcissism and penchant for fads, one more ephemeral than the next (Kohl 1985: 111), recourse to world systems terminology seems yet another example of this same excessive, tiresome tendency.

Perhaps. But there remain cogent reasons for at least attempting the exercise of determining the *degree of applicability* of the world systems concept for antiquity. First, it can be argued that the new Anglo-American archaeology, which began during the sixties and still continues to dominate the discipline at least in North America, suffers from a peculiar ahistoricism or refusal to consider the data and discipline of history seriously. This chapter cannot document this observation in the detail it deserves; reference to Binford's disparagement of cultural history and insistence on a clear dichotomy between historical and evolutionary perspectives must suffice.[9] Ragin and Chirot have suggested that one of the reasons for the immense appeal of Wallerstein's world systems approach has been its use of long-range, detailed historical data in a discipline – American sociology – that effectively "thirsted for concrete historical knowledge" (Ragin and Chirot 1984: 278). One possible merit of discussing the relevance of the world systems concept for prehistory is that it will compel archaeologists working in the American tradition to read macro-historians and historical sociologists and, in so doing, abandon their grossly misleading caricature of history as an atheoretical, narrowly focused discipline.

Secondly, Wallerstein's qualitative divide between modern and ancient times can be questioned on both theoretical and empirical grounds. At one level, the existence of such a divide practically devolves into a typological (and to that extent – as every archaeologist knows – arbitrary) problem. Depending upon their criteria, historians have placed the beginnings of the modern era as early as the late eleventh and as late as nearly the mid-nineteenth century.[10] While it is impossible to deny that capitalism in the modern industrial age differs fundamentally from those social formations characteristic of previous periods, important aspects of continuity can still be traced, and, as in the somewhat misguided, if unresolved, substantivist-formalist controversy in economic anthropology, a position that altogether rejects any correspondences between capitalist and pre-capitalist or Western and non-Western societies often tends to distort our vision of the present and idealize that of the past (Godelier 1972). Schneider's intelligent and generally laudatory review of Wallerstein's original study criticizes the book precisely for its perpetuation of this great divide between modern and ancient medieval times:

> From the point of view of social science, Wallerstein's most significant
> contribution is the suggestion that processes of interaction and unequal
> exchange might explain events not only in Third World areas transformed
> by European hegemony in the nineteenth and twentieth centuries, but in
> earlier periods within Europe itself. This establishes a unity of theory
> between Western and non-Western peoples, the absence of which has long
> been problematic in unilineal models of change whose ethnocentrisms are
> consistent with their inability to account for the disparity between
> Europe's precocious advances and other peoples' "lag" . . . *The Modern
> World System* suffers from too narrow an application of its own theory.
> For, although Wallerstein admires Owen Lattimore's description of the
> differentiation process according to which ancient Chinese civilization
> "gave birth to barbarism" . . . he does not view the pre-capitalist world as
> systematically integrated through the operations of world economic forces.
>
> (Schneider 1977: 20)

According to Schneider, Wallerstein too easily dismisses the external economic linkages forged by non-Western political empires, denigrates the effects and importance of earlier long-distance trade in luxury goods, and, consequently, fails to explain adequately or understand the motivations and stimuli that led to the Great Discoveries and the beginnings of the modern era. The initial trade for luxuries, such as pepper and spices, not only was critical for European expansion and the emergence of the modern world system, but also transformed itself over time as former luxuries (for example, sugar) later became staples and were mass-produced on industrial-like plantations, a development which, in turn, partially set the stage for the later industrial take-off of the late eighteenth century (compare the elegant study of Mintz [1985]). The book suffers, in short, from an unnecessary, self-limiting ethnocentrism that bestows special status upon modern European development.

One should also note that as the search for the divide between modern and premodern times can be arbitrary and even counter-productive, discussions of pre-capitalist economies often founder on misleading, overly compartmentalized dichotomies, such as distinctions between local and long-distance exchange; a trade in luxuries versus a trade in staples; considerations of land versus maritime transport; or political/ideological as opposed to economic factors operative in early imperial expansion. That such distinctions can be meaningful and illuminate real differences is clear, but they hardly ever describe absolutely distinctive phenomena. Unconscious utilization of such distinctions may lead to the rigid and artificial separation of complex entities that simultaneously encompass both sides of the dichotomy. For example, among other goods, particularly textiles, early Mesopotamian civilization exchanged staple foodstuffs for so-called luxuries or prestige goods. Such goods often were imported via maritime routes along the Arabian/Persian Gulf, then re-exported farther inland by both land and riverine/canal routes. Imperial expansion during Akkadian times certainly was associated with the extension of a political/military bureaucracy, as well as the self-glorification and ultimately deification of Akkadian rulers, but it was also a quest for raw materials lacking in the southern alluvium, some of which, like copper, had been transformed over time from luxury/prestige to utilitarian/essential goods.

One cannot determine how ancient economies or, if you will, ancient world systems differed from those of the modern era until one has attempted the comparison. Differences, as well as similarities, should be sought for the purpose of better understanding of both the present and the past. If the concept of a world system, as employed by Wallerstein and his followers, has limited utility for understanding the broad pattern of development that culminated in the emergence of complex archaic societies throughout West Asia, it is important to spell out why the concept cannot be employed uncritically. Models that only partially succeed or even fail also instruct – often in very important ways.

Finally, there seems to be almost an internal theoretical inconsistency in world systems advocates' apparent disinterest in the nature of pre-sixteenth century A.D. world economies. Makkai (1983: 441) justifiably has argued that in his writings Wallerstein has replaced the fundamental Marxian concept of a mode of production with that of the world economy. The merits or faults of such a replacement need not concern us here, but, as this observation is true, it is obvious that scholars writing from this perspective must investigate world economies and systems for the past as well. That is, history did not begin in the sixteenth century A.D.; throughout antiquity societies were structurally integrated with others through external relations that were not fortuitously but systemically structured in forms that demand further analysis. Indeed, the once overused and much maligned concept of diffusion has frequently been criticized for its connotation of the nearly accidental character of the processes by which traits are borrowed. One final potential for prehistory of the world systems approach is its insistence upon structure and upon the unequal relations that develop among the different societies participating in the system.

The ancient political economy and the scale of its activities
Before turning to some of the archaeological and linguistic evidence suggestive of a Bronze Age West Asian world system, it is useful to enumerate and critically examine some of the features that supposedly distinguish ancient from modern economies. Two of the most sophisticated "primitivists," M. Weber (1976) and M. I. Finley (1973, 1978), have generalized about the nature of the ancient economy primarily from their extensive knowledge of the classical or Graeco-Roman world (though Weber, of course, also exhaustively studied ancient Israel, China, and India). One should

remember that classical sources are incomplete, peculiarly biased, and relatively impoverished compared to ancient Near Eastern cuneiform sources for direct and sustained accounts recording ancient economic practices. Yet the differences they listed between ancient and modern economies remain formidable. While Weber acknowledged the existence of commodity production and large-scale interregional exchange in classical Greece and Rome, he stressed that these similarities were superficial and insisted that the ancient world was structured in a fundamentally different manner from that of medieval Europe (his Great Transformation took place earlier than Wallerstein's) or modern times. Land transportation systems were exorbitantly expensive relative to sea and water transport, a factor that explained the maritime orientation of cities of the classical world – though not of most cities of the ancient Near East. Credit facilities were thought to be so poorly developed or so thoroughly integrated with state structures that private capital formation was negligible and development was more stifled than stimulated by ubiquitous government contract.[11] Craft guilds were not autonomous organizations, jealously guarding their rights as in medieval Europe, but were controlled by the state, and modern "factories" or sizable organizations separate from extended households and businesses, like joint stock companies, were unknown. Classical cities were centers of consumption, not production, and stores of precious metals were generally hoarded in capital treasuries and not reinvested for further capital accumulation. The tremendous role played by unfree, particularly slave, labor in classical times also retarded development. The system was technologically stagnant and supported public works projects, rather than production for markets. Moreover, reliance on slave labor meant that more capital needed to be invested in simply assembling and maintaining the work force, a feature that led to a slowdown in capital turnover and capital formation.

M. I. Finley has extended Weber's list of differences. According to him one must always insist upon the agrarian base of the ancient world and recognize that the scale of its productive activities was incomparably minuscule relative to modern times. Thus, for example, one of the largest workshops (*ergasteria*) producing *terra sigillata* ware in Arezzo employed only 58 slaves, hardly an industrial giant compared to the assembly line plants of today. He further argued that the concept of class is inappropriate for antiquity where more inclusive ranking criteria emphasizing social and political status structured social relations.[12] Different, generally unfavorable values were accorded commercial activities that were usually conducted by freedmen and foreigners, not by the aristocracy. Following Weber, Finley emphasizes the negligible role of manufacturing and the lack of autonomous guild associations comparable to those that built the great guildhalls or bourses of medieval Europe. Economic activities related to capital formation and investment operated on an incomparably smaller scale and were structured differently, if they existed at all. The list of absences in ancient economies is impressive and telling: no cyclical business cycles due to supply and demand operations in a money market; no bankruptcy laws to mitigate the effects of disastrous business ventures; no machinery from the creation of credit through negotiable interests; no clear distinctions between capital costs and labor costs; no clear plowing back of profits nor long-term loans for productive purposes; no taxes as economic levers nor reexamination of them if they failed to stimulate the economy; and no mercantilist devices for encouraging enterprises, such as patents, charters, or subsidies.

Finally, Finley explicitly rejects the concept of a "world market" for antiquity. "To be meaningful," he writes (1973: 34) the term "must embrace something considerably more than the exchange of some goods over long distances." Similarly, colonization and imperialism in the ancient world did not function in a manner comparable to the modern world system. Thus, expansion of the Roman Empire took place without exploiting the provinces or denying the local inhabitants the opportunity to become wealthy landowners themselves.

Given the nature of the ancient economy, two of the most important and most profitable forms of modern imperialist exploitation were ruled out. I refer to cheap labor and cheap raw materials: in more technical language, the employment, by compulsion if necessary, of colonial labor at wages well below the market wage at home, and the acquisition, again by compulsion if necessary, of raw materials for production at prices substantially below the market prices at home. I am not saying that labor in the subject territories was not profitably exploited, or that provincial sources of raw materials were not exploited. My point is that the rate of exploitation was not essentially different from that "at home."

(Finley 1978: 64; cf. also 1973: 158)

Finley's generalization for the classical world also seems to characterize Pharaonic Egyptian expansion into Nubia.[13] Ironically, W. Adams's detailed and historically informed analysis of Egyptian imperialism essentially documents the same point, despite the fact that the major thesis of his entire study is the striking similarity between modern and ancient imperialism. Thus, for example, W. Adams (1984: 69) observes:

The Nubians under Egyptian rule had acquired a taste for certain kinds of Egyptian manufactured goods, but many of these were now being produced on Nubian soil either by natives or by expatriate Egyptian craftsmen. What the Egyptians had not done in Nubia was to create an economy dependent on exports, and hence they were able to exert no real influence in their former colony once their political control was gone. Militarily they were weaker than the Nubians themselves; indeed, their own frontiers were now guarded largely by Nubian mercenary troops.

The extent to which wealth was transferred from colony to imperial seat and the nature of the dependencies created by ancient empires may constitute – *contra* W. Adams's intensive search for parallels – an important difference between ancient and modern empires.

However, not all "international" movements of materials and peoples during the Bronze Age took place under the aegis of an expanding imperial power (Lamberg-Karlovsky 1975: 361). At least from Early Dynastic times onwards, Near Eastern texts refer to merchants (*damgar*) engaged in a long-distance trade that was often financed at least partially by state or public institutions; many of these merchants prospered and accumulated wealth from their participation in these exchange networks. To adopt the vernacular, "killings" could be made, and wealth transferred on a substantial scale, since the prices of commodities differed from one area to another, making such accumulation possible. Documentation is simply inadequate to try to quantify the exact scale of this transfer of wealth, this "exploitation" of peripheral areas by centers, for the purpose of detecting basic similarities between ancient and modern economies. Negative evidence does not necessarily imply a real difference, and occasional references to the scale of past activities suggests that, at times within specific exchange networks, actual economic exploitation occurred resembling *grosso modo* that of modern times.

Explicit also within this primitivist critique is the dominance of political/ideological over strictly economic considerations in the ancient world. As many have observed, the concept of an economy as a separate sphere of activity – or subsystem of the social system – is unique to modern times, and, for Finley, the lack of such a concept in Greece and Rome was not an "intellectual failing" but "a consequence of the structure of ancient society." Such an observation, of course, raises the legitimate and central materialist query as to the degree to which consciousness determines social being. If the ancient Near East truly lacked narrators of past events, such as Herodotus or, even more, Thucydides, this "intellectual failing" by no means suggests that ancient Near Eastern societies were not formed by understandable, natural historical processes which can and indeed must be reconstructed. In short, most of the supposedly unique features of the ancient world can be reduced to differences in scale, which, in turn, must be evaluated through the application of consistent criteria as to whether they actually constitute differences in kind or only in degree. Some of the previously cited distinctions must be more critically scrutinized by reference to the more complete picture of the ancient economy that can be derived from consideration of linguistic and archaeological evidence from the ancient Near East.

Reference to the "embeddedness" of ancient or precapitalist economies relative to those of our day makes a qualitative and exceedingly problematic distinction that is almost impossible to quantify. Analytical separation of political/ideological from economic factors is never straightforward, since both in antiquity and today such factors nearly always operate in tandem; the opposite belief in a separate, relatively autonomous sphere where modern economic activities occur forms the cornerstone of the dominant ideology of Western society – that based on a free marketplace. How should one, for example, conceptualize the expansion of the British Empire? When was economic growth supplanted by political consolidation and further advance – only after the Great Mutiny of 1857? Merchants and missionaries essentially marched together with the machinery of the expanding state, though one, of course, can distinguish relatively mercantile from relatively imperial phases.[14] If there is a sense in which politics were *relatively* more important or – to use the Althusserian term – "dominant" than today, if the ancient economy was *relatively* less disembedded, it is ultimately related to the fact that large-scale productive activities, such as the textile industries of southern Mesopotamia, were under tighter state or public supervision and control, that the state or public sector, at least initially and in most cases, was primarily responsible for organizing surplus production and production for export (Diakonoff 1982b).

Categoric assertions that deny the presence of supply/demand mechanisms for regulating prices or reject the notion of business cycles in antiquity, insisting on the absolute decoupling of exchange and production decisions, are usually based on negative evidence, which, in turn, bespeak more the real problem of documentation than any absolute feature of the ancient economy. Occasional textual references that allow one to establish the relative price of goods for the ancient Near East support reconstructions that are more complex and modern-looking. For example, barley prices are known to have fluctuated widely on an annual basis depending upon the relative scarcity or abundance of grain before or after the harvest,[15] and the prices of land, houses, and temple offices in ancient Nippur during the Old Babylonian period are thought to have been manipulated by wealthy landowners interested in accumulating wealth and power (Stone 1977). The relative value of silver to gold is known to have fluctuated, depending presumably upon the relative abundance or scarcity of these two imported metals. Thus, for example, the value of silver to gold during the period of the royal archives at Ebla was set roughly at 5:1, a ratio that changed dramatically with the beginnings of the Old Akkadian period when the price of silver dropped to c. 9:1 (G. Pettinato, personal communication); similarly the price of silver increased from roughly 9:1 to 3:1 over a course of three generations during the late nineteenth and early eighteenth centuries B.C. (Farber 1978: 3–5). Farber's detailed study of prices during the Old Babylonian period shows a consistent pattern for the long-term fluctuation of the relative prices of basic commodities such as barley, oil, land, and slaves, revealing a sharp rise in prices and wages during the reign of Abi-eshuh (early seventeenth century B.C.); interestingly, the one basic commodity that failed to follow the general movement of prices was wool, the price of which apparently was artificially supported by the central government. Such price controls, needless to say, were not unique to ancient times.

Wallerstein's distinction between the modern world system and earlier world empires also emphasizes the economic nature of the former and the political nature of the latter. For him, ancient world empires expanded by incorporating new territories and obtained necessary resources and materials through the coercive imposition of tributes and taxes. Goods flowed to the political center and – in classic Polanyi-like fashion – were redistributed by the state according to its own specific rules of allocation. Earlier world economies may have existed, but they always were transformed into political empires. It is certainly true that ancient political empires levied tributes on conquered areas and imposed taxes, either of labor services or goods, on their subjected citizenry. Many early civilizations may have expanded politically, as Wallerstein suggests, to incorporate areas from which they obtained essential resources. Although known almost exclusively from archaeological data, the Harappan or Indus Valley civilization may have expanded in precisely this fashion. Unlike the Old Assyrian settlement at Kanesh (see below), where traders adopted the local material culture, entire Harappan colonies, containing exclusively Harappan materials, have been discovered well beyond the confines of the Indus Valley. The Harappan settlements at Shortughai on the Ai Khanoum plain of northeastern Afghanistan provide the most striking illustration of this difference (Francfort and Pottier 1978). J. Shaffer (1982: 44–5) has suggested that the distributional evidence from Harappan sites indicates that foreign trade was unimportant to this early civilization, for Harappans built their complex social order through elaborate internal exchange networks that redistributed local resources throughout their vast domains; others, like Lamberg-Karlovsky (n.d.) and Miller (1985), have recently attempted to explain the peculiar features of Harappan remains primarily in terms of organizational principles, such as the endogamous caste structures, of the historic Hindu or Buddhist South Asian traditions.

Regardless of whether or not these interpretations are correct, Harappan materials have always been considered enigmatic, if not unique, and Harappa's pattern of expansion is not shared by the best documented early civilization: Mesopotamia. Indeed, consideration of the development of early Mesopotamian civilization reveals that, at least, two features of Wallerstein's analysis are incorrect: (a) world economies and political empires were not always commensurate with one another; and (b) there existed no irreversible trend for the former to transform itself into the latter. Mesopotamian civilization developed over the course of roughly three millennia: political empires and periods of expansion alternated with periods of breakdown, nomadic or semi-nomadic incursions, and times of intense competition and struggle between local, culturally related, but politically autonomous city-states. Individual cities remained the basic building blocks of state formation in Mesopotamia at least through the third and into the second millennium B.C. At a slightly later period during the early second millennium B.C., the well-documented example of the old Assyrian trading network[16] clearly demonstrates how the economic life and prosperity of a city, Assur, depended upon its middleman role in the long-distance exchange primarily of silver and gold from Anatolia for tin and textiles from regions to the east and south. This profit-motivated trade extended far beyond the political borders of any state and connected areas stretching from the Anatolian plateau to southern Mesopotamia east across the Iranian plateau, possibly to western Afghanistan (Cleuziou and Berthoud 1982), into a single world system. Similarly, the earlier royal archives from Ebla in northern Syria unequivocally demonstrate that even when cities expanded into kingdoms of considerable size they still engaged in essential "international" exchange, transporting raw materials, luxury goods, textiles, and even livestock and agricultural products, such as olive oil, across recognized political boundaries (Pettinato 1981: ch. 7).

An even earlier reliance on intercultural exchange can be reconstructed from archaeological materials dated to Early Dynastic times. Sumerian civilization, of course, developed on an alluvial plain that was noteworthy for lacking most essential natural resources besides clay, bitumen, reeds, possibly salt, and fish and birds. The trade that developed partly as a result of this deficiency cannot be dismissed as the relatively unimportant luxury exchange of status markers among participating elites.

Since trade was one means by which the competing city-states of Early Dynastic Sumer obtained non-indigenous resources, it was essential for them to produce commodities that could be exchanged. Textual and archaeological evidence together confirm that they succeeded primarily by engaging in the surplus production of woollen textiles or a production for exchange that was intimately related to the internal structure of Sumerian society. That is, the control of a dependent, semi-free, largely female labor force by the so-called "great" public organizations, the temples and the palaces, not only resulted in production for exchange, but also helped create and continually reinforce the nascent state institutions themselves (cf. Zagarell 1986b). Analyses of the distribution of certain classes of archaeological materials dated to the mid-third millennium have demonstrated that finished commodities, as well as raw materials, were imported into Sumer (Kohl 1978, 1979). In other words, the intercultural trade that developed between resource-poor southern Mesopotamia and the resource-rich highland areas of Anatolia and Iran necessarily transformed the productive activities of all the societies participating in the exchange network without the development of an overarching polity or empire. For example, a specialized center for the production of elaborately carved soft stone vessels has been excavated at the small, non-urban settlement of Tepe Yahya in southeastern Iran. There is no evidence to suggest that this center was incorporated into a larger political unit encompassing the urban centers that imported its vessels.

It has also been proposed that Sumerian and other lowland cities held a competitive advantage in this exchange at least in so far as that they could obtain commodities and natural resources from multiple, isolated, and autonomous communities, such as Tepe Yahya, while the highland communities came to rely exclusively upon the goods – textiles and possible foodstuffs – that they received from Mesopotamia and Khuzistan (Kohl 1978: 471–2); the highland settlements or other peripheral zones occasionally became locked into unequal exchange relationships for both internal and external reasons. Utilizing textual references to sizable quantities of grain, such as 2380 *kur* (over 425,000 liters) of barley, which are mentioned possibly in reference to the Arabian/Persian Gulf trade, Edens (n.d.: 25) has calculated that the entire estimated population of the major settlement on Bahrain in the early second millennium B.C., Qala'at al-Bahrain City II, could have been sustained for roughly more than half a year on the basis of such imports. Some real dependencies might have been created in those peripheral zones along the Gulf, which are known to have supported significant populations but which lacked, above all, sufficient sources of fresh water. Needs and demands, of course, were in part artificially created, and, importantly, the small communities that engaged in the procurement of raw materials and/or the production of highly crafted commodities were themselves internally transformed as a result of their participation in this system. Emergent elites who directed these productive activities came to depend upon the continuance of the trade to maintain their newly acquired privileged positions within society.

No one can deny that the scale of economic activities, such as international trade, in the late twentieth century A.D. far exceeds, indeed qualitatively surpasses, that of the remote past, but certain qualifications still must be made. First, the remarkably small workshops of the Graeco-Roman world seem less striking when one considers the size of industrial establishments today in developing countries which are thoroughly integrated into the modern world system. For example, over 95 percent of the manufacturing establishments in Iran in 1972 or during the heyday of the Shah's unrealistic and ill-fated march to become an industrial power employed less than ten people (Halliday 1979: 182). Secondly, attempts at quantifying the volume of long-distance trade for the early modern period also reveal surprisingly small-scale activities. Portuguese presence in the east from Hormuz to Macao and Nagasaki is estimated at only 10,000 settlers for the entire sixteenth century A.D. or, in other words, completely dwarfed by the Islamic commercial penetration of the Indian Ocean which had begun centuries earlier. Indeed, Steensgaard (1973) believes that the Portuguese simply took over and/or coexisted with earlier Asian systems of trade; for him, earlier transcontinental caravan and peddling trading systems were only decisively interrupted and transformed after the fall of Hormuz (1622) and the large-scale establishment and penetration of major North West European trading companies. Consideration only of the *scale* of European involvement in the Far East makes it impossible to understand its rapid success and conquests.[17]

A basic problem for reconstructing the scale of activities for even more remote periods of the past, particularly antiquity, is, as already noted, one of documentation (see Adams 1979b: 395). Occasionally, however, when textual documents mention the size of specific shipments of goods or the number of laborers in a dependent work force, one cannot help but be impressed by their considerable extents, not qualitatively distinct from those characteristic of the early modern periods. Individual shipments of at least twenty tons of copper have been recorded, and Larsen conservatively estimates that some 100,000 textiles and 80 tons of tin may have been exported from Assur to the small town of Kanesh over a 50-year period during Old Assyrian times (Gledhill and Larsen 1982: 206, 212). R. McC. Adams (1981: 147–9) calculates a total of c. 2,350,000 head of sheep in southern Mesopotamia during the heavily state-controlled Ur III period at the end of the third millennium, or c. 53 percent more than is estimated for roughly the same area of southern Iraq in 1952–3 A.D., when the human population of the area was roughly three times as great; such figures bespeak not only the large-scale ritual slaughter of livestock for cultic purposes (again underscoring the indissoluble link between ideological and economic factors), but also indicate the importance and size of surplus woolen textile production in southern Mesopotamia which was essential for their acquisition of imported raw materials. Dependent work forces far exceeded the few dozen Finley suggests was exceptional for classical times. Iron Age Achaemenid treasury tablets from Persepolis refer to rations being issued to crews of 694, 702, and 677 dependent male workers (*kurtash*); there are frequent references to several hundred workers, and one tablet even mentions the payment in silver to 957 Babylonian(?) stone quarry workers (Dandamaev and Lukonin 1977: 186–202; see also Adams's discussion (1974a: 274) citing Jacobsen's 9000 slave employees at Ur's textile establishment). G. Pettinato (1981:134), epigraphist of the pre-Sargonic Ebla archives, has calculated that the roll of work superintendents, each of whom controlled twenty persons, consisted of

11,700 individuals, suggesting a total population of over 200,000, a figure, which, he claims, is corroborated by an economic document of barley rations for 260,000 people. Although there is considerable disagreement on the exact extent of the Ebla kingdom and the nature of its relations with southern Mesopotamia (Michalowski 1985), it seems clear that it controlled numerous outlying settlements and that its wealth was to a surprising degree based on trade and on the surplus production of wool (Gelb 1985). All dependents at Ebla seem to have been paid both in barley and silver, a fact that highlights the incipient monetization of the Ebla economy, which, apparently, was based on the international standard of the Dilmun (most likely, the island of Bahrain) shekel. The Ebla texts also record annual outlays of up to 2000 kg of silver, and one text refers to 1740 *minas* (870 kg) of gold and another to 300 kg of gold stored in the form of vessels in the state treasury as non-invested wealth (Pettinato 1981: 166–7; 195–6).

From an archaeological perspective, it is important to note that the site of Ebla itself only slightly exceeds 50 ha in size. Clearly, the figures for dependents cited above cannot represent the population of the city alone but must refer to the entire commercial kingdom which controlled several hundred towns and villages encompassing most of Syria and Palestine. Granted this, however, Pettinato still estimates a population at Ebla itself of c. 40,000 or a total considerably in excess of a figure derived from the commonly cited, primarily village-derived demographic conversion factor of c. 100 or even the more liberal figure of 200 persons/ha.[18] Pettinato's calculations differ from these by a factor of anywhere from four to eight and recall the much larger population estimates originally favored by H. Frankfort (1948: 396, n. 23) and L. Woolley (1963: 428), which for Ur convert to a figure of between 400–600 persons/ha. McGuire Gibson (personal communication) likewise believes that we have grossly underestimated the population of Mesopotamian cities, noting that all calculations must consider the possibility of significant numbers of peoples migrating into cities for economic and political reasons and living in extended families often in the upper storeys of houses that excavations have occasionally revealed were packed closely together.[19] Most researchers concede that the use of a single density estimator for Mesopotamian hamlets, villages, towns, and cities masks reality; unfortunately, continued reliance on the conservative estimates often creates a spurious sense of accuracy.

Though arguably more deficient than textual sources on the scale of past activities, archaeological data likewise suggest that ancient economic activities took place on an exceedingly complex and large scale. For example, Edens (n.d.: 13) has calculated the relative frequency of shell from the Arabian/Persian Gulf as a raw material for the production of cylinder seals – objects which, of course, were essential for administrative/accounting purposes. More than half the cylinder seals found at Ur during late Early Dynastic times were made of shell from the Gulf (n=190), and roughly 36 per cent of cylinder seals for Akkadian times (n=644) from Ur, the Diyala, Kish, and Susa were made of shell. While cylinder seals, of course, are small objects, use on this scale must at least imply regular access to sources for shell in the Gulf. The recent work of G. Weisgerber at the Maysar sites in Oman (most likely, ancient Magan) corroborates the textually derived picture of regular, sizable shipments of copper up the Gulf to Mesopotamia. More copper ingots were recovered from the c. 1 ha site of Maysar 1 in a few seasons of excavation than have been recovered in nearly 150 years of excavation on all other third millennium sites in the Near East (Weisgerber 1983: 274). More than 100 copper deposits and more than half a million tons of slag, mostly dating to Early Islamic times, were recorded by the German team. Although the Early Islamic mining and smelting activities often destroyed evidence for third millennium workings and made it impossible to estimate the scale of ancient copper production, Weisgerber has recovered evidence for third millennium production at the two Early Islamic sites that he has excavated and believes that the same evidence would appear at a "large number" (that is, the vast majority) of the c. 100 medieval mining sites (Hauptmann and Weisgerber 1980: 137).

Archaeological discoveries and cuneiform texts together have abundantly confirmed that precious stones, such as lapis lazuli, were highly coveted, prestige goods destined for consumption in Mesopotamia in public architecture or elite burials. Yet the equivalency lists compiled from the Ebla texts reveal that for several years a shekel of lapis lazuli was only one-third the price of a shekel of silver or was less expensive than all but the poorest quality textiles produced at the site (Pettinato 1981: 198–9). Even tin, which also most likely was imported from far to the east, possibly western Afghanistan, and which was essential for the production of bronzes (a single text from Ebla records the production of nearly 20 kg of tin bronzes), was valued at only two-thirds the price of silver, or, in other words, it was still less expensive than most textiles (cf. Muhly 1985: 280–1). Such figures also minimally suggest the regular movement of non-local materials along long-distance, undoubtedly, in some cases, overland, trade routes that stretched for thousands of kilometers over vast stretches of West Asia.

West Asian Bronze Age "world" systems: the problems of multiple cores and transferrable technologies

Let us turn to what perforce must be a more descriptive account of the interacting, politically heterogeneous world system(s) of West Asia from the late fourth through the early second millennium B.C. This description is not arranged chronologically, nor meant to read as a history that traces the various contractions, expansions, and shifts in the locations of various centers and peripheries of this interlocking system. Such a work still needs to be done and would require synthesizing an exceedingly vast corpus of archaeological materials extending from the Balkans and the Nile Valley in the west to Central Asia and the Indian subcontinent in the east; such materials would then have to be integrated with the political and economic histories that have been reconstructed for those exceptional literate areas – Egypt, Syria, and Mesopotamia – of this related Bronze Age world. Our more limited present aim is simply to show that this area can be considered at some level as a unit, that it formed some form of complex, multi-centered world system(s).

Different types of archaeological evidence, such as the well-documented exchange in obsidian, spread of domesticates or the distribution of types of ceramics and specific features of ceramic technology, demonstrate that extensive areas of Anatolia, Syria-Palestine, Mesopotamia, and Iran participated in certain primitive, presumably overlapping exchange networks at least as early as during the Early Neolithic Period (c. 8000–6000 B.C.). Archaeological data also suggest that over time increasingly larger areas were associated at some level of sociopolitical integration and interacted with or expanded into other areas (for example, the Halaf and Ubaid cultures or ceramic horizons). It is also clear that the scale of such interaction increased exponentially during the late fourth millennium B.C. or beginning of the period that Childe appropriately dubbed "the urban revolution." Late Uruk settlements or colonies, such as Habuba Kabira, are found in northern Mesopotamia and even probably along the upper stretches of the Euphrates as far as Malatya in what is today southeastern Turkey (for instance, at Arslantepe). Mesopotamian and West Asian materials have been recognized in late predynastic Gerzean contexts in Egypt and include objects such as cylinder seals, the characteristic authenticating device for Mesopotamia. Intriguingly, a primitively executed, but unmistakable cylinder seal, dating possibly to the early third millennium B.C., has also been recovered at a site along the upper Zeravshan River, c. 45 km east of Samarkand in Soviet Tadjikistan, and a similarly shaped, possibly earlier, seal was found north of Maikop in Ciscaucasia (Nekhaev 1986). While examples of such correspondences could be extended almost indefinitely, their significance varies from case to case; certainly alone, such archaeologically attested links do not document integration into some overarching, tightly structured, systemically integrated exchange network. It is not really until the Early Dynastic Period (c. 2900–2400 B.C.) in Sumer that one can combine both textual and archaeological data to reconstruct interregional networks suggestive of a Wallersteinian-like world system. Even this latter evidence, however, still does not permit us to trace an outline as nuanced as that which has been drawn for the sixteenth century A.D. One could speculate that certain areas, such as the western Zagros, functioned during specific periods as semi-peripheries within a system dominated by the Mesopotamian core, but our knowledge of Bronze Age West Asian economic interconnections is far too incomplete to confirm such hypotheses.

Multiple cores and bonds of dependency

That interconnections existed on some substantial scale is clear, but their detailed structure still eludes convincing analysis. If one refuses to despair, the only way to proceed is first to comprehend the whole area that was engaged in some form of regular interregional exchange during the Bronze Age. A quick glance at any reasonably complete map of known third millennium archaeological sites in West Asia reveals several dense concentrations of hierarchically structured settlements, normally centered around major riverine systems, that are separated by more sparsely populated zones. Cultural evolution throughout the greater Middle East during the third and second millennia B.C. was not exclusively nor even dominantly related to developments within Mesopotamia.[20] Reference has already been made to the geographically more extensive and culturally more uniform Harappan civilization, and any complete discussion must consider Egypt and, as shall be examined below, southern Central Asia. To use world systems terminology, multiple core areas coexisted and intermittently came into direct or indirect contact with one another. Each core manipulated an adjacent hinterland which at times it may have attempted to control. Egypt's relations with Nubia, the Levantine coast, and the Sinai peninsula provide a striking illustration of such a regionalized system. Meluhhan or Indus villagers may have resided in Mesopotamia (Parpola et al. 1977), and now direct archaeological evidence suggests that the Harappans, like the Sumerians, were interested in the copper resources of Oman (Weisgerber 1984). Bronze Age sites in southern Central Asia (western Turkestan) exchanged some materials with Harappan centers, as is evident from the discoveries of Indus seals, ivory sticks, and etched carnelian beads at Altyn-depe in southern Turkmenistan (Masson 1981). Sites along the piedmont strip of southern Turkmenistan and in the lowland plains of Bactria and Margiana contain numerous objects made from materials such as lapis lazuli, turquoise, and various metals, which were not available locally but which existed in adjacent regions and which must have been procured through some regularized intercultural exchange network. In short, the Bronze Age world system of the late third and early second millennia B.C. was characterized not by a single dominant core region economically linked to less developed peripheral zones, but by a patchwork of overlapping, geographically disparate, and politically autonomous core regions or foci of cultural development, each of which primarily exploited its own immediate hinterland.

The existence of such multiple cores in sporadic contact with one another is not a peculiar anomaly of the Bronze Age world system but points to a basic disconformity between this system and that postulated by Wallerstein for the modern era. Specifically, peripheries situated between cores were far from helpless in dictating the terms of exchange; they could develop or terminate relations depending upon whether or not these relations were perceived to be in their best interest. For example, recent archaeological excavations in the United Arab Emirates and Oman at sites such as Hilu (Cleuziou 1980, 1981), Bat (Frifelt 1976), and Maysar (Weisgerber 1980, 1981) have revealed the existence of a fairly uniform late third/early second millennia culture characterized by distinctive architecture, ceramics, and mortuary practices which, at least at Maysar, was engaged in the large-scale production of copper for exchange.[21] The archaeological data are consistent with cuneiform documents recording extensive trade with Magan, a region that exported copper and diorite to Mesopotamia, but ceramics, ingot forms, and an excavated triangular-shaped seal from Maysar also indicate metallurgical relations with South Asia (Weisgerber 1980: 106, fig. 77; 1984). Although it is still too early to determine whether or not this prehistoric Omani culture maintained exchange relations simultaneously or successively with Sumer and Harappa, it seems impossible to refer to the systematic underdevelopment of this autonomous culture. If anything, prehistoric Oman appears to have prospered or been sustained at a more complex level of cultural development than would have been possible in the absence of these exchange relations. While circumstantial, this evidence seems to contradict a model of exchange so unequal as to foster "the development of underdevelopment."

There is little reason to doubt that patterns of dependency or, perhaps better, interdependency were established as a result of intercultural exchange in the Bronze Age world system. Less developed peripheral societies were probably more strongly affected by participation in this exchange than were the more densely populated, internally differentiated civilizations that emerged on lowland alluvial plains. Dependency could lead to exploitation, and, if later myths, such as Enmerkar and the Lord of Aratta, are a guide (see Kohl 1978: 472 and criticisms on 476–84; and discussion above), it is possible that in exceptional circumstances – during a drought or famine – the more powerful urban societies could dictate the terms of the exchange. But the relations between ancient cores and peripheries were not structurally analogous to those that underdevelopment theorists postulate are characteristic of First–Third World relations today. Unless conquered (that is, incorporated into a larger polity), ancient peripheries typically could have followed one of several options ranging from withdrawal from the exchange network to substitution of one core partner for another. Archaeological and historical evidence converge to suggest that most intercultural exchange systems in antiquity were fragile, lasting at most a few generations before collapsing. This inherent instability is related to the relative weakness of the bonds of dependency that existed between core and peripheral partners.[22]

Transferrable technologies and shifts in power

Peripheral societies of the Bronze Age not only had more options available to them, but they also did not necessarily suffer from a technological gap that doomed them to politically and militarily inferior positions *vis-à-vis* civilized cores. That is, consideration of the technological base of these early Bronze Age civilizations also reveals a fundamental structural discrepancy between ancient and modern world systems. It is not that the scale of intercultural trade in the late third/early second millennia B.C. was a fraction of that which united the world in the sixteenth century A.D., nor that the speed, reliability, and capability of transportation and communication systems in the Bronze Age were greatly circumscribed relative to the systems which developed at the beginning of the modern era. These are relative phenomena. Rather, a qualitative difference exists because critical technologies, such as metal working and later horse breeding, were not controlled by core areas alone. Bronze Age technologies could not be monopolized but quickly diffused from one area to another or, in this sense, were transferrable. Moreover, important technologies often initially developed or were further refined in peripheral areas close to the natural sources of the necessary resources.

The uses to which transferrable technologies could be put varied from society to society depending upon their needs and internal structure. Major technological innovations that made possible new forms of social organization and that had the potential to alter existing balances of power often appeared in peripheries or along the frontiers of civilized society. Peripheral societies not only exercised a considerable range of options in dealing with more powerful trade partners but, in certain times and places, also developed new techniques or applied nearly universal skills in a broadly "progressive" fashion that ultimately had far-reaching social and political consequences. This characteristic potential for innovation in peripheral areas in the Bronze Age world system is well illustrated by consideration of Late Bronze Age developments in areas peripheral to the Mesopotamian core, such as the eastern Mediterranean (Childe 1957: 8–9) or southern Central Asia.

Let us consider briefly Late Bronze Age developments in the latter area. Recent discoveries of numerous Bronze Age settlements in Margiana and Bactria suggest that earlier theories of barbarian invasions or total breakdowns in interregional exchange networks that led to a near total abandonment of long-occupied urban settlements in southern Turkmenistan (Masson and Sarianidi 1972) are incorrect; a crisis in urbanization or social devolution in southern Central Asia (and by extension throughout areas farther to the south) never occurred. Urban life did not collapse, but settlements *shifted* in Central Asia to the lowland plain formed by the lower Murghab and to the southern and northern Bactrian plains. These settlements were clearly related in terms of their material features to the earlier settlements in southern Turkmenistan, but they were also different. Sites were obviously planned and fortified; burial practices changed; and more numerous and advanced metal tools and weapons were produced on the Margiana and Bactrian sites. Known area of occupation in Margiana alone during its so-called Gonur or second stage of development is roughly double that documented in southern Turkmenistan or the core area during its period of urban florescence (NMG V). If southern and northern Bactria are also considered, the estimated area of *expansion*, not contraction or collapse, doubles once more. That is, present evidence suggests that settled life minimally was four times as extensive in Bactria and Margiana during the Bronze Age than in southern Turkmenistan.[23] While chronological correlations between the different regions need further clarification, it is obvious that the development of settled life in Bactria and Margiana cannot be accounted for solely or even primarily on the basis of emigration from southern Turkmenistan. In addition, hundreds of archaeological sites or stations, composed chiefly of lithic remains, have been documented north of Margiana in the Kyzyl Kum desert (Vinogradov and Mamedov 1975) and immediately north of the Bronze Age sites in southern Bactria (Vinogradov 1979). It is likely that the relatively sudden appearance of planned Bronze Age sites on these lowland plains also involved the incorporation of these less technologically advanced peoples. The known core area of southern Turkmenistan was replaced by new centers in Bactria and Margiana at the end of the third and beginning of the second millennium. The cultures that developed in these newly settled areas clearly were related to the earlier cultures that evolved over several millennia in southern Turkmenistan but also exhibited new features, perhaps reflecting their mixed origins.

These Central Asian materials cannot easily be incorporated into an unmodified Wallersteinian world systems model. Rather, significant discrepancies emerge: an older core (southern Turkmenistan) appears to have been quickly displaced immediately after its florescence through a large-scale expansion onto formerly uncultivated, naturally fertile plains; the new settlements appear to have been remarkably self-sufficient and well-organized, though less internally differentiated than the earlier urban centers of southern Turkmenistan; at the same time, metallurgical technology, in particular, and the scale of subsistence and craft-related productive activities seem to have increased substantially. Peripheral frontier areas were transformed into cores which were both more and less developed than the societies that they replaced. In addition, the recorded shifts in settlements appear to have been accompanied by significant changes in methods of transportation related to the introduction of the horse and utilization of the spoked wheel.

Horse bones are found at Kelleli 1 and/or Taip (Kuzmina 1980: 27, 33) and at the later Takhirbai 3 site in Margiana and in Late Bronze Age contexts at Tekkem-depe and Namazga-depe in the piedmont strip. The horse, which initially was domesticated somewhere on the south Russian steppe (see Anthony 1986) probably in the fourth millennium B.C., was introduced into Central Asia on a significant scale during the Late Bronze Age period. Such an introduction or contact might be suggested by the presence of diagnostic incised "steppe" ceramics on many of the sites in the lower Murghab and at Tekkem-depe; in addition, a clay model head of a horse was found at Namazga-depe. Although one cannot confidently speak of the advent of mounted pastoral nomadism or the extent of true horsemanship at this time, it seems likely from what is known of immediately succeeding periods (for example, at Pirak to the south [Jarrige and Santoni 1979]) that riding skills were developing at the end of the third and the beginning of the second millennia and that these must have profoundly affected the entire area of southern Central Asia. The evidence for spoked, as opposed to solid, wheels consists of a model wheel with four brown painted spokes and an emphasized hub from Namazga, a wheel with six red painted spokes from Tekkem, and another spoked wheel from El'ken-depe (Kuzmina 1980: 27). The significance of this development is unclear, though it too presumably led to increased mobility and ease of wheeled transport for hauling goods and/or for military purposes.[24]

The new settled societies in Bactria and Margiana, some of which may have moved farther south into Baluchistan and eastern Iran, adopted pre-existing, easily transferable technologies in strikingly innovative and politically significant ways. This adoption, possibly analogous to that postulated by Childe (1957) for his "progressive" European barbarians, resulted in the abandonment of an older core area and indeed may have been partly responsible for the collapse of early urban civilization in South Asia.[25] Core areas, in short, were not terribly stable, and critically important technologies, capable of transforming political relations among interacting areas, were readily transferrable to less developed regions, some of which were situated closer to natural source deposits or breeding plains for live resources, such as horses.

Technologies, of course, did not diffuse automatically, and their importance, even use, differed from one social context to the next. But the model of a world system, which Wallerstein defined for the modern era, only imperfectly describes structured interactions in antiquity. Economic development and dependency were not linked phenomena during the Bronze Age in the manner postulated by contemporary critical theory for – to paraphrase their terminology – the development of underdevelopment in the Bronze Age was sharply constrained or itself underdeveloped. Critical technologies, such as metal working, could diffuse relatively easily and new means of transportation and sources of power, such as horses, could be raised in peripheral zones and radically restructure this ancient world system. Technological gaps, which dependency theorists argue pervade First/Third World relations today, simply did not exist in the Bronze Age in a manner that signified permanent political dominance or subjugation. Foraging and nomadic stockbreeding populations on the Central Asian steppes or on the previously uncultivated plains of Margiana and Bactria rapidly adopted and transformed technologies that developed elsewhere, and these innovations made it possible – not inevitable – for them to alter established methods of interaction and political relations throughout many disparate regions of the greater Middle East.

Central Asia clearly interacted with South Asia and Iran in the late third millennium, but it was neither a core, periphery, nor semi-periphery in terms of economic exchange with any of these areas. Contact was at best indirect and sporadic with Mesopotamia and non-existent with the eastern Mediterranean. A stray chlorite weight carved in an immediately recognizable "Intercultural Style" from Soviet Uzbekistan or the discovery of etched carnelian beads in Thailand, and Southeast Asian spices in second millennium Mesopotamian contexts do not demonstrate the existence of a unified world system in any meaningful economic sense; materials and ideas simply could have diffused throughout Eurasia in a variety of ways. For Wallerstein's model to apply one must demonstrate economic dependency, and this one can do for only separate, apparently politically independent, areas of Eurasia during the third and early second millennia B.C.

The Bronze Age world system consisted, in fact, of overlapping systems that constantly shifted and modified their boundaries due to unpredictable historical events, technological changes, or the formation and dissolution of larger political units and alliances. Thus, in the early to mid-third millennium, southern Iran, extending the length of the Zagros, was united into a world system dominated by Khuzestan and possibly south-central Iran at the site of Anshan. The Namazga civilization of southern Central Asia formed part of another world system, perhaps spatially resembling that defined by Biscione and Tosi as prehistoric Turan (1979). Relations with South Asia and its Harappan-dominated world system changed during the latter part of the third millennium, possibly related to a shift from overland to maritime long-distance exchange and to the development of metallurgy, particularly the production of weapons, and the introduction of horses.

Successful, extensive, culturally heterogeneous, and relatively long-lived political empires, such as, above all, that formed by the Achaemenids in Iron Age times, emerged later and were explicitly distinguished by their politically imposed unity from the world system of modern times. Moreover, developments that occurred in Bronze Age peripheries soon transformed these less socially complex societies, as on the plains of Bactria and Margiana and, perhaps, at Shah-dad in southeastern Iran, into core areas of their own. Expansion and colonization during the Bronze Age into largely unsettled areas continuously stimulated development and may have been structurally similar to the Greek overseas ventures of the seventh and sixth centuries B.C. However, the Bronze Age colonies, as in Bactria, soon became more advanced than their homelands for they quickly achieved, if they did not originally possess, political autonomy and could develop relatively freely of limiting historical and social constraints.

Yet, if one adopts a sufficiently broad temporal perspective, it is also clear that this contrast with the modern world system can be overdrawn. Shifts in the status of modern core states, notably the decline of British and rise of American hegemony, are easy to discern. Conversely, the reemergence of core areas in antiquity should not be overlooked. The political ascendancy of southern Mesopotamia clearly waxed and waned over the centuries; the so-called Dark Ages not only reflect an absence of texts, but also refer to periods of real political decline. Time and again, however, the southern Mesopotamian core reasserted itself both in economic and *cultural* respects. Babylonia formed the wealthiest Persian satrapy, and the capitals of later empires from the Parthians to the 'Abbasid caliphate were consciously located within this fertile alluvial heartland. Easy access to and control of millennia-old long-distance trade routes partially explain these renewals, but probably even more important were the yields obtained from intensive, irrigation-dependent agriculture that periodically was renewed on a large scale by the local centralized state. The cultural legacy of southern Mesopotamia also survived these periodic political and economic upheavals well beyond the decline of the cuneiform literary tradition. It is perhaps not irrelevant to note that the amorphously defined borders of the overlapping Bronze Age world systems coincide to a surprising extent with the area encompassed by the initial spread of Islam. The fit is not perfect, and the nature and significance of connections between Bronze Age practices and later features of Islam cannot yet be traced, but coincidence usually has an explanation, and, as Nolte (1982: 49–50) has persuasively argued for *Christian* Europe, categories of religious history are often helpful for the definition of an extensive, spatially and temporally situated world system. The original Bronze Age world systems did not simply collapse, but left a complex, web-like legacy of political, economic, and, in the broadest sense, cultural interconnections which, in turn, were acted upon and influenced later historical developments.

Total history and cultural evolution: in search of a synthesis

Once-fashionable regional ecosystemic perspectives on the development of early civilizations represented an advance over earlier diffusionary theories, for they compelled one to consider long-term structural phenomena and undeniably significant infrastructural features; they still failed to satisfy, however, because they often refused to acknowledge the importance of historical events and the coming together of different cultural systems (see Kohl 1984a). As this chapter hopefully has helped demonstrate, it is notoriously difficult to assess the scale and evaluate the significance of the exchange of materials and ideas among prehistoric societies. Archaeological data, however, unequivocally demonstrate that contacts among societies at different levels of cultural development occurred, and it is reasonable to assume that in many cases their effects were substantial. Utilization of Wallerstein's concept of a world system has the singular advantage of emphasizing that such contacts were based on fundamental economic considerations that were not necessarily to every society's adaptive advantage, but were the products of stronger societies or elites within those societies attempting to impose their will and desire for material gain upon less developed peripheral areas. For both modern and ancient times, Wallerstein's mode of an interacting world system raises the essential, though often overlooked, problem of determining the most appropriate spatial and temporal unit of analysis. One cannot deny the open-ended nature of social systems in the past any more than one can ignore the interconnections among societies in the modern era (Wolf 1982). Moreover, because such interconnections have intensified during modern times, it is obvious that cultural evolution must primarily be reconstructed from archaeological, not ethnological, evidence. That Wallerstein's model cannot be applied literally to the Bronze Age does not mean that the search for interconnections and structured interaction is unproductive. Rather, the task now is to determine how and why interactions at different, archaeologically attested stages of cultural development both resembled and differed from those of today. The model cannot be applied literally to earlier social formations, but its necessary alteration may help us to understand better the development and character of pre- and early-state societies and force us to write total histories of the past. Where the data suggest meaningful contact, separate evolutionary sequences must be brought together and analyzed within a broader overarching "world" framework. Such procedures inevitably will reduce the number of genuine examples of independent state formation, but such a necessary sacrifice is a small price to pay for a richer, more deeply textured picture of a largely shared evolutionary and historical past.

Notes

1 An earlier version of this chapter appears in *Archaeological Advances in Method and Theory*, vol. 11 (1987), Academic Press.
2 See Trigger 1984d: 282–90 for a perceptive discussion of the current dissatisfaction and bibliography; for an intelligent critique of evolutionary theory largely specific to the Near East, see Yoffee (1979).
3 See Lamberg-Karlovsky and Sabloff (1979: 188) for an explicit rejection of the "pristine" evolution of any single West Asian Bronze Age civilization.
4 Though, for the American southwest, see now McGuire in press; Plog et al. 1982; Plog 1983; and Upham 1982.
5 See Wallerstein 1974, 1979, 1980; issues of the journal *Review*; and Ragin and Chirot 1984 for an assessment and general bibliography.
6 It is noteworthy that in Braudel's concluding volume, *The Perspective of the World*, to his magisterial survey of the development of capitalism and the emergence of the modern world, there are numerous references to non-European, pre-modern world systems. While the bulk of Braudel's discussion is concerned with the successive replacement of one European center by another – from Venice to England – he ventures out from this peninsular (i.e. European) focus to consider non-Western "world-economies", such as those dominated by the Russians, Ottomans, and the greatest fourth "world economy" of the Far East, encompassing Islam, India, and China. Braudel's terminology is very loose and the theoretical discussion somewhat unclear and open to the same criticisms of creating suprahistorical forces and systems that have been levelled at Wallerstein. For present purposes, while Braudel explicitly adopts Wallerstein's formulation, he likewise explicitly departs from the latter's qualitative distinction between world empires and world economies and systems (1984: 54–5) and the unique character of modern times, thus admitting a series of overlapping world economies, which resembles, to some extent, our depiction of contemporaneous, competing centers spread across West Asia during the Bronze Age.

7   E.g. Kellenbenz 1976; Brenner 1977; Hunt 1978; George 1980; Chirot 1985; for a balanced but critical assessment, cf. Wolf 1982: 21–3.
8   For a classic exposition of diffusion throughout West Asia, see Childe 1953: 238–4.
9   E.g. Binford 1972: 114–21; 1983b: 59–60; also Trigger 1984d: 288–90 on the need for a general *rapprochement* between anthropological archaeology and documentary history; and Trigger, this volume.
10 For the former see Berman 1983; for the latter the classic exposition is Polanyi's *Great Transformation* (1957).
11 For a counter example from the ancient Near East, see Larsen's detailed analysis (1977) of the *naruqqu*-contract.
12 See, however, de Ste Croix's generally persuasive, though dauntingly monumental rebuttal (1981) of Finley's narrow understanding of the presence and significance of classes in the ancient Graeco-Roman world.
13 See Kemp 1978; and R. McC. Adams's perceptive comments on Kemp's observations denying the massive flow of wealth and produce from the peripheral Nubian colony to Egypt (1979b: 394–5).
14 See also Steensgaard's discussion (1973: 81–95) of the contradictory or mixed nature of the Spanish–Portuguese *Estado da India*.
15 See Farber 1978: 19 and Silver 1983: 798; the latter study, written by an economic historian, who, like Polanyi, was not trained in Assyriology, attempts to cull somewhat randomly from the secondary literature instances which refute Polanyi's general interpretation of the ancient Near Eastern economy.
16 See most recently the summary article by Gledhill and Larsen 1982.
17 Braudel 1984: 488–511; for a discussion of pre-European trade in the Far East and a comparison of the scale of pre-modern and post-Industrial Revolution trade across the Indian Ocean, see also Chaudhuri 1985: 34–62, 182–220; also Hodges and Whitehouse 1983: 130–49 for a graphic description of the 'Abbasid expansion of regular trade with China in the late eighth and early ninth centuries A.D.
18 Adams 1965b: 24–5, 123; 1981: 69; see also the figures for Near Eastern villages recorded in Kramer 1982: 159–60 and her discussion on pp. 116–26, 155–68.
19 See also the 1917 figures for Baghdad and Najaf cited by Adams 1981: 349–50, ch. 4, n. 1.
20 See also Lamberg-Karlovsky (1972: 99) for an early statement on broad "interaction spheres" linking different areas within West Asia.
21 For a general overview to developments in prehistoric Arabia, see Tosi 1986.
22 Cf. Larsen (1979a: 99), who also seems to believe in the inherent fragility of interconnections throughout the ancient world.
23 See Kohl 1984b: 117–19; 135–8; 143–6; 151–4; 159–60 for these estimates.
24 Similarly – to turn briefly to another area – a somewhat later but equally dramatic example of the significance of developments in transportation technology is provided by the introduction of the dromedary for hauling goods across the Syrian desert. In a provocative, far-reaching article, Gibson (n.d.) associates the historically attested shift in traditional political (and, correspondingly, economic) alliances among Assyrians, Elamites, and Babylonians, which occurred in the ninth century B.C., with the wide-scale adoption of the dromedary as a pack animal. Once Babylonia could be linked to the Mediterranean and Egypt by camel caravan, Assyrian incursions along the middle Euphrates (for example, at Mari) became far less significant, and Elam and Babylonia abandoned their traditional relations as rivals and became allies interested in maintaining this trading connection to the west. The subsequent political history of this part of West Asia is intimately associated with these changes.
25 For a defense of the older, perhaps prematurely discredited theory of external invasions and the collapse of the Indus civilization see Allchin and Allchin 1982: 298–308; also the recent establishment of the chronological relations between indigenous, Harappan, and "Central Asian" materials at the foot of the Bolan pass in Pakistani Baluchistan at the sites of Mehrgarh, Sibri, and now Naushara is consistent with the replacement of an expansive Harappan presence by peoples exhibiting close material culture parallels with the Margiana/Bactrian sites to the north, though the excavator, J.-F. Jarrige (1986: 119–22), is inclined to see more an expansion north from Baluchistan to Bactria, rather than the reverse. I wish to thank Dr. Richard Meadow for providing me with this information.

15

Mesopotamia, Central Asia and the Indus Valley: so the kings were killed

C. C. LAMBERG-KARLOVSKY

. . . down in the dust lay the ancient majesty of thrones, the haughty sceptres. The illustrious emblem of the sovereign head, dabbled in gore and trampled under the feet of the rabble, mounted its high estate.

Lucretius

The earliest civilizations in the three regions of our concern have been termed Sumerian (Mesopotamia), Namazga (Central Asia), and Harappan (Indus Valley). Archaeologists, almost as one, hold firm to the conviction that *each* of the above civilizations is at least partly the result of an indigenous, autonomous process of development. In each case the distinctive nature of their material remains, their geographical separation, and most particularly the differing cultural traditions so apparent in the material culture that characterized each area *prior* to the emergence of urban complexity provide substantial support for their indigenous emergence. This is not to say, however, that particular forms of social relations, particularly of a commercial nature, did not provide an integrative force with their adjacent frontiers. The chronological priority of the Sumerian civilization over the Harappan is simply not sufficient for claiming that "it can at least be averred that, however translated, the *idea* of civilization came to the Indus from the Euphrates and Tigris, and gave the Harappans their initial direction, or at least informed their purpose" (Wheeler 1968b: 135).

Our evidence for the evolution of a complex society is best seen in Mesopotamia. The earliest Mesopotamian civilization, the Sumerian, was restricted to the southern-most regions of modern-day Iraq (c. 3500 B.C.). Remains of immediately antecedent cultures (Ubaid) have been excavated in the same area and still older cultures recovered in the surrounding Zagros mountain valleys of Iran and Iraq.

It is important to realize that *prior* to the emergence of "civilization" Mesopotamian communities already exhibited temples, urban centers, trade, militarism, craft specialization, art, monumental architecture and mechanisms for the regulation of both the production and distribution of resources. Thus all attributes of a complex society are present save for the existence of writing. This simply underscores the often unstated fact that quantitative distinctions in the above categories (that is, a lot more of the same) make for qualitative differences. Although Sumerian civilization evolved out of a prolonged millennium of "processual development," its dawn was in fact a relatively rapid appearance. In less than 300 years (3500–3200 B.C.) independent city-states emerge that are dominated first by temples and then palaces, which become, and remain, the pre-eminent architectural feature on the Mesopotamian landscape for three thousand years.

The Mesopotamian city-state was dominated politically and economically by the twin pillars of its religious temples and secular palaces. These two institutional entities, often in competition with each other for political and economic dominance, were the principal forces of production and distribution. It was only in the rare instance that the individual city-states of Mesopotamia fell under the hegemony of a single ruler. Centripetal forces of empire formation characterized Mesopotamian history in only a few instances, chiefly the Akkadian Dynasty (2350–2150 B.C.); the Ur III (2100–2000 B.C.); Old Babylonian kingdom (1900–1600 B.C.) and the Assyrian empire (800–614 B.C.).

Far more typical were the centrifugal forces tending toward a disunity. We are reminded in this context of Wallerstein's view, which suggests that European success in the formation of the capitalist system was due to an *absence* of European political unity. In like manner Mesopotamian merchants were able to keep clear of the confiscating clutches of imperial rule and to operate within a considerable degree of mobility in face of competing city-states. Competition between the productive forces of the priestly temples and royal palaces on the one hand, and between them and the private manorial estates on the other hand, allowed for a sustained tension between the principal forces of economic production. The inability of either the temple or the palace to accede to absolute authority *within* the confines of its own city-state hindered the opportunity of either institution to extend its hegemony beyond its own boundaries. When such an occasion did take place, it was the direct result of a powerful king who through military conquest vanquished his neighbors.

Mesopotamian texts indicate that the earliest cities were conceived of as estates belonging to the gods, maintained by humans, and ruled over by their priests. Controversy centers around the degree to which the social order was directed by a theocracy and the economy controlled by the temples (Nissen 1983). It is clear that in the Early Dynastic Period (c. 2900–2500) the city temples directed most of the production and redistribution of goods. Large staffs of primary producers, craftsmen, laborers, attendants, and scribes were attached to the temples; only later did the secular palaces successfully challenge the primacy of this theocratic structure.

Thus, if the origins of Sumerian civilization are to be found along the banks of the Tigris–Euphrates, what of the origins of the Indus civilization? The situation here is more complex. The Indus civilization is found along the Indus River and its tributaries, but only in its *mature* stage; the earlier stages leading to its formation appear to take place somewhere else. Mughal (1971) in his influential unpublished doctoral thesis has suggested that the earliest stages in the formation of the Indus civilization are to be found in the villages of northern Baluchistan. The factors in the rise of this civilization have been much studied and remain embroiled in controversy (Possehl 1982). One feature is apparent: its formation and distribution appears as the result of a relatively rapid process. In this respect it appears to replicate the relative speed (c. 300

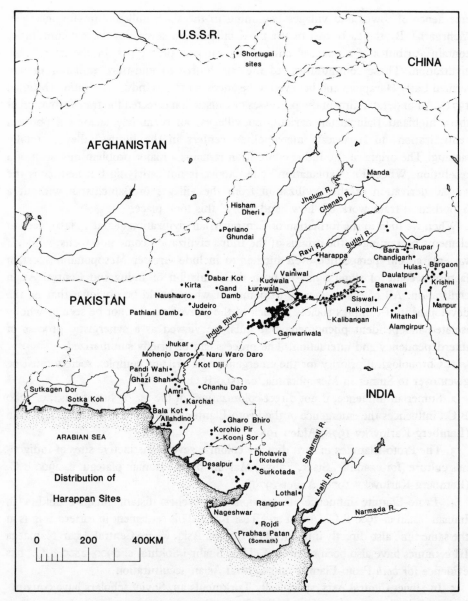

Fig. 15.1. Distribution of archaeological settlements of the Indus civilization c. 2000 B.C. (*Courtesy Gregory Possehl*)

years) that characterized the emergence of the Sumerian civilization. In regions adjacent to the Indus Valley c. 2600 B.C. there were only negligible settlements, whereas by 2300–2200 large cities appear and by 2100 B.C. Indus communities are spread from the Iran–Pakistan border to the Ganges and from the Oxus River to the Gujarat peninsula, the most expansive geographical distribution of any of the Old World civilizations (see Fig. 15.1).

Archaeologists look to the hill country of northern Baluchistan and see there the emergence of towns and villages beginning in the sixth millennium (for instance, Mehrgarh). By the early part of the third millennium several of these communities contain attributes of a material culture that suggest prototypes for the later Indus civilization. These communities, of the late fourth to mid-third millennium, are termed Early Harappan and believed to be ancestral to the Indus civilization (Mughal 1971). An understanding of the processes or causes that directed the transformation of these highland Baluchistan agricultural villages, all seemingly lacking a political centralization, to large-scale metropolitan centers in the Indus Valley is totally lacking. The origin of the Indus civilization remains a major problem in search of a resolution. Wheeler's "explanation" cited above is not satisfying but neither is the simple derivation of this civilization from the villages of Baluchistan without a hypothetical framework of "how" and "why" this took place.

When we turn to the formation of Central Asian civilization (Kohl 1984b), certain elements pertaining to the origins of the Indus civilization come into focus; while, if we enlarge our perspective even further to include Greater Mesopotamia, certain factors become of significance to both the formation of Indus and Central Asian civilization. All of this is merely to point out what should be obvious, that is, the development of complex society in each of the above areas cannot be seen as wholly isolated independent phenomena but must be viewed as a synergistic process of interdependency and interaction. The process can be briefly summarized.

1. Chronological priority for the emergence of a pristine complex society must be given over to Sumer in Mesopotamia, c. 3500 B.C.

2. Sumerian influence, if not direct colonization, of the major site of Susa, c. 3200 B.C., influences the emergence of the Proto-Elamite civilization in southwestern Iran (Lamberg-Karlovsky 1978, Alden 1982).

3. The Proto-Elamites in turn directly colonize several distinctive sites of indigenous culture (for example, Sialk, Yahya, Malyan) on the Iranian plateau, c. 2900 B.C. (Lamberg-Karlovsky 1978; Amiet 1979).

4. Proto-Elamite influence unquestionably reaches distant Shahr-i Sokhta in Iranian Sistan c. 2900 B.C. (Amiet and Tosi 1978). This settlement in eastern Iran is at the same time also directly influenced by Central Asia, where Central Asian Namazga III ceramics have also been recovered. Thus Shahr-i Sokhta, c. 2900–2800 B.C., has evidence for *both* Proto-Elamite and Central Asian acculturation.

5. In Soviet Central Asia, specifically Turkmenistan, Soviet scholars have convincingly shown the presence of an indigenous series of farming communities utilizing irrigation technology in the second half of the fourth millennium, the Geoksyur Complex (Kohl 1984b). The Turkmenian ceramics of the late fourth/early third millennium as well as anthropomorphic figurines, certain metal artifacts, stamp seals, and burial patterns are identical in many instances to those of (a) the Quetta culture of northern Baluchistan and (b) the Helmand Valley of Afghanistan (Shahr-i Sokhta to Mundigak). Both of the above regions were recognized long ago as central to the origin of the Indus civilization (Piggott 1950b).

Recapitulating the above points we see an initial Mesopotamian (Sumerian) colonization of Susa (the later Elamite capital), which results in the secondary formation of a

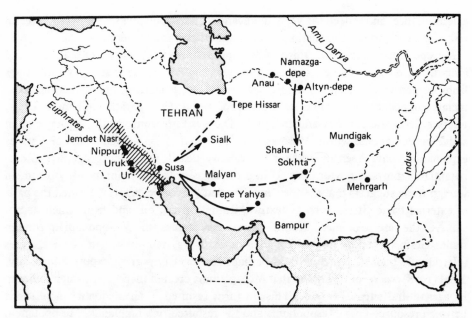

Fig. 15.2. The movement of the Proto-Elamite culture from southwestern Iran onto the Iranian plateau c. 3000 B.C.

Proto-Elamite state in south-western Iran (Wright and Johnson 1975). This Proto-Elamite state colonizes distant sites on the Iranian plateau, its influence being felt at distant Shahr-i Sokhta, where at the same time Central Asian influences are abundantly evident (Fig. 15.2). That a pattern of communication united the region from Mesopotamia to Central Asia c. 2900–2600 B.C. can be readily documented (Lamberg-Karlovsky and Tosi 1973). Similar evidence suggests a pattern of communication that connected Central Asia and Baluchistan which preceded the formation of the Indus civilization.

We argue that following the pristine origin of Mesopotamian civilization a synergistic process of increasing complexity and acculturation assisted in the formation of complex societies throughout the region, from the Euphrates to the Indus. This view is distinctly different from the more typical approach of treating these regions as distinctive unrelated processes of development and requires the formation of new research strategies to address the patterns and causes for the evolution of interactive networks.

In recent years several authors have highlighted the role of "center–periphery" relations and/or the development of "world systems" in the third millennium of the ancient Near East (Ekholm and Friedman 1985; Kohl 1979; Larsen 1979a). Such an approach is heavily influenced by modern "dependency" theorists who see the rise of the West as based on its ability to conquer and exploit a periphery (Wallerstein 1974). Though one may intuitively sense a reality in Ekholm and Friedman's (1985) argument for a substantive existence of a kind of capital accumulation in Mesopotamia, based on center–periphery relations, it remains entirely debatable as to the extent, nature, and indeed the very significance of Mesopotamia's accumulated wealth as being based on the production and/or exploitation of a wider area.

Mesopotamian texts of the third millennium address the presence of both local and long-distance trade. The existence of a thriving intercity trade is attested in the texts from numerous city-states, for instance from Lagash textiles, grain, fish, animals, metals (copper, tin, lead, silver), fats, oils, and wood were all traded to Umma, Uruk, Nippur, Der, and Adab (Lambert 1953). There is little doubt of the existence of an active intercity trade within Mesopotamia, but what of long-distance trade? Various explanations have been offered for the relative dearth of evidence detailing Meso- potamian exports. Crawford (1973) in a review of third millennium Mesopotamian foreign trade suggests that the texts indicate that "invisible exports" formed the basis of external trade. Items such as textiles, leather, grain, oil, and fish, which do not survive the archaeological record, form the staples of Mesopotamian foreign trade. Grain, a commodity which Mesopotamia was famous for in classical times (Herodotus: book I, line 193), was perhaps the most important export commodity. Kohl (1978) has recently argued that Mesopotamia created markets in which to dump its agricultural surplus (grain). This, in turn, resulted in an inequality of relations between resource-poor Mesopotamia and the resource-rich highlands. Mesopotamia, it is argued, maintained a dominance of relations by being able to manipulate the foreign markets. This conception, ultimately derived from André Gunder Frank (see Brenner 1977), argues for a unitary process in the economic relations of cores and peripheries, wherein the core expropriates the resources of the periphery, which remains underdeveloped for lack of access to its own resources. This perception, informed by the economics of modern underdevelopment, when transferred to the third millennium of Mesopotamia, has little to commend it. Neither textual nor archaeological evidence is sufficient to support this hypothesis. The unbalanced evidence for foreign trade is inherent in the distribution and nature of the texts; we have texts only from Mesopotamia and they detail items of export which do not survive the archaeological record.

Settlement pattern hierarchies

A study of settlement patterns and associated patterns of land use allows one to usefully relate the processes of social integration and fragmentation that characterized this expansive area. The presence of written texts in Mesopotamia affords a richer tapestry for understanding than is available in adjacent regions. Mesopotamian texts, in conjunction with extensive settlement surveys, provide an unparalleled opportunity to address a complex topic.

The following tables, adopted from the work of R. McC. Adams (1981), indicate the complexity of the shifting urban and non-urban settlement patterns over two thousand years of Mesopotamian history. Table 15.1 indicates the consistent decline in urban communities correlated with a substantial increase in the number of smaller non-urban settlements from 2500 B.C. to 700 B.C. How does one account for a decrease of 62 percent (from 78 to 16 percent) in the number of urban settlements? Are people moving from the cities to inhabit the smaller villages and towns? Does this urban emigration account for the increase of a 54 percent settlement increase in the number of smaller communities? Table 15.2 breaks down the fluctuations of settlement size and dramatically indicates the extent of the urban crisis.

Table 15.1 *Declining proportion of urban settlement in the third and second millennia B.C.*

	Percentage non-urban (10 ha or less)	Percentage large urban (more than 40 ha)
Early Dynastic II/III	10.0	78.4
Akkadian	18.4	63.5
Ur III–Larsa	25.0	55.1
Old Babylonian	29.6	50.2
Kassite	56.8	30.4
Middle Babylonian	64.2	16.2

Table 15.2 *Totals of assumed site areas in hectares, by size category and historic period*

	"Village"					"City"	
	1 ($\pm$2ha)	2 ($\pm$7)	3 ($\pm$15)	4 ($\pm$30)	5 ($\pm$100)	6 ($\pm$200)	Total
Late Early Dynastic	52	112	75	120	1100	200	1659
Akkadian	66	175	135	120	900	—	1416
Ur III–Larsa	286	399	240	300	1100	400	2725
Old Babylonian	216	315	150	210	700	200	1791
Kassite	330	413	105	60	400	—	1308
Middle Babylonian	200	196	30	90	100	—	616

Ha: 1 hectare = 2.47 acres
Early Dynastic II/III: 2750–2334; Akkadian: 2334–2154; Ur III–Larsa: 2113–1763; Old Babylonian 1894–1595; Kassite: 1550–1150; Middle Babylonian: 1100–700.

Source: R. McC. Adams 1981: 138, 142.

How do we explain these fluctuations within an overall trend of decreasing urban populations? Although Mesopotamia provides the best evidence for dramatic settlement and demographic shifts these also characterize Central Asia and the Indus Valley (see below). The repetitive pattern of integration–fragmentation–integration that characterized Mesopotamia, Central Asia, and the Indus are neither related, nor chronologically coincident. The repetitive pattern indicates, however, the fragility of the early urban system within each area and the likelihood that it was subject to certain uniform processes.

In Soviet Central Asia scholars have documented a parallel case of urban crisis followed by sustained village life (Biscione 1977: 1979). During the period from 2100 to 1850 B.C. (the Namazga V period), urbanization in Soviet Turkmenistan reaches its peak. Two settlements, referred to as "capitals," Altyn-depe and Namazga-depe, have surface areas of 35 and 48 hectares respectively (see Fig. 15.3). Excavations at

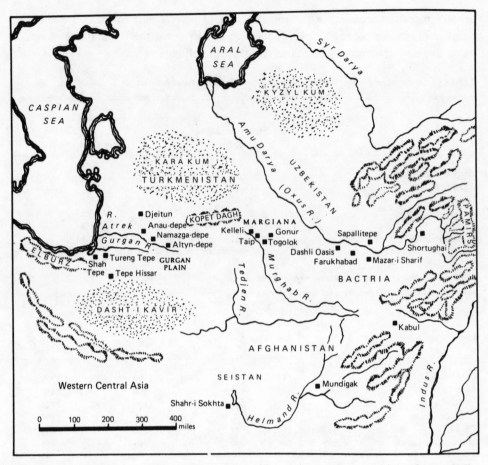

Fig. 15. 3. Distribution of principal archaeological sites of Bronze Age western central Asia. (*Courtesy Holly Pittman*)

Altyn-depe have uncovered fortification walls, "palaces," "temples," monumental buildings, craft and "priest" quarters, as well as long-distance trade with the Indus Valley and Mesopotamia (Kohl 1984b).

Complementing these two "capitals" are only a few towns of approximately 10 hectares and numerous villages of 1–2 hectares. In short, we seem to have a settlement hierarchy dominated by two urban capitals, a limited number of towns, and numerous villages.

Around 1850 B.C. there is an abrupt and dramatic transformation within the settlement system. Altyn-depe appears to be completely abandoned, Namazga-depe shrinks to 2 hectares as villages appear once again to be the sole settlement form. This urban crisis, for which several "explanations" have been advanced (climatic change, failure of the irrigation systems, and nomadic (Andronovo culture) incursions), remains without understanding. An interesting hypothesis suggested by Biscione (1977) argues for the occurrence of a "settlement segmentation" resulting from "the structure of the socio-economical organization of the proto-cities which could not support the increasing pressure of aggregating populations. Forces of production and social structure being inadequate, the population was forced to split into smaller units of decentralized communities." An alternative explanation, and one not necessarily exclusive of the above, is the hypothesis involving large-scale migratory movements. Contemporaneous with the demise of the Turkmenistan urban communities is the initial settlement of a previously uninhabited area; the Murghab and Bactrian regions to the east. The Soviet scholar Sarianidi (1981) has proposed the existence of large-scale tribal movements throughout the first half of the second millennium, involving the entire region of northeast Iran, Turkmenistan, Uzbekistan and Tadjikistan; attesting to these urban disruptions archaeological artifacts characteristic of the Murghab-Bactrian culture have been recently recovered from the settlement at Sibri and the nearby graves of Mehrgarh in Pakistan at the southern entrance of the Bolan Pass (Santoni 1984). There can be little doubt that from the beginning of the second millennium there was a considerable movement of both peoples and ideas over exceptionally wide geographical regions of Central Asia.

When confronting the Indus civilization the archaeologist has only the poorest understanding of its settlement pattern. As in Central Asia and Mesopotamia an urbanization crisis occurs in the Indus; its consequences appear to lead to a total reorientation of the civilization. Two important observations have been made concerning the Indus urban crisis and collapse. Recent archaeological surveys along the dry bed of the Hakra River in Bahawalpur state, Pakistan, revealed an area of the densest Harappan settlement for the entirety of the Indus civilization (Figure 15.1). An extensive settlement distribution of over 400 Indus sites, from villages to cities the size of Mohenjo Daro (for example, Ganwariwala), have been discovered in this region (Mughal, n.d.). Evidence suggests that hydrographic changes beginning in the third millennium substantially reduced the water supply of the Hakra River which in turn forced the abandonment of the entire area. A shift in settlement, resulting from the above hydrographic changes, from along the tributaries of the Indus, notably the Hakra-Ghaggar, toward the Saurashtra peninsula has been documented by Possehl (1980). A second factor posited as effecting settlement change is increasing nomadism (Possehl 1979). Changes in both settlement and land use have been directly attributed to the nomadization of sedentary or semi-sedentary populations; a process which Adams (1974) conceives of as cyclical in Mesopotamia (see also Briant 1982). The process of transforming nomads into sedentary populations in the late period of the Indus civilization is presently the subject of a significant research program (Rissman 1985).

Lastly, the demise of the Indus settlement pattern, and indeed the entire Indus civilization, has been unconvincingly argued as resulting from the invasion of the Indo-Aryans (Wheeler 1968). Until some shred of evidence is conjured up in support of this hypothesis it is best ignored.

One pattern is worthy of special note for it appears to be a consistent pattern for Mesopotamia, the Indus, Central Asia, and the Iranian plateau. This pattern entails the process of colonization, an effort to establish distant colonies in "foreign areas" such as the incontestable Indus colony at Shortughai along the Oxus River in distant

Central Asia (Fig. 15.1); the recently excavated Sumerian colony of Habuba Kabira in northern Syria; the Proto-Elamite colony of Tepe Yahya on the Iranian plateau; or the Central Asian settlement at Sibri in Pakistan. Perhaps related to this process of colonization are the archaeologically observed shifts in settlement pattern. Demographic shifts occur which are best documented by R. McC. Adams (1981) in Mesopotamia, but as noted above are observed in each culture area at the period of primary urban development. The appearance of this pattern, in each region of urban genesis, requires an explanation. Adams (1981) has observed for Mesopotamia a phenomenon which appears true for other areas – a pattern of "hyperurbanization," a rapid nucleation into urban concentrations. It is possible that this process of hyperurbanization leads to a state of entropy; an institutional inability to maintain the energy within the closed system for sustaining the rapid development, as suggested by Biscione (1977) for Central Asia. Thus, the peripheral colonies dependent in each instance upon core developments fail to maintain themselves and demographic shifts, movements away from the "overheated" urban system, take place within the "heartland" (Lamberg-Karlovsky 1986).

It is clear that shifting settlement patterns are characteristic of each of the three principal civilizations under review (Mesopotamia, the Indus, and Central Asia). The instability of these different urban regimes has been variously attributed to immigration and/or emigration, irrigation collapse, environmental change, nomadization and/or sedentarization, military invasion, or internal changes within the social institutions leading to "collapse." What R. McC. Adams (1981: 250) has written for Mesopotamia is most assuredly a truism for this broader area: "The crucial attribute is rapid adaptability in the face of either social or environmental pressure."

Temple, palace and community

In reflecting upon the Mesopotamian urban process the written texts provide insights which are denied us by the absence of writing in Central Asia and the undeciphered texts of the Indus Valley. Insights derived from these earliest texts often indicate conditions which are not expected and may be applicable beyond the confines of the Mesopotamian city-states. *Our* contemporary situation, in which patterned behavior allows for analytical approaches, has led to a large body of literature in economic geography which states bluntly that community size tends to be highly correlated with the number and complexity of urban functions (Haggett 1966: 114–42). It comes as a considerable surprise that there is no textual evidence to suggest that this was true for Mesopotamia, where size was not considered a significant variable in its own right. We must bear in mind that "there was no terminological contrast between 'city' and 'village' in the third or even in the early second millennium" (Diakonoff 1982b: 34, n. 72). The documentary materials from Mesopotamia narrowly reflect the views and preoccupations of the numerically small self-conscious elites who were wholly committed to an urban way of life. The concept of city had no gradation, it was an all-or-nothing category. The cognitive world of the urban Babylonian, as reflected in his texts, all but ignored suburban settlements. This is the more surprising in light of the considerable number and importance of the villages and towns that provided the surplus on which the well-being of the urban centers depended. This highly constraining concept, which excludes the countryside from one's urban world, is difficult for us to comprehend. Nevertheless, while some subordinate towns were involved in routinized interaction with urban centers, the majority of the suburban communities were rarely part of an articulated system of regional administration (Adams 1981: 249). If the cognitive perception of the urban Babylonian hardly deemed the surrounding countryside of importance to his circumscribed, self-enclosed urban existence, he most assuredly must have been wholly indifferent to the distant communities on the furthest reaches of his awareness: Central Asia and the Indus. The reasons for this, of course, rest in the rather limited perspective inherent in the written texts. Marvin Powell (1977:25) has correctly emphasized that in dealing with the archival records there are two fundamental points to keep in mind:

(1) The overwhelming majority of all third-millennium records derive from the archives of great estates associated with the temple or central government. (2) Accounting on these estates is done purely from the standpoint of the estate itself. They are internal records which concern themselves with what takes place outside only insofar as it directly concerns the expenditure and income of the estate itself.

The urban dwellers of Mesopotamia, while seemingly indifferent to the inhabitants of suburban communities, were far from casual in their treatment of nomads. The Mari archive, not the only, but merely the fullest extant texts (c. 1800 B.C.) detailing city–nomad relations, attest to an ever-present tension that characterized such relationships (Matthews 1978).

Even though the texts reflect the ideology and biases of the tribute-exacting city-states, the Mari archives indicate that "tribal groups" (1) received tribute from the king, (2) provided mercenaries and possibly surplus livestock to the city-states, (3) were engaged in agriculture as well as pastoralism. They also indicate (4) what Ibn Khaldun noted 2500 years later, namely, that leaders of "tribal" military forces living on the borders of kingdoms could take advantage of a weakening of city-state power to extend their control over neighboring regions; and lastly (5) that both groups were continuously involved in exchanges involving a complex network of political, military, and matrimonial alliances pertaining to intratribal and tribal–state relations. One is forced to conclude that peripheral villages and/or towns, as well as nomads, received scant attention simply because there was no assurance of retaining any durable relationship with them. The smaller communities remained pawns (perhaps even more so than the nomads) in the internecine competition, which characterized the rapid hyperurban process of the late fourth millennium (Adams 1981). As H. Gaube (1979) has argued for the Iranian city of more recent times, so also the Sumerian city can be defined as (1) the seat of government; (2) the center of intellectual and religious life; (3) the locus of economic activity and (4) the dwelling place of those engaged in the above.

Thorkild Jacobsen (1970) has argued that Sumerian myths described the political system prior to the rise of kingship and depict a form of "primitive democracy." Suggesting that the anthropomorphic world of the gods which is described in the myths reflects earlier political institutions, Jacobsen offers the following reconstruction for the rise of Sumerian kingship. Political authority originally rested in an assembly of free adult males. In times of stress, the assembly elected a temporary war leader, who, returning from military campaigns, refused to relinquish authority to the assembly. Kingship thus evolved as the result of a warlord retaining absolute power. Such a view, though speculative, can be supported by Sumerian texts. Jacobsen's hypothetical reconstruction for the rise of kingship continues to hold a powerful influence on our understanding of early Sumerian political formation.

From ancient texts, too, we learn that the functioning of the universe was governed by divine laws. Over a hundred of these laws, called *mes*, are known. To the Sumerian, these laws defined the only reality – the universe and everything in it, including the activities and institutions of human society. All was immutable, established by law, never subject to change. The *mes* were originally given by Enki (the god of water) to the city of Eridu. E-Anna stole them and gave their knowledge to others, the *mes* concludes, "since which time nothing else has been invented." This statement, referring to the earliest memory of Sumerian history, summarizes that culture's view of the unchanging nature of the universe.

The Mesopotamian temple-palace dominated the skyline of the Sumerian city. Its construction represented an enormous expenditure of human labor: it is estimated that 1500 laborers working a ten-hour day would have spent five years building one of the temple terraces at Uruk. Large temples or palaces are, however, exceedingly rare to the east of Mesopotamia. At Altyn-depe in Central Asia a large stepped "temple" has been excavated (Masson 1981a) and at Mundigak, in Afghanistan, a large structure identified as a "temple" has also been uncovered. These exceptional buildings nevertheless attest to the relative rarity of monumental architecture to the east of Mesopotamia.

The Mesopotamian temples represented the physical homes of their deities, where citizens believed presided a numinous spirit allowing for success in all human endeavor. All citizens belonged to a particular temple as one would to a household. The temple "community" comprised a cross-section of the population: officials, priests, merchants, craftsmen, food producers, and slaves. It also assumed community responsibilities – for example, for the care of orphans, widows, the blind, and indigent citizens unable to care for themselves (Gelb 1972b).

Under the patronage of temple deities, an enormous concentration of manpower was harnessed to produce both the goods and the agricultural surplus required by the growing city-state. The temple was the first institution to accumulate a substantial surplus capital. This was used, in turn, to build public works, undertake foreign trade, support military activity, and the development of the crafts associated with the temple complex. While the temple served as the first institution of credit capital, the populations attached to the temple lands acted as sharecroppers, forfeiting the land's productive surplus, the *usus fructus*, to the temple. Those populations not attached to the temples, the non-institutionalized sector, retained a simple subsistence economy.

Merchants obtained goods from the temples on consignment, returning to the temple a 20 percent profit while pocketing additional profit as their own. The later laws of Hammurabi are quite precise in their protection of investors from being cheated by merchants. Exact records of transactions were required. Merchants who failed to report their real profit were punished by having to repay double the amount borrowed, while those who denied borrowing, but were found guilty of lying, repaid threefold. Shamash, patron deity of justice and commerce, who offers Hammurabi the laws, is sponsor of weights and measures, providing explicit punishment for falsifying the state's standard units. Creditors were assured a right to repay loans in goods of equivalent value "in accordance with the ratio [to silver] fixed by the ruler" (Driver and Miles 1955: 186–92).

The early laws are of special interest in their recognition of "acts of God." Debtors unable to make restitution because of a crop failure due to natural events such as storms, merchants suffering a robbery of their loaned goods, or leasors of animals killed by lions, had part or all of their debts waived. Judges, witnesses and prosecutors adjudicated the specific attributes of each case before rendering a decision. The early laws were strongly opposed to extortionate practices and clearly solicitous of debtors' problems. It is of interest to point out that the debtor-oriented spirit of the palace laws is frequently the topic of editorial commentary by modern scholars, who in the spirit of capitalism find favor with the creditor rather than with the debtor. To Driver and Miles (1955: 177) it seems unfair to punish creditors by their forfeiting their entire claim merely because they attempted to extort more than the legal rate of interest: "This is hardly logical for he had no right to the illegal interest but had a right to be repaid his capital sum." The earliest legal compilations of Entemena (2404–2375 B.C.), Urukagina (2351–2342 B.C.), Ur-Nammu (2112–2095 B.C.), Lipit Ishtar (1934–1924 B.C.) and Hammurabi (1792–1750 B.C.) do not add up to a legal philosophy, much less to an economic analysis of profit, interest, rent, and so on, but they assuredly do show a strong commitment to protect the economically threatened and impoverished from the avaricious and powerful by explicitly penalizing individual and institutional economic abuses. These early laws were *ad hoc* case rulings intended to extend the palace's sway over the communal sector (the *awilu*) by championing the causes of the oppressed. The legal codes provided the bases for adjudicating tax liabilities, the duration and conditions of debt servitude, as well as the extent of personal liability of corrupt or incompetent officials, servants, doctors, and so on. The benevolence expressed in these legal codes masks the net effect and purpose of the laws, the strengthening of the palace authority;

that the strong might not oppress the weak,
that justice might be dealt the orphan (and) widow . . .
I wrote my precious words on my stela . . .
to give justice to the oppressed . . .

Let any oppressed man who has a cause
come into the presence of the statue of me, the king of justice,

and then read carefully my inscribed stela
and hear my precious words,
and may my stela make the case clear to him;
may he understand his cause;
may he set his mind at ease.

(Meek 1955: 178)

The increasing centralization of economic activity demanded the development of a complex recording system. The thousands of account tablets, presumably recording receipts and expenditures, reflect the temple's role as an administrative unit concerned with the management of surplus, collection of taxes, and the procurement of resources through the organization of long-distance trade. Indeed, the presence of professional scribes illustrates the high caliber of individuals maintained by the temple and/or palace. "The Great Organizations," as Leo Oppenheim (1977: 95) called the twin pillars of bureaucratic management, were the temples and palaces that trained and supported craftsmen, and which by the end of the third millennium monopolized the production of not only agriculture but crafts, including metallurgy, textiles, cylinder-seal production, and ceramics. The Sumerian city-state was the political center of gravity, exercising at most a variable control over neighboring autonomous tribes and a not wholly integrated village countryside. The focus of the state was the individual city, while its focal point was first the temple(s) and later the palace – dual and distinctive entities of constant tensions embodying reciprocal actions often of a competitive nature.

The temple and palace were but two pillars of the tripod which structured Sumerian civilization. From an evolutionary perspective at the dawn of Sumerian emergence the temple and the "community" could not be differentiated. The "community" consisted of those members affiliated with the temples who had by the end of the third millennium

the right to own real property and to take part in self-government, as well
as to share in all possible community incomes and in other material and
non-material benefits likely to come into the possession of the territorial
community. Concurrently, there were certain duties towards their
territorial community and their fellow-citizens.

There were duties of mutual aid (co-operation), mainly of political, but
partly of economic nature – participation in the discussion of community
affairs at popular assemblages or in the council, in the defense of the
community, in labour that benefited, or was regarded as benefiting, the
entire community – such as construction of the city walls, or buildings for
religious worship, as digging of canals, construction of roads, etc.

(Diakonoff 1982b:32)

The "community" consisted, in turn, of numerous "family communes," households of agnates – father, mother, unmarried sons and daughters as well as married sons, wives, and children. A "family commune" could at times include an entire village of kinsmen. Several related or unrelated "family communes" normally formed a "territorial community." The "family commune" was headed by a senior patriarch, whereas the "territoral community" had a collective government headed by a council of elders composed of the most important headmen of the "family communes." Diakonoff (1982: 53–62) has shown that before the separation of the temple-palace economy from the community, the two forms were indistinguishable. In fact, it could be suggested that the increasing bureaucratic dealings structuring the relations of power between the council of elders, temples, and headmen of family communities may well have formed the primary cell for the creation of the state sector. The "family communes" and "territorial communities" were increasingly absorbed into the more powerful patronage of the temple economies and "houses" of the rulers and nobility. By the end of the third millennium only the temple and royal estates were large enough to separate consistently the full-time specialization of the crafts from agricultural work. Craftsmen obtained carefully allocated raw resources for the manufacture of their products while the finished goods were strictly accounted for by the bureaucracy of the temple or palace. No data exist for the *free* outside sale of finished products manufactured by the artisans of the temples and/or palaces before the mid-second millennium; both production and distribution were in the hands of the "Great Organizations." The transition from the dyad of "territorial-community" and temple to that of palace and kingship has been summarized thus by Diakonoff (1982: 64–5):

The struggle for the control over the temples was also a struggle for reserve and export grain funds (and, consequently, for imported raw materials); for supremacy in matters of communal irrigation; and, finally, for ideological prestige ensuing from the temple's role of intermediary between the community and the deity, held to be responsible for the former's well-being or its ruin.

In the 25–24th centuries the Sumerian temple estates (beginning with the largest) fell increasingly into the possession of the ruler and the members of his family, becoming, at least in practice but sometimes also technically, their property. This was made possible by the fact that the ruler, as early as the ED III period, combined the functions of the military (*lugal*) and civilian leader (*ensi*) with that of the priest (*en*), and the supreme priest of the entire city-state or *sanga*. Control over the temple estates and their personnel gave the ruler independent military power; and if he happened to be in opposition to the local military and priestly aristocracy (as was apparently the case with Sargon of Akkad), he was also capable of relying on the backing of a numerous light *militia* of the communities. Thus the historical process led to the subordination of the city-states throughout the Mesopotamian basin to the autocratic power of the king.

Using archaeological and textual evidence from the second half of the third millennium, a number of interactive developments – both pressures and responses –

transformed the "Great Organizations" of territorial community, temple and palace into a unified city-state.

First, the temple expanded throughout the third millennium in all of its aspects, including enlargement of its buildings, diversification of activities, and the growth of administrative duties and staff. The consolidation of agricultural territories fell increasingly under the control of the temple-palace bureaucracy, as did the training and recruitment of specialists in various crafts. There was an increasing institutionalization of power in the hands of the ruling elite and within the palace personnel and its corps of retainers. The differences in wealth may well have resulted from an incipient shortage of arable land brought about by the presence of a slowly increasing population. The "Uruk Lament," a hymn of royal propaganda to curry divine and popular favor (dated to the late third millennium) has as its central theme god's wrath over man's offensive overpopulation (Green 1984: 254).

The shifting nature of land ownership, nevertheless, underscores the evolution from the "community-temple" polity to the "royal-domain." A comparison of the structure of land ownership within the "community temple" (c. 2500 B.C.) with that of the "royal-domain" (c. 1800 B.C.) is highly instructive. In the city-state of Lagash all "community-temple" land was divided into three categories: (1) *nig-en(-n)a*, the land owned by the priests which was cultivated by temple labor (paid by rations-in-kind) and used to feed its livestock and personnel, while surplus was used for exchange to obtain timber, metal, stone, and so on; (2) *kur*, land allotments given by the "territorial community" to minor officials (not priests), favored agricultural workers, craftsmen, leaders of the temples' military force, administrators, scribes, and so on; and lastly, (3) *uru-lal* land; this land appears to have been free to rent by any inhabitant of Lagash able to pay a rent-in-kind (Deimel 1931; and full bibliography in Diakonoff 1982b). In contrast, by the first centuries of the second millennium lands belonged to the following categories of the "royal-domain": (1) royal lands, property of the king; (2) lands allocated by the king to individuals: royal officials, craftsmen, service laborers; and (3) lands allotted through royal supervisors to unfree agricultural workers. Temples maintained their separate estates although now these properties were controlled by administrators representing the king.

The question of land ownership, the control over the principal means of production, has often involved the question of slavery, its very existence or degree, in Mesopotamia. Western scholars often portray periods of Mesopotamian society as characterized by a state feudal structure (with kings and serfs), while Soviet scholars perceive the same periods as having an economic structure of society based on slavery (Gelb 1972a). The laws of Hammurabi (1792–1750 B.C.) and an epistle-decree of the Hittite King Hattusilis III (1275–1250 B.C.) are not without significance in this regard: the former divides society into *awilu*: citizens and proprietors with full rights; the *muske nu*: "the royal men," those in the service of the king; and the *wardu*: the slaves. The later Hittite document divides society into the king's slaves, the royal servants, and the "sons of the city": members of the community with full civil rights; and "slaves of the slaves of the king," consisting of laborers working for royal servants; purchased and otherwise acquired slaves.

The Sumerian population consisted of five distinct social classes: the nobility (royal administrators, merchants, and priests) who owned land privately and administered temple and/or palace lands using client and slave labor. Second, members of the "community," who worked plots of family-held lands. Third, well-to-do clients of the temples or palace consisting mostly of artisans who *temporarily* received allotments of temple or palace lands in return for their craft production. Fourth, and numerically the largest, those who owned no lands whatsoever and whose labor was undertaken for the above three classes and paid by rations-in-kind; and lastly slaves, often prisoners of war, and never numerically large. The lines of separation between the classes were often far from clear. The development of the Sumerian economy occurred through a cumulative increase in the powers and wealth of the nobility and the concomitant reduction of other classes to a client relationship. By the end of the third millennium the need for credit gave rise to usurious rates of interest and large debts often leading to bond slavery; an increase in the number of individuals involved in communal labor service, and increasing numbers of fugitive outlaws: the dispossessed who looted at the edges of the large cities, the so-called "Hapiru."

The exploitation of debtors and the employment of slave labor increased as capital fell more and more into the hands of the larger estates. Labor services in the large estates were paid by rations-in-kind or by service land allotments. The production of consumable commodities, craftwork, and international trade fell entirely into the hands of the state sector by Ur III times (2113–2006 B.C.). The private estates could neither compete with the state in agricultural nor in large-scale handicraft production, such as textiles, which formed one of the principal export commodities.

A frequent occurrence, from the mid-third and throughout the second millennium, was the cancellation of private debts and the declaration of reform laws. These royal decrees were palace efforts to "level" society, prevent usury, punish corrupt officials, and not incidentally attain greater support from the population. From the time of Entemena (2424–2375 B.C.), the texts document a continuous process in which the state, by declaring a cancellation of debts (*misharum*) and penalties against avaricious private entrepreneurial behavior, attempted to effect "equity and justice in the land" (Speiser 1953: 874). Far from being entirely altruistic these freedom decrees strengthened the power of the rulers. It appears clear that two important attributes of a ruler were to be just (*nig.gina*) and equitable (*nig.sisa*). Whether in the texts of Ur-Nammu (2112–2035 B.C.), founder of the all-powerful Third Dynasty of Ur, or in the laws of Hammurabi, powerful kings were ever-eager to establish their claim as just and equitable by periodically cancelling all debts and taxes and ruling against their own overzealous administrators who ignored or exploited the rights and labor of the masses. (For debt cancellations see Kraus 1958 and Edzard 1957.)

Figure 15.4 points to the inverse relationship that exists in the evolution of the private and "institutional" sectors of production. "Private" refers to materials or objects of production whether agricultural, commercial, or industrial owned by individuals, families, or private corporations unaligned to state institutions. "Institutional" refers to those social formations which at different times were sociopolitically dominant. Thus, the Kin Community, c. 3500 B.C. consisting of ex-

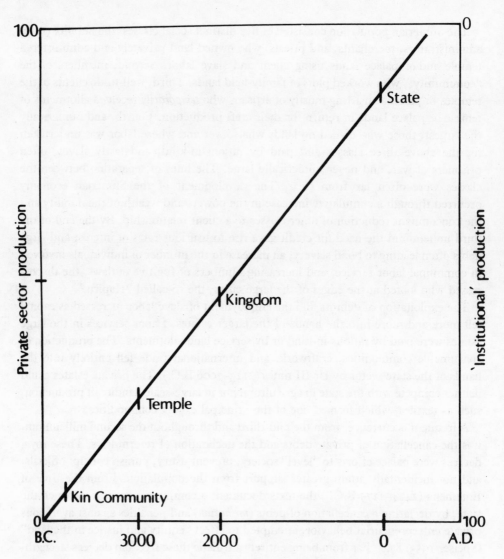

Fig. 15.4. An approximation of the relationship between private and institutional production in the preindustrial era.

tended families, lineages, clans, and so on was the "institutional" form which owned the majority of the means of production; private individual ownership of production was virtually absent. With the later evolution of the centralized temples, when unrelated families worked the agricultural lands and/or produced goods under temple authority, the ownership of the means of production, lands, animals, and implements was largely in the hands of, and controlled by, the temple bureaucracy.

Toward the end of the third millennium, secular kingdoms, ruled over by an emergent nobility, shared with the temples an institutional sector of economic productivity. Texts nevertheless clearly indicate that a considerable sector of the productive economy was increasingly in the hands of a private sector (Adams 1974b).

The Assyrian trading colonies in Anatolia (c. 1900 B.C.) provide a clear example of commerce in the hands of private family corporations (Larsen 1979a), unaligned to either the temple or palace, which, nevertheless, still owned a very considerable proportion of the means of production. A comparison of the emergence of the ancient oriental economy, with its mix of private versus institutional ownership of production (indicating nevertheless a trend toward increasing productivity and ownership in the hands of private individuals), with the later Classical world is instructive. The emergence of Classical civilization sees the full emergence of private capital, well elucidated in Finley's (1973: 28–9) useful volume:

There are private holdings of land in the Near East, privately worked;
there were "independent" craftsmen and pedlars in the towns. Our
evidence does not permit quantification, but I do not believe it is possible
to elevate these people to the prevailing pattern of economy, whereas the
Graeco-Roman world was *essentially and precisely one of private ownership*,
whether of a few acres or of the enormous domains of Roman senators and
emperors, a world of private trade, private manufacture [emphasis mine].

The world of ancient Mesopotamia and that of the Graeco–Roman is of course an abstraction. Within that abstraction rests the reality of the slow, gradual transformation of social orders dependent upon communally owned means of production to the emergence of privately owned capital.

The market network

A key factor in the transformation of the temple-palace was the growing development of a market economy. Differential wealth within the community was based primarily on the evidence of an increasing number and value of objects in the hands of different classes. We can safely link this trend with the concurrent expansion of the crafts.

Exchange of commodities through a town market, mostly in the form of barter, *must* have existed from the late fourth millennium. The fact is, however, that archaeological evidence for the existence of marketplaces has not been uncovered and the texts offer few hints to corroborate their existence. The economic operations of the market must have been limited, primarily for two reasons: (1) objects of exchange were bartered without the mediating function of money, although specific units of silver served as direct equivalents of goods (Snell 1982); and (2) the production of agriculture was seasonal in character, requiring the development of credit systems, which, as mentioned above, became evident, usuriously so, in the second millennium.

Expansion of crafts further intensified social differences by providing alternatives to the agricultural means of production and new avenues to status and wealth. By increasing a segment of the community's dependence on scarce and expensive imports, new tensions in the competition for supply and demand are created. These tensions in turn create serious motivations for warfare, increasing militarism being well documented throughout the third millennium. Sanctions for war in more distant areas, also documented in late third millennium texts, were found in the need for raw material. "By developing new productive forces and corresponding relations of production, man develops an historical nature which determines for him the character of living nature and the spiritual as well as the political character of society" (Sahlins 1976: 133).

In Marshall Sahlins's view, production represents a dialectic between self and others. In the process of satisfying their own needs, people produce new needs; this has the effect of altering the structure of social relations. The development of the distinctive Sumerian community-temple-palace economy represents a particular form for organizing production; alternative forms outside of temple-palace institutions existed for craft production that developed on the Iranian plateau, Central Asia and the Indus Valley.

At the heart of this dialectic was the different character of each area. The historian Ferdinand Braudel has hypothesized that areas of geographical uniformity (for instance, the Mesopotamian alluvial plain) led to centralization and population clustering, while areas of geographical diversity (such as the mountain regions of the Iranian plateau) tend to remain decentralized. His hypothesis receives confirmation in the scattered settlement distribution and lesser centralization of production on the Iranian plateau when compared to the settlements of Mesopotamia.

Relations between Mesopotamia and the Iranian plateau were characterized by the same sharp dichotomy outlined by Braudel. The urban Mesopotamian centers, situated in the alluvial plains, depended on irrigation agriculture to produce surplus foodstuffs; they established settlements along major waterways and canals with nucleated centers and centrally organized authority. In contrast to this, the highland communities of the Iranian plateau, Baluchistan and regions of Central Asia existed in regions characterized by dry farming with a lower agricultural productivity, less nucleated areas of settlement, a lower population density, and a relative autonomy and isolation from neighboring areas (Lamberg-Karlovsky and Beale 1986).

This dichotomy served as the basis for the establishment of an important trade network. The needs of one area suited the needs of the other; what brought them into a dialectical relationship was their complementarity. The highland communities were rich in resources; a list of their products includes copper, turquoise, carnelian, lapis, chlorite, wood, and animals, especially horses. In return for these resources, the tablets of lowland centers inform us that perishable food commodities and manufactured goods, like textiles, were exported to the highlands (Kohl 1979).

Sumerian texts referring to long-distance trade in the Early Dynastic Period indicate that the temple-palace played a dominant role in directing traffic in *finished* objects and the transshipment of natural resources between the communities of the Iranian plateau and Mesopotamia. The pursuit of private gain (or, as Adam Smith called it, man's inherent motivation to "truck and barter") was combined with the state directive to stimulate expansion of long-distance trade. Particularly instructive in relation to long-distance trade is the Sumerian epic "Enmerkar and the Lord of Aratta" (Cohen 1973).

Enmerkar, king of Uruk (2800 B.C.), in his drive to embellish the temple of his patron deity E-Anna, dispatched a messenger to the Lord of Aratta. The city of Aratta, undiscovered by archaeologists, is reported to be east of Sumer across "seven mountain ranges" and rich in mineral resources, particularly lapis lazuli. Enmerkar's emissary was sent to Aratta to exchange the "stones from the mountains" in return for Sumerian grain. The Lord of Aratta, however, did not need grain, and so rejected the offer. Soon after, his lands suffered from a severe drought, believed to be inflicted by E-Anna. After an exchange of threats the Lord of Aratta capitulated, the drought broke, and the "stones of the mountain" were shipped to Sumer in return for grain. It is significant that despite the cultural differences of Sumer and the Iranian highlands, the might of the Sumerian deity, E-Anna, was recognized and feared in the distant Iranian periphery. The shared religious ideology of Enmerkar and the Lord of Aratta facilitated trade and the veiled threat of E-Anna's might substituted for open warfare.

Two distinctive examples for the existence of widespread communication networks can be indicated by two recent studies on (1) carved chlorite bowls and (2) a distinctive type of black-on-grey ware ceramic. The distribution of a highly stylized and complex iconography carved on chlorite bowls has been long noted (Frankfort 1955: 18–19). This product, long thought to be a Sumerian art form, is distributed from Mesopotamia to the Indus and from Soviet Central Asia to the islands of the Persian Gulf in the last half of the third millennium (see Fig. 15.5). Recent analyses of these chlorite bowls indicate the existence of several centers of production, of which Tepe Yahya in southeastern Iran was but one (Kohl et al. 1979). Chlorite bowls containing characteristic designs referred to as the "intercultural style" have been found in elite contexts on virtually every Mesopotamian site. Their production at Tepe Yahya, however, challenges the view that they were exclusively Sumerian

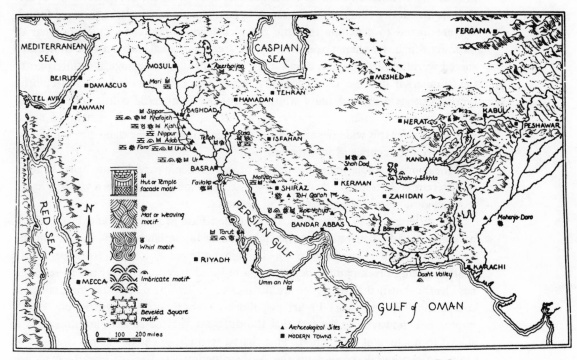

Fig. 15.5. Distribution of chlorite bowls containing motifs of the Intercultural Style c. 2400–2200 B.C.

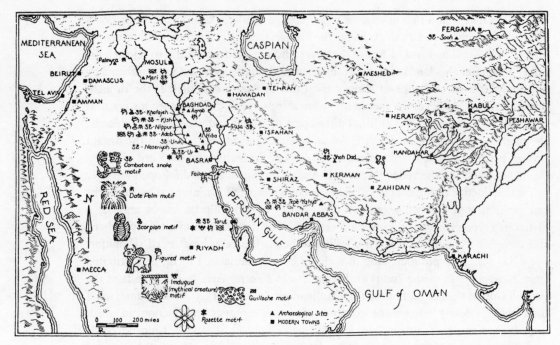

Fig. 15.6. Distribution of chlorite bowls containing motifs of the Intercultural Style c. 2400–2200 B.C.

products. The function of these bowls remains elusive; significant however is the fact that an identically complex iconography appears on them wherever they are found. We are forced to conclude that the complex iconography contains a grammar of meaning which was shared over a very wide area. This single artifact type indicates a shared world of ideology over a vast area, providing an archaeological counterpart to the "Enmerkar and the Lord of Aratta" epic. The evidence of the carved chlorite bowls suggests a level of unity while the distinctive material culture of "pots and pans" suggests a greater diversity. It is difficult to fathom the extent of social interaction over this wide region, yet clearly different views are attained by emphasizing different categories of information.

If the above example suggests a degree of shared ideology within the belief systems of different archaeological "cultures," our second example suggests a widely shared technological base in the production of ceramics.

Two different types of ceramic, the so-called Faiz Mohammed and Emir wares, have a very wide distribution in the Indo-Iranian borderlands in the last half of the third millennium (Fairservis 1956). Though both ceramic types are superficially similar, having black painted designs on a reduced grey ware body, recent research has clearly shown that the types are distinctive in design, shape, and mineralogical composition (Wright 1984). Figure 15.7 illustrates the distinctive stylistic spheres. Of importance, however, is the fact that the different stylistic spheres are united by a shared technology of production. This shared technology extends across the Gulf of Oman to contemporary sites on the Arabian peninsula. Various lines of evidence support the contention that these two ceramic types were an important medium of exchange. A complex of technical features was required for their production, suggesting an increased communication of craft specialists toward the end of the third millennium (Wright 1984).

Archaeological research has made it increasingly clear that by the middle of the third millennium a very large geographical expanse must be considered in order to explain developments within parts of it. The city-states of Mesopotamia, the disparate communities of the Iranian plateau and Central Asia and the poorly understood but impressive urban manifestation of the Indus civilization form individual links of an interconnected chain of social relations that brought these regions into contact for the first time.

Mesopotamian texts of the third and second millennium refer to the region of the Indus Valley/Baluchistan as the land of Meluhha. These texts detail the trade and resources obtained from Meluhha, including both manufactured and raw materials, ores and metal objects, precious metals, specific types of stone and stone objects, semi-precious stones, trees and wooden objects, plants, and animals. That there were direct relations between the elites of Mesopotamia and the Indus Valley is attested by the gift of a stone statuette of a Meluhha dog to King Ibbi-Sin of Ur (2028–2004 B.C.). Equally significant is the presence of a cylinder seal depicting a Meluhhan translator sitting on the knee of an Akkadian king and acting as an interpreter for two envoys. Lastly, the Mesopotamian texts refer to the presence of an actual Meluhhan village within Mesopotamia (Parpola et al. 1977). This fascinating text suggests the presence of a Meluhhan (Indus) colony in Mesopotamia. Indus–Mesopotamian relations are clearly attested in the Mesopotamian texts and are enriched by the

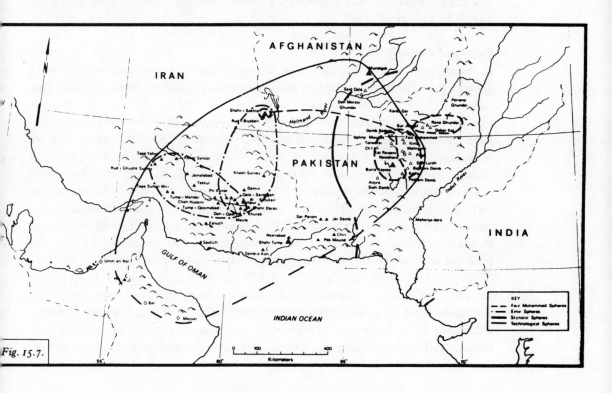

Fig. 15.7.

numerous archaeological remains of the Indus civilization that have been found in Mesopotamia.

Similarly, with the formation of the Indus civilization we can trace its direct expansion and influence into Central Asia. The recent discovery of the site of Shortugai on the Oxus River in Afghanistan attests to the establishment of an Indus colony far to the north of their known cultural distribution (see Fig. 15.3) (Francfort and Pottier 1978). Shortugai, an Indus colony in an area of distinctly indigenous population, thus appears to be in Central Asia what the Meluhhan villages are reported to be in Mesopotamian texts – colonies in foreign lands. The rich and typically Indus material culture recovered from Shortugai has suggested to the excavator that the colony was established as a frontier community for extending commercial relations deeper into Central Asia. The proximity of this site to the lapis lazuli mines of Badakshan may also be of significance. This commodity was in great demand, being considered the diamond of antiquity by the elites of Mesopotamia. Further evidence for Central Asian–Indus interrelations can be seen in the presence of two Indus seals, containing written signs, recovered from Altyn-depe in recent Soviet excavations (Masson 1981a).

There can be little doubt that by the end of the third millennium a vast network of communication united the elites from the eastern Mediterranean to the Indus Valley. Within this vast region the city-states of Mesopotamia appear politically and economically to have been the lynch-pin that was, at times, directed toward expansive empire directly affecting distant peoples and, at other times, barely able to sustain a hegemony over the immediately surrounding communities of their own city-state. The tendency toward unity and diversity characterizes the entirety of this area from 3000 B.C. to Islamic times.

Unity and diversity

In recent years several scholars have forcefully argued for a West Asian "world system" that characterized the late third millennium (Lamberg-Karlovsky and Tosi 1973; Kohl 1979). The "world economy" at the end of the third millennium incorporated a "set of sets," focusing upon Mesopotamia, the Indus and Central Asia. Each region occupied a geographical space which reached a boundary when the costs of exchange outweighed the gain or where extensions of kin involvement lost a critical mass of significance; each had urban centers as their pivot of gravity which were relatively autonomous in dealing with the outside world and which dominated the surrounding countryside. This view suggests that from the Mediterranean to the Indus Valley a network of interregional behavior connected the elites of distant and distinctive cultures. Furthermore, this view assigns to Mesopotamia the role of the principal actor within the network. Mesopotamian (Babylonian) centrality was only diminished toward the end of the second millennium by the incursions of new ethnic elements, the Kassites, Hurrians, and Hittites, who by military means conquered Babylonia. With the defeat of the Assyrian empire (by the Medes from northwestern Iran in 614 B.C.) the fortunes of Mesopotamia once again waxed brightly under such militaristic Babylonian kings as Nebuchadrezzar. The end of Babylonian power, however, followed ironically its most extensive imperial success; it was vanquished by Cyrus the Great of Persia, founder of the Achaemenid empire, in 539 B.C. Mesopotamia, once the very lynch-pin of Western Asia, now became a mere province of a wholly new imperial system which was to transform the entire region toward one of increasingly centralized political unity within a consistently diversified ethnic and cultural mosaic.

Mesopotamian historiographic tradition in its earliest form clearly asserts an *ideal* of unity – the ideal of a centralized political entity within Mesopotamia (van Seters 1985). The Sumerian king list reports that "kingship descended from heaven" to five principal cities. Each city was ruled by a dynasty of kings; hegemonic kingship was said to pass from one city to the next. This orderly sequence of dominant cities, each taking its turn ruling Mesopotamia, does not accurately reflect historical events. Dynasties listed sequentially were often contemporary, powerful dynasties of unmentioned cities are totally ignored while less powerful dynasties are given exaggerated significance. Mesopotamian historiographers made every effort to project a Mesopotamian unity, a unity wherein one sovereign from one city-state ruled over the entire countryside. Sargon of Akkad (2350–2300 B.C.) by conquest forged the first Mesopotamian empire. Political unity was the exception throughout the millennia of Mesopotamian history rather than the norm. Sargon of Akkad did, nevertheless, create one of the enduring *symbols* of unity. He installed his daughter as high priestess of the moon-god in the city of Ur. This office, always occupied by a female, became the symbol of Mesopotamian unity. Only one ruler, the sovereign of Ur, had the right to appoint the high priestess; she could not be removed – even if a new overlord of Ur was proclaimed. Although there appears to be a strong cultural ideal that Mesopotamia was a politically united land, the historical reality fell far short of this ideal. Sargon's political hegemony lasted about a hundred years (each of his successors having to reunify the land by suppressing the revolts of local city-states). Unified control of the Ur III kings (2100–2000 B.C.) lasted less than a century, while Hammurabi's unification (1792–1750 B.C.: undertaken late in his reign) did not even survive his son's lifetime.

The Mesopotamian world did, however, project a unity in a most important respect. This unity was predicated on the abstract notions of a divinely structured cosmos which was, in turn, to be mirrored by a structured social order. Religious festivals were of vital importance in Mesopotamian economic life. Throughout Mesopotamian history festivals doubled as market occasions and as auspicious moments for handing down justice. The New Year's festival was a period of not only revitalizing the natural order of the cosmos but of reconstituting an equilibrium within the social order. The New Year's festival was an occasion for the king to cancel debts and taxes, punish corrupt administrators, free slaves, and exercise the three qualities that judged him to be a good ruler: *ama.ar.gi, nig.sisa,* and *nig.gina.* An understanding of these terms is of quintessential significance to an understanding of Mesopotamian "unity" and political philosophy: *ama.ar.gi* meant freedom or liberty; literally, "returning a child to its mother," rather than leaving it in the hands of a creditor or wealthy purchaser. Lambert (1956:173–84) argues that its early meaning in the time of Entemena (2424–2375 B.C.) simply meant "exemption from taxes," while in time it came to imply overall "freedom" from debtors and "liberty" in the face of administrative or state patterns of exploitation. For an overall discussion of the "freedom" proclamations see Lemche (1979). The terms *nig.sisa* (equity) and *nig.gina* (justice) were considered as essential to the immutable nature of both the cosmic and social order. Speiser (1953) has described how the term *kittum* (Sumerian *nig.gina*) represents "that which is firm, established, true in the sense of timely reforms to meet specific circumstances, while *misharum* (Sumerian *nig.sisa*) means 'equity, justice' in the same sense of timely reforms to meet specific circumstances. The two terms are mutually complementary . . . An immutable aspect of cosmic order *kittum* is semantically the same as Biblical *'met* (from **'amint*), the original force of which still survives in the common loan-word 'Amen.' The independent function of a ruler, whether divine or human, is confined in *misharum*, that is, just and equitable implementation." In an effort to reconcile the lunar and solar calendar, the Babylonian New Year's festival reaffirmed harmony and order in the cosmos. While affirming such harmony the king through his declarations cancelling debt, taxes, freeing slaves and punishing recalcitrant administrators also reconstituted a new harmony in the social universe. The Babylonian king's obligation to be equitable, just, and to protect the freedom and liberty of the masses had a profound impact on later civilization. Such concepts as freedom, equity, and justice, which entail a specific social and legal philosophy balancing the rights and obligations of the ruler and the ruled, are unknown beyond the Mesopotamian frontiers of the third and second millennium. Identical concepts, however, are evident (and derived from Babylonia) in the Iron Age of the kingdom of Israel. A social philosophy supported by legal codes that define the rights of the people and the obligations of the ruler (state) has obvious adaptive advantages in maintaining a social equilibrium. In the Mesopotamian contexts the adaptive advantages of such a social philosophy served to establish a harmony between the tripartite structure of Mesopotamian society: the temple, palace, and community. In fact, it may be that the essential balance of power between these three institutional components brought about and necessitated such concepts as equity, justice, and freedom. In Egypt where temple, palace, and community were all subordinated to the rule of a divine pharaoh such concepts were entirely foreign.

The unity of Mesopotamia, in so far as it existed at all, was addressed by Driver (1955:9): "the conclusion that there was a customary law throughout the fertile crescent seems irresistible; and this common law was to a considerable extent written law." The eight-foot stela on which the laws of Hammurabi are inscribed is capped by a scene depicting the god Shumash, god of justice and patron deity of merchants, instructing, or delivering, the laws to his earthly steward, Hammurabi. In a metaphorical sense Shumash the cosmic god of justice offers to Hammurabi laws for social harmony and in so doing establishes a worldly unity of cosmic dimension. The harmony of earthly and cosmic rulers required justice, equity, and freedom, evident in the proclamations freeing slaves and cancelling debts, first evident in the texts of Entemena (2424–2375 B.C.) and concisely expounded in the later Babylonian laws and Wisdom Literature.

If a theological perspective for social justice provides a sense of unity in the

Mesopotamian city-states, what can one say about collapse? In Mesopotamian literature we are informed how Sargon of Akkad rose to power with the assistance of the goddess Inanna and the god Enlil. Naram-Sin, great-grandson of Sargon, was reluctant to accept the divine decrees, defied Enlil and plundered his holy city of Nippur. In response to this act of desecration the god Enlil called forth the Guti, inhabitants of the Zagros Mountains, "with human instincts but canine intelligence and monkey's features," to devastate the Akkadian capital. Other lamentations over the collapse of the city-states continues this theological perspective on the causes of collapse. Interestingly, the vehicle that implements the will of the deities is inevitably the portrayal of foreigners as the agents of destruction.

Clearly Mesopotamian, Indus, and the Central Asian civilizations were from the mid-fourth millennium amalgams of interacting ethnic and linguistic diversity. In none of the regions, excepting Mesopotamia, did there develop a successful political ideology that transcended wholly local aspects of political behavior.

Over five hundred years ago Ibn Khaldun penned his majestic macro-history of the Arab world, the *Muqaddimah*. For Ibn Khaldun the cyclical view of civilizational history was conceived of as a process of growth and integration of increasingly larger units:

> Family and local kin
> Religious community
> Kingdom
> Civilization

The last level is achieved when an office exists apart from the person who occupies it, that is to say, when the structural role of an office becomes separated from the person that occupies that position. In the end to Ibn Khaldun civilization contains in its very abstractness an internal weakness bringing about eventual decay:

> As men adopt each new luxury and refinement, sinking deeper and deeper
> into comfort, softness and peace, they grow more and more estranged
> from the life of the desert and the desert toughness. Finally they come to
> rely for their protection on some armed force other than their own.
>
> (Ibn Khaldun 1958: III, 341–2)

Historical continuity, in archaeological terms, makes the past ambiguous, perhaps even invisible. It is only in the utter collapse of a civilization that its contours become visible. After 4000 years of a near extinction from human memory the Bronze Age civilizations of Mesopotamia, the Indus Valley, and Central Asia have been exhumed and subjected to a tentative understanding. One cannot help but be struck by the categories of Ibn Khaldun and the categories developed by today's ancient historians for an understanding of the origins of "Oriental" civilization:

Ibn Khaldun	*Modern formulations*
Family and Local Kin	Territorial Community
Religious Community	Temple
Kingdom	Palace
Civilization	Civilization

16

New tracks on ancient frontiers: ceramic technology on the Indo-Iranian Borderlands

RITA P. WRIGHT

Over the past several decades, the study of production and exchange has taken a central place in research on the development of complex societies (Sabloff and Lamberg-Karlovsky 1975; Johnson 1973; Wright 1972; Earle and Ericson 1977; R. McC. Adams 1974a; Kohl 1978; Hirth 1984). These studies have been a welcome corrective to the anti-diffusionist views that had dominated anthropology and archaeology, in that they have shown that aspects of diffusion are a powerful force in generating cultural change. By focusing on production and exchange as they ramify on institutional structures (Adams 1974a: 240), they have made significant progress toward refining our understanding of their relationship to different socioeconomic settings.

This chapter falls within the above tradition, but it does so from a broadened perspective. First, I have used the term "exchange" in preference to "trade" since it encompasses a wider range of institutional settings than is presumed by trade. In particular, it leaves open the question of whether exchange relations are aligned with political, social or economic institutions. Second, I have distinguished between two types of diffusion: (1) the exchange of material goods and (2) the transmission of technical knowledge. By technical knowledge I refer to the steps taken in producing a product as they are discernible from archaeological materials; and by its transmission, the sharing of a particular technology within and between cultural groups. Although the two – exchange of material goods and transmission of technical knowledge – are obviously related, analytically separating them allows one to trace their shifting relations.

These distinctions are essential to the following discussion, since I conceive of production and exchange as operating in several different ways. First, exchange takes place within different contexts: in the case to be discussed the exchange of material goods or the transmission of technical knowledge. Second, it exists geographically and can be local, intraregional or interregional. And finally, it has a temporal component, in that relationships are subject to shifts over time. In the following discussion, I outline the implications of these shifts to different institutional settings.

The usefulness of the approach is illustrated through the laboratory analysis of two fine ware ceramics distributed throughout the Indo-Iranian Borderlands in the third millennium B.C. Principal forms of evidence are distributional data derived from neutron activation analysis, and macroscopic and microscopic analyses of details of technical procedures in ceramic manufacture. Since combining distributional *and* technological data is new to archaeology, the first section of the chapter presents an overview of the analytical techniques and the rationale for their implementation.

In a subsequent section, I present my interpretation of the evidence and its relevance to production and exchange relations in the Borderlands. This region, which encompasses eastern Iran, Afghanistan and Pakistani Baluchistan, is an ideal setting for such a study, as it was subject to numerous influences. Although some of these influences came from outside of the Borderlands, the evidence presented here concentrates on exchange networks that had developed within it.

Laboratory analysis of archaeological ceramics

Analytical studies that are integrated with archaeological evidence have the potential to refine our understanding of a variety of forms of exchange. In addition, they offer a previously unexploited resource that will usher in new directions of research. On the one hand, they afford us with the tool to test hypotheses derived from interpretations well ensconced in the archaeological literature and, on the other, to formulate new ones.

Although laboratory analyses of prehistoric ceramics have a long history, it is only recently that archaeologists have conducted both archaeological field work and laboratory analysis. This is especially true in the Near East, where studies previously have been carried out by archaeometrists, not directly involved in the archaeological research.[1] Hence while these studies frequently yielded interesting results, they were rarely properly integrated into the archaeological record. Nevertheless, the recognition of their potential led to the development of several research laboratories in anthropology departments, where programs have been developed to train archaeologists in archaeometric techniques.[2]

The most productive research projects to which laboratory analyses of ceramics have been applied fall within the broad categories of production and exchange. They include the study of long-distance and local exchange, the organization of production and craft specialization, and the comparison of technologies within regional and interregional settings. In the study of ceramics, I have found it essential to develop research programs in which standard archaeological questions, such as typological and stylistic analyses, are combined with the new questions made possible by archaeometric techniques. For example, technological and stylistic traits may be used together to infer the presence of craft specialization (Wright 1984), or, when conceptualized as separate phenomena, their independent influences can be traced (Wright 1985).

Figure 16.1 presents a general outline of the most commonly used techniques along with specific topics that can be addressed. In the figure, trade and exchange are highlighted on the right and technology on the left; specific archaeometric techniques are listed at the center. The darkened lines to the left and right correlate each technique with technology or exchange. As is evident, several different techniques can be used for each factor, and they should be employed simultaneously in order to develop converging lines of evidence. The line at the bottom indicates sample size,

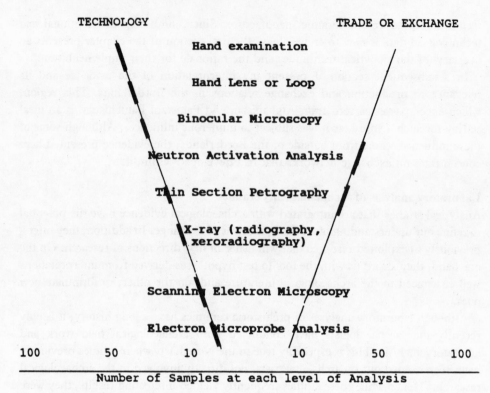

TECHNOLOGY   TRADE OR EXCHANGE

Hand examination

Hand Lens or Loop

Binocular Microscopy

Neutron Activation Analysis

Thin Section Petrography

X-ray (radiography, xeroradiography)

Scanning Electron Microscopy

Electron Microprobe Analysis

100   50   10   10   50   100

Number of Samples at each level of Analysis

Fig. 16.1. Archaeological contexts and archaeometric techniques

where increasingly smaller numbers of samples are used as one moves from macro- to microscopic levels. The methodology implies the use of multiple types of evidence, beginning with macroscopic handling of the ceramics and converging on smaller sample-size as microscopic levels are reached. It also calls for developing comprehensive programs in which the factors, exchange and technology, are viewed as interacting phenomena.

The most frequently used techniques in archaeometric studies of *exchange* are neutron activation analysis and thin-section petrography. Neutron activation analysis[3] gives determinations on a trace element level for individual samples. The trace elements of individual samples are then compared in order to discern similarities in their chemical compositions. The probability of the similarities having validity are statistically assessed, and, if valid, form the basis for delineating individual production loci. With thin section petrography, ceramic samples are grouped according to mineralogical assemblages and percentages of coarse fraction (temper or natural inclusions). Source areas are based on comparisons of the mineral assemblages of the samples with local geological histories. Analyses of local clays also may be studied and matched with the archaeological samples.

Archaeometric techniques used in the study of *production technology* are noted on the left of Fig. 16.1. In describing production technology, I reconstruct several or all of the steps involved in producing a ceramic. They include the handling of clays;

primary forming processes when the clay is in the plastic state; secondary processes carried out after the clay is leather hard; decorative techniques such as incising, but also (and perhaps the research which has yielded the most fruitful evidence) the mixing of decorative paints and glazes; and firing temperatures and atmospheres.

The techniques listed will not be discussed in detail; instead I provide a few examples based on the analytical techniques used in the current study.[4] Thin-section petrography is used in determining the handling of clays, for example their pre-processing or refinement after procurement from a clay source as determined by percentages of coarse fraction or grain size. X-ray techniques and binocular microscopy provide details of primary and secondary forming processes as indicated by orientations of pores and coarse fraction or (in the case of x-rays) areas of high and low density that may reveal evidence of coil or wheel construction. Microprobe analysis of paints and glazes provides evidence of chemical composition for reconstructing paint or glaze recipes. For analysis of properties related to temperature and atmospheric conditions in the kiln, the scanning electron microscope provides high-power magnification of the microstructure of pastes and paints or glazes. For example, refiring experiments can be carried out and alterations in microstructure due to thermal expansion (when the refired sample reaches a temperature above the original kiln temperature) can be observed.

In summary, the methods described above combine observations of macrostructure, microstructure and chemical composition. This combination of methods makes it possible to determine provenience and to reconstruct in detail the production procedures in ceramic manufacture. Together, they provide converging lines of evidence for questions of exchange and production and for comparing production technologies of different ceramic types.

Ceramic production and exchange

Archaeometric studies of ceramics from the Indo-Iranian Borderlands are just beginning and come on the heels of major archaeological research conducted over the past three decades. The principal areas of discovery are depicted on Fig. 16.2. They are the districts of Kerman, Bampur, Seistan, Kalat, Quetta, Zhob, Loralai and Kachi.[5] Human habitation had begun at least 3000 years before the development of state-level societies in the region. This chapter focuses on interregional exchange networks that had developed within the Borderlands, between Kachi (on its eastern margins) and Seistan (on its western margins), and intraregional ones, between Kachi and Quetta.

Before discussing the results of this research, it is necessary to step back several decades and to examine the relationship between the two ceramics to be discussed, one which is designated Emir, and the other Faiz Mohammad. These artifacts first became known to the archaeological record in the Indo-Iranian Borderlands through the excavations and surveys of Sir Aurel Stein. Stein, who carried out extensive research throughout the Indo-Iranian Borderlands (Stein 1929, 1931, 1937) was principally interested in the region's strategic location between ancient Mesopotamia and the Indus Valley civilization.

An artifact common to this vast territory was a black-on-grey painted ceramic that

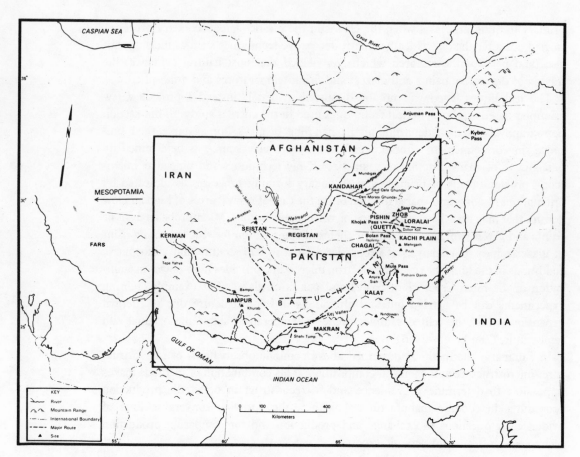

Fig. 16.2. The Indo-Iranian Borderlands.

provided one of the material links for the Borderlands. Stein, originally having found the ceramics in a burial context and considering the sophistication of their production methods, thought of them as elite goods related to a specialized ritual function. Later, painted grey wares were found in excavations and surveys at several major sites, for example, Shakr-i Sokhta in Seistan, Bampur in the Bampur Valley, and Damb Sadaat in Quetta. They were also known in smaller quantities at the site of Tepe Yahya and on, as yet, unexcavated and small sites throughout the Bampur Valley, Seistan, Kalat, Zhob, Loralai and Makran. Their areal extent is approximately represented by the region outlined in Fig. 16.2.

Later scholars (Lamberg-Karlovsky and Tosi 1973) followed Stein and outlined the material factors shared among cultures within the Borderlands. They introduced the concept of an interaction sphere, which emphasized the chronological contemporaneity of developments within the region and the importance of production and exchange as a factor in the establishment of hierarchical systems (*ibid.*: 45).

Recent excavations at the site of Mehrgarh in the Kachi district partially altered and partially corroborated these views. First, modifications of the geographical distribution of the painted grey wares were necessary in that large quantities of them were found on the Kachi plain both at Mehrgarh and at a number of other sites on the plain. The presence of large quantities of painted grey wares in Kachi and in direct association with kilns or ceramic production debris was viewed as an indication of local manufacture. Second, cross-parallels in ceramic assemblages established the contemporaneity of the painted grey wares on the Kachi plain with others within the Borderlands.[6] Moroever, the continuous occupation of Mehrgarh over several thousand years pushed back settlement on the Kachi plain to an earlier period than was previously believed based on sequences developed from highland evidence. This long period of settlement included the independent development of agriculture and husbandry (Meadow 1984). Effectively, it indicated that earlier diffusionary views that major aspects of culture, such as the origins of agriculture and husbandry and craft production (also found in the earliest levels in Kachi) were no longer valid or, at least, required re-evaluation.

Exchange of technical knowledge in the Indo-Iranian Borderlands

My own research on the painted grey wares initially involved a typological study (Wright 1984, 1987), and it was as a result of this work that the painted grey wares were divided into the two types, Faiz Mohammad and Emir. The Emir are distributed in the districts of Seistan and Bampur, and the Faiz Mohammad in Kachi, Quetta, Zhob, Loralai and Kalat. These typological divisions were based on clusters of attributes regarding vessel morphology and design elements. Although the neutron activation analysis was primarily conducted to investigate questions of exchange, it provided an additional line of evidence to the typological divisions, since the Emir and Faiz Mohammad fell into two distinct chemical compositional groups. These differences were expected, since the geological histories of the Seistan and Bampur regions differ from those of Kachi, Quetta, Kalat, Zhob and Loralai. Fig. 16.3 outlines the separate geographical distribution.

The laboratory analyses were specifically undertaken to determine whether the production technology of the two ceramics was similar or different. Observations noted while developing the typological analysis indicated that the only converging attributes of the two types were technological.

The research followed the method outlined in Fig. 16.1. First, large numbers of sherds were studied both in the field and in the laboratory for indications of the production technology. Second, specific technological factors were investigated by binocular microscopy, some of which were later subjected to more detailed microscopic studies. From the beginning, a comprehensive program was envisioned in which technological criteria and the exchange of material goods were thought of as interrelated phenomena.

Research consisted of comparing the production procedures of the Emir and the Faiz Mohammad from several districts within the Borderlands, but concentrated on Seistan (Emir), and Quetta, Kalat and Kachi (Faiz Mohammad), the districts from which the largest number of samples had been found.[7] Its purpose was to identify the technical procedures in each district as outlined in the section "Laboratory analysis of archaeological ceramics," above.[8]

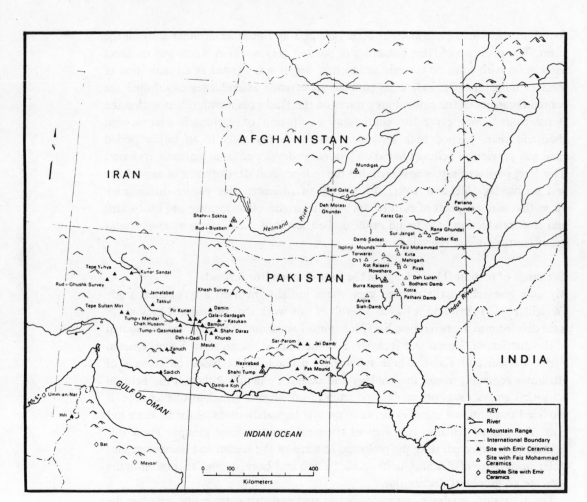

Fig. 16. 3. Location of sites and distribution of Faiz Mohammad and Emir ceramics.

The variables studied included the steps involved in manufacturing the ceramics. In contrast to the stylistic attributes of the ceramics, the production technology of the painted grey wares was found to be the same throughout the Borderlands. This uniform technology included a number of subtle details of production. First the handling of clays throughout the Borderlands was homogeneous. Both were produced with extremely fine clays with coarse fractions below the silt range and on a fast wheel. These steps were followed by a secondary process involving a thinning technique probably developed to stretch the fine clays beyond their normal workability range. Decorative paints were a mixture of fine clays and iron oxide colorants and were based on the same chemical compositions. The latter included a corresponding increase of iron oxide and alkali content along with fine particle size to produce a high color intensity. Finally, they were fired in kilns in which temperatures were in excess of 950°C and in which a two-stage firing process was used, an initial oxidizing and a final reducing one.

Of the manufacturing steps reproduced, none was unusual for Kachi. During the periods under discussion, all of the techniques used in producing the Faiz Mohammad ceramics are known from other ceramics in Kachi, although none of the other pottery there combines them as they are combined in the Faiz Mohammad. In Seistan the case is reversed. None of the contemporaneous ceramics in Seistan, particularly in the early periods, when Emir production first began, show evidence of production on a fast wheel, reduction firings, the thinning technique used to stretch the workability range of the clays, temperatures in excess of 950°C.

While there are few analogies with which to speculate on the mechanisms for the widespread sharing of technologies, they most assuredly involved craftsmen who were familiar with pottery manufacture. The techncial procedures indicate a highly sophisticated knowledge of ceramic production and it is unlikely that this type of information was transmitted by individuals not themselves acquainted with pottery technology. As I described, procedures represent a complex of related traits, not merely reduction firings. The evidence indicates that details of the technology were known and all of them were employed. The implications of this finding will be discussed in detail below.

Exchange of material goods

In this aspect of the research, I attempted to delineate exchange networks for both the Emir and the Faiz Mohammad, but only the results of the Faiz Mohammad will be discussed here.[9] These results broke down into four chemical compositional groups. They indicated that there were multiple production centers for the Faiz Mohammad and that distribution was on an intraregional and interregional basis. Three of the chemical groups corresponded to exchange between the upland zones of Quetta and Kalat and lowland sites of Kachi.[10]

This exchange of materials between uplands and lowlands appears as a more general pattern observable in other aspects of the archaeological record. The Kachi plain itself is a low-lying area, where mountain ranges of the upland zones meet the plain and rise abruptly. Access between upland and lowland is restricted to a few natural corridors. The mountain zones themselves are interspersed with narrow alluvial valleys to which some inhabitants today retreat from Kachi during the hot summer months, but which in ancient times also were inhabited by permanent settlements. Today, tribal groups come down to the Kachi plain and the Indus bringing their animals to pasture land. Our faunal and floral evidence indicate that subsistence in prehistory was much like it is today (Meadow 1984), suggesting that the flow of tribal groups between upland and lowland zones has been a constant feature of life in Baluchistan. The same pattern is obvious in the overall ceramic assemblages, where a diversity of locally manufactured styles can be documented. Thus exchange coincided with a pattern of seasonal migrations between highlands and lowlands.

The fourth chemical compositional group indicated the long-distance exchange of Faiz Mohammad ceramics between the Kachi plain and distant Seistan at the site of Shahr-i Sokhta. This exchange occurred late in the sequence and involved the transport of ceramics over a 700 km area. It will be discussed in greater detail below.

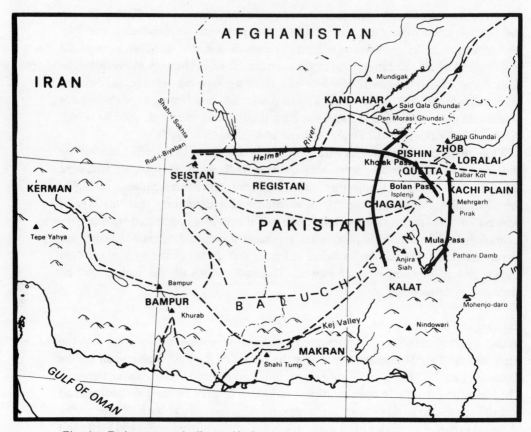

Fig. 16. 4. Exchange networks discussed in the text.

In summary, two different types of interaction have been identified. They are represented on Fig. 16.4 and are as follows: the most dominant pattern is one indicative of intraregional contact between the uplands and lowlands of Quetta, Kalat and Kachi. Interregional exchange, a second pattern, was documented between Seistan and Kachi. This exchange was not reciprocal as none of the Emir has been found in either the upland or lowland zones. The relevance of these exchange networks, their relationship to different institutional settings and the implications of temporal shifts will be discussed below.

Conclusion

When taken together, the results reveal a complex, although discernible, picture that suggests that different forms of exchange contributed differently to cultural developments. My understanding of the mechanisms involved on the contextual, geographical, and temporal levels and their impact on different institutional settings is as follows.

When we turn to the exchange of the technical knowledge required to produce the Emir and the Faiz Mohammad ceramics, there is clear evidence of a technology, the details of which were widely shared. As I indicated, the evidence does not support parallel invention, as a complex of traits is involved, not merely general principles. This example of widely shared technological information is not unusual in the archaeological record; for example, Muhly (1980) has commented upon the proliferation of metallurgical technology. Among other things this evidence indicates, as Kohl (this volume) has pointed out, that technologies were not monopolized during prehistoric periods.

The spread of technologies over cultural boundaries thus has implications for our understanding of cultural processes, namely that in prehistoric periods technological information was not subject to the same constraints as stylistic factors. Whereas the latter are traditionally believed to serve as markers of group identification (Wobst 1977) and to foster boundary maintenance between groups (Barth 1969), this study indicates that technologies do not.

A factor of additional relevance in the case of the Indo-Iranian Borderlands was the timing of the exchange of technological information. As I indicated, if we compare the relative stratigraphies from Seistan and Kachi, both the Emir and the Faiz Mohammad were produced during the same periods. In Seistan, this period comes at the beginning of the sequence at the site of Shahr-i Sokhta, where the Emir are found in large quantities. And when we compare the technology of Emir to other ceramics being produced at the site, there are few points of overlap. Missing in the production of contemporary ceramics at Shahr-i Sokhta is the use of a fast wheel, thinning clays to stretch them beyond their workability range, high temperatures in excess of 950°C and firings in reduction atmospheres. In Kachi all of these procedures were known to potters from Period III (Wright 1986), some 1000 years before production of Faiz Mohammad or Emir began. It therefore seems reasonable to assume that the spread of technical knowledge was from east to west, Kachi to Seistan.

When we look at the exchange of material goods, we can observe several different exchange networks, not a single one, each of which implies different institutional settings. The upland/lowland exchange of ceramics most reasonably is related to the seasonal migrations of tribal groups between the hills and plain of Quetta and Kalat and Kachi. As such, their institutional settings as reasonably represent social or political ties as economic ones. Given the subsistence pattern and on ethnographic analogy, exchange relations may have been between kinsmen or tribal groups where its function was related to alliance formation. The exchange of ceramics to distant Seistan late in the sequence presents a different context. In view of the long distance involved between Kachi and Seistan and the fact that exchange crossed cultural boundaries, this exchange most likely occurred on an economic level.

Perhaps the most significant results of this study are revealed when they are set against a temporal and spatial framework. There, we can observe important shifts as well as regularities that reveal significant cultural processes. First, the division of the Borderlands into two separate cultural areas persists throughout the period. This pattern follows other archaeological evidence that shows two different historical trajectories, one leading to the Helmand civilization (eastern Iran) and the other to the Indus Valley civilization. Second, within the latter we find the sustained exchange of material goods from lowland Kachi to upland Quetta and Kalat. This, too, follows the other archaeological evidence, in particular faunal analyses and ceramic assemblages. The exchange of ceramics to distant Seistan is our only concrete evidence for long-distance exchange and for an economic function.

We can also observe a close link between the exchange of technological information and material goods. Here, we can clearly trace the early transmission of technological information, when the production *and* distribution of the Faiz Mohammad and the Emir conformed to separate production zones. In the initial periods of production, there is no evidence for the exchange of the Emir or the Faiz Mohammad or any other material between the two zones. Late in the sequence the context of interaction shifts, when ceramics produced on the Kachi plain are exchanged to Seistan. Viewed in this context, the transmission of technological information may be seen as a bridge – a mechanism, if you will – that led to the subsequent exchange of material goods.

The implications of the above go beyond our simple case. In the study described, I have been able to trace a number of different networks of exchange whose relationships shifted spatially and temporally during the third millennium. Different production and exchange networks, as they have been broadly defined, acted as discrete entities but also sometimes overlapped. Importantly, the transmission of ideas appears to have acted as a precursor to the later exchange of tangible goods, indicating that different types of exchange are dynamically related.

Archaeologists have traveled many miles in their attempts to provide an adequate critique of diffusion as a tool in tracing developmental processes in the growth of societies. The results of this research have shown that close analyses of different types of exchange may reveal general patterns that demonstrate their interrelationships. It also indicates that the transmission of ideas should resume its place in studies of exchange. Like others before me, I do not view diffusion or exchange as a process that is in any way automatic, in Childe's words "like infection with a disease" (1951b: 168). However, I also do not believe that it is a "non-principle" (Harris 1968: 377). The new analytical techniques, when properly integrated with the archaeological evidence, provide us with fresh territory to explore. As a device and in concert with broadened perspectives on exchange, they offer a powerful tool for forging new tracks on old frontiers.

Notes
1 The use of analytical techniques addressing specific archaeological questions is rare in the Old World. In the Near Eastern study of ceramics, Dr. Fred Matson stands out as a pioneer in combining field and laboratory studies. With the exception of Matson, however, studies have been carried out by archaeometrists.
2 Two such laboratories with which I am familiar are the Center for Materials Research in Archaeology and Ethnology at M.I.T. and the Center for Archaeological Research and Development at Harvard University. Similarly, a few archaeometry departments, for example at the Smithsonian Institution, offer post-doctoral opportunities for archaeological research. In neutron activation analyses, Drs. G. Harbottle, E. Sayre, and R. Bishop of the Brookhaven National Laboratory collaborated with many archaeologists and trained them in the technique.
3 For a description of the procedures see Harbottle (1976) and Bishop et al. (1982).
4 There are several useful references in which specific techniques are either described or

examples of their use provided. To name a few, Shephard (1971); Rye (1981); Olin and Franklin (1982); Kingery and Vandiver (1986); Rice (1987).

5 In addition to the work of Stein to be discussed below, the major surveys and excavations undertaken in these regions are Lamberg-Karlovsky (1970); de Cardi (1964, 1970); Fairservis (1956, 1959, 1961), Tosi (1969, 1983); Jarrige and Lechevallier (1979); Jarrige and Meadow (1980).

6 This chronology follows Shaffer (in press). Comparative stratigraphy for the third millennium indicates the following contemporaneous periods, based on the sequences at Shahr-i Sokhta (Seistan) and Mehrgarh (Kachi). For Seistan, Period I is contemporaneous with Period V in Kachi; Period II with Period VI and early Period VII; Period III with late Period VII. Emir ceramics are produced in Periods I, II and early III in Seistan and Faiz Mohammad in Periods V, VI, VII in Kachi. Periods VI and VII in Kachi correspond to the Early Harappan.

7 Emir ceramics from the site of Bampur also formed a part of the study of the technology. They were not studied as extensively as the Emir from Shahr-i Sokhta because of the more restricted numbers available in museum collections and because the excavations at Bampur were on a smaller scale than those at Shahr-i Sokhta.

8 Detailed descriptions of the analytical evidence have been published elsewhere. See, for example, Wright (1984, 1985, 1987).

9 Trace element divisions for the Emir are reported in Wright (1984). An in-depth study of the complete corpus of the ceramics from Shahr-i Sokhta is currently in progress.

10 An additional compositional group was found in Zhob and Loralai, indicating that Faiz Mohammad ceramics were locally produced there and exchanged within that region.

17

Pastoralism and the early state in Greater Mesopotamia

ALLEN ZAGARELL

During the period leading up to the field project described in this chapter,[1] the role of the highlands and more specialized pastoral adaptations in the emergence of Greater Mesopotamian alluvial civilization had been an area of much speculation, fueled by alluring but often obscure references to highland peoples and cultures in the documentary and literary record. Hinz had postulated the existence of a highland/ lowland symbiosis which took the political form of confederation and provided the basis for the Elamite state structure (Hinz 1964: 3–4). R. McC. Adams had discussed the continuum connecting pastoralists, agriculturalists and urban populations. The chronic flux and local instability of these populations, he believed, may have played an important role in the growth of the Mesopotamian state (Adams 1974b: 3). A similar, integrated view of nomad and settled in the Mesopotamian heartland during the formative state phase was suggested by Nissen (1971). Others raised the possibility that highland nomadic pastoralists provided the impetus, in the form of military pressure, which pushed Elamite chiefdoms to transform themselves to state-level societies (Wright et al. 1975).

Although some of the speculative suggestions were statically ecological in nature, some scholars, particularly Lees and Bates, building on Adams's model, suggested a more historically based ecological picture (Lees and Bates 1974). They hypothesized that an increasing and specialized nomadic sector could not exist outside and independent of a specialized agricultural sector. The demands of irrigation cultivation and maintenance restricted the mobility of agriculturalists formerly engaged in multi-resource exploitation. These restrictions and the production of surplus grain led to the emergence of specialized pastoralists (nomadic), also freed from the necessity of producing their own grains.

The data base available for determining or contributing to a regional solution to the genesis and effects of Greater Mesopotamian nomadism was relatively weak. Little actual archaeological field work had been carried out in the highlands themselves. The work by Braidwood and others, focusing on the Neolithic, was largely confined to the "hilly flanks" of the Zagros, where it was believed the food-production revolution had occurred. Hints of what could be expected were provided by the wide-ranging field trips of Aurel Stein (1940) and by several excavations (Guran: Meldgard et al. 1964; Giyan: Contenau and Ghirshman 1935; the work of Hole et al. in the Deh Luran (1969); and Hole and Flannery in the Khoramabad plain: 1967). The pioneering work

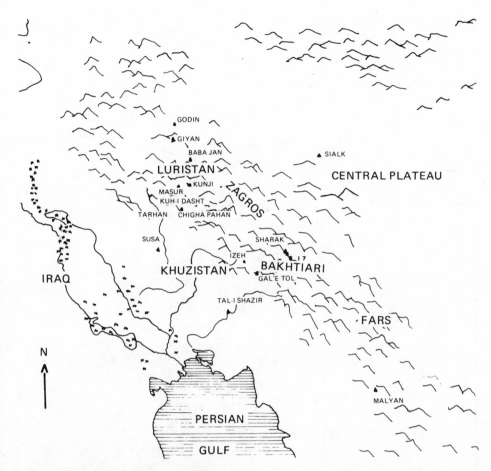

Fig. 17.1. Zagros highlands and surrounding regions.

of Van den Berghe in Fars Province and, less intensively, in Greater Luristan (Luristan proper and the Bakhtiari region), Goff-Meade's pathmaking survey of the Pish-e Kuh section of Luristan (1971), and several less intensive surveys and reconnaissances (Shippman 1970; Nissen 1971; Nissen and Redman 1971; Gropp and Nadjmbadi 1970) all indicated that sections of the Central Zagros highlands were settled at a very early date. However, few of the surveys in the deep mountain zone were of an intensive nature and none was equipped conceptually to deal with the question of nomadic pastoral emergence.

Given the new questions and the limited data base, several archaeologists, including myself, independently began projects in various sections of the Zagros highlands. My project centered on the eastern section of the Bakhtiari mountains, while Henry Wright carried out a project in the southern section. Other projects included those of Louis Levine and Cuyler Young in the Kangavar and Mahi Dasht, William Sumner in Fars, Louis Van den Berghe in the Posht-e Kuh and Peder Mortensen in the Hulailan section of the Pishe-e Kuh area of Luristan. This work, continuing until the Iranian revolution in 1979, produced a mass of new information, much of which has been published only recently. This work, in combination with research projects dedicated

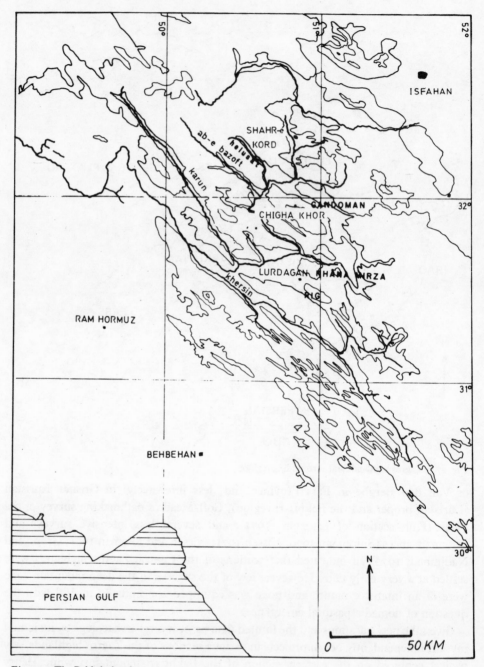

Fig. 17.2. The Bakhtiari region.

to elucidating pastoral adaptations in other regions of the world, has provided some criteria for the identification of pastoralists (see particularly Chang and Koster 1986). Moreover, recently a series of new explanatory models for nomadic pastoralist specialization has been suggested (Sherratt 1981, 1983; Gilbert 1983; Sumner 1986).

The project

Geography

My own project was to take place in the Bakhtiari section of the Iranian Central Zagros. This region was in many ways ideal for an investigation of late prehistoric and early historical highland pastoralist adaptations and their possible relationship to alluvial centers of civilization. The Bakhtiari mountains, immediately northeast of the Khuzistan alluvial plain, the historical lowland center of Elamite civilization, are part of a chain of connected highland zones inhabited by some of the Middle East's major pastoralist tribes; these include the Feili Lurs, Kurdish remnants, more numerous north of Kermanshah, the Kuhgilu, the eclectic Hamseh confederation, and the powerful Qashqai and Bakhtiari confederations.

The geography and ecology of the mountain zone were encouraging to such an investigation. The mountains border the relatively arid alluvial lowlands but retain their own character and permit autonomous modes of behavior to develop within them. The mountains form a series of parallel chains running northwest/southeast, generally allowing less arduous movement from valley to valley within the mountains, but limiting access from the outside. Reaching heights of 4000 m, they are interspersed by increasingly high connecting valley systems. The high mountain zone offers a surprisingly variable array of environmental conditions. The mountains receive between 1000 and 350 mm of precipitation per year, largely confined to the winter months, overwhelmingly in the form of snow and consequent runoff. The highland margins experience a serious drop in precipitation. Contemporary conditions in neighboring valleys may present totally different pictures. For example, the Ardal region is arid, eroded, desolate, and covered by dunes, while the Helusat River area is lush and wooded. Seasonal lakes cover large stretches of some valleys, such as the Chogha Yurd plain; in others, like Lurdagan, natural springs spew forth water adequate for irrigation and even significant wet rice cultivation. Soils vary from richer alluvial soils to rocky arid stretches barely suited to the most extensive forms of exploitation.

The high mountains, with their limited points of access and traverse, sufficiently buffer the highland regions for the surrounding lowland and central high plateau zones to have allowed a high degree of political and social-organizational autonomy throughout much of their history. The difficulties of military penetration and occupation in the face of determined opposition were and are many, and therefore attempts at direct control of these regions were relatively limited (see below). However, all the major routes connecting coastal and alluvial Iran, and most connecting Mesopotamia proper with the central Iranian Plateau and Central Asia, pass through this section of the Zagros (for sources see Zagarell 1982a: 9). Together with the highlands themselves, these more easterly regions represent important resource areas for the Greater Mesopotamian alluvial centers. Thus, the region was unlikely to have remained a neglected backwater, bypassed and unnoticed by the newly emerging state systems.

Recent historical forms of highland resource exploitation

The next stage of the work was to determine the actual system of highland exploitation by its more recent late historical inhabitants in order to define the criteria for the interpretation of earlier material cultural remains. Although much had been written about Iranian highland nomadism, difficulties abounded. Much of the best, anthropologically sophisticated work was only published or carried out after my work had already begun (Digard 1978, 1981; Ehmann 1975; Garthwaite 1978, 1983). Moreover, although environmental conditions might be presumed to have remained the same, the dominant modes of production, dominant property and political forms, and conditions characterizing and affecting highland life could not be presumed to have remained unchanged.[2]

The literature indicated a rather fluid complex picture of highland ethnic, economic and social adaptations. The tribal confederations were not ethnic confederations or tribes, but rather consisted of various language groups, all united under the political banner of the tribal confederation (more about this will be said below). The ecological diversity to some extent reflected the very different highland modes of subsistence to be found. Some of this diversity was tied to ethnic diversity; for example, the Arab Gomish "tribe" of the Bakhtiari confederation was more likely to be involved in marsh-buffalo herding than other mountain tribal groups. Much more common was the variation in degree of sedentariness, economic mix of subsistence modes, and emphasis of herding stock. Each variant could of course be classified according to anthropological systems of identification (see, for example, Huetteroth 1959: 37–47 or Khazanov 1984: 40–69). In fact, within the Central Zagros highlands, groups can be found spanning the entire spectrum of categories, although the predominant form clearly revolved around so-called semi-nomadic and semi-sedentary adaptations. Forms, or formal categories, which exist cheek to cheek within the highlands are: (1) *"pure" nomadism*, where the entire ethnic unit takes part in migratory movements, and where the group is only involved in pastoral subsistence activities; (2) *semi-nomadism*, where the entire ethnic unit takes part in migratory movements, but where subsidiary agriculture plays a significant role; (3) *semi-sedentarism* (including Yahla peasantry), where the entire group takes part in short-range movements, but where agriculture is dominant and pastoral activities are an important, but subsidiary, economic sector; (4) *transhumance*, when societies are involved in agricultural and pastoral activities, and specialized herders care for the flocks; (5) *fully sedentary communities*, which are completely sedentary. Categories (1) and (5) are relatively rare in the Zagros highlands. Category (2) makes up the majority of the Zagros "nomadic" groups, and categories (3) and (4) represent typical village communities, although there are many variations.

However, although these forms can be categorized it is not obvious that the categories are anything more than descriptions, and to delineate them does not actually convey the systemic unity behind the categories. Particular social units were able to move from one category to another, and the regional continuum of categoric adaptations could change emphasis depending upon historical and economic circumstances. I have identified numerous examples of groups changing their economic strategy, becoming more or less nomadic depending upon herding success, agricultural disaster, cattle/flock epidemics, external military threats, and so forth. Moreover, more mobile pastoral units were often kin to more sedentary units with whom they left their summer or winter tents, in turn occasionally taking the flocks of their more sedentary relatives with them on seasonal migrations (see Zagarell 1982a: chapter 4). Thus the picture that emerged was an adaptation of long-term variation of forms which facilitated movement along a continuum from one category into another, depending upon economic and political fortune, while at the same time providing access to grains and social support in a relatively stable environment.

The interconnectedness of forms indicates the difficulties involved in identifying changes in levels of pastoral mobility and the proliferation of nomadic activities during specific historic periods, but not for the reasons many archaeologists had surmised. Pastoral encampments, however temporary, were not necessarily signs of specialized nomadism. They could simply be Yahla camps, or even the summer encampments of fully sedentary villagers who left their village in order to escape the ravages of summer vermin (Porter 1821–2, I: 479). Moreover, longer-term sedentary settlement within a region did not preclude mobile pastoralism; rather, I expected the two forms, camp and village, to be found within reasonable proximity of one another, given the many material, economic and often kin ties between them. I concluded that any investigation into nomadic adaptations would have to be regional in nature. Evidence for increasing or decreasing pastoral mobility (pastoral nomadic specialization) could not be primarily small-scale incidents, but would have to be found in changing patterns of "settlement," including changing location, size, ecology and interrelationships of sites over time.

The regional approach called for more intensive site settlement survey approaches, rather than an emphasis on more intensive excavation. Moreover, because of severe monetary restrictions, each stage of the project had to be seen as a self-contained unit, with its own set of questions and with only limited labor available to answer them. The first stage of the project was the intensive survey of one valley, Khana Mirza, in which a guide, a mule and I walked the entire valley. The immediately surrounding valleys (Rig and Lurdagan) were more extensively covered by motorcycle. The second season included small excavations of two of the sites discovered during the first season and a more extensive auto survey of several valleys (Gandoman, Eman Qeis, Chogha Yurd) on one of the possible thoroughfares connecting the alluvial lowlands with the Iranian Central Plateau and beyond. The third season was represented by a very extensive reconnaissance of several of the important mountain crossroads and of many important valley systems (from Lurdagan, Malamir, and the Abe-Vanak), again carried out by myself, a mule, and a guide. The interrupted fourth season (1978) included a moderately intensive survey of the Shahr-e Kord plain in the northern reaches of the Bakhtiari mountains, on the main road leading into the central plateau, and a small site sounding (Qal'e Geli) in the Lurdagan plain. During all these surveys, sites were divided up into sectors, with both "blind" and "fossil-type" collections of pottery made from all sites. The pottery types were counted and diagnostic sherds were drawn and photographed, as were other small finds. The appearance and prevalence of pottery of the various periods would provide the crude indicators of periods and extents of habitation.

The prehistoric environment

Little is known about the prehistoric environmental conditions of the Bakhtiari region of the Zagros. Analysis of pollen cores from Zeribar and Mir-abad indicates forestation of the Central Zagros region beginning in approximately 8000 B.C., first as oak/pistachio/almond savannah, becoming thicker oak forest during the Late Chalcolithic (see Bender 1975 and Henricksen 1985). It has suggested that a warming trend took place, reaching its high point approximately 3500 B.C. (Nuetzel 1975, 1976). The only relevant independent information I have for the Bakhtiari mountains is an analysis of the pollen from the sounding of the Neolithic site of Qal'e Rostam. The pollen indicates a local environment similar to the present one. However, tree pollen is very rare, suggesting either that forestation has yet to have taken place at altitudes of 2000 m or that human activities are responsible for forest removal (Zagarell 1982a: 54).

Results of the Bakhtiari survey: patterns of settlement

A continuous pattern of Bakhtiari highlands use can be discerned from the epi-Paleolithic/proto-Neolithic onwards. From 2000 m and above, the region seems to have experienced its own indigenous transition from hunting-gathering to agricultural production, in tandem with other sections of the Zagros. Cave sites, apparently late epi-Paleolithic and proto-Neolithic in date, have been found in various sections of the Bakhtiari and particularly in the Shahr-e Kord region (Zagarell 1982a: 18–20). These sites seem to have been involved in hunting/gathering subsistence activities, as reflected in tool types (blade-sections, micro-blades, scrapers). Evidence of an aceramic Neolithic phase can be discerned at several sites, although nowhere unmixed with other materials. At the tiny (c. 70 × 60 m) early Neolithic hamlet site of K 100, Qal'e Rostam, in the Khana Mirza plain, at the lowest sounding level, obsidian and micro-blades were found unassociated with pottery, although the cleared area was represented by only two 1 × 5 m trenches (for literature see Zagarell 1982a/b; Nissen and Zagarell 1976). Early Neolithic pottery sites, on the other hand, can be found throughout much of the Bakhtiari highlands. The three Neolithic cultures of the northeast Bakhtiari highlands are clearly local and indigenous. In fact, there are very significant differences between the Neolithic cultures of the southwest Bakhtiari mountains and those of the northeast. Moreover, the final Rostam phase seems to be rare in other sections of the northeastern mountains. The earliest phase (Qal'e Rostam III) is represented by open forms, heavily fiber tempered with black cores and mottled surfaces. The pottery often carries a layer of fine clay on the outer surface, frequently covered with fine cracks. It is difficult to compare this pottery directly to known complexes, but it seems related to early pottery experimentation in other areas. The middle phase (Q.R. II) consists of a red-polished ware, similar to that which may be found at many Iranian highland sites (for example, at Guran: Mortensen 1964: 31; and Sialk I: Ghirshman 1938: 14). The latest phase (Q.R.I), represented by a distinctly local pottery group, consists of heavy chaff-tempered, polychrome decorated ware. The stone tools, overwhelmingly composed of blades and blade sections, frequently microliths and occasionally sporting silica sheen, indicate continuity from the epi-Paleolithic and earlier Neolithic phases of development.

The inhabitants of the sites seem to have been engaged in a multi-resource exploitation of the highland valleys. Some of the Shahr-e Kord sites sit in the plain's center, far from the hilly valley edge, indicating an emphasis on agricultural activities. At Qal'e Rostam, querns, mortars, pestles, blade sections with silica sheen all suggest agricultural, vegetal food-processing activities. On the other hand, the placement of many of the sites at points where various pastoral, agricultural, hunting and gathering activities might all have been pursued offers a picture of a more mixed economy. Shellfish remnants suggest the exploitation of marsh resources. The faunal evidence, although still only superficially examined, provided evidence for pastoral activities. Moreover, several cave-sites appear to have been in use during the later Neolithic period. In particular, the contemporary combination of the cave-shelter site of Eshkafte-Kharaji and the open air site, S 2. in the Shahr-e Kord plain suggests an agricultural/pastoral economy, with possible cave-to-open-air movement.

In several other Central Zagros highland regions there is strong evidence of similar mixed economies, including economies with a significant mobile pastoral sector. The basal levels of Tepe Guran in the Hulailan Valley seem to have constituted a seasonal herding encampment. Within the Hulailan, short-range movements from nearby caves to open-air sites would seem to reflect the herding aspect of relatively mixed communities (Mortensen 1964, 1972). At Tepe Tula'i, a mound on the northern edge of the Khuzistan plain, a pastoral herding site has been identified (Hole 1975, 1979). It has been suggested that this was not a specialized herding site *per se*, but rather a herding camp of a larger, agro-pastoral community (Wheeler-Pires-Ferreira 1975–7). Similar open-air/cave combination-sites can be found in other sections of the Zagros (for example, at Shanidar cave; Solecki 1952, 1958, 1979). Thus, mobile pastoral activities certainly played a role during the Neolithic phases of development, but in the context of a mixed economy, where they represented one resource among many.

The political structure appears to have been decentralized. On the community level, there are no archaeological indications of internal stratification or significant status hierarchies. On the intercommunity level sites do not seem to have formed complex site hierarchies, nor are they agglomerated, indicating that these smaller, village/hamlet sized sites were autonomous communities. Hamlets do not seem to have competed for space; rather, there appear to have been more than adequate available resources for all.

During the following Early Chalcolithic period (Eskandari phase), the local Neolithic pottery material culture aspect was replaced by pottery with definite lowland connections (X ware and Susiana a) apparently emanating from the Khuzistan plain. A similar intrusion is known somewhat earlier from the Deh Luran/Poshte-kuh section of the Zagros. In the lowlands this pottery group is connected with rather rudimentary irrigation experimentation (Oates 1972). In the Bakhtiari section of the Zagros, however, there is little evidence of a shift in settlement or a radical shift in

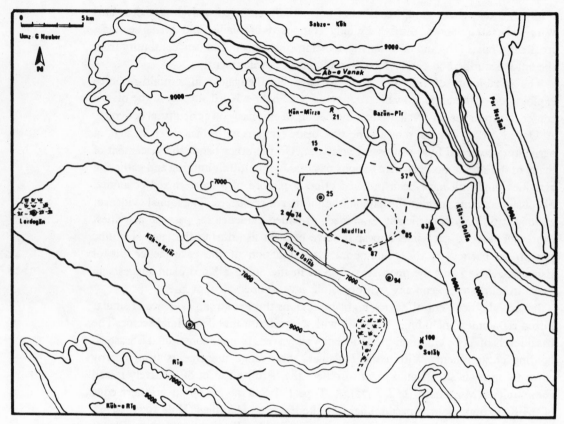

Fig. 17.3. Khana Mirza plain. Middle Chalcolithic.

economic strategy and therefore this new pottery complex does not *necessarily* connote any significant movement of populations. There may have been a subtle shift towards areas more supportive of a largely agricultural economy, but many of the sites inhabited had been utilized by earlier, local Neolithic populations. However, cave use seems to decrease sharply, not only in the Bakhtiari region, but also in other Zagros highland regions, indicating that mobile pastoral activities, as part of a total mixed economy strategy, declined in importance (this Early Chalcolithic shift is particularly apparent in the Hulailan plain; see Mortensen 1976). On the political level, there continued to be little evidence of highland social stratification, either in the distribution of sites or in the types of finds. In fact, the distribution of sites and the small village dimensions of these sites suggest that we continue to confront politically independent, largely self-sufficient communities, still largely undifferentiated internally.

During the subsequent Middle Chalcolithic (Chellegah and Afghan phases) there is a very significant increase in the number and size of sites. This increase is probably the result of moister climate, the expansion of small-scale irrigation techniques and the utilization of natural irrigation regimes. Almost every valley shows some evidence of habitation during this time-period (see the discussion in Wright 1979; Shippman

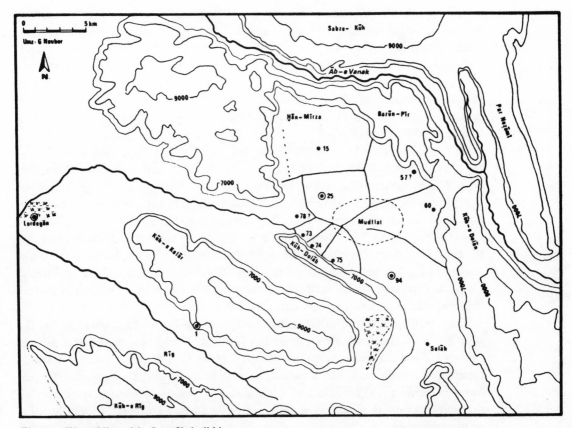

Fig. 17.4. Khana Mirza plain. Late Chalcolithic.

1970; Zagarell 1982a: 59–62). The distribution of sites argues for a very strong agricultural orientation. In the Khana Mirza plain sites are fairly evenly distributed over the entire valley, although they favor the agriculturally richer sections. This is indicated by the illustration of Figs. 17.3 and 17.4, where I have evenly divided the distances between each site and arbitrarily ascribed the consequent areas to the various sites. Each site appears to have had a total potential use area of approximately 18 sq. km. Although site size remains within the village range, some of the Khana Mirza sites, essentially equally spaced throughout the Rig and Lurdagan plains, appear to have been larger than their neighbors and would seem to represent some limited form of site hierarchy. In the northern Shahr-e Kord plain, increase in site size is corroborated by the site of S12, 158 × 128 m, part of the larger Choghate–Eskandari complex. Another member of the Choghate-Eskandari complex, approximately 100 m away, is S13, c. 85 × 58 m, also covered with Middle Chalcolithic wares, perhaps once constituting a single settlement with S12, although there are also chronological differences indicated for the collected complexes as a whole. On the fringes of the Central Zagros, in the Behbehan section of Kuhgiluyah, still larger sites have been found dating to this time-range (Tepe Sohz: Nissen 1971; Nissen and Redman 1971; Dittmann 1984), suggesting the emergence of ranking and authority systems within the highlands. Similar site differentiation can be found in other sections of the Central Zagros (Fars, Luristan, Lower Bakhtiari). The highlands were clearly becoming more socially complex, with fledgling systems of authority and differential site functioning emerging as characteristic for the region as a whole.

In many highland regions evidence of small-scale irrigation networks dating to the Middle Chalcolithic has been uncovered. Often these systems appear to have represented no more than the utilization of natural water regimes and temporary seasonal lake beds (in the Bakhtiari – Khana Mirza, Gandoman, Emam Qeis plains, and sites along the Khersan and Helusat rivers: Zagarell 1982a/b: 62; Deh Luran: Wright et al. 1975; use of marsh in the Kur basin of Fars: Sumner 1972: 240, 247; in the Behbehan plain: Nissen 1983: 57; Zagarell 1982a/b: 86; Luristan: Mortensen 1975: 30–1; Young 1975: 25; in the Doulat-Abad plain, near Tepe Yahya: Prickett 1976). In general, the use of subsidiary irrigation parallels developments in the surrounding alluvial lowlands (in Khuzestan: Hole 1968: 250), although the technology utilized differed. In the highlands, irrigation efforts were often characterized by a combination of small-scale terracing and natural irrigation regimes. Whereas in the lowlands such systems could be expanded significantly with relatively low levels of labor input, in the highland valleys expansion possibilities were limited.

Thus, through much of the Middle Chalcolithic the Zagros highlands seem to be progressing in the same direction as the lowlands. Larger, agricultural sites are emerging. Sites are becoming differentiated, presumably reflecting progressive inter-community stratification. The highlands seem to be developing their own indigenous forms of authority. The extent of such authority systems (chiefdoms) cannot be determined, but may have, in some cases, united several valleys. In viewing the developments one would have every right to believe that the highlands would continue to develop in a similar direction as that of the lowlands. This was not to be the case.

During the early phases of the Middle Chalcolithic, the pottery complexes closely parallel those of the alluvial lowlands. Significantly, towards the latter half of this period the highland pottery complexes diverged increasingly from lowland ones. During the latter half of the Middle Chalcolithic there is some evidence of a more mobile mode of life, not seen since the Neolithic, presaging the much greater importance of such mobility during the following phase. In the northern Bakhtiari zone this is only indicated by the reutilization of caves. In the Poshte-Kuh section of Luristan, the earliest Luristan graveyards of Parchinah and Hakalan may represent pastoral cemeteries situated along migration routes, as suggested by the excavator (see Van den Berghe 1973, 1975).

During the following Late Chalcolithic (contemporary with the Mesopotamian Uruk period), we find significant changes in the Bakhtiari section of the highlands. Although the larger sites continue to be inhabited, many of the smaller village sites have been abandoned; one's first impression is of a significant decline in population. The agricultural, evenly dispersed pattern has vanished. A new type of site – the slope site – appears. These sites are very small, no more than 0.4 ha, situated along the hilly slopes, often in areas not conducive to agriculture, and are poor, at least today, in water resources. They sit where narrow ravines cut into the stony hillsides. In contrast to the Middle Chalcolithic pattern, these sites are not allotted maximum available valley surface. On these sites heavy sherdage patterns are associated with boulder accumulations, representing some type of limited construction. The best recent comparisons for these archaeological sites are several slope sites utilized by modern pastoralists. The modern sites include one with a house and a corral and another consisting of several stone sheep-corrals. I am suggesting that these are sites of more mobile pastoralists, although the degree of mobility remains uncertain. Cave utilization continues during this phase, although in other regions it expands considerably. Both the larger, clearly village communities and the slope sites contain the same pottery – a red ware with affinities to the highland Banesh complex of Fars province. The sharing of the same material culture by larger village and slope sites indicates not merely the lack of an opposition between the two forms, but their high level of social integration.

A third form of contemporary settlement can be found, but only along the outer fringes of the Bakhtiari mountains. These are settlements with clear lowland and/or Central Plateau pottery affinities. The sites of Sharak (S10) and S17, in the Shahr-e Kord plain, sit on the major cross-mountain route, connecting the alluvial plain and Central Plateau. Both of these sites are characterized by large numbers of beveled rim bowls, low, crude trays, and flanged open bowls. Nevertheless, they do not represent a unified material culture. Rather, at Sharak these vessels are accompanied by sizable amounts of painted and plain Sialk 7b, Godin VI wares, which indicate Central Plateau connections, as well as Bakhtiari Late Chalcolithic red wares. S17, on the other hand, is accompanied by bent spouts, pierced ear lugs and by painted wares typical of the Banesh complex of Fars province. However, despite the differences in pottery complexes, the sites may still be contemporary, although I suspect that the S17 complex is slightly later than that of S10. Similar non-local sites appear along the southern margins of the Bakhtiari fringe (Wright 1979; Zagarell 1986a, n.d.a). Significantly, however, this non-local pottery complex appears only rarely within the heart of the Bakhtiari high-mountain zone; it is only found on some of the larger sites. This limited appearance within the mountain heartland, in contrast to the full complex along the mountain fringes, suggests that the highlands were relatively independent of their more socially complex alluvial and Central Plateau neighbors. Moreover, the appearance of small amounts of this non-local ware on only some of the larger sites suggests differential access/contact of highland sites with such outposts and, indeed, suggests differential authority adhering to those communities.

Similar *apparent* population declines and site-types can be found within other sections of the Zagros. Slope sites, thought to be the communities of semi-sedentary or semi-nomadic peoples – that is, more mobile pastoral economies – coexisting with more urban alluvial complexes are to be found in Fars province (Sumner 1986). In Luristan, the high mountain graveyards divorced from settlement continue. Small open-air sites, thought to be camps, have been identified in the Hulailan plain (Mortensen 1975, 1976). Moreover, cave sites become utilized increasingly, occasionally accompanied by corrals, suggesting a strong connection with pastoral

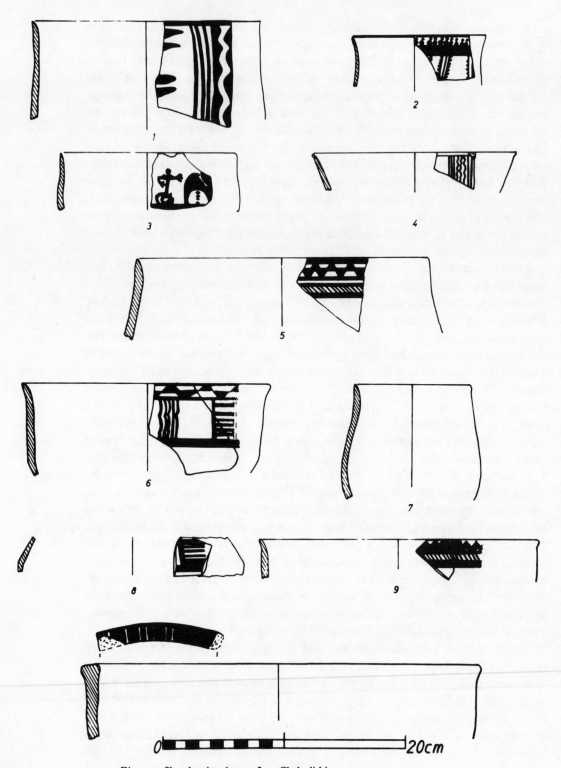

Fig. 17.5. Sharak painted ware. Late Chalcolithic.

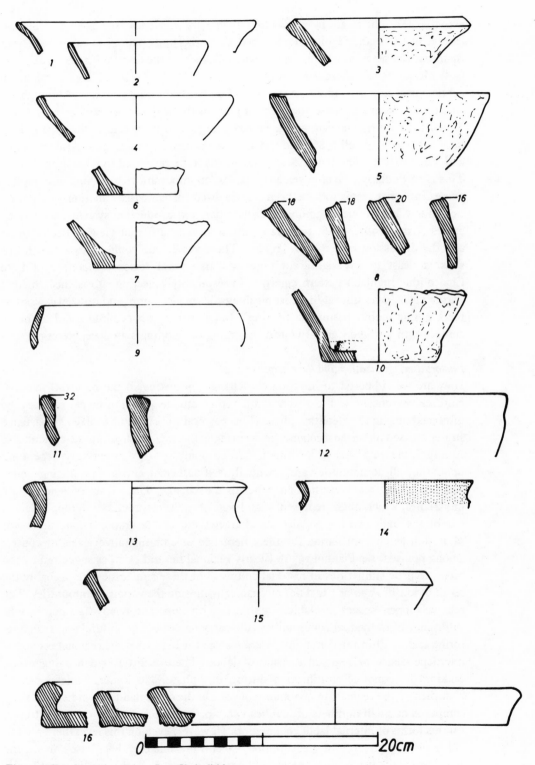

Fig. 17.6. Sharak unpainted ware. Late Chalcolithic.

activities (Wright et al. 1975; Zagarell 1982a: 83–4; Henricksen 1985:29). Significantly, in Luristan, despite the fact that the indigenous pottery is clearly different
than that characterizing either the alluvial lowlands or the Central Plateau group (see
Goff-Meade 1971), there are several sites which do have close Plateau or alluvial
connections, similar to those we have found in the Bakhtiari mountains. Although the
situation is complex, these sites seem to sit on the major thoroughfare connecting
Khuzistan with the plateau, and seem to be larger and more central than the strictly
local sites (see Zagarell 1986b and n.d.a. for a discussion of these sites. Also see Weiss
and Young 1975). The lowland complex seems to be restricted to a handful of sites.
This is particularly true of beveled rim bowls, an important element of that complex,
possessing what seems to have been a specialized, urban-based function (apparently
tied to lowland public/communal redistribution and production systems; see among
others Nissen 1980b:95–6, 1983:92–3, the somewhat different view of Beale [1978]
and the discussion by Le Brun [1980]). These vessels are confined to a handful of
sites, at least in any significant numbers. In several regions, therefore, a Late
Chalcolithic highland pattern emerges – presumably reflecting subsistence changes
(larger village/agricultural-life existing alongside smaller camps and utilized cave sites,
representing mobile pastoral camp sites). In all areas this is combined with intimate
contact with lowland/Central Plateau emerging or budding state-level societies.

Pastoralism, civilization and the emerging state
How are we supposed to interpret the changes occurring in the highland material
culture? Significant is the determination that mobile pastoralism can already be
discerned during the Neolithic phase. This pastoralism is part of a mixed subsistence
strategy based upon an economy of hunting/gathering/herding/limited agriculture.
Although the emphasis within this mixed economy strategy might vary depending
upon site, all communities are essentially self-sufficient and are producing goods
destined for internal consumption rather than exchange. There is no evidence of site
hierarchies, which might represent high levels of multi-community interdependence,
nor of the high density populations characteristic of "saturation" conditions (for
saturation as an explanation for the emergence of administrative levels of control
among nomads, see Planhol 1976). Clearly regional ties did exist, as suggested by the
broad stylistic similarities in material culture, but these similarities are probably the
result of kinship and/or ritual ties mechanically uniting the various communities. The
relatively open spaces available, combined with apparent relative economic self-
sufficiency of individual communities (the carrying out of agricultural and manufacturing tasks within the community), argues against high levels of regional economic
interdependence or regional division of labor. There is little evidence suggesting
ranking or economic stratification during this phase. No leaders (chiefs) can be
identified on the regional or community level. On the other hand, the individual sites,
composed of small numbers of families, were probably much more dependent upon
various forms of internal labor cooperation. However, even on this level there are few
indicators of high levels of specialization, except, presumably, those based on sex and
age. Moreover, quite often in the ethnographic record, flocks are personal/family

Fig. 17.7. Nomadic camps and flocks. Rig Valley.

property, rather than the property of the larger group (Markov 1978). Truncated forms of family flock ownership combined with the self-sufficiency of most households, that is, their ability to carry out many of their production tasks without institutionalized forms of cooperation, suggest the possibility that individual family units were atomized to some degree, although the level of self-sufficiency of family units, in the context of self-sufficient communities, either as production or consumption units, has yet to be determined. The accounting tools and storage facilities of some communities, and existence of community buildings, more evident towards the latter half of the Neolithic, all indicate some level of internal cooperation. Many smaller, rural communities consisted of only a handful of families. Certainly within these communities family groups must have cooperated and shared food during difficult times, but each family unit was probably engaged in the same economic activity.

Thus, regional cooperation was certainly necessary for the survival of communities and family groups – avoidance of hostilities; mutual respect for resources, particularly water and pasture, utilized by several groups; probable mutual support during famines and epidemics, most likely facilitated by gift exchange and marriage alliances, all reflected in the broad sharing of material cultural attributes – but such intergroup cooperation must have been *perceived* as voluntary, rather than as a precondition for production. Pasture and agricultural resources must have appeared bounteous. Standardized, particularly long-distance migration routes would have been superfluous. Under these conditions there was no need of managerial institutions to facilitate interaction between sedentary and nomadic groups, or to direct and allocate pasture to the various herding groups, and in fact there were none. We are dealing

Fig. 17.8. S7. Sangiyan. Epipaleolithic cave site in Shahr-e Kord plain.

with economically autarkic groups, engaged in a mixed economic strategy under non-competitive conditions. This largely parallels the condition of East African mixed economy societies described by Bonte. Bonte (1974) has persuasively argued that these East African mixed pastoral and agricultural communities represent a form of production quite similar to that described by Marx under "Germanic mode of production" (Marx 1965:75–80). This form of pastoral activity differs significantly in context from that of more recent Zagros societies practicing mobile pastoralism, whose herds, flocks and animal products are often produced for exchange, possessors of more complex systems of institutional leadership (centralized tribes/confederations), in close contact with more sedentary peoples. Indeed, there seems to have been an historical break between this form of pastoralism and the form which later characterized much of the Central Zagros, separated by a rather extended period dominated by agricultural strategies.

More mobile pastoral groups, alongside sedentary highland settlements, seem to begin to proliferate during the latter half of the Middle Chalcolithic and become very common during the Late Chalcolithic. Until this point highland and lowland developmental pathways were parallel; the late Middle Chalcolithic/Late Chalcolithic phases represent the periods of highland/lowland material culture differentiation, presumably reflecting the diverging regional socio-organizational and ecological adaptations. The dominant social relations and modes of production of highland and lowland regions were becoming quite different in character.

The lowlands, and presumably the Central Plateau, had developed a society based on the integration of several coexisting production modes; a lineage based mode, based on extended family production (for a discussion of this mode see Terray 1975), an emerging private sector, becoming evident during the Early Dynastic Period (often having ties to the state apparatus), and a dominant public/communal, eventually state-organized system of production, based on storage and the exploitation of various forms of dependent labor (see Diakonoff 1976, 1982a, 1982b, Gelb 1972a, 1972b, 1973, 1982, and Zagarell 1986b). Although storage and storage controls begin no later than the late Neolithic/Early Chalcolithic, the system of centralized production only becomes evident during the earliest stage of the Late Chalcolithic, perhaps beginning during the late Middle Chalcolithic, although in a very limited form (Zagarell 1986b).

The highlands had earlier developed a mode of subsistence largely based on rain-supported agriculture, with limited subsidiary use of small-scale irrigation during the Middle Chalcolithic. The emergence of a more mobile pastoral sector, in the context of a largely sedentary society, may have been the consequence of several contributing factors. The highlands, despite the differences in environment, were broadly developing along the same pathway as the lowlands. However, given the limited possibilities of expanding highland irrigation systems, it is likely that production increases became associated increasingly with the pastoral sector (see Bonte 1981b for the connection between mobile pastoralism and increasing levels of production). This, in turn, may have been encouraged by changing climatic conditions. This new emphasis on mobility, however, did not repeat the conditions of Neolithic times, for it occurred in context of highland sedentary subsistence agricultural communities, which had already developed some system of indigenous authority, thus facilitating interaction between communities and camps which probably were kin-related. As discussed below, this authority, and its confederational institutional form, was probably augmented by the external contact with alluvial and Central Plateau centers of civilization.

Clearly, the Central Zagros highlands were in close contact with the lowlands and the Central Plateau during the Late Chalcolithic. The appearance of non-local sites along the mountain fringes (Sharak, S17, Godin, Qal'e Tol, and so on) testify to contact with highland groups and the utilization of routes through these regions, presumably related to exchange systems. However, at least for the Bakhtiari section of the Zagros, there is no evidence of such sites in the mountainous heartland, although small amounts of non-local pottery on some of the larger highland sites suggest selective contact with these fringe communities. This makes it likely that the fringe sites are "ports of trade," contact points with a largely autonomous, politically independent highland zone. This system of contact is thus segmented, consisting of independent lowland, highland and Central Plateau components. Moreover, there are several fringe sites, at different exit and entrance points throughout the highlands, suggesting alternate routes, in turn indicating that no single lowland community dominated the lowlands. This, in turn, suggests a more fragmented lowland society during the Late Chalcolithic. The various centers were probably ritually rather than *politically* united (for a fuller discussion of these routes, "segmentation" and "colony" sites, see Zagarell 1986b and n.d.a). This contradicts the earlier assumption of a centralized Khuzistan state system during the Late Chalcolithic, which was based on settlement survey data (Johnson 1973; for a discussion of the question of the proposed

Khuzistan/Mesopotamian Late Chalcolithic state system see R. McC. Adams 1981 and Zagarell 1986a).

The segmented nature of the system is the result, reflection, and cause of several historical and structural conditions. It reflects the different developmental pathways taken by highlands and lowlands. The highlands were structured by a more dispersed production system, probably founded upon smaller kin-group production of goods, rather than being dominated by a system of centralized production and distribution centers as were the lowlands. Comparative historic and ethnographic evidence suggests that tribal (confederational) leaders would have had only limited power to enforce their will, since the economic power base of such pastoral confederations would have been unstable and not easily transformed into political power (see, among others, Garthwaite 1978, 1983 and Zagarell n.d.b). However, given the Middle Chalcolithic emergence of highland authority systems, the now more dense pastoral populations, with more limited pasture available and periodic regional saturation points being approached, must have actively sought alliances and support for leaders who would aid them in the defense of, or would provide, protected pasture. In fact, historically, such alliances, and consequent confederations (tribes), are not kin-organizations on the upper levels. Rather they are political entities, utilizing a kin-idiom to describe the relationship of the various component groups to one another and to the various levels of leadership.

This process of emerging confederational leadership would have been encouraged by contact with the lowlands and the Central Plateau. The increasing social complexity of those regions provided impetus for the development of broad exchange systems and migration of populations. However, the highlands are not easily controlled. They are difficult of access, given to internal resistance, and almost impossible to occupy. The production system is dispersed and difficult to exploit directly, which may have encouraged its still greater dispersal (see Henricksen 1985). In fact, control over the region has been traditionally indirect. In general, the great advantage of highland tribal societies *vis-à-vis* more centralized state systems is the lack of a single, regional, tribal leader. When there is no single head to be struck off, short of genocide there is no way to avoid the reemergence of independent, "unruly", constituent tribal groups. This is not an ideal situation for states having to deal with such regions. Without any individual or limited group having access to sufficient coercive resources, a deal made with one "leader" binds no one else, and, in fact, encourages other petty leaders to make impossible any agreement without similar agreements being concluded with them. Therefore state leaders have traditionally encouraged the development of semi-autonomous tribal leaders, making them responsible for controlling their populations and intervening in internal tribal affairs to overthrow those same leaders when they became too powerful and threatened the power of the state (see, for example, Briant 1982, Garthwaite 1983 and Zagarell n.d.b).

Lowland society during the Late Chalcolithic, despite its powerful new bureaucracy, its ability to store, control, produce, and distribute goods, must also be understood as administratively weak. The coercive powers and structures of lowland communities were still limited. This is reflected in the inability of later Early Dynastic societies to develop effective administrative forms of intercommunity control; that is, placing those loyal to the dominant, state apparatus over other, dependent communities. Rather, lowland leaders dominated other, independent communities, which remained under the administration of their own local leaders, through an unstable hegemony and periods of temporary military and economic advantage (see Zagarell 1986a). Even internally, it has been suggested, because of limited forms of military advantage, there were difficulties in enslaving male prisoners of war, which encouraged a preponderance of women in the early dependent labor force (see particularly, Diakonoff 1976:67; Gelb 1972b; Adams 1984:114–17; and Zagarell 1986b). Only during the still later Akkadian and Ur III periods was a stable administrative state system imposed upon dependent centers. Thus, given the still greater relative weakness of lowland society during the Late Chalcolithic, the city-state competitive condition, and the already existing system of highland hierarchy, it is probable that authorities within the alluvial and plateau centers accepted these realities and actively supported the highland centralizing process as a way of exercising control within the highlands without the high levels of expense and risk occupation forces would have entailed. The system of "colonies" itself, interfacing with independent zones, consciously or unconsciously encouraged the emergence and strengthening of tribal centers of authority (see, for example, Barth 1961:130). The contact and exchange zone provided economic incentives for individuals able to negotiate and to enforce decisions, and it provided economic resources for coercive activities.

Encouragement of political consolidation and periodic regional intervention did not introduce the social conditions of the civilizational centers into the highlands, but rather paradoxically, encouraged the further social divergence of the regions. The highlands, in contrast to their Neolithic phase with its "Germanic-like" dispersed production mode, were now more likely characterized by confederational leaders dispensing pasture and by the apparent necessity of recognized communal ownership of pasture as the precondition of production. Traditionally, on the pastoral level, the political leadership has only minimal control over the labor process *per se*. In fact, there is often little to differentiate the immediate labor process from that of its Neolithic pastoral predecessor. However, loyalty to a group in the form of loyalty to its leader (traditionally to a khan) represented the precondition for appropriation. This structure has many similarities to Marx's description of the "Asiatic mode of production", despite significant differences. Thus, in sharp contrast to lowland economic existence, highland society developed a system of dispersed production and central hierarchy based on a combination of an organizationally dominant, centralized and somewhat more dispersed production form. I have previously argued that this developed form of highland and pastoral authority is only possible given state or highly centralized institutional interference in highland affairs (Zagarell n.d.b and Khazanov 1984).

Conclusions

The evidence, I contend, indicates two periods of high-level pastoral activity within the Zagros highlands: the Neolithic period, with its dispersed, mixed economy and relatively undifferentiated, acephalous society, during the Early Chalcolithic, and a Late Chalcolithic pastoralism characterized by the coexistence of sedentary village and mobile pastoral camp site and shared material culture. While highland production is still dispersed, the various component sectors are more specialized and differentiated in comparison with the Neolithic phase. The coexistence of camp and village sites in the highlands indicates that there is no automatic antagonistic opposition between pastoral and sedentary sectors. In fact, I see the range of variation possible under such a system, alongside its increased productive capacity, as a significant positive adaptation.

I can see no support for the assertion that highland pastoralists *pushed* lowland society across the state threshold. The threat of nomadic incursions and conquest, while real (see for example, Ibn Khaldun 1958), is rarely simply an opposition between settled and nomadic modes of life. Rather, it is a reflection of the non-state (unruly, untamed, uncivilized, *unexploitable*) character of these groups *vis-à-vis* the dominant class (see Adams 1974b and Briant 1982). Moreover, historically the nomadic threat has been closely linked to nomadic mobility. This mobility and consequent raiding is largely based on the horse or camel, forms of transportation apparently not available during the Chalcolithic periods. Mobile pastoralists on foot, even those involved in regular migratory patterns, would have had minimal advantage over free village dwellers, particularly if these pastoralists were only engaged in short-distance movements. They are as vulnerable as sedentary tribal villagers (see, for example, Rowton 1974).

Clearly, there were contacts and negotiations between highlands and lowlands, and lowland society was affected by that contact but it was not obviously more affected than by contact with other societies. Of course, in so far as tribal groups and more mobile ways of life are decentralized alternatives to state forms of organization, they provide a counterweight, and in that sense a threat, to emerging centralized structures. State structures were faced with the necessity of curtailing, in one way or another, the freedom of movement of their own populations, creating their own forms of social circumscription (see Carneiro 1970 for a discussion of the role of circumscription in the state-building process). But, in general, it is more likely that the highlands were radically transformed by contact with centralized alluvial societies.

The forces transforming the highlands, creating the socio-economic "endform," were multidimensional, combining social-structural, ecological, and historical factors. Socio-structural conditions include the developing social differentiation among kin-based societies in highlands and lowlands, the coexistence of lineage and public/communal centralized production within the lowlands in contrast to similar differentiation in context of more dispersed economies of the highlands. The ecological conditions include the encouragement of irrigation techniques and the ability more easily to expand and develop the agricultural and irrigation aspects of the economy in the lowlands. This stood in sharp contrast to the favorable conditions for the expansion of the pastoral sector and the difficulties involved in the expansion of irrigation regimes in the highlands. History, structure in motion, includes the non-predictable condition that the highlands had given birth to a system of limited authority before the emergence of strongly centralized administrative institutions within the lowlands. All these combined to create different paths of development in highlands and lowlands, characterized by very different dominant production modes. The structural conditions alone, without analysis of the actual relationship of forces and the effects of particular variants, are insufficient to predict regional directions of development. The functions of various societal structures are not, and cannot be, inherent in those structural components themselves, but only take on such functions through the integration of those structural elements into a broader system of structural relations.[3]

Notes

1 The field work was variously funded by the Freie Universität of West Berlin, the National Geographic Society and the Deutsche Forschungsgemeinschaft.
2 For example, more recently many agricultural, sedentary groups are tenants, not tribally organized, kin-owners of their own means of production. This would not have been the case during the late prehistoric/early historic periods discussed in this chapter. This has to have affected the relationship between pastoral nomad and settled. Moreover, most Middle Eastern pastoral nomads have become enmeshed in developed commodity networks, which directly affect their aspirations, goals and behaviors.
3 See Lewins and Lewontin 1985: Conclusion, and the discussion of Marx (1982:384–406) about the very different structural positions and functions of peasantry in Western Europe and Russia, given the different historical and consequent structural circumstances facing these societies.

References

Aberle, D.F. et al. 1950. The functional prerequisites of a society. *Ethics* 60:100–11.

Acsadi, G. and J. Nemeskeri. 1970. *History of Human Lifespan and Mortality*. Budapest, Akademei Kiado.

Adams, R.E.W., ed. 1977. *The Origins of Maya Civilization*. Albuquerque, University of New Mexico Press.

    1980. Swamps, canals, and locations of ancient Maya cities. *Antiquity* 54:206–14.

    1981. Settlement patterns of the Central Yucatan and Southern Campeche regions. In W. Ashmore, ed., *Lowland Maya Settlement Patterns*, 211–58. Albuquerque, University of New Mexico Press.

    1983. Ancient land use and culture history in the Pasion River region. In E.Z. Vogt and R.M. Leventhal, eds., *Prehistoric Settlement Patterns, Essays in Honor of Gordon R. Willey*, 319–36. Albuquerque, University of New Mexico Press.

    1986. Rio Azul. *National Geographic*.

Adams, R.E.W., W.E. Brown Jr. and T.P. Culbert. 1981. Radar mapping, archaeology, and ancient Maya land use. *Science* 213:1457–63.

Adams, R.E.W. and R.C. Jones. 1981. Spatial patterns and regional growth among classic Maya cities. *American Antiquity* 46:301–22.

Adams, Richard N. 1976. *Energy and Structure*. Austin, University of Texas Press.

Adams, Robert McC. 1965a. *The Evolution of Urban Society*. Chicago, Aldine.

    1965b. *Land Behind Baghdad: A History of Settlement on the Diyala Plains*. Chicago, University of Chicago Press.

    1966. *The Evolution of Urban Society*. Chicago, Aldine.

    1969. The study of ancient Mesopotamian settlement patterns and the problem of urban origins. *Sumer* 25:111–24.

    1972. Patterns of urbanization in early Southern Mesopotamia. In P. J. Ucko, R.Tringham and G.W. Dimbleby, eds., *Settlement and Urbanism*. London, Duckworth.

    1974a. Anthropological perspectives on ancient trade. *Current Anthropology* 15(3): 239–58.

    1974b. The Mesopotamian social landscape: a view from the frontier. In C.B. Moore, ed., *Reconstructing Complex Societies*, 1–12, Supplement to the *Bulletin of the American Schools of Oriental Research*, 20.

    1977. World picture, anthropological frame. *American Anthropologist* 79:265–79.

    1979a. Late prehispanic empires of the New World. In Mogens Trolle Larson, ed., *Power and Propaganda. A Symposium on Ancient Empires*, 59–73. Mesopotamia; Copenhagen Studies in Assyriology 7. Copenhagen, Akademisk Forlag.

    1979b. Common concerns but different standpoints: a commentary. In M.T. Larsen, ed., *Power and Propaganda: A Symposium on Ancient Empires*, 393–404. Copenhagen, Akademisk Forlag.

    1981. *Heartland of Cities*. Chicago, Chicago University Press.

    1984. Mesopotamian social evolution: old outlooks, new goals. In T. Earle, ed., *On the*

Evolution of Complex Societies: Essays in Honor of Harry Hoijer 1982, 79–129. Malibu, Undena Publications.

Adams, Robert McC. and Hans J. Nissen. 1972. *The Uruk Countryside: The Natural Setting of Urban Societies*. Chicago, University of Chicago Press.

Adams, W. 1984. The first colonial empire; Egypt in Nubia, 3200–1200 B.C. *Comparative Studies in Society and History* 26(1):36–71.

Alden, J.R. 1982. Trade and politics in proto-Elamite Iran. *Current Anthropology* 23(6):613–40.

Alexander, R.D. 1974. The evolution of social behavior. *Annual Review of Ecology and Systematics* 5:325–83.

   1975. The search for a general theory of behavior. *Behavorial Science* 20:77–100.

   1979. *Darwinism and Human Affairs*. Seattle, University of Washington Press.

Allchin, B. and R. Allchin. 1982. *The Rise of Civilization in India and Pakistan*. Cambridge, Cambridge University Press.

Allison, Marvin. 1984. Paleopathology in Chilean and Peruvian populations. In M.N. Cohen and G.J. Armelagos, eds., *Paleopathology at the Origins of Agriculture*, 515–30. New York, Academic Press.

Amiet, P. 1979. Archaeological discontinuity and ethnic duality in Elam. *Antiquity* 53 (209): 195–204.

Amiet, P. and M. Tosi. 1978. Phase 10 at Shahr-i Sokhta: excavations in Square XDV and the late fourth millennium B.C. assemblage of Sistan. *East and West* 28 (1–4): 9–31.

Amin, S. 1974. *Accumulation on a world scale*. New York, Monthly Review Press.

Andrews, E.W. IV and E.W. Andrews V. 1980. *Excavations at Dzibilchaltun, Yucatan, Mexico*. Middle American Research Institute Publication 48. New Orleans, Tulane University.

Angel, J.L. 1984. Health as a crucial factor in the changes from hunting to developed farming in the Mediterranean. In M.N. Cohen and G.J. Armelagos, eds., *Paleopathology at the Origins of Agriculture*, 51–74. New York, Academic Press.

Anthony, D. 1986. The "kurgan culture": a reconsideration.

Ashmore, Wendy. 1981a. Some issues of method and theory in lowland Maya settlement archaeology. In W. Ashmore, ed., *Lowland Maya Settlement Patterns*, 37–70. Albuquerque, University of New Mexico Press.

   1981b. ed. *Lowland Maya Settlement Patterns*. Albuquerque, University of New Mexico Press.

   1986. Peten cosmology in the Maya southeast; an analysis of architecture and settlement patterns at Classic Quirigua. In P.A. Urban and E.M. Schortman, eds., *The Prehistoric Southeast Maya Periphery: Problems and Prospects*, edited by P.A. Urban and E.M. Schortman. Austin, University of Texas Press.

Ashmore, Wendy and Gordon R. Willey. 1981. A historical introduction to the study of lowland Maya settlement patterns. In W. Ashmore, ed., *Lowland Maya Settlement Patterns*, Albuquerque, University of New Mexico Press.

Athens, J. Stephen, 1977. Theory building and the study of evolutionary process in complex societies. In L.R. Binford, ed., *For Theory Building in Archaeology*, 353–84. New York, Academic Press.

Azzi, Corry. 1974. Comment on Harris. *Current Anthropology* 15: 317–21.

Bahn, P. 1986. No sex, please, we're Aurignacians. *Rock Art Research* 3(2):99–120.

Ball, Joseph W. 1977. The rise of the northern Maya chiefdoms: a socioprocessual analysis. In R.E.W. Adams, ed., *The Origins of Maya Civilization*, 101–32. Albuquerque, University of New Mexico press.

Barnard, N. 1961. *Bronze Casting and Bronze Alloys in Ancient China*. Monumenta Senica Monograph 14, Tokyo.

Barth, F. 1961. *Nomads of South Persia*. Boston, Little, Brown.

   1969. *Ethnic Groups and Boundaries*. Boston, Little, Brown.

Bashilov, V.A. and E.N. Loone. 1986. On the levels of knowledge and cognitive aims of archaeology. *Sovetskaja Archeologiya* 3: 192–202 (in Russian).

Baudrillard, J. 1980. Forgetting Foucault. *Humanities in Society* 3:(1):103–14.

Beale, T. 1978. Bevelled rim bowls and their implications for change and economic organization in the later fourth millennium B.C. *Journal of Near Eastern Studies* 37:289–313.

Beard, C. 1934. Written history as an act of faith. *American Historical Review* 39: 219–29.

Beaton, J.M. 1983. Comment. Does intensification account for change in Australian Holocene archaeological record? *Archaeology in Oceania* 18:94–7.

1985. Evidence for a coastal occupation time-lag at Princess Charlotte Bay, North Queensland and implications for coastal colonization and population growth theories for aboriginal Australia. *Archaeology in Oceania* 20:1–20.

Becker, C. 1932. Everyman his own historian. *American Historical Review* 37:221–36.

Becker, Marshall J. 1986. El patron de asentamiento en Tikal, Guatemala, y otros sitios mayas de las tierras bajas; implicaciones para el cambio cultural. *Mayab* 2:7–21. Madrid.

Bender, Barbara. 1975. *Farming in Prehistory*. London, John Baker.

1978. Gatherer-hunter to farmer; a social perspective. *World Archaeology* 10: 204–22.

1981. Gatherer-hunter intensification. In A. Sheridan and G. Bailey, eds., *Economic Archaeology: Towards an Integration of Ecological and Social Approaches*, 149–57. Oxford, BAR International Series 96.

1985. Emergent tribal formations in the American midcontinent. *American Antiquity* 50:52–62.

Bender, M.M., D.A. Baerris and R.L. Steventon. 1981. Further light on carbon isotopes and Hopewell agriculture. *American Antiquity* 46:346–3.

Bender, Thomas. 1985. Making history whole again. *New York Times* Book Review, 6 October: 1, 42–3.

Benfer, Robert. 1984. The challenges and rewards of sedentism: the preceramic village of Paloma, Peru. In M.N. Cohen and G.J. Armelagos, eds., *Paleopathology at the Origins of Agriculture*, 531–58. New York, Academic Press.

1986. Middle and Late Archaic adaptation in Central Coastal Peru. Paper presented to the Annual Meeting of the Society for American Archaeology, New Orleans.

Bennike, Pia. 1985. Paleopathology of Danish skeletons. Copenhagen, Akademisk Forlag.

Berdan, Frances. 1975. Trade, tribute, and market in the Aztec empire. Ph.D. dissertation, Department of Anthropology, University of Texas, Austin.

Berkhofer, R.F., Jr. 1978. *The White Man's Indian: Images of the American Indian from Columbus to the Present*. New York, Knopf.

Berlin, Henry. 1958. El glifo "emblema" en las inscripciones mayas. *Journal de la Société des Americanistes* n.s. 47:111–19, Paris.

Berman, H. 1983. *Law and Revolution: The Formation of the Western Legal Tradition*. Cambridge, MA: Harvard University Press.

Berthelot, Jean. 1986. The extraction of precious metals at the time of the Inka. In J.V. Murra, N. Wachtel and J. Revel, eds., *Anthropological History of Andean Polities*, 69–88. Cambridge, Cambridge University Press.

Bezdek, James C. 1981. *Pattern Recognition with Fuzzy Objective Functions*. New York, Plenum Press.

Binford, L.R. 1962. Archaeology as anthropology. *American Antiquity* 28:217–25.

1965. Archaeological systematics and the study of culture process. *American Antiquity* 31:203–10.

1968a. Archeological perspectives. In S.R. and L.R. Binford, eds., *New Perspectives in Archeology*, 5–32. Chicago, Aldine.

1968b. Post Pleistocene adaptations. In S.R. and L.R. Binford, eds., *New Perspectives in Archeology*. Chicago, Aldine.

1972. *An Archaeological Perspective*. New York, Seminar Press.

1977. Introduction. In L.R. Binford, ed., *For Theory Building in Archaeology*, 1–13. New York, Academic Press.

1978. *Nunamiut Ethnoarchaeology*. New York, Academic Press.

1980a. *Bones: Ancient Men and Modern Myths*. New York, Academic Press.

1980b. Willow smoke and dogs' tails: hunter-gatherer site systems and archaeological site formation. *American Antiquity* 45:4–20.

1983a. *In Pursuit of the Past*. New York, Thames & Hudson.

1983b. *Working at Archaeology*. New York, Academic Press.

1984. *Faunal Remains from Klasies River Mouth*. New York, Academic Press.

1986. In pursuit of the future. In eds., D. Meltzer, D. Fowler and J. Sabloff *American Archaeology Past and Future*, 459–79. Washington, Smithsonian Institution Press.

Binford, L.R., and S.R. Binford 1966. A preliminary analysis of functional variability in the Mousterian of Levallois facies. *American Anthropologist* 68:238–95.

Binford, S.R. and L.R. Binford. 1968. *New Perspectives in Archeology*. Chicago, Aldine.

Birdsell, Joseph. 1968. Some predictions for the Pleistocene based on equilibrium studies among recent hunter gatherers. In R.B. Lee and I. DeVore, eds., *Man the Hunter*, 229–40. Chicago, Aldine.

Biscione, R. 1977. The crisis of Central Asian urbanization in II millennium B.C and villages as an alternative system. In *Le Plateau iranien et l'Asie centrale des origines à la conquête islamique*, 113–27. Paris.

1979. Centre and periphery in late proto-historic Turan: the settlement pattern. In H. Hartle, ed., *South Asian Archaeology*, 203–16. Berlin, Deitrich Reimer.

Biscione, R. and M. Tosi. 1979. *Protoistoria degli Stati Turanici*. Supplement 20, *Annali dell' Istituto Universitario Orientale* 39:3. Naples.

Bishop, Ronald L., G. Harbottle and E.V. Sayre. 1982. Chemical and mathematical procedures employed in the Maya fine past ceramics project. In G. Willey, ed., *Excavations at Siebal*, 272–82. Memoirs of the Peabody Museum of Archaeology and Ethnology, Harvard University, 15 (2).

Black, F.L. et al. 1974. Evidence for persistence of infectious agents in isolated human populations. *American Journal of Epidemiology* 100:230–50.

Blakely, Robert. 1971. Comparison of mortality profiles of Archaic, Middle Woodland, and Middle Mississippian populations. *American Journal of Physical Anthropology* 34:43–54.

Blakely, R.L. and B. Detweiler. 1986. Odontological evidence of differential stress at the King and Etowah sites in 16th century Georgia. *American Journal of Physical Anthropology* 69:176.

Blanton, Richard E. 1976a. Anthropological studies of cities. *Annual Review of Anthropology* 5: 249–64.

1976b. The role of symbiosis in adaptation and sociocultural change in the Valley of Mexico. In E.R. Wolf, ed., *The Valley of Mexico*. 181–202. Albuquerque, University of New Mexico press.

1978. *Monte Alban: Settlement Patterns at the Ancient Zapotec Capital*. New York, Academic Press.

1980. Cultural ecology reconsidered. *American Antiquity* 45: 145–51.

Blanton, R.E., S.A. Kowalewski, G.M. Feinman and J. Appel, eds. 1981. *Ancient Meso-america: A Comparison of Change in Three RRegions*. Cambridge, Cambridge University Press.

Bloch, Maurice, 1983. *Marxism and Anthropology*. Oxford, Oxford University Press.

Blute, M. 1979. Sociocultural evolutionism: an untried theory. *Behavioral Science* 24:46–59.

Boas, F., ed., 1938. *General Anthropology*. War Department Education Manual EM 226. U.S. Armed Forces Institute, Madison, Wisconsin.

Bonner, J.T. 1980. *The Evolution of Culture in Animals*. Princeton, Princeton University Press.

Bonte, P. 1974. Non-stratified social formations among pastoral nomads. In J. Friedman and

M.J. Rowlands, eds., *Evolution of Social Systems*, 173–200. Pittsburgh, University of Pittsburgh Press.

1981a. Theory and anthropological analysis; the study of pastoral nomadic societies. In J.S. Kahn and J.R. Llobera, eds., *The Anthropology of Pre-Capitalist Societies*, 22–56. Atlantic Highlands, N.J., Humanities Press.

1981b. Ecological and economic factors in the determination of pastoral specialization. *Journal of Asian and African Studies* 16:33–49.

Boquet-Appel, J.-P. and C. Masset. 1982. Farewell to paleodemography. *Journal of Human Evolution* 11:321–33.

1985. Paleopathology: resurrection or ghost? *Journal of Human Evolution* 14:107–11.

Boserup, Ester. 1965. *The Conditions of Agricultural Growth*. Chicago, Aldine.

Box, George E.P. and George C. Tiao. 1973. *Bayesian Inference in Statistical Analysis*. Reading, MA, Addison-Wesley.

Boyd, C.C. 1986. *An evolutionary approach to the prehistory of Upper East Tennessee and adjacent areas*. Ph.D. dissertation, University of Tennessee, Knoxville.

Boyd, R. and P.J. Richerson. 1985. *Culture and the Evolutionary Process*. Chicago, University of Chicago Press.

Braithwaite, M. 1984. Ritual and prestige in the prehistory of Wessex c. 2200–1400 BC: a new dimension to the archaeological evidence. In D. Miller and C. Tilley, eds., *Ideology, Power and Prehistory*, 93–110. Cambridge, Cambridge University Press.

Brandes, M.A. 1979. *Siegelabrollungen aus den archaischen bauschichten in Uruk-Warka*. Vol. I. Wiesbaden, Franz Steiner.

Braudel, F. 1966. *La Méditerranée et le monde méditerranéen à l'époque de Philippe II*, 2nd ed. 2 vols., Paris, Lib. Armand Colin.

1984. *The Perspective of the World (Civilization and Capitalism 15th–18th Century*, vol. 3). New York, Harper & Row.

Braun, D.P. and S. Plog. 1982. Evolution of "tribal" social networks: theory and prehistoric North American evidence. *American Antiquity* 47:504–25.

Braverman, Harry. 1974. *Labor and Monopoly Capitalism*. New York, Monthly Review Press.

Bray, Warwick. 1978. Civilizing the Aztecs. In J. Friedman and M.J. Rowlands, eds., *The Evolution of Social Systems*, 373–98. London, Duckworth.

1983. Landscape with figures: settlement patterns, locational models, and politics in Mesoamerica. In E.Z. Vogt and R.M. Leventhal, eds., *Prehistoric Settlement Patterns, Essays in Honor of Gordon R. Willey*, 167–94. Albuquerque, University of New Mexico Press.

1984. Ideology in archaeology: a review of *Religion and Empire* by Geoffrey Conrad and Arthur Demarest. *Nature* 311: 281–2.

Brenner, R. 1977. The origins of capitalist development; a critique of Neo-Smithian Marxism. *New Left Review* 104:25–93.

Brew, J.O. 1946. *The Archaeology of Alkali Ridge, Southern Utah*. Papers of the Peabody Museum of Archaeology and Ethnology, Harvard University, 24. Cambridge, MA.

Briant, P. 1982. *Etat et pasteurs au moyen orient ancien*. Cambridge, Cambridge University Press.

Bridges, Patricia. 1983. Subsistence activity and biomechanical properties of long bones in two Amerindian populations. *American Journal of Physical Anthropology* 60:177.

Bronowski, Jacob. 1971. Symposium on technology and social criticism: Introduction – Technology and culture in evolution. *Philosophy of the Social Sciences* 1:195–206.

Bronson, Bennet. 1966. Roots and the subsistence of the ancient Maya. *Southwestern Journal of Anthropology* 22:251–79.

1978. Angkor, Anuradhapura, Prambanan, Tikal: Maya subsistence in an Asian perspective. In P.D. Harrison and B.L. Turner II, eds., *Pre-Hispanic Maya Agriculture*, 255–300. Albuquerque, University of New Mexico Press.

Brooks, A.S., A. Crowell and J.E. Yellen. 1979. ‡ Gi: A Stone Age archaeological site in the

Northern Kalahari Desert, Botswana. In R.E. Leakey and B. Ogot, eds., *Proceedings of the VIII Pan-African Congress of Prehistory and Quaternary Studies, Nairobi, Sept. 1–3, 1977,* 304–9.

Brooks, A.S., D. Gelberd and J.E. Yellen. 1984. Food production and culture change among !Kung San: implications for prehistoric research. In J.D. Clark and S. Brandt, eds., *From Hunters to Farmers,* 289–306. Los Angeles, University of California Press.

Brothwell, D.R. 1963. Macroscopic dental pathology of some earlier human populations. In D.R. Brothwell, ed., *Dental Anthropology.* Oxford, Pergamon.

Brothwell, Don, and Eric Higgs, eds. 1970. *Science in Archaeology.* New York, Praeger.

Brown, J.A. ed. 1971. *Approaches to the Social Dimensions of Mortuary Practices.* Washington, Memoirs of the Society for American Archaeology, No. 25.

Brown, R.H. 1978. Symbolic realism and sociological thought; beyond the positivist-romantic debate. In R.H. Brown and S.M. Lyman, eds., *Structure, Consciousness and History,* Cambridge, Cambridge University Press.

Brumfiel, Elizabeth M. 1976. Regional growth in the eastern Valley of Mexico: a test of the "population pressure" hypothesis. In K.V. Flannery, ed., *The Early Mesoamerican Village,* 234–49. New York, Academic Press.

1980. Specialization, market exchange, and the Aztec state: a view from Huexotla. *Current Anthropology* 21: 459–78.

1983. Aztec state making: ecology, structure, and the origin of the state. *American Anthropologist* 85:261–84.

Brumfiel, Elizabeth and Timothy K. Earle, eds. 1987. *Specialization, Exchange, and Complex Society.* Cambridge, Cambridge University Press.

Buikstra, Jane, ed. 1981. *Prehistoric Tuberculosis in the Americas.* Northwestern University Archaeological Program Scientific Papers 5.

1984. The Lower Illinois River region: a prehistoric context for the study of ancient diet and health. In M.N. Cohen and G.J. Armelagos, eds., *Paleopathology at the Origins of Agriculture,* 217–36. New York, Academic Press.

Buikstra, Jane and D.C. Cook. 1980. Paleopathology: an American account. *Annual Review of Anthropology* 9:433–70.

Buikstra, Jane and L. Konigsberg. 1985. Paleodemography: critiques and controversies. *American Anthropologist* 87:316–33.

Buikstra, J. and N. Van der Merwe. 1986. Diet, demography and health: human adaptation and maize agriculture in the Eastern Woodlands. Paper presented to the 19th Chacmool Conference, University of Calgary.

Buikstra, Jane et al. 1985. Diet sedentism and demographic change; the identification of key variables. *American Journal of Physical Anthropology* 66:151.

Bulkin, V.A., Leo S. Klejn and G.S. Lebedev. 1982. Attainments and problems of Soviet archaeology. *World Archaeology* 13(3): 272–95.

Bullard, W.R., Jr. 1960. Maya settlement pattern in northeastern Peten, Guatemala. *American Antiquity,* 25:355–72.

Bumstead, M.P. et al. 1986. Multielement enhancement of 13c/12c dietary interpretation: pilot study. Paper presented to the 19th Chacmool Conference, University of Calgary.

Butzer, Karl W. 1982. *Archaeology as Human Ecology.* Cambridge, Cambridge University Press.

Caldwell, J.R. 1958. *Trend and Tradition in the Prehistory of the Eastern United States.* American Anthropological Association, Menasha: Memoir series 88.

1959. The New American Archaeology. *Science* 129:303–7.

1964. Interaction spheres in prehistory. In J. R. Caldwell and R.L. Hall, eds., *Hopewellian Studies,* 133–43. Springfield, State Museum Scientific Papers, 12.

Campbell, K. and J.W. Wood. In press. Fertility in traditional societies. In P. Diggory and S.

Teper, eds., *Natural Human Fertility: Social and Biological Mechanisms*. London, Macmillan.

de Cardi, Beatrice. 1964. British expedition to Kalat, 1948 and 1957. *Pakistan Archaeology* 1:20–39.

1970. *Excavations at Bampur, a Third Millennium Settlement in Persian Baluchistan, 1966.* New York, The American Museum of Natural History. Anthropological Papers 51 (3).

Carneiro, R.L. ed. 1967. *The Evolution of Society: Selections from Herbert Spencer's Principles of Sociology*. Chicago, University of Chicago Press.

1970. A theory of the origin of the state. *Science* 169:733–8.

Carr, Christopher, ed. 1985. *For Concordance in Archaeological Analysis: Bridging Data Structures, Quantitative Techniques, and Theory*. Kansas City, Missouri, Westport.

Carr, E.H. 1962. *What is History?* London, Vintage.

Carrasco, Pedro, and Johanna Broda, eds. 1978. *Economia, Politica e Ideologia en el Mexico Prehispanico*. Mexico, Centro De Investigaciones Superiores.

Cartmill, Matt, D. Pilbeam and G. Isaac. 1986. One hundred years of paleoanthropology. *American Scientist* 74:410–20.

Caso, Alfonso. 1945. *La Religion de los Aztecas*. Mexico, Secretaria de Educación Publica.

Cassidy, C.M. 1984. Skeletal evidence for prehistoric subsistence adaptation in the central Ohio River Valley. In M.N. Cohen and G. T. Armelagos, eds., *Paleopathology at the Origins of Agriculture*, 307–46. New York, Academic Press.

Caute, David. 1978. *The Great Fear: The Anti-Communist Purge under Truman and Eisenhower*. New York, Simon & Schuster.

Cavalli-Sforza, L.L. and M.W. Feldman. 1981. *Cultural Transmission and Evolution: A Quantitative Approach*. Princeton, Princeton University Press.

Caws, P. 1968. What is structuralism? *Partisan Review* 35 (1): 75–91.

Chang, C. and H.A. Koster. 1986. Beyond bones: toward an archaeology of pastoralism. In M. Shiffer, ed., *Advances in Archaelogical Method and Theory* 9:97–148. New York, Academic Press.

Chang, K.C. 1962. China. In R.J. Braidwood and G.R. Willey, eds., *Courses Toward Urban Life*, 177–92. Chicago, Aldine.

1976a. *Early Chinese Civilization*. Cambridge, MA, Harvard University Press.

1976b. Towns and cities in ancient China. In K.C. Chang, *Early Chinese Civilization*, 61–71. Cambridge, MA, Harvard University Press.

1980. *Shang Civilization*. New Haven and London, Yale University Press.

1983a. The origins of Shang and the problem of Xia in Chinese archaeology. In George Kuwayama, ed., *The Great Bronze Age of China: a Symposium*. Los Angeles, County Museum of Art.

1983b. *Art, Myth, and Ritual: Paths to Political Authority in Ancient China*, Cambridge, MA, Harvard University Press.

1985. Concerning the concept of the early Chinese 'city' (in Chinese). *Wenwu* 2:61–7.

1987a. *The Archaeology of Ancient China*. 4th edn. New Haven and London, Yale University Press.

1987b. The ancient Chinese *cong* and its significance (in Chinese). In *Treatises on Archaeology and Cultural Relics; Papers in Celebration of the Thirtieth Anniversary of the Founding of the Wenwu Press*, 252–60. Peking, Wenwu Press.

In preparation. *Continuity and Rupture: Ancient China and the Rise of Civilizations*.

Chapman, Robert, Ian Kinnes and K. Randsborg, eds. 1981. *The Archaeology of Death*. Cambridge, Cambridge University Press.

Charlton, Thomas H. 1986. Review of *Ritual Human Sacrifice in Mesoamerica*, edited by Elizabeth Boone and *Religion and Empire* by G. Conrad and A. Demarest. *Archaeology* 39(1): 68–70.

Chase, A.F. and P.M. Rice, eds. 1985. *The Lowland Maya Postclassic*, Austin, University of Texas Press.

Chaudhuri, K.N. 1985. *Trade and Civilisation in the Indian Ocean: An Economic History from the Rise of Islam to 1750*. Cambridge, Cambridge University Press.

Chernoff, Miriam. 1982. *Empirical Bayes Estimation of Ceramic Proportions at Teotihuacan*. Paper for the Annual Meeting of the Society for American Archaeology, Minneapolis, 1982. Department of Anthropology, Brandeis University, Waltham, MA.

Childe, V.G. 1936. *Man Makes Himself*. London, Watts.

1942. *What Happened in History*. Harmondsworth, Penguin.

1950. The urban revolution. *Town Planning Review* 21 (1):3–17.

1951a. *Man Makes Himself*. New York, Mentor.

1951b. *Social Evolution*. New York, Schuman; London, C.A. Watts.

1952. *New Light on the Most Ancient East*. Rev. edn. New York, Praeger.

1953. *New Light on the Most Ancient East*. New York: Norton.

1957. The Bronze Age. *Past and Present* 12: 2–15.

1958. *The Prehistory of European Society*. Harmondsworth, Penguin.

Chippindale, Christopher and Fekri Hassan, eds. In preparation. *Design Grammars in Archaeology and Anthropology*.

Chirot, D. 1985. The rise of the West. *American Sociological Review* 50:181–95.

Chollot, M. 1964. *Musée des Antiquités Nationales – Collection Piette*. Paris, Musées Nationaux.

1980. *Les Origines du graphisme symbolique. Essai d'analyse des écritures primitives en préhistoire*. Paris, Singer-Polignac.

Cieza de León, Pedro. 1967 [1553]. *El señorío de los Incas. Segunda parte de la crónica del Perú*. Lima, Instituto de Estudios Peruanos.

1984 [1553]. *La crónica del Perú. Primera parte*. Lima, Instituto de Estudios Peruanos.

Claessen, Henri and Peter Skalnik, eds. 1978. *The Early State*. The Hague, Mouton.

Clark, Geoffrey. 1976. More on contingency table analysis, decision making criteria, and the use of log linear models. *American Antiquity* 41: 259–73.

Clarke, D.L. 1972. A provisional model of an Iron Age society and its settlement system. In D.L. Clarke, ed., *Models in Archaeology*. London, Methuen.

Cleuziou, S. 1980. Three seasons at Hili: toward a chronology and cultural history of the Oman peninsula in the 3rd millennium B.C. *Proceedings of the Seminar for Arabian Studies* 10: 19–32.

1981. Oman peninsula in the early 2nd millennium B.C. In H. Hartel, ed., *South Asian Archaeology 1979*, 279–93, Berlin.

Cleuziou, S. and T. Berthoud. 1982. Early tin in the Near East: a reassessment in the light of new evidence from western Afghanistan. *Expedition* 25(1): 14–25.

Clifford, J. and G.E. Marcus. 1986. *Writing Culture: The Poetics and Politics of Ethnography*. Berkeley, University of California Press.

Coale, A. and P. Demeny. 1983. *Regional Model Life Tables and Stable Populations*. 2nd edn. New York, Academic Press.

Cockburn, T.A. 1971. Infectious diseases in ancient populations. *Current Anthropology* 12:45–62.

Coe, M.D. 1968. *America's First Civilization*. New York, Van Nostrand.

1978. *The Lords of the Underworld; Masterpieces of Classic Maya Ceramics*. Princeton, Princeton University Press.

Coe, W.R. 1965. Tikal: ten years' study of a Mayan ruin in the lowlands of Guatemala. *Expedition* 8:5–56.

Cohen, M.N. 1977. *The Food Crisis in Prehistory*. New Haven, Yale University Press.

1981. Pacific Coast foragers: affluent or overcrowded? In S. Koyama and D.H. Thomas, eds., *Affluent Foragers*. Osaka, Senri Ethnological series, 9.

1985a. Prehistoric hunter-gatherers: the meaning of social complexity. In T.D. Price and J.A. Brown, eds. *Prehistoric Hunter-Gatherers: the Emergence of Cultural Complexity*, 99–112. New York, Academic Press.

1985b. Research, development and circumscription in the stone age. Paper presented to the Annual Meeting of the American Anthropological Association.

1987. The significance of long term changes in human diet and food economy. In M. Harris and E. Ross, eds., *Food*. Philadelphia, Temple University Press.

In preparation: *Civilization and Health*.

Cohen, M.N. and G.J. Armelagos, eds. 1984. *Paleopathology at the Origins of Agriculture*. New York, Academic Press.

Cohen, Ronald. 1981. Evolutionary epistemology and human values. *Current Anthropology* 71: 658–87.

Cohen, S. 1973. Enmerkar and the Lord of Aratta. Ph.D. dissertation. University of Pennsylvania, Philadelphia.

Collier, George A., Renato I. Rosaldo and John D. Wirth, eds. 1982. *The Inca and Aztec States 1400–1800: Anthropology and History*. New York, Academic Press.

Conkey, M. 1978a. Style and information in cultural evolution: toward a predictive model for the Paleolithic. In C.L. Redman et al., eds., *Social Archaeology*, 61–85. New York, Academic Press.

1978b. An analysis of design structure: variability among Magdalenian engraved bones from northcoastal Spain. Ph.D. dissertation, University of Chicago.

1980a. Context, structure, and efficacy in paleolithic art and design. In M.L. Foster and S. Brandes, eds., *Symbol as Sense*, 225–48. New York, Academic Press.

1980b. The identification of prehistoric hunter-gatherer aggregation sites: the case of Altamira. *Current Anthropology* 21 (5): 609–30.

1981. What can we do with broken bones? Paleolithic design structure, archaeological research, and the potential of museum collections. In *The Research Potential of Anthropological Museum Collections*, edited by A–M. Cantwell, J.B. Griffen, and N. Rothschild. *Annals*, New York Academy of Sciences, 376:35–52.

1982. Boundedness in art and society. In I. Hodder, ed., *Symbolic and Structural Archaeology*, 115–28. Cambridge, Cambridge University Press.

1985. Ritual communication, social elaboration, and the variable trajectories of paleolithic material culture. In T.D. Price and J.A. Brown, *Prehistoric Hunter-Gatherers: the Emergence of Social and Cultural Complexity*, 299–323. New York, Academic Press.

n.d. New approaches in the search for meaning? A review of research in paleolithic art. To appear in *Journal of Field Archaeology*.

Conkey, Margaret W. and Janet D. Spector. 1984. Archaeology and the study of gender. *Advances in Archaeological Method and Theory* 7: 1–37.

Conrad, Geoffrey W. 1977. Chiquitoy Viejo: an Inca administrative center in the Chicama Valley, Peru. *Journal of Field Archaeology* 4:1–18.

1981a. Cultural materialism, split inheritance, and the expansion of ancient Peruvian empires. *American Antiquity* 46:3–26.

1981b. Reply to Paulsen and Isbell. *American Antiquity* 46: 38–42.

Conrad, Geoffrey W. and Arthur A. Demarest. 1984. *Religion and Empire; The Dynamics of Aztec and Inca Expansionism*. Cambridge, Cambridge University Press.

Contenau, G. and R. Ghirshman. 1935. *Fouilles de Tepe Giyan près de Nehavand*. Paris, Geuthner.

Cook, D.C. 1984. Subsistence and health in the lower Illinois Valley: osteological evidence. In M.N. Cohen and G.J. Armelagos, eds., *Paleopathology at the Origins of Agriculture*, 237–70. New York, Academic Press.

Cook, Sherburne F. 1946. Human sacrifice and warfare as factors in the demography of precolonial Mexico. *Human Biology* 18: 81–102.

Cooke, C.W. 1931. Why the Mayan cities in the Peten district were abandoned. *Journal of the Washington Academy of Science* 21: 283–7.

Cordell, L.S. and F. Plog. 1979. Escaping the confines of normative thought: a reevaluation of Puebloan prehistory. *American Antiquity* 44:405–29.

Costin, Cathy L. 1984. The organization and intensity of spinning and cloth production among the Late Prehispanic Huanca. Paper presented at the Annual Meeting of the Institute of Andean Studies, Berkeley, California.

1986. From chiefdom to empire state; ceramic economy among the Prehispanic Wanka of Highland Peru. Ph.D. dissertation, University of California, Los Angeles. Ann Arbor, University Microfilms.

Covarrubias, Miguel. 1957. *Indian Art of Mexico and Central America*. New York, Knopf.

Cowgill, George L. 1975a. On causes and consequences of ancient and modern population changes. *American Anthropologist* 77: 505–25.

1975b. Population pressure as a non-explanation. In A.C. Swedlund, ed., *Population Studies in Archaeology and Biological Anthropology: A Symposium*, 127–31. Society for American Archaeology Memoirs, 30.

1977. The trouble with significance tests and what we can do about it. *American Antiquity* 42: 350–68.

1979. Teotihuacan, internal militaristic competition, and the fall of the Classic Maya. In N. Hammond and G.R. Willey, eds., *Maya Archaeology and Ethnohistory*, 51–62. Austin, University of Texas Press.

1986. Archaeological applications of mathematical and formal methods. In D. Meltzer, D. Fowler, and J. Sabloff, eds., *American Archaeology Past and Future*, 369–93. Washington, DC, Smithsonian Institution Press.

In press. The concept of diversity in archaeological theory. In G. Jones and R. Leonard, eds., *The Concept and Measurement of Archaeological Diversity*. Cambridge, Cambridge University Press.

Crawford, H.E.W. 1973. Mesopotamia's invisible exports in the third millennium. *World Archaeology* 5 (2): 232–41.

Culbert, T.P. ed. 1973. *The Classic Maya Collapse*, Albuquerque, University of New Mexico Press.

Culler, J. 1975. *Structuralist Poetics: Structuralism, Linguistics and the Study of Literature*. London, Routledge & Kegan Paul.

D'Altroy, Terence N. 1981. Empire growth and consolidation: the Xauxa region of Peru under the Incas. Ph.D. dissertation, University of California, Los Angeles. Ann Arbor, University Microfilms.

1987. Introduction. *Ethnohistory* 34 (1), Special Issue: Inka Ethnohistory (in press).

D'Altroy, Terence N. and Ronald Bishop, n.d. The production of provincial Inka ceramics. Ms.

D'Altroy, Terence N. and Cathy L. Costin. 1983. Producción de cerámica durante el Horizonte Tardío en el Mantaro superior. Report submitted to the Instituto Nacional de Cultura, Lima.

D'Altroy, Terence N. and Timothy K. Earle. 1985. Staple finance, wealth finance, and storage in the Inka political economy (including Comment and Reply). *Current Anthropology* 26(2):187–206.

D'Altroy, Terence N. and Christine A. Hastorf. 1984. The distribution and contents of Inca state storehouses in the Xauxa region of Peru. *American Antiquity* 49(2): 334–49.

Dandamaev, M.A. and V.G. Lukonin. 1977. *Kul'tura i ekonomika drevnego Irana*. Moscow, Nauk.

Daniel, Glyn. 1950. *A Hundred Years of Archaeology*. London, Duckworth.

1968. *The First Civilizations*. New York, Crowell.

Darwin, C. 1859. *The Origin of Species*. London, John Murray.

Davis, W. 1986. The origins of image-making. *Current Anthropology* 27 (3): 193–215.

Dawkins, R. 1976. *The Selfish Gene*. Oxford, Oxford University Press.

Deevey, E.S. et al. 1979. Maya urbanism: impact on a tropical karst environment. *Science* 206: 298–306.

Deetz, J. 1977. *In Small Things Forgotten. The Archaeology of Early American Life*. Garden City, NY; Anchor Press/Doubleday.

De George, R.T. and M. Fernande. 1972. *The Structuralists: from Marx to Lévi-Strauss*. New York, Anchor Press/Doubleday.

Deimel, A. 1931. Die sumerische Tempelwirtschaft zur Zeit Urukaginas und seiner Vorgänger, *Analecta Orientalia* 2. Rome.

Delporte, H. 1979. *L'Image de la femme en préhistoire*. Paris, Picard.

Demarest, Arthur A. 1976. The ideological adaptation of the Mexica Aztec. In G.R. Willey, ed., *Advanced Seminar on Mesoamerican Archaeology*. Department of Anthropology, Harvard University.

1978. Interregional conflict and "situational ethics" in Classic Maya warfare. In Marco Giardino, Barbara Edmonson and Winifred Creamer, eds., *Codex Wauchope; A Tribute Roll*, 101–11. New Orleans, Tulane University Press.

1981. *Viracocha, the Nature and Antiquity of the Andean High God*. Monographs of the Peabody Museum, 6. Cambridge, Peabody Museum Press.

1984. Mesoamerican human sacrifice in evolutionary perspective. In E. Boone and J. Soustelle, eds. *Ritual Sacrifice in Pre-Columbian Mesoamerica*, Washington, Dumbarton Oaks.

1986. *The Archaeology of Santa Leticia and the Rise of Maya Civilization*. Middle American Research Institute, 52. New Orleans, Tulane University.

1987. The archaeology of religion. In Mircea Eliade, ed., *the Encyclopedia of Religion*. New York, MacMillan.

In press. Ideology in ancient Maya cultural evolution: the dynamics of galactic polities. In A. Demarest and G. Conrad, eds., *Ideology and Cultural Evolution in the New World*. Cambridge, Cambridge University Press.

Demarest, Arthur A. and Geoffrey W. Conrad. 1983. Ideological adaptation and the rise of the Aztec and Inca empires. In Richard Leventhal and Alan Kolata, eds., *Festschrift in Honor of Gordon R. Willey*, 373–99. Albuquerque, University of New Mexico Press.

In press. eds. *Ideology in the Evolution of Pre-Columbian Civilizations. A School of American Research Advanced Seminar*. Cambridge, Cambridge University Press.

Denbow, J.W. 1984. Prehistoric herders and foragers of the Kalahari: the evidence for 1500 years of interaction. In C. Schrire, ed., *Past and Present in Hunter Gatherer Studies*, 175–93. New York, Academic Press.

Denbow, J.W. and E.N. Wilmsen. 1986. Advent and course of pastoralism in the Kalahari. *Science* 234 (4783): 1590–15.

Devereux, George. 1967. A typological study of abortion in 350 primitive, ancient, and preindustrial societies. In H. Rosen, ed., *Abortion in America: Legal, Anthropological, and Religious Considerations*, 97–152. Boston, Beacon Press.

Diakonoff, I.M. 1976. Slaves, helots and serfs in early antiquity. In J. Harmatta and G. Komoroczy, eds., *Wirtschaft und gesellschaft im alten Vorderasien*. Budapest, Akademiai Kiado.

1982a. Chapters 1,2,3 (pp. 5–78) in I.M. Diakonoff, ed., *Istorija drevnovo mira I. Rannija drevnost*. Moscow, Glavnaja Redaksii Voctocnoj Literaturi.

1982b. The structure of Near Eastern society before the middle of the 2nd millennium B.C. *Oikumene* 3:7–100.

Dickel, David. 1985. Growth stress and Central California pre-historic subsistence shifts. *American Journal of Physical Anthropology* 63:152.

Dickel, David et al. 1984. Central California: prehistoric subsistence changes and health. In M.N. Cohen and G.J. Armelagos, eds., *Paleopathology at the Origins of Agriculture*, 439–62. New York, Academic Press.

Diener, Paul. 1980. Quantum adjustment, macroevolution, and the social field: some comments on evolution and culture. *Current Anthropology* 21: 423–43.

Diener, Paul and Eugene Robkin. 1978. Ecology, evolution, and the search for cultural origins; the question of Islamic pig prohibition. *Current Anthropology* 19: 493–540.

Diener, Paul, Kurt Moore and Robert Mutaw. 1980. Meat, markets, and mechanical materialism: the great protein fiasco in anthropology. *Dialectical Anthropology* 5: 171–92.

Diener, Paul, Donald Nonini and Eugene Robkin. 1978. The dialectics of the Sacred Cow: ecological adaptation versus political appropriation in the origins of India's cattle complex. *Dialectical Anthropology* 3: 221–38.

1980. Ecology and evolution in cultural anthropology. *Man* 15: 1–31.

Diez de San Miguel, Garci. 1964 [1567]. *Visita a la Provincia de Chucuito por Garci Diez de San Miguel en el año 1567. Documentos Regionales para le Etnología y Etnohistoria Andina.* Lima, Casa de Cultura.

Digard, J.P. 1978. The segmental system: native model or anthropological construction? Discussion of an Iranian example. In W. Weissleder, ed., *The Nomadic Alternative*, 315–17. Hague, Mouton.

1981. *Techniques des nomades baxtyari d'Iran.* Edition de la Maison des Sciences. Cambridge, Cambridge University Press.

Dittmann, R. 1984. *Eine Randebene des Zagros in der Frühzeit. Ergebnisse des Behbehan-Zuhreh surveys.* Berliner Beiträge zum Vorderen Orient 3. Berlin, Dietrich Reimer.

Donisi, M.P. 1983. The incidence and pattern of long bone fractures in selected prehistoric human skeletal series from the central Tennessee River Valley of Alabama. *American Journal of Physical Anthropology* 60:189.

Doran, Jim. 1986. Formal methods and archaeological theory: a perspective. *World Archaeology* 18 (1): 21–37.

Doyle, Michael W. 1986. *Empires.* Ithaca, Cornell University Press.

Dragoo, D. 1963. *Mounds for the Dead: An Analysis of the Adena Culture.* Annals of the Carnegie Museum, 37. Pittsburgh, PA.

Dray, W.H. 1957. *Laws and Explanation in History.* London, Oxford University Press.

1966. *Philosophical Analysis and History.* New York, Harper and Row.

Drennan, R.D. 1976. Religion and social evolution in formative Mesoamerica. In K.V. Flannery, ed., *The Early Mesoamerican Village*, 345–68. New York, Academic Press.

Drinnon, Richard. 1980. *Facing West: The Metaphysics of Indian-Hating and Empire Building.* Minneapolis, University of Minnesota Press.

Driver, G.R. and J.C. Miles. 1955. *The Babylonian Laws.* Oxford, Oxford University Press.

Duby, George. 1985. Ideologies in social history. In J. LeGoff and P. Nora, eds., *Constructing the Past: Essays in Historical Methodology*, 151–65. Cambridge, Cambridge University Press.

Dumont, L. 1986. *Essays on Individualism: Modern Ideology in Anthropological Perspective.* Chicago, University of Chicago.

Dunnell, R.C. 1971. *Systematics in Prehistory.* New York, The Free Press.

1972. *The Prehistory of Fishtrap Kentucky.* Yale University Publications in Anthropology, 75. New Haven, CT.

1978a. Natural selection, scale, and cultural evolution: some preliminary considerations. Paper presented at the 77th Annual Meeting of the American Anthropological Association, Los Angeles, CA.

1978b. Style and function: a fundamental dichotomy. *American Antiquity* 43:192–202.

1980. Evolutionary theory and archaeology. In M.B. Schiffer, ed., *Advances in Archaeological Method and Theory*, 3:35–99. New York, Academic Press.

1982. Science, social science, and common sense: the agonizing dilemma of modern archaeology. *Journal of Anthropological Research* 38:1–25.

1986. Methodological issues in Americanist artifact classification. In M. Schiffer, ed., *Advances in Archaeological Method and Theory*, 9: 149–207. Orlando, Florida, Academic Press.

Dunnell, R.C. and R.J. Wenke. 1980. An evolutionary model of the development of complex society. Paper presented at the 1980 Annual Meeting of the American Association for the Advancement of Science, San Francisco.

Durham, W.H. 1976. The adaptive significance of cultural behavior. *Human Ecology* 4: 89–121.

Eagleton, T. 1983. *Literary Theory*. Minneapolis, University of Minnesota Press.

Earle, Timothy K. 1977. A reappraisal of redistribution: complex Hawaiian chiefdoms. In T.K. Earle and J.E. Ericson, eds., *Exchange Systems in Prehistory*, 213–29. New York, Academic Press.

1978. *Economic and Social Organization of a Complex Chiefdom: the Halelea District Kaua'i, Hawaii*. Anthropological Papers, Museum of Anthropology, University of Michigan 63.

1985. Community exchange and markets in the Inca state: recent archaeological evidence. In Stuart Plattner, ed., *Markets and Marketing*, 369–97. Monographs in Economic Anthropology, No. 4. University Press of America.

1987. Specialization and the production of wealth: the Hawaiian chiefdoms and the Inka empire. In Elizabeth Brumfiel and Timothy K. Earle, eds., *Specialization, Exchange, and Complex Society*. Cambridge, Cambridge University Press.

Earle, Timothy K. and Cathy L. Costin. 1986. Inka imperial conquest and changing patterns of household consumption in the Central Andes. Paper presented at the Annual Meeting of the Society for Economic Anthropology. Champaign-Urbana, Illinois.

Earle, Timothy K. and Terence N. D'Altroy. 1982. Storage facilities and state finance in the Upper Mantaro Valley, Peru. In J. Ericson and T. Earle, eds., *Contexts for Prehistoric Exchange*, 265–90. New York, Academic Press.

Earle, Timothy K. and J.E. Ericson. 1977. *Exchange Systems in Prehistory*. New York, Academic Press.

Earle, Timothy K and Robert W. Preucel. 1987. Processual archaeology and the radical critique. *Current Anthropology* 28(4): 501–38.

Earle, Timothy K., Terence N. D'Altroy, Catherine J. LeBlanc, Christine A. Hastorf and Terry Y. Levine. 1980. Changing settlement patterns in the Upper Mantaro Valley, Peru. *Journal of New World Archaeology* 4:1–49.

Earle, Timothy K., Terence N. D'Altroy, Christine A. Hastorf, Catherine J. Scott, Cathy L. Costin, Glenn S. Russell, and Elsie Sandefur. 1987. *Archeological Field Research in the Upper Mantaro, Peru 1982–83: Investigations of Inka Expansion and Economic Change*. Los Angeles, University of California, Institute of Archaeology (in press).

Edens, C. n.d. Consumption and exchange; history of the Gulf trade c. 3000–1500 B.C.

Edzard, E. 1957. *Die zweite Zwischenschaft babyloniens*. Wiesbaden.

Ehmann, D. 1975. *Bahtiyaren – Persische Bergnomaden Im Wandel der Zeit*. Wiesbaden, Reichert.

Ehrmann, J. 1970. *Structuralism*. New York, Anchor Press/Doubleday.

Eisenberg, L.E. 1985. Bioarchaeological perspectives on diseases in a "marginal" Mississippian population. *American Journal of Physical Anthropology* 66:166–7.

1986. The patterning of trauma at Averbuch: activity levels and conflict during the late Mississippian. *American Journal of Physical Anthropology* 69: 197.

Ekholm, K. and Jonathan Friedman. 1985. Towards a global anthropology. *Critique of Anthropology* (1): 97–119.

El Najjar, M.Y. 1977. Maize, malaria and the anemias in the pre-Columbian New World. *Yearbook of Physical Anthropology* 28:329–37.

Espinoza Soriano, Waldemar. 1973. Colonias de mitmas multiples en Abancay, Siglos XV y XVI: Una información inédita de 1575 para la etnohistoria Andina. *Revista del Museo Nacional* 39:225–99.

Fabian, J. 1984. *Time and the Other: How Anthropology Makes its Object*. New York, Columbia University Press.

Fagan, Brian M. 1986. American archaeology: past and future. *Antiquity* 60: 210–13.

Fairservis, Walter A. Jr. 1956. *Excavations in the Quetta Valley, Pakistan.* Anthropological Papers of the American Museum of Natural History, 45(2): 169–402. New York.

1959. *Archaeological Surveys in the Zhob and Loralai Districts, West Pakistan.* Anthropological Papers of the American Museum of Natural History, 47(2). New York.

1961. *Archaeological Studies in the Seistan Basin of Southwestern Afghanistan and Eastern Iran.* Anthropological Papers of the American Museum of Natural History, 48(1): 1–129. New York.

1976. *Excavations at Allahdino I – Seals and Inscribed Material. Papers of the Allahdino Expedition.*

1977. *Excavations at Allahdino III – The Graffiti: A Model for the Decipherment of the Harappan Script. Papers of the Allahdino Expedition,* 9–25. Poughkeepsie, N.Y.

1982. Allahdino: an excavation of a small Harappan site. In G. Possehl, ed., *Harappan Civilization: A Contemporary Perspective,* 107–12. New Delhi, Oxford and IBH Publishing Co. in collaboration with American Institute of Indian Studies. pp. 107–112.

1988. *The Fourth River.* New York, A. Knopf.

Fairservis, W.A. and Southworth, Franklin C. 1986. Linguistic archaeology and the Indus culture. Paper read at the American Anthropological Association meeting, November 1986.

Farber, H. 1978. A price and wage study for northern Babylonia during the Old Babylonian period. *Journal of the Social and Economic History of the Orient* 21(1): 1–51.

Fash, W.L., Jr. 1983. Maya state formation: a case study and its implications. Ph.D. dissertation, Tozzer Library, Harvard University.

Fei, H.T. 1952. *China's Gentry.* Chicago, University of Chicago Press.

Feigl, H. and May Brodbeck. 1953. *Readings in the Philosophy of Science.* New York, Appleton –Century–Croft.

Fine, A. 1987. *The Shaky Game. Einstein, Realism and Quantum Theory.* Chicago, University of Chicago.

Finley, M.I. 1973. *The Ancient Economy.* London, Chatto & Windus.

1978. Empire in the Graeco–Roman world. *Review* II(1): 55–70.

Fisher, R.A. 1930. *The Genetical Theory of Natural Selection.* Oxford, Clarendon Press.

Fitzhugh, W.W., ed. 1985. *Cultures in Contact: The Impact of European Contacts on Native American Cultural Institutions, A.D. 1000–1800.* Washington, Smithsonian Institution Press.

Flam, Louis. 1984. The palaeogeography and prehistoric settlement patterns of the Lower Indus Valley, Sind, Pakistan. In K.A.R. Kennedy and G.L. Possehl, eds., *Studies in Archaeology and Palaeoanthropology of South Asia,* 77–82. New Delhi, Oxford and IBH Publishing Co. for American Institute of Indian Studies.

Flannery, K.V. 1965. The ecology of early food production in Mesopotamia. *Science* 147: 1247–56.

1967. Culture history vs. culture process. *Scientific American* 217: 119–22.

1968. The Olmec and the Valley of Oaxaca: a model for interregional interaction in formative times. In Elizabeth P. Benson, ed., *Dumbarton Oaks Conference on the Olmec.* Washington, DC, Dumbarton Oaks.

1969. The origins and ecological effects of early domestication in Iran and the Near East. In P.J. Ucko and G.W. Dimbleby, eds., *The Domestication and Exploitation of Plants and Animals.* 73–100. London, Duckworth.

1972a. The cultural evolution of civilizations. *Annual Review of Ecology and Systematics* 3:399–426.

1972b. Archaeology with a capital S. In C.L. Redman, ed., *Research and Theory in Current Archaeology,* 47–53. New York, Wiley.

1976. *The Early Mesoamerican Village.* Academic Press, New York.

1983. Divergent evolution. In K.V. Flannery and J. Marcus, eds., *The Cloud People: Divergent Evolution of the Zapotec and Mixtec Civilizations*, 1–14. New York, Academic Press.

Flannery, Kent V. and Joyce Marcus. 1976a. Formative Oaxaca and the Zapotec Cosmos. *American Scientist* 64: 374–83. New Haven, CT.

1976b. Evolution of the public building in formative Oaxaca. In Charles Cleland, ed., *Cultural Change and Continuity*. New York, Academic Press.

1983. eds. *The Cloud People: Divergent Evolution of the Zapotec and Mixtec Civilizations*. New York, Academic Press.

Flood, Josephine. 1976. *The Moth Hunters*. Canberra: Australian Institute for Aboriginal Studies.

Ford, Annabel. 1985. Maya settlement pattern chronology in the Belize River area and the implications for the development of the Central Maya Lowlands. *Belcast Journal of Belizean Affairs* (2): 13–31.

Ford, J.A. 1954. The type concept revisited. *American Anthropologist* 56:42–54.

Ford, R.I. 1973. Archeology serving humanity. In C.L. Redman, ed., *Research and Theory in Current Archeology*, 83–93. New York, John Wiley.

Fowler, Don D. 1987. Uses of the past; archaeology in the service of the state. *American Antiquity* 52(2): 229–48.

Fox, R.G. 1985. *Lions of the Punjab: Culture in the Making*. Los Angeles, University of California Press.

Francfort, H.-P. and M.-H. Pottier. 1978. Sondage préliminaire sur l'établissement proto-historique Harapéen et post-Harapéen de Shortugai (Afghanistan du N.–E.). *Arts Asiatiques* 34: 29–79.

Frank, A.G. 1967. *Capitalism and Underdevelopment in Latin America: Historical Studies of Chile and Brazil*. New York, Monthly Review Press.

Frankenstein, Susan and Michael J. Rowlands. 1978. The internal structure and regional context of early Iron Age society in south-western Germany. *Bulletin of the Institute of Archaeology, University of London* 15: 73–112.

Frankfort, H. 1948. *Kingship and the Gods*. Chicago, University of Chicago Press.

1955. *The Art and Architecture of the Ancient Orient*. Harmondsworth, Penguin.

Frayer, David. 1981. Body size, weapon use and natural selection in the European upper paleolithic and mesolithic. *American Anthropologist* 83: 57–73.

Freeman, L.G. Jr. 1968. A theoretical framework for interpreting archaeological materials. In R.B. Lee and I. DeVore eds., *Man the Hunter*, 262–7. Chicago, Aldine.

Freidel, David A. 1979. Culture areas and interaction spheres: contrasting approaches to the emergence of civilization in the Maya Lowlands. *American Antiquity* 44: 36–54.

1981a. Civilization as a state of mind; the cultural evolution of the Lowland Maya. In G.D. Jones and R.R. Kautz, eds., *The Transition to Statehood in the New World*, 188–227. Cambridge, Cambridge University Press.

1981b. The political economics of residential dispersion among the lowland Maya. In W. Ashmore, ed., *Lowland Maya Settlement Patterns*, 311–32. Albuquerque, University of New Mexico Press.

1986. Maya warfare: an example of peer polity interaction. In C. Renfrew and John Cherry, eds., *Peer Polity Interaction and Socio-Political Change*, 93–108. Cambridge, Cambridge University Press.

In press. The trees of life "ahau" as idea and artifact in Classic lowland Maya civilization. In A. Demarest and G. Conrad, eds., *Ideology and Cultural Evolution in the New World*. Cambridge, Cambridge University Press.

Freidel, D.A. and L. Schele. 1986. *Symbol and Power; A History of the Lowland Maya Cosmogram*. Princeton, Princeton University Press.

Fried, Morton. 1967. *The Evolution of Political Society*. New York, Random House.

1975. *The Notion of Tribe*. Menlo Park, Cummings.

Friedman, Jonathan. 1974. Marxism, structuralism and vulgar materialism. *Man* 9: 444–69.

1975. Tribes, states, and transformations. In M. Bloch, ed., *Marxist Analyses and Social Anthropology*, 161–202. New York, Wiley.

1987. Prolegomena to the adventures of phallus in blunderland: an anti-anti-discourse. *Culture and History* 1: 31–49.

Friedman, Jonathan and M.J. Rowlands. eds. 1978a, *The Evolution of Social Systems*. London, Duckworth.

1978b. Notes towards an epigenetic model of the evolution of "Civilization." In J. Friedman and M.J. Rowlands, eds., *The Evolution of Social Systems*, 201–76. London, Duckworth; Pittsburgh: University of Pittsburgh Press.

Friedrich, M.H. 1970. Design structure and social interaction. *American Antiquity* 35: 332–43.

Frifelt, K. 1976. Evidence of a third millennium B.C. town in Oman. *Journal of Oman Studies* 2: 57–73.

Fritz, J.M. 1973. Relevance, archeology and subsistence theory. In C.L. Redman, ed., *Research and Theory in Current Archeology*, 59–82. New York, Wiley.

1978. Paleopsychology today: ideational systems and human adaptation in prehistory. In C.L. Redman et al., *Social Archaeology: Beyond Subsistence and Dating*, 37–60. New York, Academic Press.

1986. Vijayanagara: authority and meaning of a south Indian imperial capital. *American Anthropologist* 88: 44–55.

Fritz, John M. and Fred T. Plog. 1970. The nature of archaeological explanation. *American Antiquity* 35: 405–12.

Full, William E., Robert Ehrlich and James C. Bezdek. 1982. Fuzzy Q-model: a new approach for linear unmixing. *Journal of Mathematical Geology* 14 (3).

Furst, P.T. 1972. Hallucinogens and the shamanic origins of religions. In P.T. Furst, ed., *Flesh of the Gods*. New York, Praeger.

1973–4. The roots and continuities of shamanism, *Arts Canada* 185–7.

1976. Shamanistic survivals in mesoamerican religion. *Actas del XLI Congreso Internacional de Americanistas*, 3. Mexico.

Gall, Patricia L. and Arthur A. Saxe. 1977. The ecological evolution of culture: the state as predator in succession theory. In T.K. Earle and J.E. Ericson, eds., *Exchange Systems in Prehistory*, 255–68. New York, Academic Press.

Gamble, C. 1982. Interaction and alliance in Paleolithic society. *Man*, n.s. 17: 92–107.

Gardin, Jean-Claude. 1980. *Archaeological Constructs: An Aspect of Theoretical Archaeology*. Cambridge, Cambridge University Press.

Gardiner, P. 1959. *Theories of History*. New York, The Free Press.

Gardner, H. 1973. *The Quest for Mind: Piaget, Lévi-Strauss and the Structural Movement*. New York, Knopf.

Garn, Stanley M. 1979. The noneconomic nature of eating people. *American Anthropologist* 81:902–3.

Garn, Stanley M. and Walter D. Block. 1970. The limited nutritional value of cannibalism. *American Anthropologist* 72: 106.

Garthwaite, G.R. 1978. Pastoral nomadism and tribal power. *Iranian Studies* II:173–93.

1983. *Khans and Shahs: A Documentary Analysis of the Bakhtiyari in Iran*. Cambridge, Cambridge University Press.

Gaube, H. 1979. *Iranian Cities*. New York: New York University Press.

Geertz, C. 1980. *Negara, the Theatre-State in Nineteenth-Century Bali*. Princeton, Princeton University Press.

1984. Anti-anti relativism. *American Anthropologist* 86: 263–78.

Gelb, I.J. 1972a. From freedom to slavery, pp. 81–92. *Bayerische Akademie der Wissenschaften* A(6) Munich.

1972b. 'The Arua Institution', *Revue d'Assyriologique et d'archéologique Orientale* 66: 2–32.

1973. Prisoners of war in early Mesopotamia. *Journal of Near Eastern Studies* 32:70–98.

1979. Household and family in early Mesopotamia. In E. Lipinski, ed., *State and Temple Economy in the Ancient Near East*, 1:1–97, Katolieke Universiteit te Leuven.

1982. Terms for slaves in ancient Mesopotamia. In *Societies and Languages of the Ancient Near East. Studies in Honor of I.M. Diakonoff*. Warminster, England, Aris & Phillips.

1985. Ancient society and economy. *The Oriental Institute 1984–1985 Annual Report*, 51–3.

Gellner, E. 1982. What is structuralism? In C. Renfrew, M. Rowlands and B.A. Seagraves, eds., *Theory and Explanation in Archaeology*, 97–123. New York, Academic Press.

1985. *Relativism and the Social Sciences*. Cambridge, Cambridge University Press.

1987. *Culture, Identity and Politics*. Cambridge, Cambridge University Press.

George, C.H. 1980. The origins of capitalism: a Marxist epitome and a critique of Immanuel Wallerstein's modern world-system. *Marxist Perspectives* 10: 70–101.

Gero, Joan M. 1983. Gender bias in archaeology: a cross-cultural perspective. In J.M. Gero et al., eds., *The Socio-Politics of Archaeology*, 51–7. Amherst, University of Massachusetts Department of Anthropology, Research Report 23.

1985. Socio-politics and the woman-at-home ideology. *American Antiquity* 50: 342–50.

Gero, Joan and Dolores Root. 1986. Public presentations and private concerns: archaeology in the pages of *National Geographic*. Paper delivered at the World Archaeological Congress, Southampton, England.

Gero, J.M., D.M. Lacy and M.L. Blakey, eds. 1983. *The Socio-Politics of Archaeology*. Amherst, University of Massachusetts, Department of Anthropology, Research Report 23.

Ghirshman, R. 1938. *Fouilles de Sialk près de Kashan*. Vol. I. Paris, Geuthner.

Gibson, Eric. 1986. Diachronic patterns of lithic production, use and exchange in the southern Maya Lowlands. Doctoral dissertation, Tozzer Library, Harvard University.

Gibson, M. n.d. Duplicate systems of trade, a key element in Mesopotamian history. Earlier version of a paper to be published by CNRS (Paris).

Giddens, A. 1984. *The Social Constitution of Society: Outline of a Theory of Structuration*. Cambridge, Polity Press.

Gilbert, A.S. 1975. Modern nomads and prehistoric pastoralists; the limits of analogy. *Journal of the Ancient Near Eastern Society of Columbia University* 7:53–71.

1983. On the origins of specialized nomadic pastoralism in Western Iran. *World Archaeology* 15:105–19.

Gilbert, R.I. and J. Mielke. 1985. *Techniques for the Analysis of Prehistoric Diet*. New York, Academic Press.

Gilman, Antonio. 1976. Bronze Age dynamics in southeast Spain. *Dialectical Anthropology* 1: 307–19.

1981. The development of social stratification in Bronze Age Europe. *Current Anthropology* 22: 1–23.

1984. Explaining the Upper Palaeolithic revolution. In M. Spriggs, ed., *Marxist Perspectives in Archaeology*, 115–26. Cambridge, Cambridge University Press.

Gilman, Antonio and John B. Thornes. 1985. *Land-Use and Prehistory in South-East Spain*. London, Allen & Unwin.

Glassie, H. 1975. *Folk-Housing in Middle Virginia: A Structural Analysis of Historical Artifacts*. Knoxville, University of Tennessee Press.

Gledhill, J. and M.T. Larsen. 1982. The Polanyi paradigm and a dynamic analysis of archaic states. In A.C. Renfrew, et al., eds., *Theory and Explanation in Archaeology*, 197–229. New York.

Godelier, Maurice. 1972. *Rationality and Irrationality in Economics*. London, New Left Books.

1977. *Perspectives in Marxist Anthropology*. Cambridge, Cambridge University Press.

1978a. Economy and religion: an evolutionary optical illusion. In J. Friedman and M.J. Rowlands, eds., *The Evolution of Social Systems*, 3–12. London, Duckworth.

1978b. Politics as 'infrastructure': an anthropologist's thoughts on the example of Classical Greece and the notions of relations of production and economic determinism. In J. Friedman and M.J. Rowlands, eds., *The Evolution of Social Systems*, 13–28. London, Duckworth.

1978c. Infrastructures, societies, and history. *Current Anthropology* 19: 763–71.

1984. To be a Marxist in anthropology. In Jacques Maquet and Nancy Daniels, eds., *On Marxian Perspectives in Anthropology: Essays in Honor of Harry Hoijer 1981*, 33–57, Malibu, Undena.

Goff-Meade, C. 1971. Luristan before the Iron Age. *Iran* 9:91–151.

Goodman, A. et al. 1984a. Health changes at Dickson Mounds, Illinois (A.D. 950–1300). In M.N. Cohen and G.J. Armelagos, eds., *Paleopathology at the Origins of Agriculture*, 271–306. New York. Academic Press.

1984b. Indications of stress from bone and teeth. In M.N. Cohen and G.J. Armelagos, eds., *Paleopathology at the Origins of Agriculture*, 13–50. New York, Academic Press.

Gordon, D.H. 1958. *The Pre-Historic Background of Indian Culture*. Bombay, N.M. Tripathi.

Gordon, R.J. 1984. The !Kung in the Kalahari exchange; an ethnohistorical perspective. In C. Schrire, ed., *Past and Present in Hunter Gatherer Studies*, 195–224. New York, Academic Press.

Gould, Richard. 1980. *Living Archaeology*. Cambridge, Cambridge University Press.

Gould, S. J. 1979. Shades of Lamarck. *Natural History* 88(2):22–8.

1980. Is a new and general theory of evolution emerging? *Paleobiology* 6:119–30.

Green, M.W. 1984. The Uruk lament. *Journal of the American Oriental Society* 104 (2): 253–79.

Griffin, J.B. 1943. *The Fort Ancient Aspect: Its Cultural and Chronological Position in Mississippi Valley Archaeology*. Ann Arbor, University of Michigan Press.

1960. Climatic change: a contributory cause of the growth and decline of northern Hopewellian culture. *Wisconsin Archaeologist* 41:21–33.

Gropp, G. and S. Nadjmbadi. 1970. Bericht über eine Reise im West und Südiran. *Archaeologische Mitteilungen aus Iran* n.s. 3:173–231.

Guaman Poma de Ayala, Felipe. 1980. *El primer nueva corónica y bien gobierno. Edición crítica de John V. Murra y Rolena Adorno*. Mexico: Siglo Veintiuno.

Gunn, J. and R.E.N. Adams. 1981. Climate change, culture, and civilization in North America. *World Archaeology* 13:87–101.

Haas, Jonathan. 1982. *The Evolution of the Prehistoric State*. New York, Columbia University Press.

Habermas, Jurgen. 1971. *Knowledge and Human Interest*. Boston, Beacon Press.

Haggett, Peter. 1966. *Locational Analysis in Human Geography*. New York, St. Martin's Press.

Haldane, J.B.S. 1932. *The Causes of Evolution*. New York, Harper.

Halliday, F. 1979. *Iran: Dictatorship and Democracy*. New York, Penguin.

Hamblin, N.L. 1985. The role of marine resources in the Maya economy: a case study from Cozumel, Mexico. In Mary Pohl, ed., *Prehistoric Lowland Maya Environment and Subsistence Economy*, 159–74. Peabody Museum Papers 77, Harvard University, Cambridge, MA.

Hammond, Norman. 1974. The distribution of late Classic Maya major ceremonial centers in the Central Area. In N. Hammond, ed., *Mesoamerican Archaeology, New Approaches*, 313–34. London, Duckworth.

Hammond, Norman and Wendy Ashmore. 1981. Lowland Maya settlement: geographical and chronological frameworks. In W. Ashmore, ed., *Lowland Maya Settlement Patterns*, 19–36. Albuquerque, University of New Mexico Press.

Hammond, N., D. Pring, R. Wilk, S. Donaghey, E. Wing, A.V. Miller, F.P. Saul and L.H. Feldman. 1979. The earliest lowland Maya? Definition of the Swasey phase. *American Antiquity* 44: 92–110.

Handsman, Russell G. 1980. The domains of kinship settlement in historic Goshen: signs of a past cultural order. *Artifacts* 9(1): 4–7.

1981. Early capitalism and the center village of Canaan, Connecticut: a study of transformations and separations. *Artifacts* 9(3): 1–21.

Handwerker, W.P. 1983. The first demographic transition: analysis of subsistence changes and reproductive consequences. *American Anthropologist* 85: 5–27.

Hanson, N. R. 1958. *Patterns of Discovery*. Cambridge, Cambridge University Press.

Harbottle, Garman. 1976. Activation analysis in archaeology. *Radiochemistry* 3:33–72.

Harner, M.J. 1970. Population pressure and the social evolution of agriculturalists. *Southwestern Journal of Anthropology* 26:67–86.

1977. The ecological basis for Aztec sacrifice. *American Ethnologist* 4: 117–35.

Harris, D.R. 1978. The agricultural foundations of Lowland Maya civilization: a critique. In P.D. Harrison and B.L. Turner II, eds., *Pre-Hispanic Maya Agriculture*. Albuquerque, University of New Mexico Press.

Harris, Marvin. 1964. *The Nature of Cultural Things*. New York, Random House.

1968. *The Rise of Anthropological Theory*. New York, Thomas Y. Crowell.

1974. *Cows, Pigs, Wars and Witches: The Riddles of Culture*. New York, Random House.

1977. *Cannibals and Kings: The Origins of Cultures*. New York, Random House.

1979. *Cultural Materialism: The Struggle for a Science of Culture*. New York, Random House.

1981. *America Now: The Anthropology of a Changing Culture*. New York, Simon & Schuster.

Harrison, Peter D. 1978. *Bajos* revisited: visual evidence for one system of agriculture. In P.D. Harrison and B.L. Turner II, eds., *Pre-Hispanic Maya Agriculture*. Albuquerque, University of New Mexico Press.

1981. Some aspects of preconquest settlement in Southern Quintana Roo, Mexico. In W. Ashmore, ed., *Lowland Maya Settlement Patterns*, 259–86. Albuquerque, University of New Mexico Press.

Harrison, Peter D., and B.L. Turner II, eds., 1978. *Pre-Hispanic Maya Agriculture*. Albuquerque, University of New Mexico Press.

Hartney, P.C. 1981. Tuberculosis in a prehistoric population sample from southern Ontario. In Buikstra, J., ed., *Prehistoric Tuberculosis in the Americas*. Northwestern University Archaeological Program Scientific Papers 5.

Hassan, Fekri. 1981. *Demographic Archaeology*. New York, Academic Press.

Hassig, Ross. 1985. *Trade, Tribute, and Transportation*. Norman, University of Oklahoma Press.

Hastorf, Christine A. 1983. Prehistoric agricultural intensification and political development in the Jauja region of Central Peru. Ph.D. dissertation, University of California. Ann Arbor, University Microfilms.

Hastorf, Christine A. and Michael J. DeNiro. 1985. Reconstruction of prehistoric plant production and cooking practices by a new isotopic method. *Nature* 315:489–91.

Hastorf, Christine A. and Timothy K. Earle. 1985. Intensive agriculture and the geography of political change in the Upper Mantaro region of Central Peru. In I.S. Farrington, ed., *Prehistoric Intensive Agriculture in the Tropics*, 569–95. Oxford, BAR International Series 232.

Hauptmann, A. and G. Weisgerber. 1980. Third millennium B.C. copper production in Oman. *Révue D'Archéometrie* 3: 131–8.

Haviland, W.A. 1965. Prehistoric settlement at Tikal, Guatemala. *Expedition* 7(3): 14–23.

1966. Maya settlement patterns: a critical review. *Archaeological Studies in Middle America*, Middle American Research Institute, Publication 26, Tulane University, New Orleans.

1967. Stature at Tikal, Guatemala: implications for ancient Maya demography and social organization. *American Antiquity* 32:316–25.

1969. A new population estimate for Tikal, Guatemala. *American Antiquity* 34: 429–33.

Hawkes, Kristen and J.F. O'Connell. 1985. Optimal foraging models and the case of the !Kung. *American Anthropologist* 87:401–5.

Hawkes, T. 1977. *Structuralism and Semiotics*. Berkeley, CA, University of California Press.

Hayden, Brian. 1981. Research and development in the Stone Age. *Current Anthropology* 22:519–48.

Helgren, D. and A. Brooks. 1983. Geoarchaeology of ‡Gi, a Middle Stone Age and Later Stone Age site in the Northwest Kalahari. *Journal of Archaeological Science* 10: 181–7.

Hempel, Carl G. 1966. *Philosophy of Natural Science*. New York, Prentice-Hall.

Hempel, Carl G. and P. Oppenheim. 1948. Studies in the logic of explanation. *Philosophy of Science* 15: 135–75.

Henricksen, E. 1985. The early development of pastoralism in the Central Zagros Highlands (Luristan). *Iranica Antiqua* 20: 1–42.

Hesse, M. 1978. Theory and value in the social sciences. In C. Hookaway and P. Pettit, eds., *Action and Interpretation: Studies in the Philosophy of the Social Sciences* 1–16. Cambridge, Cambridge University Press.

Hexter, J.H. 1971. *The History Primer*. New York, Basic Books.

Higgs, Eric S. and Michael R. Jarman. 1975. Palaeoeconomy. In E. S. Higgs, ed., *Palaeoeconomy*, 1–7. Cambridge, Cambridge University Press.

Hill, James N. 1965. Broken K: a prehistoric society in Eastern Arizona. Ph.D. dissertation, Department of Anthropology, University of Chicago, Chicago.

1977. Systems theory and the explanation of change. In J.N. Hill, ed., *Explanation of Prehistoric Change*, 59–103. Albuquerque, University of New Mexico Press.

Himes, N.E. 1963. *Medical History of Contraception*. New York, Gamut Press.

Hinsley, C.M., Jr. 1981. *Savages and Scientists: The Smithsonian Institution and the Development of American Anthropology, 1846–1910*. Washington, Smithsonian Institution Press.

1985. From shell-heaps to stelae: early anthropology at the Peabody Museum. In George W. Stocking, Jr., ed., *Objects and Others: Essays on Museums and Material Culture*, 49–74. Madison, University of Wisconsin Press.

Hinz, W. 1964. *Das Reich Elam*. Stuttgart, Kohlhammer.

Hirth, Kenneth G. 1984. *Trade and Exchange in Early Mesoamerica*. Albuquerque, University of New Mexico Press.

Hodder, I. 1982a. *Symbols in Action: Ethnoarchaeological Studies of Material Culture*. Cambridge, Cambridge University Press.

1982b. *The Present Past*. London, Batsford.

1982c. *Symbolic and Structural Anthropology*. Cambridge, Cambridge University Press.

1982d. Theoretical archaeology: a reactionary view. In I. Hodder, ed., *Symbolic and Structural Archaeology*, 1–16. Cambridge, Cambridge University Press.

1984. Burials, houses, women and men in the European Neolithic. In D. Miller and C. Tilley, eds., *Ideology, Power and Prehistory*, 51–68. Cambridge, Cambridge University Press.

1986. *Reading the Past*. Cambridge, Cambridge University Press.

Hodges, R. and D. Whitehouse. 1983. *Mohammed, Charlemagne and the Origins of Europe*. Ithaca, NY, Cornell University Press.

Hole, F. 1968. Evidence of social organization from Western Iran. In S. and L. Binford, eds., *New Perspectives in Archaeology*, 245–66. Chicago, Aldine.

1975. The sondage at Tappeh Tula'i. In F. Bagherzadeh, *The Proceedings of the 3rd Annual Symposium on Archaeological Research in Iran*, 63–76. Tehran, Iranian Centre for Archaeological Research, Muzeh-e Iran Bastan.

1977. *Studies in the Archaeological History of the Deh Luran Plain. The Excavation of Chagha Sefid*. Museum of Anthropology, Memoirs 9. Ann Arbor, University of Michigan.

1979. Rediscovering the past in the present: ethnoarchaeology in Luristan, Iran. In C. Kramer, ed., *Ethnoarchaeology: Implications of Ethnography for Archaeology*, 192–218. New York, Columbia University Press.

Hole, F. and K. Flannery. 1967. The prehistory of southwestern Iran: a preliminary report. *Proceedings of the Prehistoric Society* 33:147–206.

Hole, F., K. Flannery and J. Neely. 1969. *Prehistory and Human Ecology of the Deh Luran Plain*.
Museum of Anthropology, Memoirs 1. Ann Arbor: University of Michigan.
Horwich, P. 1987. *Asymmetries in Time: Problems in the Philosophy of Science*. Cambridge, MA, MIT Press.
Houston, Stephen D. and Peter Mathews. 1985. The dynastic sequence of Dos Pilas, Guatemala. *Precolumbian Art Research Institute*. Monograph 1, San Francisco.
Howell, Nancy. 1979. *Demography of the Dobe !Kung*. New York, Academic Press.
  1982. Village composition implied by a paleodemographic life table: the Libben site, Ohio. *American Journal of Physical Anthropology* 59:263–70.
  1986. Feedback and buffers in relation to scarcity and abundance: studies of hunter gatherer populations. In Coleman and Schofield, eds., *State of Population Theory*. London, Blackwell.
Huetteroth, W.D. 1959. *Bergnomaden und Yaylabauern im Mittleren Kurdischen Taurus*. Marburg, Selbstverlag des Geographischen Institutes der Universität Marburg.
Huffman, T. 1981. Snakes and birds: expressive space at Great Zimbabwe. *African Studies* 40: 131–50.
Hunt, V. 1978. The rise of feudalism in Eastern Europe: a critical appraisal of the Wallerstein world system thesis. *Science and Society* 42 (1): 43–61.
Huss Ashmore, R. et al. 1982. Nutritional inference from paleopathology. *Advances in Archaeological Method and Theory* 5: 395–474.
Hyslop, John. 1984. *The Inka Road System*. New York, Academic Press.
  1985. *Inkawasi: The New Cuzco*. Oxford, BAR International Series 234.

Ibn Khaldun. 1958. *The Muqaddimah: An Introduction to History*, 1. (tr. Franz Rosenthal.) New York, The Bollingen Foundation.
Isaac, G.Ll. 1971. The diet of early man: aspects of archaeological evidence from Lower and Middle Pleistocene sites in Africa. *World Archaeology* 2:278–98.
Isbell, William H. 1976. Cosmological order expressed in prehistoric ceremonial centres. *Andean Symbolism Symposium*. Paris, International Congress of Americanists.
  1978. Environmental perturbation and the origin of the Andean state. In C.L. Redman et al., eds., *Social Archaeology: Beyond Subsistence and Dating*, 303–13. New York, Academic Press.
Iversen, Gudmund R. 1984. *Bayesian Statistical Inference*. Beverly Hills, CA, Sage.

Jacobsen, T. 1970. Primitive democracy in ancient Mesopotamia. In W.L. Moran, ed., *Toward the Image of Tammuz*. Cambridge, MA, Harvard University Press.
Jameson, F. 1972. *The Prison-House of Language*. Princeton, Princeton University Press.
Jarrige, J.-F. 1986. Excavations at Mehrgarh-Nawsharo. *Pakistan Archaeology* 18–22 (1974–1986): 63–131.
Jarrige, J.-F. and M. Lechevallier. 1979. Excavations at Mehrgarh, Baluchistan: their significance in the prehistorical context of the Indo-Pakistan Borderlands. In M. Taddei, ed., *South Asian Archaeology 1977*, 1:463–535. Naples, Istituto Universitario Orientale.
Jarrige, J.-F. and R.H. Meadow. 1980. The antecedents of the Harappan civilization. *Scientific American* 243 (2): 122–33.
Jarrige, J.-F. and M. Santoni. 1979. *Fouilles de Pirak*, vols. I and II. Paris, Diffusion de Boccard.
Jennings, J.D. ed., 1979. *The Prehistory of Polynesia*. Cambridge, MA, Harvard University Press.
Jochim, M.A. 1976. *Hunter-Gatherer Subsistence and Settlement*. New York, Academic Press.
  1983. Paleolithic cave art: some ecological speculations. In G. Bailey, ed., *Hunter-gatherer Economy in Prehistory: A European Perspective*, 212–19. Cambridge, Cambridge University Press.

Johansson, S.R. and S. Horowitz. 1986. Estimating mortality in skeletal populations; influence of the growth rate on the interpretation of levels and trends during the transition to agriculture. *American Journal of Physical Anthropology* 71:233–50.

Johnson, G.A. 1973. *Local Exchange and Early State Development in Southwestern Iran*. Museum of Anthropology, Anthropological Papers 51. Ann Arbor, University of Michigan.

1981. Monitoring complex system integration and boundary phenomena with settlement size data. In S.E. van der Leeuw, ed., *Archaeological Approaches to the Study of Complexity*, 143–88. Amsterdam, University of Amsterdam Press.

Johnston, Kevin. 1985. Maya dynastic territorial expansion: glyphic evidence from classic centers of the Pasion River, Guatemala. In *Fifth Palenque Round Table, 1983*. Merle Greene Robertson, gen. ed. San Francisco, Pre-Columbian Art Research Institute.

Jones, George T. and Robert D. Leonard, eds. In press. *The Concept and Measurement of Archaeological Diversity*. Cambridge, Cambridge University Press.

Jones, George T., Donald K. Grayson and Charlotte Beck. 1983. Sample size and functional diversity in archaeological assemblages. In R. Dunnell and D. Grayson, eds., *Lulu Linear Punctate: Essays in Honor of George Irving Quimby*, 55–73. Museum of Anthropology, Anthropological Papers 72. Ann Arbor, University of Michigan.

Joralemon, P.D. 1971. A study of Olmec iconography. In *Dumbarton Oaks Studies in Pre-Columbian Art and Archaeology* 7. Trustees for Harvard University, Washington, DC.

Joyner, Stephanie P., ed. 1983. *SUGI Supplemental Library User's Guide*. Cary, NC, SAS Institute Inc.

Julien, Catherine. 1982. Inca decimal administration in the Lake Titicaca region. In Collier et al., eds., *The Inca and Aztec States 1400–1800: Anthropology and History* 119–51. New York, Academic Press.

Kaogu 1980 (1): 18–31; 1983 (1): 30–42; 1983(6): 531–6; 1984(12): 1069–71, 1068.

Kaogu Xuebao 1980(3): 329–84.

Katzenberg, M.A. 1984. *Chemical Analysis of Prehistoric Human Bone from Five Temporally Distinct Populations in Southern Ontario*. Archaeological Survey of Canada, Mercury Series 129. Ottawa, National Museum of Man.

Keene, Arthur S. 1983. Biology, behavior, and borrowing: a critical examination of optimal foraging theory in archaeology. In J.A. Moore and A.S. Keene, eds., *Archaeological Hammers and Theories*, 137–55. New York, Academic Press.

Keesing, Roger M. 1987. Anthropology as interpretive quest. *Current Anthropology* 28: 161–76.

Keightley, David N. 1978. *Sources of Shang History*. Berkeley and Los Angeles, University of California Press.

Kellenbenz, H. 1976. The modern world-system: capitalist agriculture and the origins of the European world economy in the sixteenth century. *Journal of Modern History* 48: 685–92.

Kelley, D.H. 1976. *Deciphering the Maya Script*. Austin, University of Texas Press.

Kemp, B.J. 1978. Imperialism and empire in New Kingdom Egypt. In P.D.A. Garnsey and C.R. Whittaker, eds. *Imperialism in the Ancient World*, 7–57. Cambridge, Cambridge University Press.

Kennedy, Brenda. 1981. *Marriage Patterns in an Archaic Population*. Archaeological Survey of Canada, Mercury Series 104. Ottawa, National Museum of Man.

Kennedy, Kenneth. 1984. Growth, nutrition and pathology in changing paleodemographic settings in South Asia. In M.N. Cohen and G.J. Armelagos, eds. *Paleopathology at the Origins of Agriculture*, 169–92. New York, Academic Press.

Kenoyer, Jonathan M. 1984. Shell working industries of the Indus civilization: a summary. *Paleorient* 10(1): 49–63.

Khazanov, A.M. 1984. *Nomads and the Outside World*. Cambridge, Cambridge University Press.

Kingery, W. David and P. Vandiver. 1986. *Ceramic Masterpieces*. New York, Free Press.

Kintigh, Keith W. 1984. Measuring archaeological diversity by comparison with simulated assemblages. *American Antiquity* 49: 44–54.

Kintigh, Keith W. and Albert J. Ammerman. 1982. Heuristic approaches to spatial analysis in archaeology. *American Antiquity* 47 (1): 31–63.

Kirch, Patrick Vinton. 1984. *The Evolution of Polynesian Chiefdoms*. Cambridge, Cambridge University Press.

Kluckhohn, Clyde. 1940. The conceptual structure in middle American studies. In C.L. Hay et al., eds., *The Maya and their Neighbors*, 41–51. New York, Appleton-Century.

  1955. Anthropology. In J.R. Newman, ed., *What is Science?* New York, Simon & Schuster.

Kobayashi, K. 1967. Trend in length of life based on human skeletons from prehistoric to modern times in Japan. *Journal of the Faculty of Science* 3:2. University of Tokyo.

Koerner, B.D. and R.L. Blakely. 1985. Degenerative joint disease, subsistence, and sex roles at the protohistoric King site in Georgia. *American Journal of Physical Anthropology* 66:190.

Kohl, Philip L. 1975. The archeology of trade. *Dialectical Anthropology* 1:43–50.

  1978. The balance of trade in southwestern Asia in the third millennium B.C. *Current Anthropology* 19(3): 463–92.

  1979. The "world economy" of West Asia in the third millennium B.C. In M. Taddei, ed., *South Asian Archaeology 1977*, 55–85. Naples, Istituto Universario Orientale.

  1981a. Materialist approaches in prehistory. *Annual Review of Anthropology* 10:89–118.

  1981b. *The Bronze Age Civilization of Central Asia: Recent Soviet Discoveries*, ed. and with an introduction ("The Namazga civilization: an overview", vii–xxxviii). Armonk, NY, M.E. Sharpe.

  1984a. Force, history and the evolutionist paradigm. In M. Spriggs, ed., *Marxist Perspectives in Archaeology*, 127–34. Cambridge, Cambridge University Press.

  1984b. *Central Asia: Palaeolithic Beginnings to the Iron Age*. Paris: Editions Recherche sur les Civilisations, "Synthèse" 14.

  1985. Symbolic cognitive archaeology: a new loss of innocence. *Dialectical Anthropology* 9:105–17.

Kohl, Philip L. and Rita P. Wright. 1977. Stateless cities; the differentiation of societies in the Near Eastern Neolithic. *Dialectical Anthropology* 2: 271–83.

Kohl, P., G. Harbottle and E.V. Sayre. 1979. Physical and chemical analyses of soft stone vessels from Southwest Asia. *Archaeometry* 21: 131–59.

Kolakowski, Leszek. 1976. *La Philosophie positiviste*. Paris, Denoël.

  1978. *Main Currents of Marxism, III: The Breakdown*. Oxford, Oxford University Press.

Kramer, C. 1982. *Village Ethnoarchaeology: Rural Iran in Archaeological Perspective*. New York, Academic Press.

Kraus, F.R. 1958. *Ein Edikt des Königs Ammi-saduga von Babylon*. Leiden.

Kristiansen, Kristian. 1981. Economic models for Bronze Age Scandinavia: towards an integrated approach. In A. Sheridan and G. Bailey, eds., *Economic Archaeology: Towards an Integration of Ecological and Social Approaches*, 239–303. Oxford, BAR International Series 96.

Kroeber, A. 1948. *Anthropology*. Rev. edn. New York, Harcourt, Brace & World.

Kroeber, A.L. and C. Kluckhohn. 1952. *Culture: A Critical Review of Concepts and Definitions*. Papers of the Peabody Museum of American Archaeology and Ethnology, Harvard University, 47. Cambridge, MA.

Kroker, Arthur. 1984. *Technology and the Canadian Mind: Innis/McLuhan/Grant*. Montreal, New World Perspectives.

Kroker, A. and D. Cook. 1986. *The Postmodern Scene: Excremental Culture and Hyper-Aesthetics*. New York, St. Martin's Press.

Kruskal, J. B. 1964. Nonmetric multidimensional scaling. *Psychometrika* 29:1–27, 115–29.

Krzanowski, Andrzej. 1978. Yuraccama, the Settlement Complex in the Alto Chicama Region (Northern Peru). In J. Krzysztof Kozlowski, ed., *Polish Contributions in New World Archaeology*, 29–58. Krakow, Zaklad Narodowy in Ossolinskich.

Kuhn, T.S. 1962. *The Structure of Scientific Revolutions*. Chicago, University of Chicago Press.

Kurjack, E.B. and T. Silvia Garza. 1981. Pre-Columbian community form and distribution in the Northern Maya area. In W. Ashmore, ed., *Lowland Maya Settlement Patterns*. 287–310. Albuquerque, University of New Mexico Press.

Kurtz, Donald V. 1978. The legitimation of the Aztec state. In H. Claessen and P. Skalnik, eds., *The Early State*, 169–89. The Hague, Mouton.

Kus, Susan. 1982. Matters material and ideal. In I. Hodder, ed., *Symbolic and Structural Archaeology*, 47–62. Cambridge, Cambridge University Press.

1983. The social representation of space: dimensioning the cosmological and the quotidian. In J.A. Moore and A.S. Keene, eds., *Archaeological Hammers and Theories*, 277–98. New York, Academic Press.

1984. The spirit and its burden. In M. Spriggs, ed., *Marxist Perspectives in Archaeology*, 91–107. Cambridge, Cambridge University Press.

Kuttner, Robert. 1985. The poverty of economics. *The Atlantic Monthly* (February): 75–84.

Kuzmina, E.E. 1980. Etapi razvitiya kolesnogo transporta Srendei Azii v epokhu eneolita i bronzi. *Vestnik Drevnei Istorii* (4): 11–35.

La Lone, Darrell. 1982. The Inca as a nonmarket economy: supply on command versus supply and demand. In J. Ericson and T. Earle, eds., *Contexts for Prehistoric Exchange*, 291–316. New York, Academic Press.

La Lone, Mary B. and Darrell La Lone. 1987. The Inka state in the Southern Highlands: State administrative and production enclaves. *Ethnohistory* 34 (1) (in press).

Lamberg-Karlovsky, C.C. 1970. *Excavations at Tepe Yahya, Iran*. Cambridge, MA, American School of Prehistoric Research Bulletin 27.

1972. Tepe Yahya 1971 – Mesopotamia and the Indo-Iranian borderlands. *Iran* 10: 89–100.

1974. Urban interaction on the Iranian plateau: excavations at Tepe Yahya, 1967–1973. *Proceedings of the British Academy* 59: 1–43.

1975. Third millennium modes of exchange and modes of production. In J.A. Sabloff and C.C. Lamberg-Karlovsky, eds., *Ancient Civilization and Trade*, 341–68. Albuquerque, University of New Mexico Press.

1978. The Proto–Elamites on the Iranian Plateau. *Antiquity* 52 (205): 114–20.

1986. The long durée of the Ancient Near East. In L. Huot, ed., *De l'Indus aux Balkans, Recueil Deshayes*. Paris, Editions Recherche sur les Civilisations.

n.d. Caste or class formation within the Indus civilization. To appear in Beatrice de Cardi felicitation volume, ed. E.C.L. During-Caspers.

Lamberg-Karlovsky, C.C. and Thomas W. Beale. 1986. Conclusion: Yahya in the context of a wider core-periphery interaction sphere in the fifth and fourth millennium B.C. In C. C. Lamberg-Karlovsky, ed., *Tepe Yahya: The Early Periods*. Cambridge, MA, Peabody Museum, Harvard University.

Lamberg-Karlovsky, C.C. and J.A. Sabloff. 1979. *Ancient Civilizations: The Near East and Mesoamerica*. Cummings.

Lamberg-Karlovsky, C.C. and M. Tosi. 1973. Shahr-i Sokhta and Tepe Yahya: tracks on the earliest history of the Iranian plateau. *East and West*, n.s. 23 (1–2):21–53. Rome, IsMEO.

Lambert, J.B. et al. 1984. Ancient human diet from inorganic analysis of bone. *Accounts of Chemical Research* 17:298–305.

Lambert, M. 1953. Textes commerciaux de Lagash. *Revue d'Assyriologie* 43: 57–69, 105–20.

1956. Les "Reforms" d'Urukagina. *Revue d'Assyriologie* 50: 168–89.

Laming–Empèraire, A. 1962. *La Signification de l'art rupestre paleolithique*. Paris, Picard.

Lane, M. 1970. *Structuralism, a Reader*. London, Cape.

Lange, F.W. 1971. Marine resources: a viable subsistence alternative for the prehistoric Lowland Maya. *American Anthropologist* 73: 619–39.

Langer, William L. 1974. Infanticide: a historical survey. *History of Childhood Quarterly* 1: 353–66.

Langley, James. 1986. *Symbolic Notation of Teotihuacan: Elements of Writing in a Mesoamerican Culture of the Classic Period.* Oxford, BAR International Series 313.

Larrain, J. 1979. *The Concept of Ideology.* London, Hutchinson.

Larsen, Clark. 1983. Deciduous tooth size and subsistence change in prehistoric Georgia Coast populations. *Current Anthropology* 24:25–6.

  1984. Health and disease in prehistoric Georgia. In M.N. Cohen and G.J. Armelagos, eds., *Paleopathology at the Origins of Agriculture,* 367–92. New York, Academic Press.

Larsen, M.T. 1977. Partnerships in the Old Assyrian trade. *Iraq* 39 (1): 119–45.

  1979a. *Power and Propaganda: A Symposium on Ancient Empires.* Copenhagen, Akademisk Forlag.

  1979b. The tradition of empire in Mesopotamia. In M.T. Larsen, ed., *Power and Propaganda: A Symposium on Ancient Empires,* 75–103. Copenhagen, Akademisk Forlag.

Lavallée, Danielle and Michèle Julien. 1983. *Asto: curacazgo prehispanico de los Andes Centrales.* Lima, Instituto de Estudios Peruanos.

Leach, E. 1976. *Culture and Communication: The Logic by which Symbols are Connected.* Cambridge, Cambridge University Press.

LeBlanc, Catherine J. 1981. Late prehispanic Huanca settlement patterns in the Yanamarca Valley, Peru. Ph.D. dissertation, University of California, Los Angeles. Ann Arbor, University Microfilms.

Le Brun, A. 1980. Les "Ecuelles Grossieres": état de la question. In *L'Archéologie de l'Iraq du debut de l'époque néolithique à 333 avant notre ère.* Paris, Editions du Centre National de la Recherche Scientifique.

Lechtman, Heather. 1984. Andean value systems and the development of prehistoric metallurgy. *Technology and Culture* 25:1–36.

Lee, Richard B. 1972. The intensification of social life among the !Kung Bushmen. In B. Spooner, ed., *Population Growth: Anthropological Implications,* 343–50. Cambridge MA, MIT Press.

  1979. *The !Kung San: Men Women and Work in a Foraging Society.* Cambridge, Cambridge University Press.

Lee, R.B. and I. DeVore. 1968. *Man the Hunter.* Chicago, Aldine.

Lees, S. and D. Bates. 1974. The origin of specialized nomadic pastoralism: a systemic model. *American Antiquity* 39: 188–93.

LeGoff, Jacques. 1985. Mentalities: a history of ambiguities. In J. LeGoff and P. Nora, eds., *Constructing the Past: Essays in Historical Methodology,* 166–80. Cambridge, Cambridge University Press.

LeGoff, Jacques, and Pierre Nora, eds. 1985. *Constructing the Past: Essays in Historical Methodology.* Cambridge, Cambridge University Press.

Legros, Dominique. 1977. Chance, necessity, and mode of production: a Marxist critique of cultural evolutionism. *American Anthropologist* 79: 26–41.

Legros, Dominique, Donald Hunderfund and Judith Shapiero. 1979. Economic base, mode of production, and social formation: a discussion of Marx's terminology. *Dialectical Anthropology* 4: 243–9.

Lemche, N.P. 1979. *Andurarum* and *Misharum*: comments on the problems of social edicts and their application in the ancient Near East. *Journal of Near Eastern Studies* 38(1): 11–18.

Leonard, R.D. and G.T. Jones. 1986. Elements of an inclusive evolutionary model for archaeology. *Journal of Anthropological Archaeology* (In press).

Leone, M.P. 1972. Issues in anthropological archaeology. In M.P. Leone, ed., *Contemporary Archaeology.* Carbondale, Southern Illinois University Press.

1975. Views of traditional archaeology. *Reviews in Anthropology* 2: 191–9.

1977. The new Mormon temple in Washington, D.C. In L. Ferguson, ed., *Historical Archaeology and the Importance of Material Things*, 43–61. Special Publication Series, 2. Society for Historical Archaeology.

1981a. Archaeology's relationship to the present and the past. In R.A. Gould and M.B. Schiffer, eds., *Modern Material Culture: The Archaeology of Us*, 5–14. New York, Academic Press.

1981b. The relationship between artifacts and the public in outdoor history museums. *Annals of the New York Academy of Sciences* 376: 301–13.

1982. Some opinions about recovering mind. *American Antiquity* 47: 742–60.

1984. Interpreting ideology in historical archaeology: using the rules of perspective in the William Paca Garden in Annapolis, Maryland. In D. Miller and C. Tilley, eds., *Ideology, Power and Prehistory*, 25–35. Cambridge, Cambridge University Press.

Leon-Portilla, M. 1963. *Aztec Thought and Culture, A Study of the Ancient Nahuatl Mind*. Norman, University of Oklahoma Press.

1968a. *Quetzalcoatl*. Fondo de Cultura Economica, Mexico.

1968b. *Trempo y Realidad en el Pensamento Maya*. Mexico City.

Leroi-Gourhan, A. 1958. Répartition et groupement des animaux dans l'art parietal paléolithique. *Bulletin de la Société Préhistorique Française* 55: 515–27.

1965. *Treasures of Paleolithic Art*. New York, Abrams.

1966. La Religion des grottes: magic ou metaphysique? *Sciences et Avenir* 228. (Reprinted in Leroi-Gourhan 1983).

1968. *The Art of Prehistoric Man in Western Europe*. London, Thames & Hudson.

1972. Considérations sur l'organisation spatiale des figures animales dans l'art parietal paléolithique. In *Santander Symposium*. Santander, Spain, Actas del symposium internacional de arte prehistorico.

1978. The mysterious markings in the Paleolithic cave art of France and Spain. *CNRS Research* 8:26–32.

1982. *The Dawn of European Art*. Cambridge, Cambridge University Press.

1983. *Le Fil du temps: Ethnologie et préhistoire, 1935–1970*. Paris, Librairie Arthème Fayard.

1986. The religion of the caves; magic or metaphysic? Translated from the French by A. Michelson. *October* 37: 7–17.

Leroi-Gourhan, A. and J. Allain. 1979. *Lascaux inconnu*. Paris, Editions Centre National de Recherche Scientifique.

LeVine, Terry Y. 1987. Inka labor service at the regional level: the functional reality. *Ethnohistory* (1) (in press).

Lévi-Strauss, C. 1958. *Anthropologie structurale*. Paris, Plon.

1962a. *Le Totemisme aujourd'hui*. Paris, PUF.

1962b. *La Pensée sauvage*. Paris, Plon.

1964. *Le Cru et le cuit*. Paris, Plon.

1966. *The Savage Mind*. Chicago, University of Chicago Press.

Lewins, R. and R. Lewontin. 1985. *The Dialectical Biologist*. Cambridge, MA, Harvard University Press.

Lewis, R. Barry. 1986. The analysis of contingency tables in archaeology. In M. Schiffer, ed., *Advances in Archaeological Method and Theory*, 9: 277–310. Orlando, Florida, Academic Press.

Lewis-Williams, J.D. 1982. The economic and social context of southern San rock art. *Current Anthropology* 23 (4): 429–49.

1983a. Introductory essay: science and rock art. In *New Approaches to Southern African Rock Art*, South African Archaeological Society, Goodwin Series, 4: 3–13.

1983b. *Rock Art of Southern Africa*. Cambridge, Cambridge University Press.

Lewontin, R.C. 1970. The units of selection. *Annual Review of Ecology and Systematics* 1:1–18.

1974a. *The Genetic Basis of Evolutionary Change*. New York, Columbia University Press.

1974b. Darwin and Mendel – the materialist revolution. In J. Neyman, ed., *The Heritage of Copernicus; Theories pleasing to the Mind*, 166–83. Cambridge, MA, MIT Press.

Li, Hui-lin. 1974. The origins and use of *Cannabis* in Eastern Asia: Linguistic and cultural implications. *Economic Botany* 28.

Longacre, William A. 1963. Archaeology as anthropology: a case study. Ph.D. dissertation, Department of Anthropology, University of Chicago, Chicago.

Lorblanchet, M. 1980. Peindre sur les parois des grottes. *Dossiers de l'Archéologie* 46: 33–9.

Lourandos, H. 1983. Intensification: a late Pleistocene–Holocene archaeological sequence from Southwestern Victoria. *Archaeology in Oceania* 18: 81–94.

1985. Intensification in Australian prehistory. In T.D. Price and J.A. Brown, eds., *Prehistoric Hunter Gatherers*. New York, Academic Press.

Lovejoy, C.O. and K.G. Heiple. 1981. The analysis of fractures in skeletal populations with an example from the Libben site, Ottowa Co. Ohio. *American Journal of Physical Anthropology* 55:529–41.

Lovejoy, C.O. et al. 1977. Paleodemography at the Libben Site, Ottowa Co. Ohio. *Science* 198:291–3.

Lovejoy, C.O. et al. 1985. Multifactorial determination of skeletal age at death. *American Journal of Physical Anthropology* 68: 1–14.

Lowie, Robert H. 1937. *The History of Ethnological Theory*. New York, Holt, Rinehart & Winston.

Lumsden, C.J. and E.O. Wilson. 1981. *Genes, Mind and Culture. The Coevolutionary Process*. Cambridge, MA, Harvard University Press.

Lundell, C.L. 1940. The 1936 Michigan Carnegie Botanical Expedition to British Honduras. *Botany of the Maya Area, Miscellaneous Paper* 14. Carnegie Institute of Washington, Publication 522, Washington, DC.

Luttwak, Edward N. 1976. *The Grand Strategy of the Roman Empire*. Baltimore, Johns Hopkins University Press.

McCall, D.F. 1964. *Africa in Time-Perspective*. Boston, Boston University Press.

McDonald, William L. 1965. *The Architecture of the Roman Empire. Vol. I. An Introductory Study*. New Haven, Yale University Press.

McGhee, R. 1977. Ivory for the sea woman: the symbolic attributes of a prehistoric technology. *Canadian Journal of Archaeology* 1: 141–59.

McGovern, Thomas H. 1980. Cows, harp seals, and churchbells: adaptation and extinction in Norse Greenland. *Human Ecology* 8: 245–75.

McGuire, R.H. In press. Prestige economies in the prehistoric southwestern periphery. In F.J. Mathian and R.H. McGuire, eds., *Ripples in the Chichimec Sea: New Considerations of Southwest-Mesoamerican Interactions*. Carbondale, Ill., Southern Illinois University Press.

Mackay, E.J.H. 1938. *Further Excavations at Mohenjo Daro*. 2 vols. New Delhi, Government of India.

1943. *Chanhu-Daro Excavations, 1935–36*. American Oriental Series, 20. Boston, Museum of Fine Arts.

1948. *Early Indus Civilization*. 2nd enlarged and rev. edn. by D. Mackay. London, Luzac.

Macksey, R. and E. Donato. 1970. *The Structuralist Controversy: The Language of Criticism and the Sciences of Man*. Baltimore and London, Johns Hopkins University Press.

McNeill, W.H. 1986a. *Polyethnicity and National Unity in World History*. Toronto, University of Toronto Press.

1986b. *Mythistory and Other Essays*. Chicago, University of Chicago Press.

MacNeish, Richard. 1972. *The Prehistory of the Tehuacan Valley*. Austin, University of Texas.

MacNeish, R.S., S.J.K. Wilkerson and A. Nelken-Turner. 1980. *First Annual Report of the Belize Archaic Archaeological Reconnaissance*, R.S. Peabody Foundation, Andover.

Mahadevan, I. 1970. Dravidian parallels in Proto-Indian script. *Journal of Tamil Studies* 2(1).

Majumdar, N.G. 1934. *Exploration in Sind*. Memoirs of the Archaeological Survey of India 48. Calcutta.

Makkai, L. 1983. Ars Historica: on Braudel. *Review* 6 (4): 435–54.

Makkreel, R. 1975. *Dilthey: Philosopher of the Human Studies*. Princeton, Princeton University Press.

Mamdani, Mahmood. 1974. The myth of population control. *Development Digest* 12: 13–28.

Mandelbaum, Maurice. 1977. *The Anatomy of Historical Knowledge*. Baltimore, Johns Hopkins University Press.

Marcus, George and Michael M.J. Fisher. 1987. *Anthropology as Cultural Critique*. Chicago, University of Chicago Press.

Marcus, Joyce. 1973. Territorial organization of the Lowland Classic Maya. *Science* 180: 911–16.

1976. *Emblem and State in the Classic Maya Lowlands*, Dumbarton Oaks, Washington, DC.

1983a. Lowland Maya archaeology at the crossroads. *American Antiquity* 48:454–88.

1983b. On the nature of the Mesoamerican city. In E.Z.Vogt and G.R. Willey, eds., *Prehistoric Settlement Patterns, Essays in Honor of Gordon R. Willey*. 195–242. Albuquerque, University of New Mexico Press.

Markov, G.E. 1978. Problems of social change among the Asiatic nomads. In W. Weissleder, ed., *The Nomadic Alternative*. The Hague, Mouton.

Marks, J. and E. Staski. 1986. Individuals and the evolution of biological and cultural systems. *American Anthropologist* (in press).

Marshack, A. 1972. *The Roots of Civilization*. New York, McGraw–Hill.

Marshall, Sir John. 1931. *Mohenjo Daro and the Indus Civilization*. 3 vols. London, A. Probsthain.

Marshall, L. 1976. *The !Kung of Nyae Nyae*. Cambridge, MA, Harvard University Press.

Martin, Deb et al. 1984. The effects of socioeconomic change in prehistoric Africa: Sudanese Nubia as a case study. In M.N. Cohen and G.J. Armelagos, eds., *Paleopathology at the Origins of Agriculture*, 193–216. New York, Academic Press.

Martin, P.S. and Fred Plog. 1973. *The Archaeology of Arizona*. Garden City, Natural History Press.

Martin, P.S., G.I. Quimby and D. Collier. 1946. *Indians Before Columbus*. Chicago, University of Chicago Press.

Marx, Karl. 1965 [1857–8]. *Pre-Capitalist Economic Formations*. New York, International Publishers.

1967 [1894]. *Capital. Vol III: The Process of Capitalist Production as a Whole*. New York, International Publishers.

1968a. [1845] Theses on Feuerbach. In K. Marx and F. Engels, *Selected Works in One Volume*, 28–30. New York, International Publishers.

1968b. [1859] Preface to *A Contribution to the Critique of Political Economy*. In K. Marx and F. Engels, *Selected Works in One Volume*, 181–5. New York, International Publishers.

1982. Entwuerfe einer Antwort auf den Brief von V.I. Sassulitsch. In *Marx-Engels Werke*, 19: 384–406. Berlin, Dietz.

Marx, Karl and F. Engels. 1962. *Selected Works in Two Volumes*. Moscow, Foreign Languages Publishing House.

1970. *The German Ideology*, ed. C.J. Arthur. New York, International Publishers.

Mason, R.J. 1981. *Great Lakes Archeology*. New York, Academic Press.

Masson, V.M. 1981a. *Altyn Tepe*. (In Russian) Moscow, Akademia Nauk.

1981b. Seals of a proto-Indian type from Altyn-depe. In P.L. Kohl, ed., *The Bronze Age Civilization of Central Asia: Recent Soviet Discoveries*. Armonk, NY, M.E. Sharpe.

Masson, V.M. and V.I. Sarianidi. 1972. *Central Asia: Turkmenia before the Achaemenids*. London, Thames & Hudson.

Matheny, Raymond T., ed. 1980. *El Mirador, Peten, Guatemala: An Interim Report*. Papers of the New World Archaeological Foundation 45. Provo, UT, Brigham Young University.

1987. Early states in the Maya lowlands during the late Preclassic period: Edzna and El Mirador. In E. Benson, *The Maya State*. Rocky Mountain Institute for Precolumbian Studies.

Mathews, Peter and Gordon R. Willey. 1986. Prehistoric polities of the Pasion region: hieroglyphic texts and their archaeological settings. Paper presented at a seminar. Santa Fe, New Mexico, October.

Matthews, V.H. 1978. *Pastoral Nomadism in the Mari Kingdom*. Cambridge, American School of Oriental Research.

Maynard Smith, J. 1976. Group selection. *Quarterly Review of Biology* 51:277–83.

Maynard Smith, J. and N. Warren. 1982. Models of cultural and genetic change. *Evolution* 36:620–7.

Mayr, E. 1959. Typological versus population thinking. In B. Meggers, ed., *Evolution and Anthropology: A Centennial Appraisal*, 409–12. Washington DC., Washington Anthropological Society.

1970. *Populations, Species, and Evolution*. Cambridge, MA, Harvard University Press.

Meadow, Richard H. 1984. Animal domestication in the Middle East: a view from the eastern margin. In J. Clutton-Brock and C. Grigson, eds., *Animals and Archaeology: Early Herders and their Flocks*. Oxford, BAR International Series 202:309–37.

Meek, T.J. 1955. The Code of Hammurabi. In J.B. Pritchard, ed., *Ancient Near Eastern Texts Relating to the Old Testament*. Princeton, Princeton University Press.

Meiklejohn, C. et al. 1984. Socioeconomic change and patterns of pathology and variation in the mesolithic and neolithic of Western Europe: some suggestions. In M.N. Cohen and G.J. Armelagos, eds., *Paleopathology at the Origins of Agriculture*, 75–100. New York, Academic Press.

Meldgard, J., P. Mortensen and H. Thrane. 1964. Excavations at Tepe Guran, Luristan. *Acta Archaeologia* 34: 97–133.

Mellaart, James. 1975. *The Neolithic of the Near East*. London, Thames & Hudson.

Meltzer, David J. 1981. Ideology and material culture. In R.A. Gould and M.B. Schiffer, eds., *Modern Material Culture: The Archaeology of Us*, 113–25. New York, Academic Press.

1983. The antiquity of man and the development of American archaeology. In M.B. Schiffer, ed., *Advances in Archaeological Method and Theory* 6: 91–142. New York, Academic Press.

Meltzer, David J., Don D. Fowler and Jeremy A. Sabloff. 1986. Editors' Introduction. In D. Meltzer, D. Fowler, and J. Sabloff, eds., *American Archaeology Past and Future*, 7–19. Washington, DC., Smithsonian Institution Press.

Mensforth, Robert. 1985. Relative long bone growth in the Libben and Bt-5 prehistoric skeletal populations. *American Journal of Physical Anthropology* 68: 247–62.

1986. The pathogenesis of periosteal reactions in earlier human groups, diagnostic epidemiological and demographic considerations. Paper presented to American Association of Physical Anthropologists, Albuquerque.

n.d. Paleodemography of the skeletal population from Carlston Annis (Bt–5). Ms.

Michalowski, P. 1985. Third millennium contacts: observations on the relationships between Mari and Ebla. *Journal of the American Oriental Society* 105 (2); 293–302.

Michelson, A. 1986. In praise of horizontality: André Leroi-Gourhan, 1911–1986. *October* 37: 3–5.

Mignon, Molly R. 1986. Review of *Ritual Human Sacrifice in Mesoamerica*, edited by E.P. Benson. *American Antiquity* 51: 199–200.

Milanich, J.T. and C.H. Fairbanks. 1980. *Florida Archaeology*. New York, Academic Press.

Miller, D. 1985. Ideology and the Harappan civilization. *Journal of Anthropological Archaeology* 4: 34-71.

Miller, Daniel and Christopher Tilley, eds. 1984. *Ideology, Power and Prehistory*. Cambridge, Cambridge University Press.

Millon, Rene. 1973. *Urbanization at Teotihuacan, Mexico*, vol. 1. *The Teotihuacan Map*, part 2: Text. Austin, University of Texas Press.

Mintz, S. 1985. *Sweetness and Power: The Place of Sugar in Modern History*. New York, Viking.

Molnar, S. and I. Molnar. 1985. Observations of dental diseases among prehistoric populations of Hungary. *American Journal of Physical Anthropology* 67: 51–63.

Monk, M.A. and J. Fasham. 1980. Carbonized plant remains from two Iron Age sites in central Hampshire. *Proceedings of the Prehistoric Society* 46: 321–44.

Morley, Sylvanus G. 1956. *The Ancient Maya*. 3rd edn., revised by George W. Brainerd. Stanford, Stanford University Press.

Morris, Craig. 1967. Storage in Tawantinsuyu. Ph.D. dissertation, University of Chicago. Ann Arbor, University Microfilms.

1982. The infrastructure of Inka control in the Central Highlands. In G. Collier et al., eds., *The Inca and Aztec States 1400–1800*, 153–70. New York, Academic Press.

1986. Storage, supply, and redistribution in the economy of the Inka state. In J.V. Murra, N. Wachtel and J. Revel, eds., *Anthropological History of Andean Polities*, 59–68. Cambridge, Cambridge University Press.

In press. Architecture and the structure of space at Huánuco Pampa. In G. Gasparini and L. Margolies, eds., *Tecnologia, Urbanismo, y Arquitectura de los Inca*.

Morris, Craig and Donald Thompson. 1985. *Huánuco Pampa*. London, Thames & Hudson.

Mortensen, P. 1964. Additional remarks on the chronology of early villages in the Zagros. *Sumer* 20: 28–36.

1972. Seasonal camps and early villages in the Zagros. In P. Ucko, R. Tringham and G. Dimbleby, eds., *Man, Settlement and Urbanism*, 293–7. London, Duckworth.

1975. A survey of prehistoric settlements in Northern Luristan. *Acta Archaelogica* 45: 1–47.

1976. Chalcolithic settlements in the Hulailan Valley. In F. Bagherzadeh, ed., *The Proceedings of the 4th Annual Symposium on Archaeological Research in Iran*, 42–62. Tehran, Iranian Centre for Archaeological Research, Muzeh-e Iran Bastan.

Moseley, Michael E. 1975. *The Maritime Foundations of Andean Civilization*. Menlo Park, CA, Cummings.

1978. Pre-agricultural coastal civilizations in Peru. *Carolina Biology Readers* 90. Burlington, NC, Carolina Biological Supply Company.

Mosteller, Frederick and John W. Tukey. 1977. *Data Analysis and Regression: A Second Course in Statistics*. Reading, MA, Addison–Wesley.

Mote, F. 1971. *Intellectual Foundations of China*. New York, Knopf.

Mughal, M.R. 1971. The Early Harappan Period in the Greater Indus Valley and northern Baluchistan. Ph.D. dissertation, University of Pennsylvania. Ann Arbor, University Microfilms.

1982. Recent archaeological research in the Cholistan Desert. In G. Possehl, ed., *Harappan Civilization: A Contemporary Perspective*. New Delhi, Oxford and IBH Publishing Co. in collaboration with American Institute of Indian Studies, 85–96.

n.d. *Archaeological Surveys in Bahalwapur*. To be published by Department of Archaeology and Museums, Karachi.

Muhly, James D. 1980. The Bronze Age setting. In T.A. Wertime and J.D. Muhly, eds., *The Coming of the Age of Iron*. New Haven, Yale University Press.

1985. Sources of tin and the beginnings of bronze metallurgy. *American Journal of Archaeology* 89: 275–91.

Muller, J. 1966. An experimental theory of stylistic analysis. Ph.D. dissertation, Department of Anthropology, Harvard University.

1971. Style and culture contact. In C.L. Riley, J.C. Kelley, C.W. Pennington and R.L. Rands, eds., *Man across the Sea*, 66–78. Houston, University of Texas Press.

1977. Individual variation in art styles. In J.N. Hill and J. Gunn, eds., *The Individual in Prehistory*. New York, Academic Press.

1979. Structural studies of art styles. In J. Cordell, ed., *The Visual Arts: Plastic and Graphic*, 212. The Hague, Mouton.

Muller, Viana. 1985. Origins of class and gender hierarchy in northwest Europe. *Dialectical Anthropology* 10: 93–105.

Munn, N. 1962. Walbiri graphic signs: an analysis. *American Anthropologist* 64: 972–84.

Murchison, M. et al. 1983. Transverse line formation in protein-deprived rhesus monkeys. Paper presented to the Paleopathology Association, Indianapolis.

Murdock, G.P. 1949. *Social Structure*. New York, Free Press.

1959a. *Africa: its Peoples and their Culture History*. New York, McGraw-Hill.

1959b. Evolution in social organization. In B.J. Meggers, ed., *Evolution and Anthropology*, 126–43. Washington, The Anthropological Society of Washington.

Murra, John V. 1960. Rite and crop in the Inca state. In S. Diamond, ed., *Culture in History*, New York, Columbia University Press.

1962. Cloth and its functions in the Inca State. *American Anthropologist* 64: 710–28.

1972. El "control vertical" de un máximo de pisos ecológicos en la economía de las sociedades andinas. In *Visita de la Provincia de León de Huánuco en 1562* 2:429–76. Huánuco, Universidad Hermilio Valdizan.

1975. Formaciones económicas y políticas del mundo andino. Lima, Instituto de Estudios Peruanos.

1980 [1956]. *The Economic Organization of the Inka State*. Westport, JAI Press.

1982. The *Mit'a* obligations of ethnic groups to the Inka State. In Collier et al., eds., *The Inca and Aztec States 1400–1800*, 237–62. New York, Academic Press.

1985. Comment on D'Altroy and Earle, *Staple Finance, Wealth Finance and Storage in the Inka Political Economy. Current Anthropology* 26 (2): 200.

Nance, Jack G. 1983. Regional sampling in archaeological survey. The statistical perspective. In M. Schiffer, ed., *Advances in Archaeological Method and Theory*, 6: 289–356. Orlando, Florida, Academic Press.

Nardi, Bonnie Anna 1981. Modes of explanation in anthropological population theory: biological determinism vs. self-regulation in studies of population growth in Third World countries. *American Anthropologist* 83: 28–56.

Needham, Joseph. 1958. *The Development of Iron and Steel Technology in China*. London, Newcomen Society.

Nekhaev, A.A. 1986. Pogrebenie maikopskoi kul'turi iz kurgana u seal krasnogvardeiskoe, *Sovetskaya Arkheologiya* 1: 244–48.

Nelson, B.K. et al. 1986. Effects of diagenesis on strontium, carbon, nitrogen and oxygen concentrations and isotopic composition of bone. *Geochimica et Cosmochimica Acta* 50: 1941–9.

Nelson, D.A. 1984. Bone density in three archaeological populations. *American Journal of Physical Anthropology* 63: 198.

Netherly, Patricia. 1978. Local level lords on the north coast of Peru. Ph.D. dissertation, Cornell University. Ann Arbor, University Microfilms.

Netting, Robert McC. 1977. Maya subsistence; mythologies, analogies, possibilities. In R.E.W. Adams, ed., *The Origins of Maya Civilization*, 299–334. Albuquerque, University of New Mexico Press.

Nicholson, Henry B. 1971. Religion in prehispanic Central Mexico. In G. Ekholm and I. Bernal, eds., *Handbook of Middle American Indians*, 10:395–445. Austin, University of Texas Press.

Nickens, Paul R. 1976. Stature reduction as an adaptive response to food production in Mesoamerica. *Journal of Archaeological Science* 3:31–41.

Nissen, H.J. 1971. The expedition to the Behbehan region. *Oriental Institute Report for 1970/71*:9–12.

1980a. The mobility between settled and nonsettled in early Babylonia; theory and evidence. In *L'Archéologie de l'Iraq du début de l'époque néolithique à 333 avant notre ère*, 225–32. Paris, Editions du Centre National de la Recherche Scientifique.

1980b. Commentaires. In *L'Archéologie de l'Iraq du début de l'époque néolithique à 333 avant notre ère*. Paris, Editions du Centre National de la Recherche Scientifique.

1983. *Grundzüge einer Geschichte der frühzeit des vorderen orients*. Darmstadt, Wissenschaftliche Buchgesellschaft.

Nissen, H. and C. Redman. 1971. Preliminary notes on an archaeological surface survey in the plain of Behbehan and the Lower Zurah Valley. *Bastan Chenassi va Honar-E Iran* 6:48–50.

Nissen, H. and A. Zagarell. 1976. The 1975 season of the Free University of Berlin Expedition to the Zagros Mountains. In F. Begherzadeh, ed., *Proceedings of the 4th Annual Symposium on Archaeological Research in Iran*. Tehran, Iranian Centre for Archaeological Research, Muzeh-e Iran Bastan.

Nöel Hume, Ivor. 1969. *Historical Archaeology*. New York, Alfred A. Knopf.

Nolte, H.-H. 1982. The position of eastern Europe in the international system in early modern times. *Review* 6(1): 25–84.

Norr, Lynette. 1984. Prehistoric subsistence and health status of coastal peoples from the Panamanian Isthmus of lower Central America. In M.N. Cohen and G.J. Armelagos, eds., *Paleopathology at the Origins of Agriculture*, 463–90. New York, Academic Press.

1986. Skeletal responses to stress in prehistoric Panama. *American Journal of Physical Anthropology* 69:247.

Nuetzel, W. 1975. The formation of the Arabian Gulf from 14000 B.C. *Sumer* 31:101–10.

1976. The climate changes of Mesopotamia and bordering areas. *Sumer* 32: 11–24.

Oates, J. 1972. Prehistoric settlement patterns. In P. Ucko, R. Tringham and G. Dimbleby, eds., *Man, Settlement and Urbanism*. London, Duckworth.

Olin, Jacqueline S. and A.D. Franklin. 1982. *Archaeological Ceramics*. Washington, DC, Smithsonian Institution Press.

Opler, Morris. 1961. Cultural evolution, southern Athapaskans, and chronology in theory. *Southwestern Journal of Anthropology* 17: 1–20.

Oppenheim, A. Leo 1977. *Ancient Mesopotamia*. (Rev. edn. completed by E. Reiner). Chicago, University of Chicago.

Oppenheimer, Martin. 1985. *White Collar Politics*. New York, Monthly Review Press.

Orlove, Benjamin S. 1980. Ecological anthropology. *Annual Review of Anthropology* 9: 235–73.

Ortiz de Montellano, Barnard R. 1978. Aztec cannibalism: an ecological necessity? *Science* 200: 611–17.

Ortiz de Zúñiga, Iñigo. 1967. *Visita a la Provincia de León de Huánuco en 1562*. Huánuco, Universidad Hermilio Valdizan.

Ortner, Donald and W. Putschar. 1981. Identification of pathological conditions of human skeletal remains. *Smithsonian Contributions in Anthropology* 28.

Ortner, S. 1984. Theory in anthropology since the sixties. *The Comparative Study of Society and History* 10: 126–66.

O'Shea, J.M. 1984. *Mortuary Variability: An Archaeological Investigation*. New York, Academic Press.

Owen, Bruce. 1986. The role of common metal objects in the Inka State. Master's paper, Department of Anthropology, University of California, Los Angeles.

Palerm, Angel. 1972. *Agricultura y Sociedad en Mesoamerica*. Mexico, Centro de Investigaciones Superiores.

Palkovich, Ann. 1984. Agriculture, marginal environments and nutritional stress in the prehistoric Southwest. In M.N. Cohen and G.J. Armelagos, eds., *Paleopathology at the Origins of Agriculture*, 425–38. New York, Academic Press.

Parkington, J. 1969. Symbolism in paleolithic cave art. *South African Archaeological Bulletin* 24: 3–13.

Parpola, S., A. Parpola and R.H. Brunswig, Jr. 1977. The Meluhha village: evidence of acculturation of Harappan traders in late third millennium Mesopotamia? *Journal of the Social and Economic History of the Orient* 20(2): 129–65.

Parsons, Jeffrey R. 1974. The development of a prehistoric complex society: a regional perspective from the Valley of Mexico. *Journal of Field Archaeology* 1: 81–108.

1976. The role of Chinampa agriculture in the food supply of Aztec Tenochtitlan. In C.E. Cleland, ed., *Cultural Change and Continuity*, 233–62. New York, Academic Press.

Parsons, J.R. et al. 1982. Prehistoric settlement patterns in the southern Valley of Mexico: the Chalco-Xochimilco region. Museum of Anthropology, Memoirs 18. Ann Arbor, University of Michigan.

Patterson, Thomas C. 1986a. Ideology, class formation, and resistance in the Inca state. *Critique of Anthropology* 6(1): 75–85.

1986b. The last sixty years: toward a social history of Americanist archeology in the United States. *American Anthropologist* 88: 7–26.

Paulsen, Allison C. 1976. Environment and empire; climatic factors in prehistoric Andean culture change. *World Archaeology* 8:121–32.

Paynter, Robert. 1983. Field or factory? Concerning the degradation of archaeological labor. In J.M. Gero et al., eds., *The Socio-Politics of Archaeology*, 17–29. Department of Anthropology, Research Report 23. Amherst, University of Massachusetts.

1985. Surplus flow between frontiers and homelands. In S.M. Green and S.M. Perlman, eds., *The Archaeology of Frontiers and Boundaries*, 163–211. Orlando, Academic Press.

Pearson, M.P. 1982. Mortuary practices, society and ideology. In Ian Hodder, ed., *Symbolic and Structural Archaeology*, 99–113. Cambridge, Cambridge University Press.

Pease, Franklin. 1982. The formation of Tawantinsuyu: mechanisms of colonization and relationship with ethnic groups. In Collier et al., eds., *The Inca and Aztec States 1400–1800*, 173–98. New York, Academic Press.

Perzigian, A. et al. 1984. Prehistoric health in the Ohio River Valley. In M.N. Cohen and G.J. Armelagos, eds., *Paleopathology at the Origins of Agriculture*, 347–66. New York, Academic Press.

Pettinato, G. 1981. *The Archives of Ebla: An Empire Inscribed in Clay*. New York, Doubleday.

Pettit, P. 1977. *The Concept of Structuralism*. London, Gill and MacMillan.

Pfeiffer, J. 1982. *The Creative Explosion*. New York, Harper & Row.

Pfeiffer, Susan. 1984. Paleopathology in an Iroquoian ossuary with special reference to tuberculosis. *American Journal of Physical Anthropology* 65: 181–9.

Piaget, J. 1968. *Le Structuralisme*. Paris, PUF.

1971. *Structuralism*. London, Routledge & Kegan Paul.

Piggott, Stuart. 1950a. *William Stukeley: An Eighteenth-Century Antiquary*. Oxford, Oxford University Press.

1950b. *Prehistoric India*. Baltimore, Penguin.

Pires-Ferreira, Jane W. and K. Flannery. 1976. Ethnographic models for formative exchange. In Kent V. Flannery, ed., *The Early Mesoamerican Village*, 286–91. New York, Academic Press.

Pittman, H. 1984. *Art of the Bronze Age, Southeastern Iran, Western Central Asia and the Indus Valley*. New York City, Metropolitan Museum of Art.

Planhol, X. 1976. Saturation et sécurité. In *Pastoral Production and Society. Proceedings of the International Meeting on Nomadic Pastoralism. Paris 1–3 December 1970*. Ed. L'Équipe Ecologie et Anthropologie des Sociétés Pastorales. Cambridge, Cambridge University Press.

Plog, F. 1974. *The Study of Prehistoric Change*. New York, Academic Press.

1983. Political and economic alliances on the Colorado plateaus, AD 400 to 1450. *Advances in World Archaeology* 2: 289–330.

1986. Presentation at Third USA–USSR Archaeological Symposium, Smithsonian Institution, Washington DC. May 4–9.

Plog, F., S. Upham and P.C. Weigand. 1982. A perspective on Mogollon–Mesoamerican interaction. In *Mogollon Archaeology: Proceedings of the 1980 Conference*. Ramona, Acoma Books.

Plog, Stephen. 1976. Measurement of prehistoric interaction between communities. In K.V. Flannery, ed., *The Early Mesoamerican Village*, 255–72. New York, Academic Press.

1978. Social interaction and stylistic similarity: a reanalysis. In Michael B. Schiffer, ed., *Advances in Archaeological Method and Theory*, 143–82. New York, Academic Press.

1980. *Stylistic Variation in Prehistoric Ceramics; Design Analysis in the American Southwest*. Cambridge, Cambridge University Press.

Pohl, Mary. 1985a. The privileges of Maya elites: prehistoric vertebrate fauna from Seibal. In M. Pohl, ed., *Prehistoric Lowland Maya Environment and Subsistence Economy*, 133–46. Peabody Museum Papers 77. Cambridge, MA, Harvard University.

1985b. ed. *Prehistoric Lowland Maya Environment and Subsistence Economy*, Peabody Museum Papers 77. Cambridge, MA, Harvard University.

Pohl, Mary and C.H. Mikcisek. 1985. Cultivation techniques and crops. In M. Pohl, ed., *Prehistoric Lowland Maya Environment and Subsistence Economy*, 9–20. Peabody Museum Papers, 77. Cambridge, MA, Harvard University.

Polanyi, K. 1957. *The Great Transformation*. Boston, Beacon.

Polgar, Steven. 1971. Culture history and population dynamics. In S. Polgar, ed., *Culture and Population: A Collection of Current Studies*, 3–8. Chapel Hill, Carolina Population Center.

1972. Population history and population policies from an anthropological perspective. *Current Anthropology* 13: 203–11.

1975. Birth planning: between neglect and coercion. In M. Maz, ed., *Population and Social Organization*, 174–203. The Hague, Mouton.

Pollock, H.E.D., R.L. Roys, T. Proskouriakoff and A.L. Smith. 1962. *Mayapan, Yucatan, Mexico*, Carnegie Institution of Washington, Publication 619. Washington DC.

Porter, R.K. 1821–2. *Travels in Georgia, Persia, Armenia, Ancient Babylonia during the Years 1817, 1818, 1819 and 1820*. vols. I and II. London, Langman, Hurst, Rees, Orme, Brown.

Possehl, G.L. 1979. Pastoral nomadism in the Indus civilization: a hypothesis. In *South Asian Archaeology 1977*, 537–52. Naples, Istituto Universitario Orientale.

1980. *Indus Civilization in Saurashtra*. Delhi, B.R. Publishing.

1982. *Harappan Civilization*. New Delhi, Oxford/IBH.

1984. A note on Harappan settlement patterns in the Punjab. In Kenneth A.R. Kennedy and Gregory L. Possehl, eds., *Studies in the Archaeology and Paleoanthropology of South Asia*. New Delhi, Oxford/IBH.

Powell, M. 1977. Sumerian merchants and the problem of profit. *Iraq* 23: 23–9.

Powell, M.L. 1984. Health, disease, and social stress in the complex Mississippian chiefdom at Moundville, Alabama. *American Journal of Physical Anthropology* 63:205.

Price, Barbara. 1977. Shifts in production and organization: a cluster-interaction model. *Current Anthropology* 18:209–33.

1978a. Demystification, enriddlement, and Aztec cannibalism: a materialist rejoinder to Harner. *American Ethnologist* 5: 98–115.

1978b. Secondary state formation: an explanatory model. In Ronald Cohen and Elman Service, eds. *Origin of the State*, 161–86. Philadelphia, Ishi.

1982. Cultural materialism: a theoretical overview. *American Antiquity* 47(4): 709–41.

Price, T.D. and J.A. Brown, eds., 1985. *Prehistoric Hunter Gatherers: The Emergence of Social and Cultural Complexity*. New York, Academic Press.

Prickett, M. 1976. Tepe Yahya project; Upper Rud i Gushk survey. *Iran* 9:175–6.

Puleston, D.E. 1974. Intersite areas in the vicinity of Tikal and Uaxactun. In N. Hammond, ed., *Mesoamerican Archaeology: New Approaches*, 303–12. London, Duckworth.

1978. Terracing, raised fields, and tree cropping in the Maya Lowlands: a new perspective on the geography of power. In P.D. Harrison and B.L. Turner II, eds., *Pre-Hispanic Maya Agriculture*, 225–46. Albuquerque, University of New Mexico Press.

Pyne, N.M. 1976. The fire-serpent and were-jaguar in formative Oaxaca: a contingency table analysis. In K.V. Flannery, ed., *The Early Mesoamerican Village*, 272–82. New York, Academic Press.

Quilter, Jeffrey, and Terry Stocker. 1983. Subsistence economics and the origin of Andean complex societies. *American Anthropologist* 85: 545–62.

Raab, L. Mark, Timothy C. Klinger, Michael B. Schiffer and Albert C. Goodyear. 1980. Clients, contracts, and profits: conflicts in public archaeology. *American Anthropologist* 82: 539–51.

Rabinow, P. 1986. Representations are social facts; modernity and postmodernity in anthropology. In J. Clifford and G.E. Marcus, eds., *Writing Culture*. Berkeley, University of California Press.

Ragin, C. and D. Chirot. 1984. The world system of Immanuel Wallerstein: sociology and politics as history. In T. Skocpol, ed., *Vision and Method in Historical Sociology*, 276–312. Cambridge.

Rands, R.L. 1967. Ceramic technology and trade in the Palenque region, Mexico. In C.L. Riley and W.W. Taylor, eds., *American Historical Anthropology: Essays in Honor of Leslie Spier*. Carbondale, Southern Illinois University Press.

1969. *Mayan Ecology and Trade; 1967–1968, Research Records of the University Museum, Southern Illinois University*, Mesoamerican Studies 2. Carbondale.

Rao, S.R. 1973. *Lothal and the Indus Civilization*. New York, Asia Publishing House.

Rappaport, Roy A. 1978. Maladaptation in social systems. In J. Friedman and M.J. Rowlands, eds., *Evolution of Social Systems*. 49–71. London, Duckworth.

Rathbun, T.A. 1984. Skeletal pathology from the Paleolithic through the metal ages in Iran and Iraq. In M.N. Cohen and G.J. Armelagos, eds., *Paleopathology at the Origins of Agriculture*, 137–68. New York, Academic Press.

Rathje, W.L. 1975. The last tango in Mayapan: a tentative trajectory of production-distribution systems. In J.A. Sabloff and C.C. Lamberg-Karlovsky, eds., *Ancient Civilization and Trade*, 409–48. Albuquerque, University of New Mexico Press.

Read, Dwight W. 1974. Some comments on typologies in archaeology and an outline of a methodology. *American Antiquity* 39: 216–42.

Redman, Charles L. 1987. Surface collection, sampling and research design: a retrospective. *American Antiquity* 52(2): 249–65.

Redman, C.L., M.J. Berman, E.V. Curtin, W.T. Langhorne Jnr., N.M. Versaggi and J.C. Wanser. 1978. *Social Archeology*. New York, Academic Press.

Renfrew, Colin. 1972. *The Emergence of Civilisation*. London, Methuen.

1982a. Polity and power; interaction, intensification and exploitation. In C. Renfrew, ed., *An Island Polity: The Archaeology of Exploitation in Melos*, 264–90. Cambridge, Cambridge University Press.

1982b. Towards an archaeology of mind. Disney Professor Inaugural Lecture. Cambridge, Cambridge University Press.

Renfrew, Colin and J. Cherry. 1986. *Peer Polity Interaction and Sociopolitical Change*. Cambridge, Cambridge University Press.

Renfrew, A.C. and S. Shennan, eds. 1982. *Ranking, Resource and Exchange: Aspects of the Archaeology of Early European Society*. Cambridge, Cambridge University Press.

Rice, D.S. and D.E. Puleston. 1981. Ancient Maya settlement patterns in the Peten, Guatemala. In W. Ashmore, ed., *Lowland Maya Settlement Patterns*, 121–56, Albuquerque, University of New Mexico Press.

Rice, Prudence M. 1987. *Pottery Analysis: A Sourcebook*. Chicago, University of Chicago Press.

Ricketson, O.G., Jr. and E.B. Ricketson. 1937. *Uaxactun, Guatemala, Group E, 1926–31*, Carnegie Institution of Washington, Publication 477, Washington, DC.

Ricoeur, P. 1986. *Lectures on Ideology and Utopia*, ed. G.H. Taylor. New York, Columbia University Press.

Rindos, D. 1980. Symbiosis, instability, and the origins and spread of agriculture; a new model. *Current Anthropology* 21:751–72.

1984. *The Origins of Agriculture. An Evolutionary Perspective*. Orlando, Academic Press.

1986a. The evolution of the capacity for culture: sociobiology, structuralism, and cultural selection. *Current Anthropology* 27:315–31.

1986b.The genetics of cultural anthropology: toward a genetic model for the origin of the capacity for culture. *Journal of Anthropological Archaeology* 5:1–38.

Rissman, P.C. 1985. Migratory pastoralism in Western India in the second millennium B.C.: the evidence from Oriyo Timbo (Chiroda). PhD. dissertation, University of Pennsylvania, Department of Anthropology.

Ritchie, W.A. 1944. *The Pre-Iroquoian Occupations of New York State*. Rochester: Rochester Museum of Arts and Sciences, Memoir l.

1965. *The Archaeology of New York State*. Garden City, Natural History Press.

Robbins, L.M. 1978. The antiquity of tuberculosis in prehistoric peoples of Kentucky. *American Journal of Physical Anthropology* 48:429.

Robey, D. 1973. *Structuralism: An Introduction*. Oxford, Clarendon Press.

Rodin, Miriam, Karen Michaelson and Gerald M. Britan. 1978. Systems theory in anthropology. *Current Anthropology* 19: 747–62.

Rose, Jerome et al. 1984. Paleopathology and the origins of maize agriculture in the lower Mississippi Valley and Caddoan culture areas. In M.N. Cohen and G.J. Armelagos, eds., *Paleopathology at the Origins of Agriculture*, 393–424. New York, Academic Press.

ed. 1985. Gone to a better land. *Arkansas Archaeological Survey Research Series* 25.

Roth, E.A. 1985. A note on the demographic concomitants of sedentism. *American Anthropologist* 87: 38–82.

Rouse, I.B. 1939. *Prehistory in Haiti: A Study in Method*. Yale University Publications in Anthropology 21. New Haven, CT.

1972. *Introduction to Prehistory*. New York, McGraw-Hill.

Rowe, John H. 1946. Inca culture at the time of the Spanish conquest. In Julian Steward, ed., *Handbook of South American Indians*. Bureau of American Ethnology, Bulletin 143, vol. 2. *The Andean Civilizations*, 183–330. Washington, DC.

1982. Inca policies and institutions relating to the cultural unification of the Empire. In G.A. Collier, et al., eds., *The Inca and Aztec State 1400–1800*, 93–118. New York, Academic Press.

Rowton, M.B. 1974. Enclosed nomadism. *Journal of the Economic and Social History of the Orient* 17:1–30.

Rudney, Joel. 1983. Dental indicators of growth disturbance in a series of ancient lower Nubian populations; changes over time. *American Journal of Physical Anthropology* 31:295–302.

Runes, D. 1962. *Dictionary of Philosophy*. Totowa, New Jersey, Littlefield, Adams.

Russell, Glenn. 1985. Lithic evidence for Wanka household response to the imposed Inka economy. Paper presented at the 50th Annual Meeting of the Society for American Archaeology. Denver.

Rye, Owen S. 1981. *Pottery Technology*. Washington, DC, Taraxacum.

Sabloff, J.A. and E.W. Andrews V, eds. 1986. *Late Lowland Maya Civilization, Classic to Postclassic*. Albuquerque, University of New Mexico Press.

Sabloff, J.A. and C.C. Lamberg-Karlovsky. 1975. *Ancient Civilization and Trade*. Albuquerque, University of New Mexico Press.

Sabloff, J.A., T.W. Beale and A.M. Kurland, Jr. 1973. Recent developments in archaeology. *The Annals of the American Academy of Political and Social Science* 408: 103–18.

Sabloff, J.A., L.R. Binford and P.A. McAnany. 1987. Understanding the archaeological record. *Antiquity*, 61: 203–10.

Sackett, J.R. 1977. The meaning of style in archaeology: a general model. *American Antiquity* 42:369–80.

1982. Approaches to style in lithic archaeology. *Journal of Anthropological Archaeology* 1:59–112.

1983. From deMortillet to Bordes; a century of French paleolithic research. In G. Daniel and O. Klindt–Jensen, eds., *Towards a History of Archaeology*, 59–112. London, Thames & Hudson.

1986a. Style, function and assemblage variability: a reply to Binford. *American Antiquity* 51:628–34.

1986b. Isochrestism and style. *Journal of Anthropological Archaeology* 5:266–77.

Sahlins, Marshall D. 1968. *Tribesmen*. Englewood Cliffs, Prentice-Hall.

1972. *Stone Age Economics*. Chicago, Aldine.

1976. *Culture and Practical Reason*. Chicago, Chicago University Press.

1978. Culture as protein and profit. *New York Review of Books*, November 23: 45–53.

Sahlins, M.D. and E.R. Service, eds. 1960. *Evolution and Culture*. Ann Arbor, University of Michigan Press.

de Ste Croix, G.E.M. 1981. *The Class Struggle in the Ancient Greek World*. London, Duckworth.

Saitta, Dean J. 1983. The poverty of philosophy in archaeology. In J.A. Moore and A.S. Keene, eds., *Archaeological Hammers and Theories*, 299–304. New York, Academic Press.

Salmon, M.H. 1982. *Philosophy and Archaeology*. New York, Academic Press.

Salomon, Frank L. 1986. *Native Lords of Quito in the Age of the Incas*. Cambridge, Cambridge University Press.

1987. A North Andean status trader complex under Inka rule. *Ethnohistory* 34:1 (in press).

Sanders, William T. 1957. *'Tierra y agua' (Soil and Water): A Study of Ecological Factors in the Development of Meso-American Civilization*. Cambridge, MA, Harvard University Press.

1968. Hydraulic agriculture, economic symbiosis and the evolution of states in Central Mexico. In B.J. Meggers, ed., *Anthropological Archeology in the Americas*, 88–107. Washington, Anthropological Society of Washington.

1972. Population, agricultural history, and societal evolution in Mesoamerica. In B. Spooner, ed., *Population Growth: Anthropological Implications*, 101–53. Cambridge, MA, MIT Press.

1977. Environmental heterogeneity and the evolution of Lowland Maya civilization. In R.E.W. Adams, ed., *The Origins of Maya Civilization*, 287–97. Albuquerque, University of New Mexico Press.

1981. Classic Maya settlement patterns and ethnographic analogy. In W. Ashmore, ed., *Lowland Maya Settlement Patterns*, 351–70, Albuquerque, University of New Mexico Press.

Sanders, William T. and Barbara J. Price. 1968. *Mesoamerica: The Evolution of a Civilization*. New York, Random House.

Sanders, William T., Jeffrey R. Parsons and Robert S. Santley. 1979. *The Basin of Mexico: Ecological Processes in the Evolution of a Civilization*. New York, Academic Press.

Santoni, M. 1984. Sibri and the south cemetery of Mehrgarh: third millennium connections between the northern Kachi Plain (Pakistan) and Central Asia. In B. and R. Allchin, eds., *South Asian Archaeology 1981*. Cambridge, Cambridge University Press.

Sarianidi, V.I. 1981. Margiana in the Bronze Age. In P.L. Kohl, ed., *The Bronze Age Civilization of Central Asia*. Armonk, NY, M.E. Sharpe.

Sattenspiel, Lisa and H. Harpending. 1983. Stable populations and skeletal age. *American Antiquity* 48: 489–98.

Saul, Frank P. 1972. *Human Skeletal Remains from the Altar de Sacrificios*. Peabody Museum Papers. Cambridge, MA, Harvard University.

Schaedel, Richard P. 1978. Early state of the Incas. In H. Claessen and P. Skalnik, eds., *The Early State*, 289–320. The Hague, Mouton.

Schele, Linda. 1976. Accession iconography of Chan-Bahlum in the group of the cross at Palenque. In Merle Greene Robertson, ed., *The Art, Iconography, and Dynastic History of Palenque*. Mesa Redonda de Palenque, part 3: 9–34. Pebble Beach, California.

1984. Human sacrifice among the Classic Maya. In E. Boone, ed., *Ritual Human Sacrifice in Mesoamerica*, 6–48. Washington, DC, Dumbarton Oaks.

Schele, Linda, and Mary Ellen Miller. 1986. *The Blood of Kings: Dynasty and Ritual in Maya Art*. Fort Worth, Kimbell Art Museum.

Schiffer, M.B. 1976. *Behavioral Archeology*. New York, Academic Press.

Schneider, J. 1977. Was there a pre-capitalist world system? *Peasant Studies* 6(1): 20–9.

Schoeninger, Margaret J. et al. 1983. 15n/14n ratios of bone collagen reflect marine and terrestrial components of prehistoric human diet. *Science* 220:1381–3.

Schrire, Carmel, ed. 1980. An inquiry into the evolutionary status and apparent identity of San hunter-gatherers. *Human Ecology* 8: 9–32.

1984. *Past and Present in Hunter-Gatherer Studies*. New York, Academic Press.

Schuyler, Robert. 1976. Images of America: the contribution of historical archaeology to national identity. *Southwestern Lore* 42(4): 27–39.

Schwartz, B.I. 1985. *The World of Thought in Ancient China*. Cambridge, MA, Harvard University Press.

Sciulli, P.W. 1977. A descriptive and comparative study of the deciduous dentition of prehistoric Ohio Valley Amerindians. *American Journal of Physical Anthropology* 47: 71–80.

1978. Developmental abnormalities of the permanent dentition in prehistoric Ohio Valley Amerindians. *American Journal of Physical Anthropology* 48:193–8.

Seler, Eduard. 1960–1. *Gesammelte Abhandlungen*. 5 vols. Graz, Austria, Akademischen Druk- und Verlagsanstalt.

Service, E.R. 1962, 1967, 1971. *Primitive Social Organization*. New York, Random House.

1975. *Origins of the State and Civilization*. New York, Norton.

Shaffer, James G. 1974. Allahdino and the mature Harappan. Ms.

1982. Harappan culture; a reconsideration. In G.L. Possehl, ed., *The Harappan Civilization: A Contemporary Perspective*, 41–50. New Delhi: IBH Publishing Co.

In press. The Indus Valley, Baluchistan and Helmand traditions: Neolithic through Bronze Age. In R.W. Ehrich, ed., *Chronologies in Old World Archaeology*. 3rd edn. Chicago, University of Chicago Press.

Shanks, M. and C. Tilley. 1982. Ideology, symbolic power and ritual communication: a reinterpretation of Neolithic mortuary practices. In I. Hodder, ed., *Symbolic and Structural Archaeology*. Cambridge, Cambridge University Press.

1987. *Reconstructing Archaeology: Theory and Practice*. Cambridge, Cambridge University Press.

Shennan, S. 1982. Ideology, change and the European Early Bronze Age. In I. Hodder, ed., *Symbolic and Structural Archaeology*. Cambridge, Cambridge University Press.

Shephard, Anna O. 1971. *Ceramics for the Archaeologist*. Washington, DC, Carnegie Institute of Washington, Publication 609.

Sherratt, A.G. 1981. Plough and pastoralism: aspects of the secondary products revolution. In I. Hodder, G. Isaac and N. Hammond, eds., *Patterns of the Past: Studies in Honour of David Clarke*. Cambridge, Cambridge University Press.

1983. The secondary exploitation of animals in the Old World. *World Archaeology* 15:90–104.

Shipman, P. et al. 1985. *The Human Skeleton*. Cambridge, MA, Harvard University Press.

Shippman, K. 1970. Notizen einer Reise in den Bachtiaribergen. *Archaeologische Mitteilungen aus Iran*. n.s. 3:231–8.

Siemens, A.H. and D.E. Puleston. 1972. Ridged fields and associated features in Southern Campeche: new perspectives on the Lowland Maya. *American Antiquity* 37: 228–39.

Sieveking, A. 1979. *The Cave Artists*. London, Thames & Hudson.

Sillen, A. and M. Kavanaugh. 1982. Strontium and paleodietary research: a review. *Yearbook of Physical Anthropology* 25: 69–90.

Silver, M. 1983. Karl Polanyi and markets in the ancient Near East: the challenge of the evidence. *The Journal of Economic History* 43(4): 795–829.

Silverberg, Robert. 1968. *Mound Builders of Ancient America: The Archaeology of a Myth*. Greenwich, New York Graphic Society.

Simoons, Frederick J. 1973. The sacred cow and the constitution of India. *Ecology of Food and Nutrition* 2: 281–96.

1979. Questions in the sacred-cow controversy. *Current Anthropology* 20: 467–93.

Singh, Gurdip. 1974. Late quaternary history of vegetation and climate of Rajasthan Desert, India. In *Philosophical Transactions of the Royal Society*, London, 267:491.

Smith, A. Ledyard. 1950. Uaxactun, Guatemala; Excavations of 1931–1937, Carnegie Institution of Washington, Publication 588. Washington DC.

1972. *Excavations at Altar de Sacrificios*, Peabody Museum Papers 62. Cambridge, MA, Harvard University.

Smith, C.S. 1980. *From Art to Science*. Cambridge, MA, MIT Press.

1981. *A Search for Structure*. Cambridge, MA, MIT Press.

Smith, Michael E. 1986. The role of social stratification in the Aztec Empire: a view from the provinces. *American Anthropologist* 88: 70–91.

Smith, Patricia et al. 1984. Archaeological and skeletal evidence for dietary change during the late Pleistocene/early Holocene in the Levant. In M.N. Cohen and G.J. Armelagos, eds., *Paleopathology at the Origins of Agriculture*, 101–36. New York, Academic Press.

Snell, D.C. 1982. *Ledgers and Prices: Early Mesopotamian Merchant Accounts*. New Haven, Yale University Press.

Snow, D.R. 1980. *The Archaeology of New England*. New York, Academic Press.

Sober, E. 1980. Evolution, population thinking, and essentialism. *Philosophy of Science* 47:350–83.

Solecki, R.S. 1952. A Paleolithic site in the Zagros Mountains of northern Iran: report on a sounding at Shanidar Cave. *Sumer* 8: 127–92.

1958. The 1956–57 season at Shanidar, Iraq. *Sumer* 14: 104–8.

1979. Contemporary Kurdish winter-time inhabitants of Shanidar Cave, Iraq. *World Archaeology* 10: 318–30.

South, Stanley. 1977. *Method and Theory in Historical Archaeology*. New York, Academic Press.

Spaulding, A.C. 1953. Statistical techniques for the discovery of artifact types. *American Antiquity* 18:305–14.

1968. Explanation in archeology. In S.R. and L.R. Binford, eds., *New Perspectives in Archeology*, 33–9. Chicago, Aldine.

1976. Multifactor analysis of association: an application to Owasco ceramics. In C. Cleland, ed., *Cultural Change and Continuity; Essays in Honor of James Bennett Griffin*, 59–68. New York, Academic Press.

1977. On growth and form in archaeology: multivariate analysis. *Journal of Anthropological Research* 33: 1–15.

Speiser, E.A. 1953. Early law and civilization. *The Canadian Bar Review* 31: 867–83.

Spencer, H. 1857. Progress: its laws and causes. *Westminster Review* 67: 445–85.

Spencer, W.B. and F. Gillen. 1899. *The Native Tribes of Central Australia*. London, Macmillan.

Spiro, M. 1986. Cultural relativism and the future of anthropology. *Cultural Anthropology* 1 (3): 259–86.

Spooner, Brian, ed. 1972. *Population Growth: Anthropological Implications*. Cambridge, MA, MIT Press.

Spriggs, Matthew, ed. 1977. *Archaeology and Anthropology*. Oxford, BAR Reports, Supplementary Series, 19.

1984. *Marxist Perspectives in Archaeology*. Cambridge, Cambridge University Press.

Stanley, S.M. 1979. *Macroevolution. Pattern and Process*. San Francisco, W. H. Freeman.

Stebbins, G.L. and F.J. Ayala. 1981. Is a new evolutionary synthesis necessary? *Science* 213: 961–71.

Steensgaard, N. 1973. *The Asian Trade Revolution of the Seventeenth Century: The East India Companies and the Decline of the Caravan Trade*. Chicago, University of Chicago Press.

Stein, A. 1940. *Old Routes of Western Iran*. London, Macmillan.

Stein, (Sir) Mark Aurel. 1929. *An Archaeological Tour in Waziristan and Northern Baluchistan*. Memoirs of the Archaeological Survey of India 37.

1931. The Indo-Iranian borderlands: their prehistory in the light of geography and recent explorations. *Royal Anthropological Institute of Great Britain and Ireland Journal*, 64: 179–202. London.

1937. *Archaeological Reconnaissances in Northwestern India and Southeastern Iran*. London, Macmillan.

Steinbock, R.T. 1976. *Paleopathological Diagnosis and Interpretation*. Springfield, C.C. Thomas.

Stevens, A. 1975. Animals in paleolithic cave art; Leroi-Gourhan's hypothesis. *Antiquity* 49: 54–7.

Steward, Julian H. 1937. Ecological aspects of southwestern society. *Anthropos* 32:87–104.

1955. *Theory of Culture Change*. Urbana, University of Illinois Press.

Steward, J.H. and F.M. Setzler. 1938. Function and configuration in archaeology. *American Antiquity* 4:4–10.

Stiles, D. 1979. Paleolithic cultures and culture change: experiment in theory and method. *Current Anthropology* 20:1–21.

Stocking, G.W. 1974. *A Franz Boas Reader: The Shaping of American Anthropology*, 1883–1911. Chicago, University of Chicago Press; New York, Basic Books.

Stodder, A.W. 1986. The paleoepidemiological transition in the Mesa Verde region Anasazi, A.D. 600–1725. *American Journal of Physical Anthropology* 69:260.

Stone, E. 1977. The social role of the Naditu women in Old Babylonian Nippur. *Journal of the Social and Economic History of the Orient* 25(1): 50–70.

Storey, Rebecca. 1985. An estimate of mortality in a pre-Columbian urban population. *American Anthropologist* 87:519–35.

Stout, Sam. 1978. Histological structure and its preservation in ancient bone. *Current Anthropology* 19:600–4.

Stuart-Macadam, P. 1986. Nutrition and anemia in past human populations. Paper presented to the 19th Chacmool Conference, Calgary.

Sumner, C. 1979. *Reading Ideologies*. London, Academic Press.

Sumner, W. 1972. *Cultural Development in the Kur River Basin, Iran*. Ph.D. dissertation, University of Pennsylvania.

1986. Proto-Elamite civilization in Fars. In U. Finkbeiner and W. Roellig, eds., *Gamdat Nasr Period or Regional Style?* Wiesbaden, Ludwig Reichert.

Symes, Steven. 1984. Harris lines as indicators of stress; an analysis of tibiae from the Crow Creek Massacre. *American Journal of Physical Anthropology* 63: 226.

Tambiah, Stanley J. 1976. *World Conqueror and World Renouncer: A Study of Religion and Polity in Thailand against a Historical Background*. Cambridge, Cambridge University Press.

1977. The galactic polity: the structure of traditional kingdoms in Southeast Asia. *Annals of the New York Academy of Sciences* 293:69–97.

Taylor, W.W. 1948. *A Study of Archaeology*. American Anthropological Association, Memoir 69. Washington.

Terray, Emmanuel. 1975. Classes and class consciousness in the Abron Kingdom of Gyaman, tr. Anne Bailey. In M. Bloch, ed., *Marxist Analyses and Social Anthropology*, 85–136. London, Malaby.

1978. Event, structure, and history: the formation of the Abron Kingdom of Gyaman (1700–1780). In J. Friedman and M.J. Rowlands, *The Evolution of Social Systems*, 279–301. London, Duckworth.

Thapar, B.K. 1973. New traits of the Indus civilization at Kalibangan: an appraisal. In N. Hammond, ed., *South Asian Archaeology*, 84–104. Park Ridge, Noyes Press.

Thomas, Prentice M. Jr. 1981. *Prehistoric Maya Settlement Patterns at Becan, Campeche, Mexico*, Middle American Research Institute, Publication 45. New Orleans, Tulane University.

Thompson, J.E.S. 1931. *Archaeological Investigations in the Southern Cayo District, British Honduras*, Field Museum of Natural History, Anthropological Series 17 (3). Chicago.

Tilley, Christopher. 1984. Ideology and the legitimation of power in the Middle Neolithic of Southern Sweden. In D. Miller and C. Tilley, eds., *Ideology, Power and Prehistory*, 111–46. Cambridge, Cambridge University Press.

Toledo, Francisco de. 1940 [1571]. Información hecha por orden de don Francisco de Toledo en su visita de las provincias del Perú . . . In Robert Levillier, ed., *Don Francisco Toledo, supremo organizador del Perú, su vida, su obra* [1515–1582], II:65–98. Buenos Aires, Espasa–Calpe.

Tolstov, S.P. 1948. *Drevnii Khorezm; opyt Istoriko-arkheologicheskogo issledovaniia*. Moscow.

Tosi, Maurizio. 1969. Excavations at Shahr-i Sokhta. Preliminary Report on the Second Campaign, September–December 1968. *East and West*, n.s. 19 (3–4): 283–386.

1983. *Prehistoric Sistan I*. Rome, IsMEO.

1986. The emerging picture of prehistoric Arabia. *Annual Review of Anthropology* 15: 461–90.

Tourtellot, Gair III. 1970. The peripheries of Seibal: an interim report. In W.R. Bullard, Jr., ed., *Monographs and Papers in Maya Archaeology*, Peabody Museum Papers 61. Cambridge, MA, Harvard University.

In press. *Excavations at Seibal: Peripheral Survey and Excavations; Settlement and Community Patterns*, Memoir 16, Peabody Museum, Cambridge, MA, Harvard University.

Townsend, Richard F. 1979. *State and Cosmos in the Art of Tenochtitlan*. Washington, DC, Dumbarton Oaks.

Trautman, T.R. 1981. *Dravidian Kinship*. Cambridge, Cambridge University Press.

Trigger, B.G. 1968. *Beyond History: the Methods of Prehistory*. New York, Holt, Rinehart & Winston.

1978. *Time and Tradition: Essays in Archaeological Interpretation*. New York, Columbia University Press.

1980. Archaeology and the image of the American Indian. *American Antiquity* 45:662–76.

1982. Archaeological analysis and concepts of causality. *Culture* 2(2): 31–42.

1984a. Alternative archaeologies; nationalist, colonialist, imperialist. *Man* 19: 355–70.

1984b. Marxism and archaeology. In J. Macquet and N. Daniels, eds., *On Marxian Perspectives in Anthropology: Essays in Honor of Harry Hoijer 1981*, 59–97. Malibu, Undena Publications.

1984c. Childe and Soviet archaeology. *Australian Archaeology* 18:1–16.

1984d. Archaeology at the crossroads: what's New? *Annual Review of Anthropology* 13: 275–300.

1985. Marxism in archaeology: real or spurious? Reviews in *Anthropology* 12:114–23.

Tukey, John W. 1977. *Exploratory Data Analysis*. Reading, MA, Addison-Wesley.

Turner, B.L. II. 1974. Prehistoric intensive agriculture in the Mayan Lowlands. *Science* 185:118–24.

1979. Prehispanic terracing in the Central Maya Lowlands; problems of agricultural intensification. In N. Hammond and G.R. Willey, eds., *Maya Archaeology and Ethnohistory*, 103–15. Austin, University of Texas Press.

Turner, B.L. and P.D. Harrison. 1978. Implications from agriculture for Maya prehistory. In P.D. Harrison and B.L. Turner II, eds., *Pre-Hispanic Maya Agriculture*, Albuquerque, University of New Mexico Press.

  1983. *Pulltrouser Swamp, Ancient Maya Habitat, Agriculture, and Settlement in Northern Belize*. Austin, University of Texas Press.

Turner, E.S., N.I. Turner and R.E.W. Adams. 1981. Volumetric assessment, rank ordering, and Maya civic centers. In W. Ashmore, ed., *Lowland Maya Settlement Patterns*, 71–88. Albuquerque, University of New Mexico Press.

Tu Wei-ming. 1985. The continuity of being: Chinese versions of Nature. In Tu Wei-ming, *Confucian Thought*. Albany, State University of New York Press.

Tyler, S.A. and G.E. Marcus. 1987. Comment on: Out of context: the persuasive fictions of anthropology, by Marilyn Strathern, in *Current Anthropology* 28 (3): 251–70.

Ubelaker, Douglas. 1984. Prehistoric human biology of Ecuador: possible temporal trends and cultural correlations. In M.N. Cohen and G.J. Armelagos, eds., *Paleopathology at the Origins of Agriculture*, 491–514. New York, Academic Press.

Ucko, P. and A. Rosenfeld. 1967. *Paleolithic Cave Art*. New York, McGraw-Hill.

  1972. Anthropomorphic representations in paleolithic art. In *Santander Symposium*, 149–211. Actas del symposium internacional de arte prehistorico. Santander, Spain.

Upham, S. 1982. *Polities and Power*. New York, Academic Press.

Van den Berghe, L. 1973. Le Nécropole de Hakalan. *Archéologia* 57:48–59.

  1975. Le Nécropole de Dum Gar Parchinah. *Archéologia* 79:46–61.

Van den Berghe, P.L. and D.P. Barash. 1977. Inclusive fitness and human family structure. *American Anthropologist* 79: 809–23.

Vandiver, P. n.d. *Paleolithic Pigment Processing: A Soft Stone Technology*. Chicago, University of Chicago Press (forthcoming).

Van Gerven, D.P. and G.J. Armelagos. 1983. Farewell to paleodemography: a reply. *Journal of Human Evolution* 12: 352–66.

Van Seters, J. 1985. *In Search of History*. New Haven, Yale University Press.

Vico, G. 1725. *The New Science*. Rev. edn. of the 3rd edn. by T.G. Bergin and M.H. Frisch. Ithaca, Cornell University Press (1968).

Vinnicombe, P. 1967. Rock painting analysis. *South African Archaeological Bulletin* 22: 129–41.

  1976. *People of the Eland*. Pietermaritzburg, Natal University Press.

Vinogradov, A.V. 1979. Issledovaniya pamyatnikov kammenogo veka v severnom Afganistane. *Drevnaya Baktriya* 2: 7–62.

Vinogradov, A.V. and E.D. Mamedov. 1975. *Pervobitniii Lyavlyakan*. Moscow, Nauka.

Vishnu-Mittre and Savithri, R. 1982. Food economy of the Harappans. In G. Possehl, ed., *Harappan Civilization: A Contemporary Perspective*, 205–22. New Delhi, Oxford and IBH in collaboration with American Institute of Indian Studies.

Wachtel, Nathan. 1976. *The Vision of the Vanquished*. Tr. Ben and Sian Reynolds. New York, Barnes & Noble.

  1982. The *Mitimas* of the Cochabamba Valley: the colonization policy of Huayna Capac. In G.A. Collier et al., *The Inca and Aztec States 1400–1800*, 199–235. New York, Academic Press.

Wagley, Charles. 1973. Cultural influences on population: a comparison of two Tupi tribes. In D.R. Gross, ed., *Peoples and Cultures of Native South America*, 145–56. Garden City, Doubleday.

Walker, P.L. 1985. Anemia among prehistoric Indians of the American Southwest. In C. Merbs and R.J. Miller, eds., *Health and Disease in the Prehistoric Southwest*, 139–64. Arizona State University, Archaeological Research Papers 34.

  1986. Porotic hyperostosis in a marine dependent California Indian population. *American Journal of Physical Anthropology* 69: 345–54.

n.d. Enamel hypoplasia during 5000 years of Southern California prehistory. Ms.

Walker, P.L. and M. de Niro. 1986. Stable nitrogen and carbon isotope ratios in bone collagen as indices of prehistoric dietary dependence on marine and terrestrial resources in Southern California. *American Journal of Physical Anthropology* 71:51–62.

Wallerstein, I. 1974. *The Modern World-System: Capitalist Agriculture and the Origins of the European World-Economy in the Sixteenth Century.* New York, Academic Press.

1979. *The Capitalist World-Economy.* Cambridge, Cambridge University Press.

1980. *The Modern World-System. Vol 2. Mercantilism and the Consolidation of the European World-Economy 1600–1750.* Cambridge, Cambridge University Press.

Washburn, D.K. 1977. *A Symmetry Analysis of Upper Gila Area Ceramic Design.* Peabody Museum Papers 68, Cambridge, MA, Harvard University.

1983. Symmetry analysis of ceramic design: two tests of the method on neolithic material from Greece and the Aegean. In D.K. Washburn, ed., *Structure and Cognition in Art*, 38–65. Cambridge, Cambridge University Press.

Watson, P.J. 1979. The idea of ethnoarchaeology. In Carol Kramer, ed., *Ethnoarchaeology: Implications of Ethnography for Archaeology*, 227–87. New York, Columbia University Press.

Watson, P.J., S. LeBlanc and C.L. Redman. 1971. *Explanation in Archaeology: An Explicitly Scientific Approach.* New York, Columbia University Press.

Webb, Stephen. 1984. Prehistoric stress in Australian Aborigines. Thesis, Department of Prehistory, Australian National University.

Weber, M. 1976. *The Aquarian Sociology of Ancient Civilizations*, London, New Left Books.

Webster, David L. 1976. Lowland Maya fortifications. *Proceedings of the American Philosophical Society* 12:361–71.

1977. Warfare and the evolution of Maya civilization. In Richard E. W. Adams, ed., *The Origins of Maya Civilization*, 335–72. Albuquerque, University of New Mexico Press.

1987. Copan as a Classic Maya center. In E. Boone and G.R. Willey, eds., *The Southeastern Classic Maya Zone.* Washington DC, Dumbarton Oaks.

Weisgerber, G. 1980. '. . . und kupfer in Oman'. *Der Anschnitt-Zeitschrift für Kunst und Kultur im Bergbau* 32(2–3): 61–110.

1981. Mehr als Kupfer in Oman – ergebnisse der Expedition 1981. *Der Anschnitt-Zeitschrift für Kunst und Kultur im Bergbau* 33(5–6): 174–263.

1983. Copper production during the third millennium B.C. in Oman and the question of Makan. *Journal of Oman Studies* 6(2): 269–76.

1984. Makan and Meluhha – third millennium B.C. copper production in Oman and the evidence of contact with the Indus valley. In B. Allchin, ed., *South Asian Archaeology 1981*,

196–201. Cambridge, Cambridge University Press.

Weiss, H. and C. Young, Jr. 1975. The merchants of Susa. *Iran* 13: 1–17.

Weiss, K.M. 1973. *Demographic Models for Anthropology.* Memoir, Society for American Archaeology 27.

Welinder, Stig. 1979. Prehistoric demography. *Acta Arch. Lundensia*, Series IN8 Minore 8. Bonn: Rudolf Habelt.

Whallon, Robert. 1984. Unconstrained clustering for the analysis of spatial distributions in archaeology. In H. Hietala, ed., *Intrasite Spatial Analysis in Archaeology*, 242–77. Cambridge, Cambridge University Press.

Wheeler, R.E.M. 1953. *The Indus Civilization.* 1st edn. Supplement to the *Cambridge History of India.* Cambridge, Cambridge University Press.

1968a. *The Indus Civilization.* 3rd edn. Supplement to the *Cambridge History of India.* Cambridge, Cambridge University Press.

1968b. *Early India and Pakistan.* London, Thames & Hudson.

Wheeler-Pires-Ferreira, J. 1975–7. Tepe Tula'i: faunal remains from an early campsite in Khuzistan, Iran. *Paléorient* 3:275–80.

White, Christine. 1986. Mayan diet and health status at Lamanai, Belize. Paper presented to the 19th Chacmool conference, Calgary.

White, Hayden V. 1973. *Metahistory: The Historical Imagination in Nineteenth Century Europe.* Baltimore, Johns Hopkins University Press.

White, Leslie A. 1949. *The Science of Culture. A Study of Man and Civilization.* New York, Farrar, Strauss.

1959a. *The Evolution of Culture.* New York, McGraw-Hill.

1959b. The concept of evolution in anthropology. In B.J. Meggers, ed., *Evolution and Anthropology: A Centennial Appraisal,* 106–24. Washington DC, Anthropological Society of Washington.

Whitebrook, Joel. 1976. Reflections on the evolutionist controversy. *Dialectical Anthropology* 1: 181–5.

Whyte, Anne. 1978. Systems as perceived: A discussion of 'Maladaptation in social systems'. In J. Friedman and M.J. Rowlands, eds., *The Evolution of Social Systems,* 73–8. London, Duckworth.

Willer, D. and J. Willer. 1974. *Systematic Empiricism: Critique of a Pseudoscience.* Englewood Cliffs, N.J, Prentice-Hall.

Willey, Gordon R. 1953. *Prehistoric Settlement Patterns in the Virú Valley, Peru.* Bureau of American Ethnology Bulletin no. 155. Washington, DC., U.S. Government Printing Office.

1956. The structure of ancient Maya society. *American Anthropologist* 58: 777–82.

1961. Review of *Evolution and Culture,* edited by M.D.Sahlins and E.R. Service. *American Antiquity* 26: 441–3.

1966. *An Introduction to American Archaeology: Vol. 1. North and Middle America.* Englewood Cliffs, NJ, Prentice-Hall.

1976. Mesoamerican civilization and the idea of transcendence. *Antiquity* 50: 205–15.

1978. Pre-Hispanic Maya agriculture: a contemporary summation. In P.D. Harrison and B.L. Turner II, eds., *Pre-Hispanic Maya Agriculture,* 325–36. Albuquerque, University of New Mexico Press.

1981. Maya lowland settlement patterns: a summary review. In W. Ashmore, ed., *Lowland Maya Settlement Patterns,* 385–416. Albuquerque, University of New Mexico Press.

1985. Technology and style in ancient ceramics. In W.D. Kingery, ed., *Ceramics and Civilization, Ancient Technology to Modern Science,* 1: 5–25. Columbus, OH, The American Ceramic Society, Inc.

Willey, G.R. and P. Phillips. 1958. *Method and Theory in American Archaeology.* Chicago, University of Chicago Press.

Willey, G.R. and J.A. Sabloff. 1980. *A History of American Archaeology.* 2nd edn. San Francisco, Freeman.

Willey, G.R., W.R. Bullard, Jr., J.B. Glass and J.C. Gifford. 1965. *Prehistoric Maya Settlements in the Belize Valley,* Peabody Museum Papers 54. Cambridge, MA, Harvard University.

Willey, G.R., R.M. Leventhal and W.L. Fash, Jr. 1978. Maya settlement in the Copan Valley, *Archaeology* 31 (4): 32–44.

Willey, G.R., A. Ledyard Smith, Gair Tourtellot III and Ian Graham. 1975. *Excavations at Seibal. Introduction: The Site and its Setting.* Memoir 13, Part 1, Peabody Museum. Cambridge, MA, Harvard University.

Williams, J.A. 1985. Evidence of pre-contact tuberculosis in two Woodland skeletal populations from the northern plains. *American Journal of Physical Anthropology* 66: 242–3.

Wilmsen, E.N. 1978. Prehistoric and historic antecedents of a contemporary Ngamiland community. *Botswana Notes and Records* 10: 5–18.

Wilson, D. 1981. Of maize and men: a critique of the maritime hypothesis of state origins on the coast of Peru. *American Anthropologist* 83(1): 93–120.

Wilson, E.O. 1975. *Sociobiology: A New Synthesis.* Cambridge, MA, Harvard University Press.

1978. *On Human Nature.* Cambridge, MA, Harvard University Press.

Winch, P. 1958. *The Idea of a Social Science*. London, Routledge & Kegan Paul.

Wobst, H. Martin. 1976. Locational relationships in Paleolithic society. *Journal of Human Evolution* 5: 49–58.

1977. Stylistic behavior and information exchange. In C.E. Cleland, ed., *Papers for the Director. Research Essays in Honor of James B. Griffin*, 317–42. Anthropological Papers, Ann Arbor, University of Michigan.

1978. The archaeo-ethnology of hunter-gatherers or the tyranny of the ethnographic record in archaeology. *American Antiquity* 43:303–9.

Wolf, Eric R., ed., 1976. *The Valley of Mexico*. Albuquerque, University of New Mexico Press.

1982. *Europe and People without History*. Berkeley, University of California Press.

Woodburn, James. 1968. An introduction to Hadza Ecology. In R.B. and I. DeVore, eds., *Man the Hunter*, 49–55. Chicago, Aldine.

Woolley, L. 1963. The beginnings of civilization. In J. Hawkes and L. Woolley, *Prehistory and the Beginnings of Civilization*, 359–839. New York.

Wright, Henry T. 1972. A consideration of interregional exchange in Greater Mesopotamia; 4000–3000 B.C. In E.N. Wilmsen, ed., *Social Exchange and Interaction*, 95–105. Anthropological Papers 46. University of Michigan.

1977. Recent research on the origin of the state. *Annual Review of Anthropology* 6: 379–97.

1979. ed., *Archaeological Investigations in Northeastern Xuzestan, 1976*. Museum of Anthropology, Ann Arbor, University of Michigan.

1984. Prestate political formations. In T. Earle, ed., *On the Evolution of Complex Societies: Essays in Honor of Harry Hoijer 1982*, 41–77. Malibu, Undena Publications.

1988. The Susiana hinterlands during the era of primary state formation. In F. Hole, ed., *Archaeological Perspective on Western Iran*. Washington, Smithsonian Institution.

Wright, H.T. and G.A. Johnson. 1975. Population exchange and early state formation in southwestern Iran. *American Anthropologist* 77: 267–89.

Wright, H., J. Neely, G. Johnson and J. Speth. 1975. Early fourth millennium developments in southwestern Iran. *Iran* 13: 129–47.

Wright, Mary. 1961. The social sciences and the Chinese historical record. *Journal of Asian Studies* 20.

Wright, Rita P. 1984. Technology, style and craft specialization: spheres of interaction and exchange in the Indo-Iranian Borderlands, third millennium B.C. Ann Arbor, University Microfilms.

1985. Technology and style in ancient ceramics, In W.D. Kingery, ed., *Ceramics and Civilization*, 1:5–25. Columbus, OH, The American Ceramic Society.

1986. The boundaries of technology and stylistic change. In W.D. Kingery, ed., *Ceramics and Civilization*, II:1–20. Columbus, OH, The American Ceramic Society.

1987. The frontiers of prehistoric Baluchistan and the development of the Indus Civilization. In K.M. Trinkaus, ed., *Polities and Partitions: Human Boundaries in Ancient Societies*, 61–82. Arizona State Research Paper 36.

Wrigley, Edward A. 1969. *Population and History*. New York: McGraw-Hill.

Wylie, M. Alison. 1982. Epistemological issues raised by a structuralist archaeology. In I. Hodder, ed., *Symbolic and Structural Archaeology*, 39–46. Cambridge, Cambridge University Press.

1985a. Between philosophy and archaeology. *American Antiquity* 50: 478–90.

1985b. Putting Shakertown back together: critical theory in archaeology. *Journal of Anthropological Archaeology* 4: 133–47.

1985c. Facts of the record and facts of the past; Mandelbaum on the anatomy of history "proper." *International Studies in Philosophy* 17:71–85.

Wynn, T. 1979. The intelligence of later Acheulian hominids. *Man* 14:371–91.

Y'edynak, Gloria and Sylvia Fleisch. 1983. Microevolution and biological adaptability in the transition from food collecting to food production in the Iron Gates of Yugoslavia. *Journal of Human Evolution* 12: 279–96.

Yellen, J. E. 1971. Archaeological excavations in Western Ngamiland. *Botswana Notes and Records* 3: 276.

1977. *Archaeological Approaches to the Present*. New York, Academic Press.

1986. Optimization and risk in human foraging strategies. *Journal of Human Evolution* 15:733–50.

Yoffee, N. 1979. The decline and rise of Mesopotamian civilization. *American Antiquity* 44:3–35.

Young, T.C. Jr. 1975. An archaeological survey of the Kangavar Valley. *Proceedings of the 3rd Annual Symposium on Archaeological Research in Iran*, 80–90. Ed. F. Bagherzadeh. Tehran, Iranian Centre for Archaeological Research.

Zadeh, L. 1965. Fuzzy sets. *Information and Control* 8: 338–53.

Zagarell, A. 1982a. *The Prehistory of the Northeast Bahtiyari Mountains, Iran. The Rise of a Highland Way of Life*. Beihefte zum Tübinger Atlas des Vorderen Orients (42). Weisbaden, Reichert.

1982b. The political economy of Mesopotamian and South Indian temples: the formation and reproduction of urban society. *Comparative Urban Research* 9:8–27.

1986a. Structural discontinuity – a critical factor in the emergence of Primary and Secondary states. *Dialectical Anthropology* 10:155–77.

1986b.Trade, women, class and society in ancient Western Asia. *Current Anthropology* 27:415–30.

n.d.a. Regional and social borders in the Bakhtiari and Luristan Highlands of Iran. To appear in K. Maurer-Trinkaus, ed., *Polities and Partitions: Human Boundaries in Ancient Societies*. Tempe, Arizona, Anthropological Research Papers 35.

n.d.b. Interfacing modes of production. Urban and rural life in Greater Mesopotamia. A critique of cultural evolutionary and cultural materialist approaches (Ms).

Zivanovic, S. 1982. *Ancient Diseases* (English translation). London, Methuen.

INDEX